CANADA YEAR BOOK 2009

Statistics Canada

Published by authority of the Minister responsible for Statistics Canada

Available in Canada through authorized bookstore agents and other bookstores or from:

Statistics Canada
Finance Division
R.H. Coats Building., 6th Floor
150 Tunney's Pasture Driveway
Ottawa, Ontario K1A 0T6
Phone (Canada and United States): 1-800-267-6677
Fax (Canada and United States): 1-877-287-4369
E-mail: Infostats@statcan.gc.ca

September 2009
Catalogue no. 11-402-XPE
ISSN 0068-8142
ISBN 978-0-660-19908-5
Frequency: Annual
Ottawa
Cette publication est disponible en français sur demande (nº 11-402-XPF au catalogue).

Note of appreciation
Canada owes the success of its statistical system to a long-standing partnership between Statistics Canada, the citizens of Canada, its businesses, governments and other institutions. Accurate and timely statistical information could not be produced without their continued co-operation and goodwill.

The paper used in this publication meets the minimum requirements of American National Standard for Information Sciences – Permanence of Paper for Printed Library Materials, ANSI Z39.48 – 1984.
∞

Printed in Canada
Tri-Graphic Printing (Ottawa) Limited

Library and Archives Canada Cataloguing in Publication Data
Canada year book
Issued also in French under title: Annuaire du Canada.
ISBN 978-0-660-19908-5 (paper)
ISBN 978-1-100-12555-8 (PDF)
CS11-402-XPE
CS11-402-XIE
1. Canada – Statistics. I. Statistics Canada. Communications and Library Services Division.
HA744 S81 2009 317.1

Statistics Canada

Canada Year Book
2009 edition

A compact almanac for reference about Canada, with a focus on tables, charts, maps and succinct analytical articles that cover 31 subject areas, plus a list of sources and a glossary of technical terms.

Please visit www.statcan.gc.ca/canadayearbook to discover the *Canada Year Book* online collection, which presents digitized archival material from previous *Canada Year Books* going back to the first one published in 1867. Consult www.statcan.gc.ca to explore all of Statistics Canada's online resources.

Acknowledgements

This *Canada Year Book* is the result of the work of dozens of people over many months. In addition to the production team, listed below, we would like to thank the many Statistics Canada employees who helped to make this volume possible.

Production team

Writers

- Andrew Bisson, Judy Hosein, Craig Pratt, Tim Prichard, Penny Stuart, Tom Vradenburg

Fact-checking

- Brian Drysdale, Craig Pratt

Analyst

- Jacqueline Tebbens

Tables editor

- Catherine Pelletier

Charts editor

- Brian Drysdale

Table and chart production

- Danielle Baum, Juli-Ann Rowsell

Mapping

- Allan Rowell

Senior English editors

- Tim Prichard, Tom Vradenburg

Senior French editor

- Christine Duchesne

Editing and proofreading

- David Blouin, Geneviève Corbin Geoffroy, Edelweiss D'Andrea, Brodie Fraser, Paula Gherasim, Elizabeth Irving, Jennifer Kerr, Luc Moquin, Julie Morin, Robin Redmond, Christopher Warnock

Translation

- Official Languages and Translation Division

Cover design

- Rachel Penkar, Jennifer Pfitzer

Composition and graphics

- Sandra Garrison, Juli-Ann Rowsell

Indexing

- Patricia Buchanan (English), François Trahan (French)

Printing procurement

- Steeven Cryans, Anne-Marie Fleury

Marketing

- Marc Bazinet

Management

- Gabrielle Beaudoin, Bernie Gloyn, Eric St. John

Penny Stuart
Editor-in-chief

Abbreviations and symbols

Provinces and territories	
Newfoundland and Labrador	N.L.
Prince Edward Island	P.E.I.
Nova Scotia	N.S.
New Brunswick	N.B.
Quebec	Que.
Ontario	Ont.
Manitoba	Man.
Saskatchewan	Sask.
Alberta	Alta.
British Columbia	B.C.
Yukon	Y.T.
Northwest Territories	N.W.T.
Nunavut	Nvt.

Symbols

The symbols described in this document apply to all data published by Statistics Canada from all origins including surveys, censuses and administrative sources, as well as straight tabulations and all estimations.

.	not available for any reference period
..	not available for a specific reference period
...	not applicable
0	true zero or a value rounded to zero
0^s	value rounded to zero where there is a meaningful distinction between true zero and the value that was rounded
p	preliminary
r	revised
x	suppressed to meet the confidentiality requirements of the *Statistics Act*
E	use with caution
F	too unreliable to be published

When the figure is not accompanied by a data quality symbol, it means that the quality of the data was assessed to be 'acceptable or better' according to the policies and standards of Statistics Canada.

In some tables, figures may not add to totals because of rounding.

Note: All data are in current dollars unless otherwise stated.

The statistics in this edition are the most up-to-date available at the time of its preparation. For more recent data, visit Summary Tables at www.statcan.gc.ca.

Contents

Aboriginal peoples

1

Canada's Aboriginal population is younger and faster-growing than its non-Aboriginal one. In 2006, the median age for Aboriginal people was 27 years, compared with 40 years for non-Aboriginal people.

From 1996 to 2006, the Aboriginal population increased 45%, nearly six times faster than the 8% growth rate for the non-Aboriginal population.

Growing population

In 2006, 1,172,790 people identified themselves as an Aboriginal person, either as North American Indian (or First Nations people), Métis or Inuit.

Demographic trends, such as high birth rates, are one factor of the high growth rate. As well, more people are identifying themselves as an Aboriginal person, and more reserves participated in the 2006 Census than in previous censuses.

Aboriginal people make up a growing share of Canada's population, representing 3.8% of people enumerated in the 2006 Census, up from 3.3% in 2001 and 2.8% in the 1996 census.

In 2006, First Nations people accounted for 60% of the total Aboriginal population in Canada, the Métis 33%, and the Inuit 4%. Most First Nations people are Status Indians, meaning they are registered under the *Indian Act*. In 2006, 564,870 First Nations people reported they were registered Indians; they made up 81% of the total First Nations population.

Despite some improvements, Canada's Inuit, Métis and First Nations people do not share the levels of socio-economic well-being of the general population. Aboriginal people are less likely to complete high school, and their path to postsecondary education is less direct, as they tend to

Chart 1.1
Population, by Aboriginal identity, 2006

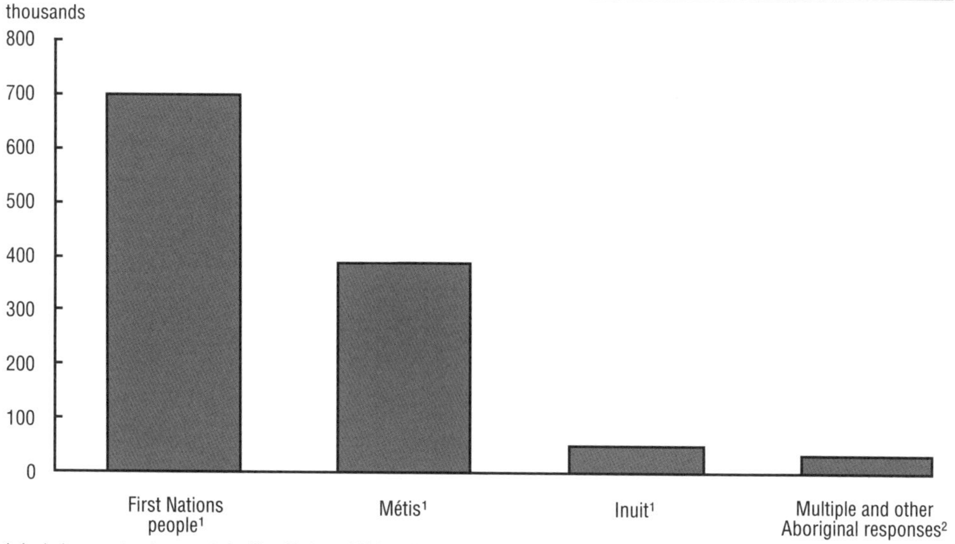

1. Includes people who reported a First Nations, Métis or Inuit identity only.
2. Includes people who reported more than one Aboriginal identity group and those who reported being a registered Indian and/or band member without reporting an Aboriginal identity.

Source: Statistics Canada, 2006 Census of Population.

return to school later in life. They are also less likely to be employed and more likely to live with low incomes.

Also, Aboriginal people are less likely to be in good health. For example, 58% of Métis aged 15 and older reported their health as excellent or very good in 2006, compared with 62% of Canada's entire population.

In addition, Inuit adults are less likely to have contact with a medical doctor than the rest of the Canadian population: 56% of Inuit adults had contact with a medical doctor in the 12 months prior to a 2006 survey, compared with 79% of adults in the total Canadian population, after controlling for age differences. Life expectancy for Inuit in the North is about 15 years shorter than for the general population.

Crowded conditions, major repairs needed

Over the past decade, the share of Aboriginal people living in crowded homes has declined. In 2006, 11% of Aboriginal people lived in homes with more than one person per room, down from 17% in 1996. However, nearly one in four lived in homes requiring major repairs in 2006, unchanged from 1996. Aboriginal people are almost four times as likely as non-Aboriginal people to live in a crowded dwelling. They are also three times as likely to live in a home in need of major repairs.

Crowding is especially common on Indian reserves or settlements. One-quarter (26%) of on-reserve First Nations people lived in crowded conditions in 2006.

Table 1.a
Aboriginal population in Canada, the territories and selected provinces, 2006

	% of total population
Canada	**3.8**
Nunavut	85.0
Northwest Territories	50.3
Yukon	25.1
Manitoba	15.5
Saskatchewan	14.9

Source: Statistics Canada, Census of Population, 2006.

Chart 1.2
Aboriginal and non-Aboriginal people living in a crowded dwelling

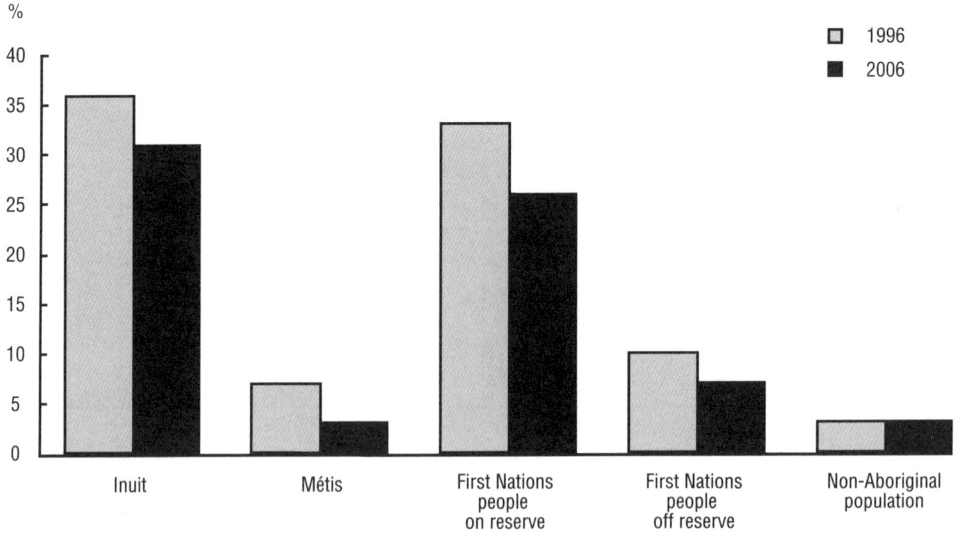

Source: Statistics Canada, censuses of population, 1996 and 2006.

Employment rates

Aboriginal people saw better employment rates in 2006 than in 2001. However, employment rate gaps remain between Aboriginal and non-Aboriginal people.

In 2006, the employment rate for Aboriginal people of core working age (aged 25 to 54) was 66%, up from 61% in 2001. This compares with 82% for non-Aboriginal people in 2006, up from 80% five years earlier.

First Nations people saw a greater gain in employment rates off reserve than on reserve. In 2006, 52% of the on-reserve First Nations population aged 25 to 54 was employed, compared with 50% in 2001.

Off reserve, 66% of the First Nations population was employed, up from 61% in 2001. The employment rate for Aboriginal people aged 25 to 54 was highest in Alberta, 78% in 2007. Alberta had the narrowest employment rate gap between Aboriginal and non-Aboriginal people. Saskatchewan, with rates of 66% for the Aboriginal population and 88% for non-Aboriginal people, had the widest employment gap.

Chart 1.3
Employment and unemployment rates, by Aboriginal identity

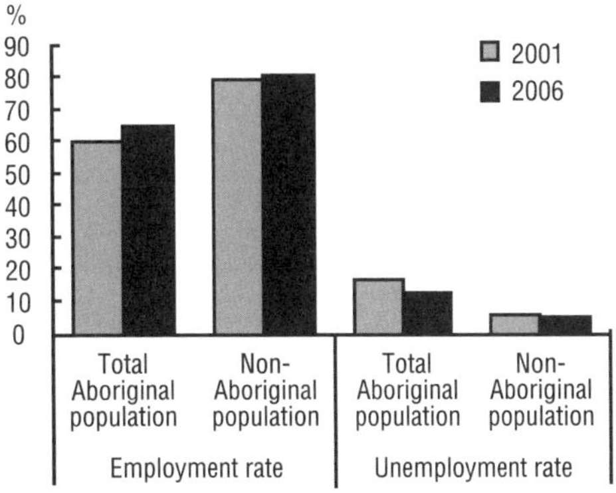

Note: Population aged 25 to 54.
Source: Statistics Canada, censuses of population, 2001 and 2006.

Young Aboriginal children living in larger families

Aboriginal children aged 6 and younger are growing up in larger families than non-Aboriginal children. In 2006, 28% of Inuit children, 17% of First Nations children living off reserve, and 11% of Métis children were living in families with four or more children. This compares with 8% of non-Aboriginal children in Canada.

Many people, including extended family and community members, are involved in raising young Aboriginal children. In 2006, 67% of young First Nations children living off reserve received focused attention from grandparents at least once a week; the shares were 69% for Métis children and 71% for Inuit children.

As well, 26% of young First Nations children living off reserve, 24% of Métis children, and 35% of Inuit children received focused attention from Elders (other than grandparents) at least once per week.

Chart 1.4
Living arrangements of Aboriginal children aged 14 and younger, 2006

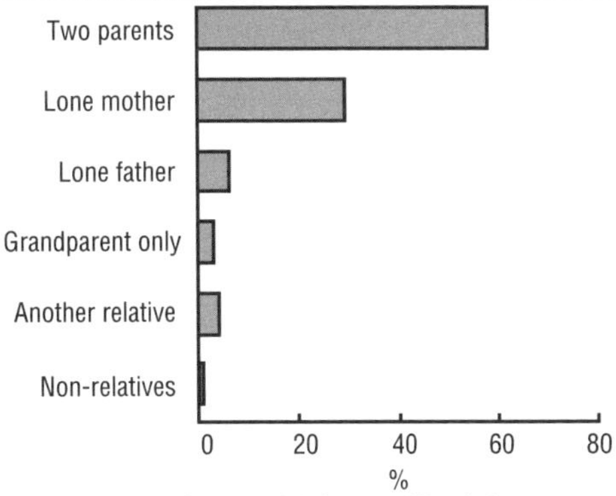

Source: Statistics Canada, 2006 Census of Population.

Table 1.1 Aboriginal identity population, by sex and by province and territory, 2006

	Canada	Newfoundland and Labrador	Prince Edward Island	Nova Scotia	New Brunswick
	number				
Both sexes					
Aboriginal identity population[1]	**1,172,790**	23,450	1,730	24,175	17,655
North American Indian	**698,025**	7,765	1,230	15,240	12,385
Métis	**389,785**	6,470	385	7,680	4,270
Inuit	**50,480**	4,715	30	320	185
Non-Aboriginal population	**30,068,240**	477,155	132,475	878,915	701,995
Males					
Aboriginal identity population[1]	**572,090**	11,525	760	11,770	8,645
North American Indian	**338,050**	3,820	565	7,320	5,810
Métis	**193,500**	3,170	145	3,940	2,450
Inuit	**25,025**	2,365	10	140	70
Non-Aboriginal population	**14,754,175**	232,445	64,230	423,800	342,505
Females					
Aboriginal identity population[1]	**600,695**	11,925	970	12,405	9,010
North American Indian	**359,975**	3,950	660	7,915	6,575
Métis	**196,280**	3,310	245	3,740	1,815
Inuit	**25,455**	2,345	20	180	110
Non-Aboriginal population	**15,314,065**	244,715	68,245	455,115	359,495

1. The Aboriginal identity population comprises the Aboriginal groups (North American Indian, Métis and Inuit), multiple Aboriginal responses and Aboriginal responses not included elsewhere.

Source: Statistics Canada, 2006 Census of Population.

Quebec	Ontario	Manitoba	Saskatchewan	Alberta	British Columbia	Yukon	Northwest Territories	Nunavut
number								
108,430	242,490	175,395	142,045	188,215	196,075	7,580	20,665	24,890
65,085	158,400	100,645	91,550	97,130	129,575	6,275	12,640	105
27,980	73,605	71,810	48,120	85,500	59,445	805	3,580	130
10,950	2,040	565	220	1,610	795	255	4,190	24,610
7,327,475	11,786,405	958,115	811,960	3,067,990	3,878,310	22,610	20,445	4,380
53,525	117,590	85,720	69,640	91,670	94,855	3,665	10,180	12,545
31,690	75,955	48,715	44,530	47,155	63,190	3,035	6,210	55
14,305	37,030	35,615	23,945	41,985	28,595	400	1,860	60
5,475	940	280	110	790	335	100	1,990	12,405
3,592,455	5,760,285	471,200	399,840	1,539,125	1,903,530	11,545	10,790	2,425
54,905	124,905	89,675	72,400	96,545	101,215	3,915	10,480	12,345
33,395	82,440	51,935	47,020	49,970	66,390	3,245	6,430	50
13,680	36,580	36,185	24,175	43,515	30,855	400	1,715	65
5,480	1,095	280	105	820	455	150	2,200	12,205
3,735,020	6,026,115	486,915	412,120	1,528,860	1,974,780	11,070	9,655	1,960

Table 1.2 Aboriginal identity population, by age group, by sex and by province and territory, 2006

	Canada	Newfoundland and Labrador	Prince Edward Island	Nova Scotia	New Brunswick
	number				
Both sexes, all ages	**1,172,790**	**23,450**	**1,730**	**24,175**	**17,655**
0 to 4	**108,895**	1,445	230	1,745	1,350
5 to 9	**114,765**	1,805	210	2,080	1,605
10 to 14	**125,235**	2,145	160	2,480	1,490
15 to 19	**118,105**	2,300	170	2,430	1,695
20 to 24	**93,905**	1,920	100	1,905	1,240
25 to 34	**161,570**	3,035	235	3,220	2,195
35 to 44	**169,465**	3,675	230	3,630	2,870
45 to 54	**143,285**	3,395	215	3,515	2,645
55 to 64	**81,090**	2,175	100	1,930	1,445
65 and older	**56,465**	1,545	75	1,230	1,105
Males, all ages	**572,090**	**11,525**	**760**	**11,770**	**8,645**
0 to 4	**55,380**	700	120	880	690
5 to 9	**58,910**	920	95	1,060	815
10 to 14	**64,120**	1,135	75	1,240	715
15 to 19	**60,250**	1,150	65	1,170	885
20 to 24	**45,390**	940	70	945	615
25 to 34	**76,220**	1,375	120	1,455	1,040
35 to 44	**79,205**	1,735	70	1,690	1,390
45 to 54	**67,540**	1,735	85	1,715	1,310
55 to 64	**39,420**	1,140	30	1,020	720
65 and older	**25,650**	695	30	595	460
Females, all ages	**600,695**	**11,925**	**970**	**12,405**	**9,010**
0 to 4	**53,515**	745	110	870	660
5 to 9	**55,860**	885	110	1,015	795
10 to 14	**61,110**	1,005	80	1,240	780
15 to 19	**57,855**	1,150	105	1,260	810
20 to 24	**48,510**	980	35	960	625
25 to 34	**85,350**	1,660	115	1,770	1,155
35 to 44	**90,260**	1,940	160	1,940	1,480
45 to 54	**75,745**	1,660	125	1,805	1,335
55 to 64	**41,670**	1,040	70	910	720
65 and older	**30,810**	855	50	635	645

Source: Statistics Canada, 2006 Census of Population.

Quebec	Ontario	Manitoba	Saskatchewan	Alberta	British Columbia	Yukon	Northwest Territories	Nunavut
				number				
108,430	**242,490**	**175,395**	**142,045**	**188,215**	**196,075**	**7,580**	**20,665**	**24,890**
8,680	19,815	18,810	16,600	18,315	16,195	640	1,875	3,195
9,185	21,075	19,180	16,540	19,300	18,005	690	1,950	3,135
9,650	23,435	20,200	17,510	20,945	21,045	735	2,355	3,070
9,590	22,335	17,910	16,130	19,630	19,945	700	2,290	2,980
8,200	18,540	14,250	11,990	16,535	14,875	550	1,590	2,200
14,440	33,680	23,830	19,365	28,730	25,605	990	2,770	3,475
16,005	37,935	23,720	17,845	26,510	29,615	1,230	3,020	3,175
14,775	33,720	19,215	13,705	20,420	26,425	1,045	2,350	1,850
9,910	19,340	10,940	7,115	10,695	14,420	580	1,330	1,100
7,995	12,615	7,340	5,240	7,125	9,930	420	1,125	705
53,525	**117,590**	**85,720**	**69,640**	**91,670**	**94,855**	**3,665**	**10,180**	**12,545**
4,460	10,150	9,585	8,395	9,405	8,130	315	920	1,630
4,560	10,685	10,100	8,655	9,930	9,155	345	990	1,590
5,015	11,840	10,475	8,925	10,625	10,960	370	1,190	1,550
4,840	11,600	8,805	8,275	9,940	10,400	395	1,170	1,550
3,975	8,925	6,630	5,770	8,105	7,180	280	850	1,105
7,015	15,440	11,375	8,775	14,010	12,175	445	1,270	1,725
7,865	17,945	10,895	8,415	12,005	13,525	635	1,470	1,550
7,225	15,895	9,050	6,620	9,385	12,085	460	1,080	890
5,005	9,475	5,390	3,345	4,985	6,790	240	700	575
3,565	5,620	3,405	2,455	3,280	4,460	180	540	370
54,905	**124,905**	**89,675**	**72,400**	**96,545**	**101,215**	**3,915**	**10,480**	**12,345**
4,215	9,660	9,230	8,200	8,910	8,065	325	955	1,565
4,625	10,390	9,080	7,885	9,375	8,850	340	965	1,540
4,640	11,595	9,725	8,585	10,320	10,090	370	1,160	1,520
4,750	10,740	9,105	7,855	9,690	9,545	300	1,120	1,430
4,220	9,610	7,620	6,220	8,430	7,695	275	740	1,095
7,420	18,240	12,450	10,590	14,720	13,430	540	1,500	1,750
8,140	19,985	12,820	9,425	14,505	16,095	595	1,550	1,625
7,550	17,825	10,165	7,080	11,035	14,345	585	1,270	960
4,910	9,865	5,550	3,775	5,710	7,635	335	635	520
4,425	7,000	3,935	2,780	3,845	5,470	240	585	330

Table 1.3 Population, by Aboriginal identity, highest level of schooling and sex, 2006

	All levels	Less than high school	High school only	Trade school[1]	College[1]	University[2]	University[3]
				number			
Both sexes	**25,664,220**	**6,098,330**	**6,553,425**	**2,785,420**	**4,435,135**	**1,136,150**	**4,162,225**
Aboriginal identity population[4]	**823,890**	359,780	179,585	93,885	119,680	22,950	42,280
North American Indian	**473,235**	228,985	94,380	49,240	62,340	13,685	21,440
Métis	**291,330**	100,770	74,575	38,220	49,210	8,035	18,265
Inuit	**32,775**	19,885	4,435	3,135	3,935	505	790
Multiple Aboriginal identities	**5,590**	2,010	1,435	755	835	165	355
Other Aboriginal identity	**20,960**	8,125	4,760	2,535	3,350	555	1,410
Non-Aboriginal population	**24,840,335**	5,738,550	6,373,835	2,691,535	4,315,455	1,113,195	4,119,950
Males	**12,470,785**	**3,004,625**	**3,032,870**	**1,778,080**	**1,906,335**	**479,095**	**2,045,725**
Aboriginal identity population[4]	**393,680**	182,410	81,210	58,525	45,755	8,190	15,610
North American Indian	**223,370**	115,165	41,725	30,705	22,870	4,790	7,065
Métis	**142,840**	52,845	34,745	24,020	19,760	2,975	7,670
Inuit	**15,965**	9,795	2,005	2,020	1,660	170	260
Multiple Aboriginal identities	**2,610**	1,020	650	450	310	55	100
Other Aboriginal identity	**8,895**	3,585	2,075	1,325	1,145	190	505
Non-Aboriginal population	**12,077,100**	2,822,210	2,951,660	1,719,555	1,860,580	470,905	2,030,105
Females	**13,193,435**	**3,093,700**	**3,520,555**	**1,007,335**	**2,528,800**	**657,055**	**2,116,505**
Aboriginal identity population[4]	**430,205**	177,365	98,380	35,360	73,925	14,760	26,665
North American Indian	**249,865**	113,825	52,660	18,530	39,465	8,895	14,370
Métis	**148,490**	47,925	39,825	14,205	29,455	5,050	10,600
Inuit	**16,810**	10,090	2,430	1,110	2,270	335	540
Multiple Aboriginal identities	**2,975**	990	785	300	525	110	240
Other Aboriginal identity	**12,065**	4,540	2,680	1,210	2,210	370	910
Non-Aboriginal population	**12,763,230**	2,916,335	3,422,175	971,980	2,454,875	642,295	2,089,840

Note: Population aged 15 years and older.
1. Certificate or diploma.
2. Certificate or diploma below bachelor's degree.
3. Degree at the bachelor's level or higher.
4. The Aboriginal identity population comprises the Aboriginal groups (North American Indian, Métis and Inuit), multiple Aboriginal responses and Aboriginal responses not included elsewhere.

Source: Statistics Canada, 2006 Census of Population.

Table 1.4 Population, by Aboriginal identity, labour force characteristics and sex, 2006

	All labour force status	In the labour force	Employed	Unemployed	Not in the labour force	Participation rate	Employment rate	Unemployment rate
	number					%		
Both sexes	**25,664,220**	**17,146,135**	**16,021,180**	**1,124,960**	**8,518,085**	**66.8**	**62.4**	**6.6**
Aboriginal identity population[1]	**823,890**	519,250	442,395	76,860	304,635	63.0	53.7	14.8
North American Indian	**473,235**	278,455	228,285	50,175	194,780	58.8	48.2	18.0
Métis	**291,325**	204,165	183,785	20,375	87,165	70.1	63.1	10.0
Inuit	**32,775**	20,100	16,020	4,080	12,675	61.3	48.9	20.3
Multiple Aboriginal identities	**5,590**	3,595	3,290	310	1,990	64.3	58.9	8.6
Other Aboriginal identity	**20,960**	12,935	11,015	1,920	8,025	61.7	52.6	14.8
Non-Aboriginal population	**24,840,335**	16,626,880	15,578,780	1,048,100	8,213,450	66.9	62.7	6.3
Males	**12,470,785**	**9,020,595**	**8,431,530**	**589,065**	**3,450,190**	**72.3**	**67.6**	**6.5**
Aboriginal identity population[1]	**393,680**	264,980	222,350	42,625	128,700	67.3	56.5	16.1
North American Indian	**223,370**	141,100	113,150	27,950	82,275	63.2	50.7	19.8
Métis	**142,840**	105,790	94,720	11,070	37,050	74.1	66.3	10.5
Inuit	**15,965**	10,195	7,770	2,430	5,770	63.9	48.7	23.8
Multiple Aboriginal identities	**2,610**	1,810	1,615	195	800	69.3	61.9	10.8
Other Aboriginal identity	**8,890**	6,085	5,100	985	2,805	68.4	57.4	16.2
Non-Aboriginal population	**12,077,100**	8,755,615	8,209,180	546,435	3,321,485	72.5	68.0	6.2
Females	**13,193,435**	**8,125,540**	**7,589,650**	**535,890**	**5,067,895**	**61.6**	**57.5**	**6.6**
Aboriginal identity population[1]	**430,205**	254,270	220,040	34,230	175,935	59.1	51.1	13.5
North American Indian	**249,860**	137,360	115,135	22,220	112,505	55.0	46.1	16.2
Métis	**148,490**	98,370	89,060	9,310	50,120	66.2	60.0	9.5
Inuit	**16,810**	9,905	8,255	1,645	6,905	58.9	49.1	16.6
Multiple Aboriginal identities	**2,975**	1,785	1,670	115	1,190	60.0	56.1	6.4
Other Aboriginal identity	**12,065**	6,850	5,920	935	5,215	56.8	49.1	13.6
Non-Aboriginal population	**12,763,230**	7,871,265	7,369,605	501,660	4,891,960	61.7	57.7	6.4

Note: Population aged 15 years and older.
1. The Aboriginal identity population comprises the Aboriginal groups (North American Indian, Métis and Inuit), multiple Aboriginal responses and Aboriginal responses not included elsewhere.
Source: Statistics Canada, 2006 Census of Population.

Table 1.5 Aboriginal languages indicators for First Nations people, Canada, 2006

	Aboriginal mother tongue[1]		Knowledge of an Aboriginal language[2]	
	number	% change from 2001 to 2006[3]	number	% change from 2001 to 2006[3]
Cree	76,460	10	87,285	7
Ojibway	24,410	-2	30,255	-2
Oji-Cree	11,605	18	12,435	20
Montagnais-Naskapi	10,470	8	11,080	10
Dene	8,495	9	9,250	8
Mi'kmaq	7,685	4	8,540	0
Siouan languages (Dakota/Sioux)[4]	5,675	34	6,285	32
Atikamekw	5,140	11	5,320	12
Blackfoot	3,270	11	4,760	10
Salish languages, not included elswhere	1,990	6	2,800	-1
Algonquin	2,020	10	2,560	12
Dogrib	2,055	10	2,540	17
Carrier	1,800	29	2,320	18
South Slave	1,575	15	2,160	7

1. The first language learned at home in childhood and still understood.
2. Languages in which the respondent can conduct a conversation.
3. Data have been adjusted to account for incompletely enumerated reserves in 2001 and 2006.
4. Caution should be exercised when analysing data for Siouan languages (Dakota/Sioux) due to some overestimation in British Columbia in 2001.

Source: Statistics Canada, censuses of population, 2001 and 2006.

Agriculture

2

Canada's farm population is continuing its long-term decline and those minding the farm tend to be older.

In 2006, the farm population was 684,260: 1 in 46 Canadians now lives on a farm, compared with nearly 1 in 3 in 1931.

Canada had 327,055 farm operators in 2006, down nearly 6% from 2001. Farms may have more than one operator. In 2006, nearly 41% of these farm operators were aged 55 and older; among the self-employed labour force as a whole, 29% were 55 and older. At 51.0 years, farmers and farm managers had the highest median age of all occupations in the country. In comparison, the median age for the labour force was 41.2 years.

More operators are working off the farm: in 2006, just over 46% reported that their main occupation was something other than agriculture. The top off-farm occupation for male farm operators was running transportation equipment. For female farm operators, clerical occupations predominated.

Revenue measures industry's health

Canadian farmers generated $41.8 billion from the sale of crops and livestock in 2008, 14% more than in 2007. Receipts for crop producers totalled $23.0 billion in 2008, up nearly 26% from 2007 as a result of higher prices, driven by tight world supplies and strong demand. Revenue from Canada's two main cash crops rose in 2008.

Receipts from wheat (including durum, the wheat used for pasta) were up 49%; receipts from canola, 42%. Stronger grain and oilseed prices, particularly in the first three quarters of 2008, were the main factor behind these gains.

In the crop sector, while grain and oilseed prices climbed, so did the cost of their inputs. Fertilizer prices rose 60% and diesel fuel prices rose 37% during the

Chart 2.1
Farm Product Price Index, selected commodities

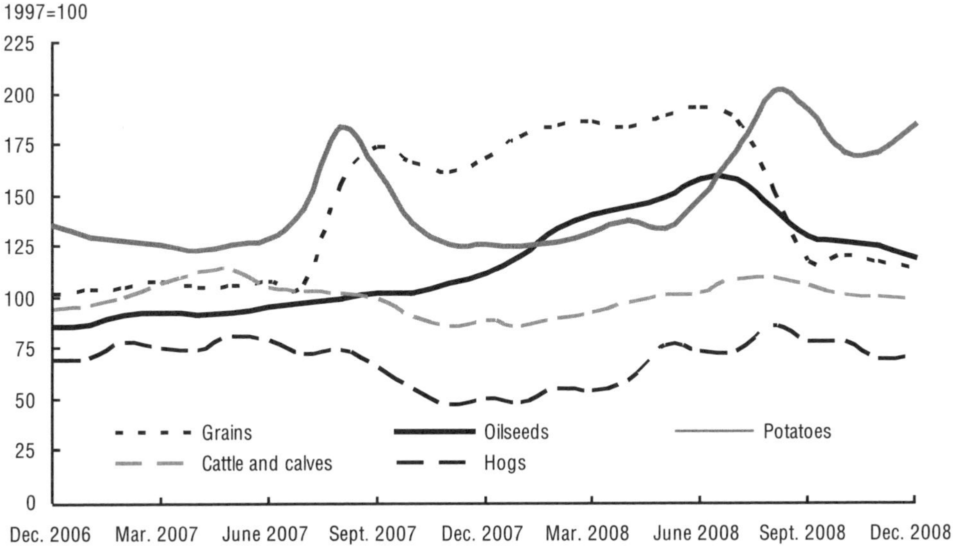

Source: Statistics Canada, CANSIM table 002-0021.

first 11 months of 2008 compared with the same period in 2007.

Livestock receipts in 2008 rose nearly 3% to $18.8 billion. Revenue from cattle and calves gained almost 3%: prices fell nearly 1%, but a record number of cattle were marketed.

Receipts from cattle and calf exports rose nearly 6% from 2007.

Both receipts and volumes rose for milk, poultry and eggs: this supply-managed sector posted a 6% increase in receipts. These commodities together accounted for 44% of total livestock receipts.

In the hog industry, receipts fell 3%, shipments, 1%, and prices, 2%.

Across the livestock sector, higher grain prices pushed up feed costs for much of the year, and profits were also hurt by a strong Canadian dollar.

The number of cattle and hogs on farms declined in 2008. Hog inventories were down more than 10% to 12.2 million, continuing a three-year decline. The number of cattle—beef and dairy—dropped 5% to 13.2 million head as of January 1, 2009.

Table 2.a
Farm population and total population, rural and urban, 2001 and 2006

	2001	2006
	number	
Total farm population[1]	**729,405**	**684,260**
Rural farm population	697,960	642,715
Urban farm population[2]	31,445	41,540
Total population	**29,914,315**	**31,511,587**
Rural population	6,053,467	6,216,135
Urban population	23,860,848	25,295,452

1. Includes all members of a farm operator's household.
2. Urban areas have a minimum population concentration of 1,000 and a population density of at least 400 per square kilometre. All other territory is considered rural.

Source: Statistics Canada, censuses of agriculture and censuses of population, 2001 and 2006.

Chart 2.2
Farm operators, by age

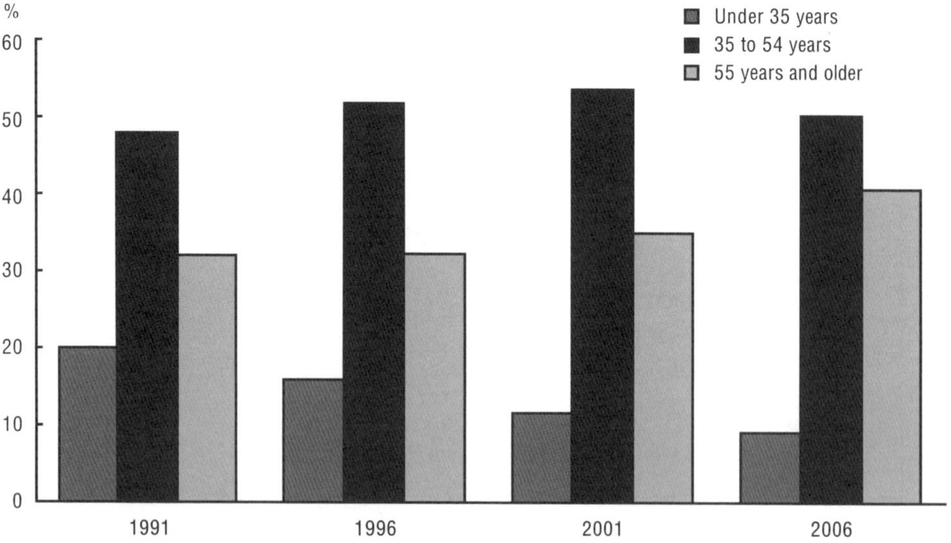

Source: Statistics Canada, Catalogue no. 95-632-X.

It's how you turn it over

The conventional wisdom on tillage, the process of turning over cropland soil with plows or other instruments, has been shifting.

Tilling the soil loosens and aerates it, enabling new plants to push their roots deeper. It also controls weeds, and helps to mix in fertilizer, manure and organic matter, such as last year's crop stubble. However, conventional tillage can lead to wind or water erosion and a loss of soil moisture, and pulling the plow uses fuel and requires more than one pass over a field.

According to the 2006 Census of Agriculture, 28% of Canada's crop acreage was tilled conventionally—a process involving turning over most of the crop residue into the soil—compared with 69% of the acreage in 1991. In 2006, 46% of the acreage was planted using the no-till method, in which seeds are pushed into the soil with minimal disturbance of the soil surface, compared with 7% in 1991.

Chart 2.3
Tillage methods

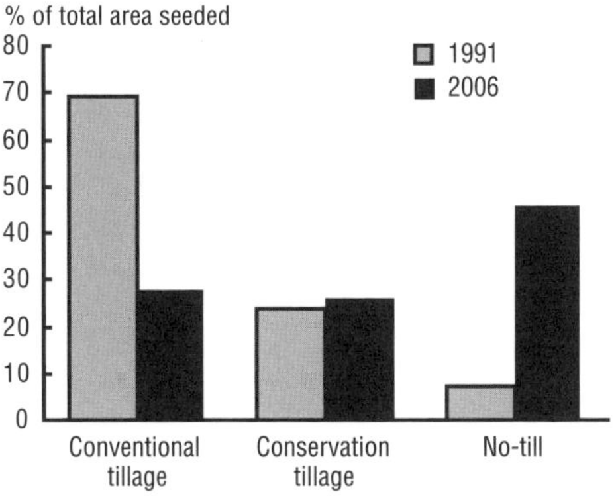

Source: Statistics Canada, Catalogue no. 16-002-X.

More 'million-dollar' farms

Canada had 5,902 'million-dollar' farms in 2006—farms with gross receipts from the sale of products totalling $1 million or more (at 2005 constant prices). The 2001 Census of Agriculture counted 4,453 such farms.

Million-dollar farms made up less than 3% of the 229,373 farms counted in the 2006 Census, but accounted for nearly 40% of total farm receipts.

Hog farms comprised less than 3% of all farm operations in Canada, but nearly 18% of them were million-dollar operations—the highest proportion of any farm type.

Conversely, field crops is Canada's most common farm type. This type of farm accounts for nearly 40% of all farms in 2006, but less than 2% of them were million-dollar operations.

Chart 2.4
Number of farms, by total gross farm receipts

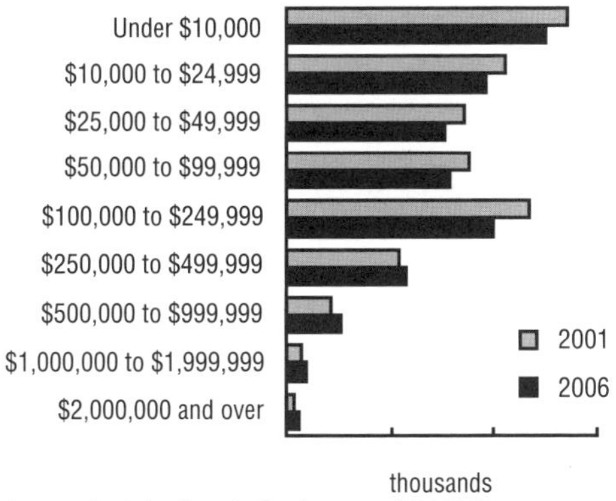

Source: Statistics Canada, Catalogue no. 95-629-X.

Most million-dollar farms seem profitable: in 2006, 86% of them reported earning enough in farm receipts to cover expenses, compared with 56% of all farms.

Table 2.1 Livestock and poultry, 1995 to 2009

	1995	1996	1997	1998	1999	2000
	thousands					
Inventory on January 1						
Cattle	12,709	13,402	13,412	13,360	13,211	13,201
Bulls[1]	249	249	246	236	225	230
Milk cows	1,245	1,237	1,231	1,184	1,157	1,103
Beef cows	4,252	4,381	4,387	4,361	4,386	4,452
Dairy heifers[2]	528	524	531	511	494	487
Beef heifers[2]	1,290	1,418	1,388	1,433	1,309	1,347
For breeding	778	814	724	687	605	645
For market	512	604	664	746	704	703
Steers[3]	775	864	981	1,004	1,197	1,267
Calves	4,370	4,728	4,648	4,631	4,443	4,315
Pigs	11,291	11,588	11,480	11,985	12,429	12,904
Breeding stock	1,195	1,152	1,195	1,287	1,304	1,346
Boars,[4] six months and older	67	61	58	58	54	49
Sows[5] and gilts,[6] six months and older	1,128	1,091	1,136	1,229	1,250	1,297
All other pigs	10,096	10,436	10,285	10,698	11,125	11,559
Under 20 kilograms	3,280	3,300	3,317	3,505	3,872	3,918
20 to 60 kilograms	3,497	3,504	3,511	3,635	3,678	3,916
Over 60 kilograms	3,319	3,632	3,457	3,559	3,576	3,725
Sheep, 1 year and older	441	456	447	465	490	543
Rams[7]	23	22	23	24	25	28
Ewes[8]	418	434	425	441	465	515
Lambs	176	187	180	197	227	251
	thousands					
Production						
Chickens	486,218	501,289	516,952	541,278	570,468	590,623
Turkeys	21,255	21,475	20,999	20,070	20,087	21,268

1. Uncastrated male bovines.
2. Female bovines that have never borne young.
3. Castrated male bovines.
4. Uncastrated male pigs.
5. Female pigs that have borne young.
6. Female pigs that have never borne young.
7. Male sheep.
8. Female sheep that have borne young.

Source: Statistics Canada, CANSIM tables 003-0004, 003-0018, 003-0019, 003-0031 and 003-0032.

2001	2002	2003	2004	2005	2006	2007	2008	2009
thousands								
13,608	13,752	13,466	14,555	14,925	14,655	14,155	13,895	13,180
239	237	239	270	273	264	245	247	243
1,091	1,084	1,066	1,055	1,041	1,019	995	984	978
4,602	4,636	4,752	5,019	5,284	5,247	5,020	4,982	4,655
498	508	512	504	518	495	480	471	456
1,475	1,518	1,453	1,558	1,583	1,615	1,551	1,578	1,362
674	654	648	688	638	628	587	595	537
801	865	805	871	945	987	964	983	825
1,222	1,195	1,174	1,203	1,160	1,147	1,145	1,102	1,058
4,482	4,574	4,270	4,945	5,067	4,868	4,720	4,532	4,430
13,576	14,375	14,745	14,725	14,810	15,110	14,907	13,810	12,180
1,406	1,512	1,569	1,615	1,634	1,605	1,579	1,512	1,395
46	44	42	39	37	35	33	30	24
1,361	1,468	1,527	1,576	1,597	1,571	1,546	1,483	1,371
12,169	12,863	13,177	13,110	13,176	13,505	13,328	12,298	10,786
4,115	4,239	4,369	4,545	4,487	4,476	4,545	4,472	3,689
4,127	4,340	4,454	4,371	4,413	4,623	4,532	3,962	3,619
3,928	4,284	4,354	4,195	4,277	4,406	4,251	3,864	3,478
606	644	641	641	633	589	584	557	546
30	29	29	27	27	26	26	24	24
576	615	613	613	606	563	558	533	522
342	349	334	354	345	305	295	269	262
thousands								
624,792	625,692	615,939	613,527	626,251	622,242	640,329	640,281	..
20,191	19,672	19,834	19,526	20,492	21,172	21,757	22,849	..

Table 2.2 Principal field crops, seeded areas, 1995 to 2009

	1995	1996	1997	1998	1999	2000	2001
	hectares[1]						
All wheat	11,365,800	12,488,361	11,576,100	10,870,600	10,469,000	11,072,200	10,950,500
Spring wheat	8,822,500	9,983,447	9,016,600	7,533,200	8,288,900	8,001,100	8,325,400
Winter wheat	358,000	441,114	327,600	403,500	395,400	428,500	460,100
Durum wheat	2,185,300	2,063,800	2,231,900	2,933,900	1,784,700	2,642,600	2,165,000
Oats	1,579,400	2,060,342	1,876,300	2,062,600	1,885,700	1,825,700	1,907,400
Barley	4,654,300	5,238,025	5,021,500	4,632,300	4,409,100	5,101,300	4,700,200
All rye	215,300	218,265	208,000	267,300	225,000	188,200	181,400
Fall rye	197,100	202,065	191,800	249,100	208,800	167,900	163,200
Spring rye	18,200	16,200	16,200	18,200	16,200	20,300	18,200
Mixed grains	321,000	291,619	317,800	275,200	278,700	290,200	364,200
Corn for grain	1,006,500	1,130,775	1,052,500	1,126,500	1,166,200	1,206,000	1,294,200
Buckwheat	17,100	17,775	15,800	14,700	13,900	15,900	15,900
Dry field peas	819,400	544,300	848,500	1,084,500	851,300	1,240,200	1,343,600
Dry white beans	61,700	42,560	47,900	39,800	79,200	80,600	84,400
Coloured beans	43,200	43,144	43,900	54,100	70,700	84,400	94,900
Flaxseed	876,100	592,900	736,600	878,200	809,400	594,900	671,800
Soybeans	826,100	875,993	1,061,700	980,600	1,004,000	1,068,700	1,081,500
Mustard seed	267,000	239,100	292,200	283,200	279,900	212,300	165,800
Canola (rapeseed)	5,344,000	3,540,311	4,905,900	5,477,400	5,598,700	4,937,000	3,826,800
Sunflower seed	48,600	36,400	50,600	68,800	85,000	74,800	72,800
Sugar beets	24,900	23,800	14,200	18,200	18,200	17,000	12,100
Tame hay	6,577,600	6,395,660	6,349,500	6,578,600	6,937,100	7,270,700	7,663,400
Fodder corn	170,700	190,523	204,600	200,200	188,600	211,500	233,800
Lentils	333,800	303,500	329,000	378,400	506,300	698,900	708,200
Canary seed	147,600	248,800	113,300	210,400	149,800	165,900	170,000
Fababeans	4,000	1,840	2,400	5,600	2,800	6,100	5,200
Triticale	23,000	25,100	23,000	56,600	74,800	70,800	47,300
Safflower	2,000	800	0	1,200	4,000	5,200	2,400
Caraway seed	..	..	..	..	..	..	7,300
Coriander seed	..	..	..	..	..	..	..
Borage seed	..	..	..	..	..	..	..
Chick peas	..	..	10,500	38,800	141,600	295,400	485,700

1. Conversion factor: 1 hectare equals 2.47 acres.
Source: Statistics Canada, CANSIM table 001-0010.

2002	2003	2004	2005	2006	2007	2008	2009
			hectares[1]				
10,370,400	10,413,300	9,885,100	9,653,900	9,852,200	8,849,500	10,192,400	10,249,000
7,454,800	7,353,900	7,116,200	6,827,300	7,585,000	6,157,200	6,621,900	7,012,200
436,900	647,400	630,200	519,900	731,200	743,700	1,130,200	917,900
2,478,700	2,412,000	2,138,700	2,306,700	1,536,000	1,948,600	2,440,300	2,262,300
2,345,900	2,033,200	1,924,100	1,767,900	2,063,500	2,188,400	1,758,400	1,600,500
5,070,200	4,989,400	4,432,100	4,142,600	3,689,900	4,396,800	3,786,600	3,834,900
159,900	246,400	258,200	207,600	276,200	171,900	168,000	188,200
143,700	228,200	242,000	207,600	276,200	171,900	168,000	188,200
16,200	18,200	16,200	0	0	0	0	..
284,000	240,700	222,400	213,700	335,700	170,700	143,400	142,500
1,299,300	1,264,600	1,184,800	1,113,100	1,093,100	1,391,500	1,204,000	1,248,200
12,100	9,300	6,100	4,000	7,200	2,000	0	..
1,209,900	1,169,300	1,282,900	1,303,000	1,260,500	1,469,000	1,616,600	1,701,700
115,300	72,900	68,800	76,900	76,900	60,700	54,700	14,200
109,700	88,800	88,900	114,800	101,300	92,500	73,600	26,200
692,000	744,600	700,000	760,800	804,800	528,000	631,300	698,100
1,030,300	1,052,800	1,223,000	1,172,400	1,213,500	1,180,100	1,202,400	1,328,900
289,300	339,800	298,600	194,100	133,800	186,200	194,200	222,600
3,876,800	4,735,700	5,218,200	5,369,900	5,283,300	6,321,600	6,539,600	6,066,100
99,500	108,400	80,900	87,000	77,000	80,900	68,800	56,700
12,100	12,100	14,200	13,800	15,700	13,800	7,300	..
7,806,500	7,879,000	8,024,500	8,169,900	8,237,000	8,239,200	8,201,600	..
226,000	233,900	234,800	222,800	270,700	246,400	252,200	245,400
540,200	513,400	738,400	802,800	566,500	580,800	651,600	797,200
279,200	259,000	347,900	184,200	135,600	178,100	167,900	113,300
5,200	4,800	6,000	4,800	8,400	6,100	0	..
87,000	78,100	72,900	53,800	57,300	48,600	34,400	16,200
2,000	..	..	..	..	..	..	..
8,100	8,100	4,000	0	5,800	8,100	0	..
8,100	8,100	10,100	10,100	..	..	..	..
2,000	2,000	4,000	0	0	2,000	..	..
192,200	62,700	46,600	78,800	129,100	174,000	44,400	0

Table 2.3 Principal field crop production, 1994 to 2008

	1994	1995	1996	1997	1998	1999	2000
	tonnes						
All wheat	22,919,500	24,989,400	29,801,400	24,299,400	24,082,300	26,959,900	26,535,500
Spring wheat	16,944,400	18,847,100	24,146,900	19,032,400	16,564,600	20,900,800	19,027,000
Winter wheat	1,340,300	1,493,900	1,027,900	915,300	1,475,800	1,718,200	1,800,000
Durum wheat	4,634,800	4,648,400	4,626,600	4,351,700	6,041,900	4,340,900	5,708,500
Oats	3,640,500	2,872,800	4,361,100	3,489,300	3,957,500	3,641,300	3,403,300
Barley	11,692,000	13,032,500	15,562,000	13,533,900	12,708,700	13,196,000	13,228,600
All rye	399,700	309,600	309,400	320,000	408,200	386,600	260,300
Fall rye	348,900	291,800	291,100	303,400	391,700	366,800	247,000
Spring rye	50,800	17,800	18,300	16,600	16,500	19,800	13,300
Mixed grains	630,900	653,300	581,900	626,400	540,000	462,800	434,900
Corn for grain	7,189,900	7,280,900	7,541,700	7,179,800	8,952,400	9,161,300	6,953,700
Buckwheat	12,400	21,200	22,200	16,500	14,800	12,500	13,600
Dry field peas	1,441,000	1,454,700	1,173,000	1,762,300	2,336,800	2,251,900	2,864,300
Dry white beans	84,800	116,200	61,200	82,600	73,900	149,100	119,300
Coloured beans	85,900	86,900	71,800	85,400	111,200	135,400	142,100
Flaxseed	967,700	1,104,900	851,000	895,400	1,080,900	1,022,400	693,400
Soybeans	2,253,700	2,297,500	2,169,500	2,737,700	2,736,600	2,780,900	2,703,000
Mustard seed	319,300	244,300	230,800	243,400	238,600	306,400	202,200
Canola (rapeseed)	7,232,500	6,434,200	5,062,300	6,393,100	7,643,300	8,798,300	7,205,300
Sunflower seed	117,000	66,200	54,900	65,100	111,800	121,900	119,300
Sugar beets	1,091,300	1,026,900	1,034,200	635,000	880,000	743,900	821,000
Tame hay	31,141,300	26,851,400	28,025,000	21,137,500	21,825,000	25,032,900	23,921,600
Fodder corn	4,743,800	4,995,700	5,375,400	5,466,600	6,425,600	6,611,500	5,890,300
Lentils	450,400	431,900	402,500	378,800	479,800	723,800	914,100
Canary seed	240,400	154,600	284,600	115,000	235,300	166,000	170,800
Fababeans	6,800	5,800	5,520	4,300	13,700	6,500	15,400
Triticale	40,700	39,900	35,200	31,000	85,300	126,200	89,700
Safflower	1,100	2,000	700	0	1,400	3,800	6,700
Caraway seed	..	..	..	..	..	..	..
Coriander seed	..	..	..	..	..	..	..
Borage seed	..	..	..	..	..	..	..
Chick peas	..	..	..	14,500	50,900	187,200	387,500

Source: Statistics Canada, CANSIM table 001-0010.

2001	2002	2003	2004	2005	2006	2007	2008
tonnes							
20,630,200	15,961,300	23,048,600	24,795,500	25,748,100	25,265,400	20,054,000	28,611,100
16,010,200	10,531,200	16,124,700	17,530,300	17,803,300	18,617,300	13,873,400	18,404,900
1,570,500	1,553,200	2,712,300	2,463,800	2,030,200	3,301,900	2,499,200	4,686,900
3,049,500	3,876,900	4,211,600	4,801,400	5,914,600	3,346,200	3,681,400	5,519,300
2,690,700	2,910,700	3,376,700	3,467,200	3,282,700	3,852,200	4,696,300	4,272,600
10,845,600	7,467,700	12,164,200	12,556,700	11,677,600	9,573,100	10,983,900	11,781,400
227,800	133,800	327,100	397,500	330,400	382,900	233,000	316,200
215,600	129,400	307,800	383,500	330,400	382,900	233,000	316,200
12,200	4,400	19,300	14,000	..	..	..	..
446,500	358,900	384,400	342,500	316,400	346,500	262,600	221,900
8,389,200	8,998,800	9,587,300	8,836,800	9,332,200	8,989,800	11,648,700	10,592,000
16,300	12,200	9,900	1,500	4,600	7,400	2,300	0
2,044,800	1,283,800	1,930,900	3,097,200	2,993,600	2,519,900	2,934,800	3,571,300
136,200	209,700	151,000	80,700	117,900	159,700	105,200	108,900
153,000	197,100	193,300	137,400	199,600	212,900	171,600	157,300
715,000	679,400	754,400	516,900	990,600	988,800	633,500	861,100
1,635,200	2,335,700	2,273,300	3,043,900	3,155,600	3,465,500	2,695,700	3,335,900
107,100	154,300	226,100	286,700	183,800	108,200	123,400	161,000
5,017,100	4,520,500	6,771,200	7,673,600	9,483,300	9,000,300	9,528,500	12,642,900
103,800	157,400	142,300	52,200	84,400	157,300	124,800	112,200
544,300	344,700	680,400	743,900	607,800	870,900	762,000	344,700
20,373,500	18,396,700	23,265,800	27,307,400	29,555,100	29,966,200	30,217,400	30,431,500
6,079,000	6,355,800	7,213,000	7,795,400	7,653,000	9,680,600	8,136,600	8,840,600
566,300	328,000	484,600	915,800	1,164,300	692,800	733,900	919,500
113,900	177,500	234,600	300,500	227,200	133,100	162,000	195,600
10,200	9,100	8,400	15,300	9,800	16,000	10,900	0
31,200	26,000	64,400	80,000	43,200	26,900	47,000	37,900
2,900	1,100	..	..	..	..	..	..
2,000	2,400	3,200	2,500	0	0	..	..
..	5,200	4,800	7,900	8,900	..	..	..
..	800	500	700	0	0	200	..
455,000	144,500	67,600	51,200	103,900	163,200	224,800	67,000

Table 2.4 Principal field crop production, by province, 2008

	Canada	Newfoundland and Labrador	Prince Edward Island	Nova Scotia	New Brunswick
	tonnes				
All wheat	**28,611,100**	.	42,900	11,700	5,800
Spring wheat	**18,404,900**	.	36,200	2,400	5,400
Winter wheat	**4,686,900**	.	6,700	9,300	400
Durum wheat	**5,519,300**	.	.	.	.
Oats	**4,272,600**	.	13,000	5,100	22,700
Barley	**11,781,400**	.	80,000	10,200	32,300
Fall rye	**316,200**	.	..	..	.
Mixed grains	**221,900**	.	7,300	..	..
Corn for grain	**10,592,000**	.	.	39,300	35,100
Buckwheat	**0**	.	.	.	.
Dry field peas	**3,571,300**	.	.	.	.
Dry white beans	**108,900**	.	.	.	.
Coloured beans	**157,300**	.	.	.	.
Flaxseed	**861,100**	.	.	.	.
Soybeans	**3,335,900**	.	17,100	.	.
Mustard seed	**161,000**	.	.	.	.
Canola (rapeseed)	**12,642,900**	.	.	.	.
Sunflower seed	**112,200**	.	.	.	.
Sugar beets	**344,700**	.	.	.	.
Tame hay	**30,431,500**	32,700	281,200	326,600	333,800
Fodder corn	**8,840,600**	.	95,300	88,900	61,700
Lentils	**919,500**	.	.	.	.
Canary seed	**195,600**	.	.	.	.
Fababeans	**0**	.	.	.	.
Triticale	**37,900**	.	.	.	.
Coriander seed	**..**	.	.	.	.
Chick peas	**67,000**	.	.	.	.

Source: Statistics Canada, CANSIM table 001-0010.

Quebec	Ontario	Manitoba	Saskatchewan	Alberta	British Columbia
			tonnes		
149,500	2,903,900	4,280,900	12,437,500	8,736,200	42,700
137,000	228,600	3,264,400	7,416,200	7,272,000	42,700
12,500	2,675,300	1,016,500	579,700	386,500	..
.	.	..	4,441,600	1,077,700	.
205,000	67,900	1,116,600	2,267,100	541,300	33,900
258,000	191,600	1,121,300	4,594,000	5,447,500	46,500
0	45,700	83,800	110,500	76,200	0
48,000	118,800	5,200	11,000	30,600	1,000
3,150,000	6,858,300	473,700	.	35,600	.
..	..	0	.	.	.
.	.	107,500	2,732,400	731,400	0
..	72,600	36,300	.	..	.
7,700	55,100	59,600	.	34,900	.
.	.	161,300	666,800	33,000	.
600,000	2,476,600	242,200	.	.	.
.	.	..	123,900	37,100	.
33,000	49,900	2,576,400	5,629,100	4,322,700	31,800
.	.	112,200	..	..	.
..	.	..	.	344,700	.
4,600,300	6,078,100	3,447,300	4,490,600	9,344,000	1,496,900
1,600,300	4,808,100	1,143,100	.	571,500	408,200
.	.	..	919,500	..	.
.	.	11,000	184,600	..	.
.	.	0	..	0	.
.	.	0	18,500	19,400	.
.	.	.	..	.	.
.	.	.	67,000	0	.

Table 2.5 Farm cash receipts, crops 1994 to 2008

	1994	1995	1996	1997	1998	1999
	$ thousands					
Total crop receipts	**11,542,606**	**13,114,105**	**14,016,229**	**14,093,889**	**13,642,036**	**13,121,182**
Wheat	2,436,389	2,823,648	3,482,441	3,521,262	2,419,075	2,338,900
Marketing board payments[1]	1,367,430	1,432,766	1,123,878	725,720	948,849	948,353
Oats	144,883	224,863	305,427	263,857	193,228	174,622
Barley	517,327	719,800	960,127	727,160	510,285	421,352
Deferred grain receipts	-772,840	-843,814	-1,036,068	-1,000,195	-951,219	-612,127
Liquidation of deferred grain receipts	356,092	772,840	843,814	1,036,068	1,000,190	965,148
Rye	24,310	30,776	38,989	34,242	19,743	17,212
Flaxseed	184,905	230,310	220,875	291,632	262,858	138,965
Canola (rapeseed)	2,111,164	1,906,362	1,968,956	2,127,750	2,663,207	1,771,011
Soybeans	506,678	661,659	626,673	814,222	800,348	618,194
Corn	505,789	704,294	808,128	696,106	642,363	742,902
Sugar beets	40,548	52,043	40,670	34,483	39,838	30,527
Potatoes	533,104	517,641	533,124	512,581	612,166	700,669
Greenhouse vegetables	..	..	218,473	270,361	376,949	438,491
Other vegetables	..	..	749,685	778,440	791,025	782,354
Vegetables	863,319	923,155	..	..	..	..
Apples	143,898	184,149	186,587	177,700	168,718	182,629
Other tree fruits	63,875	68,116	54,853	57,135	63,100	70,360
Blueberries	..	..	..	..	..	..
Strawberries	63,202	68,128	48,639	49,979	53,015	53,590
Grapes	..	..	..	..	..	..
Other berries and grapes	156,011	172,610	206,101	202,124	201,996	268,504
Floriculture, nursery and sod	883,978	941,540	999,335	1,095,216	1,059,689	1,195,407
Floriculture	..	..	..	..	..	..
Nursery	..	..	..	..	..	..
Sod	..	..	..	..	..	..
Tobacco	373,946	296,647	345,332	353,267	358,610	356,706
Mustard seed	69,075	74,553	110,974	95,161	87,716	89,486
Sunflower seed	17,396	25,742	19,607	17,166	26,282	30,326
Lentils	97,808	134,667	135,279	97,570	120,786	195,960
Canary seed	39,282	58,392	81,652	48,229	40,285	39,667
Dry beans	79,589	101,383	63,808	72,467	98,922	125,061
Dry peas	192,485	217,900	219,825	239,337	275,313	262,147
Chick peas	..	..	..	912	6,180	21,944
Forage and grass seed	45,872	46,980	66,785	77,518	87,346	84,867
Hay and clover	102,947	132,077	137,283	171,294	179,346	204,849
Maple products	100,393	90,975	121,386	131,098	137,470	147,277
Forest products	161,661	180,061	167,537	156,144	144,173	132,215
Miscellaneous crops	85,383	93,172	88,039	98,961	92,508	78,308
Ginseng	46,707	70,670	78,015	63,467	58,661	45,231
Christmas trees	..	..	..	66,884	60,318	63,413

1. Payments made directly to producers by the Canadian Wheat Board, the Ontario Wheat Producers' Marketing Board and, starting in 2006, by the *Fédération des producteurs de cultures commerciales du Québec.*

Source: Statistics Canada, CANSIM table 002-0001.

2000	2001	2002	2003	2004	2005	2006	2007	2008
				$ thousands				
12,969,706	**13,504,866**	**14,411,906**	**13,312,062**	**14,420,425**	**13,498,283**	**14,595,189**	**18,425,255**	**23,075,675**
2,354,516	2,562,831	2,459,795	2,240,026	2,130,954	1,761,947	2,183,859	2,907,627	4,325,703
811,564	1,042,085	981,534	337,267	1,007,545	842,575	728,644	1,454,342	1,578,875
196,414	273,962	305,208	243,168	231,433	257,040	332,765	426,846	564,800
477,973	621,288	505,355	370,948	455,227	343,279	353,271	685,673	776,203
-600,798	-901,715	-707,482	-720,785	-725,334	-440,888	-564,327	-956,851	-1,444,207
668,747	617,916	865,783	716,026	740,301	688,582	442,871	588,097	1,000,683
15,285	16,210	12,182	12,440	29,457	13,050	15,913	36,557	31,511
148,743	165,737	236,609	192,160	198,722	171,221	158,805	246,963	340,804
1,559,711	1,723,004	1,776,767	1,889,576	2,151,367	1,826,124	2,503,038	3,451,624	4,904,485
677,947	534,482	587,657	758,345	630,764	760,350	679,914	1,030,131	1,125,826
676,073	630,884	819,169	786,685	794,416	622,774	753,676	1,048,099	1,545,159
32,899	19,333	20,072	22,732	30,921	32,140	38,180	34,726	23,543
682,785	722,874	917,617	845,723	820,195	787,452	895,586	866,675	987,165
504,713	589,710	595,780	637,145	739,176	744,616	796,376	805,812	799,834
796,612	866,539	836,640	883,358	900,312	892,190	942,713	977,645	1,030,703
..	..	..	..	..	..	..	..	..
192,597	181,209	153,127	146,276	148,360	147,230	148,596	161,981	168,890
67,919	..	..	..	..	..	..	..	..
..	84,236	86,308	116,589	151,337	168,863	224,939	189,940	158,729
53,550	55,890	52,396	53,475	56,890	58,690	60,782	60,585	61,140
..	74,655	77,085	55,790	82,400	54,650	94,065	111,091	112,880
232,888	..	..	..	..	..	..	..	..
1,417,392	1,496,750	1,644,909	1,690,984	1,731,320	1,707,458	1,702,263	1,746,726	1,856,885
..	1,076,423	1,197,679	1,226,791	1,252,517	1,205,112	1,186,003	1,188,871	1,265,679
..	339,175	359,857	360,401	372,623	388,987	389,103	430,051	456,715
..	81,153	87,371	103,793	106,182	113,359	127,156	127,803	134,494
348,427	240,007	274,150	222,256	231,181	194,942	178,683	79,269	70,360
63,774	54,142	58,163	75,395	75,494	59,698	51,627	90,396	145,474
31,237	33,495	45,610	51,115	31,746	19,705	34,170	70,194	58,432
233,525	178,152	132,095	144,593	204,998	215,939	198,339	343,917	632,991
34,383	50,462	92,635	75,470	54,886	39,778	46,627	76,407	110,200
123,029	101,474	139,089	141,843	151,916	155,345	153,268	165,097	195,624
269,772	304,475	252,978	253,495	342,672	307,136	317,865	562,747	630,682
63,113	149,057	121,018	18,525	7,295	17,113	49,784	48,641	40,881
82,882	67,218	76,854	65,150	71,543	83,721	91,092	79,327	75,134
265,148	327,000	345,071	314,726	286,131	263,609	245,475	257,506	274,554
180,680	145,777	150,251	153,245	147,996	189,644	185,218	165,518	209,673
120,250	117,952	115,663	113,366	111,071	108,776	113,670	125,145	119,887
73,340	85,954	97,519	94,519	104,739	100,159	111,405	143,830	179,589
46,716	60,099	68,241	70,899	52,870	69,956	64,364	91,386	73,294
67,216	76,239	75,433	69,280	65,023	65,761	66,030	58,669	67,472

Table 2.6 Farm cash receipts, livestock and livestock products and direct payments, 1994 to 2008

	1994	1995	1996	1997	1998	1999
	$ thousands					
Total farm cash receipts from crops and livestock	**25,881,396**	**27,123,321**	**29,075,327**	**29,835,513**	**29,505,263**	**30,256,780**
Total receipts from livestock and livestock products	12,513,891	12,703,800	13,857,294	14,632,865	14,441,683	15,159,564
Cattle	4,256,085	4,147,003	4,358,769	4,764,242	5,149,009	5,465,302
Calves	556,845	460,186	371,990	526,849	554,635	716,237
Hogs	2,031,823	2,252,460	2,884,759	2,989,331	2,201,164	2,395,475
Sheep	2,908	3,206	3,026	3,494	4,034	4,013
Lambs	60,875	66,403	74,812	71,844	67,723	70,463
Dairy products	3,354,465	3,463,085	3,514,733	3,709,267	3,846,077	3,920,935
Hens and chickens	1,060,948	1,050,960	1,248,291	1,298,789	1,356,008	1,320,852
Turkeys	221,061	237,891	266,906	258,588	248,836	240,235
Eggs	559,998	590,826	644,956	482,874	466,165	477,591
Wool[1]	1,127	1,976	1,229	1,506	1,292	555
Honey	51,316	58,209	62,817	74,486	88,593	79,602
Furs	34,192	31,222	57,974	41,261	41,298	30,500
Miscellaneous livestock and livestock products	203,110	214,374	242,507	259,286	260,480	277,403
Hatcheries (chicks and poults)	..	..	..	28,304	32,406	30,233
Total receipts from direct payments	1,824,899	1,305,416	1,201,804	1,108,759	1,421,544	1,976,034
Crop insurance payments[2]	414,825	306,725	256,832	302,721	318,356	239,544
Private hail insurance	198,180	174,738	81,613	71,068	55,855	68,628
Western Grain Stabilization Act payments	-1,323	-626	-4,527	-582	-228	-31
Price stabilization payments	5	2	0	..	..	..
Tripartite payments	67,586	10,551	-461	5,577	-26	2,388
Provincial stabilization payments	300,472	308,128	300,359	170,846	507,947	572,776
Dairy subsidy	222,304	213,553	170,657	146,610	132,113	103,652
Other payments[3]	39,372	67,182	105,525	214,741	139,145	546,516
Net Income Stabilization Account payments	40,619	46,296	114,716	153,322	268,724	444,918
Gross Revenue Insurance Plan payments	542,859	178,867	177,090	44,456	-342	137

1. As of 2001, receipts from wool are accounted for in 'miscellaneous livestock and livestock products.'
2. Data exclude payments under private hail insurance plans.
3. Programs to deal with unusual climatic or economic conditions in the agriculture sector. Starting in 1999, payments under the Western Grain Stabilization Plan, Tripartite Plans and the Gross Revenue Insurance Plan are included in 'other payments.'

Source: Statistics Canada, CANSIM table 002-0001.

2000	2001	2002	2003	2004	2005	2006	2007	2008
				$ thousands				
32,879,399	**36,243,327**	**35,970,624**	**34,244,827**	**36,338,224**	**36,743,561**	**36,949,543**	**40,736,355**	**45,946,150**
17,100,989	18,972,521	18,129,777	16,084,649	17,055,534	18,321,856	17,820,680	18,218,193	18,742,990
6,059,487	6,989,558	6,873,961	4,574,415	4,512,524	5,655,659	5,725,507	5,691,980	5,842,930
826,579	893,228	803,334	588,460	575,359	734,945	733,001	651,155	649,545
3,355,271	3,838,667	3,240,401	3,345,475	4,217,338	3,888,679	3,367,854	3,280,010	3,184,517
5,214	4,743	3,568	4,395	4,246	6,215	6,692	6,125	5,431
81,521	92,273	99,486	96,377	80,088	104,430	125,647	121,989	118,262
4,029,833	4,142,313	4,135,287	4,480,779	4,601,909	4,852,249	4,843,231	5,207,151	5,310,510
1,368,143	1,522,302	1,453,080	1,528,417	1,579,731	1,615,170	1,547,233	1,748,631	1,987,926
263,253	262,503	258,788	262,642	267,824	271,505	278,481	320,202	388,502
511,052	547,868	563,678	566,227	560,520	540,459	560,519	567,548	607,926
780	..	..	..	..	..	..	..	..
69,489	84,868	133,024	157,184	135,384	104,317	104,494	95,645	88,021
46,209	46,203	49,971	49,914	77,512	85,314	96,599	90,174	115,491
313,315	507,216	472,049	388,120	394,396	419,464	391,388	397,181	406,412
32,729	40,778	43,152	42,248	48,703	43,449	40,031	40,399	37,517
2,808,704	3,765,940	3,428,941	4,848,116	4,862,265	4,923,422	4,533,674	4,092,907	4,127,485
451,382	917,589	1,407,047	1,707,485	755,810	820,072	600,268	570,674	598,788
159,254	123,657	86,071	104,507	108,718	116,304	138,832	188,443	316,514
..	..	..	..	..	..	..	..	..
..	..	..	..	..	..	..	..	..
..	..	..	..	..	..	..	..	..
411,180	516,476	395,673	711,321	626,336	390,763	496,919	837,851	643,780
72,666	41,885	8,758	..	..	..	..	..	..
1,258,001	1,724,622	915,707	1,601,738	2,437,261	3,153,942	2,980,709	2,223,736	2,328,657
456,221	441,711	615,685	723,065	934,140	442,340	316,946	272,203	239,746
..	..	..	..	..	..	..	..	..

Table 2.7 Farm operators, by farm type and by province, 2006

	Canada	Newfoundland and Labrador	Prince Edward Island	Nova Scotia
	number			
All operators[1,2]	**327,055**	**715**	**2,335**	**5,095**
Farm type[3]				
Dairy cattle and milk production	**25,770**	55	360	495
Beef cattle ranching and farming, including feedlots	**86,000**	60	475	905
Hog and pig farming	**9,245**	10	90	85
Chicken egg production	**2,680**	20	20	75
Broiler and other meat-type chicken production	**2,935**	5	15	90
Turkey production	**445**	0	5	15
Poultry hatcheries	**70**	0	0	5
Combination poultry and egg production	**240**	0	0	10
Other poultry production	**390**	0	0	0
Sheep farming	**4,260**	30	20	80
Goat farming	**1,525**	5	0	35
Apiculture	**2,170**	5	10	30
Horse and other equine production	**22,905**	15	115	260
Fur-bearing animal and rabbit production	**535**	25	15	125
Livestock combination farming	**10,860**	20	80	220
All other miscellaneous animal production	**3,770**	0	5	25
Soybean farming	**8,390**	0	10	0
Oilseed (except soybean) farming	**13,505**	0	0	0
Dry pea and bean farming	**1,590**	0	0	0
Wheat farming	**15,480**	0	15	5
Corn farming	**4,880**	0	0	10
Other grain farming	**38,145**	5	70	15
Potato farming	**2,405**	30	495	20
Other vegetables (except potato) and melon farming	**5,315**	95	70	175
Fruit and tree-nut farming	**12,185**	50	205	1,185
Mushroom production	**235**	0	0	5
Other food crops grown under cover	**1,410**	10	5	40
Nursery and tree production	**6,895**	60	25	500
Floriculture production	**4,135**	75	15	145
Tobacco farming	**910**	0	0	0
Hay farming	**24,090**	85	110	345
Fruit and vegetable combination farming	**865**	30	10	35
All other miscellaneous crop farming	**12,815**	20	90	165

Note: Each census farm is classified according to the commodity or group of commodities that accounts for 50% or more of its total potential receipts.
1. Figures may not add to totals because of rounding.
2. Farm operators are those responsible for the management decisions made in the operation of a census farm or agricultural operation. Up to three farm operators may be reported per farm.
3. Farm type is based on the North American Industry Classification System (NAICS) 2002 farm-typing categories.
Source: Statistics Canada, 2006 Census of Agriculture.

New Brunswick	Quebec	Ontario	Manitoba	Saskatchewan	Alberta	British Columbia
			number			
3,695	**45,470**	**82,410**	**26,620**	**59,185**	**71,660**	**29,870**
430	12,545	8,540	820	360	1,050	1,115
670	6,375	15,000	9,240	16,795	30,115	6,365
65	2,975	3,395	1,155	315	950	200
45	225	935	180	75	220	880
15	555	1,260	135	110	295	455
5	70	165	35	15	50	85
0	10	20	10	5	10	10
0	30	70	15	5	25	85
0	100	135	15	10	35	85
25	930	1,515	195	260	615	590
20	235	555	105	80	265	225
35	215	530	350	350	395	255
195	1,200	6,560	1,265	1,600	7,095	4,600
20	95	170	25	0	10	45
150	885	3,665	660	1,285	2,365	1,535
30	270	445	180	725	1,605	485
5	475	7,665	225	5	5	0
0	20	35	1,940	7,130	4,270	115
0	0	195	170	1,085	130	5
10	100	1,225	1,645	8,730	3,680	70
5	2,535	2,270	35	0	10	15
35	1,580	6,155	5,050	16,110	8,945	185
340	435	345	240	130	250	110
100	1,240	2,250	145	60	185	1,000
485	1,840	2,835	185	230	360	4,815
5	25	105	0	0	10	80
10	395	510	10	35	135	260
215	910	2,080	215	115	820	1,960
110	740	1,525	210	220	415	690
0	5	900	0	0	0	0
395	2,360	7,965	1,655	2,470	5,855	2,850
30	160	255	15	20	60	250
245	5,935	3,115	510	845	1,435	460

Table 2.8 Farm operators, by sex and age group, census years 2001 and 2006

	2001		2006		2001 to 2006
	number	% of total	number	% of total	% change
All operators[1,2]	**346,195**	**100.0**	**327,055**	**100.0**	**-5.5**
Under 35	39,920	11.5	29,925	9.1	-25.0
35 to 54	185,575	53.6	164,160	50.2	-11.5
55 and older	120,705	34.9	132,975	40.7	10.2
Median age	49	...	51	...	4.1
Male operators	255,015	73.7	236,220	72.2	-7.4
Under 35	29,430	8.5	22,170	6.8	-24.7
35 to 54	132,060	38.1	114,695	35.1	-13.1
55 and older	93,530	27.0	99,360	30.4	6.2
Median age	49	...	52	...	6.1
Female operators	91,180	26.3	90,835	27.8	-0.4
Under 35	10,490	3.0	7,755	2.4	-26.1
35 to 54	53,510	15.5	49,465	15.1	-7.6
55 and older	27,175	7.8	33,615	10.3	23.7
Median age	48	...	50	...	4.2

1. Figures may not add to totals because of rounding. Minor differences can be expected in figures appearing in other tables.
2. Farm operators are those responsible for the management decisions made in the operation of a census farm or agricultural operation. Up to three farm operators may be reported per farm.

Source: Statistics Canada, censuses of agriculture, 2001 and 2006.

Table 2.9 Total farm area, land tenure and land in crops, census years from 1986 to 2006

	1986	1991	1996	2001	2006
			number		
Total number of farms	**293,089**	**280,043**	**276,548**	**246,923**	**229,373**
Total farm area					
Area in hectares[1]	67,825,757	67,753,700	68,054,956	67,502,446	67,586,739
Farms reporting	293,089	280,043	276,548	246,923	229,373
Average area in hectares per farm reporting	231	242	246	273	295
Total area owned					
Area in hectares[1]	43,218,905	42,961,352	43,060,963	42,265,706	41,377,673
Farms reporting	273,963	264,837	262,152	235,131	220,513
Average area in hectares per farm reporting	158	162	164	180	188
Total area rented or leased from others[2]					
Area in hectares[1]	24,606,852	24,792,348	24,993,993	25,236,740	26,209,066
Farms reporting	118,735	111,387	111,718	103,484	97,989
Average area in hectares per farm reporting	207	223	224	244	267
Land in crops (excluding Christmas tree area)					
Area in hectares[1]	33,181,235	33,507,780	34,918,733	36,395,150	35,912,247
Farms reporting	264,141	248,147	237,760	215,581	194,717
Average area in hectares per farm reporting	126	135	147	169	184

1. Conversion factor: 1 hectare equals 2.47 acres.
2. Total area rented or leased from others includes land leased from governments, rented or leased from others and crop-shared from others.

Source: Statistics Canada, censuses of agriculture, 1986 to 2006.

Business, consumer and property services

3

A young person entering the workforce in 2008 was likely to find a job in one of Canada's many service industries. Three-quarters of Canadians work in services—from waiting on tables to designing architectural plans to selling cars and real estate.

And, in the downturn in the last quarter of 2008, jobs in services fared better than jobs in goods-producing industries. From October 2008 to April 2009, employment in the goods-producing sector declined 6.3%. By contrast, employment in the services-producing sector, which is traditionally less sensitive to economic slowdowns, slipped 0.5% over the same period.

Services generated more than $864 billion worth of output in 2008. From 1998 to 2008, the services sector grew by 40.5%, compared with 18.5% growth for goods-producing industries. Among the fastest growing service industries over this decade were administrative support, waste management and remediation services, wholesale trade, as well as professional, scientific and technical services.

Business services

With the growth of the service economy, business support services have become more important to the Canadian economy. Changes in business practices such as outsourcing have been made possible by advances in telecommunications technology. Consequently, the business support services industry—credit bureaus, telephone call centres, and document preparation and business service centres—has seen steady growth.

From 1998 to 2008, the number of jobs in business services increased 275.4%—a growth rate that has outpaced the economy's employment growth rate, (32.9% since 1998). Business services'

Chart 3.1
GDP for goods- and services-producing industries

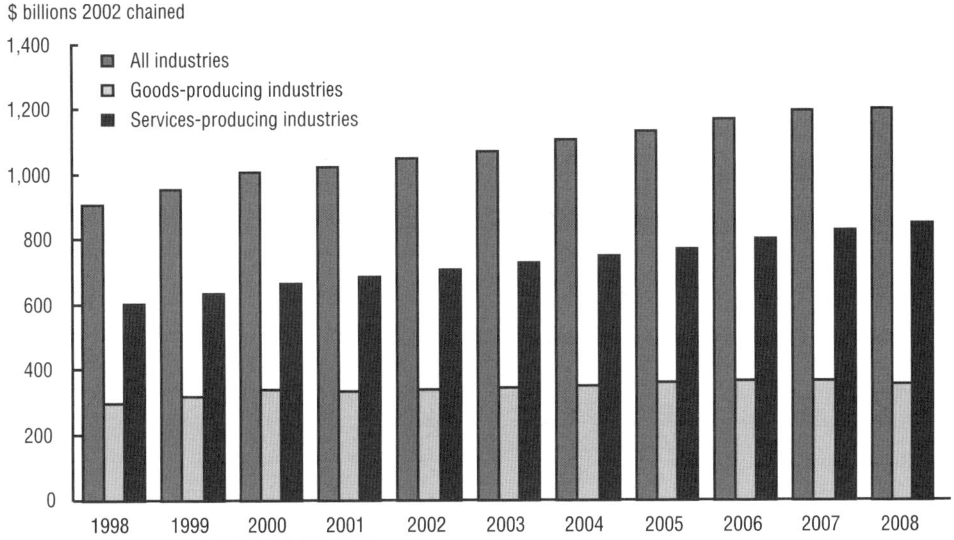

Source: Statistics Canada, CANSIM table 379-0027.

percentage of the overall employment picture nearly tripled from 0.3% in 1998 to 0.8% in 2008.

Personal services

Canadians often turn to the services sector to take care of regular chores and enjoy a little leisure and entertainment. Good economic conditions in 2007, including rising personal disposable income, helped maintain the services growth.

Firms providing personal services earned $9.1 billion in 2007, up 5.5% from 2006. Total operating revenues for the food services and drinking places industry reached $42.4 billion in 2007, up 4.1% from 2006. This continued a trend of increases started in 2004, but the pace in 2007 was more moderate than the 4.9% posted in 2006.

Real estate services

The long-term rise in residential real estate prices has benefited agents, brokers and appraisers, whose total revenues grew by 7.8% to $10.7 billion in 2007.

Real estate sales in Ontario accounted for about half of the operating revenues earned by the industry. Saskatchewan led national growth with a 34% increase in operating revenues.

Table 3.a
GDP of selected services, at basic prices

	2003	2008
	$ millions	
Real estate and rental and leasing	134,681	157,716
Administrative and support services	23,258	27,686
Personal and laundry services and private households	8,024	8,907

Note: Chained 2002 dollars.
Source: Statistics Canada, CANSIM 379-0027.

Chart 3.2
Average weekly earnings, selected services industries

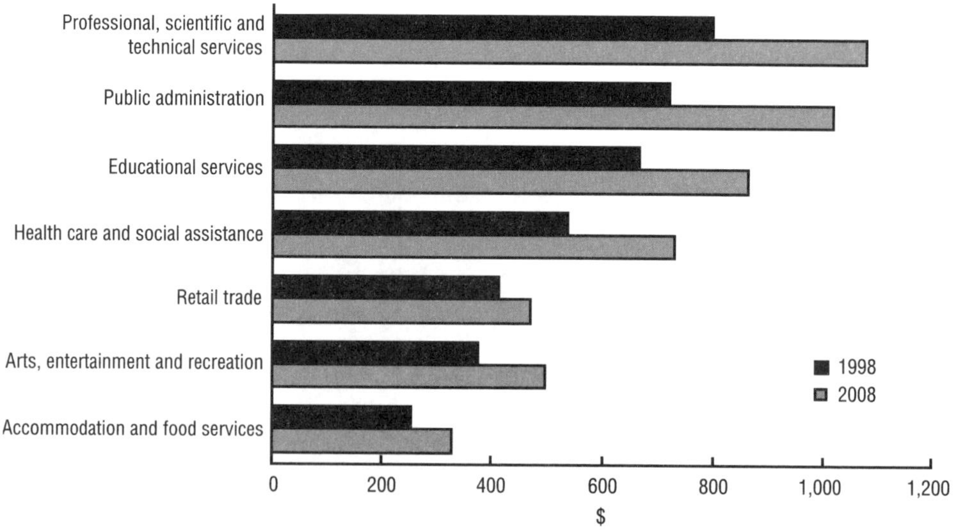

Source: Statistics Canada, CANSIM table 281-0027.

Employment services

With many companies using agencies when looking for new employees or opting to hire temporary employees, the employment services industry has grown in recent years.

Across Canada, 4,698 firms reported that they were in the employment services industry in 2007. Their operating revenues reached $8.9 billion in 2007, up 10.8% from 2006. This followed an 8.5% increase from 2005 to 2006.

Ontario accounted for the majority of the industry with a 59% share of operating revenues, down from 62% in 2002. However, operating revenues grew strongly in Western Canada, with Saskatchewan and British Columbia posting double-digit increases in 2007.

Although temporary staffing services accounted for the bulk of operating revenues earned, its share has declined. Revenue gains for the industry in 2006 and 2007 came almost entirely from permanent placements and contract staffing services.

Chart 3.3
Employment services operating revenues and expenses

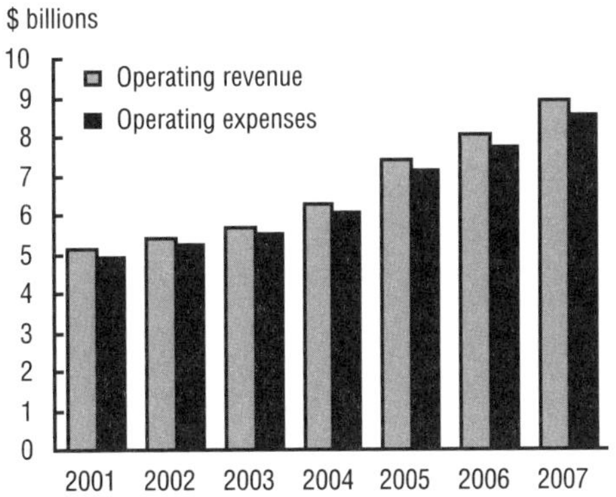

Source: Statistics Canada, CANSIM table 361-0001.

Cable's changing revenue mix

The addition of large numbers of Internet and telephony customers has led to changes in the mix of the cable industry's operating revenues.

Subscription revenues from non-traditional services accounted for 39.4% of all subscription revenues for the industry in 2007, compared with 24.3% in 2003 and 3.8% in 1999. Those revenues rose by 32.2% in 2007 to 2.7 billion, while those from subscriptions to traditional television services rose 6.4% to $4.1 billion.

From December 2006 to December 2007, the proportion of households using cable telephone services expanded from 11% to 15%.

Fewer than one in four households now uses only a traditional land-line telephone service.

Chart 3.4
Cable and satellite subscribers, by type of service

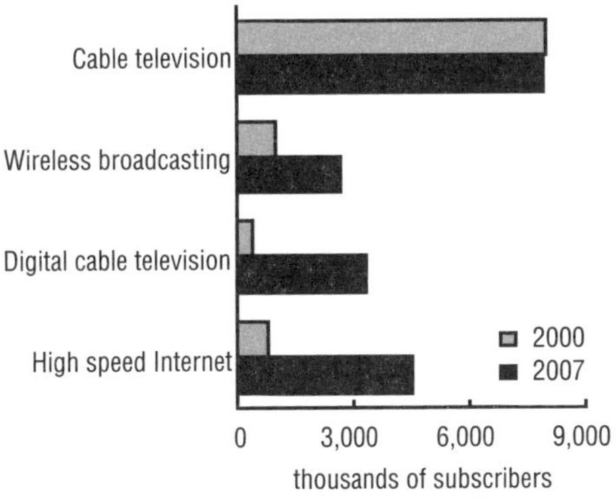

Source: Statistics Canada, CANSIM table 353-0003.

The number of cable Internet subscribers increased from 4.0 million in 2006 to 4.5 million in 2007.

Table 3.1 GDP of goods- and services-producing industries, by province and territory, 2003 to 2008

	2003	2004	2005	2006	2007	2008
			$ millions 2002 chained			
Canada						
Goods-producing industries	**350,817**	**360,281**	**368,147**	**372,320**	**374,126**	**363,863**
Services-producing industries	**740,591**	**764,791**	**787,730**	**818,097**	**846,591**	**864,371**
Newfoundland and Labrador						
Goods-producing industries	7,058	6,866	6,898	7,171	8,293	8,096
Services-producing industries	8,866	8,904	9,145	9,271	9,487	9,804
Prince Edward Island						
Goods-producing industries	910	941	962	987	1,012	998
Services-producing industries	2,499	2,572	2,628	2,684	2,749	2,803
Nova Scotia						
Goods-producing industries	6,427	6,490	6,527	6,290	6,475	6,590
Services-producing industries	18,531	18,816	19,168	19,718	20,076	20,545
New Brunswick						
Goods-producing industries	5,818	5,784	5,670	5,938	5,988	5,743
Services-producing industries	13,790	14,409	14,838	15,098	15,387	15,686
Quebec						
Goods-producing industries	72,826	74,221	74,695	74,343	75,767	75,618
Services-producing industries	153,968	158,025	160,769	165,010	169,382	173,202
Ontario						
Goods-producing industries	135,581	136,258	138,369	136,938	135,852	129,961
Services-producing industries	311,791	322,314	331,447	343,510	354,101	360,071
Manitoba						
Goods-producing industries	9,334	9,391	9,780	10,472	10,813	11,118
Services-producing industries	24,700	25,204	25,668	26,427	27,360	27,999
Saskatchewan						
Goods-producing industries	14,325	15,390	15,897	15,143	15,212	16,009
Services-producing industries	20,126	20,682	21,196	21,902	22,964	23,878
Alberta						
Goods-producing industries	64,092	68,108	70,781	73,734	73,527	70,950
Services-producing industries	84,935	88,952	93,932	100,989	106,724	110,000
British Columbia						
Goods-producing industries	32,429	34,252	35,780	37,331	36,850	35,254
Services-producing industries	97,599	101,026	104,995	109,372	114,029	115,912
Yukon						
Goods-producing industries	140	176	198	211	240	287
Services-producing industries	1,033	1,057	1,093	1,128	1,137	1,157
Northwest Territories						
Goods-producing industries	1,699	1,727	1,641	1,745	2,047	1,806
Services-producing industries	1,638	1,710	1,784	1,816	1,899	1,933
Nunavut						
Goods-producing industries	140	153	147	156	212	249
Services-producing industries	753	778	794	809	826	840

Note: North American Industry Classification System (NAICS), 2002.
Source: Statistics Canada, CANSIM tables 379-0026 and 379-0027.

Table 3.2 Average weekly earnings, by industry, 2004 to 2008

	2004	2005	2006	2007	2008
			$		
All industries (excluding unclassified)	**709.41**	**737.29**	**755.50**	**788.17**	**810.45**
Goods-producing industries	898.09	930.36	947.88	998.61	1,028.65
Forestry, logging and support	894.01	883.89	902.28	907.41	935.84
Mining and oil and gas extraction	1,278.11	1,296.35	1,325.73	1,437.44	1,527.98
Utilities	1,261.08	1,298.32	1,350.66	1,421.49	1,424.73
Construction	846.38	877.34	900.32	961.16	1,014.51
Manufacturing	862.60	896.35	904.69	940.67	949.54
Services-producing industries	658.13	685.77	705.02	734.61	757.02
Trade	547.17	567.45	584.13	598.59	612.79
Transportation and warehousing	807.78	828.07	834.40	864.51	883.28
Information and cultural industries	916.99	952.30	955.52	1,003.44	1,003.54
Finance and insurance	887.00	921.01	951.25	997.59	1,000.76
Real estate and rental and leasing	654.56	698.06	710.73	756.11	772.87
Professional, scientific and technical services	937.42	989.94	1,016.41	1,060.36	1,093.67
Management of companies and enterprises	1,012.41	1,005.19	1,050.28	1,086.16	1,087.91
Administrative and support, waste management and remediation services	546.15	583.67	600.98	648.97	673.05
Educational services	750.52	779.60	808.15	834.62	862.64
Health care and social assistance	635.03	667.40	687.72	705.55	743.94
Arts, entertainment and recreation	437.37	439.16	445.08	468.77	503.66
Accommodation and food services	287.18	288.45	299.73	318.40	331.11
Public administration	894.04	925.45	951.03	1,007.53	1,040.51
Other services	573.54	605.40	622.43	652.13	669.67

Notes: North American Industry Classification System (NAICS), 2007.
Data include overtime.
Source: Statistics Canada, CANSIM table 281-0027.

Table 3.3 Employees, by job permanency, 2003 to 2008

	2003	2004	2005	2006	2007	2008
			thousands			
Permanent employees						
All industries	**11,619.1**	**11,772.4**	**11,860.6**	**12,163.1**	**12,408.8**	**12,721.2**
Goods-producing industries	2,946.9	2,968.7	2,946.5	2,944.1	2,914.4	2,943.5
Services-producing industries	8,672.2	8,803.7	8,914.1	9,219.0	9,494.4	9,777.7
Temporary employees						
All industries	**1,651.3**	**1,721.2**	**1,797.6**	**1,823.2**	**1,842.6**	**1,775.0**
Goods-producing industries	347.8	358.4	369.9	353.9	363.3	352.8
Services-producing industries	1,303.5	1,362.8	1,427.7	1,469.3	1,479.3	1,422.2

Note: North American Industry Classification System (NAICS), 2002.
Source: Statistics Canada, CANSIM table 282-0080.

Table 3.4 Selected services operating statistics, 2003 to 2007

	2003			2004		
	Revenue	Expenses	Profit margin	Revenue	Expenses	Profit margin
	$ millions		%	$ millions		%
Personal and laundry services	8,044.7	7,199.7	10.5	8,282.7	7,641.3	7.7
Personal care	3,539.9	3,142.4	11.2	3,748.8	3,503.3	6.5
Funeral	1,399.6	1,253.0	10.5	1,425.9	1,283.1	10.0
Dry cleaning and laundry	1,920.8	1,740.8	9.4	1,881.6	1,717.7	8.7
Other personal services	1,184.4	1,063.5	10.2	1,226.4	1,137.2	7.3
Management consulting	6,634.4	5,449.6	17.9	6,683.0	5,304.4	20.6
Environmental and other scientific and technical consulting services	1,908.3	1,614.7	15.4	2,022.3	1,646.1	18.6
Offices of real estate agents and brokers	7,024.5	4,583.3	34.8	7,834.1	5,132.4	34.5
Offices of real estate appraisers	505.7	412.8	18.4	577.5	477.8	17.3
Automotive equipment rental and leasing	4,639.8	4,072.2	12.2	4,839.5	4,285.7	11.4
Consumer goods rental	1,893.4	1,766.4	6.7	1,979.0	1,834.8	7.3
General rental centres	271.0	237.1	12.5	318.3	280.0	12.0
Food services and drinking places	35,260.0	34,120.7	3.2	37,366.0	35,994.3	3.7
Full-service restaurants	15,380.0	14,998.6	2.5	16,465.6	16,016.2	2.7
Limited-service eating places	14,029.5	13,480.3	3.9	14,873.1	14,177.6	4.7
Special food services	2,973.7	2,840.0	4.5	3,095.7	2,982.2	3.7
Drinking places (alcoholic beverages)	2,876.8	2,801.7	2.6	2,931.6	2,818.4	3.9
Specialized design services	2,016.8	1,816.6	9.9	2,229.9	1,975.2	11.4
Interior design	541.6	494.6	8.7	618.1	540.3	12.6
Industrial design	209.3	196.2	6.3	222.5	210.5	5.4
Graphic design	1,135.1	1,003.8	11.6	1,246.2	1,098.6	11.8
Other specialized design services	130.7	122.0	6.6	143.1	125.7	12.1
Advertising agencies	2,151.6	1,963.7	8.7	2,231.0	1,988.7	10.9
Other advertising and advertising-related services	2,583.0	2,432.4	5.8	2,781.8	2,544.4	8.5
Architectural services	1,873.1	1,573.8	16.0	1,920.3	1,620.3	15.6
Engineering services	11,044.5	9,941.9	10.0	12,147.8	10,734.8	11.6
Surveying and mapping services	1,865.4	1,703.8	8.7	1,957.6	1,783.6	8.9
Accounting, tax preparation, bookkeeping and payroll services	8,244.0	5,837.7	29.2	8,713.3	6,082.3	30.2
Employment services	5,689.1	5,491.9	3.5	6,268.9	6,033.4	3.8
Lessors of residential buildings and dwellings (except social housing projects)	18,884.1	14,843.7	21.4	20,815.1	16,471.7	20.9
Non-residential leasing	24,735.8	18,804.0	24.0	26,347.3	20,812.4	21.0
Real estate property managers	2,771.6	2,353.7	15.1	3,450.7	2,897.8	16.0

Note: North American Industry Classification System (NAICS), 2007.
Source: Statistics Canada, CANSIM tables 352-0003, 352-0005, 352-0008, 352-0010, 355-0005, 359-0001, 360-0001, 360-0002, 360-0003, 360-0004, 360-0005, 360-0006, 360-0007 and 361-0001.

2005			2006			2007		
Revenue	Expenses	Profit margin	Revenue	Expenses	Profit margin	Revenue	Expenses	Profit margin
$ millions		%	$ millions		%	$ millions		%
8,442.5	7,621.9	9.7	8,595.0	7,726.9	10.1	9,070.4	8,144.2	10.2
3,797.0	3,446.8	9.2	3,912.7	3,468.8	11.3	4,177.1	3,708.7	11.2
1,452.9	1,285.1	11.6	1,476.0	1,322.9	10.4	1,523.0	1,363.4	10.5
1,936.7	1,758.0	9.2	1,964.6	1,814.5	7.6	2,019.8	1,852.1	8.3
1,256.0	1,132.1	9.9	1,241.7	1,120.7	9.7	1,350.5	1,220.0	9.7
7,102.7	5,570.6	21.6	7,513.5	5,982.1	20.4	7734.2	6178.6	20.1
2,373.0	1,972.0	16.9	2,842.4	2,390.9	15.9	3647.2	3022.6	17.1
8,554.1	5,237.0	38.8	9,199.5	5,943.5	35.4	9,916.2	6,556.7	33.9
651.2	548.1	15.8	721.0	615.8	14.6	777.6	664.6	14.5
5,034.0	4,558.5	9.4	4,967.8	4,525.3	8.9	5,064.6	4,611.6	8.9
2,112.1	1,995.9	5.5	2,114.3	2,002.6	5.3	2,121.9	2,029.5	4.4
366.5	322.0	12.1	385.5	357.9	7.2	411.9	381.0	7.5
38,846.7	37,387.2	3.8	40,760.1	39,004.0	4.3	42,413.7	40,713.7	4.0
17,271.3	16,743.9	3.1	18,050.0	17,492.8	3.1	18,903.4	18,340.0	3.0
15,387.3	14,638.9	4.9	16,452.6	15,532.9	5.6	17,086.6	16,211.0	5.1
3,371.9	3,280.8	2.7	3,573.6	3,418.7	4.3	3,815.2	3,634.2	4.7
2,816.2	2,723.6	3.3	2,683.8	2,559.6	4.6	2,608.5	2,528.5	3.1
2,332.9	2,071.2	11.2	2,538.9	2,230.3	12.2	2,723.3	2,384.0	12.5
682.2	616.7	9.6	814.9	731.9	10.2	928.7	819.8	11.7
228.6	207.3	9.3	243.1	213.2	12.3	x	x	x
1,265.6	1,106.8	12.6	1,311.3	1,134.7	13.5	1,349.9	1,162.1	13.9
156.5	140.4	10.3	169.5	150.5	11.2	x	x	x
2,388.8	2,186.8	8.5	2,443.1	2,211.9	9.5	2,509.3	2,262.3	9.8
2,994.7	2,766.9	7.6	3,237.4	2,954.4	8.7	3,389.9	3,070.4	9.4
2,059.0	1,708.2	17.0	2,373.0	2,017.3	15.0	2,797.5	2,332.1	16.6
13,793.5	11,919.7	13.6	15,371.7	13,576.9	11.7	17,847.9	15,552.3	12.9
2,287.3	2,052.3	10.3	2,720.1	2,387.3	12.2	2,776.9	2,402.9	13.5
9,901.2	6,920.1	30.1	11,048.5	7,773.4	29.6	11,405.6	8,114.3	28.9
7,402.0	7,130.8	3.7	8,033.7	7,752.8	3.5	8,904.0	8,542.6	4.1
22,804.4	17,901.7	21.5	23,598.0	18,942.1	19.7	..	..	..
26,029.4	19,909.1	23.5	27,659.3	21,083.9	23.8	..	..	..
3,802.3	3,131.0	17.7	4,381.9	3,673.1	16.2	..	..	..

Table 3.5 Payroll employment, by industry, provinces and territories, 2008

	Canada	Newfoundland and Labrador	Prince Edward Island	Nova Scotia	New Brunswick	Quebec
	number					
Industrial aggregate including unclassified businesses	**14,817,695**	**191,013**	**61,069**	**396,080**	**312,732**	**3,378,855**
Goods producing industries	**2,873,450**	32,705	9,621	62,483	58,448	669,366
Forestry, logging and support	**47,615**	.	.	.	x	13,430
Mining, quarrying, and oil and gas extraction	**202,225**	.	.	.	x	13,937
Utilities	**120,145**	.	.	.	..	31,116
Construction	**829,561**	10,966	4,295	20,916	18,766	158,346
Manufacturing	**1,673,904**	15,158	4,915	34,285	31,124	452,537
Services-producing industries	**11,734,158**	155,848	50,927	329,799	250,860	2,657,289
Trade	**2,652,811**	33,833	10,203	74,611	53,711	634,034
Transportation and warehousing	**691,909**	8,496	2,608	17,320	16,399	155,742
Information and cultural industries	**326,367**	3,829	.	8,690	5,994	65,368
Finance and insurance	**656,395**	5,943	1,788	17,388	11,802	147,084
Real estate and rental and leasing	**251,959**	.	742	.	.	49,066
Professional, scientific and technical services	**754,536**	5,733	1,742	13,131	9,270	162,401
Management of companies and enterprises	**124,844**	676	466	2,278	2,600	24,861
Administrative and support, waste management and remediation services	**774,009**	7,204	3,438	18,108	22,518	154,115
Educational services	**1,135,454**	19,983	x	36,429	24,972	270,977
Health care and social assistance	**1,528,013**	29,865	8,659	53,756	38,738	374,242
Arts, entertainment and recreation	**241,916**	1,620	1,397	6,028	3,897	54,792
Accommodation and food services	**1,078,596**	12,703	5,491	29,919	22,821	225,686
Other services (except public administration)	**509,590**	6,225	1,998	12,357	8,692	115,878
Public administration	**1,007,760**	17,501	6,699	32,682	25,965	223,044

Note: North American Industry Classification System (NAICS), 2007.
Source: Statistics Canada, CANSIM table 281-0024.

Ontario	Manitoba	Saskatchewan	Alberta	British Columbia	Yukon	Northwest Territories	Nunavut
number							
5,704,709	**562,486**	**435,300**	**1,776,624**	**1,942,693**	**19,493**	**26,172**	**10,468**
1,107,296	96,613	71,852	427,693	328,656	1,926	5,406	1,383
7,561	.	537	3,640	16,537	.	.	.
28,597	x	15,357	111,179	18,264	.	.	.
46,434	..	3,922	13,917	9,233	.	.	.
273,211	25,840	25,095	161,793	126,516	960	2,222	634
751,492	61,635	26,942	137,164	158,106	.	.	.
4,526,397	460,059	358,735	1,318,525	1,578,785	17,413	20,506	9,016
995,417	94,257	80,069	310,676	358,690	2,925	3,093	1,290
247,939	36,724	19,158	80,569	101,135	1,782	3,318	718
146,339	11,285	11,786	31,322	39,738	x	.	.
285,486	31,649	21,914	56,917	75,461	359	x	.
100,833	7,736	6,087	35,171	38,108	.	.	.
313,992	15,898	12,216	114,940	103,448	600	923	240
50,395	3,753	5,400	17,943	16,240	.	.	.
351,163	22,974	12,575	81,265	99,056	293	956	345
426,352	46,159	40,328	121,893	139,086	x	1,797	1,430
559,234	76,813	54,051	130,796	199,317	1,003	1,030	510
94,034	7,886	7,468	28,824	35,606	.	.	.
382,763	38,464	31,835	140,129	185,335	1,647	1,460	344
189,953	19,492	16,226	69,565	67,567	478	777	384
382,495	46,968	39,623	98,516	119,998	5,990	5,407	2,872

Table 3.6 Subscribers to cable services, by type of service and technology, 2002 to 2007

	2002	2003	2004	2005	2006	2007
	thousands					
Subscribers to basic programming services	7,625.9	7,577.7	7,616.8	7,620.2	7,790.4	7,917.3
Subscribers to digital cable services	1,146.3	1,403.7	1,810.0	2,283.0	2,776.5	3,336.7
Subscribers to high speed Internet services by cable	1,868.8	2,363.8	2,838.3	3,381.1	3,961.7	4,534.6
Subscribers to telephone services by cable	..	..	..	211.7	927.5	1,784.9
Homes with access to cable services	11,379.2	11,695.8	11,908.9	12,119.7	12,411.1	12,572.9
Homes with access to cable services	10,256.9	10,820.5	11,177.1	11,561.1	11,851.7	12,186.2
Homes with access to high speed Internet services by cable	10,046.0	10,692.4	11,119.2	11,517.9	11,916.6	12,195.1
Homes with access to telephone services by cable	..	..	..	4,346.2	8,371.9	10,095.1
Households in licenced area	11,580.4	11,882.9	12,079.8	12,295.1	12,541.6	12,704.1

Note: North American Industry Classification System (NAICS), 2007.
Source: Statistics Canada, CANSIM table 353-0003.

Business performance and ownership

4

The sharp downturn seen in the last quarter of 2008, and the years of solid results that preceded it, are reflected in the data on the performance of companies operating in Canada.

In the fourth quarter of 2008, corporations earned $62.4 billion in seasonally adjusted operating profits, down 19.2% from the third quarter—the largest quarterly decline in 16 years. About two-thirds of the major industry groups reported lower profits. Non-financial industries' profits fell 17.6% to $46.9 billion; those of the financial industries declined 23.8% to $15.5 billion.

Profits decline

Lower profits in the fourth quarter were attributable to lower revenues: oil and gas extractors, banks and other depository credit intermediaries, and manufacturers led the decline.

Manufacturers' earnings fell 20.9% to $9.5 billion in the fourth quarter of 2008; much of the decrease came from the petroleum and coal industry. Chemicals, plastics and rubber products manufacturers helped offset declines; their profits rose 5.2% to $1.9 billion despite temporary plant shutdowns in the quarter. Retailers earned $4.1 billion in the final quarter of 2008, down 2.0% from the third quarter.

Losses from trading in financial instruments caused banks to lead declines in the financial industries. Banking and other depository credit intermediaries earned $4.8 billion, down 26.4% from the third quarter.

Despite those fourth-quarter declines, corporations earned $281.7 billion in 2008, 4.3% more than in 2007. Much of the growth came from oil and gas extraction (up 54.0% to $38.0 billion) and petroleum and coal manufacturers

Chart 4.1
Operating revenue and operating profits, all industries

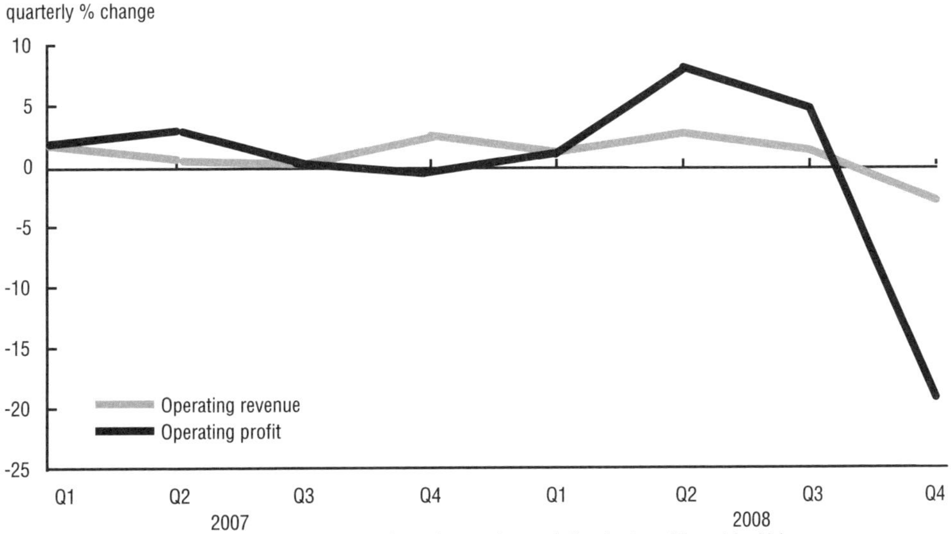

Note: All industries excluding management of companies and enterprises and other funds and financial vehicles.
Source: Statistics Canada, CANSIM table 187-0002.

(up 17.9% to $13.7 billion), because of high oil and gas prices during the first half of 2008.

Banking and depository credit intermediaries dragged down financials, as amounts set aside for future losses on investments, loans and other assets more than doubled in 2008. Banks posted profits of $22.4 billion, down 20.2% from 2007.

Corporate income taxes were higher in 2007

Corporations paid $55.7 billion in taxes in 2007; $37.9 billion to the federal government, and $17.8 billion to provincial governments.

The finance and insurance industries paid $13.8 billion in income taxes, up 11.5% from 2006. The banking and other depository credit intermediation industries accounted for $5.5 billion of that total.

Non-financial industries paid $41.9 billion in income tax in 2007, down 2.4% from the previous year.

Table 4.a
Business bankruptcies, selected industries

	2007	2008
	number	
All industries	**6,293**	**6,164**
Construction	1,091	1,073
Retail trade	895	837
Finance and insurance	87	102
Accommodation and food services	734	739

Sources: Office of the Superintendent of Bankruptcy Canada and Statistics Canada, CANSIM table 177-0001.

Chart 4.2
Operating profits, all industries

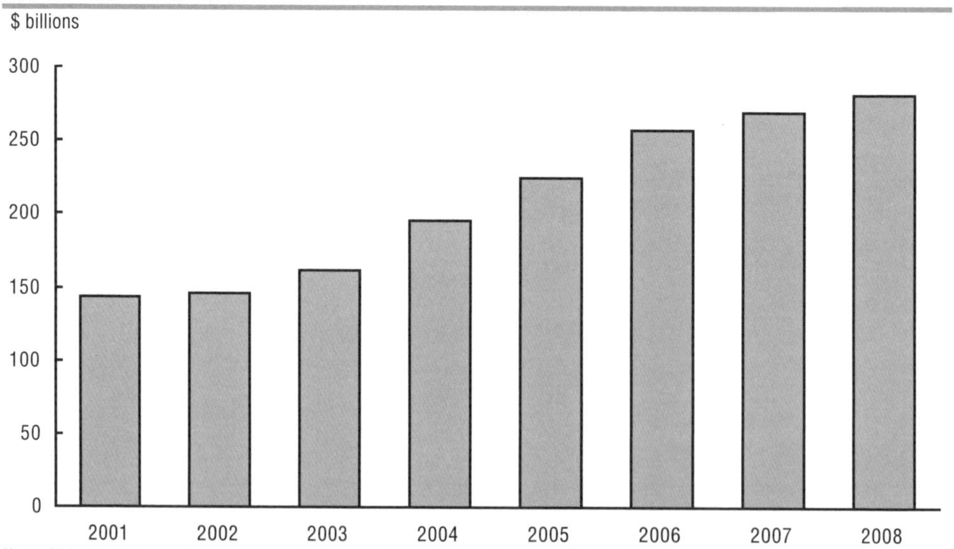

Note: All industries excluding management of companies and enterprises and other funds and financial vehicles.
Source: Statistics Canada, CANSIM table 187-0002.

Foreign firms in Canada: recent trends

Of the nearly 1.3 million corporations doing business in Canada in 2006, less than 1% were foreign-controlled—a proportion that has changed little over time. However, in 2006, foreign-controlled firms accounted for about 30% of operating revenue and 27% of operating profits, or $78.4 billion.

The United States continued to be the most common country of origin of foreign-controlled enterprises operating in Canada. In 2006, U.S.-based firms controlled 54% of all assets held by foreign-based firms; British firms controlled 13%; Netherlands firms, 7%, German firms, 6%; French firms, 4%; and Japanese firms, 4%.

Foreign control is more prevalent in the non-financial industries than in the finance and insurance industries. In the non-financial industries, 26% of assets were under foreign control in 2006, compared with 16% in the finance and insurance industries. This gap is largely the result of regulations governing foreign control in the finance and insurance industries, particularly in banking.

Chart 4.3
Foreign-controlled enterprises, 2006

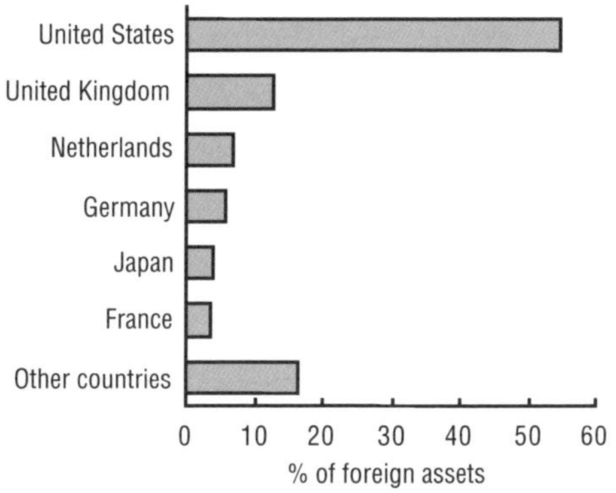

Source: Statistics Canada, CANSIM table 179-0004.

Unincorporated firms

The unincorporated sector comprises self-employed owners of farms, businesses or professional practices that are not corporate legal entities. In 2002, they accounted for about 10% of the gross domestic product generated by the business sector.

Entrepreneurs create unincorporated enterprises for many reasons: they might desire the independence of self-employment, or they might be pushed into it by a lack of jobs. It's the model of choice for many physicians, lawyers and other professionals.

The Labour Force Survey counted 2.6 million self-employed Canadians in 2008, 15,000 more than in 2007. About 65% of self-employed people were men; 35% were women. About 72% worked in services, and 28% in goods-producing industries. Less than 10% of self-employed businesses used paid help, and less than 1% used unpaid family help.

Chart 4.4
Self-employed workers

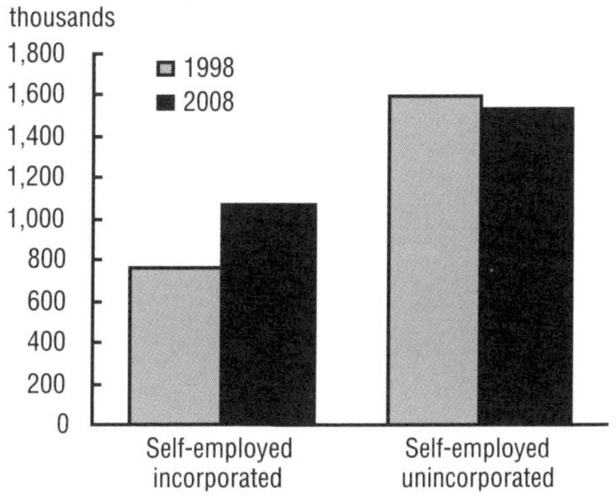

Note: Includes workers with paid and non-paid help.
Source: Statistics Canada, CANSIM table 282-0012.

Table 4.1 Businesses, by province and territory, 1995 to 2005

	Canada	Newfoundland and Labrador	Prince Edward Island	Nova Scotia	New Brunswick
	thousands				
1995	**961.4**	21.6	7.6	32.0	27.8
1996	**963.0**	20.4	7.5	31.4	27.5
1997	**983.9**	20.4	7.6	32.1	27.6
1998	**1004.0**	20.4	7.7	32.4	28.2
1999	**1016.1**	20.2	7.7	32.9	28.3
2000	**1019.8**	19.8	7.3	32.2	27.8
2001	**1031.0**	19.8	7.2	32.2	27.8
2002	**1042.2**	19.5	7.2	31.9	27.6
2003	**1056.9**	19.8	7.1	31.9	27.3
2004	**1090.5**	20.3	7.1	32.4	27.7
2005	**1120.8**	20.4	7.0	32.4	28.0

Notes: A firm may exist in more than one province and, therefore, firm counts at the provincial and at the national levels may vary. Counts include both business sector firms and non-business sector firms.
1. Includes data for Yukon, Northwest Territories and Nunavut.
Source: Statistics Canada, Longitudinal Employment Analysis Program, 1991 to 2005.

Quebec	Ontario	Manitoba	Saskatchewan	Alberta	British Columbia	Territories[1]
			thousands			
227.5	303.5	35.7	40.7	112.4	148.9	3.7
227.3	303.5	35.7	40.9	114.4	150.6	3.8
228.0	311.0	36.1	41.6	121.1	154.6	3.8
231.3	319.7	36.7	41.2	126.6	156.0	3.8
233.3	326.7	36.8	40.8	129.5	156.1	3.8
232.8	331.6	36.1	40.1	132.4	155.7	4.0
232.3	337.2	36.4	40.0	137.1	156.9	4.1
232.6	342.7	36.8	39.9	140.6	159.2	4.2
233.6	349.7	36.8	39.8	144.2	162.4	4.3
237.4	363.3	37.6	40.0	150.0	170.2	4.5
239.9	374.4	38.3	40.1	157.8	177.9	4.6

Table 4.2 Bankruptcies, by province and territory, 2004 to 2008

	2004	2005	2006	2007	2008
			number		
Canada	**8,118**	**7,517**	**6,742**	**6,293**	**6,164**
Newfoundland and Labrador	56	56	45	52	39
Prince Edward Island	39	42	41	32	14
Nova Scotia	255	276	241	206	162
New Brunswick	207	204	193	151	196
Quebec	1,958	1,709	1,832	2,034	2,157
Ontario	2,557	2,715	2,668	2,586	2,437
Manitoba	178	149	160	102	103
Saskatchewan	368	373	302	204	150
Alberta	1,565	1,195	665	449	447
British Columbia	921	786	587	470	454
Yukon	4	5	3	3	4
Northwest Territories	9	6	5	2	1
Nunavut	1	1	0	2	0

Note: North American Industry Classification System (NAICS), 2002.
Sources: Office of the Superintendent of Bankruptcy Canada and Statistics Canada, CANSIM table 177-0001.

Table 4.3 Bankruptcies by industry, 2004 to 2008

	2004	2005	2006	2007	2008
			number		
All industries	**8,118**	**7,517**	**6,742**	**6,293**	**6,164**
Agriculture, forestry, fishing and hunting	412	401	357	294	277
Mining and oil and gas extraction	66	53	35	27	31
Utilities	12	9	14	6	7
Construction	1,342	1,316	1,152	1,091	1,073
Manufacturing	740	698	570	588	626
Wholesale trade	390	338	322	313	296
Retail trade	1,201	1,096	987	895	837
Transportation and warehousing	804	693	640	607	652
Information and cultural industries	140	114	136	92	101
Finance and insurance	118	101	80	87	102
Real estate and rental and leasing	174	166	149	158	132
Professional, scientific and technical services	513	424	429	402	372
Management of companies and enterprises	39	39	39	36	31
Administrative and support, waste management and remediation services	331	341	326	270	256
Educational services	51	57	60	37	39
Health care and social assistance	136	115	74	74	72
Arts, entertainment and recreation	172	155	156	144	116
Accommodation and food services	929	833	765	734	739
Other services (except public administration)	542	565	440	430	394
Public administration	6	3	11	8	11

Note: North American Industry Classification System (NAICS), 2002.
Sources: Office of the Superintendent of Bankruptcy Canada and Statistics Canada, CANSIM table 177-0007.

Table 4.4 Businesses, by firm size, 1985 to 2005

	All businesses	0 to 19 employees	20 to 99 employees	100 to 499 employees	500 employees and over
			thousands		
1985	**810.2**	759.3	42.7	6.5	1.7
1986	**835.6**	781.5	45.3	7.0	1.8
1987	**866.3**	808.6	48.6	7.3	1.8
1988	**889.8**	829.7	50.8	7.5	1.9
1989	**908.8**	848.7	50.7	7.5	1.9
1990	**918.0**	858.2	50.4	7.5	1.9
1991	**906.7**	842.8	53.4	8.4	2.1
1992	**907.2**	845.5	51.8	7.9	2.0
1993	**909.7**	847.2	52.5	8.0	2.0
1994	**917.3**	853.5	53.3	8.4	2.1
1995	**922.2**	856.5	54.9	8.7	2.1
1996	**924.1**	857.2	56.0	8.8	2.2
1997	**943.5**	874.2	57.9	9.2	2.2
1998	**956.3**	885.3	59.2	9.5	2.3
1999	**968.4**	896.8	59.5	9.8	2.3
2000	**978.8**	904.3	61.8	10.3	2.4
2001	**988.9**	912.1	63.5	10.8	2.5
2002	**999.3**	920.4	65.4	11.0	2.5
2003	**1,013.3**	933.3	66.4	11.1	2.5
2004	**1,045.0**	964.4	66.7	11.3	2.5
2005	**1,074.9**	993.5	67.4	11.5	2.6

Notes: Data prior to 1991 were backcasted from a model.
Counts include both business sector firms and non-business sector firms.
Source: Statistics Canada, Longitudinal Employment Analysis Program, 1991 to 2005.

Table 4.5 Enterprises operating in Canada, summary statistics, by country of control, 2002 to 2006

	2002	2003	2004	2005	2006
	$ millions				
Canadian- and foreign-controlled corporations					
Assets	4,378,310	4,592,361	5,014,443	5,267,565	5,789,970
Operating revenue	2,435,923	2,517,501	2,688,160	2,855,998	3,021,925
Operating profit	170,488	189,549	224,185	256,042	287,834
	% change from previous year				
Assets	4.2	4.9	9.2	5.0	9.9
Operating revenue	1.4	3.3	6.8	6.2	5.8
Operating profit	-1.2	11.2	18.3	14.2	12.4
	$ millions				
Canadian-controlled corporations					
Assets	3,474,374	3,651,394	3,999,082	4,209,459	4,565,427
Operating revenue	1,737,962	1,780,852	1,894,500	2,008,547	2,115,752
Operating profit	122,260	135,913	158,644	182,659	209,465
Private corporations					
Assets	3,122,247	3,298,816	3,638,550	3,850,715	4,185,380
Operating revenue	1,651,698	1,691,687	1,787,787	1,896,696	1,996,454
Operating profit	96,421	108,524	130,589	152,178	177,675
Government business corporations					
Assets	352,127	352,578	360,531	358,744	380,046
Operating revenue	86,264	89,165	106,713	111,851	119,298
Operating profit	25,839	27,389	28,056	30,481	31,790
Foreign-controlled corporations					
Assets	903,935	940,966	1,015,361	1,058,107	1,224,543
Operating revenue	697,960	736,649	793,660	847,451	906,173
Operating profit	48,227	53,636	65,541	73,382	78,369
United States corporations					
Assets	549,406	552,304	593,293	609,066	665,983
Operating revenue	445,054	454,146	489,905	522,825	531,617
Operating profit	30,567	34,321	41,862	46,572	41,421
European Union corporations					
Assets	264,782	285,920	320,513	337,777	385,081
Operating revenue	163,212	186,057	199,512	212,078	240,831
Operating profit	12,670	13,620	17,255	18,816	23,048
Other foreign corporations					
Assets	89,747	102,742	101,555	111,264	173,480
Operating revenue	89,695	96,446	104,243	112,549	133,726
Operating profit	4,990	5,696	6,424	7,994	13,900

Note: North American Industry Classification System (NAICS), 2007.
Source: Statistics Canada, CANSIM table 179-0004.

Table 4.6 Operating revenue, by industry, 1992 to 2008

	1992	1993	1994	1995	1996	1997	1998
				$ millions			
All industries[1]	**1,292,263**	**1,367,380**	**1,483,080**	**1,577,326**	**1,679,437**	**1,794,991**	**1,831,780**
Total, non-financial industries[2]	1,132,719	1,208,252	1,322,397	1,401,572	1,497,030	1,607,525	1,645,645
Agriculture, forestry, fishing and hunting	20,076	22,914	24,378	22,504	22,555	28,144	23,744
Oil and gas extraction and support activities	25,066	27,444	32,084	35,129	44,574	47,351	44,444
Mining and quarrying (except oil and gas)	8,992	8,827	11,451	12,054	13,586	15,098	14,505
Utilities	13,778	13,498	17,430	16,997	16,234	23,209	26,929
Construction	104,733	101,232	104,744	90,365	94,491	96,842	106,084
Manufacturing	323,236	350,814	398,678	462,778	485,106	517,491	535,503
Wholesale trade	195,420	210,029	229,742	245,969	263,005	280,569	288,115
Retail trade	213,739	222,011	229,806	237,728	251,484	270,364	260,104
Transportation and warehousing	53,722	62,061	64,875	66,817	73,189	74,148	78,361
Information and cultural industries	29,900	32,108	36,128	39,262	43,439	48,652	54,371
Real estate and rental and leasing	31,345	33,609	35,706	35,352	37,476	37,564	37,327
Professional, scientific and technical services	32,405	35,716	40,357	39,693	46,652	53,206	55,015
Administrative and support, waste management and remediation services	22,423	25,914	30,357	28,398	32,089	33,573	34,433
Educational, health care and social assistance services	10,999	12,320	13,586	13,629	14,687	16,350	17,839
Arts, entertainment and recreation	4,381	4,756	5,163	5,068	5,175	5,594	6,024
Accommodation and food services	27,303	28,915	30,283	31,319	32,395	36,193	38,752
Repair, maintenance and personal services	15,202	16,084	17,634	18,505	20,890	23,175	24,092
Total, finance and insurance industries (excluding other funds and financial vehicles)	159,545	159,128	160,683	175,755	182,407	187,466	186,135
Depository credit intermediation	66,266	61,488	62,013	71,333	72,695	72,591	78,222
Activities related to credit intermediation	2,382	2,286	2,318	2,630	2,591	2,469	2,507
Non-depository credit intermediation	9,143	10,817	8,875	9,623	10,222	10,925	11,518
Securities, commodity contracts, and other financial investments and related activities	26,063	28,422	31,103	29,133	32,951	36,253	29,765
Insurance carriers and related activities	55,692	56,113	56,375	63,039	63,950	65,231	64,128

Notes: Non-pension funds are excluded from totals because they are largely unincorporated and, therefore, are not a reflection of incorporated business financial position and performance. In addition, these entities are excluded from the corporate sector within the Canadian System of National Accounts.
North American Industry Classification System (NAICS), 2007.
1. Excludes management of companies and enterprises and other funds and financial vehicles.
2. Excludes management of companies and enterprises.
Source: Statistics Canada, CANSIM table 187-0001.

	1999	2000	2001	2002	2003	2004	2005	2006	2007	2008
	$ millions									
	1,936,379	**2,199,690**	**2,304,118**	**2,333,286**	**2,417,617**	**2,570,770**	**2,731,901**	**2,893,491**	**3,027,616**	**3,185,145**
	1,741,764	1,984,070	2,084,864	2,125,319	2,195,320	2,336,161	2,478,681	2,604,945	2,711,950	2,878,663
	24,487	33,187	35,986	37,056	38,551	39,841	41,702	42,873	45,665	43,929
	49,482	82,953	97,767	99,868	108,906	117,623	139,054	155,345	169,328	210,320
	17,806	18,672	18,932	19,127	18,588	22,348	22,524	33,667	34,400	40,508
	30,734	50,682	67,747	47,707	52,198	56,682	62,359	65,801	63,752	69,977
	101,660	120,632	130,332	139,612	150,167	161,265	177,634	197,415	218,036	240,689
	587,901	649,238	642,674	651,800	657,546	701,237	720,710	713,505	707,656	719,305
	302,129	338,709	355,382	356,771	366,198	394,181	422,557	452,912	467,567	498,041
	268,008	283,545	308,199	337,202	349,677	361,055	380,562	393,934	417,777	440,522
	79,668	85,808	89,245	88,495	89,703	103,029	112,129	115,344	125,272	138,865
	58,590	64,392	69,572	69,940	71,629	70,343	76,402	82,897	85,653	91,309
	38,839	48,220	44,876	48,447	51,564	55,003	55,524	61,570	66,934	68,703
	58,533	72,750	75,440	76,631	79,271	84,213	86,925	98,942	108,305	110,246
	37,212	39,731	48,343	47,556	50,799	54,542	60,810	64,226	68,529	70,558
	17,860	19,189	20,823	22,250	25,468	26,645	29,145	31,687	34,972	35,920
	5,788	8,007	8,967	9,686	10,584	10,684	10,436	11,550	11,409	11,565
	38,408	43,305	46,072	48,530	49,498	50,942	52,488	54,738	57,275	59,579
	24,660	25,059	24,505	24,637	24,976	26,525	27,719	28,540	29,420	28,622
	194,615	215,619	219,252	207,966	222,297	234,610	253,221	288,544	315,667	306,483
	80,637	89,499	89,132	77,651	81,060	82,649	91,549	106,624	122,611	121,894
	3,069	3,091	3,003	2,455	2,765	2,944	3,505	4,732	4,972	4,709
	13,224	13,456	13,707	14,612	15,121	16,290	19,273	22,230	24,605	26,039
	32,362	40,236	40,159	35,462	38,216	42,995	48,801	56,352	62,161	57,751
	65,322	69,338	73,251	77,789	85,135	89,732	90,092	98,606	101,320	96,092

Table 4.7 Operating profit or loss, by industry, 1992 to 2008

	1992	1993	1994	1995	1996	1997	1998
				$ millions			
All industries[1]	**55,407**	**65,610**	**90,591**	**98,961**	**107,511**	**118,111**	**112,121**
Total, non-financial industries[2]	38,664	45,080	68,481	72,526	76,113	80,716	78,195
Agriculture, forestry, fishing and hunting	761	977	1,293	818	1,080	1,185	1,130
Oil and gas extraction and support activities	2,429	3,612	4,543	3,826	8,537	7,091	827
Mining and quarrying[3]	251	75	710	896	832	925	435
Utilities	1,693	1,759	1,974	2,051	2,072	2,039	1,984
Construction	4,901	2,423	7,194	2,892	4,325	3,193	5,458
Manufacturing	8,674	14,127	25,081	39,195	33,724	37,601	35,985
Wholesale trade	2,231	2,632	4,172	3,905	4,232	4,746	5,180
Retail trade	4,516	5,218	6,786	3,525	3,350	3,825	4,440
Transportation and warehousing	1,044	1,745	2,297	4,261	4,920	6,033	5,218
Information and cultural industries	5,162	4,847	5,061	4,782	5,594	6,783	6,960
Real estate and rental and leasing	4,013	4,541	5,188	3,262	3,981	3,605	3,885
Professional, scientific and technical services	383	500	756	1,380	1,509	1,552	1,980
Administrative and support, waste management and remediation services	92	127	187	743	918	1,240	1,081
Educational, health care and social assistance services	996	1,254	1,332	590	735	532	1,093
Arts, entertainment and recreation	78	130	233	22	49	137	214
Accommodation and food services	1,139	758	1,159	-89	-274	-438	1,601
Repair, maintenance and personal services	302	356	516	466	529	666	723
Total, finance and insurance industries[4]	16,743	20,530	22,111	26,432	31,394	37,391	33,922
Depository credit intermediation	1,637	4,552	6,660	9,966	13,011	17,078	16,018
Activities related to credit intermediation	364	381	380	381	370	391	406
Non-depository credit intermediation	2,977	2,842	2,734	2,779	2,996	2,908	2,879
Securities, commodity contracts, and other financial investments and related activities	9,204	9,396	9,045	7,789	8,395	9,573	9,268
Insurance carriers and related activities	2,561	3,359	3,292	5,520	6,623	7,442	5,353

Note: North American Industry Classification System (NAICS), 2007.
1. Excludes management of companies and enterprises and other funds and financial vehicles.
2. Excludes management of companies and enterprises.
3. Excludes oil and gas.
4. Excludes other funds and financial vehicles.
Source: Statistics Canada, CANSIM table 187-0001.

1999	2000	2001	2002	2003	2004	2005	2006	2007	2008
				$ millions					
133,714	**165,152**	**143,127**	**145,904**	**162,108**	**195,194**	**225,143**	**257,473**	**270,115**	**281,688**
99,335	127,065	106,467	112,767	118,743	141,350	163,967	184,278	187,303	207,104
395	2,365	2,589	2,139	1,406	2,098	2,578	3,015	3,793	3,060
4,858	19,126	19,567	14,686	21,137	20,407	29,856	29,191	24,697	38,037
1,295	2,354	1,537	1,676	2,205	3,328	4,031	7,823	7,187	9,777
2,528	2,233	2,917	2,504	3,320	4,333	3,204	3,886	4,293	4,819
3,615	3,407	4,315	5,063	5,082	6,512	8,417	11,395	13,727	14,686
46,185	52,381	35,667	38,061	33,075	45,079	44,306	46,128	44,436	43,644
8,530	9,437	9,906	10,187	11,002	14,086	14,790	17,496	17,691	16,808
7,428	7,044	6,989	8,302	9,276	9,884	11,402	13,436	14,048	16,372
5,060	4,789	4,167	6,462	5,741	7,610	10,007	11,230	11,434	11,848
6,403	7,615	5,051	5,922	8,125	6,340	10,765	11,785	13,358	14,456
6,109	8,876	7,031	9,068	8,923	9,035	9,459	10,553	11,898	12,456
1,165	1,050	796	1,322	1,866	3,304	4,125	5,026	6,213	6,271
1,151	1,636	1,558	1,659	2,002	2,219	2,954	3,379	3,821	3,728
1,594	1,707	2,039	2,259	2,986	3,560	4,019	4,368	5,193	5,565
118	428	208	329	250	400	335	533	600	715
1,841	1,503	1,510	1,983	1,484	1,983	2,330	3,217	3,136	3,157
1,057	1,111	623	1,144	861	1,176	1,391	1,815	1,778	1,710
34,377	38,086	36,659	33,137	43,364	53,843	61,174	73,195	82,812	74,584
15,205	15,503	14,428	11,466	18,039	21,061	23,233	26,091	30,444	25,627
380	408	460	357	353	245	522	879	1,001	691
3,757	4,198	5,321	5,822	6,067	6,554	7,612	8,819	10,180	10,303
9,598	12,272	11,457	9,778	9,954	13,909	17,705	22,691	26,449	22,739
5,436	5,707	4,994	5,712	8,952	12,075	12,103	14,716	14,740	15,223

Table 4.8 Business credit, selected sources, 2004 to 2008

	2004	2005	2006	2007	2008
	annual average ($ millions)				
All business credit	**933,319**	**988,901**	**1,048,775**	**1,119,745**	**1,185,835**
Short-term business credit	252,218	267,399	298,562	340,602	378,954
Business loans					
Chartered banks	125,688	135,757	147,619	166,498	185,035
Other institutions	27,032	29,841	33,082	35,948	41,370
Chartered bank foreign currency loans to residents	18,064	17,870	20,054	23,298	31,436
Bankers' acceptances	35,929	37,878	48,362	60,433	66,907
Adjustment to short-term business credit	-1,322	-1,634	-1,121	-1,089	-1,092
Long-term business credit	681,100	721,502	750,214	779,143	806,880
Non-residential mortgages					
Chartered banks	17,731	18,621	19,629	20,478	23,311
Trust and mortgage loan companies	668	1,039	1,275	1,780	2,458
Credit unions and *caisses populaires*	12,263	13,785	15,856	17,803	18,532
Life insurance companies	26,178	27,499	28,242	28,340	29,169
Leasing receivables					
Chartered banks	5,070	5,555	6,384	7,011	7,872
Trust and mortgage loan companies	15	46	58	60	70
Other business credit					
Bonds and debentures	248,337	258,374	255,158	262,478	274,277
Equity and other	278,775	289,167	293,561	302,184	321,637

Source: Statistics Canada, CANSIM table 176-0023.

Children and youth

5

Canada is a comparatively young country with proportionally fewer seniors and more young people in its population than many other developed countries.

In 2005, 24% of Canada's population was under age 20. That compares with 19% in Japan, 21% in 15 European countries and 28% in the United States. By contrast, 40% of the Mexican population was under age 20.

Still, our population is aging as the share of younger people has fallen over the past three decades. This trend is expected to continue over the next 50 years. In 2006, 31% of the population was under 25 compared with 48% in 1971.

A sign of the demographic shift is that, for the first time ever, the 2006 Census counted more census families comprised of couples without children aged 24 and younger present in the home (43%) than with children (41%).

On July 1, 2008, Canada had 10.2 million people aged 24 and younger. Of those, 5.6 million were under 15, 2.3 million were aged 15 to 19 and 2.3 million were aged 20 to 24.

Many women have delayed child-bearing, so a growing proportion of young children (aged 4 and younger) has a mother in her forties. In 2001, 7.8% of young children had a mother who was in her forties; this rose to 9.4% by 2006.

Health status

Fewer infants are dying from illnesses and fewer children are growing up in low-income families. Most are reaching their teens in good or excellent health.

Asthma, one of the most common chronic conditions among children, is on the rise. By 2000/2001, 13% of kids aged 11 and younger were diagnosed with asthma, up from 11% in 1994. The

Chart 5.1
Population aged 24 and younger

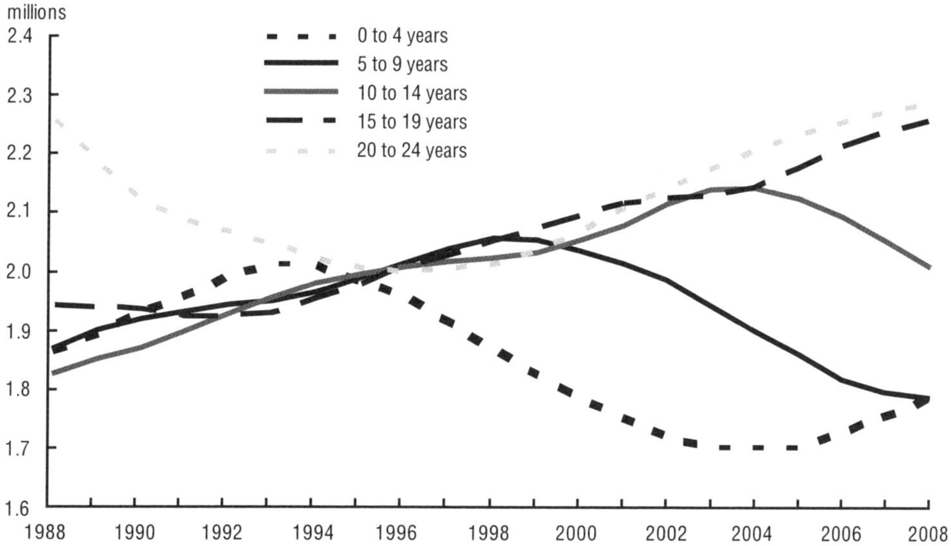

Note: Population as of July 1.
Source: Statistics Canada, CANSIM table 051-0001.

proportion with high-severity symptoms dropped from 41% to 36%. Childhood rates are highest in the Atlantic provinces and in homes with smokers.

The prevalence of obesity and being overweight doubled to 26% of children aged 14 and younger in 2006, up from 13% in 1977/1978. Children living in the lowest income neighbourhoods have the greatest likelihood of being overweight or obese. Children in rural areas weigh more than those in urban areas; however, unlike the impact of low income, this rural–urban disparity does not increase with age.

Participation in sports down

In 2005, 51% of kids aged 5 to 14 took part in organized sports in the previous 12 months, down from 57% in 1992. Soccer was the most popular sport for both boys and girls in 2005, replacing swimming, which was the most popular in 1992. Sports participation increases with household income and the education levels of parents.

Table 5.a
Population, by age and sex, 2008

	Males	Females
	number	
0 to 24	**5,201,998**	**4,935,719**
0 to 4 years	920,055	870,570
5 to 9 years	921,717	871,557
10 to 14 years	1,031,282	982,483
15 to 19 years	1,156,335	1,099,390
20 to 24 years	1,172,609	1,111,719

Source: Statistics Canada, CANSIM table 051-0001.

Children's participation in organized extracurricular activities is associated with positive social behaviours over both the short and long term. It is also linked to fewer school dropouts and lower rates of emotional and behavioural disorders.

In 2006, 200,000 families were caring for a child with disabilities. The parents of three out of five children who had some form of activity limitation said their job was affected by their child's condition. More than one-third of parents were working fewer hours, while another third had adjusted their work hours to cope.

Chart 5.2
Children who regularly participate in organized sports

Source: Statistics Canada, General Social Survey, 1992 and 2005.

Kids of older moms

Do children experience consequences when women delay motherhood until age 35 or older?

Health-wise, first-born children of older mothers are similar to children of mothers aged 25 to 29. They also reach certain developmental milestones at about the same time and they have similar average scores in cognitive development, physical aggression, emotional disorder and anxiety, and hyperactivity and inattention.

However, children of older mothers are more likely to be late to first sit up by themselves, to score lower on the Motor and Social Development Scale at ages 2 to 3, and to have lower positive behaviour scores at ages 4 to 5.

About 40% of children of older mothers are delivered by caesarean, almost twice the proportion of children of mothers aged 25 to 29 (23%). Of children of older mothers, 17% are born pre-term, compared with 11% in the younger group.

Children of older mothers are more likely to have been breastfed for more than six months: 43% versus 26% in the younger group.

Chart 5.3
First births by age of mother

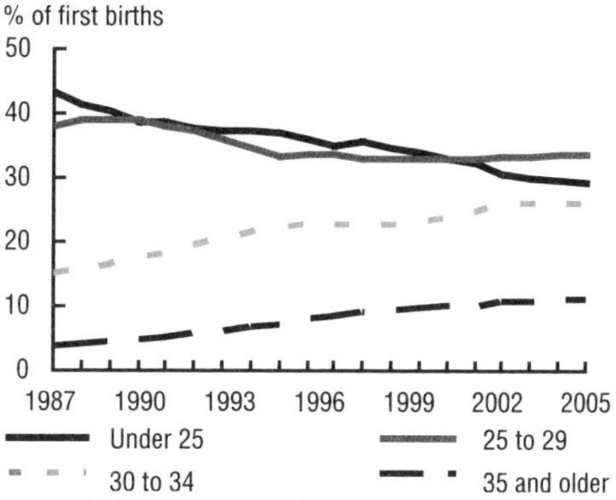

Source: Statistics Canada, Catalogue no. 89-599-M.

Teen sexual behaviour

Teens are delaying intercourse and some are more likely to use condoms than in the past. Girls account for the changes.

The number of young women aged 15 to 19 who have had intercourse at least once fell from 51% in 1996/1997 to 43% in 2005. Young men remained steady at 43%. The female rate of condom use increased from 65% in 2003 to 70% in 2005, while the male rates remained unchanged at 80%.

The proportion who had intercourse before age 15 also declined, from 12% to 8%. One in three 15- to 17-year-olds has had intercourse, compared with two in three 18- to 19-year-olds.

Quebec teenagers are sexually active at younger ages. In 2005, 58% of Quebec teenagers aged 15 to 19 reported having sexual intercourse, compared with 43% of teens living outside of Quebec.

Chart 5.4
Fifteen- to nineteen-year-olds who had sexual intercourse at least once, by province, 2005

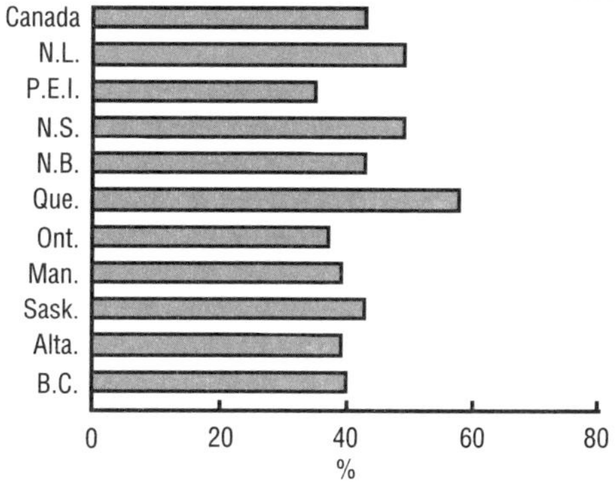

Source: Statistics Canada, Catalogue no. 82-003-X.

Table 5.1 Children and youth, by age group, selected years from 1973 to 2008

	1973		1978		1983	
	number	%	number	%	number	%
Both sexes, less than 25 years	**10,544,051**	**46.9**	**10,516,565**	**43.9**	**10,221,482**	**40.3**
Less than 1 year	341,600	1.5	355,407	1.5	370,109	1.5
1 to 4 years	1,446,566	6.4	1,411,978	5.9	1,468,806	5.8
5 to 9 years	2,082,997	9.3	1,856,999	7.7	1,793,547	7.1
10 to 14 years	2,368,189	10.5	2,129,776	8.9	1,890,627	7.5
15 to 19 years	2,272,006	10.1	2,423,548	10.1	2,191,088	8.6
20 to 24 years	2,032,693	9.0	2,338,857	9.8	2,507,305	9.9
Males, less than 25 years	**5,372,733**	**23.9**	**5,361,336**	**22.4**	**5,228,613**	**20.6**
Less than 1 year	175,772	0.8	182,358	0.8	190,270	0.8
1 to 4 years	740,914	3.3	723,303	3.0	753,415	3.0
5 to 9 years	1,065,372	4.7	953,510	4.0	918,756	3.6
10 to 14 years	1,210,738	5.4	1,090,445	4.6	970,865	3.8
15 to 19 years	1,155,890	5.1	1,233,960	5.1	1,123,436	4.4
20 to 24 years	1,024,047	4.6	1,177,760	4.9	1,271,871	5.0
Females, less than 25 years	**5,171,318**	**23.0**	**5,155,229**	**21.5**	**4,992,869**	**19.7**
Less than 1 year	165,828	0.7	173,049	0.7	179,839	0.7
1 to 4 years	705,652	3.1	688,675	2.9	715,391	2.8
5 to 9 years	1,017,625	4.5	903,489	3.8	874,791	3.4
10 to 14 years	1,157,451	5.1	1,039,331	4.3	919,762	3.6
15 to 19 years	1,116,116	5.0	1,189,588	5.0	1,067,652	4.2
20 to 24 years	1,008,646	4.5	1,161,097	4.8	1,235,434	4.9

Note: Percentage of the total population of Canada.
Source: Statistics Canada, CANSIM table 051-0001.

1988		1993		1998		2003		2008	
number	%	number	%	number	%	number	%	number	%
9,775,732	**36.5**	**9,903,650**	**34.5**	**10,023,700**	**33.2**	**10,098,745**	**31.9**	**10,137,717**	**30.4**
368,509	1.4	392,149	1.4	344,912	1.1	330,226	1.0	363,455	1.1
1,499,886	5.6	1,621,518	5.7	1,527,131	5.1	1,378,203	4.4	1,427,170	4.3
1,875,015	7.0	1,954,420	6.8	2,059,813	6.8	1,947,436	6.2	1,793,274	5.4
1,831,393	6.8	1,957,969	6.8	2,026,544	6.7	2,139,861	6.8	2,013,765	6.0
1,944,994	7.3	1,932,135	6.7	2,052,582	6.8	2,128,568	6.7	2,255,725	6.8
2,255,935	8.4	2,045,459	7.1	2,012,718	6.7	2,174,451	6.9	2,284,328	6.9
5,007,108	**18.7**	**5,071,242**	**17.7**	**5,136,490**	**17.0**	**5,174,491**	**16.4**	**5,201,998**	**15.6**
188,448	0.7	201,468	0.7	176,303	0.6	169,370	0.5	186,426	0.6
768,149	2.9	830,145	2.9	782,963	2.6	705,994	2.2	733,629	2.2
963,081	3.6	1,001,051	3.5	1,054,691	3.5	996,782	3.2	921,717	2.8
938,076	3.5	1,005,051	3.5	1,040,078	3.4	1,096,188	3.5	1,031,282	3.1
997,677	3.7	992,128	3.5	1,054,922	3.5	1,094,873	3.5	1,156,335	3.5
1,151,677	4.3	1,041,399	3.6	1,027,533	3.4	1,111,284	3.5	1,172,609	3.5
4,768,624	**17.8**	**4,832,408**	**16.8**	**4,887,210**	**16.2**	**4,924,254**	**15.6**	**4,935,719**	**14.8**
180,061	0.7	190,681	0.7	168,609	0.6	160,856	0.5	177,029	0.5
731,737	2.7	791,373	2.8	744,168	2.5	672,209	2.1	693,541	2.1
911,934	3.4	953,369	3.3	1,005,122	3.3	950,654	3.0	871,557	2.6
893,317	3.3	952,918	3.3	986,466	3.3	1,043,673	3.3	982,483	2.9
947,317	3.5	940,007	3.3	997,660	3.3	1,033,695	3.3	1,099,390	3.3
1,104,258	4.1	1,004,060	3.5	985,185	3.3	1,063,167	3.4	1,111,719	3.3

Table 5.2 Children and youth, by age group and by province and territory, 2008

	Canada	Newfoundland and Labrador	Prince Edward Island	Nova Scotia	New Brunswick
			%		
Both sexes, less than 25 years	**30.4**	**27.6**	**30.7**	**28.5**	**28.2**
Less than 1 year	**1.1**	0.9	1.0	0.9	0.9
1 to 4 years	**4.3**	3.7	3.9	3.7	3.8
5 to 9 years	**5.4**	5.0	5.4	4.9	5.1
10 to 14 years	**6.0**	5.5	6.4	5.7	5.7
15 to 19 years	**6.8**	6.5	7.4	6.7	6.5
20 to 24 years	**6.9**	6.1	6.6	6.6	6.2
Males, less than 25 years	**15.6**	**14.1**	**15.7**	**14.4**	**14.5**
Less than 1 year	**0.6**	0.5	0.5	0.5	0.5
1 to 4 years	**2.2**	1.9	2.0	1.9	1.9
5 to 9 years	**2.8**	2.5	2.8	2.5	2.6
10 to 14 years	**3.1**	2.9	3.3	2.9	3.0
15 to 19 years	**3.5**	3.3	3.7	3.4	3.3
20 to 24 years	**3.5**	3.1	3.3	3.3	3.2
Females, less than 25 years	**14.8**	**13.5**	**15.0**	**14.1**	**13.7**
Less than 1 year	**0.5**	0.4	0.5	0.4	0.5
1 to 4 years	**2.1**	1.8	1.9	1.8	1.8
5 to 9 years	**2.6**	2.4	2.7	2.4	2.4
10 to 14 years	**2.9**	2.7	3.1	2.8	2.8
15 to 19 years	**3.3**	3.1	3.6	3.3	3.2
20 to 24 years	**3.3**	3.1	3.3	3.3	3.0

Note: Percentage of the total population of Canada, the province or the territory.
Source: Statistics Canada, CANSIM table 051-0001.

Quebec	Ontario	Manitoba	Saskatchewan	Alberta	British Columbia	Yukon	Northwest Territories	Nunavut
				%				
28.6	**30.9**	**33.4**	**33.8**	**33.2**	**29.1**	**31.4**	**39.0**	**52.1**
1.1	1.1	1.2	1.3	1.3	1.0	1.1	1.6	2.4
4.1	4.4	4.8	4.9	4.9	3.9	4.5	6.2	8.9
5.0	5.6	6.2	6.1	5.8	5.0	5.7	7.0	10.8
5.8	6.2	6.8	6.7	6.2	5.7	6.1	7.5	10.8
6.5	6.9	7.4	7.6	6.9	6.6	7.0	8.8	10.2
6.3	6.9	7.0	7.3	8.0	6.9	7.0	8.0	9.1
14.7	**15.8**	**17.1**	**17.4**	**17.2**	**15.0**	**16.2**	**20.2**	**26.6**
0.6	0.5	0.6	0.6	0.7	0.5	0.6	0.9	1.2
2.1	2.2	2.5	2.5	2.5	2.0	2.4	3.3	4.4
2.5	2.8	3.2	3.1	3.0	2.6	2.9	3.4	5.6
3.0	3.2	3.5	3.4	3.2	3.0	3.0	3.8	5.4
3.3	3.5	3.8	3.9	3.6	3.4	3.8	4.6	5.4
3.2	3.5	3.6	3.7	4.2	3.6	3.5	4.3	4.6
14.0	**15.1**	**16.3**	**16.5**	**16.0**	**14.1**	**15.2**	**18.8**	**25.6**
0.5	0.5	0.6	0.6	0.6	0.5	0.5	0.7	1.3
2.0	2.1	2.3	2.4	2.4	1.9	2.1	2.9	4.4
2.4	2.7	3.0	3.0	2.8	2.4	2.8	3.7	5.1
2.8	3.0	3.3	3.3	3.0	2.8	3.1	3.7	5.4
3.2	3.4	3.6	3.7	3.4	3.2	3.2	4.2	4.9
3.1	3.4	3.4	3.5	3.8	3.3	3.5	3.7	4.5

Table 5.3 Children and youth, by age group and family structure, 2006

	Total children and youth	Family structure		
		Couple families	Lone-parent families	Not in census families
	number			
0 to 4 years	**1,765,440**	1,469,870	295,470	100
5 to 9 years	**1,819,890**	1,432,120	387,510	260
10 to 14 years[1]	**2,075,250**	1,578,080	495,820	1,350
15 to 19 years[1]	**2,273,730**	1,574,040	521,170	178,520
20 to 24 years[1]	**1,490,670**	886,320	174,290	430,060

1. Excludes those who are parents.
Source: Statistics Canada, CANSIM table 111-0010.

Table 5.4 Young parents, by family structure, 2002 to 2006

	2002	2003	2004	2005	2006
	number				
Parents aged 15 to 19 years					
Couple families	52,080	55,690	57,720	57,770	58,210
Lone-parent families	13,210	12,680	11,750	10,890	10,810
Parents aged 20 to 24 years					
Couple families	380,840	407,700	409,740	406,680	405,960
Lone-parent families	73,040	73,080	71,340	67,630	64,570

Source: Statistics Canada, CANSIM table 111-0010.

Table 5.5 Mothers of children aged 4 years and younger, by age of mother and census family status, 2001 and 2006

	All mothers		Married mothers		Common-law mothers		Lone mothers	
	2001	2006	2001	2006	2001	2006	2001	2006
	%							
Total	**100.0**	**100.0**	**100.0**	**100.0**	**100.0**	**100.0**	**100.0**	**100.0**
15 to 19 years	**1.3**	**1.1**	0.1	0.1	2.3	1.7	6.2	5.0
20 to 24 years	**10.4**	**8.8**	5.0	3.8	20.1	16.4	25.4	23.3
25 to 29 years	**23.9**	**23.2**	22.0	20.2	29.6	31.0	26.3	27.2
30 to 34 years	**33.5**	**33.7**	37.8	37.6	26.5	28.4	21.1	21.3
35 to 39 years	**23.1**	**23.8**	26.6	27.8	16.2	15.9	14.1	14.8
40 to 44 years	**6.8**	**8.2**	7.5	9.2	4.7	5.7	5.7	6.9
45 to 49 years	**1.0**	**1.2**	1.0	1.3	0.6	0.8	1.1	1.5

Source: Statistics Canada, censuses of population, 2001 and 2006.

Table 5.6 Deaths and death rates of children and youth, by age group, 1996, 2001 and 2006

	1996		2001		2006	
	number	rate	number	rate	number	rate
Less than 1 year	**2,051**	**5.6**	**1,739**	**5.2**	**1,771**	**5.0**
Males	1,155	6.1	997	5.8	983	5.4
Females	896	5.0	742	4.6	788	4.6
1 to 4 years	**461**	**0.3**	**340**	**0.2**	**284**	**0.2**
Males	257	0.3	191	0.3	163	0.2
Females	204	0.3	149	0.2	121	0.2
5 to 9 years	**297**	**0.1**	**245**	**0.1**	**198**	**0.1**
Males	158	0.2	132	0.1	111	0.1
Females	139	0.1	113	0.1	87	0.1
10 to 14 years	**339**	**0.2**	**286**	**0.1**	**275**	**0.1**
Males	206	0.2	163	0.2	160	0.1
Females	133	0.1	123	0.1	115	0.1
15 to 19 years	**1,049**	**0.5**	**1,033**	**0.5**	**985**	**0.5**
Males	730	0.7	728	0.7	674	0.6
Females	319	0.3	305	0.3	311	0.3

Note: Rate per 1,000 population.
Source: Statistics Canada, CANSIM table 102-0504.

Table 5.7 Leading causes of death of children and youth, by age group, 2003 to 2005

	2003		2004		2005	
	number	rate	number	rate	number	rate
Less than 1 year						
Perinatal conditions	981	292.7	1,019	302.3	1,037	303.1
Congenital malformations, deformations and chromosomal abnormalities	423	126.2	412	122.2	447	130.6
Sudden infant death syndrome	96	28.6	84	24.9	112	32.7
1 to 4 years						
Accidents (unintentional injuries)	86	6.3	67	4.9	74	5.4
Malignant neoplasms	29	2.1	36	2.6	28	2.1
Congenital conditions	35	2.5	38	2.8	36	2.6
5 to 9 years						
Accidents (unintentional injuries)	69	3.5	72	3.8	64	3.4
Malignant neoplasms	45	2.3	45	2.3	45	2.4
Congenital conditions	12	0.6	15	0.8	13	0.7
10 to 14 years						
Accidents (unintentional injuries)	110	5.2	90	4.2	95	4.5
Malignant neoplasms	40	1.9	52	2.5	43	2.0
Suicide (intentional self-harm)	27	1.3	28	1.3	43	2.0
15 to 19 years						
Accidents (unintentional injuries)	444	20.9	414	19.5	458	21.3
Suicide (intentional self-harm)	216	10.2	210	9.9	213	9.9
Malignant neoplasms	83	3.9	66	3.1	61	2.8

Note: Rate per 100,000 population.
Source: Statistics Canada, CANSIM tables 102-0551 and 102-0562.

Table 5.8 Current daily or occasional smokers among children and youth, by age group, selected years from 2000/2001 to 2007

	2000/2001		2003		2005		2007	
	number	%	number	%	number	%	number	%
12 to 19 years	605,558	18.7	490,404	14.8	405,109	12.1	403,212	12.0
Males	292,307	17.6	244,134	14.4	204,113	11.9	213,296	12.4
Females	313,250	19.8	246,270	15.2	200,996	12.3	189,916	11.5
12 to 14 years	69,203	6.0	43,731	3.4	30,923	2.5	31,924[E]	2.5[E]
Males	30,483	5.1	19,594	2.9	10,439	1.6	17,878[E]	2.7[E]
Females	38,720	7.0	24,137	4.0	20,485	3.5	14,045[E]	2.3[E]
15 to 19 years	536,354	25.7	446,673	21.9	374,185	17.7	371,288	17.7
Males	261,824	24.7	224,540	21.7	193,674	18.1	195,418	18.3
Females	274,530	26.7	222,133	22.1	180,511	17.2	175,870	17.1
20 to 24 years	745,446	35.0	718,612	33.2	682,127	30.5	663,526	30.7
Males	403,213	37.3	393,206	35.4	378,655	32.4	372,054	33.4
Females	342,232	32.6	325,406	30.8	303,472	28.3	291,472	27.8

Source: Statistics Canada, CANSIM tables 105-0027, 105-0227, 105-0427 and 105-0501.

Table 5.9 Alcohol consumption among children and youth, by age group, selected years from 2000 to 2007

	2000		2003		2005		2007	
	number	%	number	%	number	%	number	%
12 to 19 years	435,482	25.1	464,455	26.6	475,980	27.7	455,510	26.7
Males	269,607	30.1	295,127	32.5	292,601	33.2	278,920	31.0
Females	165,875	19.8	169,329	20.2	183,379	21.9	176,590	21.9
12 to 14 years	12,544	4.8	11,054[E]	4.2[E]	10,690	4.5	7,816[E]	3.4[E]
Males	4,347[E]	3.0[E]	5,391[E]	4.0[E]	6,262[E]	5.1[E]	F	F
Females	8,197[E]	6.8[E]	5,664[E]	4.5[E]	4,428[E]	3.9[E]	F	F
15 to 19 years	422,937	28.8	453,401	30.5	465,290	31.3	447,694	30.4
Males	265,260	35.2	289,736	37.4	286,339	37.7	275,610	36.0
Females	157,678	22.1	163,665	23.0	178,951	24.7	172,084	24.3
20 to 24 years	687,829	37.1	793,688	41.4	878,119	44.5	802,046	42.6
Males	458,213	47.1	516,697	50.9	576,782	55.3	499,663	50.5
Females	229,616	26.0	276,991	30.7	301,337	32.4	302,383	33.8

Note: Population aged 12 to 24 who drank five or more drinks at least once a month in the past year.
Source: Statistics Canada, CANSIM tables 105-0031, 105-0231, 105-0431 and 105-0501.

Table 5.10 Labour force characteristics, population aged 15 to 24, by age group and sex, 1998 and 2008

	1998			2008		
	Full-time students	Part-time students	Non-students	Full-time students	Part-time students	Non-students
	thousands					
Males 15 to 19	**819.3**	**21.3**	**188.0**	**848.6**	**32.4**	**222.6**
Labour force	285.6	15.6	153.4	344.8	25.2	187.4
Employment full-time	10.0	4.1	86.2	13.2	8.6	116.9
Employment part-time	216.8	7.9	29.5	276.5	12.1	34.8
Unemployment	58.8	3.6	37.8	55.1	4.5	35.8
	%					
Participation rate	34.9	73.2	81.6	40.6	77.8	84.2
Employment rate	27.7	55.9	61.5	34.1	63.9	68.1
Unemployment rate	20.6	23.1	24.6	16.0	17.9	19.1
	thousands					
Males 20 to 24	**327.5**	**39.3**	**637.3**	**347.6**	**50.8**	**730.4**
Labour force	133.9	34.1	590.3	161.8	42.5	675.8
Employment full-time	15.8	19.8	451.9	27.6	22.3	540.3
Employment part-time	104.0	10.5	52.8	121.9	16.5	58.1
Unemployment	14.1	3.8	85.7	12.3	3.7	77.4
	%					
Participation rate	40.9	86.8	92.6	46.5	83.7	92.5
Employment rate	36.6	77.1	79.2	43.0	76.2	81.9
Unemployment rate	10.5	11.1	14.5	7.6	8.7	11.5
	thousands					
Females 15 to 19	**802.2**	**24.7**	**149.4**	**853.6**	**37.1**	**162.4**
Labour force	307.7	18.5	108.4	416.9	29.2	128.0
Employment full-time	5.5	4.1	49.1	8.8	7.8	67.6
Employment part-time	251.6	10.5	37.4	353.3	17.5	40.0
Unemployment	50.6	3.8	21.8	54.8	4.0	20.4
	%					
Participation rate	38.4	74.9	72.6	48.8	78.7	78.8
Employment rate	32.0	59.1	57.9	42.4	67.9	66.2
Unemployment rate	16.4	20.5	20.1	13.1	13.7	15.9
	thousands					
Females 20 to 24	**341.2**	**48.9**	**579.8**	**415.4**	**59.8**	**615.1**
Labour force	161.6	41.5	475.2	226.5	50.4	524.5
Employment full-time	11.6	22.5	313.8	20.9	27.3	392.9
Employment part-time	138.6	15.6	106.5	194.9	19.8	87.7
Unemployment	11.4	3.3	54.8	10.7	3.3	43.9
	%					
Participation rate	47.4	84.9	82.0	54.5	84.3	85.3
Employment rate	44.1	78.1	72.5	52.0	78.8	78.1
Unemployment rate	7.1	8.0	11.5	4.7	6.5	8.4

Note: Labour market activity during school months.
Source: Statistics Canada, CANSIM table 282-0095.

Table 5.11 Top 10 sports for children, 1992 and 2005

	1992	2005
	% of children	
All sports	**57**	**51**
Soccer	12	20
Swimming	17	12
Hockey	12	11
Basketball	6	8
Baseball	13	5
Volleyball	5	3
Gymnastics	4	2
Karate	2E	2
Downhill skiing	6	2
Track and field / athletics	2E	2E

Note: Children aged 5 to 14 regularly participating in organized sports.
Source: Statistics Canada, Catalogue no. 11-008-X.

Table 5.12 Disability rates for children 14 years and younger, by sex and age group, 2006

	Both sexes	Boys	Girls
	number		
0 to 14 years	**202,350**	**129,210**	**73,140**
0 to 4 years	27,540	17,770	9,770
5 to 9 years	74,580	48,290	26,300
10 to 14 years	100,230	63,150	37,070
	%		
0 to 14 years	**3.7**	**4.6**	**2.7**
0 to 4 years	1.7	2.1	1.2
5 to 9 years	4.2	5.3	3.0
10 to 14 years	4.9	6.0	3.7

Notes: The sum of the values in the category may differ from the total because of rounding.
Percentage of all children under the age of 15.
Source: Statistics Canada, Catalogue no. 89-628-X.

Construction

The construction industries contributed, in real terms, $74.9 billion to Canada's gross domestic product (GDP) in 2008, up 2.7% from 2007, despite a 1.1% decline in the fourth quarter of 2008.

Each of the three construction industries—residential construction, non-residential building construction, and engineering, repair and other construction activities—posted gains in 2008. The construction sector grew each year from 2003 to 2008, though its rate of growth began to decelerate in 2007.

The construction industries are a major employer. About 1.2 million Canadians worked in construction in 2008: 1,087,300 men and 144,800 women. This accounted for 7.2% of all jobs in Canada and 30.6% of those in the goods-producing sector.

Workers in many occupations are affected when the construction industries slump because not all jobs in construction require hard hats. Besides the traditional trades such as plumbing, carpentry and masonry, there are managerial, clerical and other white-collar positions.

Employment

Historically, construction has seen higher employment peaks and deeper valleys over the business cycle than other industries. During the recession of the early 1990s, jobless rates in the trades were much higher than in other occupations.

From 2001 to 2006, when Canada led the G7 nations in annual employment growth with a rate of 1.7%, construction averaged 4.5% growth. This trend held true in the 2008 economic downturn. From March 2008 to March 2009, construction employment fell 5.3%, compared with a 1.5% loss across all industries.

Construction posted the fastest employment growth from January to October 2008; then, it experienced the steepest decline as the downturn

Chart 6.1
Employment, construction and all industries

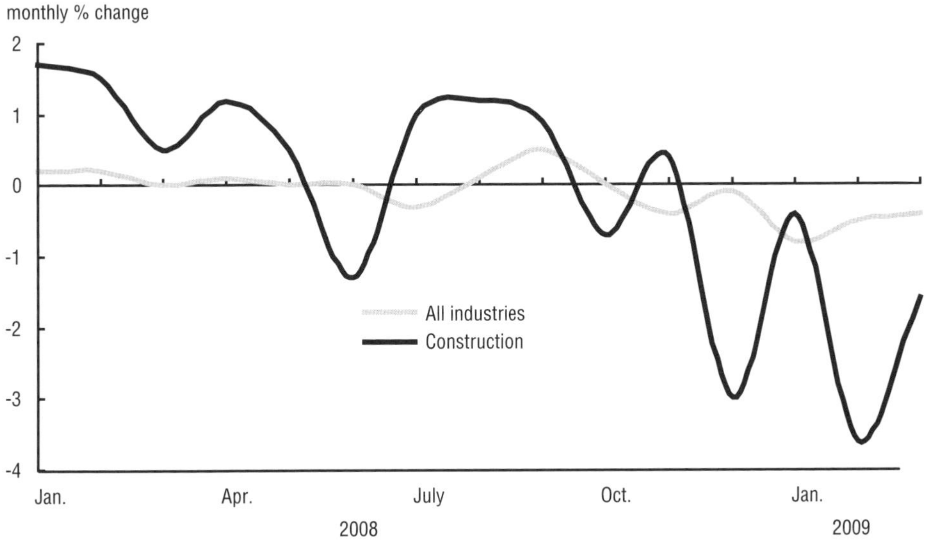

Source: Statistics Canada, CANSIM table 282-0088.

progressed. In Ontario alone, the number of workers in construction decreased 9.3% from October 2008 to May 2009.

Housing starts

Housing starts fell 7.3% over the course of 2008, decreasing more dramatically late in the year (down 11.0% in the fourth quarter). By the first quarter of 2009, starts in Western Canada had fallen 69.6% from their peak in the third quarter of 2007, reflecting the end of the commodity boom, while the average decline in the rest of Canada during the same period was 32.6%. Housing starts are used to estimate investment in residential construction.

The total value of building permits—for both residential and non-residential construction—declined 5.3% in 2008, the first annual retreat since 1995. The value of building permits fell more noticeably in the fourth quarter of 2008, declining 26.7% (unadjusted).

Table 6.a
GDP growth of the construction industry, 2003 to 2008

	2003 to 2004	2007 to 2008
	%	
Construction	6.0	2.7
Residential building construction	6.7	0.8
Non-residential building construction	2.7	1.8
Engineering, repair and other construction activites	6.6	4.2

Note: The GDP data are in chained (2002) dollars, seasonally adjusted at annual rates.
Source: Statistics Canada, CANSIM table 379-0027.

Chart 6.2
Housing starts and completions

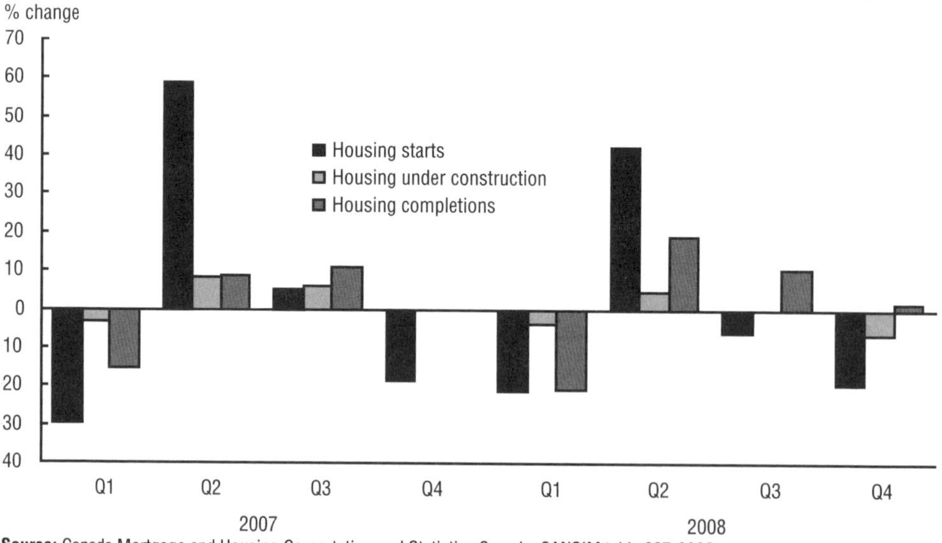

Source: Canada Mortgage and Housing Corporation and Statistics Canada, CANSIM table 027-0008.

Building materials

Slumping housing demand has depressed the lumber industry and sales of other building materials.

Sales of manufactured wood products (or shipments) fell from $3.0 billion early in 2006 to $1.5 billion in late 2008. After being one of Canada's export staples for over a century, lumber accounted for 1% of exports in January 2009.

Wholesale sales of lumber and millwork fell 15.2% in 2008. Sawn lumber production and shipments dropped 33.8% from January to December. However, thanks to positive second and third quarters, retail sales of lumber and other building supplies edged up 2.4%.

Demand for other building materials also declined in 2008. Cement production fell 27.8% from December 2007 to December 2008, while shipments of cement declined 16.7%. Asphalt shingle production rose 7.8% over the course of 2008, but fell 20.0% in the third quarter and dropped 45.7% in the fourth quarter. Shipments dropped 86.5% from January to December of 2008.

Chart 6.3
Real GDP at basic prices, all industries and construction

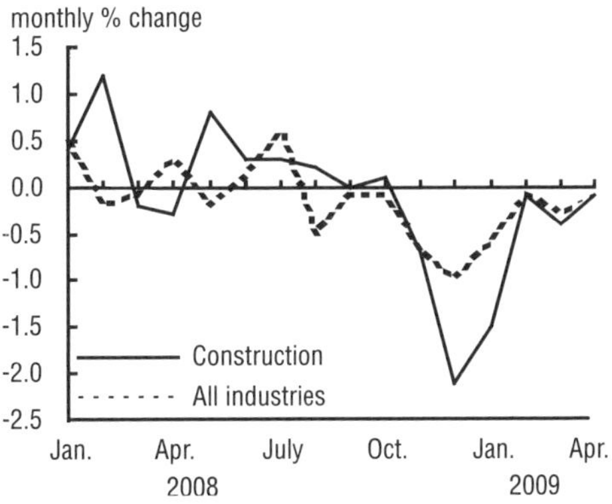

Note: Seasonally adjusted data at annual rates.
Source: Statistics Canada, CANSIM table 379-0027.

Education and skilled trades

Education and training are crucial to filling the ranks of the skilled trades. Manufacturers surveyed in 2006 and 2007 said that a lack of skilled labour was the major impediment to production.

Government programs were created to encourage youth to enter into and complete apprenticeship training, to encourage employers to hire them, and to help employed tradespersons buy tools and equipment.

The trades have consistently made up 8% of total employment. In 2007, 68% of those employed in the trades had some postsecondary education, compared with 51% in 1990.

However, there is some diversity in educational attainment among the trades. For example, 8 in 10 plumbers and electricians had postsecondary education in 2007 compared with 4 in 10 masons.

Chart 6.4
Postsecondary education of selected workers in the trades, 2007

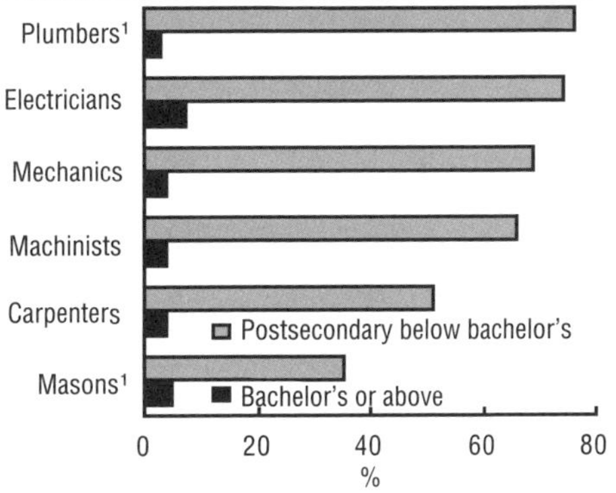

1. Data for bachelor's or above should be used with caution.
Source: Statistics Canada, Catalogue no. 75-001-X.

Table 6.1 Housing starts, by province, 1994 to 2008

	1994	1995	1996	1997	1998	1999
	number					
Canada	**154,057**	**110,933**	**124,713**	**147,040**	**137,439**	**149,968**
Newfoundland and Labrador	2,243	1,712	2,034	1,696	1,450	1,371
Prince Edward Island	669	422	554	470	524	616
Nova Scotia	4,748	4,168	4,059	3,813	3,137	4,250
New Brunswick	3,203	2,300	2,722	2,702	2,447	2,776
Quebec	34,154	21,885	23,220	25,896	23,138	25,742
Ontario	46,645	35,818	43,062	54,072	53,830	67,235
Manitoba	3,197	1,963	2,318	2,612	2,895	3,133
Saskatchewan	2,098	1,702	2,438	2,757	2,965	3,089
Alberta	17,692	13,906	16,665	23,671	27,122	25,447
British Columbia	39,408	27,057	27,641	29,351	19,931	16,309

Source: Statistics Canada, CANSIM table 027-0009.

Table 6.2 Value of building permits, by province and territory, 1994 to 2008

	1994	1995	1996	1997	1998	1999
	$ millions					
Canada	**27,636.7**	**24,589.3**	**26,155.4**	**30,838.2**	**33,340.8**	**35,736.1**
Newfoundland and Labrador	262.7	201.7	224.1	213.6	252.7	296.8
Prince Edward Island	112.7	95.2	95.8	110.0	116.1	140.9
Nova Scotia	669.2	619.6	689.0	630.7	637.1	907.2
New Brunswick	440.5	487.9	441.1	459.0	481.0	481.2
Quebec	5,898.5	4,947.4	4,938.0	5,133.2	5,897.4	5,939.6
Ontario	10,001.3	9,192.2	9,597.6	12,888.7	13,839.8	16,732.5
Manitoba	685.3	525.4	592.3	689.6	1,031.8	879.4
Saskatchewan	372.3	478.2	543.0	626.8	672.9	721.6
Alberta	2,740.5	2,506.6	2,883.1	4,446.3	5,552.2	4,801.9
British Columbia	6,317.9	5,401.4	6,053.1	5,543.8	4,739.6	4,695.5
Yukon	51.0	74.0	51.8	49.6	39.9	48.8
Northwest Territories (including Nunavut)	84.9	59.6	46.6	46.9	80.2	90.6
Northwest Territories	..	..	..	..	..	..
Nunavut	..	..	..	..	..	..

Source: Statistics Canada, CANSIM table 026-0003.

2000	2001	2002	2003	2004	2005	2006	2007	2008
				number				
151,653	**162,733**	**205,034**	**218,426**	**233,431**	**225,481**	**227,395**	**228,343**	**211,056**
1,459	1,788	2,419	2,692	2,870	2,498	2,234	2,649	3,261
710	675	775	814	919	862	738	750	712
4,432	4,092	4,970	5,096	4,717	4,775	4,896	4,750	3,982
3,079	3,462	3,862	4,489	3,947	3,959	4,085	4,242	4,274
24,695	27,682	42,452	50,289	58,448	50,910	47,877	48,553	47,901
71,521	73,282	83,597	85,180	85,114	78,795	73,417	68,123	75,076
2,560	2,963	3,617	4,206	4,440	4,731	5,028	5,738	5,537
2,513	2,381	2,963	3,315	3,781	3,437	3,715	6,007	6,828
26,266	29,174	38,754	36,171	36,270	40,847	48,962	48,336	29,164
14,418	17,234	21,625	26,174	32,925	34,667	36,443	39,195	34,321

2000	2001	2002	2003	2004	2005	2006	2007	2008
				$ millions				
36,950.1	**40,856.1**	**47,262.1**	**50,772.0**	**55,578.6**	**60,750.7**	**66,265.8**	**74,379.7**	**70,437.4**
282.9	298.3	383.3	421.0	501.2	494.1	538.4	660.1	802.5
98.8	217.2	146.2	178.1	223.8	244.0	207.0	163.8	216.9
878.5	699.9	877.3	1,014.1	1,125.8	1,188.0	1,291.4	1,288.9	1,326.7
484.6	535.1	663.8	696.3	797.3	829.0	933.3	965.2	1,113.8
6,272.0	7,571.1	8,628.4	10,090.9	11,629.6	11,288.0	11,878.3	12,973.4	13,806.7
17,556.5	19,069.3	22,281.4	23,235.2	23,905.3	24,129.6	23,292.2	26,710.4	25,414.6
853.9	739.2	888.9	1,065.0	1,150.4	1,128.5	1,378.8	1,480.1	1,636.7
609.0	703.3	708.6	772.6	770.0	905.7	1,138.6	1,646.4	2,185.8
5,296.4	5,911.7	6,846.5	6,667.2	7,327.1	10,201.7	13,875.7	15,729.7	13,141.2
4,492.0	4,954.8	5,659.4	6,394.2	7,938.7	10,182.9	11,541.5	12,544.7	10,577.2
55.5	49.8	31.3	52.6	75.9	77.3	95.6	79.6	70.0
..	..	..	..	..	..	..	..	..
23.0	76.0	91.6	86.2	105.3	68.7	37.7	74.0	87.4
47.2	30.4	55.4	98.6	28.1	13.2	57.4	63.5	58.0

Table 6.3 Investment in non-residential building construction, by census metropolitan area, 2004 to 2008

	2004	2005	2006	2007	2008
			$ millions		
All census metropolitan areas	**21,904.9**	**22,438.5**	**25,113.1**	**29,375.2**	**32,458.1**
St. John's	121.6	167.4	146.1	158.1	164.6
Halifax	235.1	328.3	385.5	335.9	338.0
Moncton[1]	..	..	78.2	176.8	185.6
Saint John	88.8	62.8	87.8	132.5	120.3
Saguenay	107.2	85.0	124.2	151.7	150.8
Québec	587.2	648.6	671.7	771.8	1,060.6
Sherbrooke	130.0	118.3	162.4	171.1	180.6
Trois-Rivières	149.5	103.6	124.8	200.4	202.6
Montréal	3,110.0	3,014.5	2,970.2	3,416.6	3,659.6
Ottawa–Gatineau	1,449.9	1,307.5	1,583.7	1,624.6	1,422.3
Kingston	146.7	150.8	119.3	194.3	301.6
Peterborough[1]	..	..	51.4	57.6	80.4
Oshawa	531.6	509.5	411.3	377.1	385.1
Toronto	6,667.6	6,577.0	6,361.0	6,739.3	7,866.5
Hamilton	791.9	609.8	672.1	554.6	838.5
St. Catharines–Niagara	416.8	314.7	312.3	274.3	266.9
Kitchener	568.6	638.9	550.3	552.2	659.2
Brantford[1]	..	..	63.5	149.8	83.1
Guelph[1]	..	..	121.2	197.1	162.1
London	565.5	578.8	473.7	516.8	655.9
Windsor	323.4	299.4	366.8	344.6	262.4
Barrie[1]	..	..	147.9	243.6	276.8
Greater Sudbury/Grand Sudbury	96.7	140.3	136.3	230.6	256.5
Thunder Bay	128.1	105.5	114.4	85.1	99.3
Winnipeg	545.5	539.2	658.0	599.1	534.3
Regina	199.7	188.2	240.5	284.7	270.8
Saskatoon	186.3	242.4	395.2	370.6	568.3
Calgary	1,467.7	1,818.1	2,537.4	4,421.9	5,029.9
Edmonton	1,075.2	1,247.9	1,608.5	1,840.2	2,202.6
Kelowna[1]	..	..	102.6	225.6	304.0
Abbotsford-Mission	84.7	138.5	232.3	247.2	229.0
Vancouver	1,747.6	2,240.8	2,735.5	3,348.8	3,279.3
Victoria	382.1	262.9	367.0	380.6	360.9

1. Became a census metropolitan area in 2006.
Source: Statistics Canada, CANSIM table 026-0016.

Table 6.4 Capital expenditures for construction, by sector, 2005 to 2009

	Actual			Preliminary	Intentions
	2005	2006	2007	2008[1]	2009[2]
	$ millions				
Canada	**171,964.8**	**195,762.9**	**214,226.8**	**231,057.3**	**220,279.5**
Agriculture, forestry, fishing and hunting	1,359.4	1,228.5	1,832.1	1,595.9	1,452.2
Mining and oil and gas extraction	39,397.4	45,800.8	48,316.4	50,195.6	36,670.2
Utilities	9,861.4	11,687.8	14,025.4	17,222.0	18,123.2
Construction	531.0	586.6	671.2	726.5	730.3
Manufacturing	2,235.7	2,665.9	3,192.6	2,277.7	2,221.5
Wholesale trade	1,106.7	1,540.7	1,486.3	1,314.3	1,439.8
Retail trade	3,665.8	4,170.7	4,886.2	4,492.4	4,030.0
Transportation and warehousing	3,966.3	5,767.2	6,201.9	8,741.6	10,461.8
Information and cultural industries	2,693.5	2,124.4	2,127.4	2,600.9	2,547.4
Finance and insurance	809.0	868.2	914.9	1,087.3	1,254.5
Real estate and rental and leasing	3,550.1	4,385.5	4,584.5	4,447.9	4,181.1
Professional, scientific and technical services	330.8	481.7	442.1	434.8	355.3
Management of companies and enterprises	26.5	44.1	26.5	46.4	34.0
Administrative and support, waste management and remediation services	248.8	384.6	453.4	413.4	353.6
Educational services	4,707.7	5,192.1	5,441.8	5,824.0	5,759.9
Health care and social assistance	3,708.7	4,506.8	4,222.4	5,480.1	5,805.7
Arts, entertainment and recreation	692.6	837.5	1,123.1	925.6	829.0
Accommodation and food services	1,508.6	1,786.2	1,853.2	2,374.2	1,054.0
Housing	73,574.9	81,708.8	89,117.7	91,632.9	89,959.1
Public administration	17,511.6	19,504.9	22,813.9	28,681.1	32,522.9
Other services (excluding public administration)	478.4	489.7	493.6	542.7	494.0

Notes: The Capital Expenditures Survey collects data on the intentions for capital investment and the expenditures for the previous two years.
North American Industry Classification System (NAICS), 2002.
1. Data reflect the preliminary actuals for capital expenditures for 2008.
2. Data reflect the intentions for capital expenditures for 2009.
Source: Statistics Canada, CANSIM table 029-0005.

Table 6.5 Payroll employment in construction, by province, 2003 to 2008

	2003	2004	2005	2006	2007	2008
	number					
Canada	**633,977**	**662,763**	**694,384**	**736,571**	**785,836**	**829,561**
Newfoundland and Labrador	8,420	8,889	9,313	9,333	10,005	10,966
Prince Edward Island	4,176	4,229	4,214	4,172	4,224	4,295
Nova Scotia	16,596	17,176	17,636	18,893	20,188	20,916
New Brunswick	14,526	15,158	15,535	16,401	16,923	18,766
Quebec	135,994	143,748	145,758	145,908	148,119	158,346
Ontario	224,392	229,585	235,345	246,906	260,174	273,211
Manitoba	19,951	20,713	21,251	22,782	24,705	25,840
Saskatchewan	17,565	18,203	19,115	20,793	23,683	25,095
Alberta	110,041	114,577	126,677	140,134	155,226	161,793
British Columbia	79,420	87,504	96,039	107,891	119,009	126,516
Yukon	629	659	858	1,062	1,007	960
Northwest Territories	1,641	1,728	2,018	1,757	2,010	2,222
Nunavut	626	595	625	538	564	634

Notes: North American Industry Classification System (NAICS), 2002.
Survey of Employment, Payroll and Hours.
Source: Statistics Canada, CANSIM table 281-0024.

Table 6.6 Production of building materials, 2004 to 2008

	2004	2005	2006	2007	2008
	thousands of cubic metres				
Dry sawn lumber	84,589.6	82,888.9	80,870.4	72,042.6	57,250.1
	thousands of bundles				
Asphalt shingles, all sizes	43,639.0	40,284.7	44,590.3	41,143.2	44,270.7
	thousands of metric tonnes				
Cement	13,862.9	14,179.4	14,335.5	15,077.6	13,672.4
Steel pipe and tubing	2,647.2	2,837.1	2,948.5	2,614.7	2,537.8

Note: Standard Classification of Goods (SCG).
Source: Statistics Canada, CANSIM tables 303-0009, 303-0046, 303-0052 and 303-0060.

Crime and justice

Based on data reported by police, Canada's national crime rate declined for the third consecutive year in 2007, continuing the downward trend in police-reported crime since the rate peaked in 1991.

The national crime rate was 7.0 crimes per 100 people—the lowest since 1978 and 32% below its 1991 peak of 10.3 crimes per 100 people.

The drop was driven mainly by decreases in high-volume, predominantly non-violent crimes, such as counterfeiting, thefts of $5,000 and under, break-ins and motor vehicle thefts. In particular, the rate of break-ins has been steadily declining since 1991. From 2006 to 2007, the rate of residential break-ins fell 9% and break-ins to businesses dropped 8%.

Among the provinces, the highest crime rates were in Western Canada and the territories, continuing a pattern observed over the past 30 years. Despite a 4% decline, Saskatchewan continued to report the highest overall crime rate, as well as the highest rate of violent crime. British Columbia had the highest property crime rate, primarily the result of a large number of thefts of $5,000 and under. For the fourth year in a row, the lowest rates occurred in Ontario and Quebec.

Impaired driving

Impaired driving and drug offences were among the few police-reported crimes to increase in 2007 from 2006. More so than other crimes, impaired driving and drug offences tend to be influenced by local police enforcement practices.

The impaired driving rate rose 3% in 2007, mainly because of a 19% increase in Alberta. Despite this recent rise, impaired driving rates have generally been declining over the past 25 years in Canada. The rate of drug offences rose 4%, driven

Chart 7.1
Crime rate

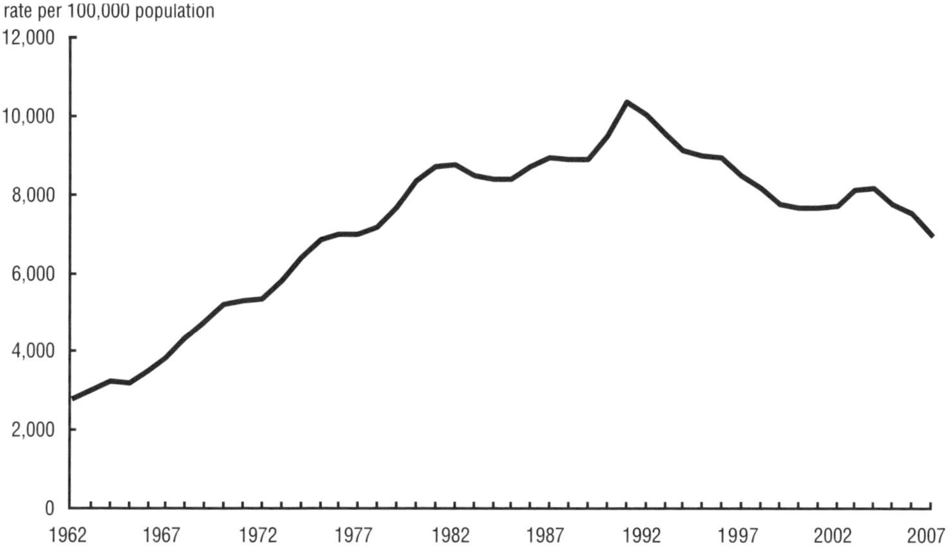

Note: Total *Criminal Code* offences, excluding traffic.
Source: Statistics Canada, CANSIM table 252-0013 and Catalogue no. 85-002-X.

by an increase in cannabis possession offences, which accounted for about half of all drug offences.

About 176,000 youth aged 12 to 17 were accused of a criminal offence in 2007. Overall, youth crime has been relatively stable for the past decade, but youth violent crime has slowly increased. In 2007, young people were charged with violent crime at a rate of 8.3 crimes per 100 youths, more than double the rate reported in the mid-1980s.

Although homicides have been generally decreasing since the mid-1970s, gang-related murders are on the rise. In 2007, police reported 594 homicides. One in five—117 deaths—were reported as gang-related homicides, which includes the deaths of gang members as well as innocent bystanders.

Firearms are used more often in gang-related homicides than in other types of murder. In 2007, just over two-thirds of gang-related homicides were committed with a firearm, compared with about 20% of homicides that did not involve gangs.

Table 7.a
Violent crimes, 1998 and 2007

	1998	2007
	rate per 100,000 population	
Crimes of violence	**992.7**	**940.9**
Homicide	2.0	1.8
Attempted murder	2.9	2.4
Assaults (Level 1 to 3)[1]	743.6	718.5
Sexual assault	90.3	65.0
Other sexual offences	12.2	8.4
Robbery	98.9	101.0
Other crimes of violence[2]	42.8	43.7

1. Level 1, or common, assault includes pushing, slapping, punching and face-to-face threats; Level 2 assault is defined as assault with a weapon or causing bodily harm; Level 3, or aggravated, assault is defined as assault that wounds, maims, disfigures or endangers the life of the victim.
2. Includes bodily harm, discharging firearms with intent, abductions, assaults against police officers and other peace or public officers, and other assaults.

Source: Statistics Canada, CANSIM table 252-0013.

Within metropolitan areas, 81% of all firearm-related homicides were committed with a handgun in 2007, compared with 29% in the rest of Canada.

Chart 7.2
Crimes, by province, 2007

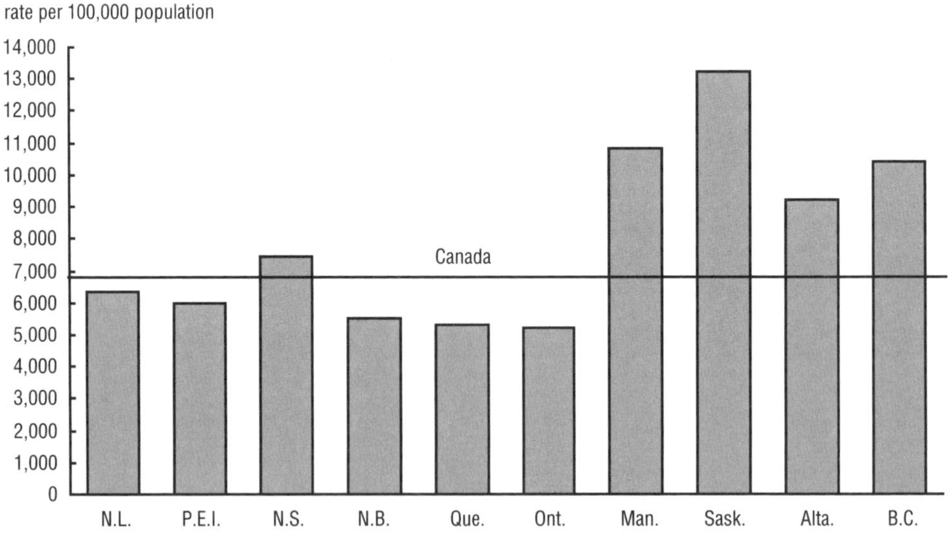

Note: Total *Criminal Code* offences, excluding traffic.
Source: Statistics Canada, CANSIM table 252-0013.

Hate crimes

Canada is among the more than 30 countries where hate crimes—violations motivated by hatred based on race, ethnicity, religion or sexual orientation—are considered a criminal offence.

In 2006, 892 hate crimes were reported by police, 0.04% of all reported crime.

More than 6 in 10 hate crimes were motivated by race or ethnicity. Blacks were targeted in almost half (48%) of the 502 hate crimes that were in this way motivated. Other targeted groups included South Asians (13%), Arabs or West Asians (12%), East and Southeast Asians (5%), Caucasians (5%) and Aboriginal people (3%).

Almost 3 in 10 hate crimes in 2006 were based on religion. Offences against the Jewish faith were the most common, accounting for 63% of 220 religion-based incidents. Another 21% were against Muslims and 6% were against Catholics.

Chart 7.3
Police-reported hate crimes, by type of motivation, 2006

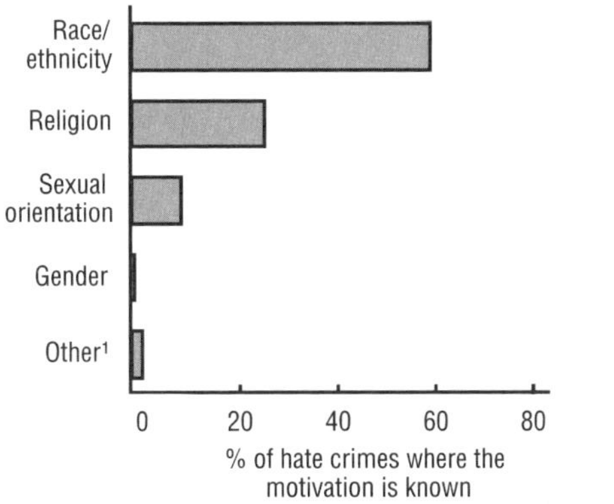

1. Includes hate crimes motivated by language, disability or other similar factor, such as professional or political beliefs.
Source: Statistics Canada, Catalogue no. 85f0033M.

About 1 in 10 incidents were motivated by sexual orientation, usually homosexuality. More than half these offences were violent; common assault was the most frequent type of violation.

Spousal violence

In almost every province and territory, victims of spousal violence were more likely to be victimized by a current spouse or common-law partner than by a former spouse or partner. In Nunavut, 97% of spousal abuse in 2006 involved current spouses. In New Brunswick, Prince Edward Island and Newfoundland and Labrador, it accounted for 72% of incidents.

In Quebec, victims of spousal violence are almost equally likely to be abused by a former spouse as a current spouse. This may reflect the province's high divorce rate, as well as the popularity of common-law relationships in Quebec and the higher probability of break-ups among common-law unions compared with marriages.

Assaults are generally higher in the western provinces and territories; in

Chart 7.4
Spousal homicide rate

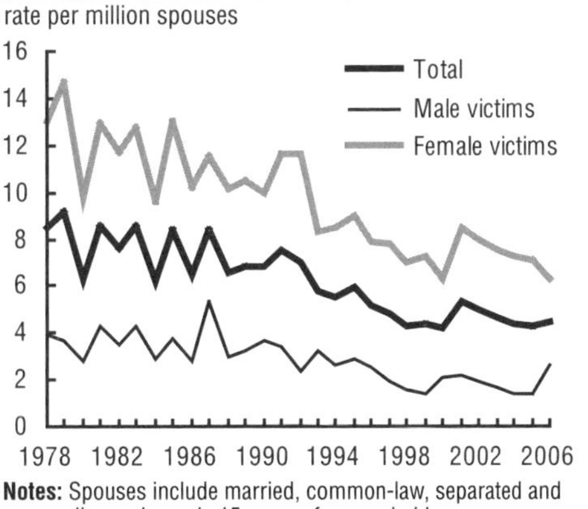

Notes: Spouses include married, common-law, separated and divorced people 15 years of age and older.
Excludes same-sex spouses.
Source: Statistics Canada, Catalogue no. 85-224-X.

Quebec, criminal harassment (or stalking) and uttering threats are more prevalent.

Table 7.1 Crimes, by type of offence and by province and territory, 2007

	Canada	Newfoundland and Labrador	Prince Edward Island	Nova Scotia	New Brunswick
	rate per 100,000 population				
All offences	**7,657.4**	**7,032.5**	**6,692.8**	**8,206.1**	**6,221.9**
Criminal Code offences (excluding traffic offences)	**6,862.7**	6,375.0	5,976.5	7,490.2	5,521.3
Crimes against the person	**940.9**	951.9	663.7	1,072.5	852.9
Homicide	**1.8**	0.6	0.0	1.4	1.1
Attempted murder	**2.4**	0.2	0.7	2.7	0.5
Assault (Level 1 to 3)[1]	**718.5**	813.6	583.6	877.7	698.3
Sexual assault	**65.0**	81.2	52.7	75.2	65.6
Other sexual offences	**8.4**	7.9	5.8	6.7	21.7
Robbery	**101.0**	29.6	10.8	70.8	30.7
Other crimes against the person[2]	**43.7**	18.8	10.1	38.1	35.0
Property crimes	**3,319.7**	2,282.8	2,659.7	3,072.3	2,305.2
Break and enter	**700.3**	717.8	509.3	662.9	511.4
Motor vehicle theft	**443.2**	119.7	120.5	200.7	179.1
Theft over $5,000	**52.7**	14.0	31.0	38.1	37.2
Theft $5,000 and under	**1,756.5**	1,173.1	1,772.4	1,672.1	1,300.4
Possession of stolen goods	**99.4**	32.8	45.5	231.1	42.4
Fraud	**267.7**	225.4	181.1	267.4	234.7
Other *Criminal Code* offences	**2,602.2**	3,140.4	2,653.2	3,345.3	2,363.2
Criminal Code traffic offences	**400.1**	340.1	533.1	350.1	363.6
Impaired driving	**241.1**	274.4	432.1	273.0	279.0
Other *Criminal Code* traffic offences[3]	**159.0**	65.8	101.0	77.1	84.6
Federal statute offences	**394.6**	317.4	183.2	365.9	337.0
Drugs[4]	**305.3**	169.3	142.1	268.3	249.7
Other federal statute offences	**89.3**	148.1	41.1	97.6	87.4

Note: A revision of populations for 2004/2006 was applied to this table in 2007. Crime rates may have been affected, and caution should be used when comparing data to any previous version of this table.

1. Level 1, or common, assault includes pushing, slapping, punching and face-to-face threats; Level 2 assault is defined as assault with a weapon or causing bodily harm; Level 3, or aggravated, assault is defined as assault that wounds, maims, disfigures or endangers the life of the victim.
2. Includes unlawfully causing bodily harm, discharging firearms with intent, abductions, assaults against police officers, assaults against other peace or public officers and other assaults.
3. Includes dangerous operation of a motor vehicle, boat, vessel or aircraft; dangerous operation of a motor vehicle, boat, vessel or aircraft causing bodily harm or death; driving a motor vehicle while prohibited; and failure to stop or remain.
4. Includes possession, trafficking, importation and production.

Source: Statistics Canada, CANSIM table 252-0013.

Quebec	Ontario	Manitoba	Saskatchewan	Alberta	British Columbia	Yukon	Northwest Territories	Nunavut
rate per 100,000 population								
5,881.3	**5,634.4**	**11,578.2**	**14,982.8**	**10,129.0**	**11,564.8**	**23,463.2**	**47,472.9**	**31,713.4**
5,119.7	5,062.6	10,868.0	13,269.6	9,213.9	10,334.2	21,320.5	43,903.2	29,997.1
744.1	745.3	1,535.7	2,036.1	1,116.6	1,185.2	2,923.6	7,071.3	7,164.2
1.2	1.6	5.2	3.0	2.5	2.0	6.5	4.7	22.5
3.0	2.2	3.1	4.1	1.9	2.4	0.0	4.7	12.9
537.9	545.7	1,167.7	1,664.2	886.8	926.3	2,639.7	6,370.1	6,142.1
56.4	56.5	105.2	121.5	64.3	69.1	193.6	492.5	668.5
12.4	4.8	8.0	16.5	6.2	9.9	9.7	25.8	77.1
91.6	92.1	202.0	158.0	110.3	126.6	48.4	58.6	38.6
41.6	42.5	44.5	68.8	44.7	49.0	25.8	114.9	202.5
2,869.0	2,635.4	4,406.5	4,313.7	4,258.9	5,176.6	4,369.3	5,795.4	4,133.3
778.7	485.9	1,037.9	1,147.4	726.9	994.3	1,100.4	2,078.0	1,883.5
470.3	271.3	1,236.3	554.3	669.2	619.0	432.4	703.6	665.3
59.3	42.2	48.0	39.8	69.9	72.9	64.5	70.4	51.4
1,316.9	1,464.4	1,826.4	2,123.6	2,258.9	3,036.7	2,362.1	2,572.9	1,218.1
39.4	105.6	72.9	128.5	175.0	118.4	83.9	105.5	96.4
204.3	266.0	185.1	320.1	359.1	335.5	325.9	265.0	218.6
1,506.6	1,681.9	4,925.8	6,919.8	3,838.4	3,972.4	14,027.6	31,036.4	18,699.6
460.7	253.0	342.4	1,068.9	580.1	436.8	1,297.2	2,028.8	1,060.7
210.5	139.4	252.2	544.8	415.6	332.6	1,119.8	1,801.3	906.4
250.3	113.7	90.2	524.1	164.5	104.2	177.5	227.5	154.3
300.9	318.8	367.8	644.4	335.0	793.8	845.5	1,540.9	655.7
264.4	242.3	207.8	286.0	261.7	653.7	674.4	1,069.5	514.3
36.6	76.5	160.0	358.4	73.3	140.2	171.0	471.4	141.4

Table 7.2 Crimes, by type of offence, 2002 to 2007

	2002	2003	2004	2005	2006	2007
	rate per 100,000 population					
All offences	**8,309.7**	**8,522.0**	**8,376.9**	**8,073.6**	**7,984.5**	**7,657.4**
Criminal Code offences (excluding traffic offences)	7,511.3	7,763.8	7,588.4	7,311.0	7,228.4	6,862.7
Crimes against the person	979.6	976.5	955.3	960.4	965.7	940.9
Homicide	1.9	1.7	2.0	2.1	1.9	1.8
Attempted murder	2.2	2.2	2.1	2.5	2.6	2.4
Assault (Level 1 to 3)[1]	751.3	747.6	732.2	732.5	737.0	718.5
Sexual assault	78.1	74.2	72.0	72.8	68.1	65.0
Other sexual offences	8.8	8.1	8.2	8.6	8.5	8.4
Robbery	95.7	101.3	96.9	100.4	106.1	101.0
Other crimes against the person[2]	41.6	41.3	42.0	41.6	41.6	43.7
Property crimes	3,973.2	4,120.6	3,969.3	3,735.8	3,596.0	3,319.7
Break and enter	878.4	899.5	862.2	808.9	769.9	700.3
Motor vehicle theft	516.1	550.0	531.3	495.2	485.9	443.2
Theft over $5,000	63.2	61.3	53.0	53.2	52.4	52.7
Theft $5,000 and under	2,127.1	2,211.8	2,106.6	1,976.6	1,892.3	1,756.5
Possession of stolen goods	95.8	104.7	111.7	106.7	110.2	99.4
Fraud	292.7	293.4	304.6	295.2	285.4	267.7
Other *Criminal Code* offences	2,558.6	2,666.7	2,663.8	2,614.8	2,666.7	2,602.2
Criminal Code traffic offences	374.8	369.7	377.1	376.3	374.3	400.1
Impaired driving[3]	255.1	245.1	251.1	242.5	233.2	241.1
Other traffic offences[4]	119.6	124.6	126.0	133.8	141.2	159.0
Federal statute offences	423.6	388.5	411.4	386.3	381.8	394.6
Drugs[5]	295.7	274.0	305.1	289.9	294.6	305.3
Other federal statute offences	127.9	114.5	106.3	96.5	87.2	89.3

Note: A revision of populations for 2004/2006 was applied to this table in 2007. Crime rates may have been affected and caution should be used when comparing data to any previous version of this table.

1. Level 1, or common, assault includes pushing, slapping, punching and face-to-face threats; Level 2 assault is defined as assault with a weapon or causing bodily harm; Level 3, or aggravated, assault is defined as assault that wounds, maims, disfigures or endangers the life of the victim.
2. Includes unlawfully causing bodily harm, discharging firearms with intent, abductions, assaults against police officers, assaults against other peace or public officers and other assaults.
3. In 2004, the Vancouver Police Department changed their scoring procedures for reporting impaired driving incidents to include all incidents of impaired driving, not just those resulting in a charge being laid: thus incidents cleared by other means, such as roadside suspension, are now included. This resulted in almost 1,900 additional incidents reported in 2004 compared with 2003. Please use caution when comparing these data with prior years.
4. Includes dangerous operation of a motor vehicle, boat, vessel or aircraft; dangerous operation of a motor vehicle, boat, vessel or aircraft causing bodily harm or death; driving a motor vehicle while prohibited; and failure to stop or remain.
5. Includes possession, trafficking, importation and production.

Source: Statistics Canada, CANSIM table 252-0013.

Table 7.3 Persons charged, by type of offence, 1997 and 2007

	1997			2007		
	Youth and adults charged	Youths charged	Adults charged	Youth and adults charged	Youths charged	Adults charged
	rate per 100,000 population[1]					
All offences	**2,526.2**	**4,922.6**	**2,268.5**	**2,218.0**	**3,442.5**	**2,096.4**
Criminal Code offences (excluding traffic offences)	1,987.1	4,539.1	1,712.6	1,679.6	2,923.4	1,556.0
Crimes against the person	548.5	908.3	509.8	494.9	826.8	461.9
Homicide	1.8	2.2	1.8	1.7	2.9	1.6
Attempted murder	2.9	2.7	2.9	2.1	1.9	2.1
Assault (Level 1 to 3)[2]	427.3	639.6	404.5	386.6	564.8	368.9
Sexual assault	40.2	61.1	38.0	27.5	45.7	25.7
Other sexual offences	4.3	6.2	4.1	2.5	5.3	2.2
Robbery	39.8	155.3	27.4	40.1	158.5	28.4
Other crimes against the person[3]	32.1	41.2	31.1	34.5	47.8	33.2
Property crimes	819.9	2,388.9	651.2	485.4	976.7	436.6
Break and enter	170.5	699.9	113.6	83.2	287.3	62.9
Motor vehicle theft	60.4	264.9	38.4	29.9	96.2	23.3
Theft over $5,000	10.9	22.1	9.7	6.1	6.5	6.0
Theft $5,000 and under	379.8	1,085.9	303.8	206.0	359.8	190.7
Possession of stolen goods	84.6	236.2	68.3	87.4	185.3	77.6
Fraud	113.8	79.9	117.5	72.9	41.6	76.1
Other *Criminal Code* offences	618.7	1,241.9	551.7	699.3	1,119.8	657.5
Criminal Code traffic offences	336.1	0.0	372.3	277.2	0.0	304.7
Impaired driving	287.5	0.0	318.5	220.5	0.0	242.4
Other *Criminal Code* traffic offences[4]	48.6	0.0	53.8	56.6	0.0	62.3
Federal statute offences	203.0	383.6	183.6	261.2	519.2	235.6
Drugs[5]	162.6	206.8	157.9	214.5	275.9	208.4
Other federal statute offences	40.4	176.8	25.7	46.7	243.3	27.2

Note: Youth are those aged 12 to 17; adults are those aged 18 and older.
1. Rate of the specific population.
2. Level 1, or common, assault includes pushing, slapping, punching and face-to-face threats; Level 2 assault is defined as assault with a weapon or causing bodily harm; Level 3, or aggravated, assault is defined as assault that wounds, maims, disfigures or endangers the life of the victim.
3. Includes unlawfully causing bodily harm, discharging firearms with intent, abductions, assaults against police officers, assaults against other peace or public officers and other assaults.
4. Includes dangerous operation of a motor vehicle, boat, vessel or aircraft; dangerous operation of a motor vehicle, boat, vessel or aircraft causing bodily harm or death; driving a motor vehicle while prohibited; and failure to stop or remain.
5. Includes possession, trafficking, importation and production.

Source: Statistics Canada, CANSIM table 252-0014.

Table 7.4 Homicides, by province and territory, 2005 to 2007

	2005		2006		2007	
	number	rate per 100,000 population	number	rate per 100,000 population	number	rate per 100,000 population
Canada	**663**	**2.1**	**606**	**1.9**	**594**	**1.8**
Newfoundland and Labrador	11	2.1	7	1.4	3	0.6
Prince Edward Island	0	0.0	1	0.7	0	0.0
Nova Scotia	20	2.1	16	1.7	13	1.4
New Brunswick	9	1.2	7	0.9	8	1.1
Quebec	100	1.3	93	1.2	90	1.2
Ontario	219	1.7	196	1.5	201	1.6
Manitoba	49	4.2	39	3.3	62	5.2
Saskatchewan	43	4.3	42	4.3	30	3.0
Alberta	108	3.3	95	2.8	88	2.5
British Columbia	101	2.4	108	2.5	88	2.0
Yukon	1	3.2	0	0.0	2	6.5
Northwest Territories	0	0.0	0	0.0	2	4.7
Nunavut	2	6.7	2	6.6	7	22.5

Source: Statistics Canada, CANSIM table 253-0001.

Table 7.5 Homicides, by method, 2005 to 2007

	2005		2006		2007	
	number	%	number	%	number	%
Shooting	223	33.6	190	31.4	188	31.6
Stabbing	198	29.9	210	34.7	190	32.0
Beating	144	21.7	119	19.6	116	19.5
Strangulation	47	7.1	48	7.9	50	8.4
Fire (burns/suffocation)	10	1.5	12	2.0	4	0.7
Other methods[1]	26	3.9	14	2.3	19	3.2
Not known	15	2.3	13	2.1	27	4.5

Note: Only one method is counted per victim.
1. Include poisoning, exposure, shaken baby syndrome, deaths caused by vehicles, and heart attacks.
Source: Statistics Canada, CANSIM table 253-0002.

Table 7.6 Solved homicides, by accused–victim relationship, 2002 to 2007

	2002	2003	2004	2005	2006	2007
	number					
Total	**470**	**433**	**479**	**495**	**459**	**414**
Spouse[1]	84	78	75	74	78	65
Parent	37	31	36	22	31	21
Other family relationship	64	33	52	62	57	50
Other intimate relationship	17	11	24	17	15	16
Acquaintance	133	161	173	159	143	135
Criminal relationship[2]	56	49	44	72	58	60
Stranger	72	61	73	87	73	66
Accused–victim relationship unknown	7	9	2	2	4	1

Note: Accused data have been revised according to updates provided by police services.
1. Comprises current and former legally married, common-law, and same-sex couples.
2. Includes male and female prostitutes, drug dealers and their clients, loan sharks and gang members.
Source: Statistics Canada, CANSIM table 253-0006.

Table 7.7 Homicides, by census metropolitan area, 1997 and 2007

	1997		2007	
	number of victims	rate per 100,000 population	number of victims	rate per 100,000 population
Population of 500,000 or more	**296**	**2.1**	**348**	**2.1**
Montréal	74	2.2	59	1.6
Québec	9	1.3	0	0.0
Ottawa–Gatineau, Ontario part	9	1.1	14	1.6
Toronto	83	1.9	111	2.0
Hamilton	11	1.7	11	1.6
Winnipeg	21	3.1	26	3.6
Calgary	9	1.0	36	3.1
Edmonton	28	3.1	36	3.3
Vancouver	52	2.7	55	2.4
Population from 250,000 to 499,999	**49**	**1.8**	**47**	**1.4**
Halifax	11	3.3	7	1.8
Ottawa–Gatineau, Quebec part	3	1.2	2	0.7
Kitchener	3	0.7	7	1.4
London	4	0.9	6	1.3
Oshawa	6	2.1	5	1.5
St. Catharines–Niagara	8	1.9	3	0.7
Saskatoon[1]	8	3.5	9	3.6
Windsor	8	2.6	4	1.2
Victoria	6	2.0	4	1.2
Population from 100,000 to 249,999	**28**	**1.9**	**24**	**1.6**
St. John's	3	1.7	1	0.6
Saint John	3	2.4	2	2.0
Saguenay	0	0.0	1	0.7
Sherbrooke	4	2.8	2	1.3
Trois-Rivières	2	1.3	4	2.7
Kingston[2]	..	..	1	0.7
Greater Sudbury/Grand Sudbury	2	1.2	4	2.5
Thunder Bay	3	2.3	2	1.6
Regina	3	1.5	5	2.5
Abbotsford–Mission[2]	..	..	2	1.2

Note: Homicide includes murder, manslaughter and infanticide.
1. Prior to 2007, Saskatoon was classified in the 100,000-to-249,999 population group.
2. Became census metropolitan areas in 2001.
Source: Statistics Canada, CANSIM table 253-0004.

Table 7.8 Adult criminal court cases, by type of decision, 2006/2007

	Total decisions	Guilty	Acquitted	Stay	Other
			number of cases		
Total cases	**372,084**	**242,988**	**13,480**	**109,863**	**5,753**
Total *Criminal Code* offences	**327,975**	214,163	12,472	96,181	5,159
Criminal Code offenses (excluding traffic)	**276,494**	173,670	9,998	88,230	4,596
Crimes against the person	**91,386**	48,329	6,288	35,064	1,705
Homicide	**288**	140	8	120	20
Attempted murder	**223**	43	12	146	22
Robbery	**4,208**	2,900	112	1,122	74
Sexual assault	**3,090**	1,519	242	1,263	66
Other sexual offences	**1,477**	722	121	603	31
Major assault[1]	**19,351**	10,536	1,552	6,953	310
Common assault[2]	**40,957**	21,837	1,995	16,562	563
Uttering threats	**16,273**	8,021	1,835	6,031	386
Criminal harassment	**2,902**	1,459	215	1,080	148
Other crimes against the person	**2,617**	1,152	196	1,184	85
Property crimes	**89,354**	59,318	1,535	27,328	1,173
Theft	**37,054**	25,119	330	11,251	354
Break and enter	**11,579**	8,293	352	2,727	207
Fraud	**14,837**	10,001	173	4,330	333
Mischief	**12,198**	7,665	418	3,984	131
Possession of stolen property	**12,940**	7,768	239	4,800	133
Other property crimes	**746**	472	23	236	15
Administration of justice	**64,927**	46,415	961	16,458	1,093
Other *Criminal Code* offences	**30,827**	19,608	1,214	9,380	625
Criminal Code traffic offences	**51,481**	40,493	2,474	7,951	563
Impaired driving	**41,233**	32,594	2,278	5,952	409
Other *Criminal Code* traffic offences	**10,248**	7,899	196	1,999	154
Other federal statute offences	**44,109**	28,825	1,008	13,682	594
Drug possession	**13,919**	7,628	30	6,186	75
Drug trafficking	**10,959**	6,051	139	4,662	107
Youth Criminal Justice Act	**1,131**	817	4	297	13
Residual federal statute offences	**18,100**	14,329	835	2,537	399

1. Includes unlawfully causing bodily harm, discharging firearms with intent, abductions, assaults against police officers, assaults against other peace or public officers and other assaults.
2. Level 1, or common, assault includes pushing, slapping, punching and face-to-face threats; Level 2 assault is defined as assault with a weapon or causing bodily harm; Level 3, or aggravated, assault is defined as assault that wounds, maims, disfigures or endangers the life of the victim.

Source: Statistics Canada, CANSIM table 252-0045.

Table 7.9 Adult criminal court cases, by type of sentence, 2006

	Total guilty cases	Prison	Conditional sentence	Probation	Fine	Restitution	Other sentences
				number			
Total offences	**242,988**	**83,043**	**9,878**	**105,415**	**73,513**	**7,490**	**118,873**
Total *Criminal Code* offences	214,163	75,460	8,008	96,967	60,218	7,369	107,316
Criminal Code offenses (excluding traffic)	173,670	68,684	7,236	90,838	29,197	7,180	78,834
Crimes against the person	48,329	15,111	2,581	35,126	4,160	781	30,663
Homicide	140	115	3	12	0	0	87
Attempted murder	43	30	1	7	1	0	18
Robbery	2,900	2,249	245	1,322	15	101	1,391
Sexual assault	1,519	753	244	999	52	7	709
Other sexual offences	722	448	100	483	12	6	284
Major assault[1]	10,536	4,485	937	7,119	925	244	5,795
Common assault[2]	21,837	3,519	661	16,953	2,227	332	16,181
Uttering threats	8,021	2,623	257	6,131	786	59	4,587
Criminal harassment	1,459	392	59	1,264	82	12	1,038
Other crimes against the person	1,152	497	74	836	60	20	573
Property crimes	59,318	24,273	3,112	31,991	9,329	5,963	24,842
Theft	25,119	9,940	1,100	12,219	4,980	1,466	10,403
Break and enter	8,293	5,031	691	5,015	340	629	2,481
Fraud	10,001	3,580	870	6,030	1,207	1,889	4,447
Mischief	7,665	1,624	109	5,057	1,387	1,590	4,717
Possession of stolen property	7,768	3,877	283	3,404	1,354	346	2,617
Other property crimes	472	221	59	266	61	43	177
Administration of justice	46,415	22,270	917	14,045	11,213	289	14,185
Other *Criminal Code* offences	19,608	7,030	626	9,676	4,495	147	9,144
Criminal Code traffic offences	40,493	6,776	772	6,129	31,021	189	28,482
Impaired driving	32,594	3,319	296	3,664	27,904	80	24,087
Other *Criminal Code* traffic offences	7,899	3,457	476	2,465	3,117	109	4,395
Other federal statute offences	28,825	7,583	1,870	8,448	13,295	121	11,557
Drug possession	7,628	1,210	81	2,342	3,818	13	4,336
Drug trafficking	6,051	2,896	1,733	1,693	535	49	4,108
Youth Criminal Justice Act	817	263	11	273	264	11	297
Residual federal statute offences	14,329	3,214	45	4,140	8,678	48	2,816

1. Includes unlawfully causing bodily harm, discharging firearms with intent, abductions, assaults against police officers, assaults against other peace or public officers and other assaults.
2. Level 1, or common, assault includes pushing, slapping, punching and face-to-face threats; Level 2 assault is defined as assault with a weapon or causing bodily harm; Level 3, or aggravated, assault is defined as assault that wounds, maims, disfigures or endangers the life of the victim.

Source: Statistics Canada, CANSIM table 252-0046.

Table 7.10 Youth court, sentenced cases, by outcome, 2006/2007

	Total guilty cases	Custody	Conditional sentence	Deferred custody and supervision
	number			
Total offences	**34,065**	**5,640**	**27**	**1,080**
Total *Criminal Code* offences	27,581	4,535	21	890
Criminal Code offences (excluding traffic)	26,695	4,448	21	871
Crimes against the person	9,164	1,591	13	422
Homicide	21	15	0	1
Attempted murder	6	5	0	0
Robbery	1,355	500	1	113
Sexual assault	459	55	1	35
Other sexual offences	272	30	0	17
Major assault[1]	2,213	429	3	117
Common assault[2]	3,404	341	7	89
Uttering threats	1,218	164	0	34
Criminal harassment	55	7	0	4
Other crimes against the person	161	45	1	12
Property crimes	11,793	1,607	2	292
Theft	4,078	423	1	73
Break and enter	3,364	635	0	112
Fraud	441	58	0	12
Mischief	2,029	159	1	40
Possession of stolen property	1,701	306	0	53
Other property crimes	180	26	0	2
Administration of justice	3,164	849	2	61
Other *Criminal Code* offences	2,574	401	4	96
Criminal Code traffic offences	886	87	0	19
Impaired driving	464	1	0	1
Other *Criminal Code* traffic offences	422	86	0	18
Other federal statute offences	6,484	1,105	6	190
Drug possession	1,050	17	4	0
Drug trafficking	730	102	2	31
Youth Criminal Justice Act	3,912	859	0	159
Residual federal statute offences	792	127	0	0

1. Includes unlawfully causing bodily harm, discharging firearms with intent, abductions, assaults against police officers, assaults against other peace or public officers and other assaults.
2. Level 1, or common, assault includes pushing, slapping, punching and face-to-face threats; Level 2 assault is defined as assault with a weapon or causing bodily harm; Level 3, or aggravated, assault is defined as assault that wounds, maims, disfigures or endangers the life of the victim.

Source: Statistics Canada, CANSIM table 252-0050.

Intensive support and supervision	Probation	Attendance at non-residential program	Fine	Community service	Reprimand	Other sentences
			number			
347	**19,953**	**213**	**1,860**	**8,120**	**724**	**11,671**
289	17,030	152	1,136	6,400	552	9,741
280	16,652	150	792	6,254	550	9,129
144	6,249	43	102	1,969	102	3,642
0	7	0	0	1	0	8
0	5	0	0	1	0	3
38	990	6	3	323	6	738
14	360	0	1	59	1	145
9	213	0	0	32	0	63
49	1,543	18	30	514	10	922
21	2,136	12	50	741	59	1,337
11	832	6	12	232	26	331
0	38	0	4	17	0	27
2	125	1	2	49	0	68
90	7,454	65	370	3,243	198	3,859
31	2,371	40	191	1,145	103	1,423
32	2,461	10	34	975	12	903
3	270	2	16	98	9	157
5	1,169	9	59	553	42	819
13	1,053	4	63	422	30	497
6	130	0	7	50	2	60
15	1,371	24	226	505	193	683
31	1,578	18	94	537	57	945
9	378	2	344	146	2	612
0	118	0	304	65	1	413
9	260	2	40	81	1	199
58	2,923	61	724	1,720	172	1,930
1	477	9	161	299	39	628
4	543	3	32	241	3	436
53	1,593	49	444	913	130	822
0	310	0	87	267	0	44

Table 7.11 Youth court, by type of decision, 2006/2007

	Total all decisions	Guilty	Acquitted	Stay	Withdrawn or dismissed	Other decisions
	number					
Total offences	**56,463**	**34,065**	**727**	**9,098**	**12,196**	**377**
Total *Criminal Code* offences	**46,907**	27,581	661	8,008	10,344	313
Criminal Code offences (excluding traffic)	**45,821**	26,695	629	7,968	10,218	311
Crimes against the person	**15,126**	9,164	369	2,177	3,315	101
Homicide	**40**	21	0	11	8	0
Attempted murder	**23**	6	2	6	9	0
Robbery	**2,228**	1,355	48	184	629	12
Sexual assault	**723**	459	42	78	139	5
Other sexual offences	**442**	272	22	45	97	6
Major assault	**3,435**	2,213	93	458	641	30
Common assault	**5,682**	3,404	89	945	1,211	33
Uttering threats	**2,137**	1,218	64	386	461	8
Criminal harassment	**135**	55	3	20	52	5
Other crimes against the person	**281**	161	6	44	68	2
Property crimes	**21,279**	11,793	175	4,540	4,650	121
Theft	**7,687**	4,078	45	1,852	1,675	37
Break and enter	**5,066**	3,364	41	712	909	40
Fraud	**817**	441	6	192	172	6
Mischief	**3,878**	2,029	41	856	948	4
Possession of stolen property	**3,505**	1,701	34	865	871	34
Other property crimes	**326**	180	8	63	75	0
Administration of justice	**4,945**	3,164	20	407	1,292	62
Other *Criminal Code* offences	**4,471**	2,574	65	844	961	27
Criminal Code traffic offences	**1,086**	886	32	40	126	2
Impaired driving	**557**	464	20	17	55	1
Other *Criminal Code* traffic offences	**529**	422	12	23	71	1
Other federal statute offences	**9,556**	6,484	66	1,090	1,852	64
Drug possession	**2,430**	1,050	8	567	797	8
Drug trafficking	**1,305**	730	26	203	340	6
Youth Criminal Justice Act	**4,795**	3,912	29	235	578	41
Residual federal statute offences	**1,026**	792	3	85	137	9

Source: Statistics Canada, CANSIM table 252-0049.

Table 7.12 Adult correctional population, 2002/2003 to 2006/2007

	2002/2003	2003/2004	2004/2005	2005/2006	2006/2007
			number		
Canada					
Total custodial admissions	**218,668**	**213,055**	**211,878**	**259,336**	**260,871**
Sentenced, custodial admissions	73,209	68,964	66,971	92,813	90,051
Remand, custodial admissions	115,489	112,744	115,385	146,494	150,696
Other statuses, custodial admissions	29,970	31,347	29,522	20,029	20,124
			%		
Sentenced admissions of females	10	10	11	11	12
Sentenced admissions of Aboriginal persons	19	19	20	23	24
			number		
Total community admissions	**111,154**	**106,075**	**108,535**	**110,474**	**108,471**
Probation, community admissions	82,678	78,098	80,436	82,232	81,644
Conditional sentence, community admissions	19,220	18,753	18,997	18,694	17,536
Conditional release, community admissions	9,256	9,224	9,102	9,548	9,291
Provinces and territories					
Total custodial admissions	**210,975**	**205,484**	**203,919**	**251,050**	**252,240**
Sentenced, custodial admissions	68,948	64,750	62,388	87,943	84,897
Remand, custodial admissions	115,489	112,744	115,385	146,494	150,696
Other statuses, custodial admissions	26,538	27,990	26,146	16,613	16,647
			%		
Sentenced admissions of females	10	10	11	11	12
Sentenced admissions of Aboriginal persons	19	19	20	23	24
			number		
Total community admissions	**103,922**	**98,703**	**101,197**	**102,803**	**100,915**
Probation, community admissions	82,678	78,098	80,436	82,232	81,644
Conditional sentence, community admissions	19,220	18,753	18,997	18,694	17,536
Conditional release, community admissions	2,024	1,852	1,764	1,877	1,735
Federal jurisdictions					
Total custodial admissions	**7,693**	**7,571**	**7,959**	**8,286**	**8,631**
Sentenced, custodial admissions	4,261	4,214	4,583	4,870	5,154
Remand, custodial admissions	.	.	.	.	.
Other statuses, custodial admissions	3,432	3,357	3,376	3,416	3,477
			%		
Sentenced admissions of females	5	5	5	6	6
Sentenced admissions of Aboriginal persons	18	18	18	19	18
			number		
Total community admissions	**7,232**	**7,372**	**7,338**	**7,671**	**7,556**
Probation, community admissions	.	.	.	.	.
Conditional sentence, community admissions	.	.	.	.	.
Conditional release, community admissions	7,232	7,372	7,338	7,671	7,556

Note: Data are for fiscal year from April 1 to March 31.
Source: Statistics Canada, CANSIM table 251-0001.

Table 7.13 Police officers, by province and territory, 2004 to 2008

	2004	2005	2006	2007	2008
			number		
Canada	**59,800**	**61,026**	**62,461**	**64,134**	**65,283**
Newfoundland and Labrador	766	776	799	838	884
Prince Edward Island	207	213	220	227	231
Nova Scotia	1,615	1,624	1,667	1,758	1,864
New Brunswick	1,302	1,297	1,291	1,326	1,355
Quebec	14,426	14,753	15,099	15,233	15,403
Ontario	23,214	23,420	23,759	24,450	24,945
Manitoba	2,266	2,256	2,313	2,409	2,419
Saskatchewan	2,010	2,011	2,030	2,046	2,124
Alberta	5,123	5,335	5,604	5,703	5,734
British Columbia	7,072	7,445	7,678	8,075	8,134
Yukon	121	120	116	119	117
Northwest Territories	171	173	171	175	178
Nunavut	123	121	122	123	119
Royal Canadian Mounted Police Headquarters and Training Academy	1,384	1,482	1,592	1,652	1,776

Source: Statistics Canada, CANSIM table 254-0002.

Table 7.14 Adult correctional services, operating expenditures for provincial, territorial and federal programs, 2002/2003 to 2006/2007

	2002/2003	2003/2004	2004/2005	2005/2006	2006/2007
			$ thousands		
Canada	**2,745,535**	**2,719,623**	**2,840,518**	**2,965,802**	**3,271,810**
Provinces and territories	1,296,580	1,272,277	1,318,697	1,389,504	1,484,563
Newfoundland and Labrador	22,843	22,908	20,278	21,294	21,809
Prince Edward Island	6,084	..	..	..	..
Nova Scotia	30,070	29,938	31,157	36,325	35,734
New Brunswick	18,389	17,998	19,612	21,004	23,838
Quebec	217,097	229,041	229,528	226,970	245,283
Ontario	553,737	523,484	562,993	603,251	626,196
Manitoba	66,670	73,358	78,319	86,477	90,495
Saskatchewan	62,976	63,543	65,329	68,900	74,249
Alberta	103,161	105,160	113,813	118,184	140,356
British Columbia	174,885	166,163	154,612	161,512	193,089
Yukon	7,761	7,848	8,272	8,782	9,339
Northwest Territories	18,299	21,860	22,423	22,322	24,175
Nunavut	14,609	10,976	12,361	14,483	..
Federal jurisdiction[1]	1,448,955	1,447,346	1,521,821	1,576,298	1,787,247

Notes: Operating expenditures are in current dollars.
Includes sums of custodial services, community supervision services, headquarters and central services, and parole boards where applicable.
Data are for fiscal year from April 1 to March 31.

1. Includes both the Correctional Service of Canada and the National Parole Board, but excludes CORCAN, the special operating agency that employs federal inmates.

Source: Statistics Canada, CANSIM table 251-0007.

Culture and leisure

Culture and leisure industries help make the country a better place to live and contribute significantly to its economy. In 2008, according to the Labour Force Survey, 759,600 Canadians, or more than 4% of the labour force, worked in jobs related to information, culture and recreation. More than half worked in Toronto, Montréal and Vancouver.

Employment in information, culture and recreation grew 20% from 1999 to 2008, surpassing the economy's overall employment growth of 19%. However, employment in these industries fell 3% from 2007 to 2008, whereas employment across the economy grew 1.5%.

The information and culture industry accounts for more than half of all employment in information, culture and recreation. Self-employment is common: 16% of information, culture and recreation workers reported themselves as self-employed in 2008.

Economic benefits

Information, culture and recreation industries contributed $56.8 billion to the economy in 2008, up 39% from 1999. The total gross domestic product (GDP) grew 26% over the same period.

Information and cultural industries—which include publishing, movie and sound recording, broadcasting and telecommunications, and news services and libraries—showed the most growth, 43%, and contributed $45.1 billion to the GDP in 2008.

Arts, entertainment and recreation industries—which include performing arts, spectator sports, museums, heritage sites, zoos, amusement parks, casinos and gaming machines, golf courses, ski hills, fitness facilities, and bowling centres—contributed $11.7 billion to the economy in 2008, an increase of 26% from 1999.

The three levels of government spent a total of $8.3 billion on culture in the

Chart 8.1
Labour force employed in the information, culture and recreation industries, selected census metropolitan areas

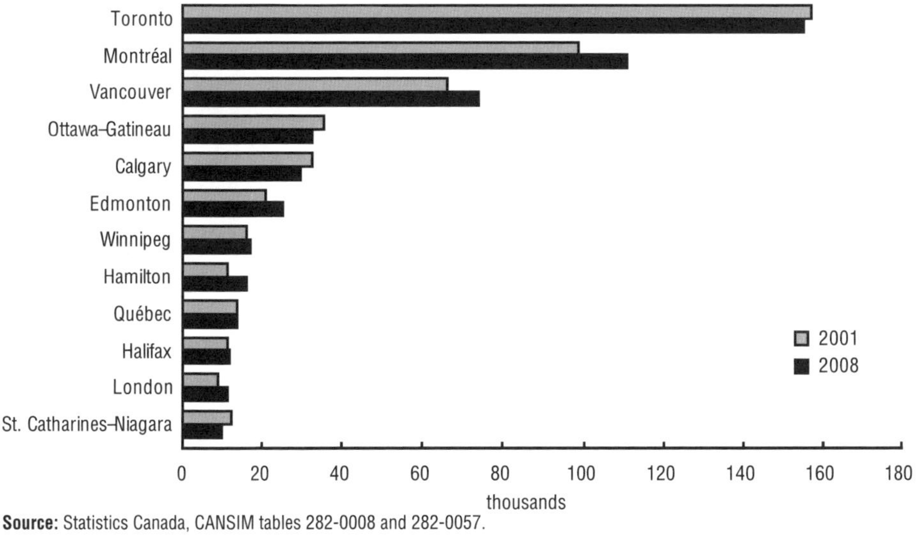

Source: Statistics Canada, CANSIM tables 282-0008 and 282-0057.

2005/2006 fiscal year, including about $444 million in intergovernmental transfers.

In 2005/2006, the federal government spent $3.5 billion on culture. Of each federal culture dollar, 47 cents supported broadcasting, 26 cents funded heritage resources—which includes museums, public archives, historic sites and nature parks—10 cents helped film and video production, 5 cents went to the performing arts, 4 cents went to literary arts and half a cent supported arts education.

Provincial and territorial governments spent $2.4 billion on culture in 2005/2006. These funds were largely directed toward libraries (37 cents of every culture dollar) and heritage institutions (28 cents). Smaller amounts went to multidisciplinary activities (about 9 cents) and the performing arts (8 cents).

Municipal governments spent $2.3 billion on culture in the 2005 calendar year. For each of their culture dollars, 70 cents funded libraries, 21 cents went to cultural centres and other activities, and 6 cents supported museums. Historic sites and parks and the performing arts each received less than 2 cents of every municipal dollar spent on culture. The remainder went to public archives.

Table 8.a
Performing arts, summary statistics, 2007

	Operating profit margin
	%
Performing arts companies	**5.9**
Theatre (except musical) companies	1.0
Musical theatre and opera companies	3.4
Musical groups and artists	14.8

Note: All establishments, by North American Industry Classification System (NAICS), 2007.
Source: Statistics Canada, CANSIM table 361-0009.

Chart 8.2
Culture expenditures by federal, provincial/territorial and municipal governments

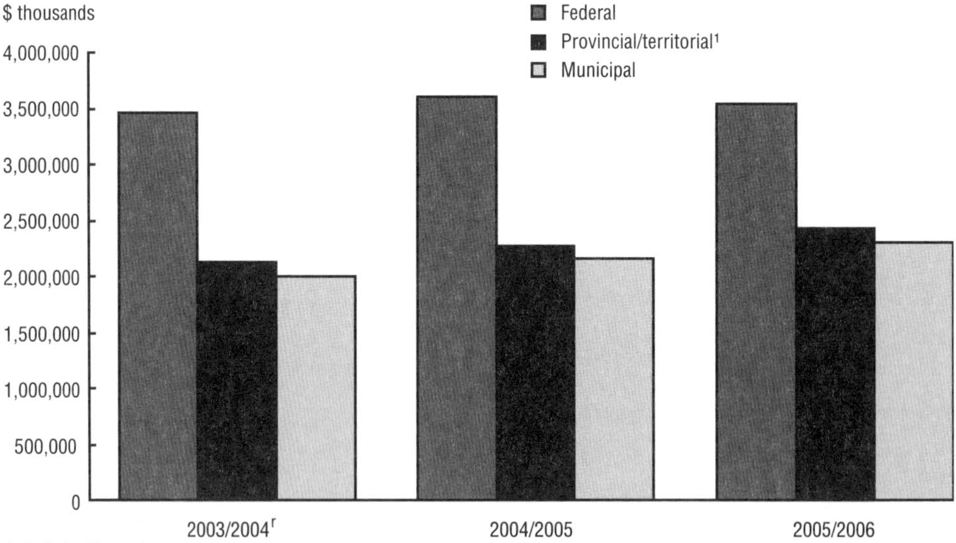

1. Excludes Nunavut.
Source: Statistics Canada, Catalogue no. 87F0001X.

What influences consumption of culture?

The higher an individual's household income or education, the more likely he or she is to go to a movie, attend a theatrical or musical performance or participate in other cultural activities.

Those in management, business, finance or an administrative occupation are nearly 9% more likely to attend a theatrical performance occasionally than those who are unemployed or working in primary industry or manufacturing.

Individuals with parents who have advanced education, such as a university degree, are significantly more likely to attend most kinds of cultural activities than those whose parents do not. The education level of a conjugal partner also positively influences higher consumption in cultural events of all kinds. For most activities, the conjugal partner's education is more important than that of the parents. Participation in cultural activities also varies by age and sex, as well as by marital status and province of residence.

Chart 8.3
Selected cultural activities participation rates, by family income, 2005

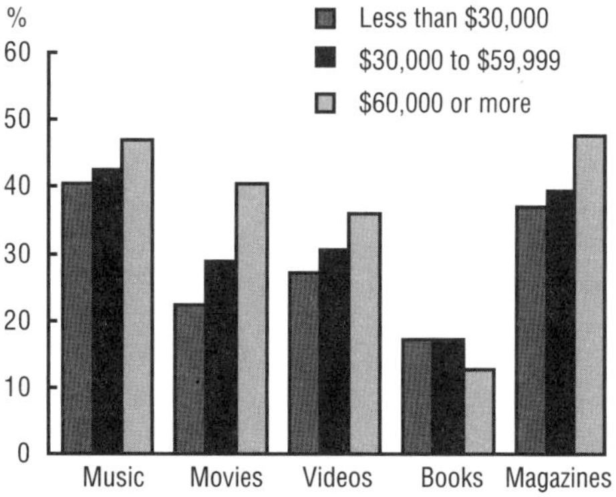

Notes: Population aged 15 and older.
Frequent participation.
Source: Statistics Canada, Catalogue no. 81-595-X.

More Canadians choosing active leisure

More Canadians are making active leisure choices in their daily lives. In 2005, 5.6 million of 22.9 million Canadians aged 20 and older participated in active leisure on a given day.

Exercising, walking and jogging rose in popularity from 1992 to 2005. The sports participation rate was about the same in both years, but Canadians are moving away from organized sports to informal sports activities.

Participation in active leisure rose to 24% in 2005, up from 21% in 1992. Participants averaged 1 hour and 46 minutes on a given day doing these activities in 2005.

People engaging in active leisure are more likely to be women, married people, university-educated people, those earning $60,000 or more, and those living in British Columbia or Quebec.

Chart 8.4
Active leisure participation

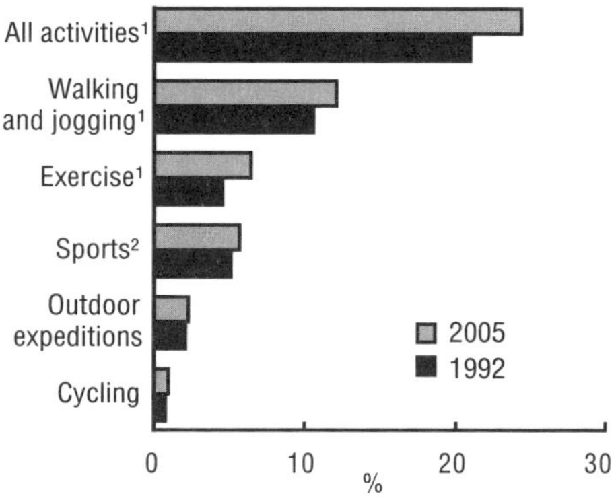

Note: Percentage participating on a given day.
1. Statistically significant difference in 2005 from 1992 at p<0.01.
2. 'Sports' refers to informal sport activity as well as organized sports.
Source: Statistics Canada, Catalogue no. 11-008-X.

Table 8.1 Federal government expenditures on culture, by cultural activity and by province and territory, 2005/2006

	Canada[1]	Newfoundland and Labrador	Prince Edward Island	Nova Scotia	New Brunswick	Quebec
	$ thousands					
All cultural activities	**3,547,062**	**47,601**	**22,269**	**103,883**	**55,614**	**1,229,535**
Libraries	**51,479**	0	0	0	0	38,378
Heritage resources	**910,305**	19,601	13,096	46,552	14,152	302,072
Arts education[3]	**18,631**	0	0	0	0	5,335
Literary arts	**133,561**	717	79	1,453	1,012	32,500
Performing arts	**188,226**	1,496	2,418	2,705	1,874	30,421
Visual arts and crafts	**19,942**	211	141	871	439	5,123
Film and video	**344,521**	3,586	262	11,606	3,085	148,491
Broadcasting[4]	**1,677,351**	20,768	5,353	38,480	32,179	587,008
Sound recording	**23,244**	15	0	23	0	2,481
Multiculturalism	**20,766**	102	82	342	330	5,356
Multidisciplinary and other activities[5]	**159,036**	1,105	838	1,853	2,544	72,370

Note: Figures may not add to totals because of rounding.
1. Total expenditures at the national level exclude intramural (operating and capital) expenditures by Human Resources and Skills Development Canada directly related to training and employment development in the culture sector.
2. Includes national organizations, foreign countries and unallocated expenditures.
3. Refers to the fine, applied and performing arts rather than to strictly academic fields such as language, history or literature. 'Arts' includes theatre, music, dance, painting, drama, photography and any other area of arts study reported by arts education institutions.
4. The Canadian Broadcasting Corporation distributes its program costs by location of production activities. Station transmission and network distribution costs are related to the geographic location of the transmitter, except for landlines and satellite channels, which are paid by Ottawa, but transferred to Toronto and Montréal network centres. Payments to private station affiliates are charged to the responsible network centres and relate also to the province where these centres are located. Administration costs and capital expenditures are distributed according to the province where the administration function is located geographically and the location of capital assets.
5. Includes financial support given to cultural facilities, centres, festivals, municipalities, cultural exchange programs and arts organizations for various cultural activities. It includes also the unallocated general and administration expenditures related to numerous cultural activities.

Source: Statistics Canada, CANSIM table 505-0003.

Ontario	Manitoba	Saskatchewan	Alberta	British Columbia	Yukon	Northwest Territories	Nunavut	Other national organizations and foreign countries[2]
				$ thousands				
1,341,907	**85,673**	**48,616**	**157,617**	**202,223**	**18,878**	**28,581**	**8,005**	**196,662**
13,102	0	0	0	0	0	0	0	0
278,086	35,740	15,940	87,812	59,731	12,428	14,622	7,470	3,002
10,395	1,090	90	1,269	453	0	0	0	0
32,151	1,756	992	3,654	7,955	114	55	12	51,110
101,261	7,177	2,277	14,054	14,131	376	351	80	9,604
6,950	709	927	1,007	3,164	92	45	141	123
71,723	6,540	3,454	6,136	35,668	263	748	91	52,867
772,036	29,241	21,219	38,607	68,875	5,120	12,491	55	45,919
831	46	3	18	478	0	0	2	19,346
10,340	329	417	546	1,244	12	0	0	1,666
45,031	3,045	3,297	4,513	10,523	472	268	153	13,025

Table 8.2 Federal government expenditures on culture, by cultural activity, 2003/2004 to 2005/2006

	2003/2004r	2004/2005	2005/2006
		$ thousands	
All cultural activities[1]	**3,461,582**	**3,597,994**	**3,547,062**
Libraries	41,949	55,104	51,479
Heritage resources	893,310	929,295	910,305
Arts education[2]	14,794	15,766	18,631
Literary arts	132,047	135,817	133,561
Performing arts	190,214	200,442	188,226
Visual arts and crafts	20,458	19,673	19,942
Film and video	359,337	350,163	344,521
Broadcasting[3]	1,609,996	1,685,824	1,677,351
Sound recording	25,476	24,076	23,244
Multiculturalism	15,857	19,187	20,766
Multidisciplinary and other culture activities[4]	158,143	162,648	159,036

Note: Figures may not add to totals because of rounding.
1. Total expenditures at the national level exclude intramural (operating and capital) expenditures by Human Resources and Skills Development Canada directly related to training and employment development in the culture sector.
2. Refers to the fine, applied and performing arts rather than to strictly academic fields such as language, history or literature. 'Arts' includes theatre, music, dance, painting, drama, photography and any other area of arts study reported by arts education institutions.
3. The Canadian Broadcasting Corporation distributes its program costs by location of production activities. Station transmission and network distribution costs are related to the geographic location of the transmitter, except for landlines and satellite channels, which are paid by Ottawa, but transferred to Toronto and Montréal network centres. Payments to private station affiliates are charged to the responsible network centres and relate also to the province where these centres are located. Administration costs and capital expenditures are distributed according to the province where the administration function is located geographically and the location of capital assets.
4. Includes financial support given to cultural facilities, centres, festivals, municipalities, cultural exchange programs and arts organizations for various cultural activities. It includes also the unallocated general and administration expenditures related to numerous cultural activities.

Source: Statistics Canada, CANSIM table 505-0003.

Table 8.3 Payroll employment, by industry, 2004 to 2008

	2004	2005	2006	2007	2008
			number		
Information and cultural industries	**300,694**	**307,647**	**313,724**	**323,886**	**326,367**
Publishing industries	81,563	85,027	85,893	90,900	93,286
Motion picture and sound recording industries	30,324	30,182	28,685	32,246	33,310
Broadcasting (except Internet)	38,233	36,908	39,880	41,527	43,030
Telecommunications	113,250	118,143	118,996	115,631	109,831
Data processing, hosting and related services	11,439	11,140	12,023	13,289	17,981
Other information services	25,884	26,247	28,248	30,293	28,929
Arts, entertainment and recreation	**228,212**	**229,076**	**236,379**	**240,519**	**241,916**
Performing arts, spectator sports and related industries	48,498	46,762	49,127	51,791	51,567
Heritage institutions	15,845	16,405	15,749	16,243	16,019
Amusement, gambling and recreation industries	163,869	165,909	171,503	172,485	174,329

Note: North American Industry Classification System (NAICS), 2007.
Source: Statistics Canada, Survey of Employment, Payrolls and Hours, CANSIM table 281-0024 and Catalogue no. 72-002-X.

Table 8.4 Government expenditures on culture, by level of government and by province and territory, 2005/2006

	Total gross expenditures	Federal government	Provincial and territorial governments	Municipal governments[1]
	$ thousands			
Total expenditures	**8,287,998[2]**	**3,547,062**	**2,432,265**	**2,308,671**
Newfoundland and Labrador	**99,783**	47,601	39,890	12,292
Prince Edward Island	**40,053**	22,269	13,757	4,027
Nova Scotia	**209,393**	103,883	70,135	35,375
New Brunswick	**136,422**	55,614	57,621	23,187
Quebec	**2,500,101**	1,229,534	773,331	497,236
Ontario	**2,997,127**	1,341,907	642,112	1,013,108
Manitoba	**269,012**	85,673	123,769	59,570
Saskatchewan	**255,723**	48,616	119,138	87,969
Alberta	**684,041**	157,617	308,900	217,524
British Columbia	**813,058**	202,223	255,337	355,498
Yukon	**34,185**	18,878	14,370	937
Northwest Territories	**39,364**	28,581	9,097	1,686
Nunavut	**13,077**	8,005	4,810	262
Other[3]	**196,662**	196,662	...	...

1. Calculated on a calendar-year basis.
2. Includes intergovernmental transfers of about $444 million.
3. Includes national organizations, foreign countries and unallocated expenditures.

Source: Statistics Canada, Catalogue no. 87F0001X.

Table 8.5 Newspaper publishing, summary statistics, 2003 to 2007

	Operating revenue[1]	Operating expenses[2]	Salaries, wages and benefits[3]	Operating profit margin[4]
	$ millions			%
2003	4,864.6	4,132.3	1,687.8	15.1
2004	5,033.9	4,317.3	1,751.2	14.2
2005	5,207.4	4,515.2	1,762.7	13.3
2006	5,353.8	4,646.2	1,801.2	13.2
2007p	5,337.7	4,557.3	1,783.2	14.6

Note: North American Industry Classification System (NAICS), 2007.

1. Excludes investment income, capital gains, extraordinary gains and other non-recurring items.
2. Excludes write-offs, capital losses, extraordinary losses, interest on borrowing, and other non-recurring items.
3. Includes vacation pay and commissions for all employees for whom a T4 slip was completed. This category also includes the employer portion of employee benefits for items such as Canada/Quebec Pension Plan or Employment Insurance premiums. Salaries and wages do not include working owners' dividends nor do they include the remuneration of owners of unincorporated businesses. Therefore, the relative level of salaries, wages and benefits will be lower in industries where unincorporated businesses are significant contributors.
4. Operating profit margin is derived as follows: operating revenue minus operating expenses, expressed as a percentage of operating revenue. The derived figure excludes corporation income tax paid by incorporated businesses and individual income tax paid by unincorporated businesses. For unincorporated businesses, operating profit margin includes unpaid remuneration to partners and proprietors, which is not recorded as salaries, wages and benefits. Therefore, the profit estimate will be higher in industries where unincorporated proprietorships and partnerships are significant contributors.

Source: Statistics Canada, CANSIM table 361-0003.

Table 8.6 Periodical and book publishing, summary statistics, by province and region, 2007

	Operating revenue[1]	Operating expenses[2]	Salaries, wages and benefits[3]	Operating profit margin[4]
	$ millions			%
Periodical publishing				
Canada	**2,283.4**	**2,026.3**	**567.3**	**11.3**
Atlantic region	48.3	42.9	13.9	11.1
Quebec	494.2	433.2	88.3	12.4
Ontario	1,308.0	1,203.1	350.8	8.0
Prairies	236.9	174.0	56.6	26.5
British Columbia and the territories	196.0	173.1	57.7	11.7
Book publishing				
Canada	**2,125.7**	**1,884.8**	**405.8**	**11.3**
Newfoundland and Labrador	2.9	2.5	0.8	14.5
Prince Edward Island	x	x	x	x
Nova Scotia	6.5	6.3	1.1	4.1
New Brunswick	4.9	4.9	2.8	1.1
Quebec	620.9	558.7	98.6	10.0
Ontario	1,362.6	1,191.8	268.4	12.5
Manitoba	5.9	6.0	1.5	-0.9
Saskatchewan	x	x	x	x
Alberta	41.0	39.0	12.3	4.8
British Columbia	79.4	74.1	19.8	6.6

Notes: Figures may not add to totals because of rounding.
North American Industry Classification System (NAICS), 2007.

1. Excludes investment income, capital gains, extraordinary gains and other non-recurring items.
2. Excludes write-offs, capital losses, extraordinary losses, interest on borrowing, and other non-recurring items.
3. Includes vacation pay and commissions for all employees for whom a T4 slip was completed. This category also includes the employer portion of employee benefits for items such as Canada/Quebec Pension Plan or Employment Insurance premiums. Salaries and wages do not include working owners' dividends nor do they include the remuneration of owners of unincorporated businesses. Therefore, the relative level of salaries, wages and benefits will be lower in industries where unincorporated businesses are significant contributors.
4. Operating profit margin is derived as follows: operating revenue minus operating expenses, expressed as a percentage of operating revenue. The derived figure excludes corporation income tax paid by incorporated businesses and individual income tax paid by unincorporated businesses. For unincorporated businesses, operating profit margin includes unpaid remuneration to partners and proprietors, which is not recorded as salaries, wages and benefits. Therefore, the profit estimate will be higher in industries where unincorporated proprietorships and partnerships are significant contributors.

Source: Statistics Canada, CANSIM tables 361-0007 and 361-0010.

Table 8.7 Sound recording and music publishing, summary statistics, by province and region, 2007

	Operating revenue[1]	Operating expenses[2]	Salaries, wages and benefits[3]	Operating profit margin[4]
	$ millions			%
Canada				
Record production and integrated record production/distribution	683.0	605.2	85.5	11.4
Music publishers	134.5	123.0	22.1	8.6
Sound recording studios	104.4	88.1	20.1	15.6
Other sound recording industries	6.1	4.5	1.5	26.8
Atlantic provinces				
Record production and integrated record production/distribution	4.2	3.5	0.4	15.2
Music publishers	.	.	.	.
Sound recording studios	3.2	2.9	0.4	10.7
Other sound recording industries	F	F	F	F
Quebec				
Record production and integrated record production/distribution	109.4	101.4	12.6	7.4
Music publishers	.	.	.	.
Sound recording studios	22.7	19.4	4.3	14.6
Other sound recording industries	F	F	F	F
Ontario				
Record production and integrated record production/distribution	501.1	435.2	65.3	13.1
Music publishers	.	.	.	.
Sound recording studios	41.6	33.7	8.4	19.0
Other sound recording industries	F	F	F	F
Prairie provinces				
Record production and integrated record production/distribution	21.2	17.2	3.0	19.1
Music publishers	.	.	.	.
Sound recording studios	6.2	5.2	1.1	15.9
Other sound recording industries	F	F	F	F
British Columbia and territories				
Record production and integrated record production/distribution	47.1	47.9	4.2	-1.6
Music publishers	.	.	.	.
Sound recording studios	30.6	26.9	5.8	12.2
Other sound recording industries	F	F	F	F

Note: North American Industry Classification System (NAICS), 2007.
1. Excludes investment income (dividends and interest).
2. Excludes write-offs, capital losses, extraordinary losses, interest on borrowing, and other non-recurring items.
3. Includes employer contributions to pension, medical/life insurance plans, and Employment Insurance for employees who have been issued a T4 statement.
4. Operating profit margin is derived as follows: total operating revenue minus total operating expenses, expressed as a percentage of total operating revenue.

Source: Statistics Canada, CANSIM table 361-0005.

Table 8.8 Spectator sports, event promoters, artists and related industries, summary statistics, 2007

	Total operating revenue[1]	Total operating expenses[2]	Salaries, wages and benefits[3]	Operating profit margin[4]
	$ millions			%
Spectator sports	2,401.4	2,356.4	991.4	1.9
Promoters (presenters) of performing arts, sports and similar events	1,890.4	1,812.2	467.8	4.1
Agents and managers for artists, athletes, entertainers and other public figures	305.5	273.0	78.3	10.6
Independent artists, writers and performers	907.2	654.3	209.6	27.9

Note: North American Industry Classification System (NAICS), 2007.
1. Excludes investment income (dividends and interest).
2. Excludes write-offs, capital losses, extraordinary losses, interest on borrowing, and other non-recurring items.
3. Includes employer contributions to pension, medical/life insurance plans, and Employment Insurance for employees who have been issued a T4 statement.
4. Operating profit margin is derived as follows: total operating revenue minus total operating expenses, expressed as a percentage of total operating revenue.

Source: Statistics Canada, CANSIM table 361-0013.

Table 8.9 Heritage institutions, summary statistics, by industry, 2005 and 2006

	Total operating revenue		Salaries, wages and benefits		Total operating expenses		Operating profit margin	
	2005r	2006r	2005r	2006r	2005r	2006r	2005r	2006r
	$ thousands						%	
For-profit establishments								
Art museums and galleries	...	...	...	...	...	...	...	...
Museums	18,919	18,292	6,271	5,025	15,426	15,029	18.46	17.84
Historic and heritage sites	4,323	4,727	1,666	1,520	3,918	4,135	9.37	12.52
Zoos and botanical gardens	94,219	104,143	39,412	50,428	83,144	97,747	11.75	6.14
Not-for-profit establishments								
Art museums and galleries	246,052	253,369	101,473	100,753	249,808	247,924	-1.53	2.15
Museums	482,774	492,851	223,256	235,991	481,905	512,229	0.18	-3.93
Historic and heritage sites	84,662	82,319	47,986	44,697	85,637	84,418	-1.15	-2.55
Zoos and botanical gardens	152,116	142,270	66,591	73,396	139,573	139,241	8.25	2.13

Note: North American Industry Classification System (NAICS), 2007.

Source: Statistics Canada, Catalogue no. 87F0002X.

Table 8.10 Heritage institutions, summary statistics, all industries, by province, 2005 and 2006

	Total operating revenue		Salaries, wages and benefits		Total operating expenses		Operating profit margin	
	2005r	2006r	2005r	2006r	2005r	2006r	2005r	2006r
	$ thousands						%	
For-profit establishments								
Canada	**117,461**	**127,218**	**47,349**	**56,973**	**102,488**	**116,926**	**12.7**	**8.1**
Newfoundland and Labrador	2,544	2,174	1,144	1,110	2,278	2,257	10.5	-3.8
Prince Edward Island	1,273	1,355	478	382	1,289	1,244	-1.3	8.2
Nova Scotia	340	1,504	493	312	468	1,348	-37.5	10.4
New Brunswick	335	428	211	269	330	526	1.7	-22.9
Quebec	15,544	18,680	7,642	8,742	13,856	17,040	10.9	8.8
Ontario	51,811	56,731	16,215	26,485	45,315	53,195	12.5	6.2
Manitoba	510	x	235	x	511	x	-0.2	x
Saskatchewan	x	x	x	x	x	x	x	x
Alberta	1,540	1,529	633	197	1,312	1,183	14.8	22.6
British Columbia	42,067	43,806	19,701	19,052	35,623	39,236	15.3	10.4
Not-for-profit establishments								
Canada	**965,604**	**970,752**	**439,306**	**454,837**	**956,923**	**983,797**	**0.9**	**-1.3**
Newfoundland and Labrador	12,933	13,317	6,187	6,255	11,992	13,053	7.3	2.0
Prince Edward Island	1,345	1,580	444	1,072	1,440	1,669	-7.1	-5.7
Nova Scotia	21,296	19,989	11,392	11,126	24,824	21,326	-16.6	-6.7
New Brunswick	18,698	15,448	10,770	8,101	19,974	14,685	-6.8	4.9
Quebec	318,176	312,301	129,851	128,491	310,020	311,938	2.6	0.1
Ontario	357,599	360,935	169,810	180,569	357,517	368,136	0.0	-2.0
Manitoba	22,179	23,341	12,142	13,452	22,923	24,578	-3.4	-5.3
Saskatchewan	17,613	20,749	8,523	10,625	17,625	21,213	-0.1	-2.2
Alberta	79,033	90,553	40,707	43,698	82,508	92,032	-4.4	-1.6
British Columbia	115,275	111,561	48,864	50,992	106,618	114,091	7.5	-2.3

Notes: Figures may not add to totals because of rounding.
North American Industry Classification System (NAICS), 2007.
Source: Statistics Canada, Catalogue no. 87F0002X.

Table 8.11 Performing arts, summary statistics, by industry and type of establishment, 2007

	Operating revenue	Salaries, wages and benefits	Operating expenses	Operating profit margin
	$ thousands			%
All establishments	**1,241,265**	**373,776**	**1,167,722**	**5.9**
Theatre (except musical) companies	333,617	132,145	330,365	1.0
Musical theatre and opera companies (including dinner theatre)	181,550	61,023	175,431	3.4
Dance companies	x	x	x	x
Musical groups and artists	362,047	62,467	308,579	14.8
Other performing arts companies (including multidisciplinary)	x	x	x	x
For-profit establishments	**628,454**	**154,044**	**555,546**	**11.6**
Theatre (except musical) companies	44,314	7,485	36,351	18.0
Musical theatre and opera companies (including dinner theatre)	102,672	39,113	99,303	3.3
Dance companies	x	x	x	x
Musical groups and artists	210,860	21,135	157,851	25.1
Other performing arts companies (including multidisciplinary)	x	x	x	x
Not-for-profit establishments	**612,811**	**219,732**	**612,176**	**0.1**
Theatre (except musical) companies	289,303	124,660	294,014	-1.6
Musical theatre and opera companies (including dinner theatre)	78,878	21,910	76,128	3.5
Dance companies	81,643	28,184	79,726	2.3
Musical groups and artists	151,187	41,332	150,728	0.3
Other performing arts companies (including multidisciplinary)	11,800	3,646	11,580	1.9

Notes: Figures may not add to totals because of rounding.
North American Industry Classification System (NAICS), 2007.
Source: Statistics Canada, Catalogue no. 87F0003X.

Table 8.12 Amusement and recreation, summary statistics, 2007

	Operating revenue[1]	Operating expenses[2]	Salaries, wages and benefits[3]	Operating profit margin[4]
	$ millions			%
Amusement parks and arcades	492.5	425.7	145.2	13.6
Other amusement and recreation industries	6,879.7	6,545.8	2,349.1	4.9
Golf courses and country clubs	2,391.8	2,284.8	885.2	4.5
Skiing facilities	946.4	857.6	312.3	9.4
Fitness and recreational sports centres	1,731.2	1,686.2	682.3	2.6
All other amusement and recreation industries	1,810.3	1,717.2	469.3	5.1

Notes: Figures may not add to totals because of rounding.
North American Industry Classification System (NAICS), 2007.
1. Excludes investment income (dividends and interest).
2. Excludes write-offs, capital losses, extraordinary losses, interest on borrowing, and other non-recurring items.
3. Includes employer contributions to pension, medical/life insurance plans, and Employment Insurance for employees who have been issued a T4 statement.
4. Operating profit margin is derived as follows: total operating revenue minus total operating expenses, expressed as a percentage of total operating revenue.
Source: Statistics Canada, CANSIM table 361-0015.

Table 8.13 Performing arts, summary statistics, all industries, by province, 2006 and 2007

	Operating revenue		Operating expenses		Salaries, wages and benefits		Operating profit margin	
	2006	2007	2006	2007	2006	2007	2006	2007
	$ thousands						%	
For-profit establishments								
Canada	**590,615**	**628,453**	**530,010**	**555,546**	**142,731**	**154,043**	**10.3**	**11.6**
Newfoundland and Labrador	5,706	6,302	5,024	4,444	904	814	12.0	29.5
Prince Edward Island	x	x	x	x	x	x	x	x
Nova Scotia	7,539	6,413	6,414	5,617	1,069	1,271	14.9	12.4
New Brunswick	x	x	x	x	497	x	x	x
Quebec	321,928	329,789	303,925	307,810	94,550	94,884	5.6	6.7
Ontario	161,485	199,623	143,601	170,389	34,982	45,603	11.1	14.6
Manitoba	11,526	11,577	9,232	9,963	2,413	2,115	19.9	13.9
Saskatchewan	4,293	3,950	3,402	3,184	655	668	20.8	19.4
Alberta	28,981	26,693	24,341	22,052	4,813	4,891	16.0	17.4
British Columbia	46,054	39,444	30,800	27,623	2,192	2,458	33.1	30.0
Not-for-profit establishments								
Canada	**617,004**	**612,809**	**609,361**	**612,177**	**213,117**	**219,734**	**1.2**	**0.1**
Newfoundland and Labrador	3,662	3,275	3,590	3,296	1,273	1,527	2.0	-0.6
Prince Edward Island	x	x	x	x	x	x	x	x
Nova Scotia	10,251	10,439	10,444	10,477	3,394	3,928	-1.9	-0.4
New Brunswick	x	x	x	x	x	x	x	x
Quebec	162,470	157,511	159,053	161,218	48,511	48,930	2.1	-2.4
Ontario	253,635	266,685	253,747	263,975	98,457	102,633	0.0	1.0
Manitoba	24,172	24,768	23,529	23,688	10,562	11,191	2.7	4.4
Saskatchewan	8,815	7,855	8,244	8,225	3,373	3,519	6.5	-4.7
Alberta	74,704	67,124	71,263	69,048	23,303	23,454	4.6	-2.9
British Columbia	73,681	70,282	73,368	67,584	22,700	22,720	0.4	3.8

Notes: Figures may not add to totals because of rounding.
North American Industry Classification System (NAICS), 2007.
Source: Statistics Canada, Catalogue no. 87F0003X.

Table 8.14 Film and video distribution, summary statistics, by region, 2005 to 2007

	Operating revenue[1]	Operating expenses[2]	Salaries, wages and benefits[3]	Operating profit margin[4]
	$ millions			%
Canada				
2005	1,664.5	1,353.7	76.6	18.7
2006	1,730.9	1,305.0	68.1	24.6
2007	1,729.9	1,460.2	96.3	15.6
Quebec				
2005	291.1	223.4	14.7	23.3
2006	235.6	225.7	13.3	4.2
2007	247.9	234.9	19.0	5.3
Ontario				
2005	1,308.5	1,110.2	59.6	15.2
2006	1,442.9	1,023.7	53.3	29.1
2007	1,336.3	1,087.6	76.4	18.6

Notes: North American Industry Classification System (NAICS), 2007.
Data for Atlantic provinces, Manitoba, Yukon, Northwest Territories and Nunavut are suppressed for confidentiality.
1. Excludes investment income (dividends and interest).
2. Excludes write-offs, capital losses, extraordinary losses, interest on borrowing, and other non-recurring items.
3. Includes employer contributions to pension, medical/life insurance plans, and Employment Insurance for employees who have been issued a T4 statement.
4. Operating profit margin is derived as follows: total operating revenue minus total operating expenses, expressed as a percentage of total operating revenue.

Source: Statistics Canada, CANSIM table 361-0014.

Table 8.15 Motion picture theatres, summary statistics, by province, 2007

	Establishments	Operating revenue[1]	Operating expenses[2]	Salaries, wages and benefits[3]	Operating profit margin[4]
	number	$ millions			%
Canada	**672**	**1,346.6**	**1,198.6**	**178.6**	**11.0**
Quebec	143	218.5	212.9	35.1	2.6
Ontario	212	582.1	524.9	77.0	9.8
Saskatchewan	37	35.0	30.0	4.6	14.1
Alberta	88	194.8	151.8	21.0	22.1
British Columbia	106	204.0	180.3	24.7	11.6

Notes: North American Industry Classification System (NAICS), 2007.
Data for Atlantic provinces, Manitoba, Saskatchewan, Alberta, and British Colimbia are suppressed for confidentiality.
1. Excludes investment income (dividends and interest).
2. Excludes write-offs, capital losses, extraordinary losses, interest on borrowing, and other non-recurring items.
3. Includes employer contributions to pension, medical/life insurance plans and Employment Insurance for all employees who have been issued a T4 statement.
4. Operating profit margin is derived as follows: total operating revenue minus total operating expenses, expressed as a percentage of total operating revenue.

Source: Statistics Canada, CANSIM table 361-0012.

Economic accounts

9

Until 2008, Canada had gone a record 16 years since its last economic downturn and had been riding a seven-year boom in commodity prices. But the economy in 2008 was unlike any in recent memory. For many younger workers and investors, 2008 was their first experience with a recession.

In the first seven months of 2008, commodity prices rose to record levels amid slow growth in North America and steady gains in Asia. Inflation dominated the headlines, while Canada's trade surplus set records. However, late in the summer, global demand and commodity prices faltered, and then fell precipitously after credit markets seized up in mid-September. These events quickly spilled over into the real economy of output and employment.

Slowing growth

By year-end, the global economy—and Canada's—was changing rapidly in response to the tumult in the global financial markets. In real terms (adjusted for inflation), Canada's gross domestic product (GDP) grew 0.5% in 2008, its slowest growth since 1991.

Despite all the turmoil, Canada's financial institutions held up well. Governments and businesses had been running large financial surpluses for the past decade, while Canadian households were less burdened with debt than those in the United States.

Canada's GDP grew in five provinces; Saskatchewan led the way with growth of 4.4%. The GDP also advanced in Yukon and Nunavut, while declining export demand contributed to lower GDP in Ontario, Alberta, British Columbia, Newfoundland and Labrador, and the Northwest Territories.

Domestic demand, the engine of economic growth since 2001, slowed

Chart 9.1
Gross domestic product and final domestic demand

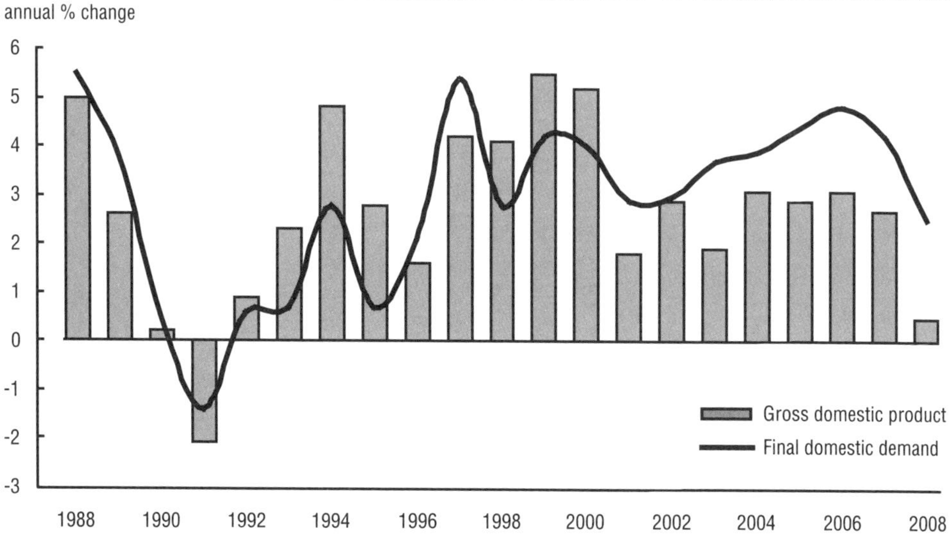

Note: Chained 2002 dollars.
Source: Statistics Canada, CANSIM table 384-0002.

from a 4.2% pace in 2007 to 2.5% in 2008, as spending on consumer goods and services weakened and the housing market softened. Declining merchandise trade and a deterioration in Canada's terms of trade—exports shrank a record 25% after October—contributed to the overall weakness in GDP.

Employment turned down decisively in November and December, falling 0.5% and 0.6%, respectively, from the same months of the previous year.

Goods production declines

Goods production declined 2.8% in 2008, the first decrease since 2001, the year of the high-technology meltdown. All goods-producing industries declined.

Building permits declined 5.3%. Permits for residential construction declined 10.2% while permits for non-residential construction increased 2.5%. Sales of existing homes posted their largest decline since 1990, falling 17.1% across the country from 2007.

Meanwhile, the services-producing industries grew 2.1%, with all sectors advancing.

Table 9.a
International investment position

	2007	2008
	% change	
Total assets	**0.9**	**24.0**
Canadian direct investment abroad	-1.8	23.6
Canadian portfolio investment	-0.5	14.8
Foreign bonds	9.1	4.8
Foreign stocks	-0.3	23.1
Foreign money market	-62.4	-53.6

Source: Statistics Canada, CANSIM table 376-0037.

Chart 9.2
Gross domestic product at market prices, by province and territory

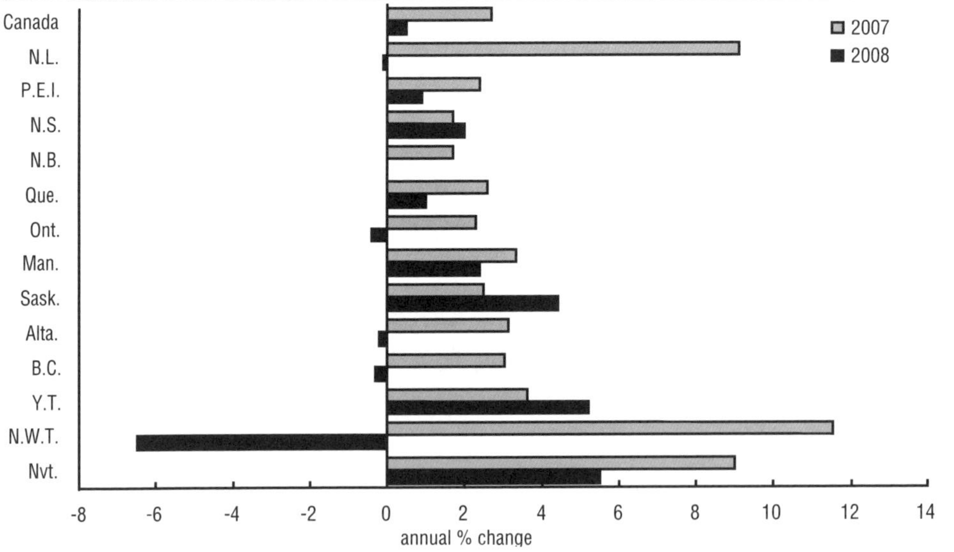

Notes: Chained 2002 dollars.
Expenditure-based estimates.
Source: Statistics Canada, CANSIM table 384-0002.

Canadians better able to pay back debt

The indebtedness of households, corporations and governments in the United States rose from 269% of GDP in 2002 to 329% in 2008. (Debt-to-GDP ratios are an indicator of the ability to meet one's financial obligations.) Household debt rose to 97% of GDP by mid-2008, fuelled by the housing boom.

In Canada, domestic debt rose from 228% of GDP in 2002 to 255% in 2008, less than half the 60-point increase in the United States. Household debt rose to 85% of GDP, while non-financial corporations and governments paid down their debt. The Canadian financial system had debt equivalent to 60% of GDP in 2008, half the American level, while avoiding the corrosive impact of subprime mortgages.

Canada consistently ran large trade surpluses over the past decade, and Canadians placed much of this surplus in direct investment abroad, avoiding opaque financial instruments. By the end of 2008, Canada had no net external indebtedness for the first time since 1926.

Chart 9.3
Domestic debt in Canada

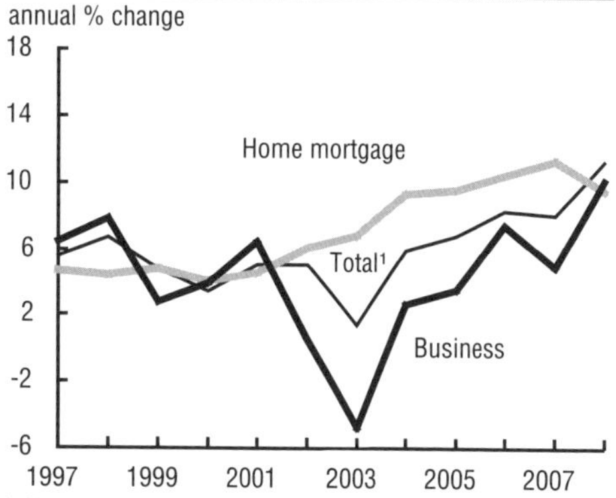

1. Household, corporate and government.
Source: Statistics Canada, CANSIM table 378-0003.

Household wealth grows

Household balance sheet data clearly show the impact of the resource and housing boom that sent household wealth climbing before 2008, and dropping in the second half of 2008, partly offsetting the increase.

From 2002 to the second quarter of 2008, household net worth rose 56%, or $2.1 trillion. Two-thirds ($1.2 trillion) of this net worth came from investments related to the soaring stock market and about one-third ($0.8 trillion) from rising homeowner net equity.

The slump in stock markets and house prices in the second half of 2008 erased 7% of household net worth—painful, but far short of the 20% reduction seen in the United States since mid-2007, when the U.S. stock and housing markets began to falter. As a result, household wealth in Canada has expanded almost twice as fast as in the United States since 2002 (45% versus 27%).

Chart 9.4
Household net worth

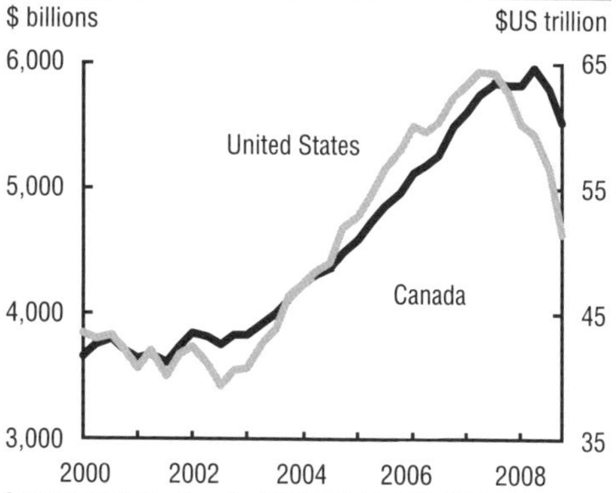

Source: Statistics Canada, CANSIM table 378-0009.

Table 9.1 Gross domestic product, expenditure-based, by province and territory, 1994 to 2008

	1994	1995	1996	1997	1998	1999
	$ millions					
Canada	**770,873**	**810,426**	**836,864**	**882,733**	**914,973**	**982,441**
Newfoundland and Labrador	10,264	10,652	10,417	10,533	11,176	12,184
Prince Edward Island	2,521	2,662	2,823	2,800	2,981	3,159
Nova Scotia	18,667	19,296	19,512	20,368	21,401	23,059
New Brunswick	15,286	16,380	16,626	16,845	17,633	19,041
Quebec	170,478	177,331	180,526	188,424	196,258	210,809
Ontario	311,096	329,317	338,173	359,353	377,897	409,020
Manitoba	25,958	26,966	28,434	29,751	30,972	31,966
Saskatchewan	24,480	26,425	28,944	29,157	29,550	30,778
Alberta	88,041	92,036	98,634	107,048	107,439	117,080
British Columbia	100,512	105,670	108,865	114,383	115,641	120,921
Yukon	910	1,047	1,128	1,107	1,087	1,085
Northwest Territories (including Nunavut)	2,387	2,400	2,525	2,691	2,652	..
Northwest Territories	..	..	..	..	..	2,292
Nunavut	..	..	..	..	..	747
Outside Canada	273	244	257	273	286	300

Note: Dollar amounts in current prices.
Source: Statistics Canada, CANSIM table 384-0002.

Table 9.2 Gross domestic product, income-based, 1994 to 2008

	1994	1995	1996	1997	1998	1999
	$ millions					
Gross domestic product at market prices	**770,873**	**810,426**	**836,864**	**882,733**	**914,973**	**982,441**
Net domestic product at basic prices	613,352	644,818	664,294	700,063	723,487	780,786
Wages, salaries and supplementary labour income	404,918	418,825	428,792	453,073	475,335	502,726
Corporation profits before taxes	65,464	76,270	80,335	87,932	86,132	110,769
Government business enterprise profits before taxes	5,827	6,709	6,143	6,653	7,080	8,401
Interest and miscellaneous investment income	52,000	50,981	50,477	48,881	47,134	47,249
Accrued net income of farm operators from farm production	1,255	2,702	3,825	1,663	1,724	1,819
Net income of non-farm unincorporated business, including rent	44,931	46,363	49,278	54,663	57,936	61,466
Inventory valuation adjustment	-5,372	-2,473	-1,596	-623	-753	-2,317
Taxes less subsidies on factors of production	44,329	45,441	47,040	47,821	48,899	50,673
Taxes less subsidies on products	56,721	59,758	61,126	66,025	68,439	72,747
Capital consumption allowances	99,631	105,021	110,818	116,574	122,659	128,999
Statistical discrepancy	1,169	829	626	71	388	-91

Note: Dollar amounts in current prices.
Source: Statistics Canada, CANSIM table 380-0016.

2000	2001	2002	2003	2004	2005	2006	2007	2008
				$ millions				
1,076,577	**1,108,048**	**1,152,905**	**1,213,175**	**1,290,906**	**1,372,626**	**1,450,490**	**1,535,646**	**1,602,474**
13,922	14,179	16,457	18,119	19,407	21,939	25,994	29,524	31,458
3,366	3,431	3,701	3,798	3,983	4,151	4,321	4,549	4,716
24,658	25,909	27,082	28,851	29,853	31,275	31,737	33,010	34,209
20,085	20,684	21,169	22,366	23,672	24,748	25,825	26,947	27,288
224,928	231,624	241,448	250,752	262,761	271,059	281,521	296,692	301,479
440,759	453,701	477,763	493,081	516,106	536,844	559,778	584,957	587,905
34,057	35,157	36,559	37,451	39,748	41,517	44,911	48,549	50,886
33,828	33,127	34,343	36,653	40,796	44,066	46,494	51,628	64,323
144,789	151,274	150,594	170,113	189,743	220,419	239,584	258,936	291,662
131,333	133,514	138,193	145,642	157,675	169,308	182,743	192,528	199,214
1,190	1,259	1,254	1,292	1,394	1,522	1,622	1,767	2,000
..	..	..	..	..	..	..	..	..
2,515	2,972	3,033	3,692	4,320	4,248	4,345	4,776	5,419
834	876	951	991	1,074	1,137	1,224	1,386	1,497
313	341	358	374	374	393	391	397	418

2000	2001	2002	2003	2004	2005	2006	2007	2008
				$ millions				
1,076,577	**1,108,048**	**1,152,905**	**1,213,175**	**1,290,906**	**1,373,845**	**1,449,215**	**1,532,944**	**1,600,081**
863,254	884,203	912,615	967,051	1,033,888	1,104,878	1,168,900	1,237,844	1,296,477
545,204	570,008	593,307	621,003	657,249	695,093	743,392	784,839	823,116
135,978	127,073	135,229	144,501	168,219	186,585	196,130	204,131	215,799
11,329	10,787	11,661	12,604	12,815	15,293	14,572	15,725	15,575
55,302	52,579	46,693	49,989	54,020	61,421	66,741	71,847	81,484
1,243	1,675	1,101	1,439	2,897	1,210	-44	433	2,808
64,944	68,857	74,292	77,181	81,313	84,024	86,651	89,974	93,438
-2,439	574	-3,584	4,262	-1,844	-730	-3,233	2,947	-6,085
51,693	52,650	53,916	56,072	59,219	61,982	64,691	67,948	70,342
76,647	75,871	84,139	84,380	89,603	93,302	95,761	98,495	94,675
137,425	147,536	155,567	161,817	167,823	176,246	185,408	195,712	207,520
-749	438	584	-73	-408	-581	-854	893	1,409

Table 9.3 Gross domestic product, expenditure-based, 1994 to 2008

	1994	1995	1996	1997	1998	1999
	$ millions					
Gross domestic product at market prices	**770,873**	**810,426**	**836,864**	**882,733**	**914,973**	**982,441**
Personal expenditure on consumer goods and services	445,857	460,906	480,427	510,695	531,169	560,884
Durable goods	54,116	56,169	59,197	67,988	71,325	77,693
Semi-durable goods	41,104	42,304	42,766	44,939	47,262	49,548
Non-durable goods	112,287	115,024	118,697	123,143	126,253	132,959
Services	238,350	247,409	259,767	274,625	286,329	300,684
Government current expenditure on goods and services	171,590	172,459	171,161	171,756	179,317	186,054
Government gross fixed capital formation	21,634	21,406	20,587	20,104	20,046	23,039
Government inventories	-1	30	-2	5	-27	-3
Business gross fixed capital formation	123,321	121,592	129,351	154,737	161,790	171,431
Residential structures	42,422	36,136	39,538	43,519	42,497	45,100
Non-residential structures and equipment	80,899	85,456	89,813	111,218	119,293	126,331
Non-residential structures	34,002	34,669	36,360	43,872	45,177	47,229
Machinery and equipment	46,897	50,787	53,453	67,346	74,116	79,102
Business investment in inventories	528	8,999	2,271	8,174	4,733	4,990
Non-farm	775	8,705	1,577	9,174	5,409	4,951
Farm	-247	294	694	-1,000	-676	39
Exports of goods and services	262,127	302,480	321,248	348,604	379,203	424,258
Goods	228,168	265,334	280,079	303,379	327,160	369,037
Services	33,959	37,146	41,169	45,225	52,043	55,221
Imports of goods and services	253,014	276,618	287,553	331,271	360,871	388,303
Goods	207,875	229,938	237,689	277,727	303,395	327,026
Services	45,139	46,680	49,864	53,544	57,476	61,277
Statistical discrepancy	-1,169	-828	-626	-71	-387	91
Final domestic demand	**762,402**	**776,363**	**801,526**	**857,292**	**892,322**	**941,408**

Note: Dollar amounts in current prices.
Source: Statistics Canada, CANSIM table 380-0017.

2000	2001	2002	2003	2004	2005	2006	2007	2008
				$ millions				
1,076,577	**1,108,048**	**1,152,905**	**1,213,175**	**1,290,906**	**1,373,845**	**1,449,215**	**1,532,944**	**1,600,081**
596,009	620,614	655,722	686,552	719,917	758,966	801,211	850,921	891,197
81,958	84,930	92,085	93,793	95,432	99,721	105,618	111,767	112,404
52,115	54,565	57,052	58,485	60,520	62,674	66,237	69,372	70,518
143,264	150,305	158,399	168,144	176,869	186,547	193,868	204,088	216,462
318,672	330,814	348,186	366,130	387,096	410,024	435,488	465,694	491,813
200,084	211,706	224,428	238,416	247,397	259,857	277,097	294,776	313,669
24,524	27,287	28,589	30,107	32,504	37,067	40,562	44,548	53,307
24	13	-45	15	21	27	-41	15	29
181,748	189,978	196,585	208,090	229,755	255,596	283,393	302,246	309,173
48,572	55,133	65,651	72,714	82,965	89,604	98,099	108,050	108,175
133,176	134,845	130,934	135,376	146,790	165,992	185,294	194,196	200,998
49,826	52,966	50,659	54,545	62,058	72,752	85,288	92,705	98,092
83,350	81,879	80,275	80,831	84,732	93,240	100,006	101,491	102,906
11,505	-4,740	-2,674	4,305	5,238	10,587	9,538	11,391	8,733
11,355	-3,745	-1,094	2,982	3,848	9,932	10,284	12,493	6,915
150	-995	-1,580	1,323	1,390	655	-746	-1,102	1,818
490,688	482,463	479,185	462,473	495,980	519,435	524,358	534,557	562,174
429,375	420,733	414,034	399,122	429,006	450,214	453,953	463,130	489,859
61,313	61,730	65,151	63,351	66,974	69,221	70,405	71,427	72,315
428,754	418,836	428,301	416,856	440,314	468,270	487,757	504,618	536,792
362,337	350,067	356,728	342,711	363,155	387,843	404,345	415,228	442,988
66,417	68,769	71,573	74,145	77,159	80,427	83,412	89,390	93,804
749	-437	-584	73	408	580	854	-892	-1,409
1,002,365	**1,049,585**	**1,105,324**	**1,163,165**	**1,229,573**	**1,311,486**	**1,402,263**	**1,492,491**	**1,567,346**

Table 9.4 Gross domestic product at basic prices, by industry, 1997 to 2008

	1997	1998	1999	2000	2001
	$ millions chained (2002)				
All industries[1]	**888,158**	**922,584**	**974,405**	**1,026,242**	**1,040,943**
Goods-producing industries					
Agriculture, forestry, fishing and hunting	22,985	24,471	26,193	26,268	24,674
Mining and oil and gas extraction	49,244	49,991	50,000	51,519	51,236
Utilities	29,045	28,554	28,982	29,050	27,384
Construction	45,421	46,928	49,053	51,757	55,542
Manufacturing	151,330	158,819	171,923	188,925	181,084
Services-producing industries					
Wholesale trade	42,823	46,221	49,396	52,519	53,438
Retail trade	44,499	47,210	49,437	52,579	55,234
Transportation and warehousing	43,048	43,905	46,603	48,921	50,176
Information and cultural industries	26,403	28,255	31,617	34,007	36,498
Finance and insurance, real estate and renting, and leasing and management of companies and enterprises	168,523	173,796	181,851	189,181	196,769
Professional, scientific and technical services	33,859	38,056	41,845	46,307	47,453
Administrative and support, waste management and remediation services	17,582	18,771	20,934	21,809	22,820
Educational services	48,904	49,000	50,162	50,394	50,675
Health care and social assistance	61,114	61,765	63,754	65,968	67,198
Arts, entertainment and recreation	8,669	8,928	9,333	9,718	10,142
Accommodation and food services	21,668	22,931	23,804	24,544	24,950
Public administration	54,293	54,909	56,674	57,968	59,705
Other services	21,262	21,886	23,335	24,627	26,101

Note: North American Industry Classification System (NAICS), 2002.

1. Aggregates are not always equal to the sum of their components from 1981 to 2001. This is caused by changing the set of relative prices when a new base year is adopted.

Source: Statistics Canada, CANSIM table 379-0027.

2002	2003	2004	2005	2006	2007	2008
$ millions chained (2002)						
1,068,765	**1,091,378**	**1,124,998**	**1,155,681**	**1,189,661**	**1,219,327**	**1,225,825**
23,293	25,478	27,669	28,214	27,648	26,478	25,945
53,488	54,979	55,672	55,796	56,699	57,288	55,305
28,883	29,057	28,993	30,613	30,181	31,344	31,137
57,775	59,871	63,453	66,611	70,805	72,890	74,852
182,736	181,349	184,814	187,806	187,041	185,311	175,609
55,226	57,767	59,990	63,159	66,622	70,256	70,390
58,483	60,515	62,666	64,535	68,420	72,391	74,570
50,066	50,270	52,169	54,148	55,690	56,624	56,756
38,229	38,631	40,813	41,888	43,227	44,349	45,114
202,959	207,544	215,074	222,475	231,381	240,536	246,941
48,481	50,797	52,099	53,618	55,963	57,874	58,505
24,853	25,722	27,363	28,500	29,989	30,948	31,109
51,593	52,566	53,764	55,561	57,108	58,863	60,522
68,142	70,324	71,589	72,826	74,940	77,035	79,227
10,398	10,365	10,791	10,873	11,454	11,716	11,727
25,408	24,881	25,656	25,998	26,680	27,146	27,742
61,523	63,314	64,085	64,548	66,134	67,463	69,417
27,230	27,894	28,729	29,632	30,565	31,542	32,518

Table 9.5 Canada's balance of international payments, 1994 to 2008

	1994	1995	1996	1997	1998	1999
	$ millions					
Current account						
Receipts	**285,601**	**330,978**	**351,038**	**385,415**	**414,777**	**461,219**
Goods and services	260,917	301,130	319,965	347,134	377,385	422,670
Goods	228,167	265,334	280,079	303,378	327,162	369,035
Services	32,750	35,796	39,886	43,755	50,223	53,636
Investment income	21,100	25,898	26,176	33,252	32,338	32,905
Transfers	3,584	3,951	4,897	5,029	5,054	5,644
Payments	**303,331**	**337,078**	**346,438**	**396,812**	**426,140**	**458,649**
Goods and services	252,285	275,869	286,650	330,346	359,947	387,298
Goods	207,873	229,937	237,689	277,727	303,399	327,026
Services	44,413	45,933	48,961	52,619	56,549	60,272
Investment income	46,990	57,089	55,571	62,133	61,965	66,518
Transfers	4,056	4,120	4,217	4,333	4,228	4,834
Balance	**-17,730**	**-6,099**	**4,600**	**-11,397**	**-11,363**	**2,570**
Goods and services	8,632	25,261	33,315	16,788	17,438	35,373
Goods	20,295	35,397	42,391	25,652	23,763	42,009
Services	-11,663	-10,136	-9,076	-8,864	-6,325	-6,636
Investment income	-25,889	-31,191	-29,395	-28,882	-29,627	-33,613
Transfers	-472	-169	680	697	826	810
Capital account, net flow	**10,241**	**6,784**	**7,957**	**7,508**	**4,934**	**5,049**
Financial account, net flow[1]	**7,520**	**-5,489**	**-20,191**	**8,256**	**-405**	**-17,531**
Canadian assets, net flow	**-49,029**	**-38,394**	**-73,306**	**-62,546**	**-67,161**	**-41,946**
Canadian direct investments abroad	-12,694	-15,732	-17,858	-31,937	-50,957	-25,625
Canadian portfolio investments	-8,927	-7,331	-19,317	-11,849	-22,497	-23,101
Foreign portfolio bonds	435	-1,085	-2,070	-6,642	-7,064	-2,477
Foreign portfolio stocks	-9,362	-6,247	-17,247	-5,207	-15,433	-20,623
Foreign money market	..	..	..	..	..	..
Other Canadian investments	-27,408	-15,331	-36,132	-18,760	6,292	6,780
Loans	123	-3,438	-4,208	-18,923	12,637	2,680
Deposits	-19,889	-7,162	-18,015	-2,898	-6,225	10,592
Official international reserves	489	-3,778	-7,498	3,389	-7,452	-8,818
Other assets	-8,131	-952	-6,411	-328	7,332	2,326
Canadian liabilities, net flow	**56,550**	**32,905**	**53,116**	**70,803**	**66,757**	**24,415**
Foreign direct investments in Canada	11,206	12,703	13,137	15,958	33,828	36,762
Foreign portfolio investments	23,312	25,233	18,668	16,181	24,779	3,738
Canadian portfolio bonds	15,995	30,730	17,953	6,166	10,337	2,602
Canadian portfolio stocks	6,412	-4,242	8,034	7,645	14,311	14,346
Canadian money market	905	-1,254	-7,319	2,369	130	-13,209
Other foreign investments	22,032	-5,032	21,311	38,664	8,149	-16,086
Loans	-137	1,129	5,994	1,873	3,181	6,641
Deposits	21,005	-6,009	16,863	34,106	3,375	-24,103
Other liabilities	1,165	-151	-1,546	2,685	1,593	1,377
Statistical discrepancy	-32	4,805	7,633	-4,367	6,833	9,912

1. A minus sign denotes an outflow of capital resulting from an increase in claims to non-residents or a decrease in liabilities to non-residents.

Source: Statistics Canada, CANSIM tables 376-0001 and 376-0002.

2000	2001	2002	2003	2004	2005	2006	2007	2008
				$ millions				
531,961	**513,754**	**514,913**	**496,899**	**539,637**	**573,774**	**595,156**	**611,294**	**637,502**
489,090	480,795	477,522	460,903	494,387	517,281	520,960	530,332	557,922
429,372	420,730	414,039	399,122	429,006	450,150	453,732	463,051	489,916
59,718	60,065	63,483	61,781	65,381	67,131	67,227	67,280	68,006
36,755	25,990	30,502	29,253	38,095	48,317	64,497	71,417	69,338
6,116	6,968	6,890	6,743	7,155	8,176	9,700	9,545	10,242
502,692	**488,649**	**495,135**	**482,250**	**509,800**	**547,321**	**574,925**	**597,686**	**627,264**
427,836	417,945	427,434	416,011	439,575	467,077	486,245	501,474	533,271
362,337	350,071	356,727	342,710	363,158	387,804	404,253	415,006	442,724
65,500	67,874	70,707	73,302	76,417	79,273	81,992	86,468	90,547
69,863	65,320	60,799	59,284	62,399	70,735	77,872	85,611	83,380
4,992	5,384	6,902	6,955	7,825	9,509	10,809	10,601	10,613
29,269	**25,104**	**19,778**	**14,649**	**29,837**	**26,453**	**20,231**	**13,607**	**10,239**
61,254	62,850	50,088	44,892	54,811	50,204	34,715	28,858	24,651
67,036	70,659	57,311	56,413	65,848	62,346	49,480	48,046	47,193
-5,782	-7,809	-7,224	-11,521	-11,037	-12,141	-14,765	-19,188	-22,541
-33,109	-39,330	-30,297	-30,031	-24,304	-22,418	-13,375	-14,194	-14,042
1,124	1,584	-12	-212	-670	-1,333	-1,109	-1,056	-371
5,314	**5,752**	**4,936**	**4,225**	**4,437**	**5,867**	**4,130**	**4,199**	**4,525**
-27,070	**-21,375**	**-22,144**	**-19,935**	**-37,246**	**-32,534**	**-21,328**	**-21,951**	**-12,928**
-142,039	**-113,930**	**-83,631**	**-67,724**	**-87,065**	**-111,305**	**-158,886**	**-170,093**	**-102,145**
-66,352	-55,800	-42,015	-32,118	-56,395	-35,891	-44,373	-57,806	-80,334
-63,927	-37,573	-29,319	-19,054	-24,369	-53,279	-78,492	-48,422	13,893
-3,963	-1,920	-6,229	-7,974	-15,290	-29,238	-43,602	-28,903	16,353
-59,965	-35,653	-21,253	-7,699	-8,092	-21,951	-28,090	-30,941	-7,672
..	..	-1,837	-3,381	-987	-2,089	-6,800	11,422	5,212
-11,759	-20,556	-12,297	-16,553	-6,300	-22,135	-36,022	-63,866	-35,704
-5,126	-8,051	-8,587	7,614	3,444	7,970	-12,314	-9,819	-888
3,973	-2,172	5,844	-19,286	-10,661	-15,817	-8,997	-41,993	-38,321
-5,480	-3,353	298	4,693	3,427	-1,653	-1,013	-4,644	-1,669
-5,125	-6,980	-9,851	-9,574	-2,510	-12,634	-13,698	-7,410	5,175
114,969	**92,555**	**61,487**	**47,789**	**49,819**	**78,770**	**137,558**	**148,143**	**89,217**
99,198	42,844	34,769	10,483	-579	32,677	71,198	116,706	49,010
14,598	37,779	18,599	19,714	54,550	9,437	31,656	-31,591	26,817
-21,458	41,002	18,297	7,870	19,238	-218	17,130	11,540	13,225
35,232	4,125	-1,531	13,491	35,742	9,133	10,814	-41,994	2,460
824	-7,349	1,833	-1,646	-429	522	3,711	-1,137	11,132
1,173	11,932	8,119	17,592	-4,152	36,657	34,704	63,027	13,390
3,396	-5,941	1,400	2,192	-2,032	5,712	14,638	10,670	1,928
-962	23,716	13,565	18,304	-531	28,951	20,384	48,574	12,947
-1,261	-5,843	-6,846	-2,904	-1,589	1,994	-318	3,783	-1,485
-7,514	-9,481	-2,570	1,062	2,973	214	-3,033	4,144	-1,836

Table 9.6 National balance sheet, market value, assets, 1994 to 2008

	1994	1995	1996	1997	1998	1999
	$ millions					
All assets	**7,448,344**	**7,898,321**	**8,601,650**	**9,270,201**	**9,811,488**	**10,663,468**
Non-financial assets	2,783,847	2,852,877	2,942,186	3,077,380	3,218,515	3,382,306
Residential structures	739,526	749,702	770,434	798,876	829,677	871,382
Non-residential structures	737,311	759,734	788,612	818,984	845,979	875,800
Machinery and equipment	280,939	291,852	295,130	316,413	343,059	362,083
Consumer durables	227,097	231,167	236,360	246,692	258,923	277,357
Inventories	131,535	146,976	151,010	158,782	170,248	179,202
Land	667,439	673,446	700,640	737,633	770,629	816,482
Financial assets	4,664,497	5,045,444	5,659,464	6,192,821	6,592,973	7,281,162
Official reserves	17,487	20,769	28,204	25,705	35,920	41,463
Currency and bank deposits	414,558	442,188	464,682	504,193	500,298	540,982
Deposits in other institutions	173,614	177,209	181,106	168,562	174,625	185,072
Foreign currency deposits	51,390	60,940	80,699	83,313	93,760	106,853
Consumer credit	111,166	116,713	124,054	132,826	144,189	158,245
Trade receivables	145,109	156,170	164,913	171,371	177,799	193,695
Bank loans	152,733	156,407	155,890	165,433	181,953	179,536
Other loans	103,787	108,681	116,467	132,026	145,558	163,978
Government of Canada short-term paper	129,356	133,524	117,851	95,038	77,955	85,482
Other short-term paper	66,829	69,965	80,505	103,581	128,194	160,587
Mortgages	433,497	443,906	459,879	478,715	497,928	519,765
Canada bonds	205,394	233,262	267,319	289,328	311,421	291,529
Provincial bonds	194,576	210,163	230,493	228,570	224,482	229,903
Municipal bonds	34,014	34,987	39,582	37,759	34,247	31,385
Other Canadian bonds	129,048	133,941	144,546	160,969	177,538	199,457
Life insurance and pensions	589,786	663,270	740,635	809,590	871,037	936,335
Corporate claims	503,729	545,557	576,758	645,998	734,715	748,271
Government claims	118,551	116,629	128,318	127,675	138,481	178,467
Shares	596,264	659,352	881,521	1,060,305	1,125,522	1,391,388
Foreign investments	135,378	155,716	202,996	248,135	290,208	385,898
Other financial assets	358,231	406,095	473,046	523,729	527,143	552,871

Source: Statistics Canada, CANSIM table 378-0009.

2000	2001	2002	2003	2004	2005	2006	2007	2008
				$ millions				
11,308,573	**11,748,672**	**12,155,289**	**12,882,008**	**13,983,191**	**15,363,956**	**16,922,813**	**18,190,275**	**18,604,618**
3,564,334	3,737,307	3,965,790	4,167,500	4,484,603	4,826,663	5,231,563	5,663,316	5,976,420
906,034	958,361	1,031,276	1,122,515	1,215,645	1,317,325	1,469,989	1,589,239	1,663,195
920,032	946,214	976,364	1,015,034	1,087,921	1,149,052	1,209,025	1,311,897	1,420,814
387,713	408,142	421,169	401,783	399,822	412,173	425,821	443,560	448,022
292,519	308,021	330,846	345,088	359,267	374,606	386,852	398,226	399,969
194,775	190,419	192,381	187,661	194,129	206,505	219,484	229,155	246,667
863,261	926,150	1,013,754	1,095,419	1,227,819	1,367,002	1,520,392	1,691,239	1,797,753
7,744,239	8,011,365	8,189,499	8,714,508	9,498,588	10,537,293	11,691,250	12,526,959	12,628,198
47,801	53,327	56,230	45,689	40,314	38,029	40,960	40,593	51,364
605,648	637,910	678,791	707,792	782,143	850,358	910,571	1,002,860	1,097,686
147,525	160,118	164,536	180,135	193,269	210,475	227,747	251,605	272,732
68,843	86,488	99,598	89,391	94,779	107,659	140,229	180,424	209,540
172,093	187,131	204,792	225,221	254,419	282,716	309,929	345,571	374,505
211,106	214,873	220,682	226,005	232,784	254,853	266,140	276,500	291,145
187,401	183,646	188,161	186,216	204,636	216,639	234,216	272,399	307,004
170,401	176,959	194,674	192,815	200,885	200,289	221,410	226,765	244,252
72,775	92,290	97,163	108,420	110,734	120,159	113,158	107,002	164,460
173,781	169,597	171,604	156,627	162,806	191,940	232,757	251,933	239,567
544,082	571,944	601,957	640,838	699,710	769,247	851,120	946,442	1,037,781
302,259	295,257	286,119	291,185	268,918	272,453	264,800	253,030	276,635
246,566	262,708	276,306	276,494	291,757	308,111	324,711	340,969	347,670
33,321	33,694	34,805	35,730	37,473	39,446	42,038	43,894	45,862
228,263	252,745	285,496	312,225	354,063	420,861	482,344	546,715	657,203
984,413	979,171	982,695	1,058,426	1,156,511	1,269,051	1,398,436	1,467,567	1,348,649
868,874	976,178	1,063,854	1,075,689	1,165,423	1,268,343	1,389,262	1,511,665	1,826,072
194,366	206,288	211,297	208,916	205,961	209,524	215,000	222,216	281,645
1,494,757	1,406,100	1,338,879	1,555,015	1,794,226	2,096,580	2,353,580	2,513,142	1,884,376
413,167	424,486	387,390	427,728	458,813	549,851	735,821	764,519	631,317
576,797	640,455	644,470	713,951	788,964	860,709	937,021	961,148	1,038,733

Table 9.7 National balance sheet, market value, liabilities and net worth, 1994 to 2008

	1994	1995	1996	1997	1998	1999
	$ millions					
Liabilities and net worth	**7,448,344**	**7,898,321**	**8,601,650**	**9,270,201**	**9,811,488**	**10,663,468**
All liabilities	4,989,023	5,383,573	5,981,264	6,489,848	6,894,097	7,489,147
Currency and bank deposits	423,528	450,727	471,893	513,500	510,176	552,014
Deposits in other institutions	173,741	177,332	181,229	168,672	174,732	185,186
Foreign currency and deposits	85,759	82,751	94,066	110,575	120,232	124,102
Consumer credit	111,166	116,713	124,054	132,826	144,189	158,245
Trade payables	147,728	158,491	165,026	171,156	175,277	191,070
Bank loans	146,186	149,012	150,255	155,889	174,593	171,523
Other loans	126,871	130,736	138,149	149,057	163,928	182,862
Government of Canada short-term paper	165,199	164,230	142,128	116,782	97,253	98,203
Other short-term paper	78,504	83,360	94,351	122,071	149,783	175,332
Mortgages	433,889	444,326	460,199	479,026	498,252	520,095
Canada bonds	277,166	323,805	368,580	387,982	406,081	390,141
Provincial bonds	342,020	371,288	391,202	390,809	401,826	376,409
Municipal bonds	39,738	41,468	46,171	44,037	40,679	36,884
Other Canadian bonds	210,701	233,020	249,059	287,349	336,986	345,775
Life insurance and pensions	589,786	663,270	740,635	809,590	871,037	936,335
Corporate claims	211,810	229,417	244,039	288,752	331,966	324,638
Government claims	118,551	116,629	128,318	127,675	138,481	178,467
Shares	957,079	1,054,533	1,329,587	1,540,149	1,653,050	2,003,387
Other liabilities	349,601	392,465	462,323	493,951	505,576	538,479
Net worth	**2,459,321**	**2,514,748**	**2,620,386**	**2,780,353**	**2,917,391**	**3,174,321**

Source: Statistics Canada, CANSIM table 378-0009.

2000	2001	2002	2003	2004	2005	2006	2007	2008
				$ millions				
11,308,573	**11,748,672**	**12,155,289**	**12,882,008**	**13,983,191**	**15,363,956**	**16,922,813**	**18,190,275**	**18,604,618**
7,906,442	8,155,543	8,386,110	8,908,536	9,673,894	10,651,954	11,653,243	12,547,584	12,574,276
618,480	654,150	692,773	722,022	798,371	866,597	931,461	1,023,402	1,122,754
147,525	160,118	164,536	180,135	193,269	210,475	227,747	251,605	272,732
93,582	110,309	120,120	107,519	103,666	116,274	133,089	170,648	186,845
172,093	187,131	204,792	225,221	254,419	282,716	309,929	345,571	374,505
211,065	219,593	227,139	227,310	229,735	251,228	263,565	278,683	292,726
177,246	173,216	178,433	180,701	196,762	207,033	218,580	254,122	280,985
185,987	187,799	199,182	196,217	210,022	204,620	221,661	243,433	250,390
84,362	99,729	107,050	118,941	118,762	129,632	126,307	117,712	183,771
189,948	183,283	186,542	166,356	173,704	202,314	241,854	261,885	253,013
544,397	572,266	602,323	641,194	700,061	769,793	851,662	946,908	1,038,293
385,677	374,083	371,421	355,265	328,593	324,540	316,670	297,513	322,342
387,334	407,815	428,799	409,876	419,073	432,455	450,720	448,475	475,390
38,374	38,346	38,514	38,995	41,201	43,488	46,326	47,980	50,500
377,831	461,379	516,649	534,437	589,034	648,256	724,984	783,985	939,678
984,413	979,171	982,695	1,058,426	1,156,511	1,269,051	1,398,436	1,467,567	1,348,649
356,884	399,148	440,710	427,029	434,054	483,763	541,667	602,585	682,414
194,366	206,288	211,297	208,916	205,961	209,524	215,000	222,216	281,645
2,189,841	2,117,604	2,079,787	2,406,760	2,747,544	3,157,667	3,517,458	3,841,696	3,213,069
567,037	624,115	633,348	703,216	773,152	842,528	916,127	941,598	1,004,575
3,402,131	**3,593,129**	**3,769,179**	**3,973,472**	**4,309,297**	**4,712,002**	**5,269,570**	**5,642,691**	**6,030,342**

Table 9.8 Canada's international investment position, 2003 to 2008

	2003	2004	2005	2006	2007	2008
			$ millions			
All assets	**921,148**	**952,790**	**996,411**	**1,188,105**	**1,198,644**	**1,486,171**
Canadian direct investments abroad	412,217	448,546	452,195	524,749	515,445	637,281
Canadian portfolio investments	253,788	265,411	292,213	371,311	369,509	424,335
Foreign bonds	45,809	58,560	82,332	124,027	135,371	141,909
Foreign stocks	197,025	195,773	196,825	227,318	226,627	278,939
Foreign money market	10,953	11,079	13,055	19,966	7,511	3,488
Other Canadian investments	255,143	238,832	252,003	292,045	313,689	424,555
Loans	50,695	49,468	45,924	72,940	77,274	94,527
Allowances	..	0	0	0	0	0
Deposits	103,583	109,442	120,813	132,220	157,898	225,190
Official international reserves	45,690	40,315	38,030	40,959	40,593	51,364
Other assets	55,174	39,607	47,236	45,926	37,925	53,473
All liabilities	**1,137,847**	**1,143,215**	**1,161,336**	**1,272,727**	**1,324,359**	**1,479,450**
Foreign direct investments in Canada	373,685	379,450	397,828	438,648	491,287	504,864
Foreign portfolio investments	507,150	521,898	502,243	532,732	502,418	584,958
Canadian bonds	401,050	402,236	387,928	409,168	384,652	454,085
Canadian stocks	84,712	100,042	93,532	99,049	95,767	95,967
Canadian money market instruments	21,388	19,621	20,783	24,515	21,999	34,906
Other foreign investments	257,012	241,867	261,265	301,348	330,653	389,628
Loans	52,398	44,149	38,219	52,997	61,184	64,550
Deposits	183,125	175,978	201,025	226,781	243,518	301,156
Other liabilities	21,489	21,740	22,021	21,569	25,952	23,921
Canada's net international investment position	**-216,699**	**-190,425**	**-164,925**	**-84,623**	**-125,716**	**6,721**

Note: Data are as of December 31.
Source: Statistics Canada, CANSIM table 376-0037.

Education, training and learning

10

Canada leads the OECD countries with the highest proportion of adults who have completed either a college or university education. In 2006, 6 out of 10 Canadians aged 25 to 64 had completed some form of postsecondary education.

Almost one in four adults aged 25 to 64—24%, or 4,156,700 people—had a high school diploma as their highest level of education; 15%, or 2,683,500, had not completed high school. Those who had not graduated from high school were concentrated in older age groups.

More university degrees

Canada had 17,382,100 adults aged 25 to 64 in the 2006 Census. The number with a university degree totalled 3,985,700, a 24% increase from 3,207,400 in 2001. In comparison, the number of adults who did not have a university degree rose 2%.

Canada ranked sixth among OECD countries in terms of the proportion of adults aged 25 to 64 who had a university degree, tied with Australia and Korea at 23%.

Young adults have a higher level of educational attainment than their older counterparts. In 2006, 29% of those aged 25 to 34 had a university degree, well above the proportion of 18% among adults aged 55 to 64.

In 2006, 44% of the Aboriginal population were postsecondary graduates: 14% had trade credentials, 19% had a college certificate or diploma and 8% had a university degree.

A higher percentage of women than men aged 25 to 34 have a university degree: 33% of women versus 25% of men in 2006. These percentages were both higher than those among older adults aged 55 to 64, where 16% of women and 21% of men had a university degree.

Educated Canadians tend to be more mobile. University degree holders

Chart 10.1
Educational attainment by age group, 2006

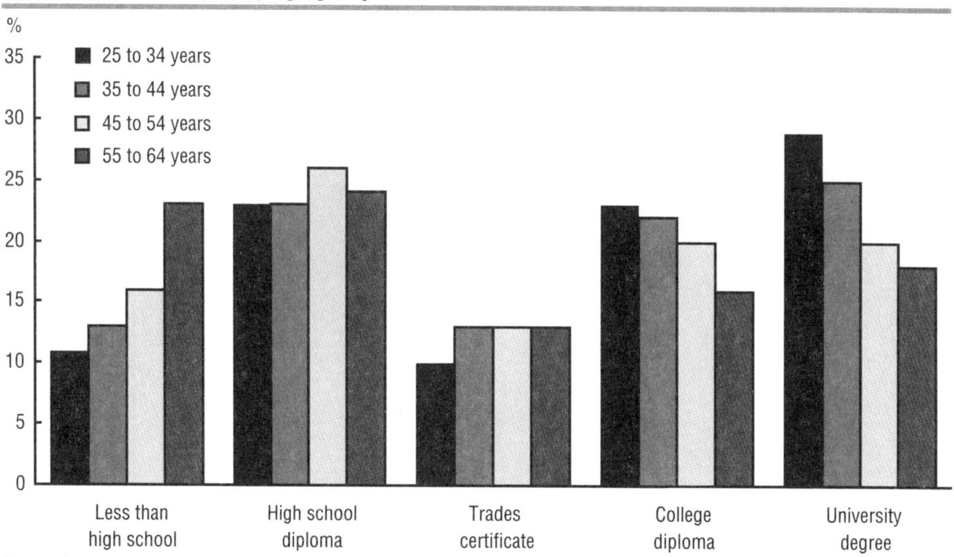

Source: Statistics Canada, 2006 Census of Population.

accounted for 23% of the adult population aged 25 to 64 in 2006, but comprised 33% of the people who moved to another province or territory from 2001 to 2006. Alberta and British Columbia had the biggest net inflows of postsecondary graduates, whereas Ontario recorded the biggest net outflows.

Fewer young adults are completing trades education than their parents. About 10% of adults aged 25 to 34 had a trade certification in 2006, compared with 13% of adults aged 55 to 64.

These young adults are also choosing different trades than the older generation of Canadians. For example, fewer young adults than older adults have a trade certificate in mechanic and repair technologies. On the other hand, more young adults than older adults have a certificate in personal and culinary services.

Immigrants highly educated

The 2006 Census counted 4,076,700 people aged 25 to 64 born outside Canada. Of these, 1,287,500, or about one-third (32%), had a university degree.

Slightly over half (51%) of recent immigrants to Canada—those who arrived from 2001 to 2006—had a university degree in 2006, compared with 28% of immigrants who arrived before 2001 and 20% of people born in Canada.

Table 10.a
Holders of a university degree, top 10 OECD countries, 2005

	%
Norway	30
United States	30
Netherlands	28
Denmark	26
Iceland	26
Australia	23
Canada	23
Korea	23
Japan	22
Sweden	21

Note: Population aged 25 to 64.
Source: Organisation for Economic Co-operation and Development, *Education at a Glance 2007, OECD Indicators.*

Chart 10.2
University graduates by age group and sex, 2006

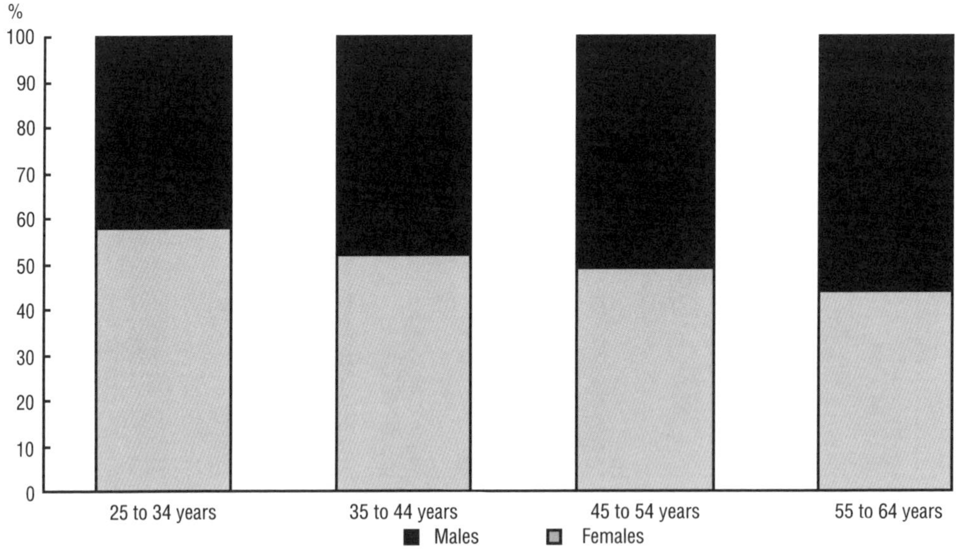

Source: Statistics Canada, 2006 Census of Population.

PhDs enrolment

Enrolment in doctoral programs in Canada has been on the rise since around 2001, but has not yet translated into more doctoral graduates.

In the 2005/2006 academic year, enrolment increased 6.1% to 36,700 candidates. This was the largest percentage increase in enrolment among all programs at the university level and it followed enrolment growth that averaged 8.1% a year over the previous three years.

However, the number of doctoral degree recipients was only slightly higher than almost a decade earlier. In 2005, 4,200 students received a research doctoral degree, compared with 4,000 in 1998.

Growth has been faster in the United States. In 2005/2006, the number of graduates from U.S. institutions increased 5.1% to 45,596 research doctoral degrees. This was 8.2% higher than the number of degrees granted in 2003/2004.

Chart 10.3
Graduate degree recipients from Canadian institutions

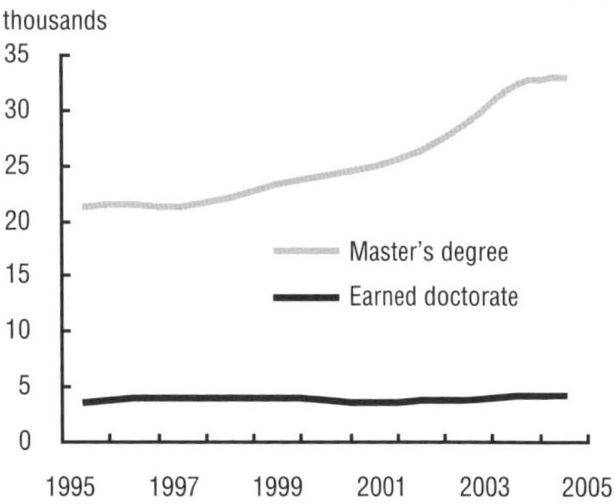

Source: Statistics Canada, CANSIM table 477-0014.

Doctoral students in Canada are more likely than those in the United States to graduate in the biological and health sciences. In contrast, the United States shows a higher proportion of graduates in humanities and education.

Education expenses

In 2007, 35% of Canadian households incurred education expenses for such items as tuition, school supplies and textbooks, spending an average of $2,949.

Their largest expenditure was by far on postsecondary tuition. Among the 15% of households that incurred these costs in 2007, average spending amounted to $4,017. Average household tuition expenses that year ranged from $1,832 in Quebec to $6,223 in New Brunswick.

Pre-elementary, elementary and secondary tuition fees were an education expense for 9% of households in 2007. These fees averaged $1,306 and ranged from $256 in New Brunswick to $2,481 in Ontario.

In 2007, 18% of households had textbook expenses and their average expenditure was $543. Spending on school supplies was the most common education expense, with 23% of households reporting such expenditures. This was, however, the lowest spending category, at a household average of $222.

Chart 10.4
Households incurring education expenses, 2007

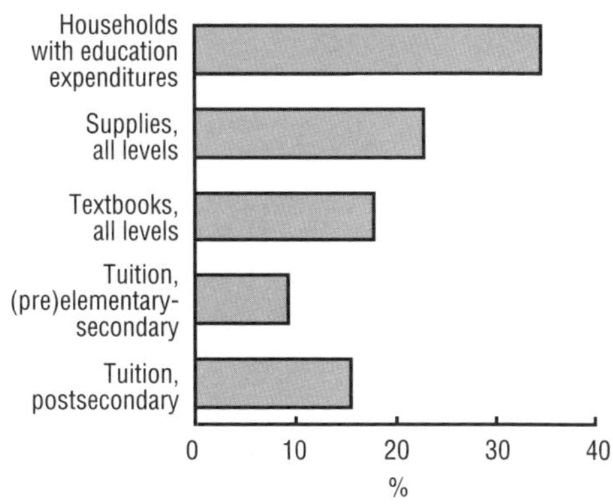

Source: Statistics Canada, CANSIM table 203-0012.

Table 10.1 Educational attainment of working-age population, by sex, 1998 to 2008

	Working-age population	0 to 8 years years of study		Some high school		High school graduate	
	thousands	thousands	%	thousands	%	thousands	%
Both sexes							
1998	**23,523**	2,646	11.2	4,444	18.9	4,460	19.0
1999	**23,787**	2,588	10.9	4,395	18.5	4,570	19.2
2000	**24,094**	2,502	10.4	4,293	17.8	4,719	19.6
2001	**24,444**	2,371	9.7	4,272	17.5	4,740	19.4
2002	**24,797**	2,322	9.4	4,205	17.0	4,811	19.4
2003	**25,107**	2,262	9.0	4,015	16.0	4,810	19.2
2004	**25,443**	2,223	8.7	3,988	15.7	4,906	19.3
2005	**25,806**	2,163	8.4	3,918	15.2	5,121	19.8
2006	**26,185**	2,122	8.1	3,954	15.1	5,208	19.9
2007	**26,553**	2,027	7.6	3,872	14.6	5,238	19.7
2008	**26,925**	1,961	7.3	3,857	14.3	5,266	19.6
Males							
1998	**11,549**	1,249	10.8	2,226	19.3	2,076	18.0
1999	**11,683**	1,227	10.5	2,210	18.9	2,134	18.3
2000	**11,843**	1,181	10.0	2,160	18.2	2,210	18.7
2001	**12,024**	1,110	9.2	2,166	18.0	2,230	18.5
2002	**12,201**	1,092	9.0	2,132	17.5	2,260	18.5
2003	**12,352**	1,056	8.5	2,053	16.6	2,266	18.3
2004	**12,515**	1,031	8.2	2,041	16.3	2,319	18.5
2005	**12,693**	1,012	8.0	2,016	15.9	2,432	19.2
2006	**12,883**	983	7.6	2,022	15.7	2,496	19.4
2007	**13,065**	943	7.2	1,995	15.3	2,524	19.3
2008	**13,252**	908	6.9	2,005	15.1	2,535	19.1
Females							
1998	**11,974**	1,397	11.7	2,218	18.5	2,385	19.9
1999	**12,104**	1,361	11.2	2,185	18.1	2,436	20.1
2000	**12,252**	1,321	10.8	2,134	17.4	2,508	20.5
2001	**12,420**	1,261	10.2	2,106	17.0	2,510	20.2
2002	**12,596**	1,230	9.8	2,072	16.5	2,551	20.2
2003	**12,755**	1,206	9.5	1,962	15.4	2,545	20.0
2004	**12,928**	1,192	9.2	1,948	15.1	2,587	20.0
2005	**13,113**	1,151	8.8	1,902	14.5	2,690	20.5
2006	**13,303**	1,140	8.6	1,932	14.5	2,712	20.4
2007	**13,488**	1,084	8.0	1,877	13.9	2,714	20.1
2008	**13,673**	1,052	7.7	1,852	13.5	2,732	20.0

Note: Population aged 15 and older based on Labour Force Survey estimates.
Source: Statistics Canada, CANSIM table 282-0004.

Some postsecondary		Postsecondary certificate or diploma		All university degrees		Bachelor's degree		Above bachelor's degree	
thousands	%	thousands	%	thousands	%	thousands	%	thousands	%
2,120	9.0	6,513	27.7	3,340	14.2	2,304	9.8	1,036	4.4
2,116	8.9	6,597	27.7	3,522	14.8	2,402	10.1	1,119	4.7
2,275	9.4	6,584	27.3	3,722	15.4	2,507	10.4	1,215	5.0
2,241	9.2	6,916	28.3	3,905	16.0	2,661	10.9	1,244	5.1
2,274	9.2	7,124	28.7	4,061	16.4	2,790	11.3	1,271	5.1
2,453	9.8	7,261	28.9	4,306	17.2	2,969	11.8	1,337	5.3
2,478	9.7	7,458	29.3	4,390	17.3	3,070	12.1	1,320	5.2
2,221	8.6	7,692	29.8	4,690	18.2	3,227	12.5	1,464	5.7
2,117	8.1	7,832	29.9	4,952	18.9	3,445	13.2	1,507	5.8
2,160	8.1	8,101	30.5	5,157	19.4	3,589	13.5	1,568	5.9
2,280	8.5	8,206	30.5	5,354	19.9	3,664	13.6	1,690	6.3
1,018	8.8	3,197	27.7	1,784	15.4	1,159	10.0	625	5.4
1,020	8.7	3,247	27.8	1,847	15.8	1,170	10.0	676	5.8
1,107	9.3	3,259	27.5	1,926	16.3	1,208	10.2	718	6.1
1,088	9.0	3,406	28.3	2,025	16.8	1,295	10.8	730	6.1
1,117	9.2	3,505	28.7	2,095	17.2	1,351	11.1	744	6.1
1,189	9.6	3,586	29.0	2,203	17.8	1,430	11.6	773	6.3
1,229	9.8	3,675	29.4	2,220	17.7	1,463	11.7	758	6.1
1,106	8.7	3,783	29.8	2,345	18.5	1,519	12.0	827	6.5
1,060	8.2	3,857	29.9	2,466	19.1	1,612	12.5	853	6.6
1,070	8.2	3,978	30.4	2,557	19.6	1,679	12.8	878	6.7
1,145	8.6	4,034	30.4	2,625	19.8	1,705	12.9	920	6.9
1,103	9.2	3,316	27.7	1,556	13.0	1,145	9.6	411	3.4
1,096	9.1	3,351	27.7	1,675	13.8	1,232	10.2	443	3.7
1,168	9.5	3,325	27.1	1,796	14.7	1,299	10.6	497	4.1
1,152	9.3	3,510	28.3	1,881	15.1	1,366	11.0	515	4.1
1,158	9.2	3,619	28.7	1,967	15.6	1,439	11.4	528	4.2
1,264	9.9	3,675	28.8	2,103	16.5	1,540	12.1	563	4.4
1,249	9.7	3,783	29.3	2,170	16.8	1,608	12.4	562	4.3
1,116	8.5	3,909	29.8	2,345	17.9	1,708	13.0	637	4.9
1,057	7.9	3,975	29.9	2,487	18.7	1,833	13.8	654	4.9
1,090	8.1	4,123	30.6	2,600	19.3	1,910	14.2	690	5.1
1,135	8.3	4,172	30.5	2,730	20.0	1,960	14.3	770	5.6

Table 10.2 School board revenue and expenditures, 1997 to 2008

	1997	1998	1999	2000
	$ thousands			
Revenue	**32,042,472**	**35,590,628**	**32,933,191**	**34,049,949**
Own-source revenue	12,157,134	9,186,870	9,593,045	9,696,626
Property and related taxes	10,926,304	7,801,048	8,009,046	7,999,391
Real property taxes	9,617,759	7,602,321	7,814,361	7,803,833
Grants in lieu of taxes	152,255	96,439	89,993	90,908
Federal government	44,341	40,772	36,637	36,802
Federal government business enterprises	1,962	2,330	2,116	1,447
Provincial and territorial governments	99,793	48,405	46,928	47,941
Provincial and territorial government business enterprises	4,054	3,148	3,026	3,367
Local governments	457	484	483	469
Local government business enterprises	1,648	1,300	803	882
Business taxes	1,047,918	26,780	28,381	29,054
Miscellaneous property and related taxes	108,372	75,508	76,311	75,596
Other taxes	651	599	650	708
Sales of goods and services	1,157,659	1,304,790	1,492,498	1,590,727
Intergovernment	382,141	457,962	483,870	547,924
General	775,518	846,828	1,008,628	1,042,803
Rentals	43,403	49,226	56,675	58,919
Other sales of goods and services	732,115	797,557	951,953	983,884
Investment income	46,592	54,598	65,691	78,818
Other interest income	5,270	4,641	5,892	5,574
Other investment income	41,322	49,957	59,799	73,244
Other revenue from own sources	25,927	25,835	25,160	26,982
Specific-purpose transfers from other government subsectors	19,885,338	26,403,758	23,340,146	24,353,323
Federal government	81,580	82,258	90,975	84,721
Provincial and territorial governments	19,650,260	26,161,478	23,088,695	24,103,915
Education transfers	18,960,162	25,637,572	22,688,501	23,723,258
Debt charges (interest)	690,098	523,906	400,194	380,657
Local governments	153,498	160,022	160,476	164,687
Expenditures	**32,212,258**	**32,091,168**	**32,700,627**	**34,142,482**
Education	31,169,335	31,309,610	31,955,580	33,416,048
Debt charges	1,042,923	781,558	745,047	726,434
Interest	1,042,534	781,414	737,104	721,368
Other debt charges	389	144	7,943	5,066
Surplus/deficit (-)	**-169,786**	**3,499,460**	**232,564**	**-92,533**

Note: Data not available for New Brunswick, Yukon and Nunavut.
Source: Statistics Canada, CANSIM table 385-0009.

2001	2002	2003	2004	2005	2006	2007	2008
$ thousands							
35,230,651	**36,895,015**	**39,085,203**	**39,494,601**	**41,742,462**	**45,465,066**	**45,964,481**	**48,226,782**
9,851,322	10,121,370	10,349,619	10,645,706	11,145,911	11,355,924	11,940,556	12,149,440
8,105,789	8,197,216	8,355,012	8,605,737	8,852,678	8,992,363	9,465,488	9,653,893
7,907,445	8,013,090	8,163,446	8,419,366	8,660,512	8,797,897	9,259,861	9,444,867
84,244	78,233	82,718	77,143	79,358	80,836	85,865	86,944
32,480	30,971	31,887	30,099	31,019	31,590	33,598	33,890
876	469	376	1,113	763	954	1,005	1,029
44,850	40,749	44,254	39,453	40,092	40,720	43,261	43,801
3,758	4,322	4,228	4,614	5,586	5,744	6,048	6,210
510	527	525	533	549	575	616	615
1,770	1,195	1,448	1,331	1,349	1,253	1,337	1,399
31,123	32,065	33,432	34,260	35,459	36,275	38,633	38,749
82,977	73,828	75,416	74,968	77,349	77,355	81,129	83,333
723	695	692	681	705	721	768	770
1,644,381	1,822,908	1,878,446	1,911,195	2,135,853	2,186,749	2,294,554	2,312,765
519,393	515,877	512,769	536,348	509,911	531,903	567,914	573,740
1,124,988	1,307,031	1,365,677	1,374,847	1,625,942	1,654,846	1,726,640	1,739,025
66,368	105,892	117,929	119,249	121,504	131,373	137,668	140,087
1,058,620	1,201,139	1,247,748	1,255,598	1,504,438	1,523,473	1,588,972	1,598,938
74,635	71,844	83,865	91,300	105,785	130,669	133,315	134,986
6,324	6,985	5,322	4,468	4,624	4,730	5,037	5,052
68,311	64,859	78,543	86,832	101,161	125,939	128,278	129,934
25,794	28,707	31,604	36,793	50,890	45,422	46,431	47,026
25,379,329	26,773,645	28,735,584	28,848,895	30,596,551	34,109,142	34,023,925	36,077,342
89,923	104,689	98,705	109,462	136,480	106,643	110,669	113,545
25,120,176	26,494,344	28,459,642	28,555,159	30,264,440	33,819,289	33,724,229	35,771,485
24,701,947	26,089,163	28,059,578	28,156,914	29,876,606	33,433,617	33,314,282	35,357,414
418,229	405,181	400,064	398,245	387,834	385,672	409,947	414,071
169,230	174,612	177,237	184,274	195,631	183,210	189,027	192,312
35,368,073	**36,873,300**	**38,264,627**	**39,398,230**	**42,979,682**	**47,199,448**	**47,712,377**	**48,751,414**
34,624,407	36,150,312	37,528,221	38,683,838	42,251,024	46,446,081	46,918,561	47,967,632
743,666	722,988	736,406	714,392	728,658	753,367	793,816	783,782
734,845	712,633	729,472	709,935	720,367	744,928	784,810	774,741
8,821	10,355	6,934	4,457	8,291	8,439	9,006	9,041
-137,422	**21,715**	**820,576**	**96,371**	**-1,237,220**	**-1,734,382**	**-1,747,896**	**-524,632**

Table 10.3 Enrolment in public elementary and secondary schools, by province and territory, 1997/1998 to 2006/2007

	Canada	Newfoundland and Labrador	Prince Edward Island	Nova Scotia[1]	New Brunswick
	number				
1997/1998	**5,352,185**	101,768	24,397	162,359	131,586
1998/1999	**5,357,244**	97,557	24,146	160,011	129,131
1999/2000	**5,372,733**	94,118	24,089	158,205	127,003
2000/2001	**5,350,773**	90,287	23,153	155,873	124,942
2001/2002	**5,360,423**	87,019	22,843	153,450	122,792
2002/2003	**5,342,883**	84,397	22,615	150,599	120,600
2003/2004	**5,283,132**	81,545	22,239	148,514	118,869
2004/2005	**5,250,032**	79,508	22,393	145,396	117,145
2005/2006	**5,206,927**	76,827	21,948	142,304	114,820
2006/2007	**5,162,963**	74,304	21,365	138,661	112,013

1. Includes enrolment in vocational programs for youth and adults.
2. Includes enrolment in adult programs and vocational programs for youth and adults.
3. Data exclude publicly funded hospitals and provincial schools, care, treatment and correctional facilities.
4. Until 2000/2001, includes enrolment in adult programs and professional training under the authority of the school boards or districts.
5. Includes enrolment in adult programs.
6. Starting in 1999/2000, Northwest Territories excludes Nunavut.

Source: Statistics Canada, Centre for Education Statistics.

Table 10.4 Graduates of public elementary and secondary schools, by province and territory, 1997/1998 to 2006/2007

	Canada	Newfoundland and Labrador	Prince Edward Island	Nova Scotia	New Brunswick
	number				
1997/1998	**208,692**	7,365	1,735	10,387	8,754
1998/1999	**212,122**	6,896	1,628	10,151	8,778
1999/2000	**304,664**	7,002	1,798	9,914	8,912
2000/2001	**305,356**	6,382	1,685	9,775	8,538
2001/2002	**314,560**	6,519	1,667	9,846	8,574
2002/2003	**333,853**	6,317	1,710	10,106	8,291
2003/2004	**315,495**	6,048	1,721	10,159	7,988
2004/2005	**318,811**	5,911	1,663	10,257	7,948
2005/2006	**315,037**	5,641	1,694	10,241	8,299
2006/2007	**310,179**	5,837	1,746	10,364	7,977

1. Data exclude publicly funded hospital and provincial schools, care, treatment and correctional facilities.
2. Historical revisions have been made to this table to exclude students that graduated from adult learning centres registered under the *Adult Learning Centres Act*, effective July 2001.
3. The number of graduates in the final year is understated by 2% to 3% because some schools had not submitted course information before the data collection cutoff for this report.

Source: Statistics Canada, Centre for Education Statistics.

Quebec[2]	Ontario[3]	Manitoba[4]	Saskatchewan[5]	Alberta	British Columbia[5]	Yukon	Northwest Territories[6]	Nunavut
number								
1,260,479	2,095,630	192,311	196,013	532,301	631,445	6,333	17,563	...
1,250,248	2,111,622	192,630	194,797	543,387	629,545	6,102	18,068	...
1,247,757	2,131,626	197,067	192,885	564,402	628,269	5,975	9,753	9,584
1,237,981	2,143,599	189,912	186,586	549,633	624,618	5,764	9,672	8,753
1,244,689	2,163,108	188,907	183,024	548,122	622,416	5,608	9,707	8,738
1,245,339	2,164,940	186,892	179,161	551,375	612,705	5,610	9,747	8,903
1,241,143	2,129,742	186,287	175,846	549,533	605,057	5,520	9,718	9,119
1,233,100	2,123,904	184,352	172,663	550,983	596,168	5,459	9,607	9,354
1,216,326	2,118,544	182,371	168,633	551,740	589,379	5,335	9,571	9,129
1,204,517	2,104,105	180,043	164,973	560,563	578,795	5,227	9,332	9,065

Quebec	Ontario[1]	Manitoba[2]	Saskatchewan	Alberta	British Columbia[3]	Yukon	Northwest Territories	Nunavut
number								
90,884	..	11,970	12,452	28,152	36,360	245	297	91
92,191	..	11,829	12,807	29,369	37,740	290	315	128
69,000	114,404	11,807	13,105	28,321	39,716	258	293	134
67,710	115,599	12,074	12,957	29,199	40,737	256	327	117
66,276	124,783	11,791	12,739	29,759	41,985	266	218	137
64,988	143,187	12,491	12,367	31,065	42,672	264	254	141
67,896	123,238	12,819	11,957	32,054	40,863	315	303	134
68,538	124,902	12,643	12,625	31,695	41,787	316	348	178
69,984	118,099	12,514	12,698	32,241	42,720	311	410	185
71,971	125,129	12,613	12,449	33,031	40,197	316	405	198

Table 10.5 University and college revenue and expenditures, 1994 to 2008

	1994	1995	1996	1997	1998	1999
	$ thousands					
Revenue	**16,419,382**	**16,759,086**	**17,260,407**	**16,729,056**	**17,389,686**	**20,064,718**
Own-source revenue	5,612,258	5,889,502	6,277,982	6,653,193	7,447,138	7,887,522
Sales of goods and services	4,349,760	4,567,345	4,843,608	5,187,833	5,699,797	6,044,702
Tuition fees	2,339,171	2,507,056	2,690,708	2,889,160	3,179,565	3,506,275
Other sales of goods and services	2,010,590	2,060,289	2,152,900	2,298,673	2,520,232	2,538,427
Investment income	367,552	366,970	427,658	408,272	556,419	476,694
Other revenue from own sources	894,945	955,187	1,006,716	1,057,088	1,190,922	1,366,126
Transfers from other levels of government	10,807,124	10,869,584	10,982,425	10,075,863	9,942,548	12,177,196
Federal government	1,095,690	1,110,639	1,090,080	1,022,516	980,566	1,112,046
Provincial and territorial governments	9,701,848	9,746,774	9,877,178	9,028,729	8,932,862	11,049,246
Local governments	9,586	12,171	15,167	24,618	29,120	15,904
Expenditures	**16,749,070**	**16,917,362**	**17,192,872**	**16,804,525**	**17,194,597**	**18,022,802**
Postsecondary education	16,451,698	16,559,462	16,747,684	16,381,240	16,762,116	17,679,221
Administration	3,103,484	3,157,017	3,361,662	3,205,490	3,251,008	3,438,931
Education	9,320,107	9,304,767	9,249,982	9,176,367	9,253,953	9,724,860
Support to students	428,626	447,082	453,669	307,665	347,649	407,889
Other	3,599,481	3,650,595	3,682,371	3,691,718	3,909,506	4,107,541
Special retraining services	..	..	..	..	..	..
Debt charges	297,372	357,900	445,189	423,285	432,481	343,581
Surplus/deficit (-)	**-329,689**	**-158,276**	**67,535**	**-75,469**	**195,089**	**2,041,916**

Notes: Fiscal year ending March 31.
Excludes Yukon College for confidentiality purposes.
Source: Statistics Canada, CANSIM table 385-0007.

2000	2001	2002	2003	2004	2005	2006	2007	2008
				$ thousands				
20,380,239	**21,732,604**	**23,262,806**	**25,359,135**	**28,096,412**	**29,484,455**	**31,396,336**	**34,074,232**	**36,723,906**
8,791,925	9,630,461	10,339,207	11,244,357	12,752,007	13,336,261	14,074,771	15,440,100	16,701,266
6,715,382	7,371,133	8,132,232	9,026,491	9,906,500	10,520,144	10,958,828	12,021,633	13,010,315
3,881,521	4,144,097	4,486,787	5,085,897	5,766,539	6,152,681	6,416,268	7,061,152	7,655,980
2,833,861	3,227,036	3,645,445	3,940,594	4,139,962	4,367,463	4,542,559	4,960,480	5,354,335
592,797	604,613	396,046	370,231	821,830	645,905	818,219	900,518	976,519
1,483,746	1,654,715	1,810,929	1,847,635	2,023,677	2,170,212	2,297,724	2,517,950	2,714,432
11,588,314	12,102,143	12,923,599	14,114,778	15,344,405	16,148,194	17,321,565	18,634,132	20,022,641
1,352,613	1,624,714	1,922,197	2,270,560	2,564,931	2,678,489	2,907,421	3,175,870	3,413,377
10,221,834	10,451,811	10,947,140	11,817,345	12,750,006	13,444,014	14,378,561	15,418,053	16,564,844
13,867	25,618	54,262	26,873	29,468	25,691	35,583	40,209	44,420
19,478,054	**21,278,479**	**23,454,251**	**25,590,341**	**27,690,208**	**29,609,613**	**31,057,720**	**33,926,786**	**36,584,388**
18,800,032	20,569,831	22,717,330	24,820,214	26,804,032	28,699,579	30,095,271	32,886,893	35,479,382
3,826,107	4,267,373	4,662,921	4,717,093	4,759,180	5,377,969	5,672,367	6,594,044	7,122,767
9,806,404	10,447,939	11,372,063	12,485,313	13,748,442	14,250,885	14,951,158	15,961,148	17,170,740
513,845	603,597	718,845	818,445	961,623	1,031,730	1,100,234	1,214,386	1,314,389
4,653,676	5,250,922	5,963,501	6,799,363	7,334,787	8,038,995	8,371,513	9,117,315	9,871,487
240,451	243,966	272,106	271,758	284,984	277,324	290,251	319,482	344,019
437,571	464,682	464,815	498,369	575,652	606,483	643,871	690,303	729,935
902,185	**454,125**	**-191,445**	**-231,206**	**406,204**	**-125,158**	**338,616**	**147,446**	**139,518**

Table 10.6 University enrolment, by instructional program, 1993/1994 to 2006/2007

	1993/1994	1994/1995	1995/1996	1996/1997
	number			
All instructional programs	**874,605**	**858,972**	**846,408**	**829,767**
Personal improvement and leisure	..	..	..	..
Education	80,010	77,472	73,290	70,428
Visual and performing arts and communications technologies	25,479	25,494	25,704	24,882
Humanities	143,907	139,254	144,522	135,750
Social and behavioural sciences and law	148,179	147,720	143,607	136,992
Business, management and public administration	130,134	123,222	120,414	121,188
Physical and life sciences and technologies	77,472	77,112	78,525	76,842
Mathematics, computer and information sciences	32,607	32,454	32,133	32,622
Architecture, engineering and related technologies	65,364	63,657	62,259	62,088
Agriculture, natural resources and conservation	14,301	14,067	15,135	15,831
Health, parks, recreation and fitness	71,730	73,131	73,884	74,694
Personal, protective and transportation services	258	210	183	189
Other instructional programs	85,167	85,173	76,752	78,255

1. Enrolment figures do not include the University of Regina.
Source: Statistics Canada, CANSIM table 477-0013.

Table 10.7 University enrolment, by program level, 1993/1994 to 2006/2007

	1993/1994	1994/1995	1995/1996	1996/1997
	number			
All program levels	**874,605**	**858,972**	**846,408**	**829,767**
Trade/vocational and preparatory training certificate or diploma	..	..	..	..
Community college certificate or diploma and other community college	3,015	2,016	2,409	2,457
Undergraduate level	668,535	658,284	648,972	639,588
Bachelor's and other undergraduate degree	596,274	586,116	580,185	575,886
Other undergraduate level	72,261	72,168	68,787	63,702
Graduate level	112,047	112,947	112,524	112,068
Master's degree	69,942	69,783	69,300	69,093
Earned doctorate	26,475	27,147	27,306	27,198
Other graduate levels[2]	15,633	16,017	15,918	15,777
Other program levels[3]	91,008	85,722	82,503	75,651

1. Enrolment figures do not include the University of Regina.
2. Includes master's qualifying year, university graduate level certificate or diploma, PhD (Doctor of Philosophy) qualifying year or probationary, internship (Postgraduate Medical Education, known as post-MD) and residency (medical, dental, veterinary).
3. Includes program levels not applicable and non-program courses (non-credit courses or courses taken without seeking a credit).
Source: Statistics Canada, CANSIM table 477-0013.

1997/1998	1998/1999	1999/2000	2000/2001	2001/2002	2002/2003	2003/2004	2004/2005	2005/2006[1]	2006/2007[1]
number									
822,774	**826,362**	**847,032**	**850,620**	**886,665**	**936,390**	**993,768**	**1,019,775**	**1,047,690**	**1,057,272**
..	..	..	0	66	69	51	117	333	234
67,623	65,673	66,282	66,483	69,492	72,042	76,875	72,786	73,977	74,520
24,984	25,359	25,410	26,922	27,915	32,331	34,200	36,867	37,221	37,524
130,038	127,392	121,395	126,813	133,149	143,193	158,115	156,204	165,066	160,521
132,135	129,795	132,378	135,111	138,552	149,577	162,972	177,153	182,613	187,302
124,626	128,556	134,169	134,784	141,534	152,295	161,235	165,243	168,435	174,714
76,536	75,537	77,289	77,082	78,255	81,804	87,261	92,199	94,497	93,564
34,407	37,473	41,490	43,053	46,035	45,837	43,977	40,764	36,600	33,900
63,438	65,223	67,299	70,038	74,847	81,096	85,785	86,529	85,503	85,755
16,731	16,362	16,419	15,504	14,943	14,592	14,769	14,925	15,264	15,501
74,781	74,826	74,832	74,643	80,991	85,293	92,397	98,643	104,235	108,450
351	345	372	1,047	1,185	1,317	1,299	1,827	1,761	2,238
77,118	79,821	89,700	79,134	79,698	76,953	74,832	76,512	82,182	83,058

1997/1998	1998/1999	1999/2000	2000/2001	2001/2002	2002/2003	2003/2004	2004/2005	2005/2006[1]	2006/2007[1]
number									
822,774	**826,362**	**847,032**	**850,620**	**886,665**	**936,390**	**993,768**	**1,019,775**	**1,047,690**	**1,057,272**
..	..	147	204	90	159	168	108	858	768
2,352	2,232	2,289	2,295	2,088	4,719	2,946	2,379	4,521	4,257
633,018	633,495	650,391	657,231	680,682	719,124	770,718	788,781	803,403	811,842
572,331	571,161	583,170	589,734	613,524	648,369	702,366	724,689	743,619	754,470
60,687	62,337	67,221	67,500	67,158	70,755	68,349	64,089	59,781	57,369
112,692	113,481	116,304	118,152	124,605	134,955	142,833	150,954	153,684	156,111
69,852	71,292	74,331	75,195	79,533	85,800	89,565	93,867	94,011	95,682
27,003	26,505	26,493	26,598	27,390	29,340	32,016	34,686	36,699	36,765
15,834	15,681	15,483	16,356	17,679	19,815	21,249	22,404	22,977	23,664
74,712	77,154	77,898	72,741	79,206	77,433	77,103	77,553	85,224	84,300

Table 10.8 University degrees, diplomas and certificates granted, 1993 to 2006

	1993	1994	1995	1996
	number			
All instructional programs	**173,850**	**178,074**	**178,065**	**178,113**
Personal improvement and leisure	..	..	..	..
Education	26,700	26,304	26,454	25,713
Visual and performing arts and communications technologies	5,124	5,310	5,241	5,199
Humanities	22,638	23,058	22,386	22,377
Social and behavioural sciences and law	38,334	39,423	39,678	38,988
Business, management and public administration	31,431	31,620	30,252	30,054
Physical and life sciences and technologies	12,015	13,119	13,662	14,631
Mathematics, computer and information sciences	6,762	6,825	7,194	6,996
Architecture, engineering and related technologies	12,135	12,999	13,293	13,341
Agriculture, natural resources and conservation	2,400	2,616	2,754	3,036
Health, parks, recreation and fitness	15,714	16,197	16,563	16,734
Personal, protective and transportation services	63	78	54	75
Other instructional programs	534	525	537	966

1. Qualifications figures do not include the University of Regina.
Source: Statistics Canada, CANSIM table 477-0014.

Table 10.9 University degrees, diplomas and certificates granted, by province, 1993 to 2006

	1993	1994	1995	1996
	number			
Canada	**173,850**	**178,074**	**178,065**	**178,113**
Newfoundland and Labrador	2,649	2,718	2,571	2,907
Prince Edward Island	498	573	585	528
Nova Scotia	7,806	8,103	7,887	7,725
New Brunswick	3,945	4,005	4,149	4,428
Quebec	56,337	57,852	56,856	56,253
Ontario	64,803	66,189	66,861	67,668
Manitoba	5,958	6,285	6,315	6,030
Saskatchewan	6,216	5,415	5,784	5,715
Alberta	11,637	12,282	12,270	12,240
British Columbia	13,998	14,652	14,784	14,616

1. Qualifications figures do not include the University of Regina.
Source: Statistics Canada, CANSIM table 477-0014.

1997	1998	1999	2000	2001	2002	2003	2004	2005[1]	2006[1]
				number					
173,934	**172,074**	**173,577**	**176,556**	**178,098**	**186,498**	**198,795**	**210,441**	**215,298**	**225,909**
..	..	..	..	..	..	..	3	33	45
23,742	21,636	22,290	22,542	22,350	23,670	24,873	25,407	25,320	26,811
5,205	5,256	5,202	5,373	5,904	6,318	6,981	7,554	7,842	8,148
20,988	20,364	19,593	20,064	20,103	20,730	22,359	22,506	24,033	25,104
37,872	37,899	36,702	36,315	35,784	36,990	38,574	41,307	42,024	45,495
29,916	30,492	31,629	33,213	34,791	37,581	40,944	44,295	45,312	45,771
15,183	15,552	14,607	14,730	14,763	14,283	14,721	15,378	15,909	17,190
6,867	6,966	7,710	8,448	9,009	10,005	10,602	11,040	9,993	9,417
12,912	13,026	12,798	13,305	13,842	14,766	16,386	17,499	17,973	18,537
3,240	3,258	3,825	4,008	3,888	3,663	3,771	3,615	3,303	3,600
16,746	16,497	16,920	16,518	16,314	17,328	18,258	20,229	21,873	23,847
102	81	90	81	228	270	270	360	327	474
1,158	1,047	2,211	1,959	1,122	900	1,050	1,248	1,356	1,473

1997	1998	1999	2000	2001	2002	2003	2004	2005[1]	2006[1]
				number					
173,934	**172,074**	**173,577**	**176,556**	**178,098**	**186,498**	**198,795**	**210,441**	**215,298**	**225,909**
2,952	3,000	3,114	2,931	2,862	2,898	2,976	3,111	3,126	3,597
570	405	540	534	606	555	624	672	750	792
7,785	7,812	7,824	7,638	7,680	7,878	8,766	9,579	9,513	10,119
4,311	4,032	3,975	4,032	4,098	4,398	4,557	4,944	5,244	5,463
53,589	51,066	50,958	50,847	51,153	54,009	57,786	61,212	62,973	62,832
65,562	65,898	65,697	67,221	68,286	71,109	76,134	80,436	84,138	89,166
5,895	5,640	5,442	5,340	5,397	5,580	5,871	6,309	6,339	6,771
5,337	5,445	5,547	5,793	5,694	5,739	5,868	5,778	3,747	3,747
12,816	13,002	13,560	14,052	15,087	16,344	17,199	18,189	18,009	19,182
15,117	15,780	16,917	18,171	17,238	17,982	19,014	20,211	21,459	24,243

Table 10.10 Employment in educational and related services, by province and territory, 2004 to 2008

	2004	2005	2006	2007	2008
			number		
Canada	**1,041,129**	**1,058,974**	**1,082,942**	**1,109,718**	**1,135,454**
Newfoundland and Labrador	19,005	18,404	18,790	18,907	19,983
Prince Edward Island	4,464	4,462	4,466	4,636	x
Nova Scotia	36,496	35,884	36,964	35,642	36,429
New Brunswick	20,626	22,621	24,327	24,249	24,972
Quebec	256,080	257,734	260,997	265,890	270,977
Ontario	383,751	393,207	403,082	415,559	426,352
Manitoba	43,750	44,710	44,242	44,592	46,159
Saskatchewan	37,977	38,603	38,818	39,897	40,328
Alberta	107,758	110,010	112,382	117,496	121,893
British Columbia	126,812	129,031	134,665	138,489	139,086
Yukon	1,156	1,200	1,234	1,300	x

Notes: Excludes owners or partners of unincorporated businesses and professional practices, the self-employed, unpaid family workers, people working outside Canada, military personnel, and casual workers for whom a T4 is not required.
Data for Northwest Territories and Nunavut are not available.
Data are based on Survey of Employment, Payrolls and Hours.
Source: Statistics Canada, CANSIM table 281-0024.

Table 10.11 Undergraduate tuition fees for full-time students, by discipline, 2006/2007 to 2008/2009

	2006/2007	2007/2008[r]	2008/2009
		average ($)	
Average undergraduate tuition fees	**4,400**	**4,558**	**4,724**
Agriculture, natural resources and conservation	3,869	4,064	4,181
Architecture and related technologies	3,839	3,999	4,246
Humanities	4,336	4,342	4,478
Business, management and public administration	4,195	4,637	4,828
Education	3,373	3,545	3,666
Engineering	4,943	5,099	5,310
Law	7,155	7,382	7,720
Medicine	9,659	10,029	10,392
Visual and performing arts, and communications technologies	3,991	4,239	4,389
Physical and life sciences and technology	4,270	4,534	4,682
Mathematics, computer and information sciences	4,650	4,746	4,947
Social and behavioural sciences	4,041	4,165	4,318
Other health, parks, recreation and fitness	4,996	4,400	4,551
Dentistry	..	12,516	12,906
Nursing	..	4,267	4,385
Pharmacy	..	4,215	4,298
Veterinary medicine	..	4,296	4,441

Note: Using the most current enrolment data available, average tuition fees have been weighted by the number of students enrolled by institution and field of study. Fees at both public and private institutions are included in the weighted average calculations.
Source: Statistics Canada, Centre for Education Statistics.

Table 10.12 Undergraduate tuition fees for full-time students, by province, 2006/2007 to 2008/2009

	2006/2007	2007/2008	2008/2009
		average ($)	
Canada	**4,400**	**4,558**	**4,724**
Newfoundland and Labrador	2,633	2,632	2,632
Prince Edward Island	4,920	4,440	4,530
Nova Scotia	6,422	6,110	5,932
New Brunswick	5,470	5,590	5,590
Quebec	1,932	2,056	2,167
Ontario	5,155	5,388	5,643
Manitoba	3,319	3,271	3,276
Saskatchewan	4,774	5,015	5,015
Alberta	4,763	5,122	5,361
British Columbia	4,740	4,922	5,040

Note: Using the most current enrolment data available, average tuition fees have been weighted by the number of students enrolled by institution and field of study. Fees at both public and private institutions are included in the weighted average calculations.
Source: Statistics Canada, Centre for Education Statistics.

Table 10.13 Public and private elementary and secondary education expenditures, 1998/1999 to 2002/2003

	1998/1999	1999/2000	2000/2001	2001/2002	2002/2003
			$ thousands		
Canada	**38,758,819**	**39,403,757**	**40,285,311**	**42,294,686**	**43,695,970**
Newfoundland and Labrador	569,287	573,908	577,319	608,376	626,405
Prince Edward Island	143,263	142,211	150,277	156,399	154,309
Nova Scotia	1,027,450	1,080,247	996,439	1,006,261	1,063,426
New Brunswick	866,150	885,836	843,565	864,441	893,478
Quebec	7,772,687	8,554,451	8,860,058	9,628,481	9,507,216
Ontario	16,191,535	15,786,513	15,842,478	16,390,755	17,122,615
Manitoba	1,690,214	1,756,112	1,821,560	1,853,923	1,976,918
Saskatchewan	1,375,143	1,389,976	1,453,208	1,490,336	1,633,710
Alberta	3,882,363	3,922,073	4,139,444	4,401,026	4,724,349
British Columbia	4,907,057	5,005,492	5,294,063	5,552,127	5,621,639
Yukon	76,779	81,178	81,289	87,159	90,812
Northwest Territories including Nunavut	208,959	..	..	..	..
Northwest Territories	..	118,246	117,625	140,288	151,824
Nunavut	..	85,416	85,439	91,986	98,458
Foreign and undistributed[1]	47,932	22,098	22,547	23,128	30,811

Note: Data are estimates for 2002/2003, budgetary for 2001/2002, and preliminary for 2000/2001.
1. Foreign and undistributed expenditures by the federal government that cannot be attributed to a particular province or territory.
Source: Statistics Canada, CANSIM table 478-0014.

Table 10.14 Registered apprenticeship training, change in registrations and completions, by major trade group, 2001/2002 to 2005/2006

	2001/2002	2002/2003	2003/2004	2004/2005	2005/2006
	annual % change				
Total major trade groups					
Registrations	7.5	8.4	6.8	9.7	11.7
Completions	-9.7	11.0	6.4	4.3	1.5
Building construction trades					
Registrations	12.9	13.2	12.6	13.4	9.9
Completions	-1.7	24.7	1.6	14.5	7.6
Electrical, electronics and related trades					
Registrations	8.8	7.0	7.1	8.8	10.0
Completions	-0.5	-8.3	24.2	6.7	9.5
Food and service trades					
Registrations	5.3	8.5	3.8	4.7	8.8
Completions	-25.5	16.6	5.7	2.5	-8.1
Industrial and related mechanical trades					
Registrations	4.9	5.9	1.0	5.7	10.2
Completions	-9.7	18.4	6.5	-4.9	1.5
Metal fabricating trades					
Registrations	5.3	5.5	3.7	10.4	13.5
Completions	-8.1	15.4	8.0	-1.1	-3.4
Motor vehicle and heavy equipment trades					
Registrations	5.0	8.1	5.9	9.3	12.4
Completions	-13.0	8.1	-3.4	8.2	-1.0
Other trades[1]					
Registrations	14.0	12.4	16.1	11.4	29.5
Completions	-3.3	24.1	0.0	1.4	21.9

1. Includes miscellaneous trades and occupations not classified elsewhere. Many of the apprenticeship trades and occupations that have been introduced since the 1990s have been added to this group. Some of these new trades and occupations include child and youth worker, early childhood educator, pork production technician and those related to motion pictures and theatres, such as assistant cameraperson, grip, and set dresser.

Source: Statistics Canada, CANSIM tables 477-0051 and 477-0052.

Energy

11

The energy sector accounted for 7% of gross domestic product (GDP) in 2008 and directly employed 363,000 people, or 2% of the labour force. High energy prices early in 2008 fuelled Canada's export revenues. According to National Energy Board figures, energy exports reached the highest value ever, $133 billion, and a record 28% of all merchandise trade. Just a year earlier, energy exports totalled $93 billion, or 21% of all exports.

In the first half of 2008, energy prices climbed to record highs amid rising demand. Oil reached US$147 per barrel in July, and natural gas prices rose to around US$13 per million British thermal units (MMBtu). The second half brought the financial and credit crisis, decreased demand for energy, significantly lower energy prices and a recession. Oil prices ended the year at US$45 per barrel, and natural gas prices dropped to less than US$6 per MMBtu.

Higher export revenues

The climbing oil prices early in 2008 also affected net energy export revenue—the value of energy exports minus the value of energy imports—lifting it to $73 billion, an increase of almost 45% over 2007. Historically, net export revenue from natural gas has been greater than net export revenue from crude oil (and its products). However, in 2008, the value of crude oil net exports surpassed the value of natural gas net exports by almost $15 billion.

Net export revenue from electricity also exceeded 2007 levels, as water conditions were favourable in the main hydro-generating provinces and electricity exports grew in Ontario. And in 2008,

Chart 11.1
Energy exports

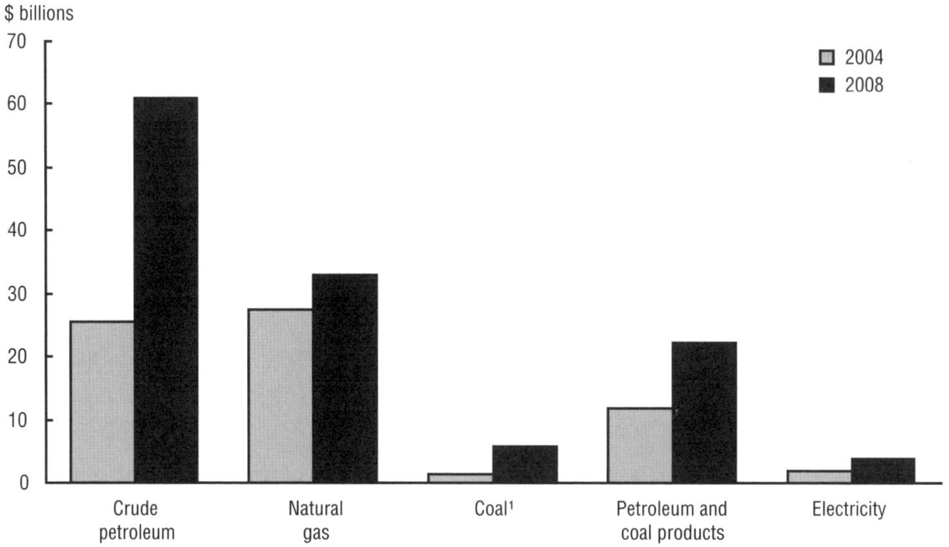

Note: On a balance of payments basis.
1. Includes coal and other crude bituminous substances.
Source: Statistics Canada, CANSIM table 228-0001.

for the first time ever, Canada became a net exporter of coal, in the amount of $360 million.

Both natural gas and oil production declined in 2008, contributing to a 2.1% drop in total Canadian energy production. Hydroelectricity production increased 10% from 2004 to 2008, whereas energy production from other sources (mainly wood) declined slightly.

Notably, investment in wind projects increased the energy produced from wind by 265% from 2004 to 2008. However, wind energy represents about 0.1% of the energy produced in Canada.

Largest consumers of energy

The United States and Canada are the largest consumers of energy in the world, consuming almost 200 gigajoules per capita—the equivalent of each Canadian and U.S. resident using 5,000 litres (32 barrels) of crude oil per year, or approximately twice the per capita energy consumed in other OECD countries. In non-OECD countries, energy consumption per capita is, on average, 23% of that consumed in the OECD countries.

From 2004 to 2008, energy consumption remained relatively stable in Canada, with transportation showing the largest increases, 5.7%. However, the population grew over this period, so per capita use of energy has fallen 1.4%. About 25% of all energy consumed by Canadians is generated using natural gas.

Table 11.a
Energy production by fuel type, 2002 and 2007

	2002	2007
	terajoules	
Coal	1,429,897	1,482,232
Crude oil	5,359,627	6,153,625
Natural gas	7,249,883	7,012,006
Natural gas liquids from gas plants	626,218	685,788
Primary electricity, hydro and nuclear	1,505,333	1,631,049
Refined petroleum products	4,592,022	4,795,930

Source: Statistics Canada, CANSIM table 128-0009.

Chart 11.2
Energy production, by primary energy source

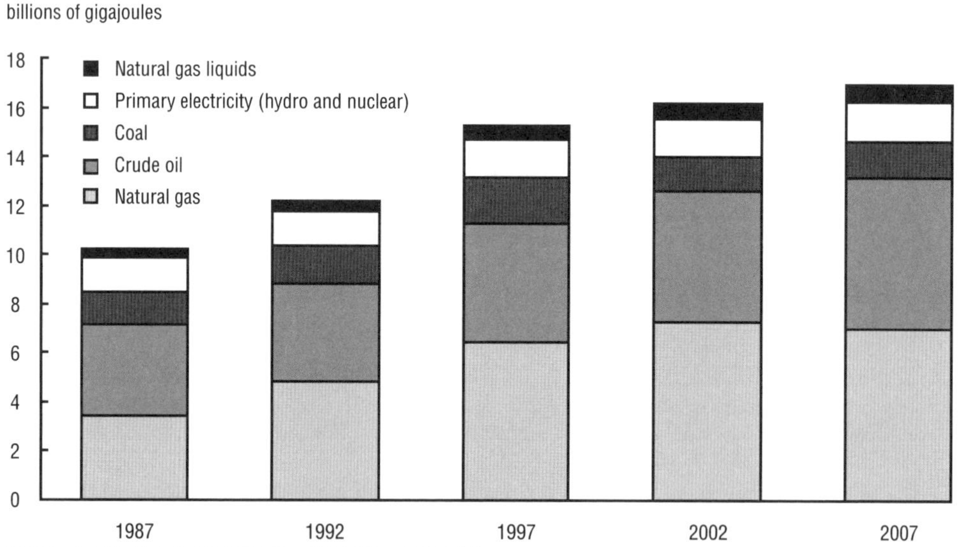

Source: Statistics Canada, CANSIM tables 128-0002 and 128-0009.

Turning down the heat

Canadian households spend a significant portion of their income on energy just to heat their homes. For some, the heating season can last up to 10 months. Adjusting the thermostat reduces heating expenses and conserves energy. Seniors are the most likely to turn down the heat.

In 2006, 90% of households were able to control their home's temperature using a thermostat. Just over half of households with a thermostat (53%) reduce the temperature while they sleep. About 7 in 10 households that programmed their thermostat lowered the temperature when they went to bed. However, less than half (46%) of households with an unprogrammed or non-programmable thermostat did so.

In the heating season, most households set the temperature between 20°C and 22°C when they are at home and awake and between 16°C and 18°C when they are sleeping.

Chart 11.3
Households with thermostats, 2006

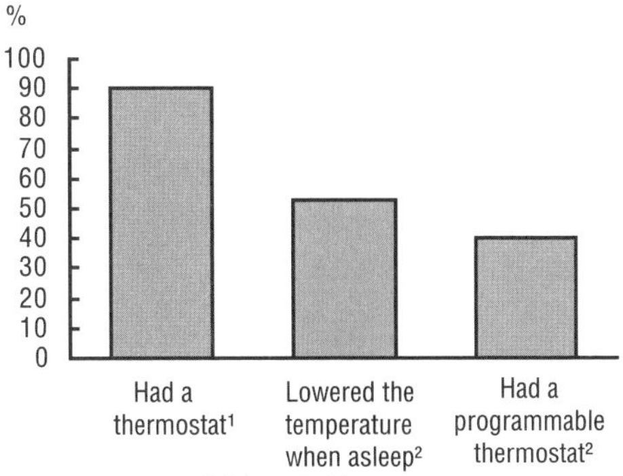

1. As a percentage of all households.
2. As a percentage of all households that had a thermostat.

Source: Statistics Canada, Catalogue no. 16-001-X.

Six out of 10 households used a forced air furnace as their primary heating system in 2006. One in four used electric baseboards, 5% had hot water radiators, and the rest used wood stoves, fireplaces, heat pumps or other equipment.

Comparing sources of electricity

The market shares of the various fuels used for generating electricity vary significantly between Canada and the United States. In Canada, hydro accounts for most of the installed power plant capacity and electricity generated, whereas coal and natural gas are the two main sources of electricity in the United States.

Coal is of particular concern because of environmental issues. In the United States, coal represents 31.9% of the country's installed generating capacity, but accounts for 49.0% of the electricity produced.

In Canada, coal-fired plants represent 13.1% of installed capacity. In 2006, 16.5% of the electric energy produced in Canada came from coal. Coal-fired plants are mainly found in Alberta, Saskatchewan, Ontario, New Brunswick and Nova Scotia, provinces with relatively less hydro power.

Chart 11.4
Electricity produced from coal, 2007

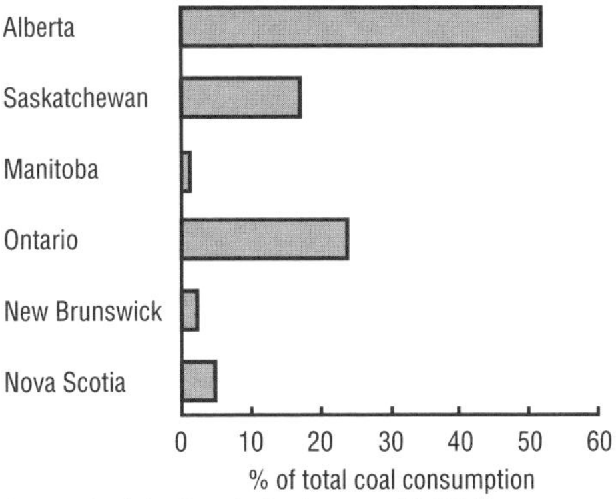

Source: Statistics Canada, Catalogue no. 57-202-X.

Table 11.1 Energy supply and demand, 1993 to 2007

	1993	1994	1995	1996	1997	1998
	petajoules					
Primary energy supply[1]						
Availability	9,314.1	9,564.3	9,695.2	10,097.2	10,200.1	10,194.9
Production	13,077.8	13,913.3	14,489.2	14,800.3	15,284.4	15,368.7
Exports	5,653.8	6,348.6	6,878.6	6,950.2	7,496.4	7,818.3
Imports	1,644.9	1,749.7	1,682.5	1,977.2	2,231.8	2,385.3
Primary and secondary energy supply						
Net supply[2]	8,165.2	8,412.4	8,583.6	8,899.6	8,927.6	8,841.3
Producer consumption	988.3	1,017.2	1,039.8	1,059.1	999.2	1,073.3
Non-energy use	729.5	740.6	758.8	800.0	833.0	811.8
Primary and secondary energy demand[3]	**6,447.4**	**6,654.7**	**6,785.0**	**7,040.4**	**7,095.5**	**6,956.2**
Industrial	1,973.2	2,053.4	2,105.6	2,180.5	2,196.9	2,149.0
Transportation	1,918.2	2,021.3	2,065.1	2,124.7	2,182.9	2,256.6
Agriculture	198.8	195.8	209.2	222.9	230.0	224.7
Residential	1,256.7	1,286.7	1,259.1	1,358.2	1,295.1	1,183.5
Public administration	132.1	143.1	143.3	134.1	135.9	130.3
Commercial and other institutional	968.6	954.4	1,002.6	1,020.4	1,054.8	1,012.3

1. Primary energy sources are coal, crude oil, natural gas, natural gas liquids, hydro and nuclear electricity.
2. Primary and secondary sources. Secondary sources are fuels, such as coal, natural gas, coke, coke oven gas, refined petroleum products, wood waste and spent pulping liquor, that are transformed to create another form of energy—for example, burning fossil fuels to create steam that turns electricity-generating turbines.
3. Final demand.

Source: Statistics Canada, CANSIM tables 128-0002 and 128-0009.

Table 11.2 Consumer Price Index, energy, 1994 to 2008

	1994	1995	1996	1997	1998	1999
	2002=100					
Electricity	87.7	87.3	88.3	89.3	90.1	90.8
Natural gas	66.7	62.6	61.9	66.5	70.6	77.5
Fuel oil and other fuel	76.2	75.1	80.3	85.2	76.5	76.8
Gasoline	76.5	80.1	83.6	85.2	77.9	84.9

Source: Statistics Canada, CANSIM table 326-0021.

1999	2000	2001	2002	2003	2004	2005	2006	2007
				petajoules				
10,518.3	10,831.0	10,950.4	11,163.5	11,478.5	11,527.5	11,307.1	11,176.9	11,654.8
15,358.2	15,768.4	15,894.9	16,171.0	16,170.9	16,553.7	16,489.9	16,815.5	16,964.7
7,824.0	8,328.4	8,443.8	8,561.9	8,499.0	8,822.7	8,662.2	8,898.6	9,269.8
2,518.5	2,852.2	3,013.4	2,923.6	3,459.8	3,107.6	3,139.2	2,977.4	3,141.0
9,190.7	9,423.7	9,303.5	9,623.1	9,829.9	10,014.0	9,946.1	9,879.6	10,354.1
1,229.3	1,257.4	1,264.9	1,344.1	1,340.0	1,303.2	1,274.0	1,282.3	1,347.9
828.9	790.3	863.2	894.3	903.4	1,029.3	983.7	1,044.9	1,048.7
7,132.5	**7,376.0**	**7,175.4**	**7,384.7**	**7,586.5**	**7,681.6**	**7,688.5**	**7,552.4**	**7,957.5**
2,177.3	2,268.6	2,166.3	2,229.5	2,318.6	2,343.2	2,312.8	2,314.0	2,465.6
2,307.3	2,279.8	2,240.4	2,250.1	2,266.3	2,347.3	2,388.8	2,372.3	2,493.1
229.9	231.9	218.1	206.8	211.8	208.9	208.5	211.4	215.0
1,232.3	1,287.8	1,240.0	1,286.7	1,338.2	1,313.0	1,296.6	1,243.4	1,344.4
124.5	131.3	126.8	125.2	128.1	131.9	136.1	127.6	123.0
1,061.4	1,176.4	1,184.1	1,286.7	1,323.8	1,337.5	1,346.1	1,283.8	1,327.6

2000	2001	2002	2003	2004	2005	2006	2007	2008
				2002=100				
91.3	92.9	100.0	98.0	102.0	104.9	110.8	112.9	113.2
94.2	122.1	100.0	130.1	127.4	136.3	140.5	131.3	146.8
108.7	108.8	100.0	114.9	126.5	158.7	165.9	172.5	225.4
103.5	100.8	100.0	106.4	117.6	132.6	139.8	146.1	164.7

Table 11.3 Gasoline prices, selected urban centres, 1994 to 2008

	1994	1995	1996	1997	1998	1999
	cents per litre					
St. John's	58.6	62.8	61.4	67.7	64.4	66.2
Charlottetown and Summerside	55.0	59.3	59.2	60.6	53.6	52.9
Halifax	52.0	54.3	54.8	60.6	57.1	60.8
Saint John	53.6	56.0	55.1	60.2	55.4	59.2
Québec	56.7	58.2	60.6	61.3	55.2	61.5
Montréal	55.2	56.8	60.6	61.9	56.3	63.0
Ottawa	52.5	53.8	55.1	56.0	51.3	56.2
Toronto	49.8	52.4	56.1	56.1	51.6	57.5
Thunder Bay	56.2	56.6	61.2	62.6	54.0	58.0
Winnipeg	52.3	54.6	56.9	57.4	53.3	57.3
Regina	55.6	57.5	59.3	60.0	55.6	60.5
Saskatoon	55.3	57.8	60.8	60.6	56.7	59.8
Edmonton	45.4	47.6	49.6	52.1	47.0	51.4
Calgary	47.4	50.0	51.7	53.2	48.9	52.6
Vancouver	55.6	58.4	59.2	58.8	50.6	54.3
Victoria	51.8	54.8	57.9	59.0	52.7	59.2
Whitehorse	58.1	63.4	67.0	67.9	66.9	67.3
Yellowknife	65.7	70.2	73.2	73.9	72.1	73.6

Note: Average annual price of regular unleaded gasoline at self-service filling stations.
Source: Statistics Canada, CANSIM table 326-0009.

Table 11.4 Household heating fuel prices, selected urban centres, 1994 to 2008

	1994	1995	1996	1997	1998	1999
	cents per litre					
St. John's	36.3	36.5	39.8	44.3	35.1	38.6
Charlottetown and Summerside	34.4	36.1	37.5	39.2	32.4	32.8
Halifax	33.8	34.0	38.5	42.8	36.9	38.9
Saint John	36.2	35.2	41.7	46.4	41.5	40.9
Québec	39.6	39.0	41.8	40.9	37.0	38.2
Montréal	36.5	33.4	34.6	36.7	32.8	33.6
Ottawa	37.3	37.3	39.6	42.8	39.2	39.3
Toronto	38.3	38.3	40.6	43.4	41.2	39.1
Thunder Bay	40.2	42.0	45.2	43.8	37.7	39.1
Winnipeg	41.8	41.9	44.4	47.8	47.0	45.6
Regina	35.6	36.9	39.7	42.7	40.9	41.4
Saskatoon	39.3	40.9	41.9	44.1	42.1	41.7
Vancouver	41.5	41.5	42.5	43.9	41.4	42.2
Victoria	39.6	39.6	40.5	44.2	40.7	42.9
Whitehorse	42.5	41.9	43.3	46.0	42.4	41.6
Yellowknife	38.7	37.9	39.6	38.9	35.0	37.1

Note: Average annual price.
Source: Statistics Canada, CANSIM table 326-0009.

2000	2001	2002	2003	2004	2005	2006	2007	2008
				cents per litre				
83.0	79.1	77.0	82.8	91.7	102.1	107.6	111.0	123.6
70.1	71.9	68.2	74.0	84.1	96.4	103.0	104.2	114.5
76.1	72.8	73.4	78.0	87.5	97.9	103.7	106.8	118.4
73.3	70.0	72.5	78.8	88.0	97.9	102.2	101.4	113.7
71.9	74.0	72.1	77.8	87.0	97.5	102.4	106.4	120.1
77.2	73.8	71.4	76.7	85.8	96.4	100.8	104.3	118.8
69.0	66.0	65.9	70.2	77.2	88.5	92.2	98.1	108.7
70.8	67.8	67.3	70.9	76.6	89.0	93.4	97.4	110.2
72.6	72.5	71.0	76.9	82.8	94.0	98.5	106.2	118.6
66.7	65.0	63.2	67.6	76.7	90.0	96.6	102.2	115.8
71.7	72.2	72.7	76.0	82.5	92.7	99.6	104.7	117.3
71.7	72.2	73.0	75.9	82.8	93.5	99.8	104.5	117.3
63.5	61.3	63.4	67.4	75.9	85.1	91.0	96.7	109.2
64.0	64.5	64.6	66.3	74.8	85.8	92.3	98.5	111.1
69.1	68.9	70.4	76.8	86.0	97.1	103.8	108.1	121.3
73.5	73.9	73.9	81.1	89.9	99.2	105.4	108.3	122.5
81.4	81.7	80.8	83.6	93.9	105.5	107.6	111.2	124.6
85.4	88.2	88.5	92.2	96.8	105.0	109.5	118.0	131.1

2000	2001	2002	2003	2004	2005	2006	2007	2008
				cents per litre				
56.1	54.5	50.1	54.8	62.4	78.6	84.8	87.6	109.4
48.8	51.3	46.5	53.4	56.8	73.8	77.6	79.3	102.3
56.1	54.7	53.3	61.4	68.5	83.6	87.9	84.0	106.3
59.4	58.7	54.9	62.4	66.0	83.2	84.7	89.7	115.1
50.2	49.1	48.8	56.3	61.3	77.2	79.0	83.3	112.6
51.3	49.9	46.3	54.3	58.6	75.0	78.6	82.0	112.2
53.4	56.8	49.2	57.2	62.9	77.4	81.6	86.8	113.0
54.3	55.9	50.8	57.9	64.0	78.0	82.2	87.6	112.7
54.3	54.6	47.9	57.1	62.9	81.4	85.5	91.0	118.0
56.1	60.2	53.0	60.8	64.4	81.6	84.0	91.5	115.8
53.3	55.2	51.8	55.7	62.4	82.0	82.6	91.8	115.3
54.0	56.5	54.6	59.3	65.3	80.0	85.5	91.5	113.4
57.1	58.1	54.2	59.2	69.4	88.1	89.0	93.5	115.6
57.9	58.0	53.6	62.9	72.3	90.8	94.1	99.9	126.3
57.0	63.1	57.5	64.5	72.3	88.4	94.1	102.3	125.6
52.3	51.9	49.0	56.5	62.0	81.3	84.8	96.4	122.6

Table 11.5 Established crude oil reserves, closing stock, 1992 to 2006

	1992	1993	1994	1995	1996	1997
	millions of cubic metres					
Canada	**590.4**	**582.2**	**544.5**	**553.0**	**526.7**	**532.2**
Newfoundland and Labrador	..	..	..	..	..	..
Ontario	1.2	1.2	2.0	1.9	1.9	1.8
Manitoba	6.7	6.5	6.3	5.6	5.1	4.7
Saskatchewan	122.6	130.2	141.9	150.1	156.8	176.6
Alberta	442.0	426.8	374.8	374.1	342.0	326.8
British Columbia	17.9	17.5	19.4	21.3	20.9	22.3

Source: Statistics Canada, CANSIM table 153-0013.

Table 11.6 Established natural gas reserves, closing stock, 1992 to 2006

	1992	1993	1994	1995	1996	1997	1998
	billions of cubic metres						
Canada	**1,929.1**	**1,859.9**	**1,832.7**	**1,840.9**	**1,725.9**	**1,620.4**	**1,562.2**
Nova Scotia	..	..	..	..	..	..	..
Ontario	16.9	17.2	13.4	12.0	12.5	12.5	12.2
Saskatchewan	78.4	84.7	86.7	86.6	81.8	76.5	71.5
Alberta	1,594.7	1,534.9	1,490.3	1,488.8	1,378.1	1,284.0	1,239.9
British Columbia	239.2	223.1	242.2	253.5	253.5	247.4	238.6

Source: Statistics Canada, CANSIM table 153-0014.

Table 11.7 Established reserves of natural gas liquids, closing stock, 1992 to 2006

	1992	1993	1994	1995	1996	1997	1998
	thousands of cubic metres						
Canada	**636,588**	**621,645**	**593,278**	**599,569**	**546,580**	**502,751**	**487,525**
Manitoba	61	56	52	46	91	0	..
Saskatchewan	1,724	2,035	2,207	2,155	2,086	1,632	1,482
Alberta	623,700	603,200	574,300	580,600	527,500	483,400	468,900
Propane	121,100	118,100	111,600	109,400	103,000	91,400	88,600
Ethane	312,000	305,000	290,000	300,000	264,000	245,000	238,000
Butane	70,600	67,100	63,900	62,900	58,500	51,900	51,100
Pentanes plus	120,000	113,000	108,800	108,300	102,000	95,100	91,200
British Columbia	11,103	16,354	16,719	16,768	16,903	17,719	17,143

Source: Statistics Canada, CANSIM table 153-0015.

1998	1999	2000	2001	2002	2003	2004	2005	2006
millions of cubic metres								
673.5	**642.5**	**667.3**	**644.7**	**606.1**	**590.0**	**603.8**	**752.3**	**712.6**
144.3	138.0	159.6	151.0	134.4	121.3	138.7	272.9	255.2
1.9	1.9	2.0	1.9	1.8	1.9	1.9	1.6	1.7
4.2	4.3	4.5	4.0	3.4	4.6	3.9	3.9	7.1
180.9	169.1	182.1	184.9	183.9	184.7	187.9	197.7	179.9
315.2	301.6	291.4	278.3	260.3	253.9	249.2	254.8	250.1
26.9	27.7	27.6	24.7	22.3	23.6	22.2	21.5	18.7

1999	2000	2001	2002	2003	2004	2005	2006
billions of cubic metres							
1,526.8	**1,614.5**	**1,547.8**	**1,529.6**	**1,469.5**	**1,497.5**	**1,553.7**	**1,577.7**
..	67.1	61.7	56.2	23.2	19.3	15.2	11.6
12.0	11.6	11.5	11.3	11.5	11.5	13.0	20.0
68.6	75.6	81.7	76.2	87.4	85.0	91.6	98.8
1,207.2	1,210.7	1,141.4	1,131.3	1,087.6	1,092.3	1,086.0	1,079.6
239.0	249.5	251.5	254.7	259.9	289.4	347.8	367.7

1999	2000	2001	2002	2003	2004	2005	2006
thousands of cubic metres							
487,339	**492,734**	**403,970**	**377,110**	**316,820**	**314,285**	**310,666**	**322,746**
..	..	..	..	..	..	..	..
1,306	1,290	1,246	1,295	1,324	1,150	1,098	1,049
469,700	473,900	463,600	359,100	298,500	295,000	289,500	296,100
82,600	85,500	84,100	79,300	69,400	71,300	69,400	72,000
256,000	252,000	252,100	165,100	124,000	122,900	120,700	125,100
48,600	50,400	49,900	46,900	41,900	41,500	40,100	40,900
82,500	86,000	77,500	67,800	63,200	59,300	59,300	58,100
16,333	17,544	17,524	16,715	16,996	18,135	20,068	25,597

Table 11.8 Energy fuel consumption, by manufacturing industry, 2002 to 2007

	2002	2003	2004	2005	2006	2007
	terajoules					
All manufacturing	**2,511,322**	**2,521,077**	**2,614,696**	**2,502,600**	**2,405,951**	**2,387,251**
Food	88,765	89,041	90,928	95,774	96,137	99,604
Beverage and tobacco products	12,896	12,237	12,266	12,475	11,046	11,419
Textile mills	8,238	8,050	8,058	7,745	7,364	6,689
Textile product mills	4,303	3,554	3,545	3,550	3,032	3,044
Clothing	4,985	4,978	3,997	2,154	1,772	1,630
Leather and allied products	966	768	568	309	228	275
Wood products	122,595	120,183	124,853	129,219	141,786	139,559
Paper	830,779	835,318	850,894	776,211	678,627	658,243
Printing and related support activities	8,548	8,765	8,521	8,878	8,608	8,969
Petroleum and coal products	366,241	368,429	405,491	358,993	367,958	381,669
Chemicals	252,056	254,575	278,149	272,915	267,188	258,289
Plastic and rubber products	32,592	35,045	37,011	37,846	35,810	40,351
Non-metallic mineral products	118,845	117,924	126,049	126,257	123,723	125,021
Primary metals	519,559	521,073	521,069	524,651	528,351	506,714
Fabricated metal products	41,361	39,784	41,647	40,979	38,701	42,401
Machinery	13,819	15,223	16,042	18,039	16,760	18,715
Computer and electronic products	3,931	4,563	5,100	5,621	5,388	6,193
Electrical equipment, appliances and components	6,011	6,708	7,107	7,282	6,883	7,243
Transportation equipment	57,134	56,725	56,267	55,896	51,485	54,618
Furniture and related products	11,308	11,521	10,908	11,645	10,175	10,995
Miscellaneous manufacturing	6,391	6,610	6,226	6,161	4,929	5,609

Note: North American Industry Classification System (NAICS), 2002.
Source: Statistics Canada, CANSIM table 128-0006.

Table 11.9 Energy fuel consumption of the manufacturing industry, by fuel type, 2002 to 2007

	2002	2003	2004	2005	2006	2007
	terajoules					
Energy consumed	**2,511,322**	**2,521,077**	**2,614,696**	**2,502,600**	**2,405,951**	**2,387,251**
Coal	46,775	50,841	55,381	51,734	53,112	56,263
Coal coke	93,299	92,236	93,389	92,869	101,622	80,886
Coke oven gas	26,824	28,019	28,333	29,530	29,339	24,749
Electricity	696,960	705,419	700,993	724,656	707,711	705,333
Heavy fuel oil	114,653	138,696	150,234	126,431	99,977	95,061
Middle distillates	19,838	18,166	19,896	19,713	17,666	17,814
Natural gas	726,312	672,564	694,866	662,426	618,186	628,920
Petroleum coke and coke from catalytic cracking catalyst	84,085	88,419	94,986	82,019	84,784	84,356
Propane	12,640	11,634	9,448	7,404	9,487[E]	8,927
Refinery fuel gas	175,149	178,996	207,558	186,407	197,698	213,258
Spent pulping liquor	290,859	292,635	299,806	258,505	216,616	223,607
Steam	41,336	47,956	48,029	50,076	60,139	60,371
Wood	182,594	195,495	211,777	210,828	209,615	187,707

Note: North American Industry Classification System (NAICS), 2002.
Source: Statistics Canada, CANSIM table 128-0006.

Each household contributes to greenhouse gas (GHG) emissions in two main ways. Direct emissions from motor-fuel use and residential-fuel use account for one-third of household emissions in Canada. Indirect emissions from industrial production of the goods and services that households consume make up the other two-thirds.

Together, direct and indirect household emissions accounted for 46% of Canada's total GHG emissions in 2004. The remaining 54% of total emissions came from industrial production of goods and services for other consumers (for example, exports to foreign countries) and from government activities.

Direct emissions

GHG emissions related to households increased 13% from 285,884 kilotonnes in 1990 to 321,727 kilotonnes in 2004. Canada ranked third among G8 countries, just behind the United Kingdom and Germany, in direct household GHG emissions per capita in 2005.

There was an insignificant change in GHG emissions per capita from 1990 to 2004, despite efficiency gains in industry and efficiency improvements in homes. Motor fuels are the largest source of households' direct GHG emissions.

Household emissions from motor-fuel use increased 29% from 55,770 kilotonnes in 1990 to 71,873 kilotonnes in 2004; this increase outpaced Canada's population growth of 16% over the same period, reflecting the popularity of larger vehicles that consume more fuel per kilometre. Sales of light-duty trucks, minivans and sport-utility vehicles climbed 74% from 1990 to 2004.

In 2004, 58% of the energy Canadians used in their dwellings came from natural gas and heating oil. Burning these two

Chart 12.1
Residential greenhouse gas emissions in G8 countries, 2005

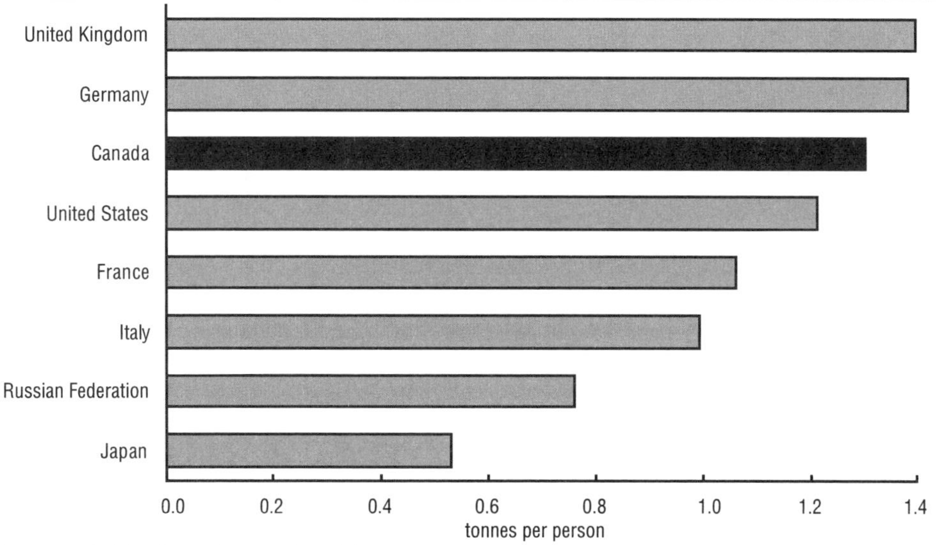

Notes: Only includes direct GHG from fuel use in the home.
GHG data from United Nations Framework Convention on Climate Change.
Source: United Nations, World Population Prospects Population Database: The 2006 Revision.

fuels accounts for 99% of the emissions from fuel use within the home. (Electricity represents 42% of total energy used in the home, but its consumption does not directly result in the release of GHGs.) Emissions from fuel use in the home remained stable from 1990 to 2004.

Households that switched from heating oil to natural gas helped stabilize those emissions. When burned, heating oil releases 47% more carbon dioxide per unit of energy than natural gas.

Indirect emissions

Two-thirds of indirect household GHG emissions, or 137,074 kilotonnes, were linked to goods production in 2004, while the remainder (72,174 kilotonnes) came from producing services. The goods and services that result in the highest indirect GHG emissions are electricity, food and beverages, restaurant meals and accommodations, and motor fuels and lubricants. These categories represented 54% of indirect GHG emissions from households in 2004 and 21% of household spending.

In 2004, the use of electricity resulted in the greatest indirect GHG emissions from households, though it represented a small portion (2%) of total household spending. This is because of the high emissions associated with the production of electricity.

Table 12.a
Greenhouse gas emissions attributable to households, 2004p

	kilotonnes	%
Total	**321,727**	**100.0**
Indirect emissions	209,249	65.0
Goods	137,074	42.6
Services	72,174	22.4
Direct emissions	112,478	35.0
In-home fuel use	40,605	12.6
Motor fuel use	71,873	22.3

Source: Statistics Canada, Catalogue no. 16-002-X.

Chart 12.2
Direct and indirect household greenhouse gas emissions

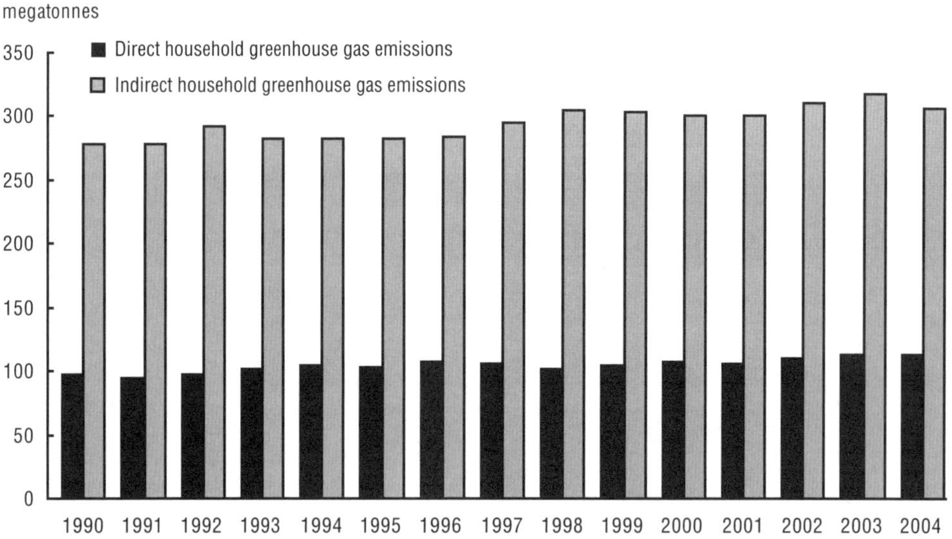

Notes: Direct household greenhouse gas emissions include all greenhouse gas emissions due to energy use in the home and for private motor vehicles.
Indirect household greenhouse gas emissions are those business-sector emissions due to the production of the goods and services purchased by households.
Source: Statistics Canada, CANSIM table 153-0046.

Environmentally active lifestyles

In 2006, 45% of Canadian households had very environmentally active lifestyles. 'Very active' means the household participates in at least four of six environmental behaviours: recycling, composting, lowering temperatures, using reduced-volume toilets, using low-flow shower heads, and using compact fluorescent light (CFL) bulbs. Practising two to three of these behaviours means a 'moderately active' environmental lifestyle; adopting zero or one suggests a 'less active' one.

In 2006, another 45% of households were moderately active, while 10% were less active. Of households with incomes above $100,000, 60% were very active in 2006, compared with 35% of households with incomes of $28,000 or less. At 54%, homeowners are more likely than renters (at 22%) to be very environmentally active.

Chart 12.3
Frequency of behaviours in environmentally active households, 2006

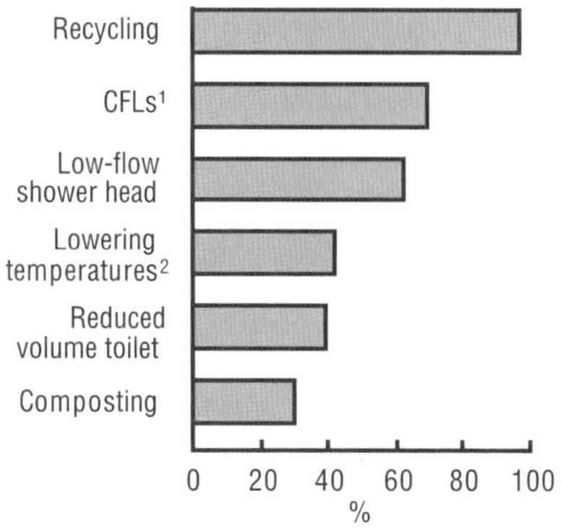

Note: As a percentage of all households that have a thermostat and have access to at least one recycling program.
1. Compact fluorescent lights.
2. Winter temperature lowered when asleep.
Source: Statistics Canada, Catalogue no. 16-002-X.

Recycling is the most common of the six environmental behaviours: 97% of households with access to it participate. The least common is composting, at 30%.

Which households drink bottled water?

In 2006, higher-income households and households with children were the most likely to use bottled water for their main source of drinking water in the home.

Almost one in four households with an income of $40,000 or less drank bottled water in the home; this rose to one in three households with an income over $91,000.

One in three households made up of working-age adults and children under 18 used bottled water as their main source of drinking water in the home.

Meanwhile, households living in apartments, households with seniors and no children, and households with at least one member with a university education were the least likely to drink bottled water.

In 2007, almost 6 in 10 Canadian households with municipally supplied water drank mainly tap water. Of those people, 54% treated the water before drinking it, up from 48% in 2006.

Chart 12.4
Households drinking bottled water, by household income, 2006

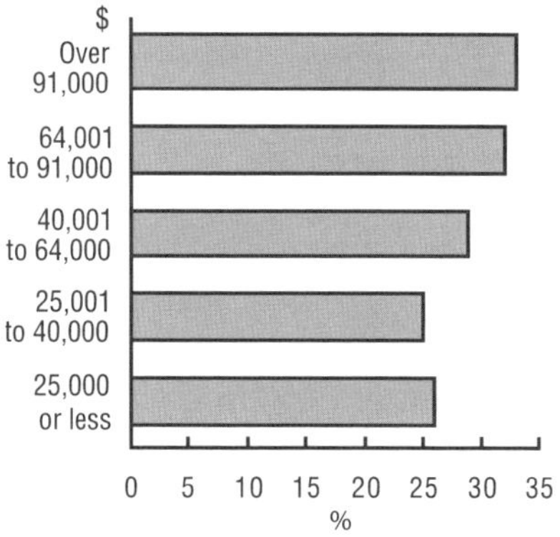

Source: Statistics Canada, Catalogue no. 16-002-X.

Table 12.1 Greenhouse gas emissions, by source, 1990 and 2006

	Cardon dioxide		Methane		Nitrous oxide	
	1990	2006	1990	2006	1990	2006
	kilotonnes					
Total[1]	**456,000**	**560,000**	**3,500**	**4,900**	**160**	**150**
Energy	425,000	519,000	1,700	2,600	30	30
Stationary combustion sources	276,000	317,000	200	200	7	8
Electricity and heat generation	94,800	116,000	1.8	4.6	2	2
Fossil fuel industries	49,700	65,200	80	100	1	1
Petroleum refining and upgrading	16,000	16,000	...	...	0.3	0.4
Fossil fuel production	34,100	49,100	80	100	0.7	1
Mining and oil and gas extraction	6,150	16,400	0.1	0.3	0.1	0.4
Manufacturing industries	54,300	45,800	3	3	2	2
Iron and steel	6,430	6,310	0.2	0.2	0.2	0.2
Non-ferrous metals	3,170	3,030	0.07	0.07	0.05	0.04
Chemical	7,060	6,450	0.15	0.14	0.1	0.1
Pulp and paper	13,500	5,650	2	2	0.8	0.8
Cement	3,680	4,840	0.07	0.1	0.04	0.04
Other manufacturing	20,500	19,500	0.4	0.4	0.4	0.4
Construction	1,850	1,290	0.03	0.02	0.05	0.03
Commercial and institutional	25,500	33,200	0.5	0.6	0.5	0.7
Residential	40,900	37,300	100	100	2	2
Agriculture and forestry	2,370	1,900	0.04	0.03	0.05	0.06
Transportation[2]	138,000	184,000	30	30	20	20
Civil aviation (domestic aviation)	6,180	8,190	0.5	0.4	0.6	0.7
Road transportation	94,900	130,000	15	9.3	10	11
Light-duty gasoline vehicles	43,800	37,700	7.8	2.9	6.2	3.6
Light-duty gasoline trucks	19,600	43,100	3.1	3.2	3.2	5.3
Heavy-duty gasoline vehicles	7,720	6,130	1.3	0.35	0.22	0.44
Motorcycles	143	254	0.14	0.17	0.00	0.01
Light-duty diesel vehicles	347	423	0.01	0.01	0.03	0.03
Light-duty diesel trucks	691	2,270	0.02	0.06	0.05	0.2
Heavy-duty diesel vehicles	20,500	39,000	1	2	0.6	1
Propane and natural gas vehicles	2,170	784	1	0.7	0.04	0.02
Railways	6,160	5,660	0.3	0.3	3	2
Navigation (domestic marine)	4,690	5,380	0.3	0.4	1	1
Other transportation	26,000	35,000	20	20	6	8
Off-road gasoline	6,000	6,000	8	8	0.1	0.1
Off-road diesel	13,000	19,000	0.7	1	6	8
Pipelines	6,700	9,390	6.7	9.4	0.2	0.3
Fugitive sources	11,000	17,000	1,500	2,400	0.1	0.1
Coal mining	...	...	90	30	...	...
Oil and natural gas	10,600	17,400	1,440	2,320	0.1	0.1
Oil	95	190	193	262	0.1	0.1
Natural gas	226	656	613	1,010	...	...
Venting	6,090	11,200	627	1,040	...	0.01
Flaring	4,400	5,900	2.6	4.1	0.00	0.01

See notes and source at the end of this table.

	Carbon dioxide		Methane		Nitrous oxide	
	1990	2006	1990	2006	1990	2006
	kilotonnes					
Industrial processes	31,000	41,000	...	...	37.8	7.88
Mineral products	8,300	9,600	...	...	...	...
Cement production	5,400	7,300	...	...	...	...
Lime production	1,700	1,600	...	...	...	...
Mineral product use[3]	1,090	600	...	...	...	...
Chemical industry	5,000	6,600	...	...	37.8	7.88
Ammonia production	5,000	6,600	...	...	...	...
Nitric acid production	...	...	...	...	3.27	3.98
Adipic acid production	...	...	...	...	35	3.9
Metal production	9,770	12,800	...	...	...	...
Iron and steel production	7,060	7,760	...	...	...	...
Aluminum production	2,700	5,000	...	...	...	...
Sulfur hexafloride used in magnesium smelters and casters	...	...	...	...	...	...
Consumption of halocarbons and sulfur hexafloride	...	...	...	...	...	...
Other and undifferentiated production	8,000	12,000	...	...	...	...
Solvent and other product use	...	...	...	...	0.56	1.0
Agriculture	...	...	980	1,300	93	110
Enteric fermentation	...	...	860	1,200	...	...
Manure management	...	...	120	160	11	15
Agricultural soils	...	...	...	...	82	96
Direct sources	...	...	...	...	45	49
Pasture, range and paddock manure	...	...	...	...	8.2	12
Indirect sources	...	...	...	...	30	30
Waste	270	190	820	950	2	2
Solid waste disposal on land	...	...	810	940	...	...
Wastewater handling	...	...	11	12	2	2
Waste incineration	270	190	0.4	0.07	0.4	0.2
Land use, land use change and forestry	-110,000	19,000	150	360	6.5	15
Forest land	-140,000	11,000	130	340	5.6	14
Cropland	13,000	-1,700	10	7	0.7	0.4
Grassland	...	...	...	...	...	...
Wetlands	4,000	2,000	0.3	0	0.01	0
Settlements	9,000	8,000	5	5	0.2	0.2

Note: Figures may not add to totals because of rounding.
1. National totals exclude all greenhouse gas emissions from the 'Land use, land use change and forestry' sector.
2. Emissions from ethanol fuel are reported within the gasoline vehicle subcategories under 'Transportation.'
3. 'Mineral product use' includes carbon dioxide emissions from the use of limestone and dolomite, soda ash and magnesite.
Source: Environment Canada, 2008, *National Inventory Report: Greenhouse Gas Source and Sinks in Canada, 1990-2006.*

Table 12.2 Household participation rates for environmental behaviours, by province, 2007

	Low-flow showerhead	Reduced-volume toilet	Compact fluorescent light bulbs	Composting[1]	Recycling[1,2]	Lowering temperatures[3]
	%					
Canada	**62**	**39**	**69**	**27**	**97**	**55**
Newfoundland and Labrador	55	28	65	21	94	60
Prince Edward Island	59	32	73	91	99	63
Nova Scotia	63	37	77	69	99	60
New Brunswick	61	31	70	32	96	54
Quebec	63	30	63	13	95	56
Ontario	65	47	76	34	98	53
Manitoba	52	38	62	23	88	49
Saskatchewan	46	37	64	27	96	59
Alberta	58	47	64	22	96	58
British Columbia	57	35	71	30	99	58

1. 2006 data.
2. Percentage of all households that had access to at least one recycling program.
3. Percentage of households that had a thermostat; temperature lowered when asleep during winter.
Source: Statistics Canada, Catalogue nos. 11-526-X and 16-001-M2008006.

Table 12.3 Capital expenditures on pollution abatement and control, by environmental milieu and by industry, 2006

	All environmental milieux	Air	Surface water	On-site contained solid and liquid waste	Noise, radiation and vibration
	$ millions				
All industries	**908.7**	**545.6**	**249.0**	**94.2**	**19.9**
Logging	**0.8**	F	F	F	F
Oil and gas extraction	**409.8**	271.2	61.8	67.4	9.4
Mining and quarrying	**174.5**	38.4	129.9	x	x
Electric power generation, transmission and distribution	**65.8**	52.5	x	x	x
Natural gas distribution	**3.0**	x	x	x	x
Food manufacturing	**12.8**	8.8	x	F	x
Beverage and tobacco product manufacturing	**x**	x	x	0.0	x
Wood product manufacturing	**30.7**	17.1	x	x	F
Paper manufacturing	**21.3**	15.7	5.2	x	x
Petroleum and coal product manufacturing	**45.7**	33.0	10.8	1.3	0.6
Chemical manufacturing	**25.8**	17.6	5.0	1.8	1.6
Non-metallic mineral product manufacturing	**16.1**	14.8	0.9	x	x
Primary metal manufacturing	**68.9**	49.5	13.0	5.1	1.2
Fabricated metal product manufacturing	**3.0**	2.2	0.1	F	x
Transportation equipment manufacturing	**15.7**	10.7	2.1	F	x
Other manufacturing industries	**12.8**	10.6	F	F	0.5
Pipeline transportation	**x**	0.2	x	x	x

Source: Statistics Canada, CANSIM table 153-0054.

Table 12.4 Capital expenditures on pollution prevention, by environmental milieu and by industry, 2006

	All environmental milieux	Air	Surface water	On-site contained solid and liquid waste	Noise, radiation and vibration	Other
	$ millions					
All industries	**1,561.1**	**885.2**	**189.2**	**203.1**	**11.4**	**272.2**
Logging	**F**	F	F	F	F	F
Oil and gas extraction	**377.1**	122.9	63.7	x	4.4	x
Mining and quarrying	**49.2**	3.2	28.1	15.0	x	x
Electric power generation, transmission and distribution	**105.9**	36.6	22.7	45.3	x	F
Natural gas distribution	**54.1**	52.6	x	1.3	x	0.0
Food manufacturing	**41.0**	5.4	F	0.9	x	F
Beverage and tobacco product manufacturing	**3.1**	x	0.4	0.7	x	x
Wood product manufacturing	**18.3**	5.9	5.4	F	F	F
Paper manufacturing	**52.0**	31.8	11.7	2.3	0.8	5.4
Petroleum and coal product manufacturing	**533.1**	508.1	18.8	x	F	x
Chemical manufacturing	**44.0**	27.5	4.9	7.6	0.1	4.0
Non-metallic mineral product manufacturing	**22.7**	12.9	3.0	3.0	F	3.5
Primary metal manufacturing	**31.1**	19.1	3.8	6.8	0.0	1.5
Fabricated metal product manufacturing	**F**	F	0.3	F	x	F
Transportation equipment manufacturing	**18.7**	7.1	1.1	F	F	F
Other manufacturing industries	**73.0**	24.7	F	F	x	F
Pipeline transportation	**39.2**	4.4	13.1	16.5	1.6	3.5

Source: Statistics Canada, CANSIM table 153-0054.

Table 12.5 Waste disposal and diversion, by province, 2002, 2004 and 2006

	2002	2004	2006	2002	2004	2006
	Total waste disposed			Total materials diverted		
	tonnes					
Canada	**24,081,371**	**25,226,766**	**27,249,178**	**6,641,546**	**7,112,735**	**7,749,030**
Newfoundland and Labrador	376,594	400,048	407,728	30,386	35,308	30,385
Nova Scotia	389,194	399,967	401,670	192,006	239,845	275,983
New Brunswick	413,606	442,173	450,238	130,728	139,262	252,174
Quebec	5,846,459	6,454,000	6,808,440	1,743,376	2,130,100	2,456,300
Ontario	9,645,633	9,809,264	10,437,780	2,265,968	2,414,552	2,396,856
Manitoba	896,556	928,117	1,024,272	215,815	157,490	152,799
Saskatchewan	795,124	794,933	833,753	116,296	114,182	106,868
Alberta	2,890,294	3,077,311	3,819,872	690,517	620,080	652,637
British Columbia	2,687,882	2,767,657	2,917,080	1,218,475	1,209,216	1,366,191

Note: Data for Prince Edward Island and the territories have been suppressed to meet the confidentiality requirements of the *Statistics Act*.
Source: Statistics Canada, CANSIM tables 153-0041 and 153-0043.

Table 12.6 Production of selected mineral commodities, 2006 and 2007

	2006	2007p
	carats	
Diamonds	13,277,703	17,007,850
	kilograms	
Gold	104,448	101,026
Platinum group	24,389	24,455
	tonnes	
Zinc	637,956	619,550
Copper	603,295	590,342
Nickel	232,948	254,413
Lead	83,096	72,774
Uranium	9,862	9,500
Molybdenum	7,723	6,841
Cobalt	7,115	8,261
Silver	995	871
Cadmium	579	452
Bismuth	214	145
Antimony	269	241
Gemstones	119	110
Tantalum	55	60
	kilotonnes	
Sand and gravel	239,895	236,906
Stone	178,424	172,699
Iron ore	34,943	32,032
Salt	14,389	11,807
Potash	8,369	11,149
Gypsum	9,789	7,640
Quartz	2,394	2,265
Peat	1,221	1,242
Nepheline syenite	738	740
Soapstone, talc, pyrophyllite	85	67
Barite	19	7

Source: Statistics Canada, Catalogue no. 26-202-X.

Ethnic diversity and immigration

13

Today, the ancestral roots of the population of Canada come from around the world. The 2006 Census identified more than 200 ethnic origins in Canada. One in three—10.1 million people—reported 'Canadian' as their origin either alone or in conjunction with other origins. After Canadian, the origins that they most often reported were English, French, Scottish, Irish, German, Italian, Chinese, North American Indian, Ukrainian and Dutch.

Visible minorities growing

Canada's visible minority population is growing at a much faster rate than its total population: 27% growth from 2001 and 2006 versus 5% in the general population. This is largely due to more immigration from Asia, Africa, the Caribbean, Central and South America and the Middle East. In 2006, about 70% of the visible minority population was born outside Canada.

In 2008, Canada accepted 247,200 immigrants, representing a rate of 8 newcomers per 1,000 people. This rate has been relatively constant since the 1990s.

From 2001 to 2006, almost 60% of newcomers to Canada came from Asia (including the Middle East). This contrasts with 35 years earlier, when Asians accounted for 12% of newcomers. Following the Second World War, most immigrants came from European countries.

The proportion of immigrants from African countries more than tripled from 3% in the late 1960s to 11% in the early 2000s. The proportion of immigrants from the United States followed an opposite trend, dropping from 11% to 3%.

Most immigrants settle in Toronto, Montréal or Vancouver. Social networks and links with family and friends influence immigrants to choose a particular location.

Wherever they settle, immigrants are about as likely as Canadian-born citizens

Chart 13.1
Immigrants to Canada

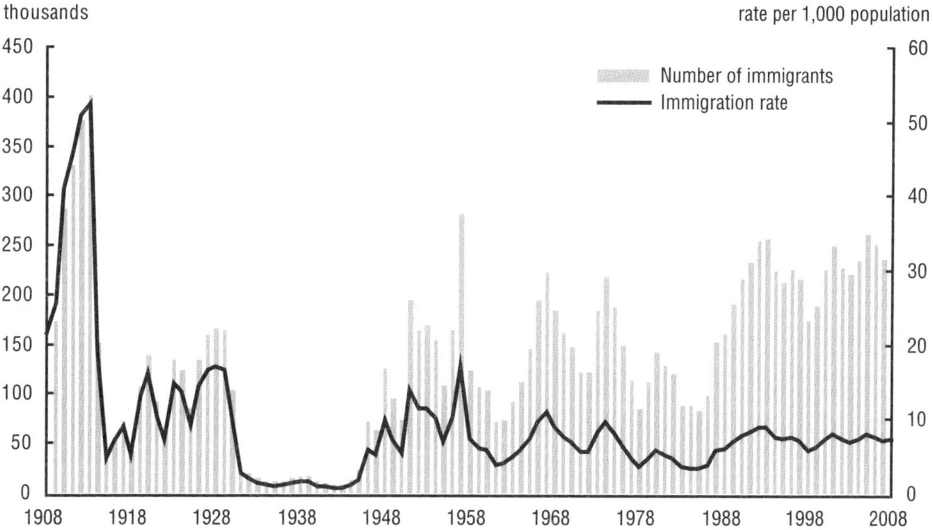

Source: Statistics Canada, Catalogue no. 91-209-X and Citizenship and Immigration Canada.

to feel safe. In 2004, 93% of foreign-born or immigrant populations reported that they were satisfied with their personal safety, compared with 95% of the Canadian-born population.

Recently-arrived immigrants also may be more likely to move about within Canada to respond to job opportunities. For example, immigrants in Canada for five years or less have noticeably higher migration rates to booming Alberta than non-immigrants. Immigrants who have been in Canada for 10 to 15 years are less likely to move to Alberta.

As immigrants integrate into the labour market here, many initially face difficulties finding jobs. For example, university-educated immigrants aged 25 to 54 who arrived in Canada within the previous five years were less likely to be employed in 2007 than their Canadian-born counterparts. This was true regardless of the country where they obtained their degree.

Table 13.a
Immigrant distribution, selected census metropolitan areas, 2006

	Total population	Total immigrant population[1]	Recent immigrants[2]
		%	
Montréal	11.5	12.0	14.9
Toronto	16.2	37.5	40.4
Vancouver	6.7	13.4	13.7
Other CMAs	65.6	37.1	31.0

1. Defined in the 2006 Census as people who are, or have been, landed immigrants in Canada.
2. Immigrants who came to Canada from January 1, 2001 to May 16, 2006.

Source: Statistics Canada, 2006 Census of Population.

Those educated in Western countries generally had higher employment rates than those educated elsewhere.

However, the gap in rates between degree-holding immigrants and their Canadian born counterparts narrows the longer an immigrant have been in Canada.

Chart 13.2
Employment rate for university-educated immigrants, 2007

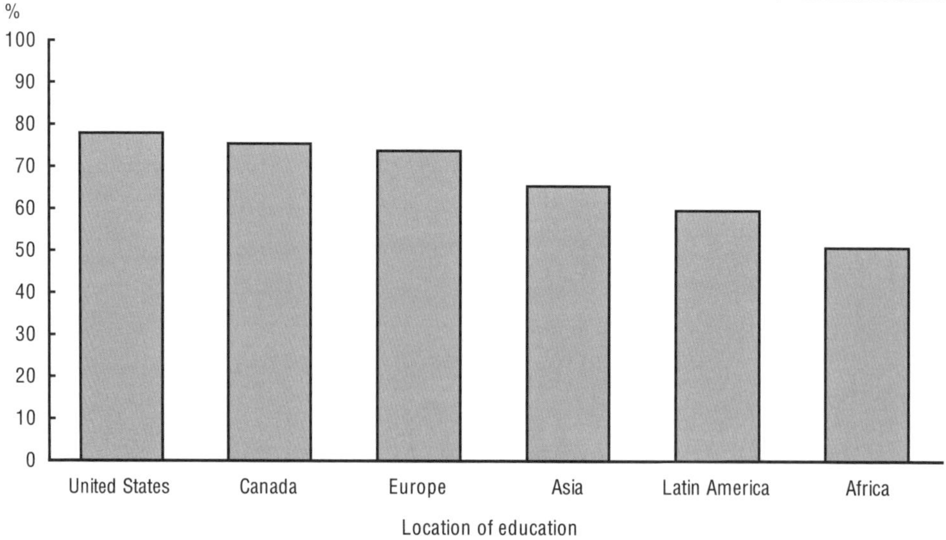

Note: Immigrants aged 25 to 54 who landed in Canada from 2002 to 2007.
Source: Statistics Canada, Catalogue no. 71-606-X.

Sending money back home

Canadians send as much as $2 billion out of the country each year to friends and family in foreign lands.

The contribution can be important. In some developing countries, including Haiti, Lesotho and Jordan, worldwide remittances account for up to 30% of their GDP. In Jamaica, the Philippines and the Dominican Republic, these money transfers account for as much as 20% of their economies.

Roughly 4 in 10 immigrants who arrived in Canada during 2000/2001 sent money to support family and friends abroad at least once during their first four years here. New arrivals from Southeast Asia, the Caribbean and Guyana are more likely than those from any other group to send money back home. The proportion is highest among immigrants from the Philippines and Haiti; it is lowest among those from France, the United Kingdom and South Korea.

Chart 13.3
Remittances by recent immigrants

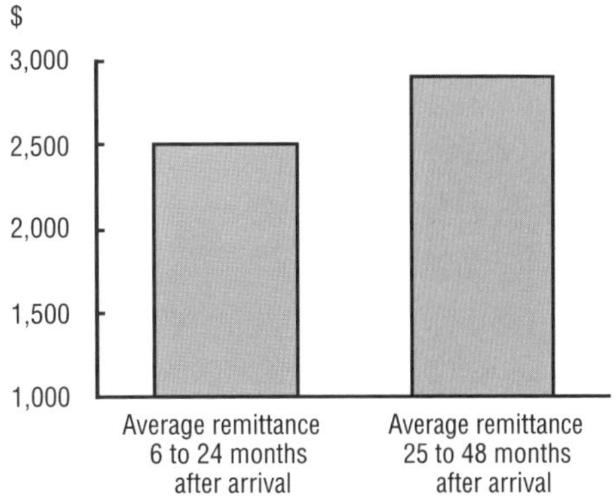

Note: Immigrants from the 2000/2001 landing cohort.
Source: Statistics Canada, Catalogue no. 75-001-X.

Familiar faces in the workplace

For a small proportion of immigrants, a job in Canada involves working alongside fellow immigrants from their homeland.

In Canada's eight largest cities, 10% of non-British and non-French immigrants work where most co-workers share their ethnic origin. The level rises to 20% among Chinese immigrants and to 18% among Portuguese immigrants. Immigrant men who work in ethnically homogeneous settings earn on average 33% less than those in more diverse workplaces. About two-thirds of this earnings gap is associated with differences in workers' education and official language proficiency as well as occupation and industry.

Immigrant workers in ethnically homogeneous settings are less likely than other immigrant workers to report low satisfaction with life. Among Canadian-born workers, sharing ethnic origins is not consistently associated with earnings or life satisfaction.

Chart 13.4
Co-ethnic concentration in the workplace, by immigration status

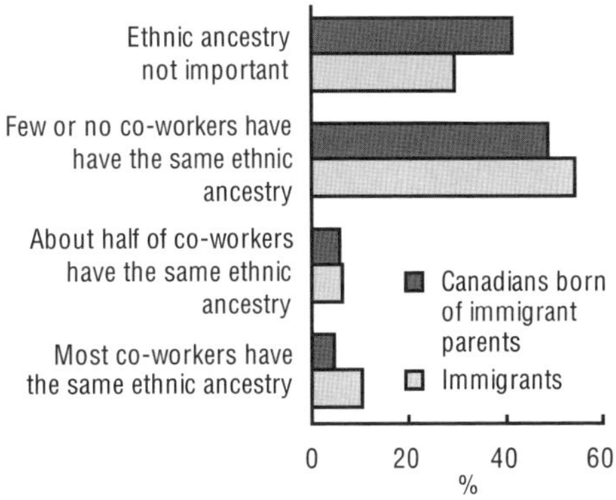

Note: Workers aged 25 to 64 in Canada's eight largest metropolitan areas.
Source: Statistics Canada, Catalogue no. 11F0019M.

Table 13.1 Immigrant population, by province and territory, 1991 to 2006

	1991	1996	2001	2006
	% of total population			
Canada	**16.1**	**17.4**	**18.4**	**19.8**
Newfoundland and Labrador	1.5	1.6	1.6	1.7
Prince Edward Island	3.2	3.3	3.1	3.6
Nova Scotia	4.4	4.7	4.6	5.0
New Brunswick	3.3	3.3	3.1	3.7
Quebec	8.7	9.4	9.9	11.5
Ontario	23.7	25.6	26.8	28.3
Manitoba	12.8	12.4	12.1	13.3
Saskatchewan	5.9	5.4	5.0	5.0
Alberta	15.1	15.2	14.9	16.2
British Columbia	22.3	24.5	26.1	27.5
Yukon	10.7	10.4	10.6	10.0
Northwest Territories	4.9	4.8	6.4	6.9
Nunavut[1]	...	...	1.7	1.6

1. Nunavut became a territory in 1999.
Source: Statistics Canada, censuses of population, 1991 to 2006.

Table 13.2 Immigrant population, by place of birth, 1991 to 2006

	1991	1996	2001	2006
	number			
Immigrant population	**4,342,890**	**4,971,070**	**5,448,480**	**6,186,950**
United States	249,075	244,695	237,920	250,535
Central and South America	219,385	273,820	304,650	381,165
Caribbean and Bermuda	232,520	279,405	294,050	317,765
Europe	2,360,425	2,332,060	2,287,550	2,278,345
United Kingdom	717,750	655,540	605,995	579,625
Other Northern and Western Europe	514,925	514,310	494,820	489,540
Eastern Europe	420,460	447,830	471,365	511,095
Southern Europe	707,285	714,380	715,370	698,080
Africa	166,175	229,300	282,600	374,565
Asia	1,069,050	1,562,770	1,989,180	2,525,160
West Central Asia and the Middle East	151,075	210,850	285,580	370,515
Eastern Asia	377,215	589,420	730,600	874,370
Southeast Asia	311,970	408,985	469,110	560,995
Southern Asia	228,795	353,515	503,890	719,275
Oceania and other[1]	46,265	49,025	52,525	59,410

1. 'Other' includes Greenland, Saint Pierre and Miquelon, the category 'Other country,' as well as immigrants born in Canada.
Source: Statistics Canada, censuses of population, 1991 to 2006.

Table 13.3 Immigrant population, by census metropolitan area, 1996 to 2006

	1996	2001	2006
		%	
Canada	**17.4**	**18.4**	**19.8**
St. John's	2.9	2.9	2.9
Halifax	7.0	6.9	7.4
Moncton[1]	3.2	2.9	3.4
Saint John	4.0	3.8	4.2
Saguenay (formerly Chicoutimi–Jonquière)	0.7	0.9	1.2
Québec	2.6	2.9	3.7
Sherbrooke	4.0	4.3	5.6
Trois-Rivières	1.6	1.5	2.2
Montréal	17.7	18.3	20.6
Ottawa–Gatineau (formerly Ottawa–Hull)	16.2	17.5	18.1
Kingston[2]	12.8	12.4	12.5
Peterborough[1]	9.3	8.8	9.4
Oshawa	16.5	15.7	16.4
Toronto	41.9	43.7	45.7
Hamilton	23.6	23.6	24.4
St. Catharines–Niagara	18.3	17.8	18.3
Kitchener	21.8	22.1	23.1
Brantford[1]	14.1	13.1	13.0
Guelph[1]	20.4	19.7	20.4
London	19.2	18.8	19.3
Windsor	20.4	22.3	23.3
Barrie[1]	11.5	11.6	12.8
Greater Sudbury/Grand Sudbury	7.5	7.0	6.7
Thunder Bay	12.2	11.1	10.4
Winnipeg	16.8	16.5	17.7
Regina	8.0	7.4	7.7
Saskatoon	7.6	7.6	7.7
Calgary	20.9	20.9	23.6
Edmonton	18.5	17.8	18.5
Kelowna[1]	13.8	13.9	14.8
Abbotsford–Mission[2]	20.3	21.8	23.7
Vancouver	34.9	37.5	39.6
Victoria	19.3	18.8	19.1

Note: Census metropolitan areas are based on the 2006 Census geography.
1. Became a census metropolitan area in 2006.
2. Became a census metropolitan area in 2001.
Source: Statistics Canada, censuses of population, 1996 to 2006.

Table 13.4 Immigrant population, by place of birth and period of immigration, 2006

	Total immigrant population	Period of immigration		
		Before 1991	1991 to 2000	2001 to 2006
	number			
Immigrant population	**6,186,950**	**3,408,415**	**1,668,550**	**1,109,980**
United States	**250,535**	168,840	42,925	38,770
Central America	**130,460**	62,100	45,080	23,275
Caribbean and Bermuda	**317,765**	200,735	82,045	34,985
South America	**250,710**	127,730	61,645	61,330
Europe	**2,278,345**	1,777,195	322,630	178,525
Western Europe	**424,640**	346,275	45,945	32,425
Eastern Europe	**511,095**	270,650	147,875	92,565
Southern Europe	**698,085**	586,540	85,950	25,590
Italy	**296,850**	289,815	4,760	2,270
Other Southern Europe	**401,235**	296,725	81,190	23,315
Northern Europe	**644,530**	573,720	42,865	27,940
United Kingdom	**579,625**	515,135	38,830	25,660
Other Northern Europe	**64,900**	58,585	4,030	2,285
Africa	**374,565**	136,235	121,115	117,215
Western Africa	**48,640**	10,070	18,645	19,930
Eastern Africa	**129,925**	59,150	39,960	30,810
Northern Africa	**134,505**	43,875	41,785	48,845
Central Africa	**22,410**	3,640	7,935	10,830
Southern Africa	**39,090**	19,500	12,790	6,795
Asia and the Middle East	**2,525,160**	898,750	979,185	647,225
West Central Asia and the Middle East	**370,520**	119,050	144,595	106,870
Eastern Asia	**874,365**	293,560	365,520	215,280
China, People's Republic of	**466,945**	133,905	177,925	155,105
Hong Kong Special Administrative Region	**215,430**	107,925	100,075	7,430
Other Eastern Asia	**191,995**	51,725	87,520	52,750
Southeast Asia	**560,995**	280,415	180,355	100,230
Philippines	**303,190**	107,760	117,550	77,880
Other Southeast Asia	**257,800**	172,650	62,805	22,345
Southern Asia	**719,280**	205,720	288,715	224,845
India	**443,690**	156,830	157,715	129,140
Other Southern Asia	**275,590**	48,895	131,000	95,700
Oceania and other[1]	**59,410**	36,825	13,925	8,655

1. 'Other' includes Greenland, Saint Pierre and Miquelon, the category 'Other country,' as well as immigrants born in Canada.
Source: Statistics Canada, 2006 Census of Population.

Table 13.5 Population, by selected ethnic origins, 2006

	Total responses	Single responses[1]	Multiple responses[2]
		number	
Total population	**31,241,030**	**18,319,580**	**12,921,445**
Canadian	**10,066,290**	5,748,725	4,317,570
English	**6,570,015**	1,367,125	5,202,890
French	**4,941,210**	1,230,535	3,710,675
Scottish	**4,719,850**	568,515	4,151,340
Irish	**4,354,155**	491,030	3,863,125
German	**3,179,425**	670,640	2,508,785
Italian	**1,445,335**	741,045	704,285
Chinese	**1,346,510**	1,135,365	211,145
North American Indian	**1,253,615**	512,150	741,470
Ukrainian	**1,209,085**	300,590	908,495
Dutch (Netherlands)	**1,035,965**	303,400	732,560
Polish	**984,565**	269,375	715,190
East Indian	**962,665**	780,175	182,495
Russian	**500,600**	98,245	402,355
Welsh	**440,965**	27,115	413,855
Filipino	**436,190**	321,390	114,800
Norwegian	**432,515**	44,790	387,725
Portuguese	**410,850**	262,230	148,625
Métis	**409,065**	77,295	331,770
British Isles, not included elsewhere	**403,915**	94,145	309,770
Swedish	**334,765**	28,445	306,325
Spanish	**325,730**	67,475	258,255
American	**316,350**	28,785	287,565
Hungarian (Magyar)	**315,510**	88,685	226,820
Jewish	**315,120**	134,045	181,070
Greek	**242,685**	145,250	97,435
Jamaican	**231,110**	134,320	96,785
Danish	**200,035**	33,770	166,265
Austrian	**194,255**	27,060	167,195

1. The respondent reported having only one ethnic origin.
2. The respondent reported having more than one ethnic origin.
Source: Statistics Canada, 2006 Census of Population.

Table 13.6 Visible minority population, by province and territory, 2006

	Total visible minority population	South Asian	Chinese	Black	Filipino
			number		
Canada	**5,068,095**	**1,262,865**	**1,216,565**	**783,795**	**410,700**
Newfoundland and Labrador	**5,720**	1,590	1,325	900	305
Prince Edward Island	**1,825**	135	255	645	30
Nova Scotia	**37,685**	3,810	4,300	19,225	700
New Brunswick	**13,345**	1,960	2,445	4,455	530
Quebec	**654,350**	72,850	79,825	188,070	24,200
Ontario	**2,745,205**	794,170	576,980	473,765	203,220
Manitoba	**109,100**	16,565	13,705	15,660	37,785
Saskatchewan	**33,895**	5,130	9,505	5,090	3,770
Alberta	**454,200**	103,885	120,270	47,075	51,090
British Columbia	**1,008,855**	262,290	407,225	28,315	88,075
Yukon	**1,220**	195	320	125	210
Northwest Territories	**2,265**	210	315	375	690
Nunavut	**420**	85	75	100	80

Source: Statistics Canada, 2006 Census of Population.

Latin American	Arab	Southeast Asian	West Asian	Korean	Japanese	Visible minority, not included elsewhere	Multiple visible minority
number							
304,245	**265,550**	**239,935**	**156,695**	**141,890**	**81,300**	**71,420**	**133,120**
485	545	120	115	60	140	75	60
215	265	30	30	70	65	65	25
950	4,505	815	780	800	505	255	1,030
715	840	440	550	620	165	155	460
89,510	109,020	50,460	16,115	5,310	3,540	4,155	11,310
147,135	111,405	110,045	96,615	69,540	28,080	56,845	77,405
6,275	2,320	5,670	1,960	2,190	2,010	1,690	3,265
2,520	1,710	2,555	1,020	735	645	405	810
27,265	26,180	28,605	9,655	12,045	11,030	3,850	13,250
28,960	8,635	40,690	29,810	50,490	35,060	3,880	25,415
100	20	145	0	10	40	10	35
85	90	355	40	15	15	30	40
20	15	10	0	10	10	10	15

Table 13.7 Visible minority population, by census metropolitan area, 2006

	Total population	Visible minority population	South Asian	Chinese	Black	Filipino
	number					
St. John's	**179,270**	3,460	890	990	620	155
Halifax	**369,455**	27,645	2,900	3,100	13,270	530
Moncton	**124,055**	2,425	350	295	1,035	100
Saint John	**120,875**	3,805	485	975	1,250	205
Saguenay	**149,600**	1,280	45	295	330	50
Québec	**704,185**	16,355	535	1,855	5,080	120
Sherbrooke	**183,635**	7,000	340	590	1,830	35
Trois-Rivières	**138,555**	2,270	50	210	625	15
Montréal	**3,588,520**	590,375	70,620	72,015	169,060	23,510
Ottawa–Gatineau	**1,117,120**	179,295	27,130	32,445	45,060	7,330
Kingston	**148,475**	8,600	1,785	2,470	1,165	485
Peterborough	**115,140**	3,095	665	730	575	110
Oshawa	**328,070**	33,700	6,195	3,690	12,605	2,155
Toronto	**5,072,075**	2,174,065	684,070	486,325	352,220	171,985
Hamilton	**683,450**	84,295	19,970	11,660	16,480	4,880
St. Catharines–Niagara	**385,035**	25,470	3,595	3,600	5,030	2,130
Kitchener	**446,495**	61,455	16,240	9,150	9,450	1,850
Brantford	**122,830**	6,715	1,785	695	1,700	655
Guelph	**126,085**	16,025	3,875	3,110	1,600	1,965
London	**452,575**	50,300	6,415	6,545	8,255	1,990
Windsor	**320,730**	51,200	10,265	7,825	9,490	3,145
Barrie	**175,335**	10,130	1,900	1,180	2,310	875
Greater Sudbury/Grand Sudbury	**156,400**	3,280	580	620	1,100	150
Thunder Bay	**121,050**	3,275	390	925	450	250
Winnipeg	**686,040**	102,940	15,290	12,810	14,470	36,935
Regina	**192,435**	12,605	1,975	3,335	2,170	1,230
Saskatoon	**230,850**	14,870	2,230	4,245	1,900	1,920
Calgary	**1,070,295**	237,890	57,700	66,375	21,060	25,565
Edmonton	**1,024,825**	175,295	40,200	47,195	20,380	19,630
Kelowna	**160,560**	8,320	2,345	1,470	660	410
Abbotsford–Mission	**156,640**	35,715	25,580	2,245	930	730
Vancouver	**2,097,965**	875,295	207,160	381,535	20,670	78,890
Victoria	**325,060**	33,870	7,210	12,330	2,360	2,760

Source: Statistics Canada, 2006 Census of Population.

Latin American	Arab	Southeast Asian	West Asian	Korean	Japanese	Visible minority, not included elsewhere	Multiple visible minority
number							
320	190	55	65	45	65	40	25
690	3,840	655	670	620	410	180	780
95	165	65	70	65	10	10	175
210	125	60	270	120	10	30	60
280	195	55	0	15	0	10	10
3,150	2,800	1,615	405	165	170	225	235
2,060	940	410	505	60	30	20	165
540	535	225	0	10	0	15	35
75,400	98,885	44,970	14,520	4,665	2,990	3,505	10,245
10,630	28,195	11,670	6,490	2,280	1,800	1,720	4,540
745	370	330	280	325	255	170	215
255	80	180	105	260	70	40	35
1,665	1,135	670	1,195	540	795	1,330	1,705
99,290	53,430	70,215	75,470	55,270	19,010	46,705	60,070
6,760	6,500	6,805	3,910	2,255	1,415	1,345	2,315
4,205	1,480	2,090	615	930	735	235	820
6,805	3,175	6,150	2,720	1,700	625	1,825	1,755
390	240	580	30	250	95	75	210
1,070	510	1,600	1,065	190	170	230	635
7,920	7,800	4,050	2,235	2,125	565	790	1,600
2,905	9,975	2,945	1,830	605	150	995	1,060
1,165	300	530	310	410	350	310	490
180	115	145	55	70	65	60	145
170	50	370	30	30	380	30	190
5,480	2,125	5,340	1,895	2,080	1,840	1,595	3,080
955	475	1,260	220	330	180	120	335
1,050	940	1,010	665	110	335	115	345
13,410	11,660	15,750	6,010	6,835	4,680	1,985	6,860
9,210	11,940	11,025	2,925	3,770	2,270	1,475	5,275
525	60	720	190	265	1,230	135	305
1,275	150	1,665	210	1,615	830	35	450
22,695	7,430	33,470	28,160	44,825	25,425	2,920	22,115
1,845	500	1,585	575	1,235	2,280	260	930

Table 13.8 Visible minority population, by age group, 2006

	All age groups	0 to 14	15 to 24	25 to 44	45 to 64	65 to 74	75 and older
	number						
Total population	**31,241,030**	**5,576,805**	**4,207,815**	**8,781,165**	**8,600,935**	**2,255,640**	**1,818,655**
Visible minority population	**5,068,095**	1,145,395	785,355	1,674,175	1,094,055	233,060	136,055
South Asian	**1,216,565**	210,930	186,925	385,525	303,440	76,060	53,680
Chinese	**1,262,865**	305,220	181,410	424,850	260,975	61,550	28,865
Black	**783,795**	221,660	130,010	244,805	142,485	29,805	15,030
Filipino	**410,700**	89,780	53,885	141,225	99,690	16,680	9,435
Latin American	**304,245**	59,915	51,885	114,620	65,015	8,360	4,450
Arab	**239,935**	55,355	38,270	80,410	51,755	8,445	5,700
Southeast Asian	**265,550**	69,650	40,985	96,010	46,560	8,125	4,210
West Asian	**156,695**	30,840	29,190	54,015	34,560	5,360	2,725
Korean	**141,890**	27,275	28,945	44,405	32,820	5,745	2,700
Japanese	**81,300**	14,900	10,290	26,860	17,600	6,005	5,630
Visible minority not included elsewhere	**71,420**	14,305	11,375	24,925	16,175	2,960	1,680
Multiple visible minority	**133,120**	45,550	22,180	36,515	22,975	3,955	1,950
Not a visible minority	**26,172,940**	4,431,410	3,422,455	7,107,000	7,506,885	2,022,585	1,682,600

Source: Statistics Canada, 2006 Census of Population.

Table 13.9 Population aged 15 and older, by visible minority group and generational status, 2006

	Total generational status	First generation	Second generation	Third generation or more
	number			
Total visible minority population	**3,922,700**	**3,273,070**	**551,740**	**97,890**
South Asian	**957,645**	820,180	132,190	5,275
Chinese	**1,005,635**	850,335	138,520	16,775
Black	**562,135**	403,955	115,090	43,095
Filipino	**320,915**	283,560	35,760	1,595
Latin American	**244,330**	219,440	22,870	2,015
Arab	**195,900**	173,015	20,300	2,585
Southeast Asian	**184,575**	159,285	23,450	1,845
West Asian	**125,855**	120,710	4,580	565
Korean	**114,615**	104,640	9,190	790
Japanese	**66,400**	28,715	18,510	19,170
Visible minority not included elsewhere	**57,115**	44,965	11,005	1,150
Multiple visible minority	**87,565**	64,260	20,270	3,035

Source: Statistics Canada, 2006 Census of Population.

Families, households and housing

14

Households have been shrinking over the past two decades and it is no surprise why: fewer people are living in large families, and more people are living alone. Families comprising couples without children outnumber those with children, and the proportion of married couples has been on the decline. Most Canadians still own their home, increasingly a condominium.

Household size is shrinking

There were 12.4 million households in Canada in 2006: 27% consisted of one person, while 9% were made up of five or more people. That makes three times as many one-person households as large households with five or more people.

From 2001 to 2006, the number of one-person households increased 12%, to reach 3.3 million. This growth continues a trend: the proportion of one-person households first surpassed that of large households in 1981.

The shrinking size of households can be attributed to several reasons including the aging baby boomers, whose adult children may have moved out, and to Generation X who are fewer in number and have lower fertility rates. In addition, smaller households may also result from increased divorce and separation rates, as well as more seniors living alone. Seniors aged 65 and older represented 34% of people who lived alone in 2006.

In 2006, for the first time ever, census families comprising couples without children outnumbered those with children. (A census family is comprised of a married or a common-law couple with or without children, or a lone parent and at least one child in the home. Children in the home are defined as people younger than 25.)

Couples without children living at home accounted for 43% of census families in 2006, whereas couples with children accounted for 41%. In 1986,

Chart 14.1
Household size, by number of people

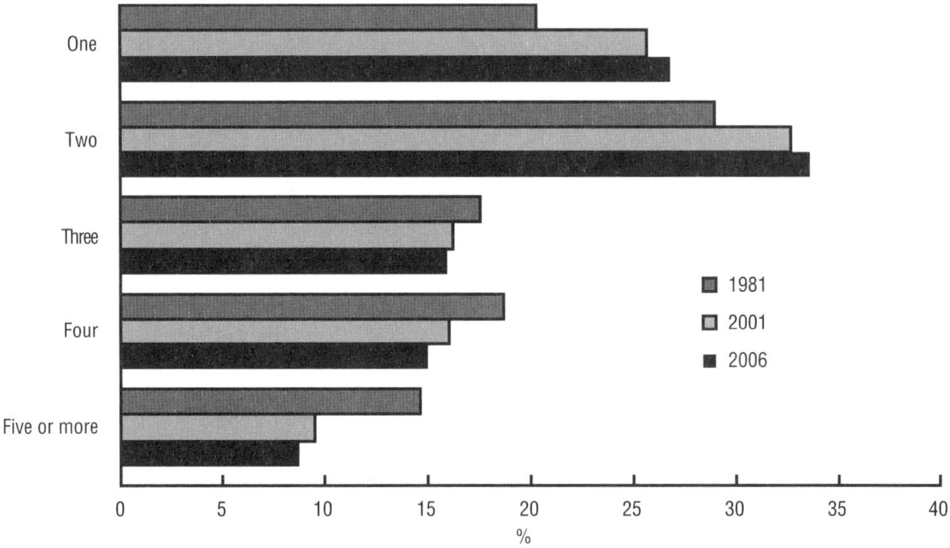

Source: Statistics Canada, 2006 Census of Population and Catalogue no. 96F0030X.

the proportions were 35% and 52%, respectively.

More than two out of three households owned their dwelling in 2006, the highest rate of home ownership since at least 1971. Of the 12.4 million households in Canada, 8.5 million owned their home.

Homeownership is rising

The increase from 2001 to 2007 continues the long-term trend of rising homeownership that began in 1991, after a period of low growth during the 1980s.

Households in the Atlantic provinces continue to have the highest homeownership rates in the country, with households in Newfoundland and Labrador ranking first, at 77%. Households in Quebec have the lowest, at 59%. This continues patterns in effect since at least 1971.

The homeownership rate for one-person households in 2006 was well below the national average but increased at a faster-than-average pace. Just under half (48%) of those who were living alone in 2006 owned their home, up from 44% in 2001.

Table 14.a
Family characteristics

	1986	2006
	number	
Families with no children at home	2,201,230	3,420,850
Families with children at home	4,532,610	5,475,990
One child at home	1,765,710	2,429,695
Two children at home	1,826,430	2,132,830
Three or more children at home	940,470	913,465
Total children at home	8,583,555	9,733,770
Average number of children at home	1.3	1.1

Note: Historical comparisons for census families must be interpreted with caution because of conceptual changes in 2001.
Source: Statistics Canada, Catalogue no. 97-553-X.

Nearly 6 out of 10 households (58%) that owned their home in 2006 had a mortgage. This is slightly higher than in 1981, when baby boomers were entering the housing market, and it marks an increase from 55% in 2001.

From 2001 to 2006, shelter costs for owner households climbed 22%, while shelter costs for renters rose 13% (both increases are based on current dollars).

Chart 14.2
Owner and renter households spending 30% or more of their income on shelter

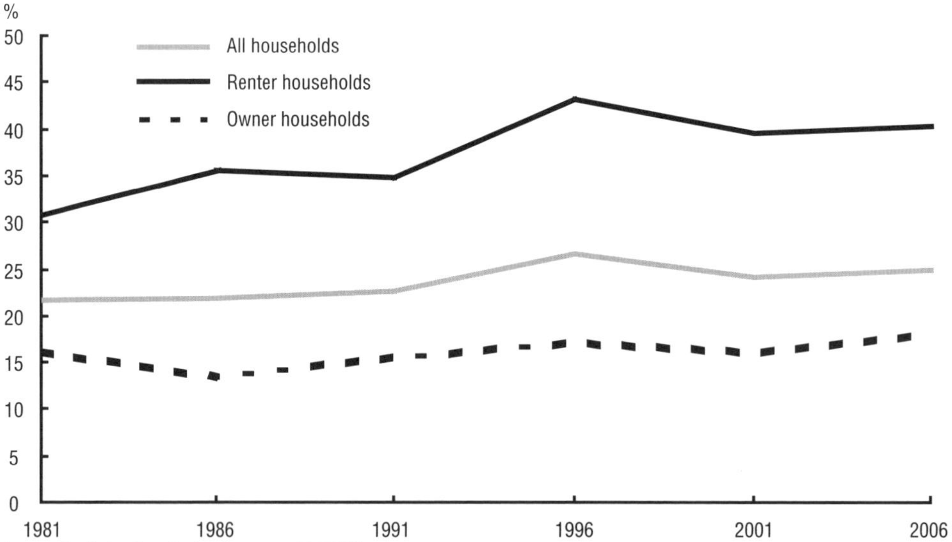

Source: Statistics Canada, Catalogue no. 97-554-X.

Condo ownership rising

Condominium ownership is growing quickly among Canadians. In 1981, less than 4% of owner households were condominium owners. By 2006, it had reached a record 11%, so that 913,000 households owned a condominium, a 37% increase from five years earlier.

Most condominiums (91%) are located in census metropolitan areas (CMAs). The percentage of condominium ownership is highest in British Columbia's four CMAs, where 2006 rates ranged from 21% in Kelowna and Victoria to 24% in Abbotsford–Mission and 31% of owner households in Vancouver.

Of the 913,000 condominium owners, 60% or 554,000 had taken out a mortgage in 2006, compared with 59% five years earlier. Households with maintainers aged 35 and younger accounted for 25% of all condominium households with mortgages in 2006, up from 22% in 2001. Over one-third (38%) of condominium owners with mortgages spent 30% or more of their household income on shelter, a substantial increase from 32% in 2001.

Chart 14.3
Owner households living in a condominium

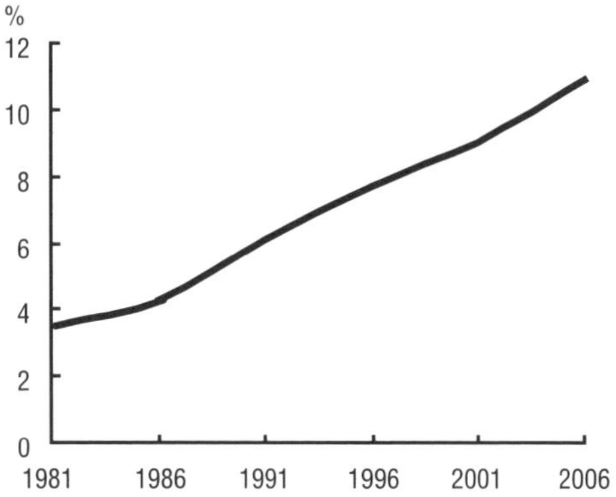

Source: Statistics Canada, censuses of population, 1981 to 2006.

I do...take two?

Divorce rates have risen sharply over the last 40 years and common-law unions have become more popular throughout the country. In 2006, divorced Canadians represented 7% of the population aged 15 and older. However, divorce affects more people than that: In 2006, 13% of Canadians aged 15 and older had experienced at least one divorce during their conjugal life, and nearly half had remarried.

Intention to remarry is an indicator of how families are changing. From 1990 to 2006, the proportion of divorced people saying they intend to remarry dropped from 26% to 22%. In 2006, 6 out of 10 divorced Canadians said they do not wish to remarry, compared with 5 out of 10 in 1990. Divorced Quebecers had the least desire to remarry in 2006: three out of four ruled out matrimony from their future relationships.

Chart 14.4
Divorced Canadians' intentions to remarry

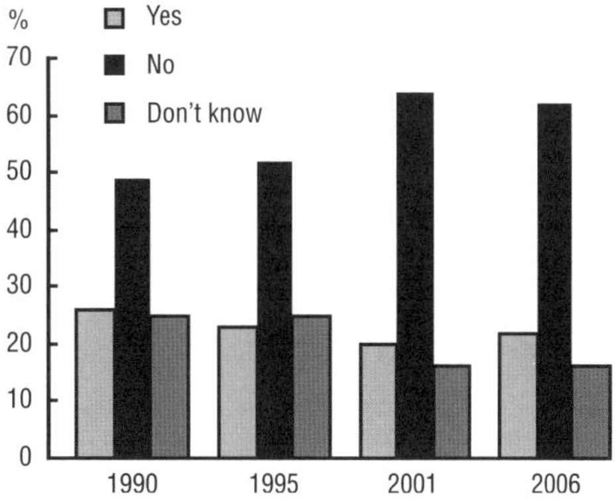

Source: Statistics Canada, Catalogue no. 89-630-X.

Table 14.1 Population, by marital status and sex, 2002 to 2007

	2002	2003	2004	2005	2006	2007
	number					
Total population	**31,372,587**	**31,676,077**	**31,995,199**	**32,312,077**	**32,649,482**	**32,976,026**
Males	15,538,572	15,688,977	15,846,832	16,003,804	16,170,723	16,332,277
Females	15,834,015	15,987,100	16,148,367	16,308,273	16,478,759	16,643,749
Never married	13,092,573	13,231,209	13,368,674	13,507,149	13,653,059	13,800,997
Males	6,999,555	7,078,089	7,155,622	7,233,428	7,314,611	7,396,835
Females	6,093,018	6,153,120	6,213,052	6,273,721	6,338,448	6,404,162
Married[1,2]	15,340,377	15,438,972	15,558,054	15,675,089	15,802,300	15,916,860
Males	7,659,734	7,701,393	7,752,882	7,803,419	7,860,087	7,910,554
Females	7,680,643	7,737,579	7,805,172	7,871,670	7,942,213	8,006,306
Widowed	1,520,850	1,532,940	1,544,226	1,553,488	1,563,856	1,573,455
Males	282,218	288,816	295,446	301,404	307,050	312,357
Females	1,238,632	1,244,124	1,248,780	1,252,084	1,256,806	1,261,098
Divorced	1,418,787	1,472,956	1,524,245	1,576,351	1,630,267	1,684,714
Males	597,065	620,679	642,882	665,553	688,975	712,531
Females	821,722	852,277	881,363	910,798	941,292	972,183

Note: Population estimates as of July 1.
1. Population aged 15 and older.
2. Includes people who are separated and people in common-law unions.
Source: Statistics Canada, CANSIM table 051-0010.

Table 14.2 Marriages, by province and territory, 2003 to 2008

	2003	2004	2005[r]	2006[r]	2007[p]	2008[p]
	number					
Canada	**147,391**	**148,585**	**148,439**	**149,792**	**151,695**	**150,423**
Newfoundland and Labrador	2,876	2,850	2,806	2,752	2,698	2,797
Prince Edward Island	823	827	829	828	831	824
Nova Scotia	4,742	4,729	4,698	4,667	4,633	4,687
New Brunswick	3,724	3,708	3,686	3,646	3,622	3,669
Quebec	21,138	21,279	22,244	21,900	22,650	22,400
Ontario	63,485	64,114	64,677	65,170	65,483	64,959
Manitoba	5,659	5,710	5,732	5,746	5,796	5,767
Saskatchewan	4,977	5,011	5,000	4,995	5,080	5,080
Alberta	17,622	17,909	18,392	19,060	19,837	19,100
British Columbia	21,981	22,080	20,007	20,660	20,697	20,770
Yukon	158	160	159	160	158	161
Northwest Territories	139	141	140	138	139	138
Nunavut	67	67	69	70	71	71

Source: Statistics Canada, CANSIM table 053-0001.

Table 14.3 Divorces, by province and territory, 2000 to 2005

	2000	2001	2002	2003	2004	2005
	number					
Canada	**71,144**	**71,110**	**70,155**	**70,828**	**69,644**	**71,269**
Newfoundland and Labrador	913	755	842	662	837	789
Prince Edward Island	272	246	258	281	293	283
Nova Scotia	2,054	1,945	1,990	1,907	2,000	1,961
New Brunswick	1,717	1,570	1,461	1,450	1,415	1,444
Quebec	17,054	17,094	16,499	16,738	15,999	15,423
Ontario	26,148	26,516	26,170	27,513	26,374	28,805
Manitoba	2,430	2,480	2,396	2,352	2,333	2,429
Saskatchewan	2,194	1,955	1,959	1,992	1,875	1,922
Alberta	8,176	8,252	8,291	7,960	8,317	8,075
British Columbia	10,017	10,115	10,125	9,820	10,049	9,954
Yukon	68	91	90	87	66	109
Northwest Territories	94	83	68	62	71	65
Nunavut	7	8	6	4	15	10

Source: Statistics Canada, CANSIM tables 053-0002 and 101-6501.

Table 14.4 Structure of census families, selected years from 1981 to 2006

	All families		Couple families		Lone-parent families	
	number	average number of children at home	number	average number of children at home	number	average number of children at home
1981	**6,325,315**	1.4	5,611,495	1.3	713,815	1.7
1986	**6,733,845**	1.3	5,880,550	1.2	853,295	1.6
1991	**7,355,730**	1.2	6,402,090	1.1	953,640	1.6
1996	**7,837,865**	1.2	6,700,355	1.1	1,137,505	1.6
2001	**8,371,020**	1.1	7,059,830	1.1	1,311,190	1.5
2006	**8,896,840**	1.1	7,482,775	1.0	1,414,060	1.5

Note: Historical comparisons for census families must be interpreted with caution because of conceptual changes in 2001.
Source: Statistics Canada, Catalogue nos. 97F0005X and 97-553-X.

Table 14.5 Family structure, by census metropolitan area, 2006

	All families			Families of married couples		
	Total	No children at home	Children at home	All married couples	No children at home	Children at home
	number					
St. John's	**52,525**	18,105	34,420	36,695	14,250	22,445
Halifax	**105,200**	42,445	62,755	72,885	32,335	40,550
Moncton	**37,130**	15,930	21,205	25,310	11,970	13,335
Saint John	**35,565**	13,740	21,825	25,010	11,395	13,615
Saguenay	**44,540**	19,065	25,470	24,780	12,890	11,890
Québec	**200,960**	86,955	114,000	100,390	51,280	49,110
Sherbrooke	**51,405**	22,345	29,055	25,795	13,650	12,140
Trois-Rivières	**39,685**	17,400	22,285	20,040	11,190	8,850
Montréal	**994,960**	366,990	627,970	562,050	237,350	324,705
Ottawa–Gatineau	**314,310**	115,535	198,770	211,590	85,020	126,570
Kingston	**42,995**	18,105	24,890	30,595	14,435	16,165
Peterborough	**33,505**	14,690	18,810	24,185	12,035	12,150
Oshawa	**94,575**	30,615	63,955	67,970	24,545	43,430
Toronto	**1,405,845**	418,550	987,295	1,059,125	349,135	709,990
Hamilton	**195,905**	70,425	125,475	144,150	58,375	85,775
St. Catharines–Niagara	**112,550**	45,170	67,380	81,640	38,515	43,125
Kitchener	**126,205**	44,365	81,840	93,250	36,255	56,995
Brantford	**35,680**	13,370	22,315	25,360	11,105	14,260
Guelph	**35,735**	13,160	22,575	25,800	10,400	15,395
London	**127,795**	49,055	78,740	91,330	39,685	51,650
Windsor	**90,350**	31,075	59,280	66,410	26,390	40,025
Barrie	**50,095**	17,400	32,700	35,580	13,680	21,905
Greater Sudbury/Grand Sudbury	**46,340**	18,625	27,715	32,115	15,235	16,880
Thunder Bay	**35,055**	13,580	21,475	24,345	11,070	13,275
Winnipeg	**189,785**	69,515	120,275	134,455	57,005	77,445
Regina	**53,720**	20,455	33,260	37,530	16,875	20,660
Saskatoon	**63,205**	24,465	38,745	45,135	20,215	24,915
Calgary	**295,345**	109,215	186,125	217,520	84,850	132,670
Edmonton	**284,400**	106,890	177,510	203,790	84,555	119,230
Kelowna	**48,280**	23,570	24,710	35,545	19,895	15,650
Abbotsford–Mission	**44,365**	16,820	27,545	33,795	14,410	19,385
Vancouver	**580,120**	207,650	372,470	433,180	166,040	267,140
Victoria	**91,935**	42,660	49,275	64,185	33,580	30,600

Notes: Census families in private households.
'Children at home' comprises all children regardless of age.
Source: Statistics Canada, 2006 Census of Population.

Families of common-law couples			Lone-parent families		
All common-law couples	No children at home	Children at home	All lone-parent families	Male parent	Female parent
number					
6,060	3,860	2,200	9,775	1,650	8,125
14,950	10,110	4,835	17,365	2,900	14,470
6,010	3,955	2,055	5,815	975	4,845
3,795	2,345	1,445	6,765	1,135	5,625
13,120	6,175	6,945	6,635	1,500	5,135
69,275	35,675	33,605	31,290	7,700	23,585
17,010	8,695	8,315	8,600	2,325	6,275
12,875	6,210	6,665	6,770	1,360	5,410
252,685	129,645	123,040	180,220	35,490	144,735
51,105	30,515	20,590	51,610	10,205	41,405
5,855	3,670	2,185	6,545	1,250	5,295
4,205	2,655	1,550	5,115	880	4,235
11,020	6,075	4,945	15,585	3,065	12,515
109,290	69,420	39,870	237,430	39,835	197,595
19,570	12,055	7,515	32,185	5,630	26,545
11,835	6,650	5,185	19,070	3,705	15,365
14,175	8,105	6,070	18,775	3,625	15,150
4,440	2,265	2,175	5,875	1,150	4,730
4,585	2,760	1,825	5,350	1,135	4,215
15,300	9,370	5,925	21,170	3,880	17,290
8,275	4,680	3,595	15,665	2,900	12,760
6,910	3,720	3,195	7,600	1,535	6,065
6,410	3,390	3,015	7,820	1,450	6,370
4,330	2,505	1,820	6,380	1,215	5,160
20,325	12,510	7,815	35,010	6,125	28,885
5,905	3,585	2,320	10,280	1,890	8,390
6,795	4,250	2,550	11,275	2,250	9,025
35,605	24,370	11,235	42,220	8,610	33,610
34,520	22,330	12,185	46,085	9,285	36,800
5,660	3,670	1,990	7,070	1,350	5,720
4,110	2,415	1,695	6,460	1,145	5,315
58,825	41,610	17,215	88,115	16,870	71,250
13,110	9,080	4,030	14,635	2,960	11,675

Table 14.6 Family structure, by province and territory, 2006

	All families			Families of married couples		
	Total	No children at home	Children at home	All married couples	No children at home	Children at home
	number					
Canada	**8,896,840**	**3,420,850**	**5,475,990**	**6,105,910**	**2,662,135**	**3,443,775**
Newfoundland and Labrador	**155,730**	61,950	93,775	114,635	53,165	61,465
Prince Edward Island	**39,185**	15,315	23,870	28,695	12,935	15,765
Nova Scotia	**267,415**	112,190	155,230	187,420	91,125	96,295
New Brunswick	**217,795**	91,300	126,490	151,210	73,435	77,775
Quebec	**2,121,610**	853,895	1,267,720	1,156,930	555,885	601,040
Ontario	**3,422,320**	1,217,845	2,204,470	2,530,560	1,008,550	1,522,015
Manitoba	**312,805**	119,575	193,230	225,880	100,490	125,385
Saskatchewan	**267,455**	110,835	156,620	194,160	95,415	98,750
Alberta	**904,850**	351,300	553,550	658,900	278,990	379,910
British Columbia	**1,161,420**	479,400	682,025	844,430	387,780	456,650
Yukon	**8,335**	3,075	5,260	4,640	2,005	2,635
Northwest Territories	**10,880**	3,130	7,750	5,555	1,830	3,725
Nunavut	**7,035**	1,040	5,995	2,890	525	2,365

Notes: Census families in private households.
Children at home comprises all children regardless of age.
Source: Statistics Canada, 2006 Census of Population.

Table 14.7 Population, by living arrangements and by province and territory, 2006

	Total population in private households	Persons in family households	Spouses, common-law partners or lone parents	Children in census families
	number			
Canada	**31,074,405**	**26,727,405**	**16,379,620**	**9,733,765**
Newfoundland and Labrador	**499,060**	447,535	287,300	150,655
Prince Edward Island	**133,330**	116,675	71,965	42,595
Nova Scotia	**899,755**	767,785	489,540	262,000
New Brunswick	**716,870**	621,700	400,000	209,190
Quebec	**7,396,275**	6,168,355	3,890,395	2,173,525
Ontario	**11,981,235**	10,542,660	6,303,925	3,977,010
Manitoba	**1,119,530**	956,425	572,400	364,255
Saskatchewan	**945,890**	802,985	490,470	297,165
Alberta	**3,228,065**	2,768,210	1,679,435	1,016,850
British Columbia	**4,054,605**	3,447,325	2,147,675	1,202,140
Yukon	**29,855**	24,750	14,940	9,130
Northwest Territories	**40,725**	35,905	19,430	15,160
Nunavut	**29,200**	27,085	12,130	14,085

Note: Population in private households.
1. Non-relatives may be present.
2. These non-relatives must constitute a census family.
Source: Statistics Canada, 2006 Census of Population.

Families of common-law couples			Lone-parent families		
All common-law couples	No children at home	Children at home	All lone-parent families	Male parent	Female parent
number					
1,376,870	**758,715**	**618,150**	**1,414,060**	**281,775**	**1,132,290**
16,935	8,785	8,150	24,160	4,420	19,740
4,085	2,380	1,705	6,405	1,135	5,265
34,700	21,060	13,645	45,290	8,010	37,280
31,000	17,865	13,130	35,585	6,435	29,150
611,850	298,005	313,845	352,825	77,940	274,890
351,040	209,300	141,745	540,715	99,605	441,105
33,715	19,080	14,635	53,210	10,275	42,930
28,855	15,425	13,430	44,445	9,270	35,170
115,685	72,310	43,370	130,265	27,715	102,555
141,830	91,620	50,205	175,160	35,390	139,770
1,970	1,065	900	1,725	445	1,280
2,990	1,300	1,690	2,330	635	1,695
2,205	515	1,690	1,940	495	1,445

Persons not in a census family, living with relatives[1]	Persons not in a census family, living with non-relatives[2]	Persons in non-family households	Living with relatives[1]	Living with non-relatives only	Living alone
number					
393,350	**220,665**	**4,347,000**	**250,670**	**769,285**	**3,327,050**
6,610	2,970	51,525	3,540	8,150	39,830
1,250	855	16,655	1,025	2,810	12,825
10,140	6,105	131,970	7,125	24,900	99,945
7,580	4,925	95,165	4,955	18,270	71,945
67,630	36,805	1,227,920	64,820	182,765	980,340
174,355	87,375	1,438,570	84,560	249,145	1,104,865
13,800	5,975	163,100	11,050	23,750	128,295
9,355	5,990	142,910	8,850	22,745	111,315
40,375	31,555	459,855	33,640	117,525	308,690
60,275	37,220	607,280	30,060	116,640	460,580
420	255	5,105	245	960	3,900
860	450	4,820	545	1,195	3,080
695	170	2,115	250	425	1,435

Table 14.8 Household equipment, 1997 to 2007

	1997	1998	1999	2000
		%		
Washing machine	80.9	81.2	80.3	80.6
Clothes dryer	77.2	78.9	77.7	78.2
Dishwasher	49.0	51.3	50.0	51.4
Refrigerator	99.8	99.8	99.7	99.8
Freezer	59.1	59.0	57.6	57.9
Microwave oven	88.1	88.7	89.6	90.8
Air conditioning	32.2	33.2	34.5	34.6
Telephone (land line or cellular)	98.5	98.6	98.8	98.8
Cellular telephone	22.0	26.5	32.5	42.0
Compact disc (CD) player	64.2	66.3	70.5	74.3
Cablevision	74.7	72.9	73.0	72.4
Satellite dish	..	..	..	..
Digital video disc (DVD) player	..	..	..	..
Compact disc (CD) writer	..	..	..	..
Digital video disc (DVD) writer	..	..	..	..
Video cassette recorders	87.2	88.0	88.7	89.9
Home computer	39.8	45.2	50.0	55.2
Internet use from home	17.4	25.0	33.4	42.6
Colour televisions	98.5	98.7	98.8	98.9
Vehicle (owned or leased)	..	82.9	83.0	83.6
Owned vehicles (automobiles, trucks, vans)	79.1	79.0	78.6	79.4
Leased vehicles (automobiles, trucks, vans)	..	8.7	8.9	9.0

Notes: All data are as of December 31 of the reference year.
In every second year starting with 2001, statistics for Canada include the territories. For the other years, Canada-level statistics include only the 10 provinces.

Source: Statistics Canada, CANSIM table 203-0020.

2001	2002	2003	2004	2005	2006	2007
			%			
80.4	80.5	81.2	81.9	82.2	81.3	82.2
79.3	78.4	78.8	79.5	80.4	80.8	81.8
52.1	54.6	55.0	56.0	57.2	57.7	59.4
99.7	99.9	99.7	99.8	99.7	99.8	99.9
56.1	56.8	56.1	55.2	56.3	53.9	53.0
91.3	92.4	93.0	93.8	94.1	93.9	93.5
35.8	37.5	39.6	41.7	44.2	48.1	48.4
98.6	98.7	98.8	98.9	98.9	99.2	99.1
47.6	51.7	54.0	58.9	64.2	67.7	71.4
71.1	73.9	76.2	79.7	80.4	81.6	81.6
68.1	66.1	64.8	66.3	65.4	65.2	64.9
18.4	21.4	22.8	22.0	22.6	24.1	23.8
19.8	35.7	51.7	68.3	77.1	83.0	85.3
19.4	27.8	32.4	38.3	43.5	47.9	51.8
..	..	..	16.0	24.5	31.7	39.4
91.6	92.1	90.2	90.0	89.1	82.0	79.0
59.8	64.1	66.6	68.7	72.0	75.4	78.4
49.9	54.5	56.9	59.8	64.3	68.1	72.7
99.2	99.1	99.0	99.2	99.0	99.0	98.9
83.0	84.0	83.1	83.8	83.6	82.5	83.1
78.2	79.3	78.2	79.1	79.0	77.3	77.6
9.8	9.8	9.8	9.9	10.1	10.8	10.8

Table 14.9 Owned dwellings, by province and territory, from 2002 to 2007

	2002	2003	2004	2005	2006	2007
				%		
Canada	**64.8**	**65.6**	**65.8**	**67.1**	**65.7**	**67.3**
Newfoundland and Labrador	76.5	77.0	76.6	79.6	78.9	77.1
Prince Edward Island	69.8	73.2	72.7	68.5	70.5	72.3
Nova Scotia	69.5	69.9	71.1	71.2	69.2	72.3
New Brunswick	71.7	73.8	76.9	76.8	76.6	75.5
Quebec	56.8	57.1	56.6	59.2	56.8	58.7
Ontario	66.7	68.0	67.6	68.8	66.7	69.3
Manitoba	68.7	70.6	68.9	73.0	69.2	71.2
Saskatchewan	73.1	72.5	73.9	74.5	72.5	74.8
Alberta	71.1	72.1	72.2	74.0	74.1	72.9
British Columbia	63.3	64.0	66.6	65.3	66.9	67.8
Yukon	..	62.2	..	62.1	..	62.1
Northwest Territories	..	51.9	..	60.9	..	59.1
Nunavut	..	26.9	..	F	..	23.2

Notes: All data are as of December 31 of the reference year.
In every second year starting with 2001, statistics for Canada include the territories. For the other years, Canada-level statistics include only the 10 provinces.
Includes owned dwellings with or without a mortgage.
Source: Statistics Canada, CANSIM table 203-0019.

Table 14.10 Average number of rooms per dwelling, by household size, 2006

	All households	One person	Two people	Three people	Four people	Five people	Six people or more
				number			
Canada	**6.4**	**4.8**	**6.3**	**6.9**	**7.7**	**8.1**	**8.2**
Newfoundland and Labrador	**7.2**	5.8	7.0	7.6	8.2	8.5	8.9
Prince Edward Island	**6.8**	5.3	6.7	7.1	7.8	8.5	8.9
Nova Scotia	**6.7**	5.3	6.6	7.3	7.9	8.4	9.0
New Brunswick	**6.7**	5.4	6.6	7.1	7.8	8.4	8.8
Quebec	**5.8**	4.4	5.8	6.4	7.2	7.7	7.9
Ontario	**6.6**	5.0	6.5	7.0	7.7	8.1	8.1
Manitoba	**6.3**	4.8	6.3	6.9	7.6	7.8	7.7
Saskatchewan	**6.8**	5.3	7.0	7.5	8.1	8.4	7.9
Alberta	**6.8**	5.2	6.7	7.3	8.0	8.3	8.5
British Columbia	**6.4**	4.7	6.4	7.0	7.8	8.3	8.6
Yukon	**5.9**	4.5	5.9	6.6	7.4	7.7	8.0
Northwest Territories	**5.6**	4.3	5.3	5.9	6.6	6.6	6.6
Nunavut	**5.0**	3.9	4.7	5.1	5.2	5.5	5.8

Source: Statistics Canada, 2006 Census of Population and Catalogue no. 97-554-X.

Geography

Sometimes, the easiest way to understand and visualize statistical data is by looking at a map.

Geographers use data from the census and from surveys to map phenomena such as the richest neighbourhoods in Toronto, the population density in Alberta or heart disease by health region.

Statistics Canada produces three different types of maps:

- Reference maps show the boundaries, names and codes of standard geographic areas, as well as the major visible features such as roads, railroads, coastlines, lakes and rivers.
- Thematic maps show the spatial distribution of a specific theme, such as population density or average annual income, for a selected geographic area.
- Interactive maps enable users to use Web-based mapping applications. Statistics Canada maintains several data products with mapping applications, such as the Aboriginal Population Profile, Agricultural Community Profiles, Community Profiles, the Federal Electoral District Profile and Crop Condition Assessment Program. A mapping tool called GeoSearch makes it easy to find places in Canada. The tool displays the appropriate map showing boundaries and other features, the population and dwelling counts for these places, as well as what kind of census geographic area it is and its relationship to other census geographic areas.

Visit Maps and geography at http://www.statcan.gc.ca to see how data can be better visualized and understood with maps.

Map 15.1
Female–male ratio by census division (CD)

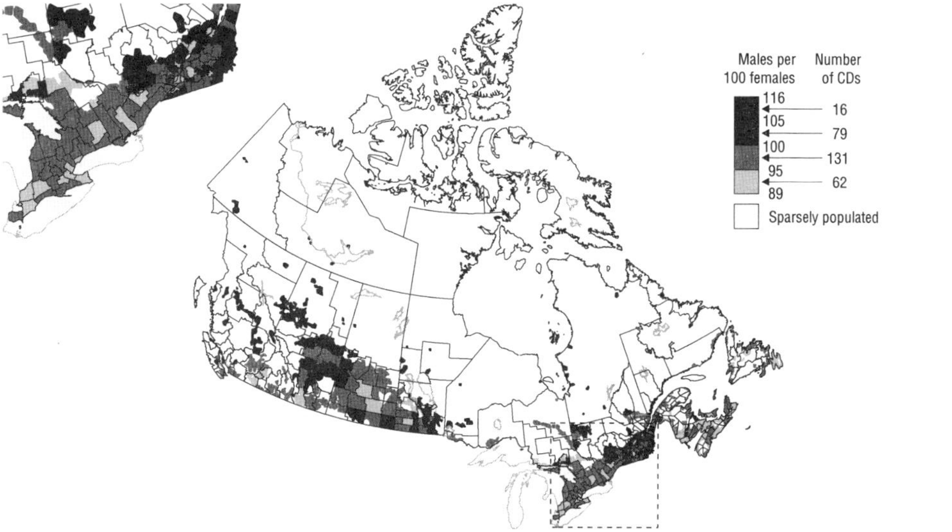

Source: Statistics Canada, Census of Population, 2006.

Map 15.2
Median 2005 earnings, by census division (CD)

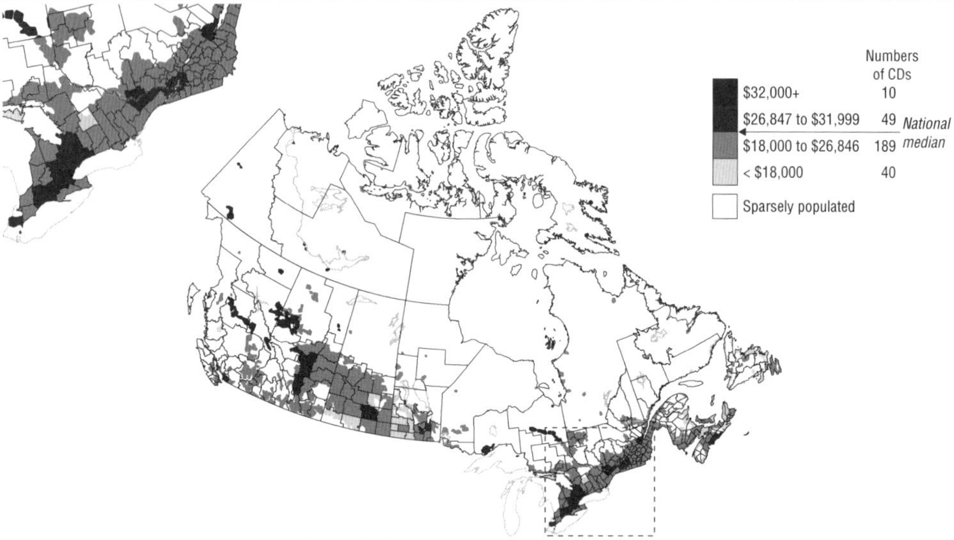

Source: Statistics Canada, Census of Population, 2006.

Map 15.3
Population earning $100,000 and over by census division (CD)

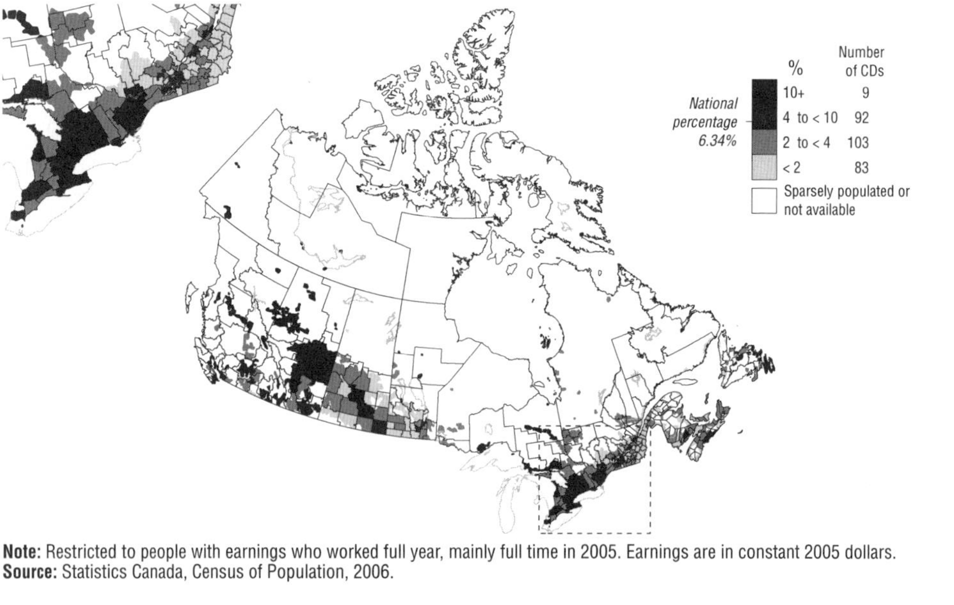

Note: Restricted to people with earnings who worked full year, mainly full time in 2005. Earnings are in constant 2005 dollars.
Source: Statistics Canada, Census of Population, 2006.

Map 15.4
Households containing couples with children aged 25 and younger at home, percentage change, 2001 to 2006, by census division (CD)

Source: Statistics Canada, Census of Population, 2006.

Table 15.1 Weather conditions, selected urban centres

	Extreme maximum temperature		Extreme minimum temperature		Rainfall[1]	Snowfall[1,2]	Precipitation[2,3]
	degrees Celsius	year	degrees Celsius	year	millimetres	centimetres	millimetres
St. John's	31.5	1983	-23.8	1986	1,191.0	322.3	1,513.7
Charlottetown	34.4	1944	-30.5	1982	880.4	311.9	1,173.3
Halifax	35.0	1995	-28.5	1993	1,238.9	230.5	1,452.2
Saint John	34.4	1976	-36.7	1948	1,147.9	256.9	1,390.3
Fredericton	37.2	1975	-37.2	1962	885.5	276.5	1,143.3
Québec	35.6	1953	-36.1	1962	923.8	315.9	1,230.3
Sherbrooke	34.0	2002	-41.2	2004	873.9	294.3	1,144.1
Trois-Rivières	36.1	1975	-41.1	1976	858.6	241.4	1,099.8
Montréal	35.6	1955	-37.2	1933	819.7	220.5	1,046.2
Ottawa	37.8	1944	-36.1	1943	732.0	235.7	943.5
Kingston	34.3	1983	-34.5	1981	794.6	181.0	968.4
Oshawa	36.5	1988	-30.5	1981	759.5	118.4	877.9
Toronto	38.3	1948	-31.3	1981	684.6	115.4	792.7
Hamilton	37.4	1988	-30.0	2004	764.8	161.8	910.1
St. Catharines	37.4	1988	-25.7	1979	745.7	136.6	873.6
London	38.2	1988	-31.7	1970	817.9	202.4	987.1
Windsor	40.2	1988	-29.1	1994	805.2	126.6	918.3
Greater Sudbury/ Grand Sudbury	38.3	1975	-39.3	1982	656.5	274.4	899.3
Thunder Bay	40.3	1983	-41.1	1951	559.0	187.6	711.6
Winnipeg	40.6	1949	-45.0	1966	415.6	110.6	513.7
Regina	43.3	1937	-50.0	1885	304.4	105.9	388.1
Saskatoon	40.6	1988	-50.0	1893	265.2	97.2	350.0
Calgary	36.1	1919	-45.0	1893	320.6	126.7	412.6
Edmonton	34.9	2002	-48.3	1938	365.7	123.5	476.9
Abbotsford–Mission	37.9	2007	-21.1	1950	1,507.5	63.5	1,573.2
Vancouver	33.3	1960	-17.8	1950	1,154.7	48.2	1,199.0
Victoria	36.1	1941	-15.6	1950	841.4	43.8	883.3
Whitehorse	34.4	1969	-52.2	1947	163.1	145.0	267.4
Yellowknife	32.5	1989	-51.2	1947	164.5	151.8	280.7
Iqaluit	26.1	2003	-45.6	1967	198.3	235.8	412.1

1. Annual average.
2. On average, one centimetre of snow equals one millimetre of rain.
3. Totals may not add up because of different densities of snow.
Source: Environment Canada, National Climate Data and Information Archives.

Table 15.2 Selected major sea islands, by region

	Area		Area
	square kilometres		square kilometres
Baffin Island	507,451	Coats	5,498
Queen Elizabeth Islands		Stefansson	4,463
Ellesmere	196,236	Mansel	3,180
Devon	55,247	Akimiski	3,001
Axel Heiberg	43,178	Richards	2,165
Melville	42,149	Air Force	1,720
Bathurst	16,042	Flaherty	1,585
Prince Patrick	15,848	Nottingham	1,372
Ellef Ringnes	11,295	Wales	1,137
Cornwallis	6,995	Rowley	1,090
Amund Ringnes	5,255	Resolution	1,015
Mackenzie King	5,048	**Pacific Coast Islands**	
Borden	2,794	Vancouver	31,285
Cornwall	2,358	Graham	6,361
Eglinton	1,541	Moresby	2,608
Graham	1,378	Princess Royal	2,251
Lougheed	1,308	Pitt	1,375
Byam Martin	1,150	**Quebec**	
Île Vanier	1,126	Anticosti	7,941
Cameron	1,059	**Prince Edward Island**	
Other Arctic Islands		Main Island	5,620
Victoria	217,291	**Newfoundland and Labrador**	
Banks	70,028	Newfoundland	108,860
Southampton	41,214	**Nova Scotia**	
Prince of Wales	33,339	Cape Breton	10,311
Somerset	24,786	**New Brunswick**	
King William	13,111	Île Lamèque	150
Bylot	11,067	Grand Manan	137
Prince Charles	9,521		

Note: A major island has a land area greater than 129 square kilometres.
Source: Natural Resources Canada, *Atlas of Canada*.

Table 15.3 Selected principal heights, by province and territory

	Elevation
	metres
Newfoundland and Labrador	
Torngat Mountains	
Mount Caubvick[1,2] (on N.L.–Que. boundary)	1,652
Torngarsoak Mountain	1,595
Cirque Mountain	1,568
Mount Erhart	1,539
Jens Haven	1,531
Innuit Mountain	1,509
Mount Cladonia	1,453
Mount Silene	1,448
Starshape Mountain	1,417
Mealy Mountains	
Unnamed peak (53°37' N, 58°33' W)	1,176
Kaumajet Mountains	
Bishops Mitre	1,113
Long Range Mountains	
Lewis Hills (48°50' N, 58°29' W)	814
Gros Morne	806
Prince Edward Island	
Queen's County (46°20' N, 63°25' W)[2]	142
Nova Scotia	
White Hill (Cape Breton Highlands) (46°42' N, 60°36' W)[2]	532
New Brunswick	
Mount Carleton[2]	817
Mount Edward	800
Mount Head	800
Quebec	
Monts Torngat	
Mont D'Iberville[1,2] (on N.L.–Que. boundary)	1,652
Mont Jacques-Rousseau	1,261
Korok Mountain (on N.L.–Que. boundary)	1,204
Appalachian Mountains	
Mont Jacques-Cartier	1,268
Mont de la Passe	1,242
Les Cones	1,196
Mont Gosford	1,192
Mont Richardson	1,185
Mont Albert	1,181
Quebec	
Mont Logan	1,151
Mont Xalibu	1,135
Mont Mégantic	1,105
Laurentian Mountains	
Mont Raoul-Blanchard	1,181
Mont Belle Fontaine	1,151
Mont de la Québécoise	1,120
Mont Tremblant	968
Mont Sainte-Anne	800
Mont Sir-Wilfrid	783
Monts Otish	
Mont Yapeitso	1,135
Collines Montérégiennes	
Mont Brome	554
Ontario	
Ishpatina Ridge[2]	693
Ogidaki Mountain	665
Batchawana Mountain	653
Tip Top Mountain	640
Niagara Escarpment (44°23' N, 80°14' W)	535
Manitoba	
Baldy Mountain[2]	832
Hart Mountain	823
Riding Mountain	610
Saskatchewan	
Cypress Hills[2] (49°33' N,109°59' W)	1,392
Wood Mountain	1,013
Pasquia Hills (53°55'N, 102°48'W)	828
Vermilion Hills	785
Alberta	
Rocky Mountains	
Mount Columbia[2] (on Alta.–B.C. boundary)	3,747
North Twin	3,733
Mount Alberta	3,620
Mount Assiniboine (on Alta.–B.C. boundary)	3,618
Mount Forbes	3,612
South Twin	3,581

1. Known as Mont D'Iberville in Quebec and as Mount Caubvick in Newfoundland and Labrador.
2. Highest point in province or territory.
3. Highest point in Canada.
Source: Natural Resources Canada, *Atlas of Canada.*

	Elevation
	metres
Alberta	
Mount Temple	3,547
Mount Brazeau	3,525
Snow Dome (on Alta.–B.C. boundary)	3,520
Mount Lyell (on Alta.–B.C. boundary)	3,504
Mount Athabasca	3,491
Mount King Edward (on Alta.–B.C. boundary)	3,490
Mount Kitchener	3,490
British Columbia	
St. Elias Mountains	
Fairweather Mountain[2] (on Alaska–B.C. boundary)	4,663
Mount Quincy Adams (on Alaska–B.C. boundary)	4,133
Mount Root (on Alaska–B.C. boundary)	3,901
Coast Mountains	
Mount Waddington	4,016
Mount Tiedemann	3,848
Combatant Mountain	3,756
Asperity	3,716
Serra Peaks	3,642
Monarch Mountain	3,459
Rocky Mountains	
Mount Robson	3,954
Mount Columbia (on Alta.–B.C. boundary)	3,747
Mount Clemenceau	3,642
Mount Assiniboine (on Alta.–B.C. boundary)	3,618
Mount Goodsir, North Tower	3,581
Mount Goodsir, South Tower	3,520
Snow Dome (on Alta.–B.C. boundary)	3,520
Mount Bryce	3,507
Selkirk Mountains	
Mount Sir Sandford	3,522
Cariboo Mountains	
Mount Sir Wilfrid Laurier	3,520
Purcell Mountains	
Mount Farnham	3,481
Monashee Mountains	
Torii Mountain	3,429

	Elevation
	metres
Yukon	
St. Elias Mountains	
Mount Logan[2,3]	5,959
Mount St. Elias (on Alaska–Yukon border)	5,489
Mount Lucania	5,226
King Peak	5,173
Mount Steele	5,067
Mount Wood	4,838
Mount Vancouver (on Alaska–Yukon border)	4,785
Mount MacAulay	4,663
Mount Slaggard	4,663
Mount Hubbard (on Alaska–Yukon border)	4,577
Northwest Territories	
Mackenzie Mountains	
Unnamed peak (61°52' N, 127°42' W)[2]	2,773
Mount Sir James MacBrien	2,762
Franklin Mountains	
Cap Mountain	1,577
Mount Clark	1,462
Pointed Mountain	1,405
Nahanni Butte	1,396
Melville Hills	
Unnamed peak (69°14' N, 121°32' W)	876
Banks Island	
Durham Heights	732
Victoria Island	
Unnamed peak (71°51' N, 112°36' W)	655
Nunavut	
Axel Heiberg Island	
Outlook Peak	2,210
Baffin Island	
Mount Odin	2,147
Unnamed peak (66°49' N, 65°20' W)	2,410
Qiajivik Mountain	1,963
Devon Island	
Summit of Devon Ice Cap	1,908
Ellesmere Island	
Barbeau Peak[2]	2,616

Table 15.4 Selected principal rivers and their tributaries

	Drainage area	Length
	square kilometres	kilometres
Flowing into the Pacific Ocean		
Yukon (International boundary to head of Nisutlin)	323,800	1,149
Porcupine	61,400	721
Stewart	51,000	644
Pelly	51,000	608
Teslin	35,500	393
White	38,000	265
Columbia (International boundary to head of Columbia Lake)	102,800	801
Kootenay	37,700	780
Kettle (to head of Holmes Lake)	4,700	336
Okanagan (to head of Okanagan Lake)	21,600	314
Fraser	232,300	1,370
Thompson (to head of North Thompson)	55,400	489
North Thompson	20,700	338
South Thompson (to head of Shuswap)	17,800	332
Nechako (to head of Eutsuk Lake)	47,100	462
Chilcotin	20,000	235
Stuart (to head of Driftwood)	16,200	415
Skeena	54,400	579
Stikine	49,800	539
Nass	21,100	380
Taku	27,500	250
Flowing into the Arctic Ocean		
Mackenzie (to head of Finlay)	1,805,200	4,241
Peace (to head of Finlay)	302,500	1,923
Smoky	51,300	492
Finlay	43,000	402
Athabasca	95,300	1,231
Pembina	12,900	547
Liard	277,100	1,115
South Nahanni	36,300	563
Fort Nelson (to head of Sikanni Chief)	55,900	517
Petitot	23,200	404
Hay	48,200	702
Peel (to head of Ogilvie)	73,600	684
Flowing into the Arctic Ocean		
Arctic Red	23,200	499
Slave (from Peace River to Great Slave Lake)	616,400	415
Fond du Lac (to outlet of Wollaston Lake)	66,800	277
Back (to outlet of Muskox Lake)	106,500	974
Coppermine	.	845
Anderson	.	692
Horton	.	618
Flowing into Hudson Bay, James Bay or Ungava Bay		
Nelson (to head of Bow)	892,300	2,575
Nelson (to outlet of Lake Winnipeg)	802,900	644
Saskatchewan (to head of Bow)	334,100	1,939
South Saskatchewan (to head of Bow)	144,300	1,392
Red Deer	45,100	724
Bow	26,200	587
Oldman	26,700	362
North Saskatchewan	122,800	1,287
Battle (to head of Pigeon Lake)	30,300	570
Red (to head of Sheyenne)	138,600	877
Assiniboine	160,600	1,070
Winnipeg (to head of Firesteel)	106,500	813
English	52,300	615
Fairford (to head of Manitoba Red Deer)	80,300	684
Churchill (to head of Churchill Lake)	281,300	1,609
Beaver (to outlet of Beaver Lake)	.	491
Thelon	142,400	904
Dubawnt	57,500	842
Kazan (to head of Ennadai Lake)	71,500	732
Moose (to head of Mattagami)	108,500	547
Abitibi (to head of Lac Loïs)	29,500	547
Mattagami (to head of Lake Minissinakwa)	37,000	443
Missinaibi	23,500	426

Source: Natural Resources Canada, *Atlas of Canada.*

	Drainage area	Length
	square kilometres	kilometres
Flowing into Hudson Bay, James Bay or Ungava Bay		
Albany (to head of Cat)	135,200	982
Severn (to head of Black Birch)	102,800	982
La Grande Rivière	97,600	893
Koksoak (to head of Caniapiscau)	133,400	874
Nottaway (via Bell to head of Mégiscane)	65,800	776
Rupert (to head of Témiscamie)	43,400	763
Eastmain	46,400	756
Attawapiskat (to head of Bow Lake)	50,500	748
Grande rivière de la Baleine	42,700	724
George	41,700	565
Harricana/Harricanaw	29,300	533
Hayes	108,000	483
Rivière aux Feuilles	42,500	480
Winisk	67,300	475
Broadback	20,800	450
Rivière à la Baleine	31,900	428
de Povungnituk	28,500	389
Innuksuac	11,400	385
Petite rivière de la Baleine	15,900	380
Arnaud	49,500	377
Nastapoca	13,400	360
Kogaluc	11,600	304
Flowing into the Gulf of Mexico		
Milk	21,600	1,005
Frenchman	5,500	341
Battle Creek	2,600	203
Lodge Creek	2,100	126

	Drainage area	Length
	square kilometres	kilometres
Flowing into the Atlantic Ocean		
St. Lawrence		
St. Lawrence (to head of St. Louis, Minnesota)	839,200	3,058
Nipigon (to head of Ombabika)	25,400	209
Spanish	14,000	338
Mississagi	9,250	266
Trent (to head of Irondale)	12,400	402
Ottawa	146,300	1,271
Gatineau	23,700	386
Rivière du Lièvre	10,400	330
Saguenay (to head of Péribonka)	88,000	698
Péribonka	28,200	451
Mistassini	21,900	298
Ashuapmushuan	15,700	266
Saint-Maurice	43,300	563
Manicouagan (to head of Mouchalagane)	45,800	560
Rivières aux Outardes	19,000	499
Betsiamites (to head of Manouanis)	18,700	444
Moisie	19,200	410
Richelieu (to outlet of Lake Champlain)	3,800	171
Saint John	35,500	673
Churchill (to head of Ashuanipi)	79,800	856
Little Mecatina	19,600	547
Romaine	14,350	496
Natashquan	16,100	410
St. Augustin	9,900	233

Table 15.5 Selected principal lakes, elevation and area, by province and territory

	Elevation	Area		Elevation	Area
	metres	square kilometres		metres	square kilometres
Newfoundland and Labrador			**Ontario**		
Smallwood Reservoir	471	6,527	Lake Simcoe	219	744
Lake Melville	tidal[1]	3,069	Rainy Lake	338	741
Nova Scotia			Big Trout Lake	213	661
Bras d'Or Lake	tidal[1]	1,099	Lake St. Clair	175	490[2]
Quebec			**Manitoba**		
Lac Mistassini	372	2,335	Lake Winnipeg	217	24,387
Réservoir Gouin	404	1,570	Lake Winnipegosis	254	5,374
Lac à l'Eau-Claire	241	1,383	Lake Manitoba	248	4,624
Lac Bienville	426	1,249	Southern Indian Lake	254	2,247
Lac Saint-Jean	98	1,003	Cedar Lake	253	1,353
Réservoir Pipmuacan	396	978	Island Lake	227	1,223
Lac Minto	168	761	Gods Lake	178	1,151
Réservoir Cabonga	361	677	Cross Lake	207	755
Ontario			Playgreen Lake	217	657
Lake Superior	184	28,700[2]	**Saskatchewan**		
Lake Huron	177	36,000[2]	Lake Athabasca	213	7,935
Lake Erie	174	12,800[2]	Reindeer Lake	337	6,650
Lake Ontario	75	10,000[2]	Wollaston Lake	398	2,681
Lake Nipigon	260	4,848	Cree Lake	487	1,434
Lake of the Woods	323	3,150	Lac La Ronge	364	1,413
Lac Seul	357	1,657	Peter Pond Lake	421	778
Lake Abitibi	265	931	Doré Lake	459	640
Lake Nipissing	196	832			

Notes: A principal lake has an area larger than 400 square kilometres.
New Brunswick and Prince Edward Island have no principal lakes.
Area of lakes includes islands.
Lakes spanning provincial or territorial boundaries are listed under the province or territory containing the larger portion.
1. Daily, monthly and seasonal variations in the time and heights of tides.
2. Area of lake found in Canada.
Sources: Natural Resources Canada, *Atlas of Canada,* and Environment Canada, Inland Waters Branch, 1973, *Inventory of Freshwater Lakes,* Ottawa.

	Elevation	Area
	metres	square kilometres
Alberta		
Lake Claire	213	1,436
Lesser Slave Lake	577	1,168
Bistcho Lake	552	426
British Columbia		
Williston Lake	671	1,761
Atlin Lake	668	775
Babine Lake	711	495
Yukon		
Kluane Lake	781	409
Northwest Territories		
Great Bear Lake	156	31,328
Great Slave Lake	156	28,568
Lac la Martre	265	1,776
Kasba Lake	336	1,341
MacKay Lake	431	1,061
Hottah Lake	180	918
Aylmer Lake	375	847
Nonacho Lake	354	784
Clinton-Colden Lake	375	737
Selwyn Lake	398	717
Point Lake	375	701
Northwest Territories		
Wholdaia Lake	364	678
Lac de Gras	396	633
Buffalo Lake	265	612
Nunavut		
Nettilling Lake	30	5,542
Dubawnt Lake	236	3,833
Amadjuak Lake	113	3,115
Nueltin Lake	278	2,279
Baker Lake	2	1,887
Yathkyed Lake	140	1,449
Aberdeen Lake	80	1,100
Napaktulik Lake	381	1,080
Garry Lake	148	976
Contwoyto Lake	564	957
Ennadai Lake	311	681
Tulemalu Lake	279	668
Kamilukuak Lake	266	638
Kaminak Lake	53	600

Table 15.6 Land and freshwater area, Canada and selected countries

	Area	Land	Fresh water
		square kilometres	
Russia	17,075,200	16,995,800	79,400
Canada	9,984,670	9,093,507	891,163
United States	9,826,630	9,161,923	664,707
China	9,596,960	9,326,410	270,550
Brazil	8,511,965	8,456,510	55,455
Australia	7,686,850	7,617,930	68,920
India	3,287,590	2,973,190	314,400
Argentina	2,766,890	2,736,690	30,200
Kazakhstan	2,717,300	2,669,800	47,500
Sudan	2,505,810	2,376,000	129,810
Algeria	2,381,740	2,381,740	0
Democratic Republic of the Congo	2,345,410	2,267,600	77,810
Saudi Arabia	2,149,690	2,149,690	0
Mexico	1,972,550	1,923,040	49,510
Indonesia	1,919,440	1,826,440	93,000
Libya	1,759,540	1,759,540	0
Iran	1,648,000	1,636,000	12,000
Mongolia	1,564,116	1,564,116	0
Peru	1,285,220	1,280,000	5,220
Chad	1,284,000	1,259,200	24,800

Source: Central Intelligence Agency, *The World Factbook*, accessed June 2009, Washington D.C.

Table 15.7 Land and freshwater area, by province and territory

	Area	Area	Land	Fresh water
	%		square kilometres	
Canada	**100.0**	**9,984,670**	**9,093,507**	**891,163**
Newfoundland and Labrador	4.1	405,212	373,872	31,340
Prince Edward Island	0.1	5,660	5,660	.
Nova Scotia	0.6	55,284	53,338	1,946
New Brunswick	0.7	72,908	71,450	1,458
Quebec	15.4	1,542,056	1,365,128	176,928
Ontario	10.8	1,076,395	917,741	158,654
Manitoba	6.5	647,797	553,556	94,241
Saskatchewan	6.5	651,036	591,670	59,366
Alberta	6.6	661,848	642,317	19,531
British Columbia	9.5	944,735	925,186	19,549
Yukon	4.8	482,443	474,391	8,052
Northwest Territories	13.5	1,346,106	1,183,085	163,021
Nunavut	21.0	2,093,190	1,936,113	157,077

Source: Natural Resources Canada, *Atlas of Canada*.

Government

The three levels of government provide Canadians with services that cannot be easily offered by private companies. The federal government is responsible for national defence and international diplomacy, the provinces and territories ensure that Canadians have access to health care and education, and local governments keep our streets clean and our communities safe.

The *Constitution Act* spells out the responsibilities of each level of government, but their accounting books show where their priorities lie and where they spend tax dollars. In 2009, the three levels of government, plus the Canada and Quebec pension plans, spent a total of $631.3 billion providing services.

All told, the federal, provincial, territorial and local governments, as well as the Canada and Quebec pension plans, closed out fiscal 2008/2009—the fiscal year ended March 31, 2009—with a surplus of $2.4 billion. Revenues for all levels of government combined were down 2.1% from the previous fiscal year; spending rose 2.5%.

Where the money goes

Provincial, territorial and local governments spent $12,517 for every man, woman and child in the country in 2009, but these averages vary widely among the provinces and territories. The costs of providing services in the North are higher; Nunavut spent $44,476 per capita. Among the provinces, per capita spending ranged from $11,372 in Ontario to $14,032 in Saskatchewan.

Social services, health and education are perennially governments' largest expenditures. In 2009, services such as social security payments, family allowances and income maintenance programs cost $190.3 billion. Health services spending totalled $121.6 billion,

Chart 16.1
Selected consolidated government expenditures, 2009

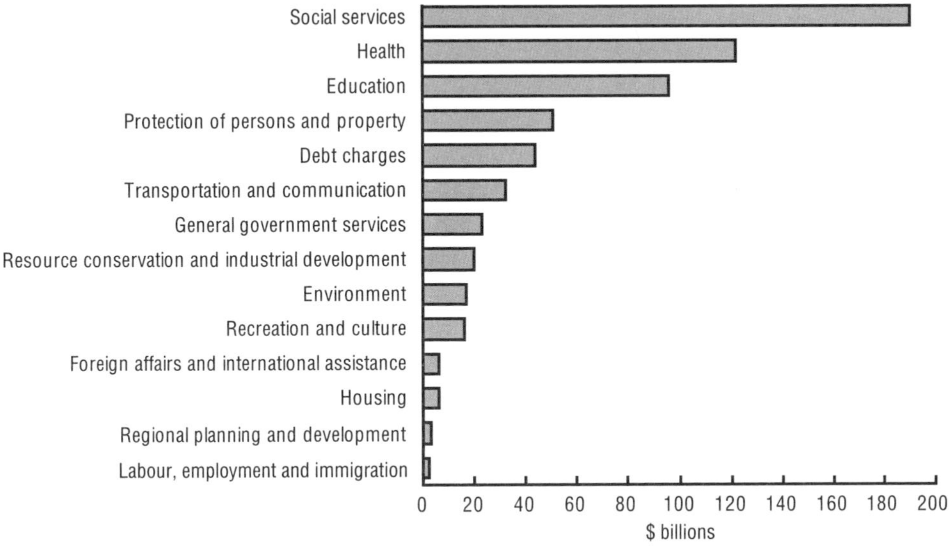

Source: Statistics Canada, CANSIM table 385-0001.

and education spending amounted to $95.7 billion. These three areas accounted for about 65% of total government spending; combined with debt charges, they accounted for nearly three-quarters (71%) of all spending.

From 2005 to 2009, government spending on health grew 29%; spending on social services, 21%; and spending on education, 24%.

Spending on foreign affairs and international assistance totalled $6.5 billion in 2009, up 4.8% from the previous year.

Debt charges have been generally declining since 2001. In 2009, they accounted for 6.9% of spending, compared with 9.3% in 2004.

Where the revenue comes from

Government spending has grown 25.8% since 2004, while consolidated government revenues have kept pace, growing 25.4%.

Table 16.a
Public sector employment, wages and salaries

	2007	2008
	number	
Employees[1]	3,382,323	3,490,747
	$ thousands	
Wages and salaries[2]	161,617,171	169,850,124

1. Annual average.
2. Annual total.
Source: Statistics Canada, CANSIM table 183-0002.

Income tax revenues grew 31.8% from 2004 to 2009; consumption taxes, 8.3%; and contributions to social security plans, 18.4%. Combined, these three revenue sources accounted for almost 70% of total government revenues in 2009.

Before 2009, the government sector posted combined surpluses of more than $20 billion for four consecutive years. The government sector has not posted a deficit since 1999.

Chart 16.2
Consolidated federal, provincial, territorial and local government revenue, 2009

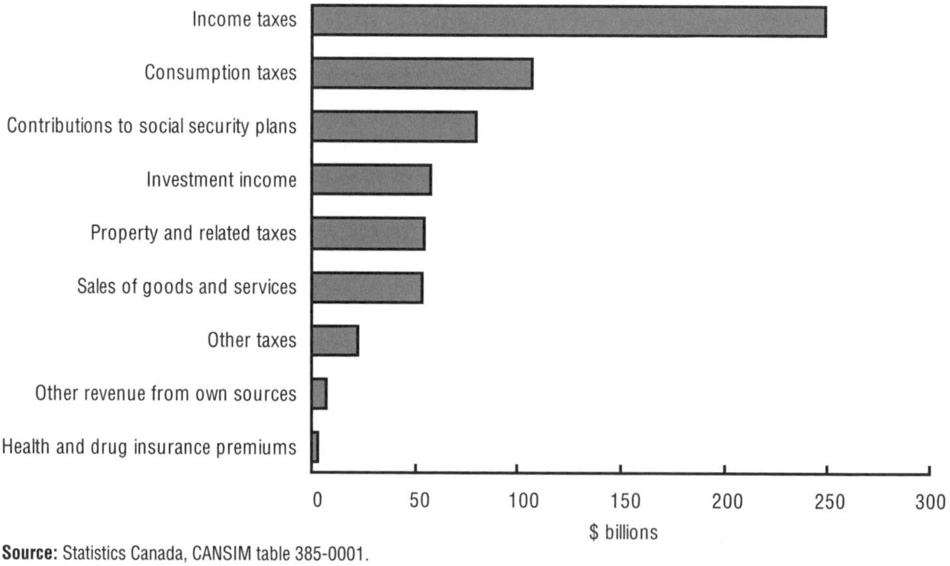

Source: Statistics Canada, CANSIM table 385-0001.

Spending outstrips revenue

Local general governments' revenue has been growing in recent years, but it has been outpaced by rising spending.

In the year ending December 31, 2008, Canada's local general governments collectively posted a $552-million deficit, equal to 0.7% of their total spending. 'Local general governments' comprise municipalities and other local entities but exclude school boards.

From 2003 to 2008, revenue grew by 42.4%; however, spending also advanced by 38.8%.

Property and related taxes were the main source of that revenue growth, advancing $9.1 billion. Transfers from provincial and federal governments increased $7.2 billion. Revenue from the sale of goods and services, mainly water and sewer services, was up $4.3 billion.

However, spending on capital (buildings and infrastructure) climbed from $11.3 billion in 2003 to $19.6 billion in 2008, as local general governments have been busy renewing infrastructure.

Chart 16.3
Local general government revenue and expenditures

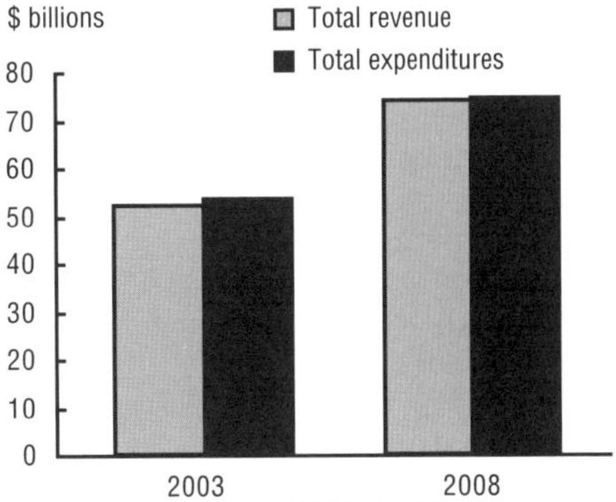

Source: Statistics Canada, CANSIM table 385-0024.

Federal public servants

The composition of federal workers is shifting toward knowledge-based jobs and in favour of women.

Knowledge-based workers—those in scientific and professional, computer systems, program and administrative, executive, administrative and foreign service categories—accounted for 58% of federal workers in the core public administration (CPA) in 2006, compared with 41% in 1995. Two out of three knowledge-based workers are in the scientific and professional categories or the program and administrative categories.

The CPA excludes the Canadian Forces, the RCMP, and agencies such as the Canada Revenue Agency. About half of federal government workers are in the CPA.

Proportionally, women eclipsed men in the CPA in 1999; women now comprise 54% of workers, while men make up 46%. In the entire labour force, men make up 53% of employed workers, and women, 47%—though the gap has narrowed gradually since 1995.

Chart 16.4
Core public administration workers, by sex

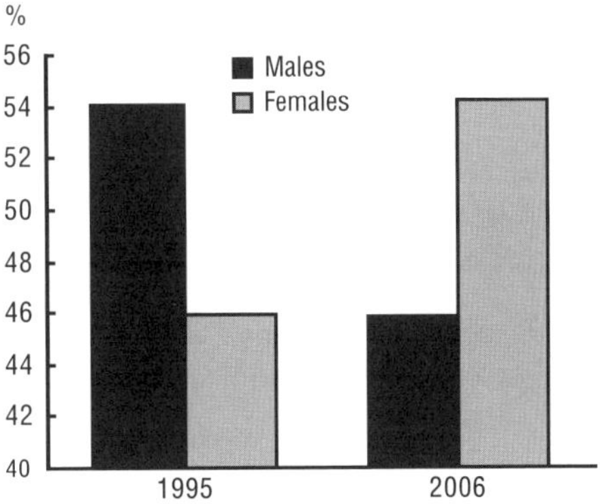

Source: Statistics Canada, Catalogue no. 11-621-X.

Table 16.1 Consolidated government revenue and expenditures, 1996 to 2009

	1996	1997	1998	1999	2000
			$ millions		
Revenue	**352,416**	**366,764**	**390,484**	**404,976**	**436,558**
Income taxes	134,343	143,578	160,204	164,593	178,423
Personal income taxes	108,649	113,750	123,029	127,763	138,443
Corporation income taxes	23,604	26,758	33,897	33,621	36,155
Mining and logging taxes	479	223	304	307	326
Taxes on payments to non-residents	1,611	2,847	2,974	2,901	3,499
Consumption taxes	66,951	69,372	73,065	76,697	80,088
General sales tax	40,320	42,222	44,620	47,566	51,323
Alcoholic beverages and tobacco taxes	5,459	5,581	5,801	6,235	6,190
Amusement tax	351	411	485	627	630
Gasoline and motive fuel taxes	10,710	10,873	11,227	11,602	11,789
Custom duties	2,971	2,677	2,766	2,359	2,104
Liquor profits	2,658	2,519	2,727	2,807	2,747
Remitted gaming profits	3,200	3,517	3,730	4,175	4,183
Other consumption taxes	1,282	1,573	1,709	1,325	1,121
Property and related taxes	35,846	36,935	38,546	38,557	40,255
Other taxes	13,039	13,080	13,333	14,054	14,334
Health and drug insurance premiums	1,579	1,648	1,700	2,018	1,950
Contributions to social security plans	43,272	45,212	45,874	49,552	51,946
Sales of goods and services	25,744	27,763	27,409	29,097	32,202
Investment income	26,285	26,153	26,377	24,560	29,588
Other revenue from own sources	5,357	3,022	3,976	5,849	7,773
Expenditures	**397,616**	**389,359**	**391,673**	**407,343**	**422,402**
General government services	12,157	12,255	12,496	13,238	13,752
Protection of persons and property	29,330	28,501	27,984	29,366	31,749
Transportation and communication	19,680	17,422	17,062	17,823	18,117
Health	53,105	53,427	56,762	59,378	64,317
Social services	118,048	120,176	122,256	126,240	129,704
Education	55,602	54,269	55,390	57,970	60,457
Resource conservation and industrial development	15,029	13,072	11,670	12,992	14,353
Environment	8,666	8,381	8,703	8,566	8,672
Recreation and culture	9,189	9,010	8,751	9,277	9,909
Labour, employment and immigration	2,805	2,237	2,930	2,996	2,951
Housing	3,948	4,053	3,733	3,816	3,519
Foreign affairs and international assistance	3,954	3,761	3,676	4,035	4,291
Regional planning and development	1,558	1,527	1,562	1,688	1,762
Research establishments	1,933	1,623	1,522	1,724	1,951
Debt charges	62,056	59,114	56,011	56,900	56,397
Other expenditures	556	530	1,166	1,334	501
Surplus/deficit (-)	**-45,200**	**-22,595**	**-1,189**	**-2,367**	**14,156**

Note: Data for the federal, provincial and territorial governments are as of March 31 and the local government data are as of December 31.
Source: Statistics Canada, CANSIM table 385-0001.

2001	2002	2003	2004	2005	2006	2007	2008	2009
				$ millions				
475,137	**468,149**	**481,412**	**505,434**	**538,265**	**573,572**	**604,592**	**647,552**	**633,672**
191,144	188,011	178,173	188,619	207,415	225,158	245,867	269,467	248,655
143,116	144,746	139,836	145,324	155,136	167,276	179,869	193,525	189,222
43,262	38,819	33,608	38,925	46,928	50,966	58,131	67,642	50,277
454	297	352	215	530	757	970	1,192	1,747
4,312	4,150	4,377	4,156	4,822	6,159	6,896	7,109	7,410
87,870	88,987	96,431	98,918	104,495	107,857	105,809	111,684	107,150
55,523	56,076	60,210	62,169	66,352	69,461	67,419	72,094	67,001
6,203	7,201	8,800	9,260	9,673	9,024	8,595	8,634	8,565
598	592	592	552	561	573	531	520	525
11,745	11,743	12,337	12,760	12,700	13,016	13,025	13,462	13,528
2,807	3,018	3,189	2,804	3,041	3,429	3,651	3,803	4,055
3,475	3,144	3,334	3,544	3,703	3,975	4,252	4,478	4,594
6,315	5,926	6,095	5,969	6,395	6,438	6,375	6,546	6,697
1,205	1,288	1,873	1,860	2,070	1,941	1,961	2,148	2,185
41,063	41,730	42,529	44,244	46,721	49,509	51,277	53,882	54,862
15,157	14,940	16,083	17,037	18,018	18,917	20,489	21,129	21,807
2,178	2,282	3,000	3,132	3,206	3,258	3,268	3,457	3,390
57,530	59,953	63,489	67,568	69,039	71,532	74,697	77,740	80,010
34,415	34,594	37,299	38,704	40,822	42,966	44,913	49,685	53,168
38,836	32,269	34,838	37,267	40,525	47,544	50,122	52,436	57,793
6,943	5,381	9,570	9,946	8,022	6,830	8,151	8,070	6,836
446,505	**461,306**	**480,915**	**501,884**	**516,576**	**547,465**	**578,174**	**616,090**	**631,251**
15,968	15,765	17,520	18,633	18,792	20,074	20,857	21,505	22,822
32,978	35,218	37,193	39,154	41,096	43,299	46,396	50,689	50,790
17,979	18,628	19,148	20,258	21,172	24,838	26,280	29,966	32,197
70,465	76,935	83,315	89,479	94,497	99,531	107,497	114,245	121,577
135,793	141,751	145,398	150,827	156,762	164,568	174,290	187,734	190,276
63,522	66,559	70,533	74,246	77,140	84,760	87,455	92,722	95,732
15,713	16,329	18,784	19,430	18,652	19,760	21,078	21,360	19,975
9,222	9,853	10,259	11,391	11,903	13,158	14,420	15,516	16,933
10,871	11,347	11,690	13,143	13,476	14,268	15,008	15,809	16,306
2,882	3,019	3,395	3,440	2,328	2,480	2,619	2,917	2,395
3,723	3,420	3,624	3,833	3,880	4,527	4,942	5,544	6,120
4,477	4,562	5,128	4,611	5,556	5,585	6,500	6,211	6,508
1,847	2,099	2,111	2,133	2,057	2,235	2,338	2,524	2,775
1,419	1,767	1,881	1,890	1,823	1,859	2,023	2,332	2,268
57,790	52,075	49,475	46,917	45,506	44,784	45,578	45,715	43,634
1,857	1,979	1,463	2,499	1,935	1,738	894	1,303	945
28,632	**6,842**	**496**	**3,550**	**21,689**	**26,107**	**26,418**	**31,461**	**2,421**

Table 16.2 Government transfer payments to individuals, 1992 to 2006

	1992	1993	1994	1995	1996	1997
	$ millions					
All levels of government	**93,077**	**98,323**	**98,495**	**98,512**	**98,865**	**100,431**
Federal government	49,317	51,600	50,166	48,879	48,752	49,234
Family and youth allowances	2,870	37	37	38	39	43
Child Tax Benefit or Credit	658	5,252	5,259	5,214	5,228	5,310
Pensions (First and Second World Wars)	856	848	864	909	914	921
War veterans' allowances	443	441	417	397	383	387
Grants to Aboriginal people	2,573	2,886	3,027	3,566	3,564	3,730
Goods and Services Tax Credit	2,557	2,655	2,833	2,810	2,866	2,905
Employment Insurance benefits	18,648	17,591	15,012	12,889	11,859	10,874
Old Age Security payments	18,776	19,479	20,170	20,622	21,221	21,798
Scholarships and research grants	726	727	780	687	686	700
Miscellaneous and other transfers	1,210	1,684	1,767	1,747	1,992	2,566
Provincial governments	23,651	24,603	24,815	25,406	25,576	25,945
Social assistance, income maintenance	9,371	9,660	9,863	9,854	9,258	8,723
Social assistance, other	1,213	2,239	2,316	2,308	2,371	2,408
Workers' compensation benefits	4,091	3,925	3,811	3,992	4,198	4,067
Grants to benevolent associations	6,848	5,506	5,577	5,962	6,123	6,714
Miscellaneous transfers	2,128	3,273	3,248	3,290	3,626	4,033
Local governments	3,410	3,899	3,949	3,738	2,950	2,640
Canada Pension Plan	12,808	14,058	15,132	15,777	16,559	17,327
Quebec Pension Plan	3,891	4,163	4,433	4,712	5,028	5,285

Source: Statistics Canada, CANSIM table 384-0009.

Table 16.3 Federal government debt, 1994 to 2008

	1994	1995	1996	1997	1998
	$ millions				
Gross federal debt	**557,604**	**595,877**	**634,939**	**651,124**	**645,725**
Unmatured debt	414,942	441,991	470,581	477,940	468,024
Marketable bonds	208,464	233,621	262,279	295,022	309,256
Treasury bills	166,000	164,450	166,100	135,400	112,300
Notes and loans	5,649	9,046	7,296	10,557	12,533
Canada Savings Bonds	31,331	31,386	31,428	33,493	30,479
Bonds issued to the Canada Pension Plan	3,498	3,488	3,478	3,468	3,456
Superannuation accounts	94,097	101,033	107,882	114,205	117,456
Dominion notes and coins in circulation	2,464	2,570	2,805	3,243	3,346
Other liabilities	46,101	50,283	53,671	55,736	56,899
Unmatured debt payable in foreign currencies	**10,668**	**16,921**	**16,809**	**23,016**	**27,183**
Financial assets	**44,385**	**45,192**	**56,221**	**62,722**	**64,144**
Net federal debt[1]	**513,219**	**550,685**	**578,718**	**588,402**	**581,581**

Note: Fiscal year ending March 31.
1. Net federal debt equals gross federal debt minus financial assets.
Source: Statistics Canada, CANSIM table 385-0010.

1998	1999	2000	2001	2002	2003	2004	2005	2006
				$ millions				
104,558	**106,006**	**110,487**	**117,633**	**121,047**	**124,775**	**130,153**	**135,897**	**145,028**
50,739	51,575	53,479	57,965	60,857	62,949	65,603	67,823	70,178
58	84	99	116	133	140	157	165	187
5,600	5,939	6,577	7,379	7,824	8,051	8,547	9,174	9,470
918	910	973	1,196	1,398	1,463	1,530	1,584	1,693
387	414	404	267	212	223	266	289	326
4,447	4,271	4,511	4,448	4,800	4,951	5,254	5,717	5,748
2,924	2,943	2,974	3,099	3,140	3,264	3,346	3,472	3,566
10,713	10,150	9,615	11,361	12,837	13,361	13,269	12,937	12,498
22,398	22,907	23,790	24,789	25,747	26,931	27,992	29,085	30,468
519	519	531	560	585	612	734	789	858
2,775	3,438	4,005	4,750	4,181	3,953	4,508	4,611	4,189
26,717	27,170	28,574	29,662	29,781	30,066	30,981	33,141	38,042
8,050	7,048	6,538	6,547	6,603	6,641	6,788	6,918	7,050
2,241	2,546	2,906	2,966	2,936	3,061	3,167	3,351	3,475
3,886	4,073	4,434	4,840	5,150	5,036	5,083	5,228	5,477
7,196	7,322	7,953	8,406	8,500	8,667	9,011	9,629	10,166
5,344	6,181	6,743	6,903	6,592	6,661	6,932	8,015	11,069
3,523	2,990	3,248	3,641	2,637	2,747	2,940	2,912	3,147
18,054	18,540	19,183	20,023	21,076	21,986	23,129	24,225	25,417
5,525	5,731	6,003	6,342	6,696	7,027	7,500	7,796	8,244

1999	2000	2001	2002	2003	2004	2005	2006	2007	2008
				$ millions					
648,389	**648,212**	**644,900**	**640,526**	**629,638**	**628,830**	**626,217**	**619,701**	**618,765**	**594,390**
461,004	457,331	447,741	444,058	441,366	437,946	432,996	428,354	419,647	394,734
315,421	315,854	316,651	314,685	303,689	292,145	276,676	269,577	264,664	259,998
96,950	99,850	88,700	94,201	104,600	113,400	127,200	131,600	134,100	117,000
16,353	11,302	12,570	7,765	7,124	7,720	6,705	6,740	3,966	3,626
28,217	26,899	26,416	24,021	22,584	21,330	19,080	17,342	15,175	13,068
4,063	3,426	3,404	3,386	3,369	3,351	3,335	3,095	1,742	1,042
122,407	128,346	129,185	126,921	125,708	127,560	129,579	131,062	134,726	137,371
3,428	3,601	3,763	3,914	4,122	4,193	4,310	4,533	4,750	4,925
61,550	58,934	64,211	65,633	58,442	59,131	59,332	55,752	59,642	57,360
36,000	**32,589**	**33,664**	**27,547**	**21,603**	**20,827**	**16,543**	**14,333**	**10,617**	**9,716**
73,921	**86,479**	**99,600**	**105,836**	**103,146**	**105,182**	**102,873**	**105,602**	**110,643**	**103,978**
574,468	**561,733**	**545,300**	**534,690**	**526,492**	**523,648**	**523,344**	**514,099**	**508,122**	**490,412**

Table 16.4 Local general government revenue and expenditures, current and capital accounts, 1994 to 2008

	1994	1995	1996	1997	1998	1999
			$ millions			
Revenue	**39,289.9**	**41,133.8**	**39,340.6**	**39,830.4**	**44,329.5**	**46,681.0**
Own-source revenue	29,310.9	30,582.4	30,515.4	31,612.1	35,448.0	37,514.5
Property and related taxes	19,055.6	19,158.7	19,545.3	20,156.4	23,202.2	24,166.1
Consumption taxes	50.1	51.1	53.8	55.0	57.7	77.8
Other taxes	374.6	368.8	388.5	440.0	457.8	511.1
Sales of goods and services	7,399.0	7,887.5	7,943.7	8,497.3	9,131.2	10,006.4
Investment income	1,988.4	2,691.7	2,153.6	2,017.8	2,108.5	2,206.7
Other revenue from own sources	443.2	424.6	430.7	445.6	490.6	546.4
Transfers, general and specific	9,979.0	10,551.3	8,825.1	8,218.4	8,881.5	9,166.6
General-purpose transfers	1,405.9	1,358.4	1,521.0	1,238.9	1,424.9	1,183.5
Specific-purpose transfers	8,573.1	9,193.0	7,304.2	6,979.5	7,456.6	7,983.0
Expenditures	**39,830.8**	**41,422.3**	**39,531.9**	**40,005.7**	**42,247.8**	**43,396.3**
General government services	3,759.4	4,006.6	3,877.0	4,014.0	4,237.6	4,711.6
Protection of persons and property	5,850.0	6,049.6	6,113.3	6,195.1	6,767.3	6,819.1
Transportation and communication	7,971.0	8,415.2	7,936.9	8,390.9	8,492.8	8,822.5
Health	760.1	812.0	723.2	674.4	860.3	763.4
Social services	5,396.9	5,186.3	4,263.1	4,213.6	5,171.3	4,983.0
Education	149.7	148.4	148.3	182.9	183.8	176.4
Resource conservation and industrial development	812.6	808.1	720.6	796.4	813.5	912.0
Environment	5,957.4	6,419.3	6,299.7	6,442.3	6,250.8	6,388.1
Recreation and culture	4,474.5	4,821.4	4,846.1	4,649.9	4,741.2	5,003.8
Housing	634.7	575.6	550.9	558.5	1,098.6	1,142.9
Regional planning and development	624.7	693.6	623.9	648.8	696.5	742.1
Debt charges	3,197.4	3,219.3	3,109.2	2,908.2	2,803.8	2,668.0
Other expenditures	242.5	267.0	319.6	330.7	130.4	263.4
Surplus/deficit (-)	**-541.0**	**-288.6**	**-191.3**	**-175.3**	**2,081.7**	**3,284.8**

Notes: Year ending December 31.
Local general governments comprise municipalities and other local entities, but exclude school boards.
Source: Statistics Canada, CANSIM table 385-0024.

2000	2001	2002	2003	2004	2005	2006	2007	2008
				$ millions				
45,707.5	**47,914.3**	**49,529.7**	**51,784.5**	**55,296.0**	**60,632.4**	**65,021.8**	**69,992.0**	**73,758.7**
38,470.1	40,344.6	41,427.2	43,191.6	45,996.6	48,895.3	51,874.9	55,983.1	57,932.9
24,347.7	25,216.0	26,066.1	27,466.9	29,153.7	31,120.7	32,765.7	35,001.1	36,519.4
83.5	91.4	96.4	97.6	98.9	103.7	110.0	113.3	116.3
513.1	555.7	619.7	631.3	716.7	773.2	817.5	911.0	939.6
10,504.0	11,217.1	11,641.5	11,720.7	12,432.8	13,301.0	14,350.8	15,764.8	16,029.3
2,363.1	2,535.1	2,261.0	2,495.9	2,777.3	2,741.8	2,888.8	3,117.4	3,220.2
658.9	729.3	742.6	779.2	817.1	855.0	942.1	1,075.6	1,108.0
7,237.4	7,569.6	8,102.5	8,592.8	9,299.4	11,737.1	13,146.9	14,008.9	15,825.9
1,165.2	1,335.7	1,474.2	1,545.6	1,657.2	1,993.8	2,336.0	2,207.5	2,476.8
6,072.2	6,234.0	6,628.3	7,047.2	7,642.2	9,743.3	10,811.0	11,801.4	13,349.1
44,911.6	**46,724.4**	**48,669.3**	**53,546.0**	**55,664.3**	**60,604.7**	**64,438.4**	**69,305.8**	**74,310.5**
3,836.9	4,359.6	5,165.1	5,853.6	5,854.1	6,244.9	6,480.1	6,592.6	7,194.2
7,194.1	7,707.3	8,096.5	8,981.8	9,232.6	9,867.6	10,392.4	11,334.5	12,124.2
8,918.1	9,094.3	9,245.7	10,186.9	10,799.3	11,794.1	12,811.5	14,426.5	15,843.3
914.9	1,142.8	1,248.7	1,342.1	1,471.7	1,656.5	1,720.5	1,802.4	1,927.0
5,532.1	5,187.9	5,285.6	5,547.7	5,777.4	6,121.0	6,316.1	6,482.2	6,684.1
190.7	223.9	202.4	206.7	210.0	230.8	230.5	236.4	239.6
940.1	970.9	937.8	1,094.2	1,155.4	1,289.2	1,387.6	1,443.5	1,526.2
6,797.0	7,168.3	7,432.8	8,591.6	9,012.2	10,254.5	11,132.3	12,020.8	12,826.6
5,538.0	5,846.7	5,751.2	6,546.5	6,774.7	7,539.0	7,914.7	8,670.2	9,188.8
1,481.7	1,721.9	1,901.0	1,950.6	2,009.4	2,199.0	2,390.7	2,498.9	2,787.5
780.7	859.5	903.4	944.3	1,013.0	1,089.6	1,234.6	1,325.2	1,381.8
2,448.3	2,328.3	2,291.3	2,222.0	2,243.8	2,212.6	2,314.4	2,367.1	2,438.8
339.0	113.0	207.8	78.0	110.7	105.8	112.9	105.5	148.3
795.8	**1,189.9**	**860.3**	**-1,761.5**	**-368.3**	**27.7**	**583.5**	**686.2**	**-551.8**

Table 16.5 Public sector employment, wages and salaries, 2004 to 2008

	2004	2005	2006	2007	2008
			number		
Employment[1]	**3,193,390**	**3,241,011**	**3,310,214**	**3,382,323**	**3,490,747**
Government	2,906,402	2,954,785	3,021,726	3,088,736	3,180,501
Federal general government[2]	366,733	370,463	386,765	387,656	400,732
Provincial and territorial general government	330,215	340,051	344,127	350,898	358,644
Health and social service institutions, provincial and territorial	745,542	749,124	764,568	783,142	800,200
Universities, colleges, vocational and trade institutions, provincial and territorial	334,440	338,228	347,527	358,138	365,137
Local general government	498,997	516,842	529,846	548,298	581,221
Local school boards	630,475	640,077	648,892	660,603	674,568
Government business enterprises	286,987	286,227	288,489	293,587	310,246
Federal government business enterprises	94,634	95,436	96,310	99,121	104,864
Provincial and territorial government business enterprises	139,293	136,074	135,621	135,876	144,755
Local government business enterprises	53,060	54,717	56,558	58,589	60,627
			$ thousands		
Wages and salaries[3]	**137,630,876**	**144,132,597**	**152,004,255**	**161,617,171**	**169,850,124**
Government	123,636,733	129,843,029	137,009,524	145,647,564	152,898,218
Federal general government[2]	21,318,866	23,641,853	24,607,267	25,502,732	27,084,707
Provincial and territorial general government	17,312,212	17,892,674	18,729,021	19,963,976	21,061,764
Health and social service institutions, provincial and territorial	30,118,472	30,864,124	33,000,612	36,256,441	37,327,219
Universities, colleges, vocational and trade institutions, provincial and territorial	13,955,698	14,798,851	15,640,855	16,634,079	17,554,257
Local general government	15,467,999	16,314,797	17,224,537	18,241,568	19,360,260
Local school boards	25,463,487	26,330,724	27,807,232	29,048,775	30,510,006
Government business enterprises	13,994,143	14,289,569	14,994,731	15,969,605	16,951,906
Federal government business enterprises	4,021,975	4,072,449	4,316,943	4,634,364	4,837,816
Provincial and territorial government business enterprises	7,283,119	7,387,818	7,693,874	8,181,295	8,785,556
Local government business enterprises	2,689,052	2,829,299	2,983,915	3,153,947	3,328,533

Notes: As of August 24, 2005, minor revisions were brought to some estimates prior to 2005: the Nunavut general government data have been revised from 2000 on; the federal government business enterprise data for Nova Scotia and Manitoba have been revised from 2003 on; the Ontario provincial government business enterprise data have been revised from 2003 on. The corresponding totals have changed for total government, total government business enterprises and total public sector. Data as of December 31.

1. Employment data are not in full-time equivalent and do not distinguish between full-time and part-time employees. The data are an annual average. Includes employees both in and outside of Canada.
2. Federal general government data include reservists and full-time military personnel.
3. Wages and salaries data are an annual sum. Includes employees both in and outside of Canada.

Source: Statistics Canada, CANSIM table 183-0002.

Table 16.6 Military personnel and pay, 2004 to 2008

	2004	2005	2006	2007	2008
	number				
Employees[1]					
Canada and outside Canada	**84,059**	**85,706**	**87,730**	**89,352**	**90,753**
Newfoundland and Labrador	1,402	1,375	1,226	1,225	1,287
Prince Edward Island	266	284	213	230	233
Nova Scotia	10,696	10,830	10,520	10,510	10,414
New Brunswick	4,959	5,084	5,300	5,798	5,812
Quebec	15,402	16,121	17,663	18,266	18,509
Ontario	27,681	28,413	29,741	29,847	30,932
Manitoba	3,908	3,927	3,824	4,012	4,013
Saskatchewan	1,104	1,150	1,108	1,112	1,105
Alberta	9,209	9,078	9,090	9,214	9,488
British Columbia	7,776	7,793	7,298	7,298	7,137
Yukon	x	x	x	x	x
Northwest Territories	153	150	166	174	156
Nunavut	x	x	x	x	x
Outside Canada	1,496	1,494	1,577	1,658	1,659
	$ thousands				
Annual wages and salaries[2]					
Canada and outside Canada	**4,130,992**	**4,635,783**	**4,738,238**	**4,833,405**	**5,209,082**
Newfoundland and Labrador	45,626	55,668	53,914	53,158	57,978
Prince Edward Island	4,840	6,299	5,862	6,224	6,682
Nova Scotia	577,901	645,756	656,543	648,200	682,110
New Brunswick	224,506	257,565	268,851	290,991	298,445
Quebec	691,147	777,348	801,439	845,349	898,147
Ontario	1,377,530	1,552,523	1,616,418	1,652,767	1,792,801
Manitoba	196,819	220,550	215,275	220,033	241,999
Saskatchewan	47,796	50,570	51,691	53,075	56,529
Alberta	433,680	483,977	485,571	484,147	556,925
British Columbia	406,287	448,902	440,776	432,545	463,146
Yukon	x	x	x	x	x
Northwest Territories	12,106	13,807	14,303	14,455	14,049
Nunavut	x	x	x	x	x
Outside Canada	112,388	122,103	126,492	129,801	137,342

Notes: Employment data are not in full-time equivalents and do not distinguish between full-time and part-time employees. Civilian employees are excluded.
1. Average annual number.
2. Wages and salaries data are an annual sum.
Source: Statistics Canada, CANSIM table 183-0004.

Table 16.7 Health and social services institutions' revenue and expenditures, 2005 to 2009

	2005	2006	2007	2008	2009
			$ thousands		
Revenue	**60,254,975**	**64,091,854**	**70,533,240**	**74,746,577**	**80,103,978**
Own-source revenue	8,985,459	10,102,819	10,592,712	11,237,972	12,107,664
Sales of goods and services	7,748,619	8,456,582	8,864,183	9,395,342	10,124,989
Investment income	115,278	158,239	180,918	193,037	208,214
Other revenue from own sources	1,121,562	1,487,997	1,547,612	1,649,594	1,774,461
Transfers from all levels of government	51,269,516	53,989,035	59,940,528	63,508,605	67,996,314
Federal government	6,868	5,707	6,508	6,848	7,361
Provincial governments	51,040,821	53,728,613	59,674,442	63,223,174	67,686,684
Local governments	221,827	254,716	259,577	278,583	302,269
Expenditures	**61,870,427**	**65,488,447**	**71,144,975**	**75,409,381**	**80,826,966**
Health	54,993,109	57,975,721	62,890,870	66,687,751	71,435,800
Hospital care	28,601,569	30,596,260	33,078,439	34,657,653	37,336,376
Medical care	13,164,745	13,367,475	14,360,351	15,393,198	16,558,004
Preventive care	1,167,437	1,309,745	1,441,885	1,512,623	1,636,130
Other health services	12,059,357	12,702,242	14,010,194	15,124,278	15,905,290
Social services	6,648,924	7,282,603	7,996,383	8,461,929	9,112,216
Social assistance	41,312	3,643	3,369	3,267	3,299
Other social services	6,607,611	7,278,960	7,993,013	8,458,662	9,108,917
Debt charges	224,556	230,123	257,723	259,701	278,949
Housing	3,838	0	0	..	..
Surplus/deficit (-)	**-1,615,452**	**-1,396,592**	**-611,736**	**-662,804**	**-722,988**

Note: Fiscal year ending March 31.
Source: Statistics Canada, CANSIM table 385-0008.

Health

About 4.1 million people, 15% of Canadians aged 12 and older, did not have a regular medical doctor in 2007, either because they were unable to find one, or because they had not looked. This proportion was up three percentage points since 1996/1997.

Of these individuals, 3.3 million people did, however, have some place to go: 64% sought treatment in a walk-in or appointment clinic, 12% went to a hospital emergency room, while 10% went to a community health centre. The remaining 14% used other types of health care facilities or services such as hospital outpatient clinics, telephone health lines or doctor's offices.

Having a regular doctor, smoking, and overweight or obesity levels are some of the indicators that can influence health.

Although smoking has declined, one-fifth of the population aged 12 and older smoked either daily or occasionally in 2007. Rates of smoking among youth aged 12 to 19 have declined since the 1990s. About 400,000 Canadians in this age group, 12% of the total, smoked daily or occasionally. In 2007, 13% of young men smoked, compared with 17% in 1998/1999. Among young women, 12% smoked compared with 22%.

Smoking rates remained highest among adults aged 20 to 44, 28% of whom smoked either daily or occasionally. One-third of men in this age group smoked, as did one-quarter of women.

Obesity increasing

Obesity levels, self-reported by Canadians, have increased: 4 million Canadians aged 18 and older, 16% of the total adult population in 2007, were in the obese category. Another 8 million Canadians, or 32%, were overweight.

Chart 17.1
Life expectancy

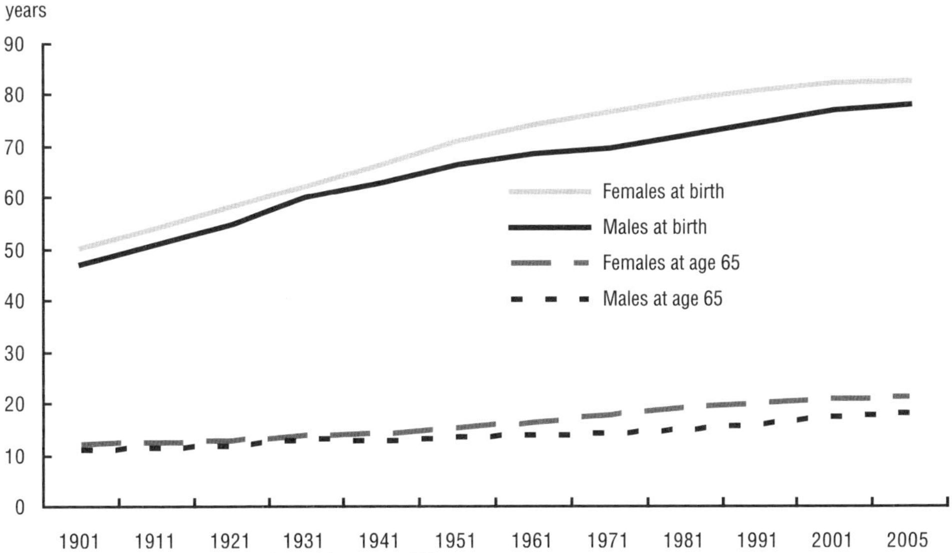

Note: Life expectancy is the estimated remaining years of life.
Source: Statistics Canada, CANSIM tables 102-0025 and 102-0511 and Catalogue no. 91-209-X.

The percentage of Canadians who are overweight or obese rose dramatically from 1985 to 1994/1995, but obesity levels appear to have stabilized in recent years.

Among the provinces, rates of obesity in 2007 were highest in Saskatchewan, Alberta and the Atlantic provinces, ranging from 18% in Alberta to a high of 22% in Newfoundland and Labrador. The lowest rates were in British Columbia, where 11% of adults were obese.

Activity levels have been linked to obesity and health. In 2007, 52% of men and 47% of women aged 12 and older were active or moderately active during leisure time.

Table 17.a
Selected health indicators, 2007

	2007		
	Both sexes	Males	Females
	% of population		
Arthritis	15.0	11.7	18.1
Diabetes	5.8	6.4	5.2
Asthma	8.0	6.7	9.4
High blood pressure	15.9	15.1	16.7
Current smoker, daily or occasional	21.9	24.6	19.4
BMI (18 and older), overweight	32.4	39.3	25.7
BMI (18 and older), obese	16.0	17.1	15.0
Influenza immunization, in past year	30.4	27.0	33.7

Note: Population aged 12 and older.
Source: Statistics Canada, CANSIM table 105-0501.

Healthy Canadians

Most Canadians today consider themselves to be healthy. In recent surveys, 60% of Canadians said their health is either very good or excellent.

A girl born in 2006 can expect to live 83.0 years, compared with 62.1 years in 1931. A boy can expect to live 78.4 years, compared with 60.0 years in 1931. Despite an aging population, death rates were constant at 7.1 deaths per 1,000 population from 2001 to 2005.

Cancer and heart disease were the two main causes of death in 2005, followed by stroke, accidents, chronic lower respiratory disease, diabetes, influenza and pneumonia, Alzheimer's disease, suicide and kidney disease.

Chart 17.2
Selected health indicators, 2007

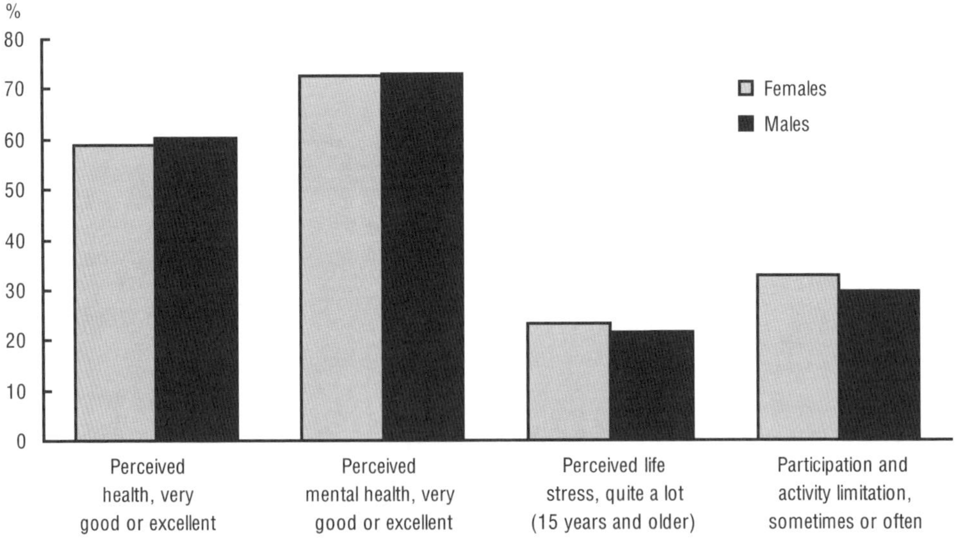

Note: Population aged 12 and older.
Source: Statistics Canada, CANSIM table 105-0501.

Health and community belonging

In 2007, 62% of Canadians reported a strong sense of community belonging. Of the 62%, 16% described their sense of belonging as very strong and 46% reported it as somewhat strong. As well, 26% felt a somewhat weak sense of community belonging, and 9% had a very weak sense of belonging.

That sense of belonging seems to bring benefits to health. Two-thirds of those who felt a very strong or somewhat strong sense of community belonging reported excellent or very good general health. By contrast, half of those with a very weak sense of belonging viewed their general health favourably.

Similarly, 81% of those with a very strong sense of community reported excellent or very good mental health, compared with 64% of those whose sense of community belonging was very weak.

Chart 17.3
Strong or somewhat strong sense of community belonging, by province

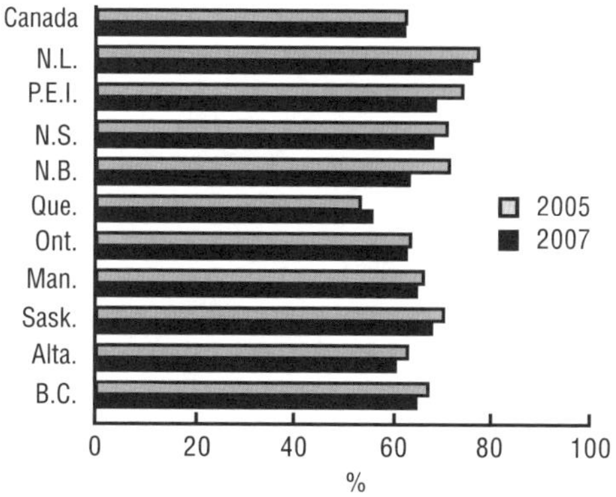

Note: Household population aged 12 and older.
Source: Statistics Canada, Catalogue no. 82-003-X.

Residents of the Atlantic provinces have the highest levels of community belonging, with people from Newfoundland and Labrador having the highest rate among all provinces at 76%.

Overweight and eating out

The higher their income, the more likely Canadian men are to be overweight.

Generally, people in higher income groups have better health than those in lower income groups, but this is less so when it comes to obesity and overweight levels among men.

Since the early 1980s, the largest increase in the prevalence of obesity has been among men in higher income groups.

A potential contributor is that men in higher household income groups are significantly more likely than those in lower income groups to eat meals away from home. People who often eat out tend to consume more calories than those who usually eat meals prepared at home.

These patterns do not hold for women. Although women from higher income households are more likely than those from lower income households to eat out, they are no more or less likely to be overweight.

Chart 17.4
Adult body mass index, 2005

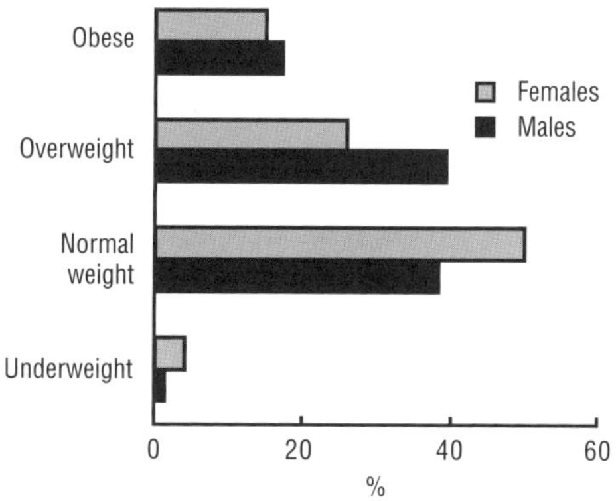

Source: Statistics Canada, CANSIM table 105-0502.

Table 17.1 Mortality rates, by selected causes and by sex, 2001 and 2005

	2001			2005		
	Both sexes	Males	Females	Both sexes	Males	Females
	rate per 100,000 population					
All causes of death	**600.8**	**756.4**	**483.2**	**563.7**	**696.7**	**460.7**
Septicaemia	**3.8**	4.4	3.3	**4.1**	4.8	3.6
Viral hepatitis	**0.9**	1.1	0.7	**1.0**	1.3	0.6
Human immunodeficiency virus	**1.3**	2.2	0.4	**1.3**	2.1	0.6
Malignant neoplasms	**178.7**	223.8	147.6	**170.3**	207.7	143.8
Colon, rectum and anus	**18.4**	22.8	14.9	**18.6**	23.7	14.6
Pancreas	**8.9**	10.3	7.8	**8.8**	9.8	7.8
Trachea, bronchus and lung	**47.3**	64.6	34.4	**46.2**	59.8	36.0
Breast	**13.9**	0.3	24.9	**12.5**	0.3	22.6
Prostate[1]	...	26.6	...	...	21.9	...
Diabetes mellitus	**19.3**	23.0	16.4	**19.1**	23.7	15.6
Alzheimer's disease	**13.9**	12.5	14.5	**12.7**	10.7	13.6
Heart diseases	**143.1**	189.7	107.6	**121.5**	160.1	91.5
Ischaemic heart diseases	**110.6**	152.8	78.4	**91.0**	125.1	64.5
Other heart diseases	**29.8**	34.5	26.2	**27.7**	32.6	23.9
Cerebrovascular diseases	**40.4**	44.6	37.1	**32.5**	35.2	30.2
Influenza and pneumonia	**12.2**	15.7	10.3	**13.2**	15.8	11.5
Influenza	**0.2**	0.3	0.2	**1.5**	1.6	1.5
Pneumonia	**12.0**	15.4	10.1	**11.7**	14.3	10.1
Chronic lower respiratory diseases	**26.3**	38.0	19.4	**25.1**	34.1	19.8
Chronic liver disease and cirrhosis	**6.5**	9.0	4.2	**6.1**	8.5	3.9
Alcoholic liver disease	**3.2**	5.0	1.5	**3.0**	4.6	1.6
Other chronic liver disease and cirrhosis	**3.3**	4.0	2.6	**3.0**	3.9	2.3
Renal failure	**8.3**	11.4	6.5	**8.3**	11.3	6.5
Certain conditions originating in the perinatal period	**4.0**	4.5	3.5	**4.4**	4.7	4.0
Congenital malformations, deformations and chromosomal abnormalities	**3.3**	3.6	3.0	**3.2**	3.4	3.1
Accidents (unintentional injuries)	**25.1**	35.3	15.6	**25.6**	35.6	16.5
Motor vehicle accidents	**8.3**	11.9	4.7	**9.2**	13.1	5.4
Falls	**4.6**	6.1	3.4	**5.4**	7.2	4.0
Accidental poisoning and exposure to noxious substances	**3.0**	4.2	1.7	**3.0**	4.2	1.8
Suicide	**11.4**	18.0	5.0	**10.9**	16.9	5.1
Homicide	**1.5**	2.2	0.8	**1.9**	2.8	0.9

Note: Rates are age standardized per 100,000 population.
1. A combined rate is not calculated for gender-specific causes of death.
Source: Statistics Canada, CANSIM table 102-0552.

Table 17.2 Life expectancy at birth and at age 65, by sex and by province and territory, 2005

	At birth		At age 65	
	Males	Females	Males	Females
	years			
Canada	**78.0**	**82.7**	**17.9**	**21.1**
Newfoundland and Labrador	75.6	80.9	15.9	19.5
Prince Edward Island	77.4	82.1	17.3	20.4
Nova Scotia	76.7	81.8	16.8	20.3
New Brunswick	77.2	82.4	17.1	20.6
Quebec	77.7	82.9	17.6	21.2
Ontario	78.5	82.7	18.1	21.0
Manitoba	76.6	81.4	17.2	20.7
Saskatchewan	76.6	82.1	17.6	21.3
Alberta	77.8	82.7	18.1	21.3
British Columbia	78.8	83.5	18.8	21.7
Territories[1]	73.5	79.9	16.1	19.3

1. Comprises Yukon, Northwest Territories and Nunavut.
Source: Statistics Canada, CANSIM table 102-0511.

Table 17.3 Residents of care facilities for the aged, by sex and by province and territory, 2001/2002 and 2006/2007

	2001/2002			2006/2007		
	Both sexes	Males	Females	Both sexes	Males	Females
	number					
Canada[1]	**171,267**	**39,145**	**99,373**	**196,261**	**46,685**	**111,478**
Newfoundland and Labrador	**3,905**	1,256	2,649	**4,795**	1,483	3,312
Prince Edward Island	**1,615**	435	1,180	**1,682**	455	1,227
Nova Scotia	**6,646**	1,735	4,911	**6,493**	1,686	4,807
New Brunswick	**5,808**	1,778	4,030	**6,466**	1,961	4,505
Quebec[1]	**32,749**	..	..	**38,098**	..	..
Ontario	**70,031**	18,834	51,197	**83,400**	23,881	59,519
Manitoba	**9,119**	2,601	6,518	**9,469**	2,729	6,740
Saskatchewan	**8,341**	2,672	5,669	**7,900**	2,457	5,443
Alberta	**13,892**	4,389	9,503	**15,904**	5,145	10,759
British Columbia	**18,953**	5,367	13,586	**21,815**	6,806	15,009
Territories[2]	**208**	78	130	**239**	82	157

Notes: Data are as of March 31.
Care facilities in which the predominant group of residents are elderly; residents are not exclusively the aged.
1. Data for Quebec are derived from administrative sources of the Ministère de la santé et des services sociaux; these sources do not provide the age and sex distribution of residents, therefore, the Canada totals for males and females exclude Quebec.
2. Comprises Yukon, Northwest Territories and Nunavut.
Source: Statistics Canada, CANSIM table 107-5504.

Table 17.4 Self-rated health status, very good or excellent, by sex, selected years from 1996/1997 to 2007

	1996/1997	1998/1999	2000/2001	2003	2005	2007
	% of males					
Canada	**65.3**	**67.3**	**62.9**	**59.5**	**60.6**	**60.2**
Newfoundland and Labrador	72.1	71.4	66.6	63.6	62.7	61.0
Prince Edward Island	65.8	66.8	64.2	67.9	54.0	56.7
Nova Scotia	62.2	61.0	58.6	55.9	56.2	55.3
New Brunswick	60.0	59.3	56.3	49.5	54.3	53.4
Quebec	66.9	67.3	63.5	58.6	59.9	60.0
Ontario	65.0	67.9	64.6	58.3	61.6	61.3
Manitoba	63.2	67.3	62.6	61.1	60.4	60.4
Saskatchewan	60.3	63.3	57.6	59.3	58.5	57.2
Alberta	65.9	75.1	62.8	66.2	61.6	60.4
British Columbia	65.3	63.4	60.4	60.9	60.3	60.1
Yukon	63.1	57.2	63.7	60.6	56.2	58.1
Northwest Territories	60.5	61.7	54.2	59.7	63.1	51.6
Nunavut	55.4	47.8	49.6	57.6	49.6	63.0
	% of females					
Canada	**61.6**	**63.2**	**59.9**	**57.3**	**59.6**	**59.0**
Newfoundland and Labrador	71.2	73.5	65.7	68.6	65.7	63.3
Prince Edward Island	66.9	68.9	64.6	62.0	61.5	61.6
Nova Scotia	62.7	64.5	60.3	60.2	59.1	58.7
New Brunswick	55.6	54.3	54.9	51.0	54.4	56.0
Quebec	61.2	63.1	58.9	55.1	58.8	58.6
Ontario	63.8	63.6	61.6	56.2	60.0	58.6
Manitoba	57.4	60.1	58.2	60.4	57.6	59.2
Saskatchewan	51.8	58.1	55.9	59.0	57.7	55.3
Alberta	61.6	66.0	60.3	61.6	62.8	64.7
British Columbia	59.1	61.9	57.6	59.2	58.5	57.1
Yukon	61.9	59.0	59.3	49.6	57.0	54.9
Northwest Territories	60.3	60.7	54.2	51.1	63.1	52.7
Nunavut	55.0	45.8	57.2	56.4	50.3	51.6

Note: Population aged 12 and older.
Source: Statistics Canada, CANSIM table 105-4022.

Table 17.5 Leisure-time physical activity, by age group and sex, selected years from 2000/2001 to 2007

	2000/2001	2003	2005	2007
		%		
Both sexes	**42.6**	**50.4**	**51.0**	**49.0**
12 to 19 years	59.5	69.9	69.6	67.9
20 to 34 years	44.5	53.7	54.8	52.1
35 to 44 years	40.0	48.6	48.1	46.3
45 to 64 years	39.5	46.5	47.3	45.7
65 years and older	34.5	38.3	40.2	38.6
Males	**44.8**	**53.3**	**53.3**	**51.5**
12 to 19 years	63.9	74.6	74.9	72.3
20 to 34 years	46.4	57.6	57.1	55.3
35 to 44 years	40.1	49.2	48.1	46.7
45 to 64 years	39.7	46.9	47.7	46.4
65 years and older	40.6	45.1	46.1	43.5
Females	**40.6**	**47.5**	**48.6**	**46.5**
12 to 19 years	54.8	65.0	64.1	63.3
20 to 34 years	42.7	49.8	52.4	48.7
35 to 44 years	39.9	47.9	48.1	46.0
45 to 64 years	39.3	46.1	46.9	45.1
65 years and older	29.7	33.1	35.5	34.6

Note: Population aged 12 and older that are active or moderately active during leisure time.
Source: Statistics Canada, CANSIM tables 105-0033, 105-0233, 105-0433 and 105-0501.

Table 17.6 Population with pain or discomfort that prevents activities, by age group and sex, selected years from 2000/2001 to 2007

	2000/2001	2003	2005	2007
		%		
Both sexes	**12.0**	**10.5**	**10.8**	**11.8**
12 to 19 years	3.2	3.3	2.4	2.9
20 to 34 years	7.2	5.9	5.4	6.6
35 to 44 years	11.3	10.1	10.0	10.9
45 to 64 years	16.2	14.1	14.9	16.0
65 years and older	20.7	17.8	18.8	19.3
Males	**9.7**	**8.0**	**8.8**	**9.5**
12 to 19 years	2.1	1.5E	2.1E	1.5E
20 to 34 years	5.6	4.3E	5.2	5.6
35 to 44 years	9.9	9.8	8.9	9.3
45 to 64 years	13.7	10.6	12.5	13.3
65 years and older	16.6	12.7	13.0	15.2
Females	**14.2**	**13.0**	**12.7**	**14.0**
12 to 19 years	4.4	5.2	2.8E	4.3
20 to 34 years	8.7	7.5	5.7	7.6
35 to 44 years	12.7	10.5	11.1	12.5
45 to 64 years	18.7	17.4	17.2	18.7
65 years and older	23.8	21.7	23.5	22.6

Note: Population aged 12 and older.
Source: Statistics Canada, CANSIM tables 105-0003, 105-0203 and 105-0501.

Table 17.7 Smoking and exposure to second-hand smoke, by sex and by province, 2007

	Canada	Newfoundland and Labrador	Prince Edward Island	Nova Scotia	New Brunswick
			%		
Daily or occasional smokers[1]	**21.9**	**25.3**	**21.5**	**24.4**	**23.3**
Males	**24.6**	29.2	26.4	25.9	27.3
Females	**19.4**	21.6	17.0	22.9	19.5
Non-smokers exposed to second-hand smoke at home[2]	**7.4**	**8.9**	**8.5**	**7.3**	**9.1**
Males	**8.3**	11.7	9.0[E]	6.6	9.8
Females	**6.6**	6.4	8.0[E]	8.0	8.5
Non-smokers exposed to second-hand smoke in vehicles[3]	**8.3**	**11.7**	**9.9**	**11.4**	**11.4**
Males	**9.1**	13.7	11.0[E]	10.7	11.2
Females	**7.5**	10.0	9.1[E]	12.0	11.6
Non-smokers exposed to second-hand smoke in public places[4]	**11.1**	**8.2**	**6.5**	**9.7**	**7.9**
Males	**11.8**	9.9	7.1[E]	9.6	8.3
Females	**10.4**	6.7[E]	6.0[E]	9.8	7.6
Smokers asked to refrain from smoking in the house	**67.0**	**69.3**	**70.5**	**69.5**	**66.8**
Males	**65.8**	66.0	65.6	69.4	64.6
Females	**68.2**	72.4	75.0	69.6	68.8

Note: Population aged 12 and older.
1. Reported currently being daily or occasional smokers.
2. Reported that at least one person smoked inside their home every day or almost every day.
3. Reported being exposed to second-hand smoke in private vehicles every day or almost every day in the past month.
4. Reported being exposed to second-hand smoke in public places every day or almost every day in the past month.
Source: Statistics Canada, CANSIM table 105-0501.

Quebec	Ontario	Manitoba	Saskatchewan	Alberta	British Columbia
			%		
25.1	**20.6**	**22.4**	**25.9**	**21.9**	**17.8**
27.4	23.6	25.0	26.7	24.9	20.1
22.8	17.8	19.9	25.1	18.9	15.5
12.0	**5.7**	**8.9**	**8.2**	**6.3**	**4.5**
14.3	6.1	8.3	9.9	6.8	4.9
10.0	5.3	9.3	6.7	5.8	4.1
9.2	**8.0**	**7.2**	**10.0**	**8.6**	**5.8**
10.5	8.7	6.3	12.4	9.9	6.5
8.1	7.4	8.0	7.8	7.4	5.2
10.1	**11.5**	**8.7**	**7.7**	**15.0**	**11.1**
10.4	12.1	8.8	10.7	17.0	11.8
9.8	11.0	8.6	4.9	13.0	10.5
49.1	**72.5**	**70.7**	**66.8**	**73.7**	**75.8**
47.8	71.4	69.3	65.9	72.8	74.5
50.3	73.7	72.0	67.6	74.7	77.0

Table 17.8 Population with a regular medical doctor, by province and territory, selected years from 2003 to 2007

	2003	2005	2007
		% of males	
Canada	**81.7**	**81.7**	**80.3**
Newfoundland and Labrador	81.3	83.7	85.9
Prince Edward Island	90.7	86.9	86.1
Nova Scotia	93.3	92.2	91.6
New Brunswick	90.3	91.2	89.6
Quebec	66.8	68.2	64.9
Ontario	89.3	89.1	88.1
Manitoba	79.6	80.0	79.3
Saskatchewan	80.8	79.3	78.4
Alberta	77.9	76.3	75.0
British Columbia	86.3	86.3	85.3
Yukon	76.5	65.6	74.4
Northwest Territories[1]	37.3	41.3	38.2
Nunavut	F	16.0[E]	10.4[E]
		% of females	
Canada	**89.9**	**89.4**	**89.1**
Newfoundland and Labrador	89.5	90.6	90.3
Prince Edward Island	94.1	92.3	89.6
Nova Scotia	96.3	96.8	96.4
New Brunswick	94.4	95.4	94.0
Quebec	81.0	81.4	81.8
Ontario	94.1	93.1	92.6
Manitoba	87.6	87.7	89.6
Saskatchewan	90.1	89.2	90.6
Alberta	89.8	88.6	88.2
British Columbia	92.2	91.6	90.5
Yukon	86.6	81.6	81.5
Northwest Territories[1]	55.0	56.9	43.5
Nunavut	F	16.0	16.6[E]

Note: Population aged 12 and older who has a regular medical doctor.
1. Estimates for 2007 for the Northwest Territories may not be comparable to estimates from previous years because of differences in the geographic and Aboriginal and/or non-Aboriginal distribution of the samples.
Source: Statistics Canada, CANSIM tables 105-0400 and 105-0501.

Table 17.9 Waiting times for specialized health services, by type of health service, selected years from 2001 to 2007

	2001	2003	2005[1]	2007
			%	
Specialist visits[2]				
Less than 1 month	46.4	47.9	46.0	45.6
1 to 3 months	41.9	40.7	41.1	40.5
Longer than 3 months	11.7	11.4	12.9	13.9
Non-emergency surgeries[3]				
Less than 1 month	39.5	40.5	40.3	40.7
1 to 3 months	41.3	42.1	40.7	41.0
Longer than 3 months	19.2	17.4	19.0	18.3
Diagnostic tests[4]				
Less than 1 month	54.7	57.5	56.4	55.4
1 to 3 months	36.1	31.1	33.3	34.1
Longer than 3 months	9.1[E]	11.5	10.2	10.5

1. Territories are included only in 2005.
2. Includes specialist visits for a new illness or condition.
3. Includes a booked or planned surgery provided on an outpatient or inpatient basis. Does not refer to surgery provided through an admission to the hospital emergency room as a result of, for example, an accident or life-threatening situation.
4. Includes selected diagnostic tests (non-emergency MRIs, CT scans, and angiographies).

Source: Statistics Canada, CANSIM tables 105-3002, 105-3003 and 105-3004.

Table 17.10 Capital and repair expenditures by the health care and social assistance sector, by province and territory, 1997, 2002 and 2007

	1997	2002	2007[p]
		$ millions	
Canada	**2,604.1**	**6,143.6**	**8,591.0**
Newfoundland and Labrador	34.2	91.9	120.8
Prince Edward Island	8.0	x	23.1
Nova Scotia	36.9	172.9	140.8
New Brunswick	66.8	81.7	173.1
Quebec	x	1,442.3	1,768.9
Ontario	965.5	2,440.4	3,345.8
Manitoba	97.0	191.1	223.7
Saskatchewan	141.6	158.5	190.7
Alberta	220.9	819.4	1,327.7
British Columbia	404.2	647.7	1,216.8
Yukon	x	14.3	9.2
Northwest Territories (including Nunavut)[1]	13.4	..	..
Northwest Territories	..	x	13.2
Nunavut	..	7.1	37.1

1. Nunavut became a territory in 1999.

Source: Statistics Canada, CANSIM table 029-0005.

Table 17.11 Health expenditures, 2004 to 2008

	2004	2005	2006[1]	2007[2]	2008[2]
			$ millions		
Health expenditures	**132,088.3**	**141,362.8**	**151,278.5**	**161,576.2**	**171,908.6**
Hospitals	38,304.7	40,373.6	42,957.5	45,456.7	48,105.9
Other institutions	14,057.3	14,665.4	15,507.1	16,365.3	17,210.5
Physicians	17,296.9	18,536.6	20,031.0	21,733.5	23,084.0
Other professionals	14,181.0	15,208.4	16,251.9	17,451.0	18,779.4
Dental services	8,971.6	9,847.0	10,313.4	11,209.8	12,116.7
Vision care services	3,066.9	3,188.0	3,440.2	3,673.4	3,946.3
Other	2,142.5	2,173.4	2,498.2	2,567.8	2,716.4
Drugs	21,894.	23,352.1	25,321.1	27,542.5	29,827.9
Prescribed drugs	17,963.8	19,268.0	21,036.6	23,063.7	25,141.1
Non-prescribed drugs	3,930.2	4,084.1	4,284.5	4,478.8	4,686.8
Other expenditures	26,354.3	29,226.7	31,209.9	33,027.2	34,901.1
			% of gross domestic product		
Health expenditures	**10.2**	**10.3**	**10.5**	**10.6**	**10.7**

1. Estimated expenditures.
2. Forecast expenditures.
Source: Canadian Institute for Health Information, *National Health Expenditures Trends 1975-2008.*

Table 17.12 Average weekly earnings of workers in the health care and social assistance sector, selected groups, 1998, 2003 and 2008

	1998	2003	2008
		$	
All health care and social assistance	**543.45**	**609.87**	**743.94**
Ambulatory health care services	501.13	586.69	735.26
Offices of physicians	464.55	574.30	807.98
Offices of dentists	501.37	560.95	744.04
Hospitals	649.05	718.40	889.65
Nursing and residential care facilities	465.97	515.29	608.18
Social assistance	414.78	506.84	608.97
Child daycare services	365.95	431.78	514.92

Notes: Data include overtime.
North American Industry Classification System (NAICS), 2007.
Source: Statistics Canada, CANSIM table 281-0027.

Income, pensions, spending and wealth

18

The job market slump and stock market declines eroded wealth in the fourth quarter of 2008, so many Canadians changed their approach to spending and saving as they faced the first recession in 16 years.

Suddenly cautious, Canadian households in the fourth quarter curtailed their net borrowing to its lowest level since 2005. Those who invest repatriated funds to the security of assets in Canada.

Personal disposable income continued to advance in the last three months of 2008 (0.4%), as increases in labour income and government transfers to people more than offset lower investment income. Labour income increased 0.7%, a similar rate to the third quarter, while average weekly earnings were up.

After decelerating since the start of the year, personal spending pulled back in the fourth quarter for the first time since the fourth quarter of 1995. Both goods and services contributed to the 0.8% decline. Spending on services was down 0.4%. This was the first decrease since the second quarter of 2001. Personal spending excluding housing fell 1.2%.

Personal spending declines

Spending on new and used vehicles dropped 5.5% in the fourth quarter of 2008, following declines earlier in the year. Still, with the stimulus of manufacturers' incentives and a one percentage point reduction in the GST early in the year, spending on motor vehicles increased 3.7% in 2008.

After 15 quarterly advances, spending on furniture, furnishings, and household equipment and maintenance fell 2.3% in the fourth quarter. Purchases of food, beverages and tobacco also fell, as did clothing and footwear purchases.

Chart 18.1
Personal savings and spending rates

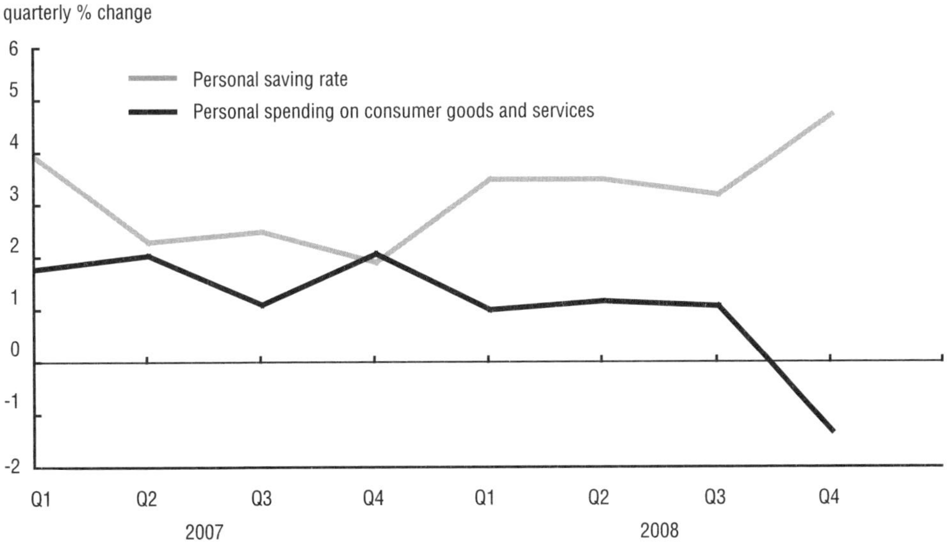

Note: Seasonally adjusted at annual rates.
Source: Statistics Canada, CANSIM table 380-0004.

Personal saving increases

The downturn in spending (in nominal terms), combined with the increase in disposable income, led to $45 billion worth of personal saving in the fourth quarter of 2008 alone, $15 billion higher than in the third quarter. This level of personal saving was the highest since the fourth quarter of 1995, and produced a saving rate of 4.7%, the highest rate recorded for Canadians since the first quarter of 2002.

Table 18.a
Spending and saving, 2008

	Q1	Q2	Q3	Q4
	$ millions			
Personal spending	891,924	901,228	889,132	886,216
Savings	31,848	29,876	47,152	45,060
Disposable income	948,596	955,512	960,852	955,260
	%			
Saving rate	3.4	3.1	4.9	4.7

Note: Seasonally adjusted at annual rates.
Source: Statistics Canada, CANSIM table 380-0004.

Spending patterns

People in the lowest income groups generally spend more of their income to provide the basics for their household. In 2007, the one-fifth of Canadian households with the lowest incomes spent an average of $22,340 on the basics.

More than half (52%) of that total spending went to food, shelter and clothing, whereas personal taxes took 3% of their budget.

By comparison, the one-fifth of households with the highest incomes spent an average of $143,360 in 2007. They spent 28% of that on food, shelter and clothing; 29% of their total spending went to pay personal taxes.

Chart 18.2
Average household spending by income group, 2007

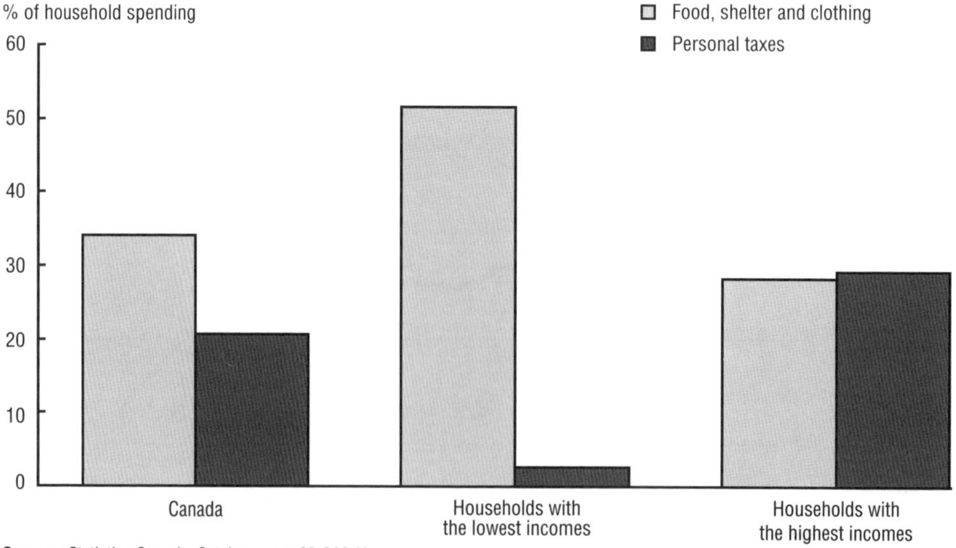

Source : Statistics Canada, Catalogue no. 62-202-X.

Household spending

Household spending averaged $69,950 in 2007, up 3.3% from the year before. This increase was sharper than the 2.2% annual rate of inflation measured by the Consumer Price Index (CPI).

Personal taxes accounted for 21% of the average household's budget in 2007, while shelter represented 20%, transportation 13%, and food 10%. These shares changed only slightly from 2006.

Spending on personal taxes averaged $14,450; spending on shelter rose to $13,640, a 5.1% increase. A 10.6% increase in mortgage payments lifted shelter spending.

Households spent an average $9,400 on transportation, up 1.7%. A 6.9% increase in spending on gasoline and other fuels was offset by a 6.3% decline in average spending for automobile purchases.

Chart 18.3
Average household spending, selected expenditures

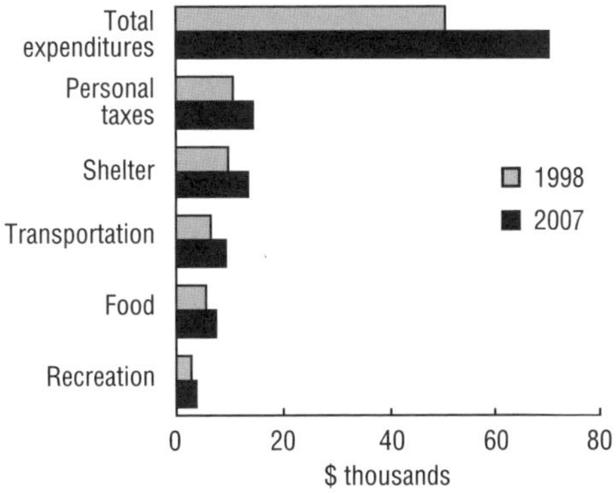

Source: Statistics Canada, CANSIM table 203-0001.

On average, households spent $7,310 on food, up 3.7%, the fastest annual increase since 2002. Food prices measured by the CPI rose 2.7%.

Are near-retirees informed about pensions?

Most Canadians nearing retirement receive financial advice and information about retirement plans and programs, but almost 3 in 10 do not. The proportion not receiving advice is far larger among lower-income households and recent immigrants.

The same holds true for knowledge of public retirement income programs. Most near-retirees say they understand the programs and the basic structure of their pension, but a significant proportion say they do not.

Almost one in six near-retirees with pension coverage (paid employees only) do not know what type of pension plan they have.

Individuals not receiving financial advice are less likely to expect their retirement income to be adequate than those who do. This is the case even when other characteristics such as income, pension coverage and registered retirement savings plan assets are taken into account.

Chart 18.4
Near-retirees' sources of financial advice, 2007

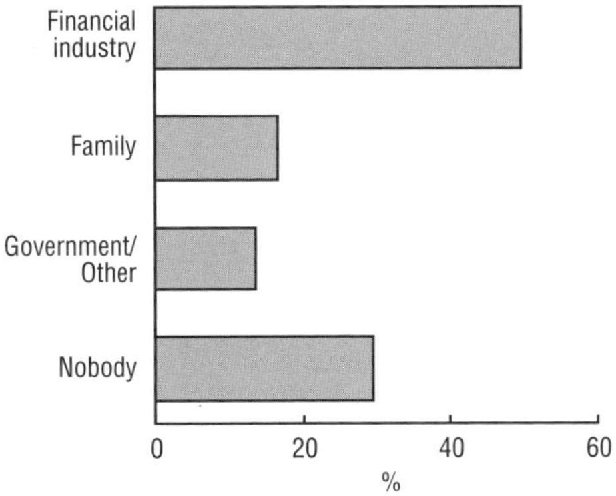

Note: Total exceeds 100% because respondents could identify more than one source.
Source: Statistics Canada, Catalogue no. 11-008-X.

Table 18.1 Average total income, by economic family type, 1993 to 2007

	1993	1994	1995	1996	1997	1998
	$ 2007 constant					
All family units	**55,700**	**56,300**	**56,500**	**56,700**	**57,100**	**59,700**
Economic families, two or more people	67,600	68,800	69,100	69,800	70,500	74,200
Elderly families[1]	50,800	51,200	53,300	51,300	52,100	51,300
Married couples	47,400	47,400	48,600	48,100	49,200	50,200
Other elderly families	58,900	60,800	65,700	60,500	60,500	55,200
Non-elderly families[2]	70,400	71,800	71,800	72,800	73,500	78,000
Married couples	67,200	67,400	67,900	69,900	70,600	76,200
No earner	32,800	33,100	32,800	34,000	33,900	34,400
One earner	53,200	55,900	55,300	59,400	56,400	60,500
Two earners	78,700	78,000	78,400	80,700	81,900	89,300
Two-parent families[3]	75,900	77,800	77,700	78,200	79,800	84,600
No earner	24,400	23,600	22,000	23,000	23,300	24,900
One earner	55,500	57,800	55,600	58,200	58,000	66,800
Two earners	79,100	81,700	81,400	81,500	83,100	87,000
Three or more earners	97,000	98,600	99,200	100,800	101,900	103,800
Married couples with other relatives	95,600	96,100	94,400	99,900	98,500	102,400
Lone-parent families[3]	33,000	34,600	34,500	32,800	33,600	35,600
Male lone-parent families	46,100	47,400	46,800	50,000	48,800	53,000
Female lone-parent families	30,800	32,500	32,500	30,100	31,000	32,500
No earner	19,300	19,400	19,500	17,600	16,900	17,400
One earner	33,900	34,600	35,100	34,800	34,200	34,700
Two or more earners	49,600	54,900	54,600	48,000	52,100	53,900
Other non-elderly families	54,900	55,400	58,000	61,200	61,100	66,700
Unattached individuals	29,000	28,900	29,400	28,700	28,800	29,400
Elderly male	28,500	32,000	30,800	30,800	30,100	31,700
Non-earner	26,900	28,600	28,400	28,400	28,000	28,100
Earner	40,700	60,300^E	50,900	48,500	44,500	53,900^E
Elderly female	22,200	22,500	24,400	23,800	23,800	24,900
Non-earner	21,600	22,000	23,400	23,200	23,200	24,000
Earner	37,600	37,200	45,900	38,200	35,600	38,200
Non-elderly male	32,700	32,900	32,600	32,100	32,400	33,000
Non-earner	13,500	14,100	13,500	12,500	12,600	11,300
Earner	38,300	37,800	37,300	37,300	37,700	38,700
Non-elderly female	28,800	27,100	28,100	26,800	26,900	26,700
Non-earner	14,400	15,900	14,200	13,900	13,600	11,900
Earner	33,600	31,700	32,800	31,600	32,200	32,700

Note: 'Average total income' refers to income from all sources, including government transfers, and before deduction of federal and provincial income taxes.
1. Families in which the major income earner is 65 years of age and older.
2. Families in which the major income earner is less than 65 years of age.
3. Families with children less than 18 years of age.
Source: Statistics Canada, CANSIM table 202-0403.

1999	2000	2001	2002	2003	2004	2005	2006	2007
				$ 2007 constant				
61,300	**63,100**	**64,000**	**64,000**	**63,700**	**64,800**	**65,400**	**66,900**	**68,800**
75,800	78,600	79,800	79,600	79,000	80,900	81,700	83,500	86,300
53,200	53,600	53,800	54,500	54,300	55,300	57,500	58,700	61,600
52,500	52,000	52,900	52,800	53,200	55,100	55,600	56,800	60,100
55,800	59,400	57,400	60,800	58,200	56,200	64,300	65,600	66,700
79,500	82,700	84,100	83,700	83,200	85,400	85,900	87,900	90,700
75,400	76,400	81,200	79,700	77,500	78,300	81,000	83,000	86,100
36,200	37,200	42,500	39,000	37,100	36,800	37,000	40,300	41,600
62,800	61,300	66,600	60,900	61,700	65,400	67,600	65,900	67,900
86,800	87,100	91,400	91,400	87,500	87,200	91,000	93,400	95,900
86,700	89,900	91,200	91,800	92,900	96,300	93,300	95,500	100,100
24,200	24,000	26,400	26,700	24,400	25,800	22,400	26,800	30,000
65,800	65,800	67,100	71,000	72,800	70,500	66,900	67,800	70,300
88,400	91,900	92,400	92,600	93,100	96,400	94,700	95,400	99,500
107,500	111,900	114,600	111,900	113,300	120,100	115,900	120,400	125,500
107,300	114,600	110,400	109,600	109,700	112,700	118,400	122,100	122,700
36,800	40,000	40,900	38,900	39,800	39,800	46,400	46,800	46,600
53,900	58,800	55,300	55,500	60,100	56,100	66,900	68,500	63,000
33,600	36,200	37,900	35,100	35,200	36,100	41,800	41,800	42,900
18,400	17,400	18,400	17,500	17,300	18,700	18,500	20,900	18,200
35,100	36,200	37,700	35,400	34,800	36,200	43,000	41,700	43,200
53,000	58,500	60,700	53,000	55,500	52,700	55,200	56,500	58,800
67,400	70,200	70,400	72,200	66,700	70,100	68,200	69,700	71,800
31,200	31,200	32,100	32,700	33,300	33,200	33,600	35,000	35,700
30,500	29,200	31,100	30,800	32,100	31,500	32,500	33,100	36,000
28,600	27,200	29,100	27,900	28,100	29,300	27,900	28,700	31,000
42,900	40,100	42,700	42,900	46,200	40,000	50,700	49,500	53,600
24,900	25,500	26,500	27,100	26,900	28,000	27,000	29,100	28,800
24,200	24,700	25,400	26,500	26,000	26,800	25,800	28,000	27,300
36,700	37,400	41,900	34,700	34,500	38,400	38,000	38,500	40,000
34,700	36,000	36,600	36,800	37,800	36,900	38,300	40,100	40,200
11,000	11,000	12,900	12,700	13,400	13,000	13,400	13,600	14,800
39,600	40,700	41,100	41,800	43,000	41,500	43,800	44,700	45,000
30,500	28,700	29,500	31,100	31,300	31,300	31,100	31,700	33,300
11,700	11,600	13,200	13,100	14,100	14,000	15,800	14,800	15,000
37,300	34,500	34,900	36,600	36,300	36,500	35,100	36,100	38,100

Table 18.2 Average total income, by economic family type and by province, 2007

	Canada	Newfoundland and Labrador	Prince Edward Island	Nova Scotia
	$ 2007 constant			
All familiy units	**68,800**	**59,200**	**56,700**	**58,200**
Economic families, two or more people	**86,300**	70,800	68,100	73,100
Elderly families[1]	**61,600**	41,400	50,700	52,100
Married couples	**60,100**	42,000	49,300	53,600
Other elderly families	**66,700**	39,900	F	47,400
Non-elderly families[2]	**90,700**	76,700	71,600	77,400
Married couples	**86,100**	69,200	69,100	72,100
No earner	**41,600**	F	F	45,800
One earner	**67,900**	60,500	50,400	63,100
Two earners	**95,900**	77,100	76,000	79,400
Two-parent families[3]	**100,100**	88,900	77,400	87,200
No earner	**30,000**	F	F	F
One earner	**70,300**	73,600	F	53,600
Two earners	**99,500**	89,800	75,500	86,700
Three or more earners	**125,500**	99,500	93,500	111,600
Married couples with other relatives	**122,700**	100,100	99,000	101,800
Lone-parent families[3]	**46,600**	39,100	37,000	39,900
Male lone-parent families	**63,000**	F	F	F
Female lone-parent families	**42,900**	35,800	36,400	36,500
No earner	**18,200**	F	F	F
One earner	**43,200**	31,000	28,700	37,700
Two or more earners	**58,800**	F	F	F
Other non-elderly families	**71,800**	67,600	59,600	71,200
Unattached individuals	**35,700**	25,400	27,100	29,600
Elderly male	**36,000**	21,300	F	34,800[E]
Non-earner	**31,000**	18,800	F	34,000[E]
Earner	**53,600**	F	F	F
Elderly female	**28,800**	20,300	27,900	27,900
Non-earner	**27,300**	20,300	27,500	27,600
Earner	**40,000**	F	F	F
Non-elderly male	**40,200**	29,600	25,700	30,900
Non-earner	**14,800**	F	F	12,800[E]
Earner	**45,000**	38,100	29,500	34,700
Non-elderly female	**33,300**	25,600	28,800	28,100
Non-earner	**15,000**	12,000[E]	F	13,700[E]
Earner	**38,100**	33,600	32,800	31,800

Note: 'Average total income' refers to income from all sources, including government transfers, and before deduction of federal and provincial income taxes.
1. Families in which the major income earner is 65 years of age and older.
2. Families in which the major income earner is less than 65 years of age.
3. Families with children less than 18 years of age.
Source: Statistics Canada, CANSIM table 202-0403.

New Brunswick	Quebec	Ontario	Manitoba	Saskatchewan	Alberta	British Columbia
			$ 2007 constant			
56,300	**58,100**	**75,600**	**63,800**	**64,300**	**83,200**	**67,300**
68,000	74,800	92,300	80,900	81,500	104,600	86,300
48,500	49,300	68,000	62,700	59,500	64,400	70,700
47,600	47,700	66,400	60,800	61,100	61,100	69,500
52,400	55,000	72,700	69,900	51,200	80,400[E]	76,000
71,700	79,300	96,800	84,000	85,800	109,900	89,300
64,700	74,200	92,800	77,700	83,700	107,600	88,300
35,900	40,000	37,600	F	F	F	F
48,000	59,200	69,900	68,600	62,600	97,300	69,300
74,700	82,500	106,400	84,100	90,300	111,700	97,900
84,100	91,600	103,800	88,800	96,100	120,700	96,100
F	F	F	F	F	F	F
51,300	63,800	63,100	62,900	80,200	116,200	74,200[E]
84,200	92,700	106,400	79,400	89,200	112,000	95,400
108,800	113,400	129,900	130,000	120,300	144,100	117,900
99,500	107,600	128,300	130,400	116,300	149,700	118,600
34,200	44,900	51,200	39,200	37,600	54,200	41,300
F	60,300	72,200	F	F	66,500	58,200
32,400	39,300	47,800	36,900	36,400	51,100	38,300
F	18,700	19,000	F	F	F	F
31,800	37,800	50,200	35,400	34,000	46,800	40,900
F	57,100	66,900	F	47,200	62,000	48,600
58,900	60,900	76,600	78,100	66,100	79,600	72,900
28,300	31,300	38,900	32,000	32,300	44,600	34,700
26,300	28,800	44,600	31,400	34,400	29,900	40,000
23,500	25,600	36,200	26,900	29,200	30,600	35,200
F	41,400	69,500[E]	F	47,200[E]	F	F
23,600	27,300	32,100	25,100	27,600	27,900	28,600
23,500	25,900	30,900	24,800	25,000	26,300	25,200
F	37,800	42,100	F	42,500[E]	F	44,100
33,400	35,200	41,600	36,800	37,700	55,400	37,100
10,900[E]	14,200	14,800	20,000[E]	F	F	15,300[E]
38,500	40,000	46,900	39,400	40,500	58,200	41,800
24,400	29,300	37,600	31,100	28,600	36,200	33,100
F	14,200	15,300	F	11,300[E]	14,200	18,600[E]
26,300	34,200	44,700	33,300	32,200	39,000	36,100

Table 18.3 Average income after tax by economic family type, 1993 to 2007

	1993	1994	1995	1996	1997	1998
			$ 2007 constant			
All family units	**45,300**	**45,600**	**45,600**	**45,600**	**45,900**	**47,900**
Economic families, two or more people	54,800	55,500	55,600	55,900	56,400	59,300
Elderly families[1]	44,400	44,500	45,900	44,100	44,700	43,800
Married couples	41,400	41,300	41,900	41,400	42,100	42,500
Other elderly families	51,400	52,800	56,200	52,100	52,400	48,300
Non-elderly families[2]	56,600	57,400	57,300	57,800	58,400	61,800
Married couples	53,200	53,300	53,600	54,400	55,100	59,100
No earner	28,500	29,100	28,900	29,200	29,000	29,500
One earner	42,900	44,700	44,200	45,800	44,600	47,700
Two earners	61,500	61,000	61,200	62,500	63,200	68,500
Two-parent families[3]	60,400	61,500	61,300	61,500	62,700	66,400
No earner	23,800	23,200	21,700	22,500	22,600	24,200
One earner	45,100	46,000	44,700	46,200	45,600	51,200
Two earners	62,400	64,000	63,500	63,800	64,800	68,100
Three or more earners	77,600	78,300	78,600	79,500	81,000	82,600
Married couples with other relatives	77,300	77,100	75,400	79,000	78,300	81,400
Lone-parent families[3]	29,400	30,600	30,400	28,900	29,600	31,500
Male lone-parent families	38,300	38,400	38,300	40,600	39,900	43,500
Female lone-parent families	28,000	29,200	29,200	27,100	27,900	29,300
No earner	19,100	19,200	19,200	17,500	16,800	17,200
One earner	30,100	30,600	30,800	30,500	30,200	30,900
Two or more earners	43,700	47,200	47,000	41,900	45,000	47,800
Other non-elderly families	45,800	46,400	48,400	51,000	51,000	55,500
Unattached individuals	24,000	23,900	24,100	23,700	23,700	24,200
Elderly male	24,700	26,700	26,100	26,100	25,800	27,000
Non-earner	23,800	24,800	24,600	24,600	24,400	24,600
Earner	32,300	42,800[E]	37,800	37,700	35,600	42,100
Elderly female	20,300	20,700	21,600	21,300	21,400	22,100
Non-earner	19,900	20,300	21,000	20,800	21,000	21,500
Earner	30,600	30,800	35,800	31,300	29,300	30,900
Non-elderly male	26,100	26,200	25,900	25,600	25,700	26,300
Non-earner	12,600	13,100	12,500	11,700	11,800	10,700
Earner	30,000	29,600	29,300	29,300	29,500	30,400
Non-elderly female	23,500	22,300	22,900	22,100	22,100	22,000
Non-earner	13,300	14,400	13,200	12,900	12,500	11,100
Earner	26,900	25,500	26,300	25,500	25,900	26,400

Note: 'Average income after tax' refers to total income, which includes government transfers, minus income tax.
1. Families in which the major income earner is 65 years of age and older.
2. Families in which the major income earner is less than 65 years of age.
3. Families with children less than 18 years of age.
Source: Statistics Canada, CANSIM table 202-0603.

1999	2000	2001	2002	2003	2004	2005	2006	2007
				$ 2007 constant				
49,500	**50,700**	**52,700**	**52,900**	**52,500**	**53,500**	**54,100**	**55,400**	**57,400**
61,100	63,000	65,500	65,600	65,000	66,600	67,500	69,100	71,900
45,700	45,400	46,900	47,600	47,300	48,200	50,200	51,200	54,200
44,700	44,000	45,800	46,100	46,200	47,800	48,300	49,300	52,700
49,200	50,300	51,300	53,000	51,300	50,100	57,200	57,900	59,300
63,600	65,900	68,600	68,500	68,000	69,800	70,500	72,300	75,000
59,100	59,900	64,700	63,900	62,200	62,900	65,300	67,200	70,000
30,400	31,000	35,700	32,000	32,100	30,400	31,900	35,000	36,500
49,500	48,500	53,700	50,000	49,800	52,400	54,500	53,700	56,400
67,500	67,800	72,300	72,800	69,900	70,000	73,100	75,300	77,500
68,600	71,100	73,700	74,500	75,000	77,800	76,100	78,000	82,000
23,700	23,200	26,100	26,000	24,200	25,500	22,100	26,600	28,700
51,900	51,900	54,100	56,900	57,700	56,900	54,900	56,100	58,700
69,500	72,200	74,400	74,800	75,000	77,500	76,800	77,500	81,400
86,200	89,900	93,300	92,200	92,700	97,500	95,500	98,800	102,500
86,200	91,300	90,900	90,000	90,400	92,600	96,800	99,800	101,100
32,600	35,200	36,600	34,900	35,600	35,700	40,500	41,100	41,800
43,500	47,000	45,800	46,400	49,300	47,000	53,700	55,700	52,100
30,500	32,800	34,600	32,200	32,500	33,200	37,500	37,800	39,500
17,800	17,400	18,300	17,500	17,200	18,600	18,500	20,500	18,000
31,500	32,500	34,200	32,400	32,200	33,100	37,900	37,200	39,300
47,900	52,200	54,600	47,700	49,700	47,900	50,300	51,400	54,200
56,700	57,100	60,200	61,700	57,400	60,300	58,800	60,400	62,500
25,400	25,600	26,800	27,400	27,700	27,600	28,100	29,100	29,800
26,100	25,100	27,000	26,900	27,700	27,400	28,100	28,500	31,000
25,000	23,900	25,700	25,100	24,900	26,100	25,000	25,600	27,600
33,800	31,800	35,100	35,000	37,400	32,100	40,500	39,000	42,800
22,200	22,500	23,900	24,400	23,900	24,800	24,100	26,100	25,800
21,700	21,900	23,000	24,000	23,300	24,000	23,200	25,300	24,700
29,500	30,600	35,700	29,600	28,400	32,200	32,100	33,000	33,800
27,600	28,800	29,700	30,100	30,700	30,000	31,200	32,400	32,700
10,400	10,300	12,100	11,700	12,400	11,900	12,100	12,100	13,400
31,200	32,200	33,100	33,900	34,500	33,500	35,300	35,900	36,400
24,300	23,400	24,600	25,800	25,900	25,900	26,200	26,600	27,800
10,500	10,500	12,200	12,000	12,900	12,800	14,400	13,600	13,700
29,300	27,700	28,800	30,000	29,700	29,800	29,400	29,900	31,500

Table 18.4 Average income after tax, by economic family type, and by province, 2007

	Canada	Newfoundland and Labrador	Prince Edward Island	Nova Scotia
	$ 2007 constant			
All family units	**57,400**	**50,000**	**48,500**	**48,700**
Economic families, two or more people	**71,900**	59,500	58,300	60,900
Elderly families[1]	**54,200**	38,300	45,800	46,300
Married couples	**52,700**	38,500	44,800	46,900
Other elderly families	**59,300**	37,900	F	44,500
Non-elderly families[2]	**75,000**	63,800	60,800	64,000
Married couples	**70,000**	57,200	57,500	58,700
No earner	**36,500**	F	F	41,600
One earner	**56,400**	49,800	43,600	51,100
Two earners	**77,500**	63,400	62,600	64,200
Two-parent families[3]	**82,000**	72,500	65,900	71,600
No earner	**28,700**	F	F	F
One earner	**58,700**	60,800	F	46,900
Two earners	**81,400**	72,500	63,600	70,600
Three or more earners	**102,500**	82,800	80,000	91,100
Married couples with other relatives	**101,100**	82,600	81,700	83,500
Lone-parent families[3]	**41,800**	35,700	34,600	35,900
Male lone-parent families	**52,100**	F	F	F
Female lone-parent families	**39,500**	33,700	34,400	34,200
No earner	**18,000**	F	F	F
One earner	**39,300**	29,400	28,000	34,900
Two or more earners	**54,200**	F	F	F
Other non-elderly families	**62,500**	59,800	53,100	60,600
Unattached individuals	**29,800**	22,200	23,300	25,300
Elderly male	**31,000**	20,200	F	31,300[E]
Non-earner	**27,600**	18,500	F	30,900[E]
Earner	**42,800**	F	F	F
Elderly female	**25,800**	19,400	24,300	24,800
Non-earner	**24,700**	19,400	23,800	24,500
Earner	**33,800**	F	F	F
Non-elderly male	**32,700**	25,000	22,000	26,000
Non-earner	**13,400**	F	F	11,800[E]
Earner	**36,400**	31,700	25,000	29,000
Non-elderly female	**27,800**	21,700	24,500	23,600
Non-earner	**13,700**	11,200[E]	F	12,800
Earner	**31,500**	27,900	27,500	26,300

Note: 'Average income after tax' refers to total income, which includes government transfers, minus income tax.
1. Families in which the major income earner is 65 years of age and older.
2. Families in which the major income earner is less than 65 years of age.
3. Families with children less than 18 years of age.
Source: Statistics Canada, CANSIM table 202-0603.

New Brunswick	Quebec	Ontario	Manitoba	Saskatchewan	Alberta	British Columbia
			$ 2007 constant			
47,900	**48,100**	**62,700**	**53,100**	**53,600**	**68,900**	**57,600**
57,800	61,800	76,600	67,100	67,700	86,600	73,700
44,100	43,800	59,300	54,500	51,800	56,900	62,400
43,300	42,200	57,700	52,800	52,700	53,900	61,400
47,500	49,700	64,100	60,900	46,700	71,500[E]	66,600
60,400	65,000	79,800	69,300	70,700	90,500	75,900
54,100	59,600	75,200	63,400	68,100	87,200	73,800
31,200	34,400	33,100	F	F	F	F
41,500	48,900	58,300	55,000	52,300	79,400	58,400
61,900	65,700	85,500	68,700	73,000	90,200	81,300
69,800	74,400	84,600	73,200	78,600	98,700	81,600
F	F	F	F	F	F	F
44,700	53,100	54,000	52,100	64,400	90,800	62,700
69,900	75,000	86,500	67,000	73,500	91,600	80,700
88,600	91,600	104,500	102,800	97,500	120,100	101,100
82,700	87,800	105,600	104,800	95,700	123,600	99,600
32,200	40,000	45,500	35,700	34,900	48,000	38,300
F	49,300	60,000	F	F	55,400	49,900
31,000	36,700	43,100	34,300	34,500	46,100	36,300
F	18,000	18,900	F	F	F	F
30,900	35,300	44,600	33,000	32,500	41,400	38,300
F	52,600	60,600	F	44,200	57,500	46,400
52,300	53,000	66,600	65,700	57,000	69,100	64,600
24,400	26,000	32,100	27,200	27,400	36,900	29,800
24,300	25,100	36,700	27,500	29,400	27,200	36,000
22,300	23,100	31,000	24,700	25,800	28,000	32,500
F	33,100	53,500	F	38,200	F	F
22,200	24,100	28,500	23,100	24,700	26,000	25,600
22,100	23,100	27,600	22,900	23,000	25,000	23,200
F	31,600	36,100	F	34,500[E]	F	36,600
27,500	28,400	34,000	30,000	30,700	44,300	31,000
10,300[E]	12,600	13,400	17,600[E]	F	F	14,300[E]
31,500	32,000	38,000	31,900	32,900	46,400	34,600
21,200	24,500	30,500	26,300	24,600	31,000	28,700
F	12,900	14,300	F	10,500[E]	13,400	15,800[E]
22,800	28,200	35,700	28,000	27,500	33,200	31,400

Table 18.5 Family characteristics and employment income, by number of children, 2006

	Families with or without children	Families with no children	Families with one child	Families with two children	Families with three or more children
			number		
Type of family					
Single-earner-male couple families	**1,198,280**	588,600	242,240	228,720	138,720
Single-earner-female couple families	**497,590**	289,530	105,860	71,400	30,800
Dual-earner couple families	**4,607,760**	1,654,780	1,148,190	1,291,310	513,480
Lone-parent families	**942,670**	.	551,370	288,080	103,220
			$		
Median employment income[1]					
Single-earner-male couple families	**30,700**	18,100	36,100	48,200	42,100
Single-earner-female couple families	**19,100**	17,000	21,600	24,300	19,100
Dual-earner couple families	**74,900**	68,500	74,400	82,300	77,400
Lone-parent families	**26,100**	.	26,700	26,900	20,800

Note: Only families with positive employment income are included in this table. Excluded families consist of: couple families where both spouses or partners reported zero or negative employment incomes; couple families where only one spouse or partner reported negative employment income; and single-parent families where the parent reported zero or negative employment income.

1. Employment income includes wages and salaries, commissions from employment, training allowances, tips and gratuities, and net self-employment income (business, professional, commission, farming and fishing income).

Source: Statistics Canada, CANSIM table 111-0020.

Table 18.6 Earnings by sex, 2002 to 2007

	2002	2003	2004	2005	2006	2007
			$			
Females						
Average earnings	27,300	26,900	27,300	27,900	28,400	29,200
Median earnings	20,600	20,700	20,700	21,100	21,300	22,000
Males						
Average earnings	43,400	42,800	43,100	43,700	43,800	44,400
Median earnings	33,700	33,600	33,600	34,100	33,800	34,300
			%			
Female-to-male earnings ratio						
Average earnings	62.8	62.9	63.4	64.0	64.7	65.7
Median earnings	61.0	61.7	61.7	61.8	63.1	64.2

Note: Includes both full-time and part-time workers.
Source: Statistics Canada, CANSIM table 202-0102.

Table 18.7 Taxfilers and dependents, by income tax, deductions and benefits, 2002 to 2006

	2002	2003	2004	2005	2006
			number		
Taxfilers and dependents[1]					
Total income	**22,798,980**	**23,070,200**	**23,408,890**	**23,715,660**	**24,113,140**
Total income taxes paid	**15,639,760**	**15,826,980**	**16,185,170**	**16,290,250**	**16,484,590**
Federal taxes	15,490,560	15,679,040	15,933,920	15,983,860	15,998,540
Provincial taxes	14,019,130	14,104,840	14,678,320	14,801,880	15,224,320
Quebec abatement[2]	3,763,520	3,805,390	3,857,230	3,837,440	3,803,250
Capital gains received[3]	1,043,090	1,220,910	1,827,800	2,220,970	2,502,180
Employment Insurance premiums	13,873,380	14,057,370	14,329,720	14,573,390	14,787,860
Canada Pension Plan and Quebec Pension Plan premiums	14,540,150	14,877,510	15,157,120	15,433,340	15,630,400
Registered pension plan premiums	3,773,640	4,056,610	4,152,860	4,236,170	4,241,760
Annual union, professional or like dues	5,257,840	5,289,240	5,359,730	5,413,350	5,493,840
Employment Insurance benefits	2,408,590	2,415,970	2,373,690	2,296,870	2,298,550
Canada Pension Plan and Quebec Pension Plan benefits	4,614,390	4,751,530	4,885,460	5,017,190	5,179,680
			$ thousands		
Amount claimed on income tax form					
Total income	**736,538,862**	**764,005,577**	**804,477,155**	**851,595,902**	**910,890,542**
Total income taxes paid	**131,945,856**	**137,361,112**	**145,807,259**	**154,372,475**	**166,405,851**
Federal taxes	86,563,273	90,164,811	94,490,517	97,827,644	105,531,361
Provincial taxes	48,317,707	50,257,718	54,509,957	59,720,213	64,176,947
Quebec abatement[2]	2,935,125	3,061,416	3,193,216	3,175,383	3,302,457
Capital gains received[3]	15,371,376	18,324,208	24,438,514	33,397,382	41,272,012
Employment Insurance premiums	7,343,744	7,183,444	6,977,046	7,089,330	6,724,261
Canada Pension Plan and Quebec Pension Plan premiums	15,110,760	16,447,784	17,174,876	18,172,785	19,084,324
Registered Pension Plan premiums	7,621,762	8,539,553	9,793,052	10,802,601	11,402,976
Annual union, professional or like dues	2,669,327	2,797,471	2,911,456	3,008,687	3,134,877
Employment Insurance benefits	12,375,522	12,611,872	12,551,987	12,317,055	12,886,696
Canada Pension Plan and Quebec Pension Plan benefits	26,007,618	27,149,428	28,750,331	30,180,437	31,692,330

Note: Taxfilers are people who filed a tax return for the reference year and were alive at the end of the year.
1. A dependent is a member of a family who did not file a personal income tax return for the reference year.
2. The Quebec abatement reduces the federal income tax payable by Quebec residents. Residents and people operating a business in Quebec are allowed a 16.5% abatement from the federal tax.
3. Capital gains are reported following the sale or disposal of property, such as the sale of real estate, farm property, corporation shares, bonds and other types of properties. Line 127 of the T1 income tax return shows taxable capital gains or three-quarters of the capital gains actually received. The information in this table has been grossed up to represent the total capital gains received.

Source: Statistics Canada, CANSIM table 111-0026.

Table 18.8 People with low income after tax, by age group, sex and economic family type, 1993 to 2007

	1993	1994	1995	1996	1997	1998
				%		
Both sexes	**14.1**	**14.0**	**14.5**	**15.2**	**15.0**	**13.7**
0 to 17 years	17.0	16.3	17.5	18.4	17.4	15.7
18 to 64 years	13.6	14.1	14.4	15.0	15.2	13.9
65 and older	10.7	8.6	8.7	9.7	9.0	8.6
Males	13.1	12.9	13.6	14.2	14.2	12.9
0 to 17 years	16.8	15.9	17.2	18.5	17.8	16.2
18 to 64 years	12.7	13.1	13.7	13.9	14.2	12.8
65 and older	6.2	4.2	4.0	5.1	5.5	5.4
Females	15.1	15.1	15.4	16.2	15.8	14.5
0 to 17 years	17.2	16.7	17.8	18.3	17.0	15.1
18 to 64 years	14.5	15.1	15.1	16.0	16.2	15.0
65 and older	14.1	11.9	12.3	13.2	11.7	11.1
Economic families, two or more people	**11.1**	**11.0**	**11.4**	**12.0**	**11.8**	**10.4**
Males	10.1	10.1	10.7	11.1	10.9	9.6
Females	12.0	11.8	12.2	12.9	12.6	11.1
Children 0 to 17 years	16.9	16.1	17.3	18.3	17.3	15.6
Children in two-parent families	10.7	10.6	11.7	11.6	11.4	10.0
Children in female lone-parent families	49.6	48.2	50.7	56.0	51.2	46.2
Children in other economic families	25.1	27.5	24.1	23.1	21.4	22.7
18 to 64 years	9.6	9.9	10.2	10.7	10.7	9.3
Males	7.9	8.5	8.9	9.1	9.0	7.8
Females	11.2	11.2	11.4	12.2	12.2	10.6
65 and older	3.0	2.3	1.9	2.3	2.8	3.3E
Males	3.1	2.2	1.8	2.0	2.9	2.7E
Females	2.9	2.5	1.9	2.6	2.8	3.9E
Unattached individuals	**35.3**	**35.0**	**35.0**	**36.1**	**36.2**	**35.2**
Males	34.4	33.0	34.1	34.7	35.6	33.8
Females	36.1	36.9	35.9	37.6	36.9	36.5
0 to 64 years	38.3	39.7	39.1	40.4	41.6	40.4
Males	36.8	36.1	37.3	37.7	38.7	36.5
Females	40.5	44.6	41.7	44.2	45.6	45.8
65 and older	27.4	22.6	24.1	25.4	22.4	20.9
Males	20.0	13.3	14.4	17.7	17.0	17.5
Females	29.9	25.6	27.3	28.1	24.3	22.1

Notes: Prevalence of low-income shows the proportion of people living below the low-income cutoffs within a given group.
After-tax low-income cutoffs (1992 base) were determined from an analysis of the 1992 Family Expenditure Survey data.
Families with incomes below these limits usually spend 63.6% or more of their income on food, shelter and clothing.
Source: Statistics Canada, CANSIM table 202-0802.

1999	2000	2001	2002	2003	2004	2005	2006	2007
				%				
13.0	**12.5**	**11.2**	**11.6**	**11.6**	**11.4**	**10.8**	**10.5**	**9.2**
14.6	13.9	12.2	12.4	12.7	13.0	11.8	11.4	9.5
13.4	12.9	11.7	12.0	12.2	11.9	11.4	11.2	9.9
7.9	7.6	6.7	7.6	6.8	5.6	6.1	5.4	4.8
12.4	11.4	10.3	10.7	11.0	10.8	10.5	10.1	9.0
14.9	13.5	12.1	12.8	13.1	13.2	12.3	11.4	9.9
12.7	11.7	10.6	10.9	11.4	11.3	11.1	10.9	9.7
4.8	4.6	4.6	4.9	4.4	3.5	3.3	3.4	3.3
13.6	13.6	12.1	12.4	12.2	11.9	11.2	10.9	9.4
14.3	14.4	12.3	12.0	12.4	12.9	11.3	11.4	9.0
14.0	14.0	12.8	13.1	12.9	12.5	11.8	11.6	10.2
10.4	10.0	8.3	9.7	8.7	7.3	8.4	7.0	6.0
9.7	**9.3**	**8.1**	**8.6**	**8.7**	**8.2**	**7.5**	**7.3**	**6.0**
9.2	8.4	7.4	8.0	8.1	7.7	7.1	6.9	5.7
10.3	10.1	8.7	9.2	9.2	8.8	7.9	7.8	6.3
14.5	13.8	12.1	12.3	12.5	12.9	11.7	11.3	9.4
9.4	9.5	8.3	7.4	7.9	8.4	7.8	7.7	6.5
41.9	40.1	37.4	43.0	41.4	40.4	33.4	32.3	26.6
24.9	14.6[E]	10.5[E]	11.2[E]	14.3[E]	14.9[E]	14.5	11.0[E]	9.5[E]
8.8	8.4	7.3	8.1	8.1	7.4	6.9	6.8	5.5
7.8	7.3	6.3	6.9	7.1	6.3	6.0	6.1	4.9
9.8	9.4	8.4	9.3	9.0	8.4	7.7	7.5	6.2
2.3[E]	2.1[E]	1.9[E]	2.4	2.2	1.7[E]	1.2[E]	1.4[E]	1.1[E]
2.1[E]	1.7[E]	1.9[E]	2.3[E]	2.0[E]	1.7[E]	1.1[E]	1.1[E]	1.2[E]
2.4[E]	2.5[E]	1.9[E]	2.4[E]	2.3[E]	1.6[E]	1.3[E]	1.7[E]	1.1[E]
34.1	**32.9**	**30.8**	**29.5**	**29.7**	**30.1**	**30.4**	**29.2**	**27.4**
33.0	30.0	28.4	27.1	28.4	29.2	29.8	28.8	27.4
35.2	35.7	33.3	32.0	30.9	31.0	31.0	29.6	27.5
38.8	37.3	35.3	33.2	33.9	35.0	34.3	33.7	32.0
35.5	32.1	30.3	29.0	30.7	32.0	32.3	31.2	29.7
43.6	44.3	42.2	39.0	38.1	39.3	37.1	37.1	35.1
21.1	20.6	18.1	19.4	17.7	15.4	18.5	15.5	13.9
17.2	17.6	16.8	15.9	14.7	11.5	13.6	14.0	13.0
22.5	21.7	18.6	20.7	18.9	16.9	20.3	16.1	14.3

Table 18.9 Average household expenditures, by province and territory, 2007

	Canada	Newfoundland and Labrador	Prince Edward Island	Nova Scotia	New Brunswick	Quebec
	$					
Total expenditures	**69,946**	**55,007**	**55,574**	**59,987**	**58,205**	**57,308**
Total current consumption	**49,766**	40,332	40,922	44,145	42,285	41,100
Food	**7,305**	6,463	6,629	6,640	6,602	7,321
Shelter	**13,643**	8,985	10,137	10,815	10,031	10,167
Household operation	**3,287**	2,968	3,097	3,304	2,945	2,601
Household furnishings and equipment	**1,964**	1,719	1,424	1,784	1,567	1,543
Clothing	**2,948**	2,588	2,112	2,412	2,312	2,368
Transportation	**9,395**	8,392	8,039	8,820	9,137	7,542
Health care	**1,932**	1,582	1,994	1,868	1,817	2,067
Personal care	**1,167**	1,008	1,027	1,048	1,000	1,089
Recreation	**3,976**	3,305	3,019	3,329	3,215	3,055
Reading materials and other printed matter	**260**	179	250	249	234	245
Education	**1,017**	579	797	1,055	1,005	633
Tobacco products and alcoholic beverages	**1,536**	1,636	1,474	1,628	1,426	1,354
Games of chance (net amount)	**251**	247	195	253	191	178
Miscellaneous	**1,081**	681	727	939	804	936
Personal income taxes	**14,447**	10,466	9,504	10,585	10,610	11,739
Personal insurance payments and pension contributions	**3,946**	3,171	3,694	3,550	3,811	3,595
Gifts of money and contributions	**1,788**	1,038	1,454	1,708	1,499	874
	% of households reporting					
Total expenditures	**100.0**	**100.0**	**100.0**	**100.0**	**100.0**	**100.0**
Total current consumption	**100.0**	100.0	100.0	100.0	100.0	100.0
Food	**100.0**	100.0	100.0	100.0	100.0	100.0
Shelter	**99.8**	99.6	100.0	100.0	100.0	99.9
Household operation	**100.0**	100.0	100.0	99.8	100.0	100.0
Household furnishings and equipment	**94.1**	93.3	95.0	95.5	94.3	90.4
Clothing	**99.2**	99.5	99.4	98.5	99.3	98.6
Transportation	**98.2**	93.3	97.3	97.3	97.8	97.7
Health care	**98.3**	97.9	97.5	98.5	98.3	98.4
Personal care	**99.8**	99.8	100.0	99.9	99.9	99.9
Recreation	**97.6**	97.3	97.5	97.8	97.8	96.1
Reading materials and other printed matter	**74.5**	66.6	78.7	77.5	75.4	71.7
Education	**34.5**	27.5	31.0	31.9	31.1	34.9
Tobacco products and alcoholic beverages	**85.2**	84.1	84.0	83.6	81.9	88.9
Games of chance (net amount)	**53.1**	52.2	54.6	55.9	55.3	56.7
Miscellaneous	**91.9**	83.6	89.8	90.5	90.6	91.6
Personal income taxes	**93.5**	81.5	92.5	88.2	89.0	90.8
Personal insurance payments and pension contributions	**84.0**	77.4	86.0	82.0	85.0	84.0
Gifts of money and contributions	**75.5**	85.6	87.3	83.1	82.2	65.6

Source: Statistics Canada, CANSIM table 203-0001.

Ontario	Manitoba	Saskatchewan	Alberta	British Columbia	Yukon	Northwest Territories	Nunavut
			$				
76,654	**63,303**	**63,944**	**85,912**	**72,621**	**76,997**	**89,075**	**73,747**
53,938	44,701	46,089	59,288	53,394	53,929	63,369	54,400
7,383	6,518	6,073	7,491	7,745	7,078	9,096	14,057
16,341	10,852	10,711	14,955	15,056	14,058	18,249	11,547
3,666	3,063	3,161	3,768	3,357	3,831	4,110	3,445
2,136	1,715	1,873	2,608	2,036	2,707	2,466	2,082
3,420	2,482	2,434	3,548	2,818	2,915	3,844	3,345
9,600	9,651	10,412	12,678	9,896	10,775	11,439	5,456
1,721	1,786	1,738	2,259	2,177	1,603	1,306	874
1,239	1,102	1,082	1,288	1,135	1,193	1,351	1,123
4,133	3,607	4,387	5,387	4,577	4,860	6,132	6,855
281	267	218	291	233	415	312	201
1,220	869	804	1,176	1,215	739	503	F
1,459	1,441	1,615	2,124	1,624	2,236	2,792	3,506
283	311	286	340	223	308	653	465
1,055	1,037	1,293	1,374	1,303	1,212	1,116	1,144
16,403	12,411	12,215	19,766	13,297	16,437	17,751	13,312
4,177	4,003	3,923	4,331	3,850	4,961	6,228	4,742
2,137	2,188	1,716	2,527	2,080	1,670	1,727	1,293
			% of households reporting				
100.0	**100.0**	**100.0**	**100.0**	**100.0**	**100.0**	**100.0**	**100.0**
100.0	100.0	100.0	100.0	100.0	100.0	100.0	100.0
100.0	100.0	100.0	100.0	100.0	100.0	100.0	100.0
99.9	99.5	99.7	99.6	99.7	99.1	98.1	99.1
100.0	100.0	100.0	100.0	100.0	100.0	97.5	99.8
96.5	93.8	92.8	94.2	94.4	97.4	90.7	91.0
99.7	99.1	99.2	99.7	98.9	100.0	98.1	98.8
98.8	98.6	98.3	99.0	98.0	98.0	96.3	81.0
98.4	98.2	98.5	98.5	97.6	98.6	92.8	82.1
99.9	99.5	99.9	99.8	99.7	99.8	96.9	97.8
98.1	98.1	98.0	98.3	98.1	99.8	97.6	95.0
74.4	78.7	77.3	79.8	74.3	84.4	78.0	48.0
32.8	34.9	34.1	37.1	38.6	31.6	29.6	F
84.0	82.5	83.7	84.2	84.5	83.9	90.4	92.9
51.0	56.8	56.2	48.8	52.6	48.5	54.4	40.8
91.6	94.1	95.4	94.8	91.7	96.3	84.8	78.1
96.9	96.2	88.5	95.3	91.7	93.8	97.7	93.6
84.2	81.8	81.1	89.2	81.9	90.8	88.2	89.7
80.6	82.8	82.5	77.3	71.4	75.1	70.0	63.7

Table 18.10 Savers' characteristics, 2002 to 2007

	2002	2003	2004	2005	2006	2007
Total savers (number)	4,524,170	4,425,850	4,385,000	4,420,570	4,707,550	5,212,320
Average age of savers (years)	54	54	55	54	54	53
Median total income of savers ($)	25,000	25,400	26,500	27,300	28,900	31,700
	%					
Males	43	44	44	44	44	43
Females	57	56	56	56	56	57
All ages	**100**	**100**	**100**	**100**	**100**	**100**
0 to 24 years	8	7	7	7	7	7
25 to 34 years	10	10	10	10	11	12
35 to 44 years	16	15	15	15	15	15
45 to 54 years	19	19	19	19	19	19
55 to 64 years	16	17	17	17	17	17
65 years and older	32	33	33	32	31	29
	$ thousands					
Total interest income	7,717,395	7,312,405	6,921,317	6,657,051	7,351,326	9,093,165
	$					
Median interest income	300	300	310	300	320	380
Male savers	300	300	270	250	280	340
Female savers	400	400	360	330	360	420
	% of interest income					
Males	41	41	41	42	42	42
Females	59	59	59	58	58	58
All ages	**100**	**100**	**100**	**100**	**100**	**100**
0 to 24 years	3	2	2	2	2	2
25 to 34 years	3	3	3	3	4	4
35 to 44 years	8	8	7	8	8	9
45 to 54 years	13	14	14	14	14	15
55 to 64 years	17	18	18	18	18	19
65 years and older	56	56	56	55	53	51

Note: Savers are defined as taxfilers who reported interest and investment income on line 121 of the personal income tax return, but no dividend income on line 120.
Source: Statistics Canada, CANSIM table 111-0036.

Table 18.11 Investors' characteristics, 2002 to 2007

	2002	2003	2004	2005	2006	2007
Investors						
Total (number)	2,952,880	2,954,330	3,141,130	3,364,620	3,494,670	3,694,370
Average age (years)	54	54	55	55	55	55
Median total income ($)	37,800	39,300	40,300	41,500	43,400	45,080
Total investment income ($ thousands)	21,781,629	22,836,519	24,341,114	27,825,737	33,554,970	37,849,705
	% of investors					
Males	51	51	50	50	50	50
Females	49	49	50	50	50	50
All ages	**100**	**100**	**100**	**100**	**100**	**100**
0 to 24 years	4	4	4	4	4	4
25 to 34 years	7	8	8	8	8	8
35 to 44 years	17	16	15	15	14	14
45 to 54 years	24	23	23	23	23	22
55 to 64 years	21	21	22	22	23	23
65 years and older	28	28	28	28	29	29
	$					
Investment income						
Median investment income	1,000	900	930	970	1,200	1,410
Males	900	800	870	910	1,170	1,380
Females	1,000	1,000	1,000	1,020	1,230	1,440
	% of investment income					
Investment income from dividends	62	61	65	68	71	68
Males	58	58	58	59	60	59
Females	42	42	42	41	40	41
All ages	**100**	**100**	**100**	**100**	**100**	**100**
0 to 24 years	2	2	2	2	2	2
25 to 34 years	3	4	4	4	4	4
35 to 44 years	13	13	13	13	13	12
45 to 54 years	21	21	21	22	23	23
55 to 64 years	23	23	24	24	24	25
65 years and older	39	38	36	35	34	34

Notes: Investors are taxfilers who reported dividend income on line 120 of their personal income tax return. They may or may not have also reported interest and other investment income on line 121.
Total income is income from all sources.
Investment income includes dividend income reported on line 120 of the tax return, or interest and other investment income reported on line 121, or both.
Dividend income consists of dividends from taxable Canadian corporations (as stocks or mutual funds). Interest and other investment income includes interest from Canada Savings Bonds, bank accounts, treasury bills, investment certificates, term deposits, earnings on life insurance policies, and foreign interest and dividend income.
Source: Statistics Canada, CANSIM table 111-0037.

Table 18.12 Consumer bankruptcies, 1993 to 2008

	Total consumer bankruptcies	Total assets	Total liabilities[1]	Total deficiency
	number	$ thousands		
1993	54,456	1,615,674	3,181,202	1,565,528
1994	53,802	1,616,605	3,033,102	1,416,498
1995	65,432	2,084,296	3,593,725	1,509,429
1996	79,631	2,386,365	4,240,090	1,853,725
1997	85,297	2,312,155	4,260,379	1,948,224
1998	75,465	2,262,007	3,950,287	1,688,279
1999	72,997	2,304,806	3,793,619	1,488,813
2000	75,137	2,477,451	4,090,506	1,613,055
2001	79,453	2,766,868	4,341,783	1,574,915
2002	78,232	2,386,961	4,421,870	2,034,909
2003	84,251	2,048,368	4,817,515	2,769,146
2004	84,426	2,020,459	4,754,302	2,733,843
2005	84,638	2,242,556	5,160,493	2,917,938
2006	79,218	2,342,350	5,146,717	2,804,367
2007	79,796	2,614,799	5,539,032	2,924,233
2008	90,610	3,807,397	7,414,488	3,607,090

1. As declared by debtors.
Sources: Office of the Superintendent of Bankruptcy Canada, and Statistics Canada, CANSIM table 177-0001.

Table 18.13 Consumer bankruptcies by province and territory, 2008

	Total consumer bankruptcies	Total assets	Total liabilities[1]	Total deficiency
	number	$ thousands		
Canada	**90,610**	**3,807,397**	**7,414,488**	**3,607,090**
Newfoundland and Labrador	2,133	65,380	127,502	62,122
Nova Scotia	3,970	195,651	292,034	96,383
Prince Edward Island	444	22,096	40,217	18,121
New Brunswick	2,655	125,898	240,920	115,022
Quebec	28,317	767,765	1,780,744	1,012,979
Ontario	36,200	1,902,984	3,454,236	1,551,251
Manitoba	2,025	72,231	137,266	65,035
Saskatchewan	1,451	60,786	101,050	40,264
Alberta	6,066	337,934	602,865	264,932
British Columbia	7,293	254,777	632,996	378,219
Northwest Territories	22	646	1,831	1,185
Yukon	27	759	1,995	1,236
Nunavut	7	491	832	341

1. As declared by debtors.
Sources: Office of the Superintendent of Bankruptcy Canada, and Statistics Canada, CANSIM table 177-0001.

Table 18.14 Registered Pension Plan members, by type of plan, contributory status and province, 2002 to 2008

	2002	2003	2004	2005	2006	2007	2008
	% of total						
Newfoundland and Labrador	**1.8**	**1.8**	**1.8**	**1.8**	**1.8**	**1.6**	**1.6**
Defined benefit	1.5	1.5	1.5	1.4	1.4	1.4	1.4
Defined contribution	3.7	3.8	3.7	3.8	3.9	2.7	2.6
Contributory	2.1	2.1	2.1	2.0	2.0	1.7	1.7
Non-contributory	1.1	1.1	1.1	0.9	1.0	1.0	1.0
Prince Edward Island	**0.3**	**0.3**	**0.4**	**0.4**	**0.4**	**0.3**	**0.4**
Defined benefit	0.3	0.3	0.3	0.4	0.3	0.3	0.4
Defined contribution	0.4	0.4	0.5	0.4	0.4	0.5	0.5
Contributory	0.4	0.4	0.4	0.4	0.4	0.4	0.4
Non-contributory	0.1	0.1	0.1	0.1	0.1	0.1	0.1
Nova Scotia	**3.0**	**2.9**	**2.9**	**3.0**	**3.0**	**2.9**	**2.9**
Defined benefit	2.9	2.8	2.9	2.9	2.9	2.8	2.8
Defined contribution	3.7	3.6	3.5	3.7	3.8	4.0	3.9
Contributory	3.3	3.1	3.1	3.2	3.2	3.1	3.1
Non-contributory	2.3	2.3	2.4	2.2	2.2	2.1	2.0
New Brunswick	**2.3**	**2.3**	**2.3**	**2.3**	**2.3**	**2.1**	**2.1**
Defined benefit	2.2	2.2	2.2	2.2	2.1	1.9	1.9
Defined contribution	2.8	2.9	2.8	3.0	3.2	3.0	3.0
Contributory	2.7	2.6	2.6	2.6	2.5	2.3	2.3
Non-contributory	1.2	1.3	1.3	1.3	1.3	1.3	1.3
Quebec	**24.4**	**24.1**	**24.8**	**25.0**	**25.1**	**25.1**	**25.0**
Defined benefit	25.9	25.8	26.7	27.0	27.2	27.1	27.4
Defined contribution	15.7	15.9	16.1	15.8	16.0	17.0	17.2
Contributory	28.2	28.0	28.9	28.7	28.2	28.2	28.1
Non-contributory	14.0	13.0	12.7	13.0	13.6	12.2	11.5
Ontario	**38.7**	**39.2**	**38.8**	**38.8**	**38.4**	**38.2**	**38.1**
Defined benefit	39.7	40.4	39.7	39.7	39.2	38.8	37.9
Defined contribution	36.6	36.6	37.6	37.9	37.1	37.7	37.3
Contributory	34.3	34.8	34.5	34.3	34.5	34.9	35.0
Non-contributory	50.7	52.1	51.9	53.6	53.3	52.1	51.6
Manitoba	**4.3**	**4.2**	**4.3**	**4.3**	**4.2**	**4.2**	**4.2**
Defined benefit	3.8	3.4	3.4	3.4	3.4	3.4	3.4
Defined contribution	6.1	5.9	5.8	5.8	6.0	5.8	5.8
Contributory	4.8	4.7	4.7	4.7	4.5	4.4	4.4
Non-contributory	3.1	2.8	2.8	2.9	3.2	3.3	3.4
Saskatchewan	**3.6**	**3.6**	**3.6**	**3.6**	**3.6**	**3.5**	**3.5**
Defined benefit	2.5	2.5	2.4	2.4	2.4	2.6	2.6
Defined contribution	10.2	10.3	10.1	10.2	10.1	8.8	9.0
Contributory	4.1	4.2	4.1	4.0	3.9	3.8	3.8
Non-contributory	2.0	2.0	2.0	2.0	2.2	2.3	2.4
Alberta	**8.9**	**9.0**	**9.1**	**9.1**	**9.4**	**9.7**	**10.0**
Defined benefit	8.6	8.8	8.9	8.8	9.3	9.5	9.8
Defined contribution	10.6	10.9	10.7	10.5	10.5	11.0	11.0
Contributory	8.4	8.5	8.5	8.5	8.7	8.6	8.8
Non-contributory	10.1	10.3	11.0	11.0	12.2	14.4	15.2
British Columbia	**12.2**	**11.9**	**11.5**	**11.4**	**11.4**	**11.7**	**11.8**
Defined benefit	12.0	11.7	11.4	11.2	11.2	11.5	11.7
Defined contribution	9.7	9.2	8.9	8.6	8.7	9.1	9.4
Contributory	11.2	10.9	10.5	11.1	11.6	11.9	11.9
Non-contributory	15.1	14.6	14.5	12.5	10.5	10.9	11.1

Note: Membership data are as of the plan's year-end in the previous calendar year.
Source: Statistics Canada, CANSIM table 280-0008.

Table 18.15 Registered Retirement Savings Plan (RRSP) contributions, by contributor characteristics, 2001 to 2007

	2001	2002	2003	2004	2005	2006	2007
				number			
Taxfilers	**21,886,860**	**21,979,210**	**22,465,770**	**22,725,310**	**23,311,690**	**23,338,370**	**23,725,970**
				%			
Male taxfilers	49	49	49	48	48	48	48
Female taxfilers	51	51	51	52	52	52	52
				number			
Total RRSP contributors	**6,241,050**	**5,991,440**	**5,948,340**	**6,002,350**	**6,135,980**	**6,196,050**	**6,292,480**
				%			
Male RRSP contributors	55	54	54	54	54	54	54
Female RRSP contributors	45	46	46	46	46	46	46
				years			
Average age of RRSP contributors	43	43	43	44	44	44	44
				%			
Age groups of RRSP contributors							
0 to 24 years	5	4	4	4	4	4	4
25 to 34 years	21	21	20	20	20	20	19
35 to 44 years	30	29	28	28	27	26	25
45 to 54 years	28	28	29	29	30	30	30
55 to 64 years	14	15	16	16	17	18	18
65 years and over	2	2	2	2	3	3	3
Income level of RRSP contributors							
less than $20,000	10	10	9	8	8	7	6
$20,000 to $39,999	..	..	..	..	..	..	25
$40,000 to $59,999	..	..	..	..	..	..	28
$60,000 to $79,999	..	..	..	..	..	..	18
$80,000 or more	13	14	15	17	19	21	23
				$ thousands			
Total RRSP contributions	**28,438,914**	**27,072,812**	**27,561,305**	**28,788,102**	**30,581,252**	**32,350,792**	**34,057,715**
				%			
Male RRSP contributors	62	61	62	62	62	62	61
Female RRSP contributors	38	39	38	38	38	38	39
Income level of RRSP contributions							
less than $20,000	3	3	3	3	2	2	2
$20,000 to $39,999	..	..	..	..	..	..	12
$40,000 to $59,999	..	..	..	..	..	..	20
$60,000 to $79,999	..	..	..	..	..	..	18
$80,000 or more	33	35	37	40	44	47	49

Source: Statistics Canada, CANSIM table 111-0039.

Information and communications technology

19

Information and communications technologies are penetrating ever more deeply into the social fabric. Canadians are using the Internet for more and more purposes, but a digital divide persists based on income, education and age.

Seventy-three percent of those aged 16 and older, or 19.2 million Canadians, went online for personal reasons in 2007, compared with 68% of those aged 18 and older in 2005.

Of Canadians in the highest income group (households earning more than $95,000), 91% used the Internet, compared with 47% of those in the lowest group (households earning less than $24,000).

Eighty-four percent of people with at least some postsecondary education accessed the Internet in 2007, compared with 58% of those with less education.

Internet use rose among all age groups from 2005 to 2007. However, 96% of young people aged 16 to 24 went online, compared with 29% of those 65 and older.

Browsing, blogging, chatting, and downloading

E-mail and general browsing are the most popular online activities at home. Finding government or health information, making travel arrangements, banking, and ordering goods and services are also popular uses of the Internet.

Moreover, 20% of home Internet users reported posting images, writing blogs, or participating in discussion forums in 2007. More than half of these content contributors were under the age of 30.

Some 50% of home Internet users used an instant messenger during 2007. Again, relatively more young people did so. The growth in broadband services has also facilitated downloading of music, movies and television shows.

Chart 19.1
Internet use, by province, 2007

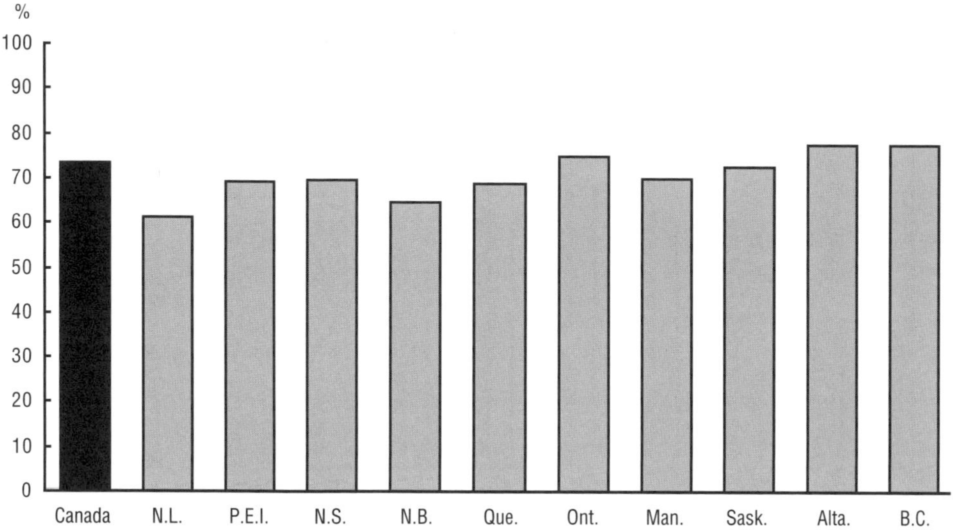

Note: Internet access from any location.
Source: Statistics Canada, CANSIM table 358-0122.

Service providers seeing growth

This ever-rising Internet use has meant sustained growth for Canada's Internet service providers.

Revenues from providing Internet services reached $5.7 billion in 2007, up 13% from 2006. The residential market was by far the largest, generating almost 64% of Internet service revenues in 2007.

High-speed service continues to gain popularity among residential users. In 2007, 90% of them chose high-speed services, up from nearly 65% in 2003. High-speed customers accounted for 94% of residential revenues in 2007, up from nearly 75% in 2003.

In 2007, 59% of high-speed subscribers chose plans with an advertised top speed of 5 megabits per second (mbps) to 9 mbps, a range that enables users to download or view online movie rentals or purchases, and may enable them to view certain low-bandwidth forms of high-definition video.

Table 19.a
Internet window-shopping, by product and service, 2007

	%
Consumer electronics	43.7
Housewares	42.8
Travel arrangements	41.5
Clothing, jewellery and accessories	40.6
Books, magazines and online newspapers	30.6
Automotive products	28.0
Other entertainment products	26.4
Music	23.7
Toys and games	21.2
Computer hardware	20.5
Videocassettes and DVDs	18.8
Real estate	18.7
Computer software	18.5
Sports equipment	16.6
Flowers, gifts	13.4
Other health and beauty products and vitamins	12.8

Note: Population aged 16 and older.
Source: Statistics Canada, CANSIM table 358-0136.

Approximately 500 Internet service providers operate in Canada, but the top five captured 77% of Internet access revenues in 2007.

Chart 19.2
Software development and computer services industries

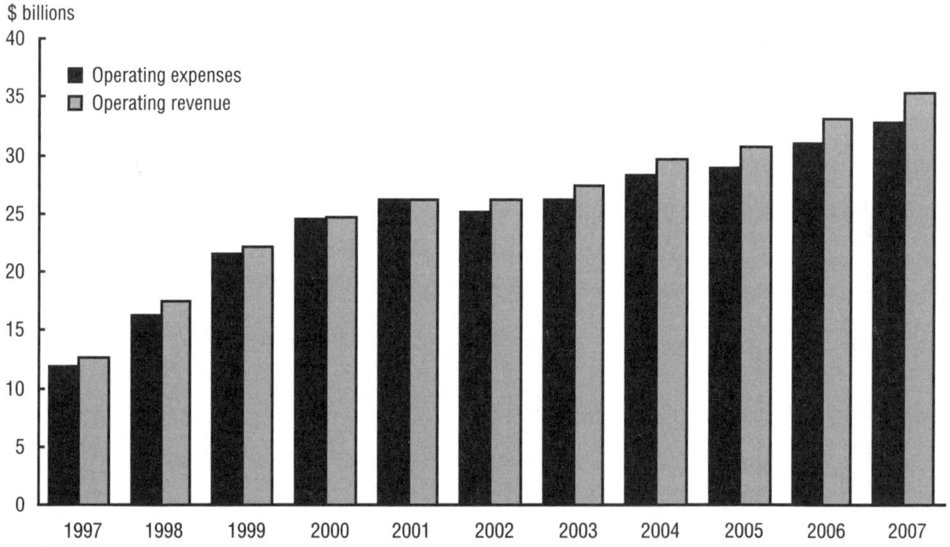

Note: Includes software publishers; data processing, hosting and related services; and computer systems design and related services industries.
Source: Statistics Canada, CANSIM table 354-0005.

Businesses online

Larger businesses tend to have stronger perceptions of the benefits of Internet presence than do smaller businesses, according to data from the Survey of Electronic Commerce and Technology.

In 2007, 47% of the large firms surveyed—manufacturing firms with more than 500 employees, or other firms with more than 100 employees—reported that doing business over the Internet had lowered their costs. Twenty-eight percent of small firms—those with fewer than 20 employees—reported such cost savings.

The Internet's arrival offered the promise of a global reach. Sixty-one percent of large firms, and 34% of small firms, reported reaching more customers by using Internet technologies. Larger firms may have more resources for developing websites and buying Web advertising, and have brand recognition in their favour.

A growing proportion of firms are turning to the Internet to better co-ordinate with suppliers, partners and customers. In 2007, 36% of firms in the private sector reported seeing this benefit, up from 20% in 2002.

Chart 19.3
Perceived benefits of Internet business for firms, by size, 2007

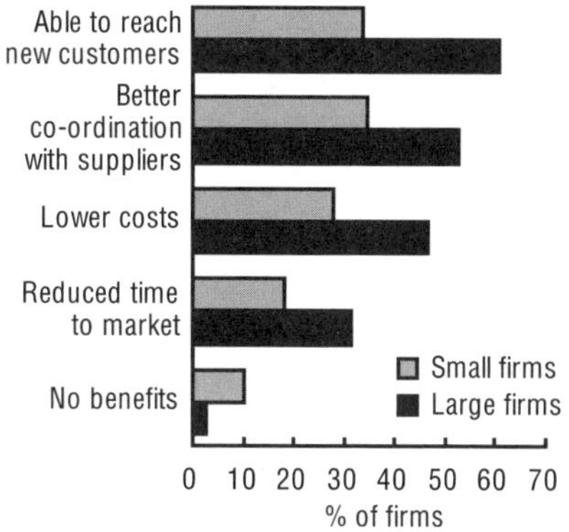

Source: Statistics Canada, Survey of Electronic Commerce and Technology, 2007.

Shopping online

Shopping online has by no means eclipsed shopping in person, but it continues to gain popularity.

More than 8.4 million Canadians aged 16 and older made an online purchase in 2007, compared with nearly 6.9 million Canadians aged 18 and older in 2005. (In 2007, online shoppers aged 16 and 17 accounted for about 2% of online orders and 1% of their dollar value.)

Canadians placed 69.9 million online orders worth almost $12.8 billion in 2007.

Many people logged on to research products. Internet 'window-shopping' complements traditional shopping: in 2007, 64% of those Canadians who window-shopped on the Internet later purchased directly from a brick-and-mortar store. The items most window-shopped for were consumer electronics, large appliances, furniture, clothing, jewellery and accessories.

Chart 19.4
Payment method used for Internet orders

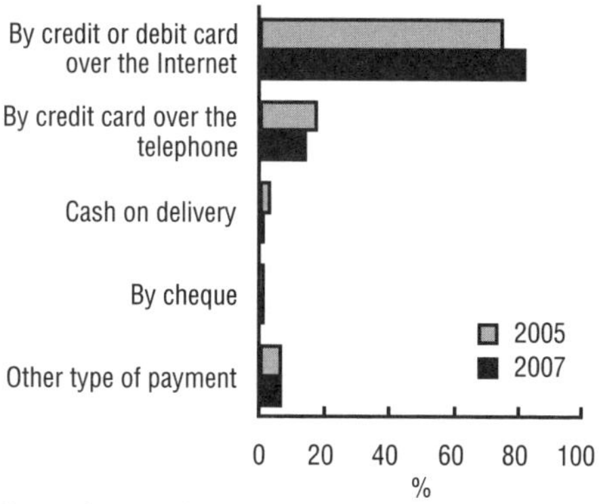

Source: Statistics Canada, CANSIM table 358-0138.

Table 19.1 Gross domestic product at basic prices, information and cultural industries, 1998 to 2008

	1998	1999	2000	2001
	$ millions 2002 chained			
Information and cultural industries	**28,255**	**31,617**	**34,007**	**36,498**
Publishing industries (except Internet)	7,174	7,860	7,992	8,566
Motion picture and sound recording industries	2,467	2,648	2,715	2,758
Broadcasting (except Internet)	..	..	..	..
Radio and television broadcasting	2,236	2,374	2,364	2,419
Pay and specialty television	..	..	..	..
Telecommunications	..	..	..	..
Cable and other program distribution	..	..	..	..
Telecommunications (except program distribution)	..	..	..	..
Other information services	..	..	..	..
Special aggregations				
All information and communication technology industries	31,244	39,652	45,684	44,592
Manufacturing of information and communication technology	7,795	10,923	13,689	8,877
Services in information and communication technology	23,693	29,050	32,399	35,810

Note: North American Industry Classification System (NAICS), 2002.
Source: Statistics Canada, CANSIM table 379-0027.

Table 19.2 Employment, information and cultural industries, 1994 to 2008

	1994	1995	1996	1997	1998
	number of employees				
Information and cultural industries	**279,777**	**284,566**	**283,051**	**288,372**	**297,503**
Publishing industries	68,555	68,679	69,542	72,250	75,475
Newspaper, periodical, book and database publishers	60,559	59,939	59,531	60,229	61,348
Software publishers	7,996	8,740	10,010	12,021	14,127
Motion picture and sound recording industries	25,210	25,234	26,895	29,912	32,735
Motion picture and video industries	23,552	23,488	24,944	27,791	30,430
Sound recording industries	1,657	1,746	1,950	2,121	2,305
Broadcasting (excluding Internet)	36,051	36,381	37,064	37,008	37,837
Radio and television broadcasting	35,071	35,429	36,098	36,074	36,897
Pay and specialty television	980	953	966	934	941
Telecommunications	121,025	125,257	119,481	119,674	122,521
Wired telecommunications carriers	84,663	87,274	83,303	83,105	85,002
Wireless telecommunications carriers (excluding satellite)	22,734	23,567	22,339	22,355	22,367
Satellite telecommunications	2,560	2,606	2,425	2,502	2,574
Other telecommunications	11,067	11,810	11,414	11,712	12,578
Data processing, hosting and related services	4,728	5,304	5,905	7,033	8,248
Other information services	24,208	23,711	24,165	22,496	20,686

Note: North American Industry Classification System (NAICS), 2002.
Source: Statistics Canada, CANSIM table 281-0024.

2002	2003	2004	2005	2006	2007	2008
			$ millions 2002 chained			
38,229	**38,631**	**40,813**	**41,888**	**43,227**	**44,349**	**45,114**
8,566	8,402	9,061	9,158	9,303	9,811	10,072
2,903	2,604	2,718	2,824	2,687	2,590	2,499
3,022	3,010	3,070	3,042	3,177	3,335	3,376
2,511	2,420	2,438	2,379	2,448	2,548	2,509
511	591	631	659	720	776	847
21,256	21,935	23,103	23,985	25,088	25,527	26,079
2,577	2,759	2,968	3,217	3,335	3,425	3,488
18,679	19,172	20,127	20,741	21,729	22,074	22,563
1,012	1,066	1,048	1,036	1,067	1,105	1,097
44,949	47,400	50,508	52,493	54,999	57,199	58,709
6,912	6,908	7,435	7,665	7,930	8,402	8,501
38,036	40,448	43,023	44,778	47,020	48,741	50,154

1999	2000	2001	2002	2003	2004	2005	2006	2007	2008
				number of employees					
304,067	**318,783**	**310,909**	**304,841**	**300,623**	**300,694**	**307,647**	**313,724**	**323,886**	**326,367**
76,656	83,152	86,406	86,230	x	81,563	85,027	85,893	90,900	93,286
59,589	62,964	62,245	62,084	x	58,475	59,001	57,411	60,101	61,960
17,066	20,188	24,161	24,146	22,599	23,088	26,026	28,482	30,800	31,326
34,306	36,622	36,250	35,490	32,417	30,324	30,182	28,685	32,246	33,310
31,954	34,213	33,932	33,268	30,061	27,706	27,451	26,280	29,988	31,182
2,351	2,409	2,318	2,222	2,356	2,619	2,731	2,404	2,259	2,128
37,453	37,634	35,562	35,856	37,491	38,233	36,908	39,880	41,527	43,030
36,550	36,764	34,158	34,292	35,609	36,296	35,023	37,830	38,904	39,586
902	870	1,404	1,564	1,883	1,938	1,885	2,050	2,622	3,444
124,379	127,934	117,341	110,380	109,216	113,250	118,143	118,996	115,631	109,831
85,603	86,991	85,133	83,402	85,111	89,848	93,472	90,964	89,465	84,401
22,257	22,837	12,443	11,917	10,436	9,212	10,115	12,681	10,327	10,352
2,571	2,641	1,742	1,756	2,371	2,893	3,128	3,370	3,450	3,492
13,948	15,464	18,023	13,306	11,299	11,296	11,427	11,981	12,389	11,587
10,233	11,939	12,294	11,808	10,977	11,439	11,140	12,023	13,289	17,981
21,040	21,502	23,056	25,077	x	25,884	26,247	28,248	30,293	28,929

Table 19.3 Software development and computer services, summary statistics, 1997 to 2007

	1997	1998	1999	2000
	$ millions			
Operating revenues				
Software publishers	3,031.0	4,243.0	5,429.1	5,348.6
Data processing, hosting and related services[1]	740.0	1,095.0	1,205.2	1,596.8
Computer systems design and related services	8,911.0	12,033.0	15,532.8	17,765.6
Operating expenses				
Software publishers	2,902.0	3,972.0	5,086.7	5,661.2
Data processing, hosting and related services[1]	672.0	1,026.0	1,110.1	1,729.3
Computer systems design and related services	8,348.0	11,253.0	15,237.0	17,188.1
	%			
Operating profit margin				
Software publishers	4.3	6.4	6.3	-5.8
Data processing, hosting and related services[1]	9.3	6.3	7.9	-8.3
Computer systems design and related services	6.3	6.5	1.9	3.2
	number			
Establishments				
Software publishers	1,489	1,745	1,882	1,849
Data processing, hosting and related services[1]	450	563	1,083	930
Computer systems design and related services	16,563	31,651	41,597	43,874

Notes: North American Industry Classification System (NAICS), 2007.
Figures may not add to totals because of rounding.
1. Prior to 2002, data refer to Code 51421 (Data processing services), North American Industry Classification System (NAICS) 1997.
Source: Statistics Canada, CANSIM table 354-0005.

2001	2002	2003	2004	2005	2006	2007
			$ millions			
5,869.2	5,383.1	5,810.5	6,276.2	6,358.3	6,272.5	6,857.3
2,275.8	2,591.0	2,650.8	2,675.3	2,815.3	2,833.5	3,046.9
17,964.9	18,205.8	18,836.1	20,727.0	21,567.4	23,994.6	25,364.7
6,399.7	5,438.7	5,924.9	5,992.3	6,231.0	5,984.0	6,471.2
2,281.8	2,439.6	2,539.1	2,451.1	2,652.2	2,493.3	2,749.3
17,492.1	17,241.6	17,741.0	19,777.4	19,923.2	22,523.8	23,524.0
			%			
-9.0	-1.0	-2.0	4.5	2.0	4.6	5.6
-0.3	5.8	4.2	8.4	5.8	12.0	9.8
2.6	5.3	5.8	4.6	7.6	6.1	7.3
			number			
2,306	1,837	1,946	2,602	1,994	1,785	2,156
1,345	1,066	1,317	1,342	1,161	1,181	1,311
43,440	42,790	45,377	51,230	47,479	51,162	53,983

Table 19.4 Internet use at home by individuals, by type of activity, 2007

	Internet users and non-users[1]	Internet users at home[2]
	%	
E-mail	63.1	92.0
Using an instant messenger	34.3	49.9
Searching for information on Canadian municipal, provincial or federal government	35.3	51.4
Communicating with Canadian municipal, provincial or federal government	17.5	25.5
Searching for medical or health-related information	40.2	58.6
Education, training or school work	34.0	49.5
Travel information or making travel arrangements	45.4	66.1
Searching for employment	22.2	32.3
Electronic banking or paying bills	42.9	62.5
Researching investments	17.5	25.5
Playing games	26.5	38.7
Obtaining or saving music	30.5	44.5
Obtaining or saving software	22.3	32.5
Viewing the news or sports	43.7	63.7
Obtaining weather reports or road conditions	47.9	69.8
Listening to the radio over the Internet	19.3	28.1
Downloading or watching television	10.8	15.7
Downloading or watching a movie	8.6	12.5
Researching community events	30.4	44.3
General browsing (surfing)	52.1	76.0
Contributing content (blogs, photos, discussion groups)	13.9	20.3
Making telephone calls	6.0	8.7
Selling goods or services (through auction sites)	6.1	8.9
Other Internet activity	1.0	1.5

1. Population aged 16 years and older.
2. Population aged 16 years and older who used the Internet in the previous 12 months for personal non-business use from home.
Source: Statistics Canada, CANSIM table 358-0130.

Table 19.5 Internet use by individuals, by location of access, 2007

	%
All locations	73.2
Home	68.6
Work	30.0
School	14.5
Public library	10.8
Other location	22.0

Note: Population aged 16 and older who used the Internet in the previous 12 months for personal non-business use from any location.
Source: Statistics Canada, CANSIM table 358-0122.

Table 19.6 Enterprises' use of information and communication technologies, 2002 to 2007

	2002	2003	2004	2005	2006	2007
	% of enterprises					
E-mail	71.2	73.9	76.6	76.2	77.5	81.1
Wireless communication	57.7	56.5	56.6	59.5	74.0	76.7
Internet	75.7	78.3	81.6	81.6	82.8	86.7
Intranet	14.9	16.4	17.6	18.8	19.7	21.2
Extranet	5.3	6.1	6.3	7.3	7.5	9.4
Sales of goods or services over the Internet	7.6	7.1	7.4	7.3	8.0	8.2
Sales over the Internet to consumers	24.6	32.3	25.2	28.6	32.5	37.7
Purchase of goods or services over the Internet	31.9	37.3	42.5	43.4	44.8	48.5

Notes: Private sector.
North American Industry Classification System (NAICS), 2007.
Source: Statistics Canada, CANSIM tables 358-0007, 358-0010 and 358-0011.

Table 19.7 Cable and wireless distribution industries, financial and operating statistics, 2002 to 2007

	2002	2003	2004	2005	2006	2007
	$ thousands					
Operating revenues	**5,215,816**	**5,820,120**	**6,351,795**	**6,828,493**	**7,926,816**	**9,109,936**
Cable television	4,269,065	4,616,485	4,997,138	5,358,078	6,198,839	7,180,033
Wireless broadcasting distribution	946,751	1,203,635	1,354,657	1,470,415	1,727,977	1,929,902
Operating expenses	**4,728,888**	**5,068,231**	**5,246,520**	**5,512,347**	**6,399,031**	**7,416,872**
Cable television	3,536,212	3,754,480	3,799,000	4,022,335	4,708,071	5,582,941
Wireless broadcasting distribution	1,192,676	1,313,752	1,447,520	1,490,012	1,690,961	1,833,931
Profit before interest and taxes	**486,927**	**751,889**	**1,105,275**	**1,316,146**	**1,527,784**	**1,693,064**
Cable television	732,853	862,006	1,198,138	1,335,743	1,490,768	1,597,092
Wireless broadcasting distribution	-245,926	-110,117	-92,863	-19,597	37,016	95,972
	thousands					
Subscribers to basic programming services	**9,645**	**9,783**	**9,942**	**10,112**	**10,419**	**10,582**
Cable television	7,626	7,578	7,617	7,620	7,790	7,917
Wireless broadcasting distribution	2,019	2,205	2,325	2,492	2,629	2,664

Note: North American Industry Classification System (NAICS), 2007.
Source: Statistics Canada, CANSIM table 353-0003.

Table 19.8 Radio broadcasting industry, financial and operating statistics, 2002 to 2007

	2002	2003	2004	2005	2006	2007
	$ thousands					
Operating revenues	**1,457,244**	**1,556,598**	**1,582,894**	**1,696,713**	**1,818,107**	**1,898,537**
Private radio broadcasting	1,106,430	1,196,514	1,234,647	1,344,417	1,420,362	1,511,208
Public and non-commercial radio broadcasting	350,814	360,083	348,247	352,297	397,745	387,329
Operating expenses	**1,302,766**	**1,354,020**	**1,454,681**	**1,513,415**	**1,597,442**	**1,663,573**
Private radio broadcasting	933,354	969,288	1,011,750	1,059,921	1,136,508	1,211,296
Public and non-commercial radio broadcasting	369,412	384,732	442,931	453,494	460,933	452,277
Profit before interest and taxes	**154,478**	**202,578**	**128,213**	**183,298**	**220,665**	**234,964**
Private radio broadcasting	173,076	227,226	222,896	284,496	283,854	299,911
Public and non-commercial radio broadcasting	-18,598	-24,649	-94,683	-101,198	-63,189	-64,948

Note: North American Industry Classification System (NAICS), 2007.
Source: Statistics Canada, CANSIM table 357-0002.

Table 19.9 Television broadcasting industry, financial and operating statistics, 2002 to 2007

	2002	2003	2004	2005	2006	2007
	$ thousands					
Operating revenues	**4,775,707**	**5,167,259**	**5,386,295**	**5,561,885**	**6,000,598**	**6,179,545**
Private conventional television	1,900,887	2,069,920	2,082,902	2,166,063	2,163,622	2,187,197
Public and non-commercial television	1,172,534	1,212,567	1,238,192	1,173,731	1,337,943	1,267,134
Pay and specialty television	1,702,287	1,884,772	2,065,201	2,222,092	2,499,033	2,725,214
Pay television	332,513	349,759	384,375	409,795	482,314	547,437
Specialty television	1,369,773	1,535,013	1,680,826	1,812,297	2,016,719	2,177,777
Operating expenses	**4,481,420**	**4,668,718**	**4,930,936**	**4,899,070**	**5,468,343**	**5,521,983**
Private conventional television	1,722,242	1,769,596	1,850,365	1,923,407	2,072,679	2,071,160
Public and non-commercial television	1,249,383	1,297,583	1,429,466	1,309,461	1,469,512	1,372,744
Pay and specialty television	1,509,795	1,601,538	1,651,105	1,666,203	1,926,152	2,078,078
Pay television	252,125	259,851	298,906	301,812	357,498	430,716
Specialty television	1,257,670	1,341,687	1,352,199	1,364,391	1,568,654	1,647,362
Profit before interest and taxes	**294,286**	**498,541**	**455,359**	**662,814**	**532,255**	**657,562**
Private conventional television	178,644	300,324	232,537	242,656	90,943	116,037
Public and non-commercial television	-76,849	-85,016	-191,273	-135,730	-131,569	-105,610
Pay and specialty television	192,492	283,234	414,095	555,889	572,881	647,135
Pay television	80,388	89,908	85,469	107,983	124,816	116,720
Specialty television	112,103	193,326	328,627	447,906	448,065	530,415

Note: North American Industry Classification System (NAICS), 2007.
Source: Statistics Canada, CANSIM table 357-0001.

International merchandise trade

20

Canada's international merchandise trade showed strong expansion in early 2008 before the global economic downturn took hold later in the year. In the fourth quarter of 2008, the goods surplus dropped to its lowest level since the first quarter of 1994.

In the first half of 2008, the loonie was hovering around par with the U.S. dollar, making Canada's exports more expensive in relation to imports. Meanwhile, commodity prices were rising—notably, oil prices neared $150 a barrel in July. The value of exported goods climbed in the first three quarters, supported by strong price gains (driven by energy) despite declining volumes.

Economic tide shifted rapidly

In August, the tide began to shift rapidly. The loonie retreated 15.8% to US$0.81 by year-end. As well, the seven-year boom in commodity prices ended, led by a drop in crude oil prices of over $100 a barrel. Commodity prices fell by more than half in just five months.

Autos and lumber were the industries that saw the largest declines. Exports of auto products dropped 9.2% in the fourth quarter of 2008 alone. The value of natural resource exports tumbled after July. Two-thirds of the decline was the result of lower prices.

Imports fell 6.4% in the fourth quarter. Imports of auto products dropped 10.8%, while those of other consumer goods declined 9.0%. Lower imports of machinery and equipment, as well as industrial goods and materials, reflected lower business investment and stalling manufacturing activity.

Still, Canada exported a record $489.9 billion worth of merchandise in 2008, up 5.8% from 2007. The gain in exports in 2008 stemmed from surging prices in the first three quarters; volumes fell 7.8%. Prices fell in the fourth quarter,

Chart 20.1
Merchandise trade

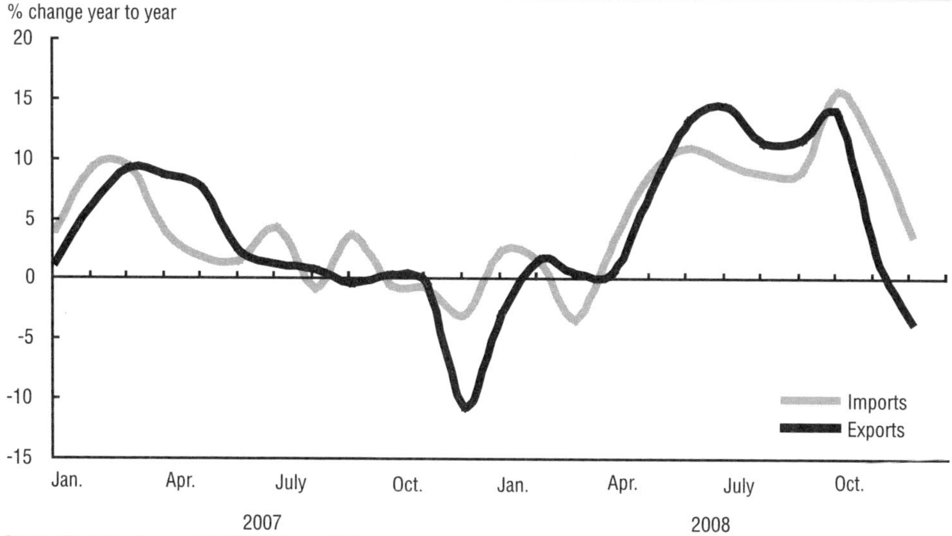

Source: Statistics Canada, CANSIM table 228-0041.

as the economic downturn began taking hold.

Energy products bolstered the overall gain in exports. Much of the increase occurred in the first six months of the year, when energy's export prices increased 51.1%.

Also rising in 2008 were exports of industrial goods and materials, as well as those of agricultural and fishing products. These outweighed export declines for automotive products, forestry products and other consumer goods.

Canada's imports topped $443.0 billion in 2008, a 6.7% increase from 2007. Energy products led the gain in imports on higher prices and volumes. As well, imports of agricultural and fishing products, industrial goods and materials, machinery and equipment, and other consumer goods increased in 2008, whereas imports of automotive and forestry products dropped.

Canada's annual merchandise trade balance with the world decreased to $46.9 billion in 2008, continuing the contraction that began in 2005. Still, Canada's trade surplus with the United States expanded to $89.1 billion in 2008 on the strength of crude oil exports.

Table 20.a
Canada's international trade partners, 2008

	Imports	Exports
	$ billions	
Total	**433.4**	**483.6**
United States[1]	227.0	375.5
United Kingdom	12.6	13.1
European Union[2]	41.5	23.3
Japan	15.3	11.1
Other OECD countries	39.5	17.7
Other countries	97.5	42.9

Note: Customs basis.
1. Includes Puerto Rico and the Virgin Islands.
2. Excludes the United Kingdom.
Source: Statistics Canada, CANSIM table 228-0003.

Chart 20.2
Merchandise trade balance

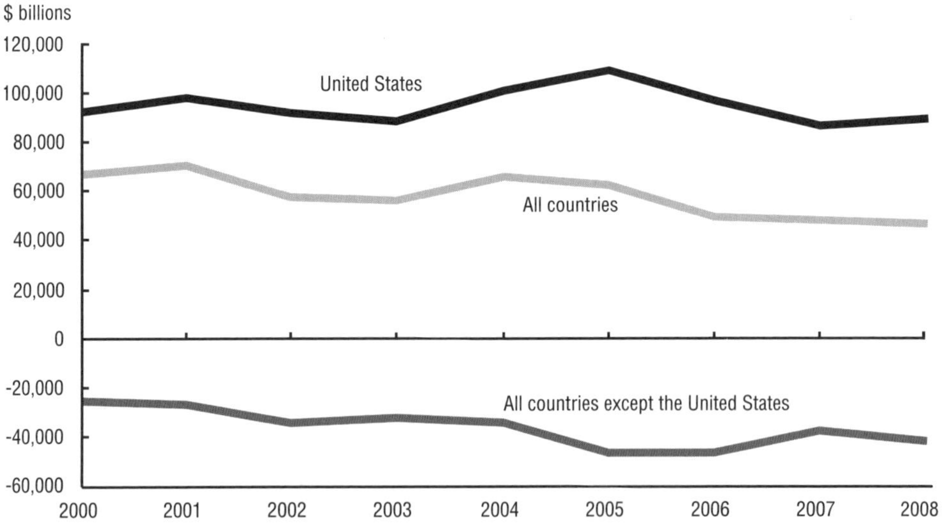

Source: Statistics Canada, CANSIM table 228-0003.

Profound changes in exports

The recession has accelerated the ongoing slump in automobile, lumber and newsprint exports.

Automobiles' and forestry products' shares of total exports continued their decade-long slide in 2008, falling to 18% of total exports, or less than half their recent high of 37% in 1999.

This trend continued into 2009, with their combined share dropping to 14% in January. Since autos manufactured in Canada have a large import component, the share of value-added exports has also fallen considerably, probably below 10%.

An export staple for over a century, lumber accounted for less than 2% of Canada's exports in January 2009, as residential construction slumped in the United States. Downsizing in the newspaper industry has added to the forestry sector's woes. Newsprint exports have tumbled 35% since 2001.

Chart 20.3
Share of all exports

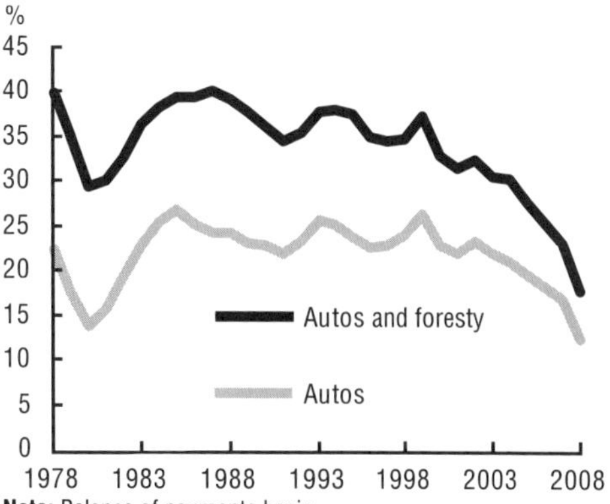

Note: Balance of payments basis.
Source: Statistics Canada, CANSIM table 228-0041.

Diversifying trade

Canada is continuing to diversify its international trade portfolio, diminishing our reliance on the United States as a trading partner. In 2008, U.S. trade accounted for 69.8% of Canada's international merchandise trade, down from 76.7% in 2003.

In 2008, the United States accounted for 65.7% of Canada's total merchandise trade on a customs basis—that is exports and imports combined—down from 74.0% in 2003.

Exports to countries other than the United States have grown to 24.5% of total exports, compared with 17.6% in 2003. Leading the gain are exports to Brazil and the Asia–Pacific countries.

Imports from countries other than the United States have also been on the rise. These now make up 36.6% of Canada's total merchandise imports. Most of the growth in non-U.S. imports in 2008 was with China and European countries.

Chart 20.4
Trade with the United States and other partners

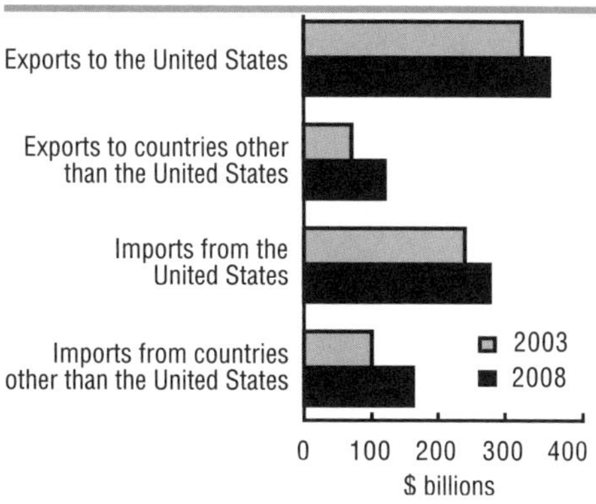

Note: Balance of payments basis.
Source: Statistics Canada, Catalogue no. 65-208-X.

Table 20.1 Merchandise imports, by commodity, 1994 to 2008

	1994	1995	1996	1997	1998	1999
	$ millions					
Imports, all merchandise	**207,872.5**	**229,936.5**	**237,688.6**	**277,726.5**	**303,398.6**	**327,026.0**
Live animals	215.4	188.3	171.1	183.8	235.0	302.7
Food, feed, beverages and tobacco	11,597.4	12,222.4	12,954.6	14,363.5	15,858.3	16,249.3
Meat and meat preparations	1,137.4	1,133.7	1,033.7	1,200.0	1,251.4	1,279.8
Fish and marine animals	1,126.4	1,286.5	1,469.6	1,434.0	1,635.8	1,869.7
Fresh fruits and berries	1,303.4	1,387.5	1,418.3	1,503.0	1,581.3	1,645.8
Dried fruits, fruits and fruit preparations	693.4	745.6	861.1	900.8	935.3	1,020.3
Fresh vegetables	949.6	1,054.4	971.7	1,112.5	1,233.8	1,213.6
Other vegetables and vegetable preparations	700.3	718.3	761.1	838.2	963.5	1,050.0
Cocoa, coffee, tea and other food preparations	2,089.3	2,056.9	2,131.7	2,589.7	2,948.9	2,865.0
Dairy produce, eggs and honey	265.5	276.1	352.0	355.0	409.7	437.8
Corn (maize), shelled	158.5	216.9	251.0	250.3	283.6	228.1
Other cereals and cereal preparations	750.1	805.1	891.1	998.0	1,136.6	1,164.1
Sugar and sugar preparations	866.5	879.4	970.7	1,035.6	1,100.9	991.6
Fodder and feed, except unmilled cereals	613.7	628.4	728.6	809.9	796.4	734.0
Beverages	872.8	959.4	1,015.3	1,214.7	1,455.8	1,669.2
Tobacco	70.4	74.2	98.6	121.6	125.2	80.3
Crude materials, inedible	9,898.0	11,531.4	13,048.1	14,171.5	12,476.7	14,316.0
Metals in ores, concentrates and scrap	2,326.2	2,989.1	2,863.0	2,950.2	2,788.4	2,747.4
Coal and other related products	548.0	591.6	751.4	910.3	1,116.3	1,098.1
Crude petroleum	4,609.3	4,833.2	6,707.8	7,189.4	5,227.4	7,160.3
Crude animal products	221.8	239.1	248.0	293.2	256.2	242.1
Crude vegetable products	663.1	815.2	843.9	949.6	939.3	965.5
Crude wood products	406.8	560.4	435.7	544.1	618.8	626.9
Cotton	101.6	149.2	168.3	154.0	221.3	138.0
Wool and man-made fibres	260.0	296.5	279.9	328.5	343.7	348.6
Crude non-metallic minerals	761.2	1,057.1	750.0	852.1	965.4	989.1
Fabricated materials, inedible	38,823.1	44,277.2	45,967.5	54,508.4	60,113.0	62,411.8
End products, inedible	136,993.1	151,331.7	153,330.6	181,930.0	202,489.8	221,180.5
Special transactions, trade	4,877.0	5,441.4	7,075.9	6,954.9	6,339.2	6,343.1
Other balance of payments adjustments	5,468.5	4,944.0	5,140.8	5,614.5	5,886.5	6,222.5

Note: On a balance of payments basis.
Source: Statistics Canada, CANSIM table 228-0003.

2000	2001	2002	2003	2004	2005	2006	2007	2008
				$ millions				
362,336.7	**350,071.2**	**356,727.1**	**342,709.5**	**363,157.8**	**387,837.8**	**404,345.5**	**415,228.7**	**442,987.9**
410.2	398.0	236.7	174.3	137.7	144.3	165.3	181.4	191.2
16,978.4	18,687.0	20,195.2	19,945.4	19,862.2	20,666.8	22,055.0	24,107.7	26,810.8
1,404.0	1,635.9	1,681.4	1,596.7	1,311.4	1,454.7	1,652.6	1,935.4	2,049.8
1,928.8	1,945.3	1,935.4	1,812.2	1,804.4	1,822.8	1,822.3	1,895.7	1,909.1
1,679.4	1,815.3	2,020.1	2,013.5	2,070.8	2,206.9	2,318.6	2,500.8	2,763.5
1,003.8	992.1	1,075.6	1,061.9	1,099.8	1,134.7	1,234.0	1,351.3	1,489.8
1,386.6	1,502.3	1,700.3	1,638.7	1,633.7	1,718.1	1,786.5	1,922.1	1,993.1
1,048.8	1,133.4	1,275.1	1,211.3	1,240.2	1,337.1	1,359.7	1,469.7	1,631.9
2,817.4	2,948.7	3,340.3	3,427.6	3,590.2	3,697.5	3,919.0	4,060.4	4,652.7
487.6	581.4	583.3	567.3	638.9	616.9	539.1	625.6	635.5
300.0	555.3	733.0	599.9	366.4	342.5	322.5	547.9	705.2
1,243.6	1,380.1	1,484.5	1,416.3	1,453.9	1,488.6	1,558.8	1,725.4	2,104.6
1,034.0	1,218.1	1,179.2	1,220.2	1,176.9	1,228.7	1,408.5	1,351.0	1,535.4
825.3	981.0	1,041.2	968.0	1,007.1	891.2	984.0	1,130.0	1,460.0
1,735.1	1,910.2	2,035.3	2,294.9	2,359.4	2,605.8	2,888.5	3,197.6	3,502.9
84.1	88.0	110.6	116.9	109.1	121.3	261.0	394.7	377.3
21,462.6	20,936.6	20,405.7	22,813.6	27,950.5	34,342.8	35,821.7	39,053.8	52,184.1
3,067.1	2,991.7	2,980.1	3,029.2	4,103.6	4,356.8	6,093.3	7,670.8	8,366.7
1,270.2	1,430.5	1,932.9	2,838.8	3,715.0	5,066.3	3,874.8	4,373.7	6,045.1
13,436.6	12,814.3	11,722.3	13,300.9	16,439.0	21,543.5	22,562.0	23,670.5	34,178.5
272.9	300.3	317.6	302.7	285.6	255.2	263.4	314.9	302.4
995.8	1,119.2	1,214.3	1,229.4	1,256.4	1,151.2	1,179.2	1,198.1	1,494.9
695.2	703.6	686.0	619.2	632.2	611.9	564.2	530.5	480.4
172.4	168.5	133.7	159.1	142.4	78.6	56.5	39.1	14.1
389.8	380.2	370.7	361.4	343.3	326.0	289.4	279.1	254.0
1,162.4	1,028.4	1,048.0	972.9	1,032.9	953.2	938.9	977.1	1,047.9
69,870.4	69,411.3	69,538.7	66,667.4	74,912.7	82,226.3	87,148.2	87,011.7	96,839.8
240,462.0	227,417.2	233,889.6	221,481.5	229,178.2	238,796.3	246,587.4	251,403.1	252,109.7
6,653.7	6,851.6	5,973.8	5,309.7	4,967.1	4,650.4	4,775.1	5,208.7	6,000.7
6,499.5	6,369.5	6,487.3	6,317.6	6,149.4	7,010.8	7,792.7	8,262.5	8,851.6

Table 20.2 Merchandise exports, by commodity, 1994 to 2008

	1994	1995	1996	1997	1998	1999
	$ millions					
Exports, all merchandise	**228,167.1**	**265,333.9**	**280,079.3**	**303,378.2**	**327,161.5**	**369,034.9**
Live animals	1,338.3	1,517.7	1,888.4	1,905.3	1,975.8	1,567.8
Food, feed, beverages and tobacco	14,890.6	17,014.1	18,884.6	20,380.4	19,814.5	21,312.6
Fish, fresh, frozen, preserved and canned	3,258.5	3,496.2	3,444.1	3,497.8	3,664.5	4,260.8
Barley	590.5	564.5	847.8	683.0	340.3	256.9
Wheat	3,547.3	4,325.2	4,658.6	5,051.5	3,642.3	3,356.2
Wheat flour	46.2	50.6	33.8	39.7	35.3	54.8
Other cereals, unmilled	250.9	318.6	432.5	489.8	348.4	400.3
Other cereal preparations	678.5	798.5	1,017.1	1,115.2	1,290.5	1,449.8
Meat and meat preparations	1,603.0	1,845.2	2,161.0	2,641.8	2,669.5	3,247.8
Alcoholic beverages	1,026.2	980.0	1,071.0	1,166.7	1,217.5	1,366.4
Other food, feed, beverages and tobacco	3,889.4	4,635.4	5,218.7	5,695.0	6,606.1	6,919.8
Crude materials, inedible	23,584.9	26,469.0	30,266.3	31,655.2	29,854.0	34,562.6
Rapeseed	1,571.5	1,265.3	1,158.0	1,126.1	1,638.5	1,332.8
Other crude vegetable products	1,013.2	1,169.0	1,236.7	1,362.1	1,610.9	1,399.1
Iron ores, concentrates and scrap	1,272.0	1,386.0	1,440.2	1,841.5	1,830.9	1,493.3
Copper in ores, concentrates and scrap	774.0	1,196.3	872.0	928.5	614.4	452.1
Nickel in ores, concentrates and scrap	592.9	981.5	1,117.7	907.3	917.4	807.1
Zinc in ores, concentrates and scrap	349.1	486.8	536.6	695.4	509.2	479.0
Other ores, concentrates and scrap	1,346.8	1,812.5	1,949.3	1,534.2	1,499.0	1,917.0
Crude petroleum	6,507.1	8,263.5	10,497.2	10,366.3	7,829.8	11,017.1
Natural gas	6,427.8	5,649.1	7,432.8	8,625.6	8,967.1	10,951.4
Coal and other crude bituminous substances	1,298.5	1,384.7	1,433.7	1,515.1	1,343.7	1,228.7
Unmanufactured asbestos	303.3	323.3	343.3	226.7	172.5	164.7
Other crude animal products	523.0	579.2	610.8	664.7	677.2	652.6
Other crude wood products	322.6	347.9	346.2	432.6	523.0	671.4
Other crude non-metallic minerals	625.9	714.1	694.5	652.9	847.4	1,496.7
Other crude materials, inedible	657.1	909.7	597.3	776.1	873.1	499.9
Fabricated materials, inedible	69,826.7	84,003.2	85,042.6	89,749.4	91,817.6	97,976.8
End products, inedible	110,410.1	127,264.6	134,806.7	149,130.3	171,731.0	199,953.3
Special transactions, trade	2,564.1	2,865.1	3,154.5	4,074.5	5,563.4	7,348.2
Other balance of payments adjustments	5,552.5	6,200.3	6,036.2	6,483.1	6,405.3	6,313.7

Note: On a balance of payments basis.
Source: Statistics Canada, CANSIM table 228-0003.

2000	2001	2002	2003	2004	2005	2006	2007	2008
				$ millions				
429,372.2	**420,730.4**	**414,038.5**	**399,122.1**	**429,005.8**	**450,210.0**	**453,951.0**	**463,126.7**	**489,856.8**
1,742.7	2,394.3	2,506.9	1,318.7	873.0	1,542.7	2,015.5	2,428.0	2,326.3
23,268.6	25,911.5	25,843.1	25,046.9	26,842.0	25,704.5	25,833.7	27,771.9	32,275.9
4,560.6	4,722.3	5,239.5	4,987.1	4,857.7	4,673.1	4,434.3	4,292.5	4,248.6
377.9	383.9	194.1	172.1	321.9	360.1	257.5	482.8	692.2
3,608.9	3,807.2	3,052.6	2,809.2	3,481.4	2,697.2	3,609.2	4,637.7	6,867.9
60.1	64.0	91.4	81.3	85.0	78.8	81.5	75.8	100.3
263.5	279.8	288.5	299.2	310.1	303.2	407.0	606.5	888.5
1,593.3	1,830.6	2,048.0	2,138.6	2,214.0	2,248.5	2,328.8	2,536.5	2,905.5
4,005.1	4,885.6	4,840.8	4,203.5	4,980.1	5,083.1	4,268.3	4,142.7	4,636.8
1,310.6	1,357.6	1,185.4	1,300.2	1,226.8	1,036.6	995.0	871.4	859.9
7,488.5	8,580.5	8,902.9	9,055.8	9,365.0	9,223.8	9,452.0	10,126.0	11,076.2
53,398.2	54,713.5	50,980.7	61,268.0	69,594.4	85,823.5	88,753.9	95,468.2	128,038.3
1,147.5	1,275.8	921.1	1,298.0	1,414.3	1,297.6	1,750.5	2,263.5	3,876.3
1,441.7	1,496.4	1,601.7	1,570.3	1,545.2	1,552.0	1,611.5	1,957.4	2,379.0
1,532.1	1,381.2	1,634.5	1,743.5	2,043.6	2,591.8	3,191.1	3,312.0	4,801.6
792.6	661.9	577.2	592.3	844.5	1,370.6	2,367.5	2,231.8	2,320.6
1,071.9	1,010.6	1,139.1	1,143.9	1,829.4	1,700.5	2,452.3	5,092.5	3,766.7
481.2	436.7	388.4	228.4	233.9	230.3	325.0	387.3	359.5
2,073.8	2,177.7	2,147.6	2,081.5	2,377.2	2,878.0	3,019.2	3,418.9	3,624.4
19,165.9	15,370.2	18,550.8	20,644.2	25,570.4	30,356.8	38,574.6	40,997.3	60,969.7
20,536.8	25,595.1	18,372.0	26,083.4	27,382.1	35,988.6	27,804.7	28,071.1	33,046.0
1,194.4	1,217.5	1,212.1	1,199.1	1,293.3	2,735.2	2,733.1	2,730.9	5,841.8
149.4	122.9	100.7	70.7	71.6	69.0	61.6	55.0	67.9
711.0	784.9	802.2	720.5	733.8	817.1	890.0	826.1	842.8
846.1	848.5	1,027.9	902.9	832.6	927.7	880.3	763.8	646.3
1,707.0	1,842.9	2,014.3	2,495.1	2,853.1	2,783.1	2,585.6	2,790.8	4,919.5
546.8	491.2	491.1	494.1	569.4	525.1	507.1	569.8	576.3
113,102.1	111,908.3	108,291.9	103,445.4	118,841.6	124,593.8	129,059.1	134,104.2	141,179.7
223,135.3	211,387.0	211,446.2	193,248.4	198,762.1	198,147.4	193,362.0	189,474.0	172,247.1
7,980.0	8,168.1	8,232.5	7,689.1	7,985.0	8,288.2	8,732.4	8,176.0	8,192.7
6,745.3	6,247.7	6,737.2	7,105.5	6,107.6	6,109.8	6,194.2	5,704.4	5,596.7

Table 20.3 Merchandise imports and exports, by origin and destination, 1994 to 2008

	All merchandise		United States[1]		United Kingdom	
	$ millions	% change from previous year	$ millions	% change from previous year	$ millions	% change from previous year
Imports						
1994	**207,872.5**	**17.4**	155,661.3	19.5	4,854.4	8.3
1995	**229,936.5**	**10.6**	172,516.5	10.8	4,899.1	0.9
1996	**237,688.6**	**3.4**	180,010.1	4.3	5,581.1	13.9
1997	**277,726.5**	**16.8**	211,450.8	17.5	6,126.5	9.8
1998	**303,398.6**	**9.2**	233,777.6	10.6	6,083.1	-0.7
1999	**327,026.0**	**7.8**	249,485.3	6.7	7,685.4	26.3
2000	**362,336.7**	**10.8**	266,511.1	6.8	12,289.3	59.9
2001	**350,071.2**	**-3.4**	254,330.7	-4.6	11,954.1	-2.7
2002	**356,727.1**	**1.9**	255,232.5	0.4	10,181.3	-14.8
2003	**342,709.5**	**-3.9**	240,356.3	-5.8	9,183.0	-9.8
2004	**363,157.8**	**6.0**	250,038.3	4.0	9,460.0	3.0
2005	**387,837.8**	**6.8**	259,332.9	3.7	9,066.5	-4.2
2006	**404,345.5**	**4.3**	265,020.2	2.2	9,554.3	5.4
2007	**415,228.7**	**2.7**	269,828.7	1.8	10,017.2	4.8
2008	**442,987.9**	**6.7**	280,773.1	4.1	11,321.2	13.0
Exports						
1994	**228,167.1**	**20.0**	181,049.3	21.4	3,677.1	14.5
1995	**265,333.9**	**16.3**	205,690.6	13.6	4,377.0	19.0
1996	**280,079.3**	**5.6**	222,461.3	8.2	4,608.5	5.3
1997	**303,378.2**	**8.3**	242,542.3	9.0	4,689.5	1.8
1998	**327,161.5**	**7.8**	269,318.9	11.0	5,323.3	13.5
1999	**369,034.9**	**12.8**	309,116.8	14.8	6,002.9	12.8
2000	**429,372.2**	**16.4**	359,021.2	16.1	7,273.3	21.2
2001	**420,730.4**	**-2.0**	352,165.0	-1.9	6,910.3	-5.0
2002	**414,038.5**	**-1.6**	347,051.8	-1.5	6,161.5	-10.8
2003	**399,122.1**	**-3.6**	328,983.3	-5.2	7,695.3	24.9
2004	**429,005.8**	**7.5**	350,576.3	6.6	9,364.0	21.7
2005	**450,210.0**	**4.9**	368,278.9	5.0	9,360.5	0.0
2006	**453,951.0**	**0.8**	361,442.1	-1.9	11,284.9	20.6
2007	**463,126.7**	**2.0**	355,743.0	-1.6	14,157.9	25.5
2008	**489,856.8**	**5.8**	369,891.1	4.0	14,206.9	0.3

Note: On a balance of payments basis.
1. Includes Puerto Rico and Virgin Islands.
Source: Statistics Canada, CANSIM table 228-0003.

European Union excluding the United Kingdom		Japan		Other Organisation for Economic Co-operation and Development countries		Other countries	
$ millions	% change from previous year	$ millions	% change from previous year	$ millions	% change from previous year	$ millions	% change from previous year
11,549.9	21.0	8,315.4	-1.9	7,364.7	57.2	20,126.9	2.2
15,390.0	33.2	8,427.6	1.3	7,942.3	7.8	20,761.0	3.2
14,994.7	-2.6	7,227.4	-14.2	9,040.6	13.8	20,834.6	0.4
18,112.9	20.8	8,711.0	20.5	11,376.7	25.8	21,948.7	5.3
19,141.2	5.7	9,671.8	11.0	11,398.8	0.2	23,326.1	6.3
20,765.8	8.5	10,592.2	9.5	13,257.2	16.3	25,240.1	8.2
21,136.5	1.8	11,729.8	10.7	19,067.6	43.8	31,602.5	25.2
23,197.1	9.7	10,571.9	-9.9	18,649.8	-2.2	31,367.6	-0.7
25,867.0	11.5	11,732.6	11.0	19,686.6	5.6	34,027.1	8.5
26,001.0	0.5	10,645.5	-9.3	19,696.9	0.1	36,826.8	8.2
27,007.0	3.9	10,094.5	-5.2	22,283.6	13.1	44,274.4	20.2
29,487.3	9.2	11,213.1	11.1	24,282.1	9.0	54,455.9	23.0
32,570.6	10.5	11,857.8	5.7	23,706.7	-2.4	61,636.0	13.2
32,409.4	-0.5	11,975.2	1.0	25,059.3	5.7	65,939.0	7.0
35,377.9	9.2	11,669.4	-2.6	27,406.9	9.4	76,439.5	15.9
9,362.7	6.4	10,788.5	17.5	4,536.0	34.9	18,753.5	13.3
13,879.3	48.2	13,286.1	23.2	4,563.4	0.6	23,537.6	25.5
12,796.3	-7.8	12,423.4	-6.5	5,087.8	11.5	22,702.0	-3.6
13,260.4	3.6	11,925.5	-4.0	8,849.0	73.9	22,111.6	-2.6
14,000.5	5.6	9,745.8	-18.3	9,120.9	3.1	19,652.2	-11.1
14,383.8	2.7	10,125.9	3.9	9,947.2	9.1	19,458.4	-1.0
16,846.3	17.1	11,297.4	11.6	12,059.0	21.2	22,875.1	17.6
16,688.9	-0.9	10,120.8	-10.4	12,172.5	0.9	22,672.9	-0.9
16,294.3	-2.4	10,115.0	-0.1	12,670.7	4.1	21,745.2	-4.1
16,423.4	0.8	9,799.5	-3.1	12,754.1	0.7	23,466.4	7.9
17,533.8	6.8	9,846.4	0.5	14,189.1	11.3	27,496.2	17.2
18,643.8	6.3	10,172.8	3.3	14,545.6	2.5	29,208.5	6.2
20,908.8	12.1	10,280.5	1.1	16,807.9	15.6	33,226.8	13.8
24,380.5	16.6	10,027.0	-2.5	19,746.2	17.5	39,072.1	17.6
25,390.4	4.1	11,872.0	18.4	21,078.7	6.7	47,417.7	21.4

Table 20.4 International trade in services, selected years from 1992 to 2007

	Receipts			
	1992	1997	2002	2007
	$ millions			
Travel	**7,898**	**12,221**	**16,741**	**16,634**
Business travel	1,547	2,461	2,737	2,890
Personal travel	6,351	9,760	14,005	13,744
Transportation	**5,232**	**8,407**	**11,060**	**12,157**
Water transport	1,470	2,004	2,391	4,072
Air transport	2,205	3,490	4,947	4,734
Land and other transport	1,557	2,914	3,722	3,350
Commercial services	**11,080**	**21,921**	**34,246**	**36,775**
Communications services	1,247	2,039	2,362	2,719
Construction services	95	187	157	159
Insurance services	2,488	2,938	5,090	3,844
Other financial services	598	1,164	1,528	2,147
Computer and information services	826	1,499	3,557	4,736
Royalties and license fees	263	1,611	3,917	3,885
Non-financial commissions	316	648	739	921
Equipment rentals	196	211	397	433
Management services	1,035	2,119	4,740	5,215
Advertising and related services	147	297	549	369
Research and development	741	1,812	2,519	2,820
Architectural, engineering and other technical services	1,171	3,045	4,075	4,268
Miscellaneous services to business	1,390	2,876	2,621	3,124
Audio-visual services	425	1,315	1,786	1,895
Personal, cultural and recreational services	140	161	209	240

Source: Statistics Canada, CANSIM tables 376-0031, 376-0032 and 376-0033.

Payments				Balance			
1992	1997	2002	2007	1992	1997	2002	2007
$ millions							
14,255	**15,873**	**18,401**	**26,663**	**-6,357**	**-3,652**	**-1,659**	**-10,029**
2,300	3,475	3,416	4,248	-752	-1,015	-679	-1,358
11,955	12,398	14,985	22,415	-5,605	-2,638	-980	-8,671
7,989	**11,417**	**14,438**	**20,032**	**-2,757**	**-3,010**	**-3,378**	**-7,875**
2,701	3,625	5,650	8,496	-1,232	-1,621	-3,259	-4,423
3,581	5,349	6,091	9,199	-1,376	-1,860	-1,144	-4,465
1,707	2,443	2,697	2,337	-150	470	1,025	1,013
14,050	**24,658**	**36,903**	**38,691**	**-2,970**	**-2,737**	**-2,657**	**-1,915**
1,207	2,236	2,305	1,958	40	-197	57	761
56	151	92	182	38	37	65	-23
2,642	4,027	6,612	5,970	-154	-1,089	-1,523	-2,127
970	1,758	2,711	3,657	-372	-595	-1,183	-1,510
527	954	2,045	2,253	300	545	1,512	2,483
2,070	3,224	7,038	8,077	-1,807	-1,613	-3,121	-4,192
370	565	634	633	-54	82	105	288
327	540	704	826	-130	-329	-307	-393
1,568	3,385	4,780	5,061	-532	-1,266	-40	154
246	520	518	532	-99	-222	31	-163
549	962	989	1,258	192	850	1,530	1,563
703	1,174	2,151	2,589	467	1,871	1,924	1,679
2,029	3,497	3,817	3,497	-639	-621	-1,197	-374
663	1,519	2,322	1,988	-238	-205	-536	-92
123	146	185	211	18	15	24	28

Table 20.5 International trade in goods and services, by province and territory, selected years from 1988 to 2008

	1988	1993	1998	2003	2008
			$ millions		
Imports to Canada	**159,117**	**219,673**	**360,871**	**416,856**	**534,096**
Newfoundland and Labrador	1,642	1,693	3,538	5,340	8,682
Prince Edward Island	242	343	652	887	1,144
Nova Scotia	3,409	4,506	7,147	8,840	10,495
New Brunswick	2,837	4,627	6,542	9,569	15,531
Quebec	33,530	47,527	72,695	84,296	112,613
Ontario	83,244	110,235	183,803	204,027	238,546
Manitoba	3,892	5,595	9,925	11,100	14,408
Saskatchewan	3,240	4,731	8,613	9,456	14,429
Alberta	11,717	16,591	33,527	43,440	64,846
British Columbia	14,431	22,763	33,200	38,377	51,071
Yukon	96	238	232	284	477
Northwest Territories (including Nunavut)	221	246	594	..	..
Northwest Territories	..	..	..	661	935
Nunavut	..	..	..	242	522
Outside Canada	616	578	403	338	396
Exports from Canada	**163,842**	**219,664**	**379,203**	**462,473**	**559,755**
Newfoundland and Labrador	2,709	2,189	3,828	6,893	14,868
Prince Edward Island	236	352	819	1,089	1,207
Nova Scotia	2,442	3,428	5,340	7,295	7,950
New Brunswick	3,447	4,011	6,215	10,274	13,759
Quebec	30,242	40,921	73,542	84,807	93,811
Ontario	76,792	108,697	193,513	218,716	215,602
Manitoba	4,402	5,263	9,829	11,356	15,204
Saskatchewan	5,481	6,740	11,760	13,601	30,166
Alberta	15,398	22,975	38,147	65,041	115,164
British Columbia	21,762	24,461	35,596	41,372	49,161
Yukon	466	237	230	171	445
Northwest Territories (including Nunavut)	342	374	371	..	..
Northwest Territories	..	..	..	1,796	2,370
Nunavut	..	..	..	59	46
Outside Canada	123	16	15	2	3

Note: Expenditure-based gross domestic product at current prices.
Source: Statistics Canada, CANSIM table 384-0002.

Labour

21

In 2008, the labour force grew at an annual rate of 1.7%, bringing the total number of people in the labour force to 18.2 million. Since peaking at 2.9% in 2002, the labour force grew by 1.6% on average over the last six years.

The employment rate—the number of people employed expressed as a percentage of the population aged 15 and older—edged down slightly in 2008, ending in December at 63.1%. This pushed the unemployment rate—the proportion of unemployed people in the labour force—up to 6.6% in December, compared with 5.9% the previous year.

The highest employment rates in 2008 were observed in Western Canada, particularly in Alberta (72.0%), Saskatchewan (66.8%), and Manitoba (66.7%).

During the last quarter of 2008, the labour market experienced some tightening as economic growth slowed. The hardest-hit sectors were agriculture, construction and manufacturing. Employment levels in those three sectors fell by 216,000 during the last quarter alone (from October to December), after gaining 317,000 in the first three quarters of the year.

The participation rate—the percentage of those aged 15 and older who had a job or were looking for one—fell to 67.6% in December from a peak of 67.9% in May, as the labour force contracted toward the end of the year.

Earnings rose

Despite employment losses, employees' average weekly wages rose 4.0% in 2008. Wages in the construction sector saw above-average growth, increasing 6.9% to $965.26; agricultural wages grew 5.2% to $543.98 on average. In manufacturing, average weekly wages grew 4.0% to

Chart 21.1
Labour force, by age and sex, 2008

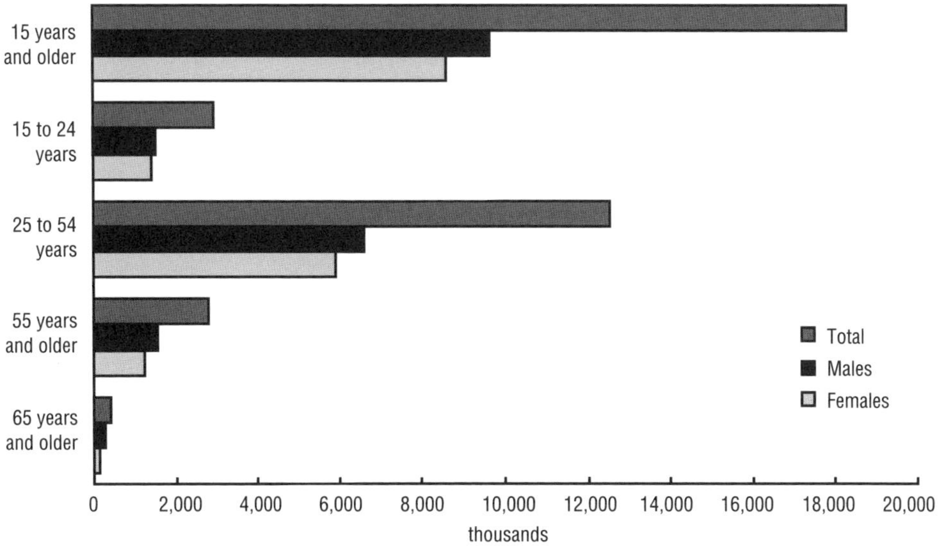

Source: Statistics Canada, CANSIM table 282-0002.

$894.24, the slowest growth of all three sectors.

The most prevalent occupations for women in 2008 were in sales and service occupations, such as retail sales people and sales clerks, cashiers, and cleaners and janitors; business, finance and administrative occupations, including secretaries and clerks; occupations in social science, education, government, service and religion, such as teachers and social workers; health occupations, including nurses and technicians; and management occupations, such as managers in retail, food and accommodation.

Men worked primarily in trades, transport and equipment operation and related occupations—mainly the construction trades, such as contractors and machinists; in sales and service occupations—primarily wholesale, retail and protective services, such as cleaners and janitors; in management occupations—mainly in retail trade, food and accommodation services; in natural and applied sciences and related occupations—mainly in professional and technical occupations; and in business, finance and administrative occupations.

Table 21.a
Labour market indicators

	2007	2008
	thousands	
Population aged 15 and older	**26,553.4**	**26,924.7**
Labour force	17,945.8	18,245.1
Employment	16,866.4	17,125.8
Unemployment	1,079.4	1,119.3
Not in labour force	8,607.5	8,679.5
	%	
Unemployment rate	6.0	6.1
Participation rate	67.6	67.8
Employment rate	63.5	63.6

Source: Statistics Canada, CANSIM table 282-0002.

Chart 21.2
Part-time employment, by reason, 2008

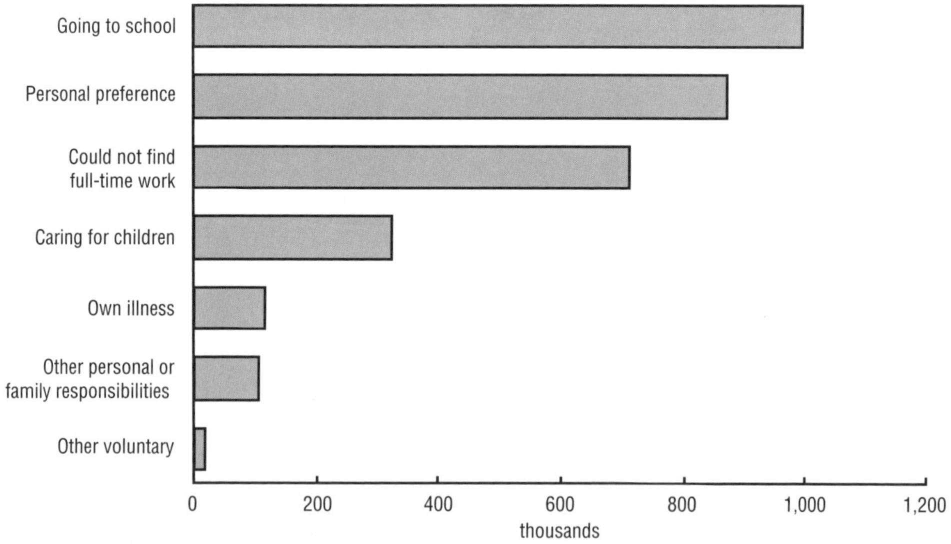

Source: Statistics Canada, CANSIM table 282-0014.

Labour mobility

Labour mobility has recently garnered attention as forecasts of future labour shortages have become more widespread. Workers moving to a new province is a signal that labour markets are responding to changing economic conditions.

An estimated 383,000 people changed their usual place of residence in favour of another province from 2007 to 2008. The migrant population tends to be younger and more educated than the non-migrant population. For most migrants, employment is a key motivation to move.

Interprovincial out-migration is more likely to occur in provinces where the unemployment rates are relatively high. The study also found that migrants generally saw greater increases in earnings than did non-migrants—particularly those leaving Quebec, Saskatchewan or any of the Atlantic provinces.

Chart 21.3
Interprovincial migration, by province and territory, 2007/2008p

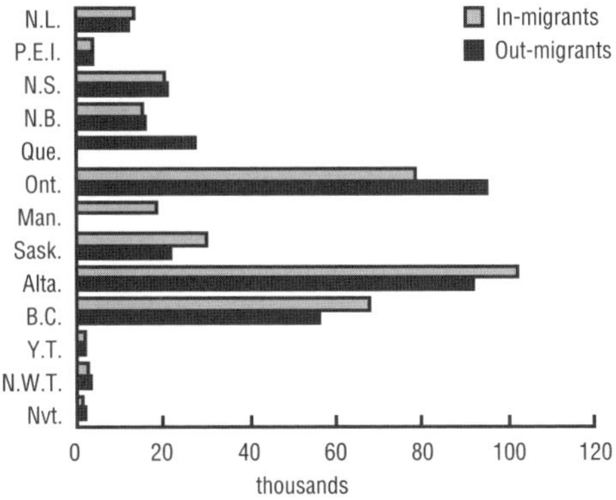

Note: July 1, 2007 to June 30, 2008.
Source: Statistics Canada, CANSIM table 051-0019.

Work arrangements

Work arrangements can take many forms other than the standard 9-to-5 day. The most common form of non-standard work arrangement in 2008 was flexible hours (that is, varying the start and end times of the workday).

According to a recent study on labour market dynamics, 36.6% of paid workers in 2005 had some flexibility in their hours of work. The next most common arrangement was weekend work (27.9%). Other arrangements include reduced work weeks, compressed work weeks, or working at home.

Workers aged 25 and younger and workers with less than a high school education are more likely to work reduced work weeks or weekends. Those 25 and older with a high school diploma or higher are more likely to work flexible hours.

Chart 21.4
Work arrangements, 2005

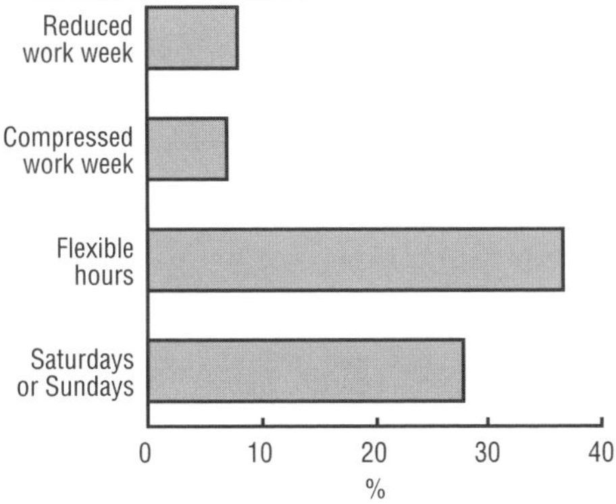

Source: Statistics Canada, Catalogue no. 71-585-X.

Almost three-quarters of paid workers who work weekends are in occupations involving marketing and sales; almost one-half of paid workers who work flexible hours are managers and professionals.

Table 21.1 Labour force characteristics, by sex and by province, 2008

	Canada	Newfoundland and Labrador	Prince Edward Island	Nova Scotia	New Brunswick
	thousands				
Population					
Both sexes	**26,924.7**	426.2	114.5	768.6	617.9
Males	**13,251.8**	207.0	55.4	370.3	301.1
Females	**13,672.9**	219.2	59.1	398.3	316.9
Labour force					
Both sexes	**18,245.1**	253.8	78.7	491.0	400.6
Males	**9,654.0**	133.2	39.8	251.9	208.3
Females	**8,591.2**	120.6	38.9	239.1	192.3
Employment					
Both sexes	**17,125.8**	220.3	70.2	453.2	366.2
Males	**9,021.3**	113.7	35.0	229.1	186.4
Females	**8,104.5**	106.6	35.2	224.1	179.8
Unemployment					
Both sexes	**1,119.3**	33.5	8.5	37.8	34.4
Males	**632.6**	19.5	4.7	22.8	21.9
Females	**486.6**	14.0	3.7	15.1	12.5
Not in the labour force					
Both sexes	**8,679.5**	172.4	35.8	277.6	217.4
Males	**3,597.8**	73.8	15.6	118.4	92.8
Females	**5,081.7**	98.6	20.2	159.2	124.6
	%				
Participation rate					
Both sexes	**67.8**	59.5	68.7	63.9	64.8
Males	**72.9**	64.3	71.8	68.0	69.2
Females	**62.8**	55.0	65.8	60.0	60.7
Employment rate					
Both sexes	**63.6**	51.7	61.3	59.0	59.3
Males	**68.1**	54.9	63.2	61.9	61.9
Females	**59.3**	48.6	59.6	56.3	56.7
Unemployment rate					
Both sexes	**6.1**	13.2	10.8	7.7	8.6
Males	**6.6**	14.6	11.8	9.1	10.5
Females	**5.7**	11.6	9.5	6.3	6.5

Note: Population aged 15 and older.
Source: Statistics Canada, CANSIM table 282-0002.

Quebec	Ontario	Manitoba	Saskatchewan	Alberta	British Columbia
thousands					
6,372.1	10,509.8	909.7	767.1	2,796.8	3,641.8
3,133.6	5,147.7	447.5	378.3	1,416.9	1,794.1
3,238.5	5,362.2	462.2	388.8	1,379.9	1,847.7
4,184.9	7,154.5	633.0	534.7	2,088.1	2,425.9
2,205.0	3,744.9	338.5	286.8	1,155.3	1,290.4
1,979.9	3,409.5	294.5	247.9	932.8	1,135.5
3,881.7	6,687.3	606.7	512.7	2,013.3	2,314.3
2,025.0	3,486.8	324.2	274.8	1,115.4	1,230.9
1,856.7	3,200.4	282.5	237.9	897.9	1,083.4
303.3	467.2	26.3	22.0	74.8	111.6
180.1	258.1	14.2	12.0	39.9	59.5
123.2	209.1	12.0	10.0	34.9	52.1
2,187.2	3,355.4	276.7	232.4	708.7	1,216.0
928.6	1,402.7	109.0	91.5	261.6	503.8
1,258.6	1,952.6	167.7	140.9	447.1	712.2
%					
65.7	68.1	69.6	69.7	74.7	66.6
70.4	72.7	75.6	75.8	81.5	71.9
61.1	63.6	63.7	63.8	67.6	61.5
60.9	63.6	66.7	66.8	72.0	63.5
64.6	67.7	72.4	72.6	78.7	68.6
57.3	59.7	61.1	61.2	65.1	58.6
7.2	6.5	4.2	4.1	3.6	4.6
8.2	6.9	4.2	4.2	3.5	4.6
6.2	6.1	4.1	4.0	3.7	4.6

Table 21.2 Labour force and participation rates, by sex and age group, 1983 to 2008

	Labour force			Participation rates		
	15 and older			15 and older		
	Both sexes	Males	Females	Both sexes	Males	Females
	thousands			%		
1983	**12,527.6**	7,319.8	5,207.8	**64.7**	76.9	53.0
1984	**12,747.9**	7,392.8	5,355.1	**65.0**	76.7	53.8
1985	**13,012.4**	7,478.9	5,533.5	**65.6**	76.7	54.9
1986	**13,272.1**	7,585.4	5,686.7	**66.1**	76.8	55.7
1987	**13,526.0**	7,680.2	5,845.8	**66.5**	76.8	56.5
1988	**13,779.1**	7,754.3	6,024.8	**66.8**	76.6	57.4
1989	**14,057.0**	7,872.4	6,184.6	**67.3**	76.8	58.1
1990	**14,244.6**	7,924.1	6,320.6	**67.1**	76.1	58.5
1991	**14,336.3**	7,924.6	6,411.8	**66.6**	75.0	58.4
1992	**14,336.1**	7,911.2	6,425.0	**65.7**	73.9	57.8
1993	**14,435.0**	7,943.2	6,491.9	**65.3**	73.3	57.7
1994	**14,573.7**	8,014.3	6,559.4	**65.2**	73.1	57.5
1995	**14,689.2**	8,049.5	6,639.8	**64.8**	72.5	57.5
1996	**14,853.5**	8,129.1	6,724.4	**64.7**	72.2	57.4
1997	**15,079.1**	8,233.8	6,845.3	**64.8**	72.2	57.8
1998	**15,316.3**	8,324.3	6,992.0	**65.1**	72.1	58.4
1999	**15,588.3**	8,457.6	7,130.7	**65.5**	72.4	58.9
2000	**15,847.0**	8,569.2	7,277.8	**65.8**	72.4	59.4
2001	**16,109.8**	8,690.9	7,418.9	**65.9**	72.3	59.7
2002	**16,579.3**	8,906.2	7,673.1	**66.9**	73.0	60.9
2003	**16,958.5**	9,067.7	7,890.9	**67.5**	73.4	61.9
2004	**17,182.3**	9,166.0	8,016.3	**67.5**	73.2	62.0
2005	**17,342.6**	9,243.7	8,098.8	**67.2**	72.8	61.8
2006	**17,592.8**	9,335.4	8,257.3	**67.2**	72.5	62.1
2007	**17,945.8**	9,492.8	8,453.0	**67.6**	72.7	62.7
2008	**18,245.1**	9,654.0	8,591.2	**67.8**	72.9	62.8

Source: Statistics Canada, CANSIM table 282-0002.

Participation rates							
15 to 24		25 to 44		45 and older		65 and older	
Males	Females	Males	Females	Males	Females	Males	Females
%							
70.6	64.5	94.0	67.6	61.3	30.8	12.1	3.7
70.8	65.0	94.1	69.4	60.3	30.8	11.8	3.9
71.1	65.6	94.2	70.9	59.4	31.8	11.8	4.1
72.3	67.0	94.4	73.1	58.6	30.9	11.1	3.4
73.0	67.5	94.3	74.0	58.1	32.0	11.2	3.3
73.1	68.0	94.2	75.3	57.5	33.0	10.7	3.6
73.8	68.5	94.2	76.6	57.4	33.4	10.5	3.9
72.4	67.3	93.8	77.7	56.8	33.9	10.8	3.6
70.1	66.1	93.1	77.8	56.3	34.6	11.1	3.4
67.8	64.5	92.0	76.8	55.9	35.4	10.6	3.4
66.5	62.2	92.1	77.1	55.5	36.1	9.7	3.5
65.9	61.9	91.8	76.9	55.9	36.6	10.7	3.4
64.9	61.3	91.6	77.1	55.4	36.9	9.9	3.4
64.1	60.3	91.6	77.8	55.4	37.1	9.8	3.4
63.6	59.2	91.9	78.4	55.8	38.1	9.8	3.6
63.4	60.2	92.2	79.0	55.8	39.3	10.2	3.5
65.3	61.5	92.2	79.6	56.4	39.9	9.8	3.4
65.9	62.8	92.1	79.9	56.7	40.9	9.5	3.3
66.1	63.2	92.1	80.4	56.9	41.6	9.4	3.4
67.8	65.3	92.3	81.3	58.1	43.2	10.3	3.8
68.3	66.5	92.5	81.7	59.2	45.0	11.5	4.2
67.8	66.2	92.4	82.2	59.6	45.5	11.8	4.4
66.1	65.8	92.3	81.8	59.9	45.9	12.1	5.0
66.4	66.4	92.0	81.8	59.6	46.8	12.1	5.2
67.4	66.5	92.1	82.6	60.0	47.8	13.0	5.6
67.8	67.0	92.4	82.1	60.5	48.6	14.2	6.8

Table 21.3 Labour force characteristics, by sex and age group, 2008

	Labour force	Employment	Unemployment	Participation rate	Employment rate	Unemployment rate
	thousands			%		
Both sexes	**18,245.1**	**17,125.8**	**1,119.3**	**67.8**	**63.6**	**6.1**
15 to 24	2,949.6	2,607.2	342.4	67.4	59.6	11.6
15 to 19	1,207.1	1,019.2	187.9	56.0	47.2	15.6
20 to 24	1,742.5	1,588.0	154.5	78.5	71.6	8.9
25 and older	15,295.5	14,518.7	776.8	67.8	64.4	5.1
25 to 44	8,076.6	7,648.0	428.6	87.3	82.6	5.3
25 to 34	3,861.8	3,646.4	215.4	86.5	81.7	5.6
35 to 44	4,214.7	4,001.5	213.2	88.0	83.5	5.1
45 to 64	6,790.3	6,454.2	336.2	75.0	71.3	5.0
45 to 54	4,428.9	4,221.4	207.6	85.7	81.7	4.7
55 to 64	2,361.4	2,232.8	128.6	60.8	57.5	5.4
55 and older	2,790.0	2,649.4	140.7	34.3	32.6	5.0
65 and older	428.6	416.5	12.1	10.1	9.8	2.8
Males	**9,654.0**	**9,021.3**	**632.6**	**72.9**	**68.1**	**6.6**
15 to 24	1,513.5	1,315.1	198.4	67.8	58.9	13.1
15 to 19	601.4	498.1	103.3	54.5	45.1	17.2
20 to 24	912.1	817.0	95.2	80.8	72.4	10.4
25 and older	8,140.4	7,706.2	434.2	73.9	69.9	5.3
25 to 44	4,280.9	4,043.3	237.6	92.4	87.2	5.6
25 to 34	2,052.1	1,929.1	122.9	91.6	86.1	6.0
35 to 44	2,228.8	2,114.2	114.6	93.0	88.3	5.1
45 to 64	3,588.9	3,399.7	189.2	80.2	75.9	5.3
45 to 54	2,306.6	2,191.5	115.1	89.8	85.3	5.0
55 to 64	1,282.3	1,208.2	74.1	67.2	63.3	5.8
55 and older	1,553.0	1,471.4	81.6	40.7	38.6	5.3
65 and older	270.7	263.2	7.4	14.2	13.8	2.7
Females	**8,591.2**	**8,104.5**	**486.6**	**62.8**	**59.3**	**5.7**
15 to 24	1,436.1	1,292.1	144.0	67.0	60.3	10.0
15 to 19	605.7	521.1	84.7	57.5	49.5	14.0
20 to 24	830.4	771.0	59.4	76.2	70.7	7.2
25 and older	7,155.1	6,812.5	342.6	62.1	59.1	4.8
25 to 44	3,795.8	3,604.7	191.1	82.1	78.0	5.0
25 to 34	1,809.7	1,717.3	92.4	81.3	77.2	5.1
35 to 44	1,985.9	1,887.3	98.6	82.9	78.8	5.0
45 to 64	3,201.4	3,054.4	146.9	70.0	66.8	4.6
45 to 54	2,122.3	2,029.8	92.4	81.7	78.2	4.4
55 to 64	1,079.1	1,024.6	54.5	54.6	51.9	5.1
55 and older	1,237.0	1,177.9	59.1	28.7	27.3	4.8
65 and older	**2,335.8**	157.9	153.3	**6.8**	6.6	3.0

Note: Population aged 15 and older.
Source: Statistics Canada, CANSIM table 282-0002.

Table 21.4 Labour force characteristics, by census metropolitan area, 2008

	Labour force	Employment	Unemployment	Participation rate	Employment rate	Unemployment rate
	thousands			%		
St. John's	106.8	98.5	8.3	69.1	63.8	7.8
Halifax	221.0	209.4	11.6	69.7	66.0	5.2
Saint John	69.3	65.0	4.3	66.2	62.1	6.2
Saguenay	75.5	69.1	6.4	60.4	55.3	8.5
Québec	410.3	391.7	18.6	67.2	64.2	4.5
Sherbrooke	88.4	83.0	5.5	63.8	59.9	6.2
Trois-Rivières	76.1	70.0	6.1	62.6	57.6	8.0
Montréal	2,052.6	1,900.1	152.6	66.9	62.0	7.4
Ottawa–Gatineau	705.8	671.7	34.1	73.3	69.7	4.8
Kingston	84.1	79.4	4.7	66.7	63.0	5.6
Oshawa	200.3	186.1	14.3	69.5	64.6	7.1
Toronto	3,138.3	2,922.8	215.4	69.0	64.2	6.9
Hamilton	399.0	374.4	24.6	66.8	62.7	6.2
St.Catharines–Niagara	213.2	197.4	15.8	64.7	59.9	7.4
Kitchener	272.4	256.1	16.3	71.1	66.9	6.0
London	262.8	244.3	18.5	68.2	63.4	7.0
Windsor	174.6	158.3	16.3	64.0	58.0	9.3
Greater Sudbury/Grand Sudbury	86.2	81.4	4.8	64.5	60.9	5.6
Thunder Bay	66.6	62.6	4.0	64.2	60.3	6.0
Winnipeg	413.8	395.9	17.9	70.9	67.8	4.3
Regina	118.8	114.2	4.6	70.9	68.1	3.9
Saskatoon	143.9	138.2	5.7	73.0	70.2	4.0
Calgary	729.5	704.1	25.5	77.1	74.4	3.5
Edmonton	644.8	621.1	23.7	73.0	70.3	3.7
Abbotsford–Mission	92.5	88.0	4.5	69.2	65.8	4.9
Vancouver	1,296.9	1,241.6	55.2	66.7	63.9	4.3
Victoria	197.5	190.9	6.6	69.0	66.7	3.3

Note: Population aged 15 and older.
Source: Statistics Canada, CANSIM table 282-0053.

Table 21.5 Full-time and part-time employment, by sex and age group, 2003 to 2008

	2003	2004	2005	2006	2007	2008
	thousands					
Total employment						
Both sexes	15,672.3	15,947.0	16,169.7	16,484.3	16,866.4	17,125.8
15 to 24	2,449.4	2,461.0	2,472.5	2,535.8	2,589.4	2,607.2
25 to 44	7,571.5	7,594.0	7,597.5	7,610.7	7,658.9	7,648.0
45 and older	5,651.4	5,892.0	6,099.7	6,337.8	6,618.2	6,870.7
Males	8,348.1	8,480.6	8,594.7	8,727.1	8,888.9	9,021.3
15 to 24	1,243.2	1,248.3	1,239.0	1,276.9	1,313.3	1,315.1
25 to 44	4,029.0	4,023.8	4,032.1	4,035.3	4,032.6	4,043.3
45 and older	3,075.8	3,208.4	3,323.6	3,414.9	3,543.0	3,662.9
Females	7,324.2	7,466.4	7,575.0	7,757.2	7,977.5	8,104.5
15 to 24	1,206.2	1,212.6	1,233.5	1,258.9	1,276.1	1,292.1
25 to 44	3,542.5	3,570.2	3,565.4	3,575.4	3,626.2	3,604.7
45 and older	2,575.6	2,683.5	2,776.2	2,922.9	3,075.2	3,207.8
Full-time employment						
Both sexes	12,705.3	12,998.1	13,206.2	13,509.7	13,803.1	13,976.6
15 to 24	1,344.3	1,361.4	1,370.2	1,419.8	1,435.1	1,438.6
25 to 44	6,624.7	6,671.2	6,684.7	6,730.9	6,774.4	6,756.1
45 and older	4,736.3	4,965.5	5,151.3	5,359.0	5,593.6	5,782.0
Males	7,423.0	7,559.3	7,664.0	7,781.0	7,909.9	8,008.0
15 to 24	774.9	781.2	782.5	809.2	828.5	825.6
25 to 44	3,832.2	3,834.1	3,832.6	3,845.6	3,840.2	3,833.2
45 and older	2,815.9	2,944.1	3,048.9	3,126.2	3,241.3	3,349.2
Females	5,282.3	5,438.8	5,542.3	5,728.7	5,893.2	5,968.7
15 to 24	569.4	580.2	587.8	610.5	606.6	613.0
25 to 44	2,792.5	2,837.2	2,852.1	2,885.3	2,934.2	2,922.9
45 and older	1,920.4	2,021.4	2,102.4	2,232.8	2,352.4	2,432.8
Part-time employment						
Both sexes	2,967.0	2,948.9	2,963.5	2,974.7	3,063.3	3,149.2
15 to 24	1,105.1	1,099.6	1,102.3	1,116.0	1,154.3	1,168.6
25 to 44	946.8	922.8	912.8	879.9	884.5	891.9
45 and older	915.0	926.5	948.4	978.8	1,024.5	1,088.7
Males	925.0	921.3	930.7	946.1	979.0	1,013.3
15 to 24	468.3	467.1	456.5	467.7	484.8	489.5
25 to 44	196.9	189.8	199.5	189.7	192.5	210.1
45 and older	259.8	264.4	274.7	288.7	301.7	313.7
Females	2,041.9	2,027.6	2,032.8	2,028.5	2,084.3	2,135.9
15 to 24	636.8	632.4	645.8	648.4	669.5	679.1
25 to 44	749.9	733.0	713.3	690.1	692.0	681.8
45 and older	655.2	662.1	673.7	690.0	722.8	774.9

Source: Statistics Canada, CANSIM table 282-0002.

Table 21.6 Reasons for part-time work, by sex and age group, 2008

	15 years and older	15 to 24 years	25 to 44 years	45 years and older
	thousands			
All people employed part time	**3,149.2**	**1,168.6**	**891.9**	**1,088.7**
Males	**1,013.3**	489.5	210.1	313.7
Females	**2,135.9**	679.1	681.8	774.9
	%			
Both sexes				
Own illness	**3.7**	0.8	3.5	7.1
Caring for children	**10.3**	0.9	30.0	4.4
Other personal/family responsibilities	**3.4**	0.7	4.7	5.2
Going to school	**31.6**	75.8	11.2	0.8
Personal preference	**27.7**	5.8	18.0	59.0
Other voluntary	**0.7**	0.4	1.1	0.8
Involuntary (no full-time work available)	**22.6**	15.6	31.6	22.7
Males				
Own illness	**4.0**	0.9	5.5	7.9
Caring for children	**1.4**	x	4.5	1.3
Other personal/family responsibilities	**1.5**	0.6	2.7	1.9
Going to school	**41.2**	76.4	19.5	0.8
Personal preference	**26.4**	6.0	20.5	62.0
Other voluntary	**1.0**	0.4	2.0	1.3
Involuntary (no full-time work available)	**24.6**	15.6	45.4	24.8
Females				
Own illness	**3.6**	0.7	2.9	6.7
Caring for children	**14.6**	1.5	37.8	5.6
Other personal/family responsibilities	**4.3**	0.8	5.4	6.5
Going to school	**27.0**	75.3	8.6	0.8
Personal preference	**28.3**	5.6	17.2	57.9
Other voluntary	**0.6**	0.4	0.8	0.6
Involuntary (no full-time work available)	**21.6**	15.6	27.3	21.9

Note: Expressed as a percentage of total part-time employment.
Source: Statistics Canada, CANSIM table 282-0014.

Table 21.7 Employment, by sector, 1994 to 2008

	1994	1995	1996	1997	1998	1999
	thousands					
All sectors	**13,058.7**	**13,295.4**	**13,421.4**	**13,706.0**	**14,046.2**	**14,406.7**
Goods-producing sector	3,397.5	3,467.6	3,476.0	3,561.0	3,657.9	3,742.5
Agriculture	437.2	419.3	422.5	417.0	424.2	406.0
Forestry, fishing, mining, and oil and gas extraction	285.6	294.8	294.0	296.7	293.5	263.8
Utilities	127.0	123.5	124.1	115.3	114.7	114.3
Construction	724.6	726.4	709.7	721.0	731.9	766.9
Manufacturing	1,823.2	1,903.8	1,925.7	2,010.9	2,093.5	2,191.5
Services-producing sector	9,661.2	9,827.7	9,945.4	10,145.1	10,388.4	10,664.3
Trade	2,061.1	2,077.5	2,087.7	2,106.1	2,125.4	2,218.2
Transportation and warehousing	644.9	660.8	674.0	694.6	712.7	737.0
Finance, insurance, real estate and leasing	832.7	846.1	861.4	865.0	847.9	859.9
Professional, scientific and technical services	642.5	674.3	706.7	777.8	849.8	900.7
Business, building and other support services	365.4	402.5	420.8	441.8	478.1	504.7
Educational services	927.2	928.3	913.0	916.6	930.0	970.7
Health care and social assistance	1,364.2	1,388.6	1,390.9	1,388.4	1,428.5	1,436.0
Information, culture and recreation	537.4	567.7	579.1	603.5	615.8	630.5
Accommodation and food services	799.1	816.1	847.9	871.0	911.4	913.6
Other services	651.9	647.2	656.0	683.0	706.8	716.5
Public administration	834.8	818.6	807.8	797.2	781.9	776.3

Notes: Population aged 15 and older.
North American Industry Classification System (NAICS), 2002.
Source: Statistics Canada, CANSIM table 282-0008.

2000	2001	2002	2003	2004	2005	2006	2007	2008
				thousands				
14,764.2	**14,946.2**	**15,310.4**	**15,672.3**	**15,947.0**	**16,169.7**	**16,484.3**	**16,866.4**	**17,125.8**
3,822.0	3,779.9	3,878.6	3,925.7	3,989.8	4,002.4	3,985.9	3,993.0	4,021.3
372.1	323.3	325.4	332.4	326.0	343.7	346.4	337.2	327.0
275.4	278.9	270.3	281.6	286.6	306.4	330.1	339.3	340.1
114.9	124.4	131.9	130.5	133.3	125.3	122.0	138.0	151.8
810.1	824.3	865.2	906.0	951.7	1,019.5	1,069.7	1,133.5	1,232.2
2,249.4	2,229.0	2,285.9	2,275.2	2,292.1	2,207.4	2,117.7	2,044.9	1,970.3
10,942.2	11,166.2	11,431.8	11,746.6	11,957.2	12,167.3	12,498.4	12,873.5	13,104.5
2,293.3	2,363.3	2,409.3	2,467.8	2,507.1	2,574.6	2,633.5	2,682.4	2,678.8
772.3	775.8	760.7	790.9	799.4	793.6	802.2	822.8	857.7
857.9	876.7	895.1	917.0	960.6	987.8	1,040.5	1,060.4	1,075.4
932.2	986.5	987.1	1,003.6	1,018.3	1,050.0	1,089.9	1,136.9	1,200.0
537.0	537.2	579.6	608.7	630.2	654.4	690.0	702.1	686.5
974.1	981.6	1,007.4	1,027.1	1,035.7	1,106.1	1,158.4	1,183.2	1,192.8
1,514.0	1,540.4	1,617.3	1,679.2	1,733.4	1,734.6	1,785.5	1,846.1	1,903.4
662.1	709.4	715.1	714.6	738.0	735.1	745.0	782.0	759.6
938.2	943.2	985.1	1,005.5	1,012.4	1,004.5	1,015.0	1,069.4	1,073.5
688.5	666.8	686.2	713.1	696.6	693.4	701.0	723.5	751.1
772.6	785.4	788.9	819.0	825.5	833.1	837.4	864.6	925.7

Table 21.8 Employment, by sector and by province, 2008

	Canada	Newfoundland and Labrador	Prince Edward Island	Nova Scotia
	thousands			
All sectors	**17,125.8**	**220.3**	**70.2**	**453.2**
Goods-producing sector	**4,021.3**	49.2	17.6	92.6
Agriculture	**327.0**	0.9	3.1	6.4
Forestry, fishing, mining, and oil and gas extraction	**340.1**	15.9	2.9	12.7
Utilities	**151.8**	1.6	0.3	3.1
Construction	**1,232.2**	16.7	5.1	31.3
Manufacturing	**1,970.3**	14.1	6.1	39.1
Services-producing sector	**13,104.5**	171.1	52.7	360.6
Trade	**2,678.8**	35.6	10.4	79.2
Transportation and warehousing	**857.7**	10.6	2.7	18.6
Finance, insurance, real estate and leasing	**1,075.4**	7.5	2.8	22.3
Professional, scientific and technical services	**1,200.0**	8.5	2.5	21.3
Business, building and other support services	**686.5**	8.2	2.6	25.9
Educational services	**1,192.8**	16.6	5.0	33.9
Health care and social assistance	**1,903.4**	32.5	8.3	60.5
Information, culture and recreation	**759.6**	8.3	2.5	19.8
Accommodation and food services	**1,073.5**	13.2	5.3	29.4
Other services	**751.1**	11.6	2.9	19.4
Public administration	**925.7**	18.6	7.6	30.3

Notes: Population aged 15 and older.
North American Industry Classification System (NAICS), 2002.
Source: Statistics Canada, CANSIM table 282-0008.

New Brunswick	Quebec	Ontario	Manitoba	Saskatchewan	Alberta	British Columbia
			thousands			
366.2	**3,881.7**	**6,687.3**	**606.7**	**512.7**	**2,013.3**	**2,314.3**
81.8	886.4	1,527.7	148.1	139.4	577.1	501.5
6.0	61.5	84.5	28.9	41.0	61.0	33.7
11.7	32.7	38.1	6.3	25.2	149.2	45.4
4.9	32.9	65.1	6.6	5.6	17.5	14.2
23.9	215.8	439.0	37.6	36.8	205.3	220.8
35.2	543.6	901.2	68.7	30.9	144.1	187.4
284.4	2,995.2	5,159.5	458.7	373.3	1,436.2	1,812.8
57.7	624.6	1,025.5	90.5	83.5	317.0	354.8
20.4	186.0	329.7	35.5	24.0	102.2	128.0
15.8	230.6	472.4	36.6	28.4	111.7	147.2
17.2	265.6	500.2	25.6	20.7	164.2	174.0
19.4	136.9	299.0	18.0	11.4	63.9	101.2
25.9	256.5	482.2	46.6	37.7	126.8	161.6
50.9	470.6	698.4	83.0	63.4	190.2	245.6
11.8	174.8	309.7	22.7	20.3	71.6	118.1
23.9	244.7	396.2	36.8	32.0	113.9	178.1
15.8	175.8	282.7	27.7	22.9	91.2	101.2
25.5	229.1	363.5	35.6	29.2	83.4	102.9

Table 21.9 Employment and average weekly earnings, public administration and all industries, 1995 to 2008

	1995	1996	1997	1998	1999
			thousands		
Employment					
All industries[1]	**11,208.7**	**11,292.5**	**11,624.9**	**11,885.4**	**12,055.8**
Public administration	746.8	722.7	707.6	702.3	705.0
Federal administration	265.0	251.9	236.8	234.7	237.9
Provincial and territorial administration	222.6	208.9	202.7	202.1	206.1
Local administration	228.4	230.1	234.8	231.5	226.6
			$		
Average weekly earnings					
All industries[1]	**598.67**	**611.01**	**623.43**	**632.72**	**640.47**
Public administration	729.83	725.35	729.12	734.05	761.05
Federal administration	804.63	801.01	813.34	830.71	886.01
Provincial and territorial administration	721.99	728.45	741.41	750.14	758.82
Local administration	678.67	670.12	666.15	657.34	671.37

Notes: North American Industry Classification System (NAICS), 2007.
Data include overtime.
1. Excludes agriculture, fishing and trapping, private household services, religious organizations and the military.
Source: Statistics Canada, CANSIM tables 281-0024 and 281-0027.

2000	2001	2002	2003	2004	2005	2006	2007	2008
				thousands				
12,460.9	**12,881.1**	**13,093.3**	**13,372.8**	**13,595.7**	**13,877.3**	**14,252.6**	**14,572.2**	**14,817.7**
713.0	837.6	839.7	888.2	897.7	921.3	945.4	961.0	1,007.8
240.9	252.0	260.7	265.6	264.9	267.2	280.7	281.5	292.2
208.0	221.4	217.5	235.2	237.1	245.3	249.7	252.5	264.7
229.9	324.1	320.4	343.9	350.2	363.4	371.1	383.6	406.5
				$				
655.55	**656.74**	**672.68**	**690.79**	**709.41**	**737.29**	**755.50**	**788.17**	**810.45**
781.15	782.01	844.53	867.71	894.04	925.45	951.03	1,007.53	1,040.51
926.60	934.05	1,006.75	1,050.21	1,077.79	1,137.76	1,145.57	1,233.71	1,286.46
767.44	800.69	837.50	885.36	925.97	953.99	1,001.42	1,048.03	1,091.16
680.57	685.09	755.43	751.61	772.87	788.08	809.12	856.34	871.63

Table 21.10 Average hourly wages of employees, by selected characteristics and professions, 2007 and 2008

	2007		2008	
	thousands	average hourly wage ($)	thousands	average hourly wage ($)
All employed people[1]	**14,251.4**	**20.41**	**14,496.2**	**21.32**
Age 15 to 24	2,500.2	11.81	2,522.1	12.39
Age 25 to 54	9,959.1	22.28	10,049.8	23.22
Age 55 and older	1,792.2	22.03	1,924.3	23.09
Males	7,185.8	22.17	7,301.6	23.18
Females	7,065.6	18.62	7,194.6	19.43
Full-time workers	11,716.2	21.73	11,910.6	22.70
Part-time workers	2,535.2	14.33	2,585.6	14.96
Union coverage[2]	4,491.5	23.51	4,527.0	24.46
No union coverage[3]	9,759.8	18.98	9,969.2	19.89
Permanent job[4]	12,408.8	21.07	12,721.2	21.98
Temporary job[5]	1,842.6	15.99	1,775.0	16.59
Management occupations	1,006.4	31.93	1,058.1	33.25
Business, finance and administrative occupations	2,753.5	19.44	2,843.9	20.28
Natural and applied sciences and related occupations	1,050.5	28.62	1,066.0	29.77
Health occupations	864.5	24.27	899.2	24.87
Occupations in social science, education, public administration and religion	1,276.5	26.29	1,325.8	27.55
Occupations in art, culture, recreation and sport	324.1	20.62	339.2	21.04
Sales and service occupations	3,686.8	13.65	3,668.2	14.22
Trade, transport and equipment operators and related occupations	2,065.9	20.38	2,155.4	21.05
Occupations unique to primary industry	293.0	17.57	279.2	18.39
Occupations unique to processing, manufacturing and utilities	930.2	17.59	861.3	18.32

Note: Data are not seasonally adjusted.
1. Those who work as paid employees of a private firm or business or the public sector. Excludes people who are self-employed.
2. Employees who are members of a union and employees who are not members of a union, but who are covered by a collective agreement or a union contract.
3. Employees who are not members of a union or not covered by a collective agreement or a union contract.
4. A job that is expected to last as long as the employee wants it (business conditions permitting) and has no predetermined end date.
5. A job that has a predetermined end date or will end as soon as a specified project is completed. This includes seasonal jobs; temporary, term or contract jobs including work done through a temporary help agency; casual jobs; and other temporary work.

Source: Statistics Canada, CANSIM tables 282-0070 and 282-0074.

Table 21.11 Average earnings, by sex and work pattern, 1993 to 2007

	All earners			Full-year, full-time workers		
	Males	Females	Earnings ratio[1]	Males	Females	Earnings ratio[1]
	$ 2007 constant		%	$ 2007 constant		%
1993	37,700	24,200	64.1	50,800	37,000	72.8
1994	39,100	24,200	61.9	52,400	36,800	70.2
1995	38,400	24,700	64.2	51,300	37,400	73.0
1996	39,100	24,900	63.6	51,800	37,700	72.8
1997	40,200	24,800	61.8	53,400	37,400	70.0
1998	41,300	25,900	62.8	55,000	39,500	71.9
1999	42,100	26,400	62.6	55,600	38,000	68.4
2000	43,500	26,800	61.7	55,600	39,300	70.6
2001	43,400	26,900	62.1	56,700	39,600	69.9
2002	43,400	27,300	62.8	56,800	39,900	70.2
2003	42,800	26,900	62.9	56,600	39,700	70.2
2004	43,100	27,300	63.4	58,700	41,000	69.9
2005	43,700	27,900	64.0	58,000	40,900	70.5
2006	43,800	28,400	64.7	58,700	42,200	71.9
2007	44,400	29,200	65.7	60,300	43,000	71.4

1. Represents female-to-male earnings ratio.
Source: Statistics Canada, CANSIM table 202-0102.

Table 21.12 Earners, by sex and work pattern, 1993 to 2007

	All earners			Full-year, full-time workers		
	Both sexes	Males	Females	Both sexes	Males	Females
	thousands					
1993	**14,900**	8,105	6,795	**8,050**	4,867	3,182
1994	**14,968**	8,175	6,793	**8,337**	5,097	3,240
1995	**15,313**	8,324	6,988	**8,532**	5,175	3,357
1996	**15,275**	8,340	6,936	**8,416**	5,155	3,261
1997	**15,616**	8,465	7,152	**8,560**	5,230	3,330
1998	**15,896**	8,599	7,298	**8,178**	4,939	3,239
1999	**16,403**	8,813	7,590	**8,497**	5,066	3,431
2000	**16,858**	9,028	7,830	**8,305**	4,956	3,349
2001	**17,226**	9,221	8,004	**8,713**	5,194	3,518
2002	**17,445**	9,324	8,121	**8,483**	5,006	3,477
2003	**17,830**	9,494	8,336	**8,725**	5,075	3,650
2004	**18,163**	9,709	8,454	**9,006**	5,263	3,743
2005	**18,393**	9,779	8,615	**9,342**	5,396	3,946
2006	**18,863**	10,013	8,850	**9,072**	5,268	3,804
2007	**19,251**	10,176	9,076	**9,266**	5,339	3,927

Note: Data before 1996 are taken from the Survey of Consumer Finances (SCF) and data from 1996 on are taken from the Survey of Labour and Income Dynamics (SLID). The surveys use different definitions and, as a result, the number of people working full year, full time in the SLID is smaller than in the SCF.
Source: Statistics Canada, CANSIM table 202-0101.

Table 21.13 Employment rate, by educational attainment, age group and sex, 2002 and 2008

	2002			2008		
	Both sexes	Males	Females	Both sexes	Males	Females
	%					
All education levels	**61.7**	**67.1**	**56.6**	**63.6**	**68.1**	**59.3**
15 to 24	**57.5**	57.4	57.6	**59.6**	58.9	60.3
25 to 44	**80.8**	85.7	75.9	**82.6**	87.2	78.0
45 and older	**47.4**	54.6	40.9	**51.7**	57.4	46.4
Less than Grade 9	**21.4**	29.6	14.1	**20.7**	28.7	13.9
15 to 24	**28.0**	31.7	23.2	**27.7**	30.8	24.0
25 to 44	**49.0**	58.0	36.9	**48.3**	58.0	35.3
45 and older	**17.2**	24.6	11.2	**16.8**	24.1	11.1
Some high school	**44.8**	52.1	37.3	**45.7**	51.8	39.0
15 to 24	**42.8**	43.4	42.0	**44.5**	43.7	45.4
25 to 44	**68.1**	76.5	57.3	**68.1**	74.7	57.9
45 and older	**34.3**	44.8	25.6	**38.2**	48.3	29.0
High school graduate	**66.3**	73.6	59.8	**64.8**	71.6	58.4
15 to 24	**70.9**	72.5	69.2	**70.1**	71.0	69.0
25 to 44	**79.5**	86.0	72.9	**79.8**	86.4	72.3
45 and older	**52.6**	60.8	46.7	**53.8**	60.8	48.7
Some postsecondary	**63.3**	66.8	59.9	**64.6**	67.2	62.1
15 to 24	**59.0**	58.6	59.4	**61.8**	60.6	62.9
25 to 44	**77.3**	82.5	72.3	**78.6**	83.1	73.4
45 and older	**53.0**	59.3	47.3	**56.0**	59.8	52.6
Postsecondary certificate or diploma[1]	**72.6**	76.7	68.6	**72.9**	76.4	69.5
15 to 24	**75.8**	76.5	75.1	**78.1**	78.1	78.0
25 to 44	**85.3**	89.4	81.4	**86.8**	91.0	82.8
45 and older	**58.0**	62.9	53.2	**60.3**	63.9	56.8
Bachelor's degree	**77.0**	79.4	74.8	**76.4**	79.1	74.0
15 to 24	**73.2**	71.0	74.5	**74.1**	74.4	73.9
25 to 44	**85.2**	88.8	82.0	**85.7**	90.4	81.9
45 and older	**65.6**	68.0	62.8	**65.0**	67.1	62.9
Above bachelor's degree	**77.2**	78.1	75.9	**76.4**	76.7	76.1
15 to 24	**63.5**	63.2	64.5	**70.2**	65.6	73.2
25 to 44	**85.7**	89.4	81.8	**85.9**	90.0	82.2
45 and older	**69.5**	69.8	69.0	**68.2**	67.6	69.1

1. Includes trades certificate.
Source: Statistics Canada, CANSIM table 282-0004.

Table 21.14 Self-employment, by sex, 1978 to 2008

	Both sexes	Males	Females
		thousands	
1978	**1,263.4**	910.3	353.1
1979	**1,324.7**	944.6	380.1
1980	**1,363.6**	971.9	391.7
1981	**1,425.2**	1,020.6	404.6
1982	**1,483.2**	1,056.7	426.5
1983	**1,543.2**	1,094.5	448.7
1984	**1,569.7**	1,096.4	473.3
1985	**1,726.0**	1,188.9	537.2
1986	**1,674.2**	1,175.6	498.5
1987	**1,699.1**	1,185.8	513.3
1988	**1,774.1**	1,233.1	541.0
1989	**1,800.3**	1,240.7	559.6
1990	**1,836.6**	1,263.6	573.0
1991	**1,895.8**	1,313.2	582.6
1992	**1,927.5**	1,316.7	610.8
1993	**2,011.1**	1,361.7	649.4
1994	**2,028.5**	1,351.7	676.7
1995	**2,083.1**	1,381.8	701.3
1996	**2,171.6**	1,426.8	744.8
1997	**2,349.4**	1,522.2	827.2
1998	**2,405.7**	1,550.6	855.1
1999	**2,433.0**	1,582.8	850.2
2000	**2,373.7**	1,538.7	835.1
2001	**2,276.7**	1,503.3	773.4
2002	**2,314.5**	1,499.7	814.7
2003	**2,401.8**	1,571.1	830.7
2004	**2,453.4**	1,614.5	838.9
2005	**2,511.6**	1,645.6	866.0
2006	**2,498.0**	1,621.4	876.6
2007	**2,615.0**	1,703.2	911.9
2008	**2,629.6**	1,719.7	909.9

Source: Statistics Canada, CANSIM table 282-0012.

Table 21.15 Days lost annually per full-time employee, by province, 2003 to 2008

	2003	2004	2005	2006	2007	2008
	number of days					
Canada	**9.2**	**9.2**	**9.6**	**9.7**	**10.2**	**10.0**
Newfoundland and Labrador	10.5	10.3	9.5	9.7	9.8	9.8
Prince Edward Island	7.7	7.6	8.6	8.5	8.4	9.0
Nova Scotia	9.8	11.0	10.8	10.7	12.0	11.4
New Brunswick	10.2	9.6	10.3	11.5	10.5	11.0
Quebec	10.8	10.8	11.2	11.5	12.0	11.6
Ontario	8.3	8.5	8.6	8.8	9.3	9.5
Manitoba	9.4	9.8	9.9	10.1	10.8	11.2
Saskatchewan	10.4	10.3	11.1	11.0	10.5	10.5
Alberta	8.0	7.5	8.6	9.0	9.0	8.3
British Columbia	9.9	8.8	10.3	9.4	10.1	9.8

Note: Excludes maternity leave.
Source: Statistics Canada, CANSIM table 279-0029.

Table 21.16 Days lost annually per full-time employee because of illness or disability, by province, 2003 to 2008

	2003	2004	2005	2006	2007	2008
	number of days					
Canada	**7.5**	**7.5**	**7.8**	**7.6**	**8.1**	**7.9**
Newfoundland and Labrador	9.1	8.8	8.1	8.2	8.2	8.2
Prince Edward Island	6.4	6.0	6.9	6.9	6.8	7.4
Nova Scotia	8.1	9.1	9.0	8.9	9.9	9.7
New Brunswick	8.8	8.0	8.5	9.7	8.8	8.8
Quebec	9.3	9.4	9.6	9.3	9.8	9.2
Ontario	6.5	6.7	6.7	6.6	7.2	7.4
Manitoba	7.8	8.0	7.9	8.1	8.7	9.0
Saskatchewan	8.6	8.1	8.9	8.7	8.3	8.1
Alberta	6.2	5.6	6.5	6.6	6.9	6.1
British Columbia	8.1	7.3	8.5	7.6	8.2	8.0

Source: Statistics Canada, CANSIM table 279-0029.

Table 21.17 Days lost annually per full-time employee, by sector, 2003 to 2008

	2003	2004	2005	2006	2007	2008
	number of days					
Goods-producing sector	**9.3**	**9.1**	**9.3**	**9.6**	**9.8**	**9.7**
Primary industries	7.9	7.9	7.6	8.3	8.5	7.7
Utilities	10.0	10.2	9.1	12.4	11.2	10.1
Construction	8.6	7.2	8.3	9.5	9.4	8.6
Manufacturing	9.7	9.9	9.9	9.7	10.2	10.7
Services-producing sector	**9.2**	**9.2**	**9.8**	**9.8**	**10.3**	**10.2**
Trade	8.1	7.6	8.2	8.5	9.3	8.8
Transportation and warehousing	11.4	11.1	12.2	11.6	12.2	12.3
Finance, insurance, real estate and leasing	8.8	7.8	8.9	7.5	8.9	8.2
Professional, scientific and technical services	5.3	5.6	5.3	5.6	6.6	6.3
Business, building and other support services	8.7	9.6	11.0	11.5	10.6	11.5
Educational services	9.5	8.8	9.8	10.7	10.6	9.7
Health care and social assistance	13.0	14.4	14.2	14.4	14.3	14.9
Information, culture and recreation	7.6	7.9	8.5	8.7	9.3	7.9
Accommodation and food services	7.8	7.9	9.1	8.2	8.1	7.3
Public administration	10.9	10.9	12.2	12.0	12.2	13.8
Other services	7.0	7.5	6.8	7.3	9.5	7.9

Notes: North American Industry Classification System (NAICS), 2002.
Excludes maternity leave.
Includes absences because of illness, disability, or personal or family responsibility.
Source: Statistics Canada, CANSIM table 279-0030.

Table 21.18 Labour force and paid workers covered by a Registered Pension Plan, by sex, selected years from 1987 to 2007

	1987	1992	1997	2002	2007
			number		
Registered Pension Plan members[1]					
Both sexes	**4,834,019**	**5,244,703**	**5,088,455**	**5,522,563**	**5,908,633**
Males	3,118,574	3,024,770	2,841,608	2,960,525	3,039,988
Females	1,715,445	2,219,933	2,246,847	2,562,038	2,868,645
			%		
Labour force covered by a Registered Pension Plans					
Both sexes	35.2	36.2	33.5	33.1	32.6
Males	39.8	37.6	34.1	32.9	31.7
Females	29.1	34.4	32.7	33.3	33.7
Paid workers covered by a Registered Pension Plan[2]					
Both sexes	42.7	45.3	41.6	39.7	38.3
Males	48.8	48.3	42.9	40.2	37.7
Females	34.8	41.8	40.1	39.2	38.8

Note: The data used from the Labour Force Survey (labour force and paid workers) are annual averages to which the number of Canadian Forces members was added.

1. Plans are established by either employers or unions to provide retirement income to employees.
2. Refers to employees in the public and private sector and includes self-employed workers in incorporated business (with and without paid help).

Source: Statistics Canada, *Pension Plans in Canada* and Labour Force Survey.

Languages

In 2006, 18.1 million Canadians, or 58% of the population, reported English as their mother tongue, a drop from 61% in 1981. Another 6.9 million, or 22% of Canadians, reported French as the language they first learned and still understand, a fall from 26% in 1981.

Allophones—those whose mother tongue is neither English nor French—numbered 6.3 million in 2006. Partly as a result of sustained immigration from around the world, the proportion of allophones increased substantially to 20% of Canadians from 13% in 1981. Of the 1.1 million immigrants who settled in Canada from 2001 to 2006, more than 80%—901,300 people—were allophones.

The linguistic portrait has also shifted because francophones are having fewer children than in the past and some francophones outside Quebec have transferred to English and are less likely to pass on the French language to their children. However, in 2006 for the first time, the majority of Quebec allophones adopted French as their main home language when using an official language most often at home.

Over 200 languages reported

Canadians reported more than 200 languages as mother tongues in the 2006 Census. These include languages associated with traditional immigration, such as German, Italian, Ukrainian and Dutch, and languages that characterize more recent immigration, particularly those spoken in Asia and Latin America, which showed the largest gains.

Chinese languages are the third largest mother-tongue group: 3% of the population reported a Chinese language as the first language learned and still understood in 2006.

Among the three largest census metropolitan areas (CMAs), Toronto has

Chart 22.1
Population by mother tongue

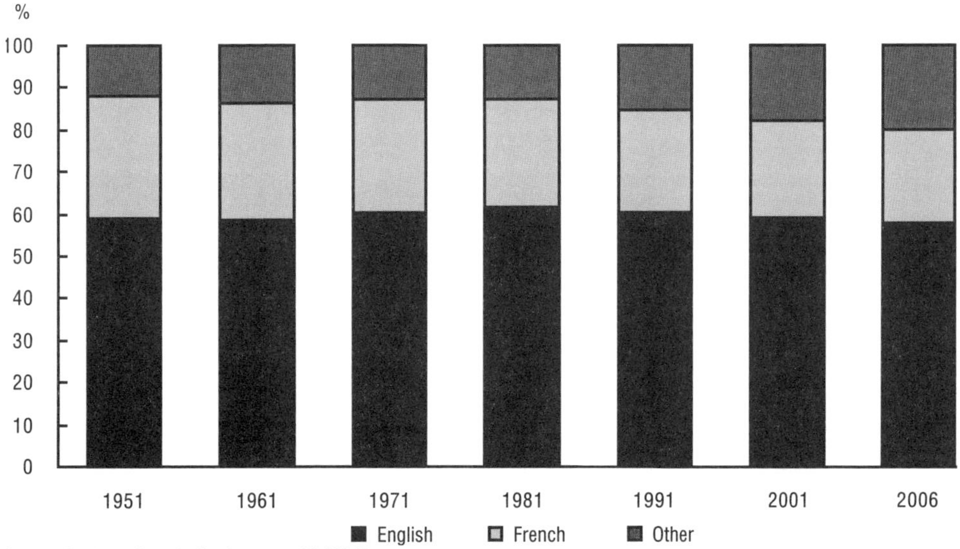

Source: Statistics Canada, Catalogue no. 91-003-X.

the highest proportion of allophones. More than 4 residents in 10 have a mother tongue other than English or French. Chinese makes up the largest portion, followed by Italian and Punjabi.

Similarly, 4 out of 10 residents of Vancouver are also allophones. Chinese is the most frequent followed by Punjabi and Tagalog.

The Montréal CMA has proportionally fewer allophones at 22%. Italian heads the list followed by Arabic and Spanish.

The 2006 Census found that 98% of the population can speak one or both official languages and that English or French is spoken 'at least regularly' at home by 94% of Canadians. As well, English or French is spoken 'most often' at home by 89% of the population, sometimes in combination with a non-official language.

About one out of every two allophones (46%) speaks English or French most often at home. The proportion rises to 68% when including allophones who speak a language other than English or French most often at home but use English or French on a regular basis as well. Two out of five allophones speak English or French exclusively at home.

The longer allophone immigrants have resided in the country, the more they are exposed to the predominant language of the host society. This tends to affect the language spoken most often at home.

The proportion of allophone immigrants speaking an official language at home was 34% for those who arrived in the 1980s and 46% for those who arrived from 1961 to 1970.

Table 22.a
Most common non-official mother tongues

	1971	2006
	number	
All Chinese languages	95,915	1,034,090
Italian	538,765	476,905
German	558,965	466,650
Punjabi	..	382,585
Spanish	23,950	362,120
Arabic	28,520	286,785
Tagalog	..	266,440
Portuguese	85,845	229,280

Source: Statistics Canada, censuses of population, 1971 and 2006.

Chart 22.2
Mother tongue, Canada less Quebec and Quebec, 2006

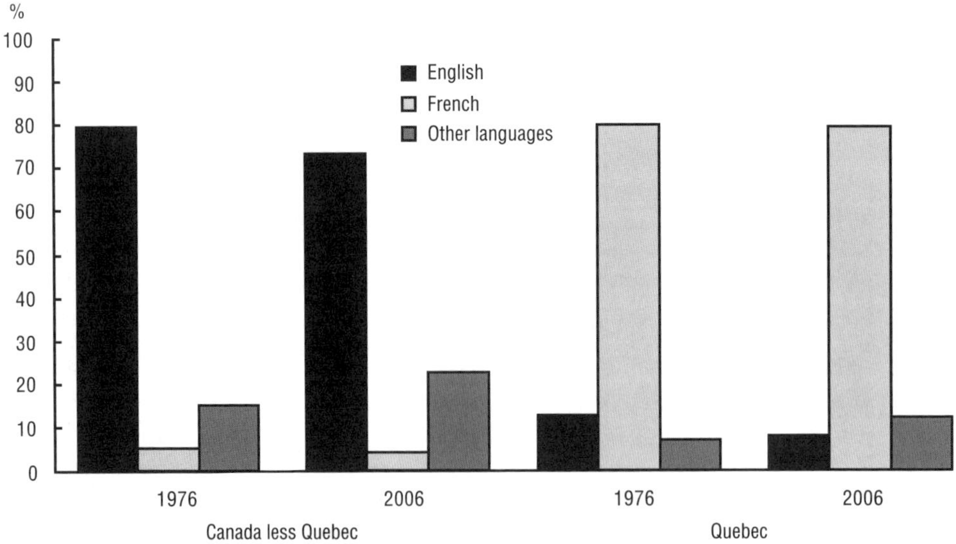

Source: Statistics Canada, censuses of popluation, 1976 and 2006.

Languages at work

While most immigrants use either English or French at work, some immigrant workers use one or more of the 200 non-official languages found in Canada.

In 2006, about 3.8 million immigrants worked or had recently worked in Canada. Of these, 16%—or 611,400 workers—used a non-official language at work.

Among those immigrants who use non-official languages at work, about one in six make no regular use of either official language. The other five use English or French along with a non-official language.

The use of non-official languages at work has been associated with a lack of official language skills, low levels of education, lower skilled jobs and lower earnings for immigrants.

The use of non-official languages at work is more common among immigrants who had arrived recently and among immigrants who had arrived at an older age.

Chart 22.3
Top 10 non-official languages used at work by immigrants, 2006

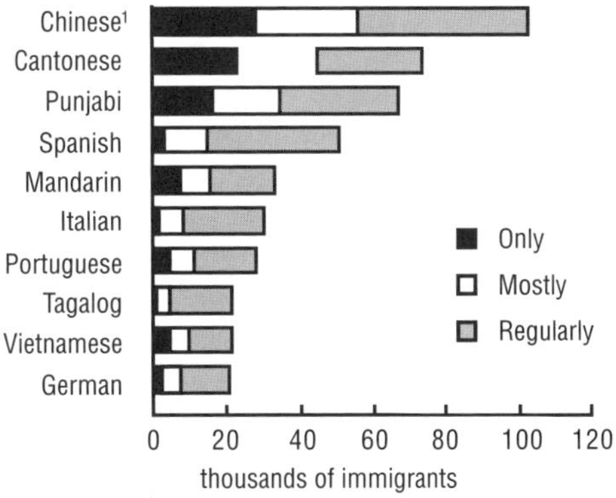

1. Unspecified Chinese languages.
Source: Statistics Canada, Catalogue no. 11-008-X.

Bilingualism among youth

By age 21, about one-third (29%) of Canadians can carry on a conversation in both French and English. Bilingualism rates, however, differ considerably by mother tongue: 65% of francophone youth said that they were bilingual in 2006 compared with 18% of non-francophones.

One reason for this is that francophones have more opportunity to use English outside of studies (at work for example) than non-francophones. The bilingualism rate among francophones living in Quebec reaches a maximum when young adults enter the workforce. Among anglophones, the rate reaches a maximum towards the end of high school.

Outside Quebec, the bilingualism rate is higher for francophones. A total of 91% of francophone youth reported being bilingual in 2006 compared with 15% of non-francophones.

Chart 22.4
Youth able to converse in both French and English at age 21, by mother tongue, 2006

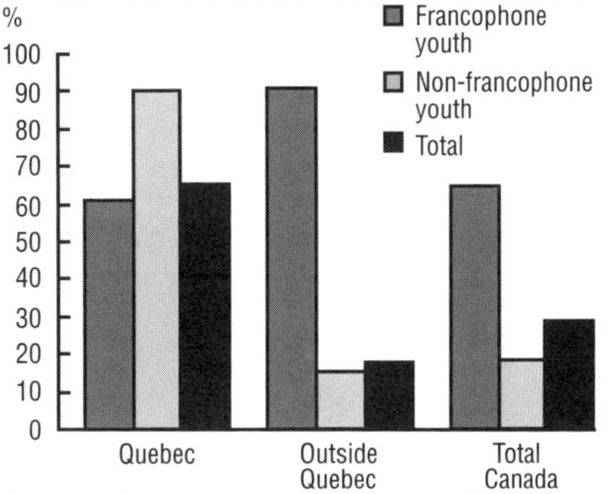

Source: Statistics Canada, Catalogue no. 81-004-X.

In Quebec, rates of bilingualism were higher for non-francophones. While 61% of francophone youth in Quebec reported that they could carry on a conversation in both languages, 90% of non-francophones said they could do the same.

Table 22.1 Mother tongue, by province and territory, 2006

	Canada	Newfoundland and Labrador	Prince Edward Island	Nova Scotia	New Brunswick
	number				
Population	**31,241,030**	**500,610**	**134,205**	**903,090**	**719,650**
Mother tongue, single response[1]	**30,848,270**	499,830	133,570	899,270	714,490
English	**17,882,775**	488,405	125,260	832,105	463,190
French	**6,817,655**	1,885	5,345	32,540	232,975
Non-official languages	**6,147,840**	9,540	2,960	34,620	18,320
Chinese	**1,012,065**	1,080	190	3,370	2,160
Cantonese	**361,450**	185	15	505	295
Mandarin	**170,950**	120	45	595	505
Hakka	**4,415**	0	0	0	10
Chinese not otherwise specified	**456,705**	760	115	2,240	1,270
Italian	**455,040**	195	55	905	590
German	**450,570**	655	275	4,045	1,935
Polish	**211,175**	115	70	1,570	220
Spanish	**345,345**	670	220	1,305	1,040
Portuguese	**219,275**	150	10	560	210
Punjabi	**367,505**	120	0	420	55
Ukrainian	**134,500**	60	20	440	140
Arabic	**261,640**	540	150	4,425	970
Dutch	**128,900**	300	865	2,440	1,290
Tagalog (Pilipino)	**235,615**	180	15	415	330
Greek	**117,285**	70	30	1,035	275
Vietnamese	**141,630**	15	10	500	205
Cree	**78,855**	20	0	15	0
Inuktitut (Inuit)	**32,380**	595	15	15	0
Other non-official languages	**1,956,060**	4,775	1,035	13,160	8,900
Mother tongue, multiple responses[2]	**392,760**	780	635	3,820	5,160
English and French	**98,625**	295	495	2,100	4,450
English and non-official language	**240,005**	435	105	1,440	560
French and non-official language	**43,335**	30	25	140	120
English, French and non-official language	**10,790**	10	10	145	30

1. The respondent reported only one language as a mother tongue.
2. The respondent reported more than one language as a mother tongue.
Source: Statistics Canada, 2006 Census of Population.

Quebec	Ontario	Manitoba	Saskatchewan	Alberta	British Columbia	Yukon	Northwest Territories	Nunavut
				number				
7,435,905	**12,028,895**	**1,133,510**	**953,850**	**3,256,355**	**4,074,385**	**30,195**	**41,055**	**29,325**
7,339,495	11,853,565	1,118,690	946,250	3,221,420	4,022,045	29,940	40,680	29,025
575,555	8,230,705	838,415	811,725	2,576,670	2,875,770	25,655	31,545	7,765
5,877,660	488,815	43,955	16,060	61,225	54,745	1,105	975	370
886,280	3,134,045	236,320	118,465	583,530	1,091,530	3,180	8,165	20,885
63,415	482,570	11,045	7,475	97,275	342,920	260	260	40
9,850	181,820	3,105	1,720	32,485	131,245	85	120	10
7,770	75,335	1,470	715	12,135	72,155	70	15	10
85	2,805	10	15	425	1,075	0	0	0
44,740	215,345	6,345	4,970	51,145	129,560	90	110	20
124,820	282,750	4,775	735	13,095	27,020	25	55	10
17,855	158,000	67,030	28,555	84,505	86,690	775	190	40
17,305	140,890	8,870	2,510	21,990	17,565	20	30	15
108,790	160,275	6,850	2,735	29,125	34,075	130	90	30
34,710	155,310	6,295	380	7,205	14,385	15	25	10
11,905	152,645	6,340	850	36,320	158,750	80	10	10
5,395	48,310	21,950	16,350	29,455	12,285	40	40	10
108,105	114,730	2,125	1,525	20,495	8,440	15	105	10
3,620	68,180	3,835	1,785	19,980	26,355	140	95	15
11,785	117,365	22,490	2,170	29,740	50,425	145	505	45
41,845	61,330	1,635	1,060	3,305	6,670	10	0	0
25,370	67,150	2,740	1,305	19,350	24,560	105	305	0
13,340	3,495	19,105	24,255	17,215	1,145	50	190	20
9,615	390	140	35	155	110	60	750	20,480
288,405	1,120,655	51,095	26,740	154,320	280,135	1,310	5,515	150
96,405	175,330	14,825	7,600	34,930	52,335	250	380	305
43,335	32,690	2,630	1,130	5,405	5,920	110	45	20
16,200	131,290	11,675	6,080	27,725	43,785	130	320	260
31,350	7,790	435	245	1,325	1,840	10	15	20
5,520	3,565	85	140	480	790	0	0	0

Table 22.2 Mother tongue, by census metropolitan area, 2006

	Total population	Single responses			
		Total	English	French	Non-official languages
	number				
St. John's	**179,270**	178,880	174,480	535	3,860
Halifax	**369,455**	367,520	337,715	10,085	19,725
Moncton	**124,055**	122,830	77,345	42,925	2,555
Saint John	**120,875**	120,300	111,215	5,510	3,570
Saguenay	**149,600**	149,230	1,100	146,435	1,700
Québec	**704,185**	700,810	10,250	671,140	19,410
Sherbrooke	**183,635**	182,345	8,850	165,115	8,385
Trois-Rivières	**138,560**	138,055	1,300	134,255	2,495
Montréal	**3,588,520**	3,514,485	425,635	2,328,400	760,445
Ottawa–Gatineau	**1,117,120**	1,096,315	550,260	360,175	185,875
Kingston	**148,475**	147,440	129,770	4,305	13,360
Peterborough	**115,140**	114,630	106,510	1,295	6,825
Oshawa	**328,070**	325,510	283,475	6,820	35,215
Toronto	**5,072,075**	4,965,405	2,746,480	58,590	2,160,335
Hamilton	**683,450**	675,780	516,360	9,725	149,695
St. Catharines–Niagara	**385,035**	381,310	307,350	13,490	60,475
Kitchener	**446,495**	441,780	334,620	5,975	101,180
Brantford	**122,825**	122,115	107,720	1,310	13,085
Guelph	**126,080**	124,875	100,365	1,755	22,755
London	**452,580**	448,750	363,885	6,055	78,805
Windsor	**320,730**	315,780	230,920	11,105	73,755
Barrie	**175,335**	174,055	154,535	3,720	15,800
Greater Sudbury/Grand Sudbury	**156,395**	154,170	99,445	42,950	11,775
Thunder Bay	**121,050**	120,185	101,305	3,100	15,780
Winnipeg	**686,040**	676,315	507,530	29,020	139,765
Regina	**192,440**	190,890	169,720	2,675	18,495
Saskatoon	**230,850**	228,865	197,260	3,490	28,120
Calgary	**1,070,295**	1,056,760	797,555	16,310	242,895
Edmonton	**1,024,820**	1,011,725	785,755	21,980	203,990
Kelowna	**160,560**	159,490	136,025	2,530	20,935
Abbotsford–Mission	**156,640**	154,770	110,265	1,625	42,885
Vancouver	**2,097,960**	2,060,350	1,190,560	24,130	845,660
Victoria	**325,065**	322,655	274,950	5,580	42,120

Source: Statistics Canada, 2006 Census of Population.

Multiple responses				
Total	English and French	English and non-offical language	French and non-official language	English, French and non-official language
number				
390	110	235	30	15
1,935	1,015	710	85	125
1,225	1,085	70	60	15
575	495	80	0	0
365	270	0	80	0
3,375	2,120	85	1,015	155
1,295	830	25	400	40
505	320	25	120	30
74,035	26,855	15,225	27,005	4,950
20,810	10,495	6,785	2,890	635
1,035	365	630	20	15
505	220	265	15	0
2,555	540	1,875	100	45
106,670	7,955	92,670	3,865	2,180
7,670	1,135	6,020	380	140
3,725	1,020	2,505	155	45
4,715	695	3,690	255	75
710	105	570	20	15
1,205	180	975	40	15
3,830	730	2,860	170	65
4,955	1,115	3,420	330	80
1,280	415	815	10	35
2,225	1,675	490	40	15
870	190	590	70	15
9,720	1,830	7,525	310	50
1,545	225	1,220	70	30
1,990	265	1,630	50	45
13,535	1,845	10,920	600	165
13,100	1,830	10,600	485	185
1,075	175	805	90	0
1,870	135	1,680	40	10
37,615	2,855	32,880	1,285	595
37,615	700	1,530	115	60

Table 22.3 Knowledge of an official language, by province and territory, 2006

	Total	English only	French only	Both English and French	Neither English nor French
	number				
Canada	**31,241,030**	**21,129,945**	**4,141,850**	**5,448,850**	**520,380**
Newfoundland and Labrador	**500,610**	475,985	90	23,675	850
Prince Edward Island	**134,205**	116,990	60	17,100	55
Nova Scotia	**903,090**	805,690	1,000	95,010	1,385
New Brunswick	**719,650**	405,045	73,750	240,085	765
Quebec	**7,435,905**	336,785	4,010,880	3,017,860	70,375
Ontario	**12,028,895**	10,335,705	49,210	1,377,325	266,660
Manitoba	**1,133,510**	1,017,560	1,930	103,520	10,500
Saskatchewan	**953,850**	902,655	485	47,450	3,260
Alberta	**3,256,355**	2,990,805	2,200	222,885	40,470
British Columbia	**4,074,385**	3,653,365	2,070	295,645	123,305
Yukon	**30,195**	26,515	105	3,440	130
Northwest Territories	**41,055**	37,010	50	3,665	325
Nunavut	**29,325**	25,830	20	1,170	2,305

Source: Statistics Canada, 2006 Census of Population.

Table 22.4 Workers who use an official language most often or regularly at work, by province and territory, 2006

	English			French		
	Total	Most often	Regularly	Total	Most often	Regularly
	%					
Canada	**85.0**	**78.3**	**6.7**	**25.7**	**21.7**	**4.0**
Newfoundland and Labrador	**99.8**	99.5	0.3	**1.5**	0.4	1.0
Prince Edward Island	**99.6**	98.7	0.9	**5.5**	1.8	3.7
Nova Scotia	**99.5**	98.4	1.2	**4.6**	1.8	2.8
New Brunswick	**88.1**	76.0	12.1	**37.5**	26.8	10.7
Quebec	**40.4**	17.1	23.2	**94.3**	86.7	7.6
Ontario	**98.6**	97.0	1.6	**5.8**	2.0	3.8
Manitoba	**98.8**	97.2	1.7	**3.6**	1.4	2.3
Saskatchewan	**99.4**	98.6	0.8	**1.2**	0.4	0.8
Alberta	**99.3**	98.6	0.7	**1.5**	0.4	1.1
British Columbia	**98.0**	96.5	1.5	**1.5**	0.4	1.1
Yukon	**99.3**	98.5	0.8	**4.0**	1.1	2.9
Northwest Territories	**99.2**	97.5	1.8	**2.7**	0.8	1.8
Nunavut	**91.2**	70.7	20.5	**2.4**	0.6	1.9
Canada except Quebec	**98.4**	96.7	1.7	**5.0**	2.1	2.9

Notes: All mother tongues (multiple responses included).
Population 15 years and older who had worked between January 1, 2005 and May 16, 2006, regardless of whether or not they were in the labour force in the reference week of May 16, 2006.
Source: Statistics Canada, 2006 Census of Population.

Manufacturing

23

The health of Canada's manufacturing sector declined by nearly every measure in 2008—from output and employment to the volume of sales and labour productivity. It was a year of contrast, featuring uneven growth over the course of the year and across industries.

Manufacturing's real gross domestic product fell for a third consecutive year, dropping 5.2% from 2007 to 2008. The motor vehicle and parts industries accounted for nearly half of the decline in output.

The value of manufacturing sales remained relatively stable in 2008, slipping 0.4% from 2007 to reach $604.7 billion. However, the volume of goods sold fell 6.8% to $546.0 billion—the third successive annual decline. Sharply reduced foreign and domestic demand during the second half of the year slowed activity in Canadian factories even further.

Industries driven by discretionary consumer spending, such as motor vehicles and wood products, saw declining sales throughout much of 2008. These were offset by exceptional price increases and strong demand for commodities during the first half of the year.

However, by the third quarter, that strong demand quickly disappeared as the global downturn spread. It continued into the early months of 2009.

Manufacturing sales drop

In 2008, 13 of 21 manufacturing industries posted sales decreases. Motor vehicle manufacturers' sales dropped 22.0% to a 14-year low. The wood products industry fared poorly for a fourth year in a row, as sales fell 13.1%.

Higher prices pushed manufacturers' sales of petroleum and coal products up 22.2% to a record high. The value of

Chart 23.1
Sales in manufacturing

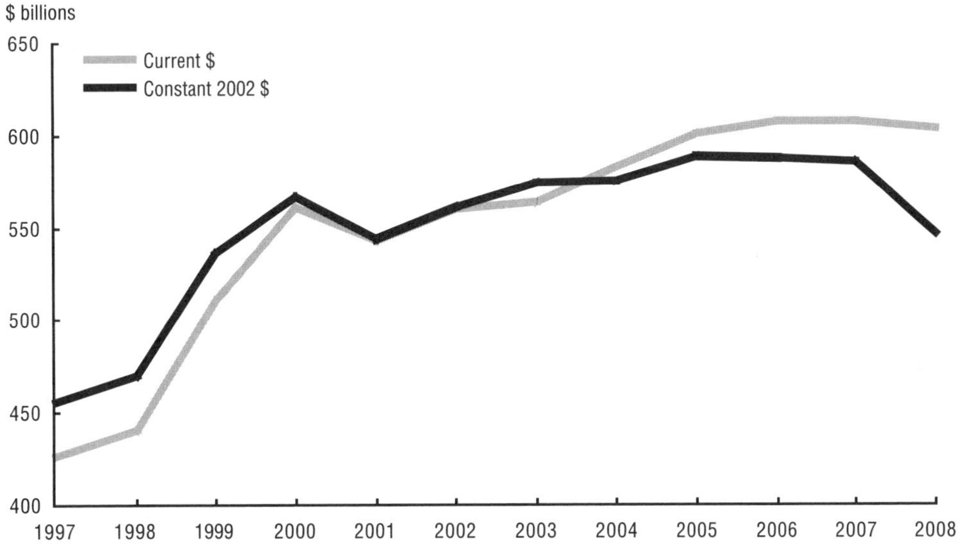

Source: Statistics Canada, CANSIM tables 304-0014 and 377-0008.

petroleum product sales surpassed that of food and motor vehicles, Canada's previous biggest players.

The primary metals and chemical products industries also benefited from robust demand for most of the year, as both industries posted sales growth of just over 4.0%.

Newfoundland and Labrador, New Brunswick, Nova Scotia, Saskatchewan and Alberta all reported sharply higher manufacturing sales. This was partly the result of high prices, as well as busy refineries and strong demand, for most of the year, for chemical and primary metal products.

In Ontario, steep declines in sales of motor vehicles and auto parts contributed to a 4.6% drop in manufacturing sales to their lowest level since 1998. In Quebec, robust growth in the aerospace and petroleum products industries contributed to a 1.8% rise in total sales.

Labour productivity was down 1.9% in 2008, the first decrease since 2001.

Table 23.a
Manufacturing sales, by region, 2008

	$ billions	% of total
Canada	**604.6**	**100.0**
Atlantic provinces	36.6	6.1
Quebec	150.9	25.0
Ontario	278.3	46.0
Prairie provinces	98.8	16.3
British Columbia	40.0	6.6

Note: Figures may not add to totals because of rounding.
Source: Statistics Canada, CANSIM table 304-0015.

Manufacturing's industrial capacity utilization rate fell from 82% in 2007 to 78% in 2008, a level not seen since the 1990 recession.

Operating profits remained almost unchanged in 2008 at $46.3 billion. Motor vehicle and parts producers lost $3.3 billion in operating profits. Excluding motor vehicles and parts, manufacturers' operating profits increased 10.7% in 2008, compared with 5.4% for the economy as a whole.

Chart 23.2
Industrial capacity utilization rate, manufacturing

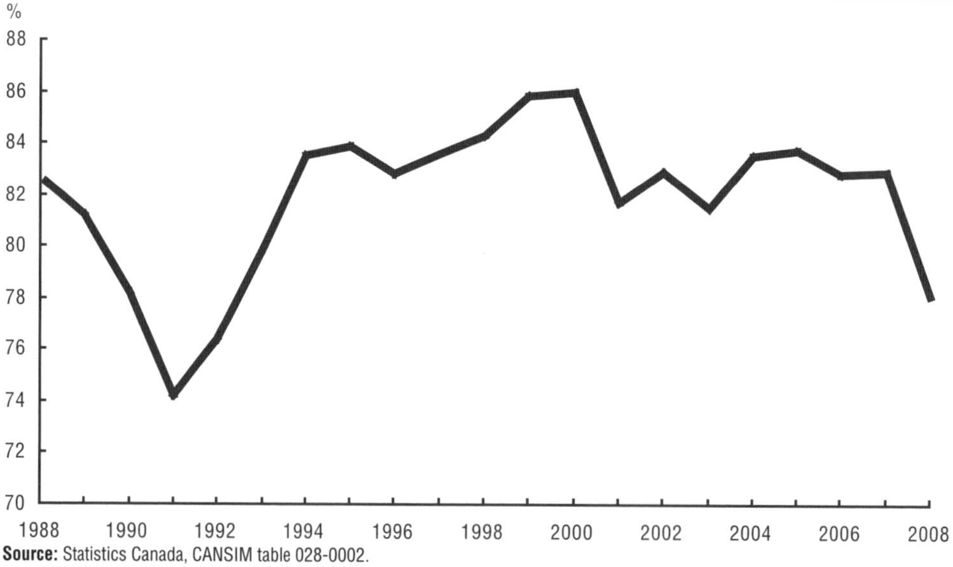

Source: Statistics Canada, CANSIM table 028-0002.

Trends in manufacturing employment

Canada lost 322,000 manufacturing jobs from 2004 to 2008, or more than one out of seven such jobs. In the rest of the economy, 1.5 million jobs were created, according to the Labour Force Survey. In 2004, manufacturing represented 14.4% of total employment; by 2008, that had shrunk to 11.5%.

Few manufacturing industries added employees from 2004 to 2008, notably transportation equipment (excluding motor vehicles and parts), petroleum and coal products, and computer and electronic products.

Some industries were hit harder. Textiles and clothing lost almost half its jobs, motor vehicle makers let go one in five employees, while motor vehicle parts manufacturers cut one in four positions.

Ontario lost the majority—198,600 jobs, or nearly one in five of the province's manufacturing jobs. Newfoundland and Labrador, New Brunswick, Quebec, British Columbia and Nova Scotia also lost more than 10% of their manufacturing jobs.

Chart 23.3
Manufacturing's share of employment

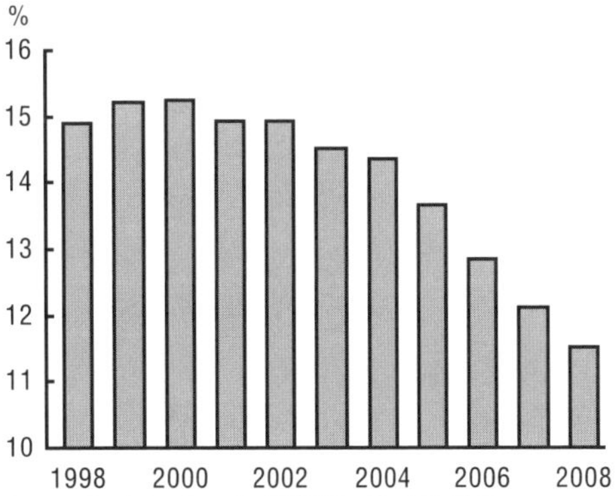

Source: Statistics Canada, CANSIM table 282-0008.

Auto sector hard hit

Canada's motor vehicle industry has seen periods of strong growth and those of sharp downturns. The year 2008 was no exception: the auto sector was hit hard by a sharp downturn in the U.S. economy.

The steep decline in the assembly of cars and light trucks, which began in December 2007, accelerated sharply in 2008. Retail motor vehicle sales in the United States fell steadily in 2008 to a 17-year low, at least partly attributable to record gasoline prices, reduced access to credit, and weakening consumer confidence. By December, retail auto sales were nearly 50% below their May 2007 peak.

Auto production at Canada's 11 assembly plants fell 20% to 2.0 million vehicles (equal to the annual output of two plants). That affected subsidiary industries such as sales of motor vehicle parts, which dropped 21%.

Chart 23.4
Motor vehicle output

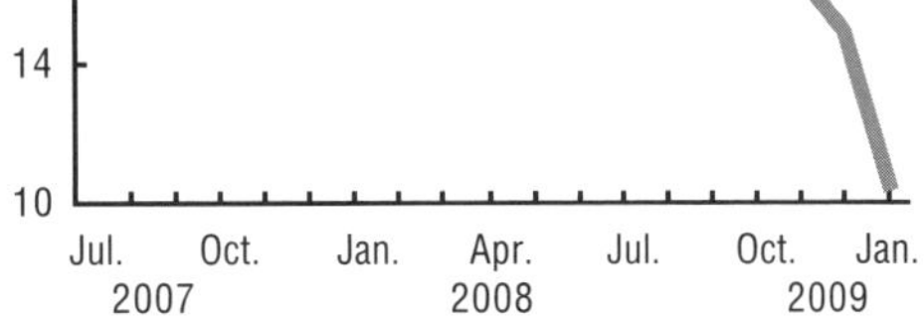

Note: 2002 constant prices.
Source: Statistics Canada, CANSIM table 379-0027.

Table 23.1 Gross domestic product at basic prices, by manufacturing subsector, 1997 to 2008

	1997	1998	1999	2000	2001
	$ millions 2002 chained				
Manufacturing sector	**151,330**	**158,819**	**171,923**	**188,925**	**181,084**
Food	14,506	15,195	15,575	16,219	17,400
Beverage and tobacco products	6,180	6,515	5,941	6,150	5,892
Textile, clothing and leather products	..	..	..	..	..
Wood products	9,047	9,510	10,219	11,334	10,835
Paper	10,709	10,434	11,469	11,893	11,295
Printing and related support activities	5,131	5,118	5,234	5,983	6,654
Petroleum and coal products	2,908	3,168	3,049	3,056	3,423
Chemicals	12,095	12,209	12,691	14,063	14,422
Plastics and rubber products	7,162	7,443	8,098	9,262	9,247
Non-metallic mineral products	3,964	4,313	4,346	4,779	4,994
Primary and fabricated metal products	19,120	20,408	21,535	25,088	24,401
Machinery	10,972	11,282	11,089	12,701	12,479
Computer and electronic products	5,828	6,754	9,460	11,430	6,764
Electrical equipment, appliance and components	3,359	3,658	3,838	4,615	4,560
Transportation equipment	28,109	29,395	35,225	35,638	32,139
Furniture and related products	3,910	4,628	5,062	5,913	6,161
Miscellaneous manufacturing	2,838	3,069	3,031	3,483	3,462

Note: North American Industry Classification System (NAICS), 2002.
Source: Statistics Canada, CANSIM table 379-0027.

2002	2003	2004	2005	2006	2007	2008
			$ millions 2002 chained			
182,736	**181,349**	**184,814**	**187,806**	**187,041**	**185,311**	**175,609**
17,296	17,071	17,159	17,696	18,630	18,986	19,303
5,878	5,633	5,636	5,748	4,854	4,644	4,603
6,761	6,266	5,671	5,032	4,461	4,116	3,426
12,079	12,232	12,789	13,398	13,053	11,678	9,656
11,865	11,910	12,042	11,872	10,835	10,328	9,445
6,232	6,040	6,145	6,042	5,576	5,364	5,286
3,477	3,477	3,432	3,297	3,338	3,339	3,245
15,124	15,657	15,409	15,671	15,823	15,823	15,570
9,979	9,991	10,109	10,350	10,348	9,916	8,955
5,096	5,375	5,570	5,684	5,992	5,961	5,718
25,149	24,607	25,029	25,511	25,788	26,313	25,235
12,158	11,788	12,738	13,043	13,375	13,578	13,617
5,821	6,249	6,573	6,792	6,979	7,238	7,253
3,860	3,073	3,360	3,416	3,384	3,378	3,291
32,007	32,579	33,491	35,292	35,703	35,272	30,809
6,098	5,596	5,837	5,604	5,476	5,529	5,166
3,857	3,905	3,993	3,889	4,030	4,184	4,354

Table 23.2 Manufacturing sales, by manufacturing subsector, 1994 to 2008

	1994	1995	1996	1997	1998	1999
	$ millions					
Manufacturing sector	**346,940.8**	**389,779.5**	**400,085.1**	**426,519.4**	**441,152.6**	**510,549.9**
Food	43,075.3	45,170.0	48,246.0	50,513.4	51,468.6	55,104.9
Beverage and tobacco products	9,175.8	9,317.9	9,610.4	10,154.4	11,190.5	11,250.8
Textile mills and textile products mills	5,303.5	5,558.6	5,621.5	5,960.2	6,371.0	6,602.4
Clothing	6,229.0	6,568.4	6,677.7	6,947.0	6,967.6	7,429.3
Leather and allied products	1,005.0	985.9	942.8	1,001.3	944.2	967.1
Paper	25,226.4	36,013.7	30,663.2	29,761.6	29,790.5	33,236.4
Printing and related support activities	7,641.3	8,447.9	8,841.4	8,961.8	9,341.9	10,436.0
Petroleum and coal products	16,677.2	17,969.3	20,688.6	20,932.8	16,325.6	21,347.3
Chemicals	27,822.1	30,074.0	30,252.6	32,486.3	31,374.1	34,194.7
Plastics and rubber products	12,504.8	14,048.1	15,045.3	16,504.1	17,362.1	21,108.8
Wood products	22,274.8	22,621.5	24,000.3	25,960.2	25,994.4	31,214.5
Non-metallic mineral products	6,794.4	7,220.7	7,851.9	8,487.7	8,930.3	9,653.4
Primary metals	24,019.4	26,178.1	26,781.9	28,743.2	29,596.9	30,755.1
Fabricated metal products	15,391.5	17,505.8	19,174.5	21,082.6	22,850.8	27,625.0
Machinery	15,407.3	18,060.8	19,548.5	21,835.9	23,097.3	24,284.6
Computer and electronic products	18,122.7	22,845.0	22,072.9	23,154.3	25,356.4	27,295.3
Electrical equipment, appliances and components	6,889.0	7,587.9	7,834.5	8,085.3	8,486.9	10,488.1
Transportation equipment	73,392.3	82,992.4	84,548.0	92,822.9	101,064.1	130,037.5
Furniture and related products	5,664.9	6,140.3	6,839.8	7,892.6	9,013.0	10,995.4
Miscellaneous manufacturing	4,324.3	4,473.0	4,843.2	5,231.8	5,626.2	6,523.2

Note: North American Industry Classification System (NAICS), 2007.
Source: Statistics Canada, CANSIM table 304-0014.

2000	2001	2002	2003	2004	2005	2006	2007	2008
				$ millions				
561,300.9	**543,272.0**	**559,902.7**	**563,634.0**	**583,081.9**	**600,349.6**	**607,380.3**	**607,343.9**	**604,743.8**
57,278.7	61,609.3	64,089.5	67,064.9	67,860.5	67,594.8	71,721.2	73,853.6	78,108.9
11,625.5	11,699.1	12,074.4	12,191.5	12,555.1	12,646.2	11,318.7	10,859.1	10,671.5
6,966.1	6,848.8	7,211.0	6,672.8	6,212.9	5,898.1	5,012.7	4,697.3	4,163.2
7,936.6	7,685.0	8,024.4	7,893.8	6,241.1	5,289.6	4,981.0	4,325.4	3,288.0
956.4	967.2	933.6	849.6	649.0	516.2	464.0	510.4	422.4
38,213.2	35,852.9	34,284.4	33,359.4	33,710.1	32,499.4	31,097.8	30,249.7	29,351.3
11,079.3	11,633.8	12,155.3	12,435.5	11,538.1	11,866.5	10,989.3	10,612.6	10,544.0
33,918.0	33,407.5	33,690.1	37,585.3	45,730.1	57,029.9	61,487.2	66,692.5	81,473.8
37,205.8	38,391.4	40,469.2	43,088.5	47,143.9	49,614.8	50,119.8	49,124.4	51,141.6
21,858.0	22,986.9	25,286.6	26,464.1	25,608.0	26,825.4	27,620.6	25,937.3	23,524.4
31,669.8	30,074.1	32,801.6	32,360.1	35,793.1	34,092.3	30,497.8	25,001.2	21,721.0
9,926.8	10,324.3	11,630.8	12,029.5	12,240.4	12,727.3	14,113.2	14,473.3	14,190.6
36,352.2	34,115.3	36,074.9	36,916.4	42,511.5	43,029.4	50,829.2	52,987.9	55,218.7
29,685.8	30,189.5	32,210.5	33,356.4	32,802.4	34,276.4	34,754.9	36,647.6	36,871.4
26,283.4	26,422.0	27,448.5	28,070.2	27,748.6	30,167.9	31,056.0	32,288.5	33,433.9
37,273.3	27,040.1	22,656.3	20,826.3	20,680.1	19,762.4	19,541.2	18,968.1	19,193.1
11,595.5	11,637.6	10,135.9	9,482.2	9,452.6	9,899.8	10,475.6	10,679.3	10,381.8
132,252.5	122,560.4	126,451.6	120,565.8	123,166.9	124,785.8	118,776.4	116,051.5	97,263.5
12,608.2	13,054.9	13,916.5	13,719.4	13,254.6	13,342.9	13,397.9	13,762.7	13,145.7
6,615.9	6,771.9	8,357.6	8,702.3	8,182.8	8,484.6	9,125.7	9,621.7	10,634.9

Table 23.3 Payroll employment, by manufacturing industry, 1994 to 2008

	1994	1995	1996	1997	1998	1999
	number					
Manufacturing sector	**1,705,673**	**1,739,096**	**1,779,368**	**1,845,808**	**1,906,843**	**1,946,466**
Food	207,152	206,340	213,999	216,006	222,195	224,202
Beverage and tobacco products	33,371	32,984	29,736	32,068	34,255	33,791
Textile mills	26,160	26,813	27,035	28,225	29,449	29,520
Textile product mills	17,864	16,512	17,890	19,845	20,500	20,417
Clothing	85,609	86,510	85,882	88,569	90,422	89,465
Leather and allied products	12,036	12,160	12,218	12,391	11,473	11,241
Paper	104,779	104,450	103,394	104,098	100,821	103,110
Printing and related support activities	75,309	80,375	76,787	76,948	79,810	82,459
Petroleum and coal products	14,488	13,414	13,990	13,747	13,753	15,454
Chemicals	89,019	88,054	86,874	88,774	89,227	91,385
Plastics and rubber products	94,063	96,902	104,354	111,754	115,525	117,688
Wood products	109,790	108,431	116,544	124,299	127,559	134,177
Non-metallic mineral products	43,880	47,077	45,687	48,554	52,166	53,286
Primary metals	102,587	102,127	101,727	98,828	100,957	100,529
Fabricated metal products	134,821	139,590	146,910	157,630	165,626	173,072
Machinery	108,551	116,450	124,562	131,871	134,419	132,486
Computer and electronic products	80,372	88,905	88,310	92,754	97,905	101,630
Electrical equipment, appliances and components	52,507	46,669	45,178	45,477	45,898	48,538
Transportation equipment	198,719	204,534	214,530	215,751	229,476	235,548
Furniture and related products	67,883	69,149	71,094	81,566	86,086	88,698
Miscellaneous manufacturing	46,713	51,648	52,668	56,652	59,319	59,772

Notes: North American Industry Classification System (NAICS), 2007.
Annual number of salaried and hourly employees on payroll.
Source: Statistics Canada, Survey of Employment, Payrolls and Hours and CANSIM table 281-0024.

Table 23.4 Manufacturing sector by establishments and production workers, by province and territory, 2005 to 2007

	Canada	Newfoundland and Labrador	Prince Edward Island	Nova Scotia	New Brunswick	Quebec
	number					
Establishments						
2005	**85,724**	765	351	1,944	1,533	23,042
2006	**83,596**	728	349	1,823	1,464	22,629
2007	**85,013**	738	369	1,904	1,497	22,319
Production workers						
2005	**1,351,014**	13,885	4,422	29,967	27,349	354,269
2006	**1,312,281**	13,231	4,886	27,741	26,583	339,129
2007	**1,273,648**	13,962	5,042	28,233	26,572	329,052

Notes: The number of establishments represents a count of locations that perform manufacturing activities. It normally corresponds to a plant, factory, or mill. It excludes sales offices and warehouses that support manufacturing activities.
Data for reference years 2004 to 2006 are based on the North American Industry Classification System (NAICS) 2002. The 2007 data are based on NAICS 2007.
Source: Statistics Canada, CANSIM table 301-0006.

2000	2001	2002	2003	2004	2005	2006	2007	2008
number								
2,036,697	**1,978,406**	**1,929,514**	**1,907,736**	**1,870,096**	**1,838,560**	**1,820,736**	**1,758,769**	**1,673,904**
232,653	231,613	233,158	233,754	235,405	232,170	233,388	229,102	226,252
35,424	35,138	34,860	33,186	31,991	28,097	28,114	26,854	26,695
30,133	26,122	23,829	22,970	20,866	17,412	14,610	12,950	10,363
20,928	19,707	19,022	18,414	18,073	17,685	16,477	15,164	12,818
93,347	82,770	76,261	71,186	62,456	51,765	46,009	40,001	32,825
12,219	9,480	8,508	7,539	6,575	5,779	5,030	4,472	3,816
110,144	103,703	95,981	96,994	93,718	87,689	83,810	79,380	73,515
85,537	83,347	79,678	78,593	73,783	72,829	73,148	72,019	70,522
15,879	15,305	15,401	15,674	15,301	15,758	16,336	16,657	17,904
95,493	93,412	92,246	92,797	92,761	93,030	90,823	88,960	88,546
123,469	125,248	126,097	125,790	127,426	125,795	124,827	118,260	107,517
141,872	135,758	134,227	133,829	137,153	135,306	130,222	122,940	110,322
56,440	53,719	51,423	51,329	51,403	51,304	53,701	52,807	52,707
104,253	91,185	90,322	85,402	79,703	78,731	80,681	78,802	69,107
183,246	184,269	181,096	180,561	176,439	176,068	179,728	175,091	171,126
136,397	134,897	137,332	137,162	136,049	140,411	144,467	139,714	138,132
106,289	105,761	95,272	89,084	87,272	85,689	85,086	83,202	83,824
53,780	48,723	45,545	45,428	43,095	42,157	42,268	42,754	41,610
244,196	242,725	233,603	231,268	229,246	229,337	222,798	215,597	199,464
94,350	98,601	98,648	98,637	93,121	94,157	90,677	85,843	79,830
60,648	56,922	57,006	58,138	58,258	57,391	58,534	58,198	57,007

Ontario	Manitoba	Saskatchewan	Alberta	British Columbia	Yukon	Northwest Territories	Nunavut
number							
34,184	2,307	1,804	7,750	11,942	59	28	15
32,723	2,266	1,775	7,740	12,014	52	21	12
33,642	2,353	1,846	8,091	12,179	48	16	11
627,182	46,185	20,699	103,828	122,776	185	183	84
602,714	45,429	21,309	108,015	122,781	204	173	86
574,094	44,512	21,682	107,968	122,093	219	175	44

Table 23.5 Industrial capacity utilization rates, 1994 to 2008

	1994	1995	1996	1997	1998	1999
	%					
All industries	**83.0**	**82.1**	**82.0**	**83.6**	**84.6**	**86.0**
Manufacturing	83.5	83.9	82.8	83.6	84.3	85.8
Food	82.0	81.6	79.6	79.0	80.7	80.1
Beverage and tobacco products	79.6	82.6	81.4	81.8	83.2	81.7
Textile mills and textile product mills	82.1	81.1	77.3	80.2	82.7	84.4
Clothing	80.4	81.0	83.0	85.1	84.1	85.6
Leather and allied products	74.9	74.0	75.4	80.1	77.6	74.1
Paper	91.1	86.7	86.4	84.5	86.5	83.9
Printing and related support activities	94.3	92.0	89.1	90.4	86.1	91.1
Petroleum and coal products	76.5	77.8	80.1	80.0	79.8	80.6
Chemicals	87.3	89.5	92.8	93.1	95.5	94.4
Plastics and rubber products	84.7	85.2	86.3	80.2	81.2	80.9
Wood products	85.0	81.0	81.6	83.2	84.4	86.8
Non-metallic mineral products	74.4	75.5	76.7	83.4	80.1	80.4
Primary metals	93.1	88.3	88.0	89.0	93.8	91.1
Fabricated metal products	80.0	78.2	79.6	80.0	80.8	85.7
Machinery	81.0	85.4	80.1	84.8	80.5	80.0
Computer and electronic products	77.3	84.9	76.2	79.3	85.0	90.8
Electrical equipment, appliances and components	82.4	79.4	83.6	85.2	91.0	93.7
Transportation equipment	81.9	86.2	84.8	86.4	86.4	89.5
Furniture and related products	79.2	80.9	81.1	82.5	83.1	84.5
Miscellaneous manufacturing	80.4	73.6	76.3	85.2	88.5	88.2

Note: North American Industry Classification System (NAICS), 1997.
Source: Statistics Canada, CANSIM table 028-0002.

2000	2001	2002	2003	2004	2005	2006	2007	2008
				%				
87.0	**84.3**	**85.4**	**84.2**	**84.8**	**84.1**	**82.8**	**82.1**	**78.0**
86.0	81.7	82.9	81.5	83.5	83.7	82.8	82.9	78.1
80.9	81.6	81.8	78.9	79.1	80.6	80.1	80.1	81.0
79.5	80.7	77.2	72.3	75.6	75.8	74.1	71.5	69.8
82.6	78.1	79.4	77.4	78.4	77.5	74.3	75.4	72.2
85.0	82.0	82.8	80.1	79.5	74.4	76.0	76.0	68.9
78.5	74.5	73.8	71.6	72.0	67.6	76.4	77.8	73.8
85.1	82.0	87.0	88.2	92.1	90.6	85.6	79.0	71.6
92.1	88.6	90.6	91.1	91.1	89.4	88.3	87.4	84.8
79.8	76.8	74.0	75.3	74.4	75.2	74.8	73.5	73.0
92.7	94.9	96.5	95.4	93.9	88.3	83.2	82.5	80.8
80.1	80.4	80.8	80.9	81.5	80.2	79.8	82.0	81.0
84.3	84.0	88.7	88.4	90.0	82.8	79.6	76.6	74.1
79.8	80.1	82.1	83.8	84.2	84.4	81.9	85.0	81.4
90.9	86.2	87.8	88.4	91.8	91.5	91.9	92.1	91.5
84.1	79.7	80.1	75.9	79.8	80.6	81.4	86.0	81.2
83.6	78.5	78.9	78.1	80.8	83.0	82.9	83.5	84.6
96.6	72.1	66.8	69.6	80.8	85.3	87.0	88.1	87.5
92.5	76.3	74.0	73.6	77.3	76.3	79.7	83.6	83.0
89.0	86.0	88.1	83.3	85.0	87.3	86.2	86.8	69.3
84.8	80.8	81.1	79.8	79.3	81.3	80.4	81.2	77.1
83.5	80.3	82.5	82.7	81.2	81.1	79.6	77.3	78.2

Table 23.6 Industrial capacity utilization rates, 2008

	1st quarter	2nd quarter	3rd quarter	4th quarter
	%			
All industries	**79.6**	**78.8**	**78.1**	**74.7**
Manufacturing	80.0	79.9	78.8	73.8
Food	81.3	82.0	81.4	79.3
Beverage and tobacco products	66.5	69.6	70.6	72.7
Textile mills and textile product mills	73.0	72.1	72.1	71.7
Clothing	70.4	66.3	68.9	70.0
Leather and allied products	74.8	72.1	70.2	78.1
Paper	85.3	85.8	86.8	81.2
Printing and related support activities	74.3	73.5	73.0	71.2
Petroleum and coal products	79.8	83.7	81.0	78.7
Chemicals	81.7	82.6	82.8	77.0
Plastics and rubber products	76.8	76.3	74.0	69.3
Wood products	72.5	72.4	72.2	69.3
Non-metallic mineral products	79.6	82.5	84.5	78.9
Primary metals	91.6	93.2	95.8	85.4
Fabricated metal products	84.3	82.1	80.6	77.8
Machinery	84.1	87.0	85.6	82.1
Computer and electronic products	87.9	88.4	87.7	85.9
Electrical equipment, appliances and components	80.6	82.0	83.9	85.5
Transportation equipment	77.3	73.4	68.4	58.1
Furniture and related products	77.8	77.9	77.8	74.9
Miscellaneous manufacturing	75.8	79.0	80.2	77.8

Note: North American Industry Classification System (NAICS), 1997.
Source: Statistics Canada, CANSIM table 028-0002.

Population and demography

Canada's population reached 33.3 million as of July 2008, a 10% increase from 30.2 million in 1998.

Largely as a result of net international migration, Canada's population growth was the highest among the G8 countries from 2001 to 2006. International migration should contribute even more to growth in coming years as the number of deaths is expected to increase with the aging of the baby boomers.

As well, Canada's fertility rate of 1.6 children per woman is well below the replacement level of 2.1. By contrast, levels in the United States have generally been at 2.1 children per woman.

Our population is aging and Canadians are living longer. In 2005, life expectancy was 78.0 years for males and 82.7 years for females.

From 1956 to 2006, the median age of the Canadian population went from 27.2 years to 38.9, a gain of more than 10 years over a span of half a century. By 2056, the median age is expected to reach 46.9 years, almost 20 years higher than it was in 1956.

Around 2015, for the first time in Canada's history, there could be more people aged 65 and older than children under the age of 15. In 2031, 8.9 million to 9.4 million Canadians will be aged 65 and older, whereas the number of children is expected to be about half that number, from 4.8 to 6.6 million.

Where the people live

Most Canadians live in a narrow corridor in the southern part of the country, near the American border. In 2008, 62% of the population lived in Quebec and Ontario, the two most populous provinces.

The Northwest Territories, Yukon and Nunavut represent 39% of the continental mass of Canada. Their inhabitants make up 0.3% of the population.

Chart 24.1
Population growth

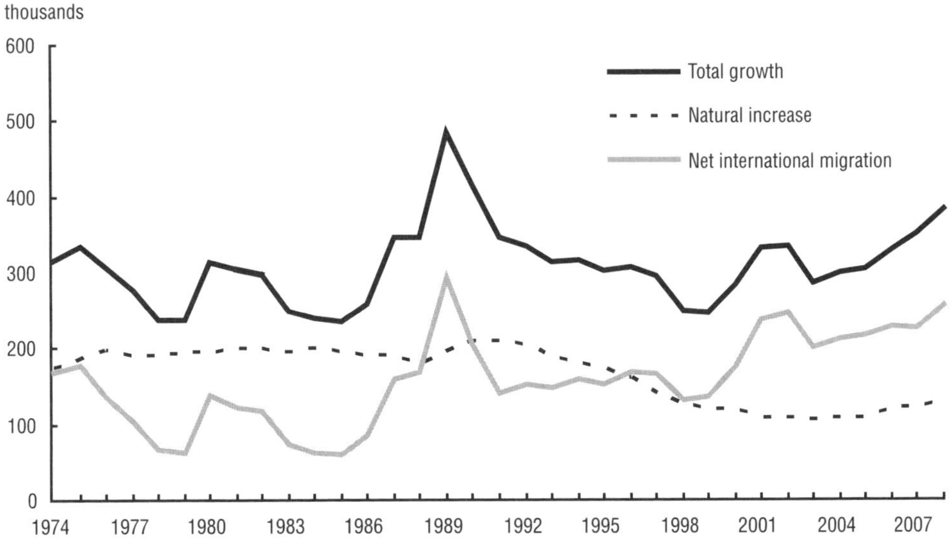

Source: Statistics Canada, CANSIM table 051-0004.

In most provinces, population growth depends mainly on immigration, whereas the population growth of Nunavut is due primarily to a total fertility rate of 2.8 children per woman, nearly twice the national rate. Although it has the highest natural growth in the country, Nunavut posted the lowest growth rate in its brief history in 2008, attributable to losses from interprovincial migration.

In 2007/2008, population growth was strongest in Canada's western provinces. Despite a decline in net interprovincial migration, Alberta's population grew 2.1%, almost twice the national average of 1.2%, and Alberta remained the province with the strongest population growth for the seventh consecutive year. British Columbia was second at 1.7%. Saskatchewan ranked third and led other provinces in the rate of interprovincial migration for the first time in recent history.

Prince Edward Island was the only province east of Ontario to exceed the national average growth. The population of Newfoundland and Labrador rose in 2007/2008, the first increase since 1991/1992.

Most Canadians live in urban areas. According to the 2006 Census, nearly 25 million people, more than 80% of Canada's population, live in cities. The majority of urban dwellers (21.5 million people) live in one of the 33 census metropolitan areas (CMAs).

Six CMAs have a population of more than 1 million—Toronto, Montréal, Vancouver, Ottawa–Gatineau, Calgary and Edmonton. Combined, these six urban areas are home to 14.1 million people, or 45% of the population.

Table 24.a
Estimated components of population growth

	2001/2002	2004/2005	2007/2008
	number		
Births	328,155	339,270	364,085
Deaths	220,494	229,906	237,202
Immigrants	256,405	244,578	249,603
Emigrants	41,897	40,811	45,049

Note: Period from July 1 to June 30.
Source: Statistics Canada, CANSIM table 051-0004.

Chart 24.2
Population growth rates, by province and territory

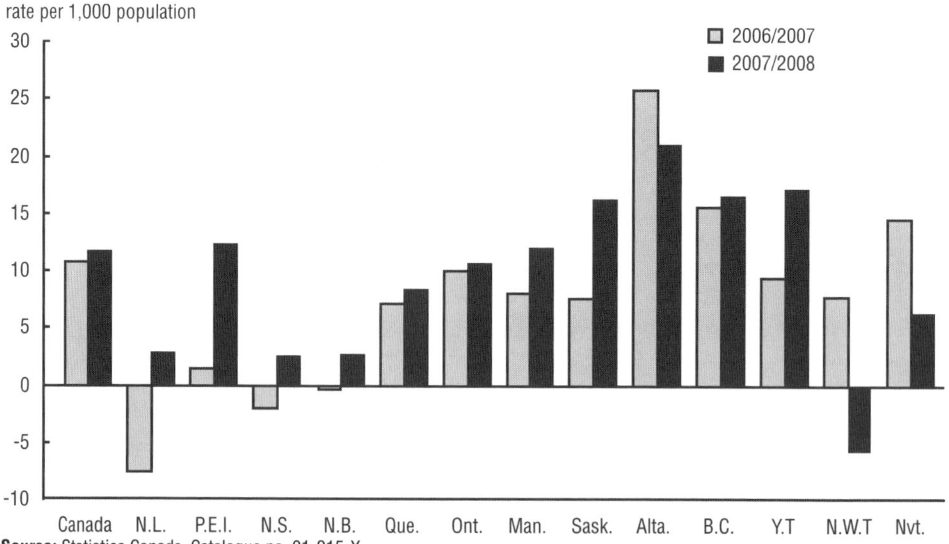

Source: Statistics Canada, Catalogue no. 91-215-X.

When Canadians migrate abroad

Canada is often thought of as an immigrant-receiving country, but it is also a player on the world stage as a source country of migrants. Whether Canadian migration abroad is temporary or permanent, long term or short term, Canadians are making their mark in other countries.

The OECD estimates that 1.1 million people who were born in Canada were residing in other OECD countries in 2000.

The United States is by far the largest recipient of Canadians on either a permanent or temporary basis. Among Canadian-born emigrants, 82% resided in the United States in 2000. The United Kingdom and Australia also welcome large numbers of Canadians. Italy and Poland, which have sent migrants to Canada in the past, are starting to see a trickle of their migrants return in their retirement years.

Chart 24.3
Average annual migrations, 2000 to 2004

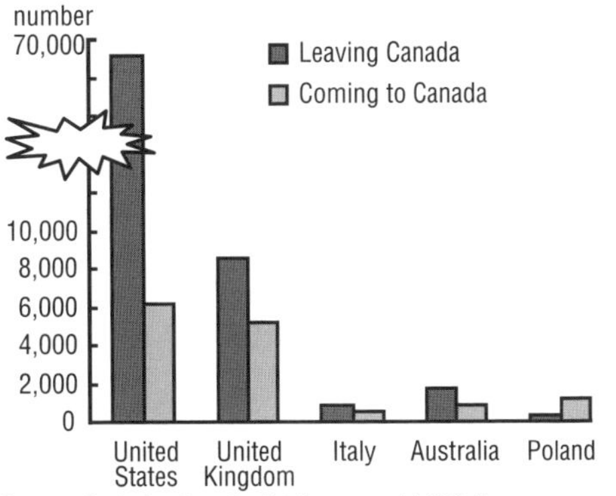

Source: Statistics Canada, Catalogue no. 11-008-X.

However, the OECD reports only on people who are Canadian-born. For example, 1% of Canadians who moved to Poland were Canadian-born, whereas 88% had actually returned to the country of their birth.

Women are having more children, but later in life

Canada's fertility rate hit a 10-year high in 2006. The average number of children per woman rose to 1.6 from 1.5 in 2005.

Alberta and Quebec accounted for 70% of the national increase in births from 2005. Births were up in every province and territory except Nova Scotia and the Northwest Territories.

The average age of women giving birth has jumped to 29 years from 27 years in 1996. For the first time, the fertility rate of Canadian women aged 30 to 34 surpassed that of women aged 25 to 29.

For more than 30 years, the total fertility rate has been below the replacement level (which is currently 2.1 children per woman). This means that, on average, Canadian couples are no longer having enough children to replace themselves.

Chart 24.4
Births and total fertility rates

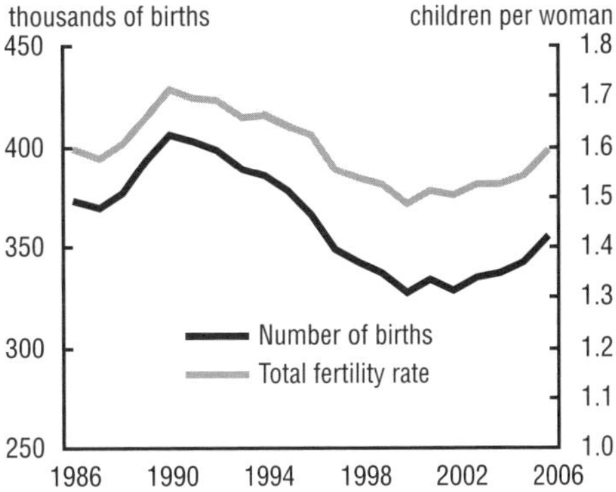

Source: Statistics Canada, Catalogue no. 84F0210X.

Table 24.1 Population, by province and territory, selected years from 1861 to 2008

	1861	1871	1881	1891	1901	1911	1921
	number						
Canada[1]	**3,229,633**	**3,689,257**	**4,324,810**	**4,833,239**	**5,371,315**	**7,206,643**	**8,787,949[2]**
Newfoundland and Labrador[1]	..	..	..	..	..	..	..
Prince Edward Island	80,857	94,021	108,891	109,078	103,259	93,728	88,615
Nova Scotia	330,857	387,800	440,572	450,396	459,574	492,338	523,837
New Brunswick	252,047	285,594	321,233	321,263	331,120	351,889	387,876
Quebec	1,111,566	1,191,516	1,359,027	1,488,535	1,648,898	2,005,776	2,360,510
Ontario	1,396,091	1,620,851	1,926,922	2,114,321	2,182,947	2,527,292	2,933,662
Manitoba	..[3]	25,228	62,260	152,506	255,211	461,394	610,118
Saskatchewan	..[3]	..[3]	..[3]	..[3]	91,279	492,432	757,510
Alberta	..[3]	..[3]	..[3]	..[3]	73,022	374,295	588,454
British Columbia	51,524	36,247	49,459	98,173	178,657	392,480	524,582
Yukon	..	..	..	..	27,219	8,512	4,157
Northwest Territories (including Nunavut)	6,691	48,000	56,446	98,967	20,129	6,507	8,143
Northwest Territories[4]	..	..	..	..	..	..	..
Nunavut[4]	..	..	..	..	..	..	..

Note: Prior to 1971, data are census counts; from 1971 on, data are estimates as of July 1 and adjusted for census net undercoverage.
1. Beginning in 1951, Newfoundland and Labrador is included in Canada total.
2. Includes 485 members of the Royal Canadian Navy whose province of residence is not known.
3. Included with Northwest Territories.
4. Prior to July 1, 1991, only data for Northwest Territories and Nunavut combined are available.
Source: Statistics Canada, CANSIM table 051-0001 and Catalogue no. 11-516-X.

Table 24.2 Population estimates, by sex and age group, and by province and territory, 2008

	Both sexes			
	All ages	0 to 14	15 to 64	65 and older
	thousands			
Canada	**33,311.4**	**5,597.7**	**23,150.6**	**4,563.1**
Newfoundland and Labrador	**507.9**	76.3	358.3	73.3
Prince Edward Island	**139.8**	23.4	95.3	21.1
Nova Scotia	**938.3**	142.7	651.1	144.4
New Brunswick	**747.3**	115.8	517.9	113.6
Quebec	**7,750.5**	1,232.2	5,385.7	1,132.7
Ontario	**12,929.0**	2,218.8	8,966.3	1,743.9
Manitoba	**1,208.0**	229.2	812.3	166.5
Saskatchewan	**1,016.0**	193.0	671.5	151.6
Alberta	**3,585.1**	654.5	2,556.4	374.2
British Columbia	**4,381.6**	686.2	3,059.1	636.4
Yukon	**33.1**	5.8	24.9	2.5
Northwest Territories	**43.3**	9.6	31.5	2.1
Nunavut	**31.4**	10.3	20.2	0.9

Note: Population as of July 1.
Source: Statistics Canada, CANSIM table 051-0001.

1931	1941	1951	1961	1971	1981	1991	2001	2008
				number				
10,376,786	**11,506,655**	**14,009,429**	**18,238,247**	**21,962,032**	**24,819,915**	**28,037,420**	**31,019,020**	**33,311,389**
..	..	361,416	457,853	530,854	575,302	579,644	522,033	507,895
88,038	95,047	98,429	104,629	112,591	123,551	130,369	136,663	139,818
512,846	577,962	642,584	737,007	797,294	854,871	914,969	932,454	938,310
408,219	457,401	515,697	597,936	642,471	706,438	745,567	749,801	747,302
2,874,662	3,331,882	4,055,681	5,259,211	6,137,305	6,547,207	7,067,396	7,396,331	7,750,504
3,431,683	3,787,655	4,597,542	6,236,092	7,849,027	8,812,286	10,431,316	11,896,663	12,928,996
700,139	729,744	776,541	921,686	998,876	1,035,545	1,109,604	1,151,439	1,207,959
921,785	895,992	831,728	925,181	932,038	975,759	1,002,713	1,000,221	1,015,985
731,605	796,169	939,501	1,331,944	1,665,717	2,291,104	2,592,306	3,058,017	3,585,142
694,263	817,861	1,165,210	1,629,082	2,240,470	2,826,558	3,373,787	4,076,264	4,381,603
4,230	4,914	9,096	14,628	18,991	23,880	28,871	30,156	33,144
9,316	12,028	16,004	22,998	36,398	47,414	..	..	..
..	..	..	..	..	..	38,724	40,844	43,283
..	..	..	..	..	..	22,154	28,134	31,448

Males				Females			
All ages	0 to 14	15 to 64	65 and older	All ages	0 to 14	15 to 64	65 and older
			thousands				
16,522.0	**2,873.1**	**11,641.1**	**2,007.9**	**16,789.4**	**2,724.6**	**11,509.5**	**2,555.2**
249.1	39.3	176.7	33.2	258.8	37.0	181.7	40.1
68.3	12.1	46.9	9.3	71.5	11.3	48.3	11.8
455.3	72.7	319.7	62.9	483.0	70.1	331.4	81.5
366.7	59.7	257.2	49.8	380.6	56.1	260.7	63.8
3,838.1	631.3	2,716.8	489.9	3,912.5	600.9	2,668.9	642.7
6,378.7	1,137.8	4,478.0	762.9	6,550.3	1,081.1	4,488.3	980.9
601.3	118.1	411.5	71.7	606.7	111.1	400.8	94.7
503.3	98.9	337.9	66.4	512.7	94.0	333.6	85.1
1,833.0	336.6	1,328.2	168.3	1,752.1	317.9	1,228.3	206.0
2,172.8	353.7	1,528.5	290.6	2,208.8	332.5	1,530.6	345.8
16.9	2.9	12.7	1.3	16.2	2.8	12.2	1.2
22.5	4.9	16.5	1.1	20.8	4.7	15.0	1.1
16.1	5.2	10.4	0.5	15.3	5.1	9.8	0.4

Table 24.3 Population, by census metropolitan area, selected years from 1987 to 2007

	1987	1992	1997	2002	2007
			number		
St. John's	165,828	176,874	176,114	177,523	183,493
Halifax	317,694	339,735	355,584	373,817	385,457
Saint John	124,989	129,276	127,509	126,137	126,382
Saguenay	161,452	164,464	162,095	156,227	151,803
Québec	624,778	667,123	686,043	701,564	728,924
Sherbrooke	139,000	146,969	152,933	158,733	166,503
Trois-Rivières	133,304	140,615	141,573	140,005	143,846
Montréal	3,150,771	3,306,109	3,395,142	3,547,112	3,695,790
Ottawa–Gatineau	872,993	977,860	1,030,052	1,118,819	1,168,788
Kingston[1]	..	..	..	154,439	154,985
Oshawa	216,731	255,310	282,306	315,800	347,999
Toronto	3,712,579	4,094,002	4,481,807	5,020,447	5,509,874
Hamilton	586,615	622,094	651,288	697,891	720,426
St. Catharines–Niagara	355,981	378,212	385,160	393,178	395,839
Kitchener	330,392	373,109	401,013	438,744	468,002
London	376,454	415,627	431,870	454,514	469,714
Windsor	271,445	279,985	298,979	325,880	331,149
Greater Sudbury/Grand Sudbury	157,929	170,381	168,596	160,987	162,653
Thunder Bay	127,388	130,639	129,389	126,205	124,109
Winnipeg	653,751	672,792	678,020	693,685	712,671
Regina	193,380	195,467	198,409	196,531	201,514
Saskatoon	210,579	216,391	226,909	231,839	241,439
Calgary	695,771	780,583	871,765	1,002,030	1,139,126
Edmonton	802,353	865,853	896,690	979,907	1,081,275
Abbotsford–Mission[1]	..	..	..	155,205	164,638
Vancouver	1,479,029	1,690,006	1,958,228	2,111,305	2,285,893
Victoria	270,990	300,444	318,471	326,774	337,411

Note: 2001 Census boundaries.
1. Abbotsford and Kingston became census metropolitan areas in 2001.
Source: Statistics Canada, CANSIM table 051-0034.

Table 24.4 Mid-size urban centres with the fastest population growth from 2001 to 2006

	2001	2006	Growth
	number		%
Okotoks, Alberta	11,689	17,145	46.7
Wood Buffalo, Alberta	42,581	52,643	23.6
Grande Prairie, Alberta	58,787	71,868	22.3
Red Deer, Alberta	67,829	82,772	22.0
Yellowknife, Northwest Territories	16,541	18,700	13.1
Lloydminster, Saskatchewan/Alberta	23,964	27,023	12.8
Canmore, Alberta	10,792	12,039	11.6
Medicine Hat, Alberta	61,735	68,822	11.5
Saint-Jean-sur-Richelieu, Quebec	79,600	87,492	9.9
Joliette, Quebec	39,720	43,595	9.8
Chilliwack, British Columbia	74,003	80,892	9.3
Fort St. John, British Columbia	23,007	25,136	9.3
Parksville, British Columbia	24,285	26,518	9.2
Lethbridge, Alberta	87,388	95,196	8.9
Courtenay, British Columbia	45,205	49,214	8.9

Source: Statistics Canada, censuses of population, 2001 and 2006.

Table 24.5 Mid-size urban centres with the fastest population decline from 2001 to 2006

	2001	2006	Decline
	number		%
Kitimat, British Columbia	10,285	8,987	12.6
Prince Rupert, British Columbia	15,302	13,392	12.5
Quesnel, British Columbia	24,426	22,449	8.1
Terrace, British Columbia	19,980	18,581	7.0
Williams Lake, British Columbia	19,768	18,760	5.1
Campbellton, New Brunswick/Quebec	18,820	17,888	5.0
North Battleford, Saskatchewan	18,590	17,765	4.4
Kenora, Ontario	15,838	15,177	4.2
Elliot Lake, Ontario	11,956	11,549	3.4
Bathurst, New Brunswick	32,523	31,424	3.4
Edmundston, New Brunswick	22,173	21,442	3.3
Cape Breton, Nova Scotia	109,330	105,928	3.1
La Tuque, Quebec	15,725	15,293	2.7
Thetford Mines, Quebec	26,721	26,107	2.3
Dolbeau–Mistassini, Quebec	14,879	14,546	2.2

Source: Statistics Canada, censuses of population, 2001 and 2006.

Table 24.6 Components of population growth, 1861 to 2006

	1861 to 1871	1871 to 1881	1881 to 1891	1891 to 1901	1901 to 1911	1911 to 1921	1921 to 1931	1931 to 1941
	thousands							
Population at end of period[2]	3,689	4,325	4,833	5,371	7,207	8,788	10,377	11,507
Population growth[3, 4]	459	636	508	538	1,836	1,581	1,589	1,130
Births	1,370	1,480	1,524	1,548	1,925	2,340	2,415	2,294
Deaths	760	790	870	880	900	1,070	1,055	1,072
Natural increase[5]	610	690	654	668	1,025	1,270	1,360	1,222
Net international migration[6]	-150	-54	-146	-130	810	311	230	-92

1. Beginning in 1951, Newfoundland and Labrador is included.
2. Before 1971 to 1976, the population at end of period represents census counts. Starting in 1971 to 1976, the population at end of period is derived from the census counts adjusted for census net undercoverage and for July 1.
3. The change in population numbers between two censuses.
4. Starting from 1971 to 1976, the difference between population growth and the sum of the natural increase and the net international migration is the result of residual deviation.
5. Natural increase is the difference between the number of births and deaths.
6. Net international migration has been calculated differently over the years. Prior to 1971 to 1976, the net international migration = immigration - emigration + residual deviation. From 1971 to 1976 to 1986 to 1991, the net international migration = immigration - emigration + net non-permanent residents + returning emigrants. From 1991 to 1996, the net international migration = immigration - (emigration + net temporary emigration) + net non-permanent residents + returning emigrants.

Source: Statistics Canada, censuses of population, CANSIM tables 051-0001, 051-0004 and 071-0001, and Catalogue no. 11-516-X.

Table 24.7 Components of population growth, by province and territory, 2007/2008

	Canada	Newfoundland and Labrador	Prince Edward Island	Nova Scotia	New Brunswick
	number				
Births	**364,085**	4,386	1,420	8,372	6,918
Deaths	**237,202**	4,663	1,206	8,333	6,216
Immigration	**249,603**	598	1,281	2,660	1,803
Emigration	**45,049**	287	65	669	484
Net temporary emigration	**20,165**	258	70	473	378
Returning emigrants	**22,615**	111	59	403	259
Net non-permanent residents	**50,130**	250	239	428	355
Net interprovincial migration	...	1,299	42	-117	-325

Note: Preliminary data for the period from July 1, 2007 to June 30, 2008.
Source: Statistics Canada, CANSIM table 051-0004.

1941 to 1951[1]	1951 to 1956	1956 to 1961	1961 to 1966	1966 to 1971	1971 to 1976	1976 to 1981	1981 to 1986	1986 to 1991	1991 to 1996	1996 to 2001	2001 to 2006
thousands											
13,648	16,081	18,238	20,015	21,568	23,450	24,820	26,100	28,037	29,610	31,019	32,576
2,141	2,433	2,157	1,777	1,553	1,488	1,370	1,280	1,937	1,573	1,409	1,557
3,186	2,106	2,362	2,249	1,856	1,760	1,820	1,872	1,933	1,936	1,705	1,682
1,214	633	687	731	766	824	843	885	946	1,024	1,089	1,129
1,972	1,473	1,675	1,518	1,090	936	977	987	987	912	616	553
169	598	482	259	463	694	493	400	965	780	844	1,107

Quebec	Ontario	Manitoba	Saskatchewan	Alberta	British Columbia	Yukon	Northwest Territories	Nunavut
number								
85,900	136,217	14,801	12,674	47,579	43,980	355	695	788
56,000	88,680	10,011	9,291	20,512	31,771	190	191	138
46,055	114,981	10,741	4,300	23,806	43,114	101	131	32
6,968	21,818	1,842	528	5,369	6,954	20	25	20
2,829	9,340	577	265	2,307	3,605	18	27	18
3,051	10,651	623	197	3,153	4,105	3	0	0
7,656	9,935	1,213	1,134	17,890	10,971	110	-30	-21
-12,399	-16,522	-503	8,067	10,010	11,458	221	-805	-426

Table 24.8 Births, by province and territory, 2002/2003 to 2007/2008

	2002/2003	2003/2004	2004/2005	2005/2006	2006/2007r	2007/2008p
	number					
Canada	**330,523**	**337,762**	**339,270**	**346,082**	**357,289**	**364,085**
Newfoundland and Labrador	4,596	4,598	4,543	4,526	4,486	4,386
Prince Edward Island	1,374	1,403	1,371	1,329	1,413	1,420
Nova Scotia	8,635	8,713	8,575	8,479	8,441	8,372
New Brunswick	7,104	7,072	6,874	6,869	6,982	6,918
Quebec	72,273	74,364	75,422	78,481	83,029	85,900
Ontario	129,256	132,873	132,795	133,775	135,753	136,217
Manitoba	13,765	13,981	14,031	14,270	14,614	14,801
Saskatchewan	11,794	12,121	11,915	12,178	12,358	12,674
Alberta	39,450	40,635	41,345	43,193	46,088	47,579
British Columbia	40,534	40,206	40,632	41,192	42,320	43,980
Yukon	322	374	340	344	360	355
Northwest Territories	658	697	705	707	687	695
Nunavut	762	725	722	739	758	788

Note: Period from July 1 to June 30.
Source: Statistics Canada, CANSIM table 051-0004.

Table 24.9 Birth rate, by province and territory, 2002/2003 to 2007/2008

	2002/2003	2003/2004	2004/2005	2005/2006	2006/2007r	2007/2008p
	crude birth rate per 1,000 population					
Canada	**10.5**	**10.6**	**10.6**	**10.7**	**10.9**	**11.0**
Newfoundland and Labrador	8.9	8.9	8.8	8.8	8.8	8.6
Prince Edward Island	10.0	10.2	10.0	9.6	10.2	10.2
Nova Scotia	9.2	9.3	9.1	9.0	9.0	8.9
New Brunswick	9.5	9.4	9.2	9.2	9.4	9.3
Quebec	9.7	9.9	10.0	10.3	10.8	11.1
Ontario	10.6	10.8	10.7	10.6	10.7	10.6
Manitoba	11.9	12.0	11.9	12.1	12.3	12.3
Saskatchewan	11.8	12.2	12.0	12.3	12.4	12.6
Alberta	12.5	12.7	12.6	12.8	13.3	13.4
British Columbia	9.9	9.7	9.7	9.8	9.9	10.1
Yukon	10.6	11.9	10.7	10.7	11.1	10.8
Northwest Territories	15.7	16.2	16.2	16.3	15.9	16.0
Nunavut	26.3	24.6	24.1	24.2	24.5	25.2

Note: Period from July 1 to June 30.
Source: Statistics Canada, CANSIM tables 051-0004 and 051-0005.

Table 24.10 Deaths, by province and territory, 2002/2003 to 2007/2008

	2002/2003	2003/2004	2004/2005	2005/2006	2006/2007r	2007/2008p
	number					
Canada	**223,905**	**228,829**	**229,906**	**225,489**	**232,534**	**237,202**
Newfoundland and Labrador	4,276	4,254	4,434	4,392	4,543	4,663
Prince Edward Island	1,217	1,225	1,126	1,165	1,181	1,206
Nova Scotia	7,944	8,269	8,372	7,968	8,166	8,333
New Brunswick	6,181	6,373	6,191	5,987	6,073	6,216
Quebec	54,896	56,411	55,857	53,373	56,406	56,000
Ontario	83,410	84,154	85,282	83,752	85,909	88,680
Manitoba	9,852	9,894	10,015	9,634	9,842	10,011
Saskatchewan	8,880	9,130	8,828	8,877	9,114	9,291
Alberta	18,098	18,776	19,066	19,560	19,933	20,512
British Columbia	28,694	29,863	30,333	30,311	30,869	31,771
Yukon	145	158	150	168	181	190
Northwest Territories	183	188	137	171	184	191
Nunavut	129	134	115	131	133	138

Note: Period from July 1 to June 30.
Source: Statistics Canada, CANSIM table 051-0004.

Table 24.11 Death rate, by province and territory, 2002/2003 to 2007/2008

	2002/2003	2003/2004	2004/2005	2005/2006r	2006/2007r	2007/2008p
	crude death rate per 1,000 population					
Canada	**7.1**	**7.2**	**7.2**	**7.0**	**7.1**	**7.2**
Newfoundland and Labrador	8.2	8.2	8.6	8.6	8.9	9.2
Prince Edward Island	8.9	8.9	8.2	8.4	8.6	8.7
Nova Scotia	8.5	8.8	8.9	8.5	8.7	8.9
New Brunswick	8.2	8.5	8.3	8.0	8.2	8.3
Quebec	7.4	7.5	7.4	7.0	7.4	7.3
Ontario	6.9	6.8	6.9	6.7	6.8	6.9
Manitoba	8.5	8.5	8.5	8.2	8.3	8.3
Saskatchewan	8.9	9.2	8.9	8.9	9.2	9.2
Alberta	5.7	5.8	5.8	5.8	5.7	5.8
British Columbia	7.0	7.2	7.3	7.2	7.2	7.3
Yukon	4.8	5.0	4.7	5.2	5.6	5.8
Northwest Territories	4.4	3.2	3.2	3.9	4.3	4.4
Nunavut	4.5	4.5	3.8	4.3	4.3	4.4

Note: Period from July 1 to June 30.
Source: Statistics Canada, CANSIM tables 051-0004 and 051-0005.

Table 24.12 Interprovincial migration, by province or territory of origin and destination, 2007/2008

	Destination				
	Newfoundland and Labrador	Prince Edward Island	Nova Scotia	New Brunswick	Quebec
	number				
Origin					
Newfoundland and Labrador	.	234	1,927	530	259
Prince Edward Island	257	.	704	609	209
Nova Scotia	1,667	796	.	2,892	932
New Brunswick	544	494	2,910	.	1,961
Quebec	257	363	984	2,189	.
Ontario	4,895	986	6,289	4,387	16,305
Manitoba	201	35	290	257	565
Saskatchewan	176	27	284	154	521
Alberta	4,323	752	4,552	3,384	3,468
British Columbia	825	286	2,351	909	3,056
Yukon	0	12	77	41	51
Northwest Territories	102	82	232	35	92
Nunavut	235	20	72	52	145

Note: Preliminary data for the period from July 1, 2007 to June 30, 2008.
Source: Statistics Canada, CANSIM tables 051-0018 and 051-0019.

Table 24.13 Interprovincial migration, by age group and by province and territory, 2007/2008

	Newfoundland and Labrador	Prince Edward Island	Nova Scotia	New Brunswick	Quebec
	number				
In-migrants, all ages	**13,482**	**4,087**	**20,672**	**15,439**	**27,564**
0 to 17	3,318	861	4,413	3,817	5,305
18 to 24	1,526	604	3,146	2,090	4,264
25 to 44	5,416	1,473	8,750	6,357	12,370
45 to 64	2,743	883	3,478	2,482	4,213
65 and older	479	266	885	693	1,412
Out-migrants, all ages	**12,183**	**4,045**	**20,789**	**15,764**	**39,963**
0 to 17	1,989	690	3,828	2,944	8,628
18 to 24	3,180	1,076	4,319	3,668	5,044
25 to 44	4,828	1,661	8,971	6,471	19,107
45 to 64	1,929	503	2,929	2,142	5,346
65 and older	257	115	742	539	1,838
Net migrants, all ages	**1,299**	**42**	**-117**	**-325**	**-12,399**
0 to 17	1,329	171	585	873	-3,323
18 to 24	-1,654	-472	-1,173	-1,578	-780
25 to 44	588	-188	-221	-114	-6,737
45 to 64	814	380	549	340	-1,133
65 and older	222	151	143	154	-426

Note: Preliminary data, period from July 1, 2007 to June 30, 2008.
Source: Statistics Canada, CANSIM table 051-0012.

Destination							
Ontario	Manitoba	Saskatchewan	Alberta	British Columbia	Yukon	Northwest Territories	Nunavut
number							
3,212	152	144	4,758	630	21	186	130
884	37	51	988	259	24	23	0
6,447	366	496	5,045	1,868	94	91	95
4,416	334	178	3,941	803	50	84	49
20,603	608	978	9,763	3,912	84	111	111
.	5,762	3,873	33,197	18,496	276	445	311
4,818	.	2,685	6,327	3,748	80	142	87
2,545	2,670	.	11,226	3,996	35	88	13
19,353	5,902	16,437	.	32,395	408	765	131
15,620	2,588	4,508	24,734	.	684	287	88
222	65	79	372	688	.	43	0
307	150	300	1,229	484	110	.	260
273	98	73	300	115	5	313	.

Ontario	Manitoba	Saskatchewan	Alberta	British Columbia	Yukon	Northwest Territories	Nunavut
number							
78,700	**18,732**	**29,802**	**101,880**	**67,394**	**1,871**	**2,578**	**1,275**
16,856	4,790	8,295	20,721	12,725	347	619	297
11,166	2,758	4,167	22,369	10,611	314	408	175
34,717	7,453	11,100	42,106	26,962	816	1,138	527
11,608	2,782	4,644	13,824	12,998	354	398	275
4,353	949	1,596	2,860	4,098	40	15	1
95,222	**19,235**	**21,735**	**91,870**	**55,936**	**1,650**	**3,383**	**1,701**
20,341	4,329	4,624	22,284	11,182	319	807	399
15,333	3,435	4,818	12,497	9,303	301	432	192
40,502	7,691	7,901	36,657	22,674	611	1,429	682
14,961	2,927	3,250	16,027	9,237	342	681	408
4,085	853	1,142	4,405	3,540	77	34	20
-16,522	**-503**	**8,067**	**10,010**	**11,458**	**221**	**-805**	**-426**
-3,485	461	3,671	-1,563	1,543	28	-188	-102
-4,167	-677	-651	9,872	1,308	13	-24	-17
-5,785	-238	3,199	5,449	4,288	205	-291	-155
-3,353	-145	1,394	-2,203	3,761	12	-283	-133
268	96	454	-1,545	558	-37	-19	-19

Table 24.14 Population projections, by age group, selected years from 2006 to 2031

	2006	2011	2016	2021	2026	2031
	thousands					
All ages[1]	**32,547.2**	**33,909.7**	**35,266.8**	**36,608.5**	**37,882.7**	**39,029.4**
0 to 4	1,697.5	1,724.7	1,781.9	1,816.8	1,812.8	1,781.3
5 to 9	1,842.6	1,780.8	1,810.7	1,871.9	1,910.9	1,910.9
10 to 14	2,084.6	1,916.4	1,858.1	1,892.0	1,956.8	1,999.4
15 to 19	2,164.8	2,170.4	2,006.4	1,952.7	1,990.3	2,058.4
20 to 24	2,252.9	2,295.3	2,304.1	2,145.8	2,096.8	2,138.2
25 to 29	2,226.1	2,330.2	2,376.7	2,391.9	2,241.4	2,198.8
30 to 34	2,222.6	2,354.8	2,462.8	2,518.1	2,542.1	2,402.7
35 to 39	2,351.1	2,327.1	2,462.6	2,576.9	2,639.6	2,671.1
40 to 44	2,698.3	2,409.3	2,390.6	2,530.6	2,649.3	2,717.1
45 to 49	2,671.5	2,711.2	2,431.6	2,418.6	2,561.7	2,683.3
50 to 54	2,363.9	2,651.5	2,695.4	2,425.9	2,417.8	2,563.0
55 to 59	2,082.5	2,327.4	2,614.1	2,662.9	2,404.5	2,401.4
60 to 64	1,583.3	2,027.9	2,272.3	2,557.8	2,612.4	2,367.8
65 to 69	1,227.3	1,513.1	1,942.1	2,184.7	2,466.6	2,527.6
70 to 74	1,044.2	1,130.8	1,401.5	1,806.8	2,044.1	2,318.2
75 to 79	878.0	907.6	993.3	1,241.0	1,610.8	1,837.3
80 to 84	638.3	692.2	724.3	804.0	1,016.1	1,332.1
85 to 89	342.8	422.2	465.5	494.6	560.3	719.8
90 to 94	137.3	169.2	211.2	237.4	257.2	299.2
95 to 99	33.1	42.4	54.4	68.6	79.0	87.4
100 and older	4.7	5.4	7.1	9.5	12.1	14.4

Note: Based on population estimates as of July 1, 2005, according to a medium growth scenario.
1. Figures may not add to totals because of rounding.
Source: Statistics Canada, CANSIM table 052-0004.

Prices and price indexes

Prices are often seen as an indicator of the state of the economy: in 2008, prices for goods and services were as volatile as any other economic indicator. Prices for many key goods and services advanced strongly in the first part of the year, but weakened in the last few months.

The advance was strong enough that prices for the goods and services in the Consumer Price Index (CPI) basket were, despite the late-year drop, an average 2.3% higher in 2008 than in 2007. Prices rose an average of 2.2% in 2007 compared with 2.0% in 2006.

Over the course of 2008, consumer prices posted the most dramatic ups and downs seen since 2003. On a seasonally adjusted monthly basis, consumer prices increased by 0.3% in the first quarter of the year, after rising 0.8% in the final quarter of 2007. In the second quarter of 2008, prices advanced 1.7%; however, in the fourth quarter, they dropped 1.2%.

Shelter, transport and food prices most active

The all-items CPI rose and fell in step with both the shelter and transportation price indexes over the year. Energy prices are a key component of the shelter and transportation indexes, and they influenced food prices.

Fuel oil and natural gas prices helped push up, then pull down, the shelter cost index. However, the cost of owned accommodation was the most significant upward contributor, the result of a strong housing market over most of 2008. Despite its year-end decline, the shelter cost index rose 4.4% over the course of 2008, accounting for about one-half the increase in the all-items CPI.

The transportation cost index, which includes costs for buying, renting and leasing vehicles; operational costs for vehicles such as gasoline, maintenance and repairs and parking fees; and public

Chart 25.1
Selected price indexes, 2008

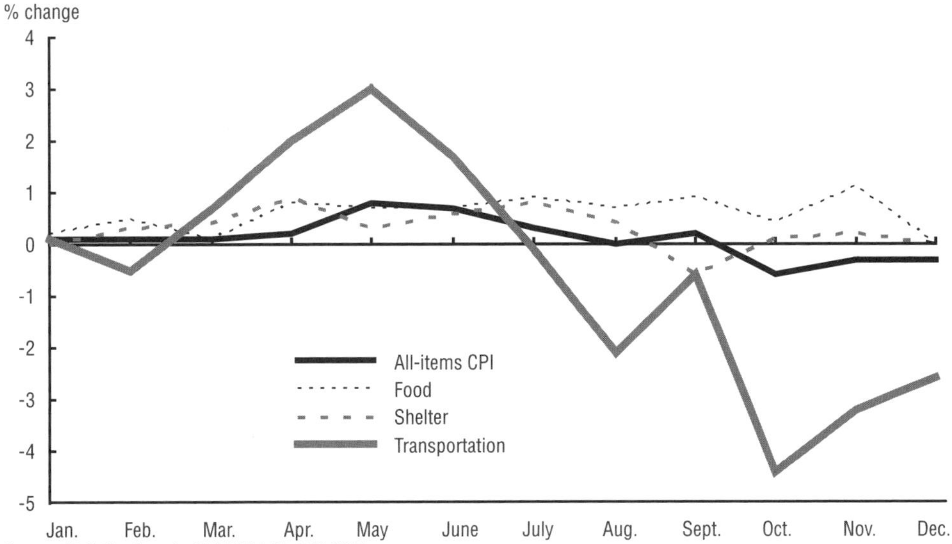

Source: Statistics Canada, CANSIM table 326-0022.

transportation, both within and between cities, rose 2.0% in 2008. Prices for purchasing passenger vehicles fell 6.9%, the largest annual decline since 1955.

Rising food prices are nothing new: food prices have outpaced growth in the all-items CPI for five consecutive years. The food cost index advanced 3.5% in 2008, reflecting worldwide agricultural supply and demand conditions and higher energy prices.

The rise was mainly the result of surging commodity prices, partly driven by growing demand for food in emerging markets, as well as rising gasoline prices, which pushed up transportation costs.

Food purchased from stores, rather than restaurants, has been the primary driver of higher consumer food prices. Prices for restaurant food rose 2.5%. Prices for food purchased from stores advanced for the fifth consecutive year, rising 3.9% in 2008 and 2.7% in 2007.

Prices for food staples such as bread, rice, flour, milk and eggs rose sharply in 2008. Price increases for bakery and cereal products were the greatest contributors, as the surge in prices for grains meant higher costs at the kitchen table. In particular, bread prices rose 15.1%; flour, 34.5%; pasta, 31.9%; and rice, 17.4%.

Table 25.a
Consumer Price Index, goods and services, 2008

	2002=100
Goods and services	**114.1**
Goods	109.4
Services	118.7

Source: Statistics Canada, CANSIM table 326-0021.

Chart 25.2
Selected food price indexes

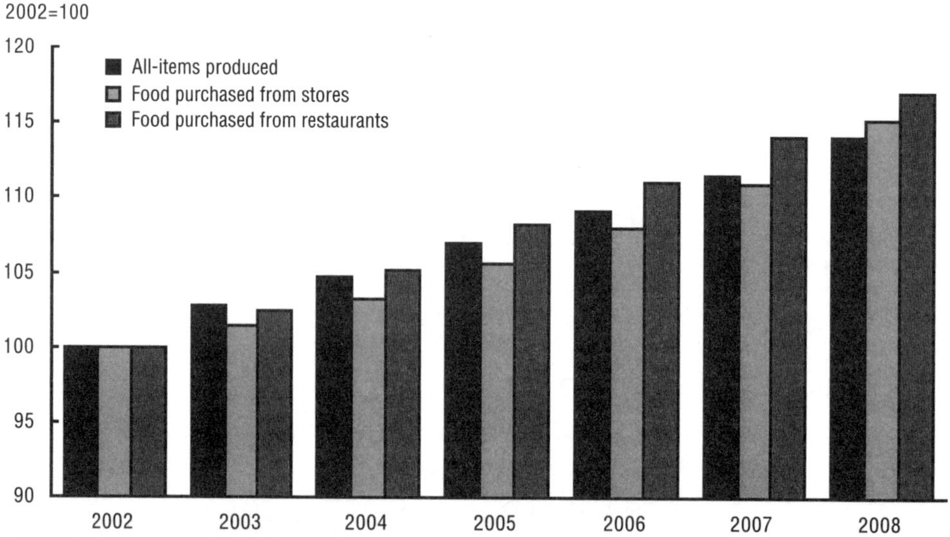

Source: Statistics Canada, CANSIM table 326-0021.

Energy prices not alone

Prices for all sorts of commodities, from grains to metals, boomed during most of 2008, then busted in the final months of the year; energy prices followed that trend.

The worldwide commodity price boom started in 2002, but was strongest from 2005 to 2008. Of all commodities, energy showed the strongest and most consistent price gains throughout the cycle.

Energy product prices, particularly those for gasoline, fuel oil and other fuels, followed similar patterns over the course of 2008. Canadian gasoline prices averaged a rise of 12.7% in 2008, more than double the 4.5% increase in 2007 and virtually matching the 12.8% rise in 2005, the year hurricanes Katrina and Rita disrupted the oil market. However, by December 2008 gasoline prices were about 26% lower than in December 2007.

Chart 25.3
Selected energy price indexes

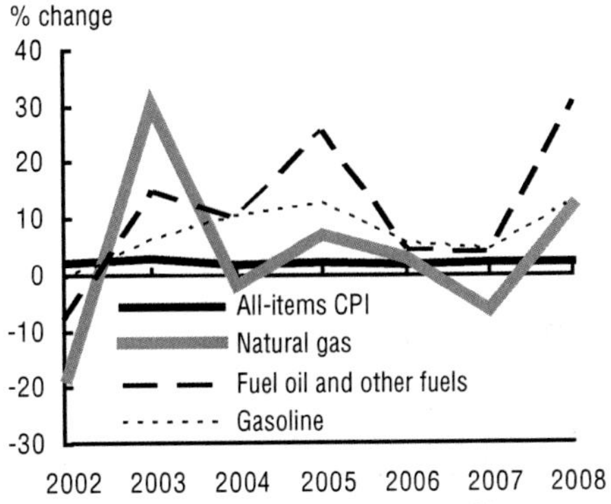

Source: Statistics Canada, CANSIM table 326-0021.

Natural gas prices rose 11.8% in 2008, after falling 6.5% in 2007. The rise in 2008 was the biggest jump since the 30.1% hike posted in 2003.

What got cheaper

Some consumer items have become cheaper, which helped temper the overall CPI increase in 2008. Many are items that have a high degree of imported content; many are also items that Canadians buy less frequently than food or gasoline.

Clothing prices fell 3.3% in 2008, and footwear prices, 2.2%, the seventh consecutive annual decline for both. Computer equipment and supplies fell a further 13.3% in 2008 after falling 17.1% in 2007 and 20.8% in 2005. Prices for photographic equipment and supplies dropped at an accelerating pace for the third consecutive year—15.0% in 2008, 9.7% in 2007 and 8.9% in 2006.

In 2008, price indexes for audio equipment fell 6.6%, and for video equipment, 9.2%, continuing on the heels of previous declines. Book prices declined 9.4%; furniture, 1.9%; and household appliances, 3.1%.

Chart 25.4
Selected price indexes

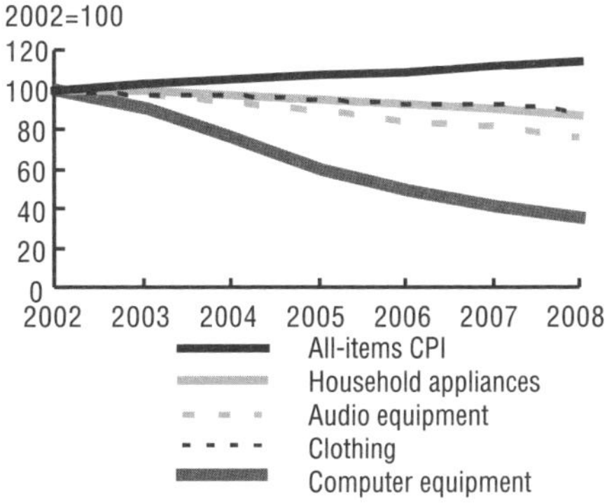

Source: Statistics Canada, CANSIM table 326-0021.

Table 25.1 Consumer Price Index, 1989 to 2008

	1989	1990	1991	1992	1993	1994	1995	1996	1997
	2002=100								
All-items	**74.8**	**78.4**	**82.8**	**84.0**	**85.6**	**85.7**	**87.6**	**88.9**	**90.4**
Food	76.5	79.6	83.4	83.1	84.5	84.9	86.9	88.0	89.4
Shelter	78.1	82.5	86.3	87.9	89.1	89.4	90.4	90.6	90.8
Household operations, furnishings and equipment	82.5	84.2	87.4	87.9	88.7	88.9	90.6	92.5	93.7
Clothing and footwear	83.7	86.1	94.3	95.1	96.0	96.8	96.7	96.4	97.7
Transportation	67.8	71.6	72.9	74.4	76.8	80.2	84.3	87.6	90.3
Health and personal care	75.5	79.1	84.7	86.6	88.9	89.7	89.6	90.1	91.7
Recreation, education and reading	70.3	73.2	78.3	79.2	81.1	83.5	86.7	88.7	91.0
Alcoholic beverages and tobacco products	59.9	65.2	76.4	81.0	82.2	68.8	68.7	70.1	72.3
Core Consumer Price Index[1]	77.2	79.8	82.1	83.6	85.3	86.9	88.8	90.3	92.0
Special aggregates									
All-items excluding food	74.4	78.1	82.6	84.2	85.7	85.9	87.7	89.1	90.6
All-items excluding shelter	73.6	76.9	81.4	82.5	84.2	84.3	86.5	88.4	90.2
All-items excluding energy	75.6	78.9	83.4	84.7	86.3	86.4	88.4	89.7	91.0
All-items excluding gasoline	..	..	..	..	..	..	..	..	..
Shelter[2]	77.9	82.2	86.0	87.5	88.7	89.1	90.4	90.6	90.8
Goods	78.4	81.6	85.7	86.4	87.8	86.8	88.4	89.9	91.2
Services	70.9	74.9	79.6	81.4	83.1	84.5	86.7	88.0	89.5
	annual % change								
All-items	**5.1**	**4.8**	**5.6**	**1.4**	**1.9**	**0.1**	**2.2**	**1.5**	**1.7**
Food	3.8	4.1	4.8	-0.4	1.7	0.5	2.4	1.3	1.6
Shelter	5.8	5.6	4.6	1.9	1.4	0.3	1.1	0.2	0.2
Household operations and furnishings	3.6	2.1	3.8	0.6	0.9	0.2	1.9	2.1	1.3
Clothing and footwear	4.0	2.9	9.5	0.8	0.9	0.8	-0.1	-0.3	1.3
Transportation	5.1	5.6	1.8	2.1	3.2	4.4	5.1	3.9	3.1
Health and personal care	4.4	4.8	7.1	2.2	2.7	0.9	-0.1	0.6	1.8
Recreation, education and reading	4.5	4.1	7.0	1.1	2.4	3.0	3.8	2.3	2.6
Alcoholic beverages and tobacco products	9.1	8.8	17.2	6.0	1.5	-16.3	-0.1	2.0	3.1
Core Consumer Price Index[1]	4.3	3.4	2.9	1.8	2.0	1.9	2.2	1.7	1.9
Special aggregates									
All-items excluding food	5.4	5.0	5.8	1.9	1.8	0.2	2.1	1.6	1.7
All-items excluding shelter	4.7	4.5	5.9	1.4	2.1	0.1	2.6	2.2	2.0
All-items excluding energy	5.1	4.4	5.7	1.6	1.9	0.1	2.3	1.5	1.4
All-items excluding gasoline	..	..	..	..	..	..	..	..	..
Shelter[2]	5.8	5.5	4.6	1.7	1.4	0.5	1.5	0.2	0.2
Goods	4.3	4.1	5.0	0.8	1.6	-1.1	1.8	1.7	1.4
Services	5.7	5.6	6.3	2.3	2.1	1.7	2.6	1.5	1.7

Note: Annual average indexes are obtained by averaging the indexes for the 12 months of the calendar year.
1. Bank of Canada definition.
2. 1986 definition.
Source: Statistics Canada, CANSIM table 326-0021.

1998	1999	2000	2001	2002	2003	2004	2005	2006	2007	2008
					2002=100					
91.3	**92.9**	**95.4**	**97.8**	**100.0**	**102.8**	**104.7**	**107.0**	**109.1**	**111.5**	**114.1**
90.9	92.0	93.3	97.4	100.0	101.7	103.8	106.4	108.9	111.8	115.7
91.1	92.3	95.6	99.1	100.0	103.2	105.8	109.2	113.1	116.9	122.0
95.1	95.8	96.7	98.6	100.0	100.7	101.2	101.7	102.2	103.2	104.6
98.8	100.1	100.3	100.7	100.0	98.2	98.0	97.6	95.8	95.7	93.8
89.6	92.6	97.2	97.3	100.0	105.2	107.7	112.0	115.2	117.1	119.5
93.6	95.4	97.0	98.9	100.0	101.4	102.8	104.6	105.9	107.3	108.8
93.0	94.7	97.0	98.4	100.0	100.8	101.1	100.8	100.6	101.8	102.2
74.9	76.5	79.0	85.0	100.0	110.1	116.0	119.1	121.7	125.5	127.5
93.2	94.5	95.7	97.7	100.0	102.2	103.8	105.5	107.5	109.8	111.7
91.3	93.0	95.8	97.9	100.0	103.0	104.8	107.1	109.2	111.4	113.8
91.3	93.0	95.3	97.3	100.0	102.5	104.1	106.1	107.6	109.4	111.2
92.3	93.6	95.0	97.3	100.0	102.4	103.8	105.4	107.2	109.5	111.3
91.9	93.2	95.0	97.6	100.0	102.6	104.2	106.0	107.9	110.1	112.1
91.3	92.7	96.1	99.4	100.0	102.7	105.0	108.1	111.8	115.7	120.6
91.4	93.1	96.0	98.4	100.0	101.9	103.4	105.8	107.1	108.0	109.4
91.1	92.6	94.8	97.1	100.0	103.6	105.9	108.2	111.1	114.8	118.7
					annual % change					
1.0	**1.8**	**2.7**	**2.5**	**2.2**	**2.8**	**1.8**	**2.2**	**2.0**	**2.2**	**2.3**
1.7	1.2	1.4	4.4	2.7	1.7	2.1	2.5	2.3	2.7	3.5
0.3	1.3	3.6	3.7	0.9	3.2	2.5	3.2	3.6	3.4	4.4
1.5	0.7	0.9	2.0	1.4	0.7	0.5	0.5	0.5	1.0	1.4
1.1	1.3	0.2	0.4	-0.7	-1.8	-0.2	-0.4	-1.8	-0.1	-2.0
-0.8	3.3	5.0	0.1	2.8	5.2	2.4	4.0	2.9	1.6	2.0
2.1	1.9	1.7	2.0	1.1	1.4	1.4	1.8	1.2	1.3	1.4
2.2	1.8	2.4	1.4	1.6	0.8	0.3	-0.3	-0.2	1.2	0.4
3.6	2.1	3.3	7.6	17.6	10.1	5.4	2.7	2.2	3.1	1.6
1.3	1.4	1.3	2.1	2.4	2.2	1.6	1.6	1.9	2.1	1.7
0.8	1.9	3.0	2.2	2.1	3.0	1.7	2.2	2.0	2.0	2.2
1.2	1.9	2.5	2.1	2.8	2.5	1.6	1.9	1.4	1.7	1.6
1.4	1.4	1.5	2.4	2.8	2.4	1.4	1.5	1.7	2.1	1.6
..	1.4	1.9	2.7	2.5	2.6	1.6	1.7	1.8	2.0	1.8
0.6	1.5	3.7	3.4	0.6	2.7	2.2	3.0	3.4	3.5	4.2
0.2	1.9	3.1	2.5	1.6	1.9	1.5	2.3	1.2	0.8	1.3
1.8	1.6	2.4	2.4	3.0	3.6	2.2	2.2	2.7	3.3	3.4

Table 25.2 Consumer Price Index, all-items, by province and territory, 2003 to 2008

	2003	2004	2005	2006	2007	2008
	2002=100					
Canada	**102.8**	**104.7**	**107.0**	**109.1**	**111.5**	**114.1**
Newfoundland and Labrador	102.9	104.8	107.6	109.5	111.1	114.3
Prince Edward Island	103.5	105.8	109.1	111.6	113.6	117.5
Nova Scotia	103.4	105.3	108.2	110.4	112.5	115.9
New Brunswick	103.4	104.9	107.4	109.2	111.3	113.2
Quebec	102.5	104.5	106.9	108.7	110.4	112.7
Ontario	102.7	104.6	106.9	108.8	110.8	113.3
Manitoba	101.8	103.8	106.6	108.7	110.9	113.4
Saskatchewan	102.3	104.6	106.9	109.1	112.2	115.9
Alberta	104.4	105.9	108.1	112.3	117.9	121.6
British Columbia	102.2	104.2	106.3	108.1	110.0	112.3
Yukon	101.9	103.0	105.3	106.8	109.5	113.4
Northwest Territories	102.3	103.8	106.2	107.7	110.8	115.2
Nunavut	100.2	101.2	102.9	104.6	107.9	110.4
	annual % change					
Canada	**2.8**	**1.8**	**2.2**	**2.0**	**2.2**	**2.3**
Newfoundland and Labrador	2.9	1.8	2.7	1.8	1.5	2.9
Prince Edward Island	3.5	2.2	3.1	2.3	1.8	3.4
Nova Scotia	3.4	1.8	2.8	2.0	1.9	3.0
New Brunswick	3.4	1.5	2.4	1.7	1.9	1.7
Quebec	2.5	2.0	2.3	1.7	1.6	2.1
Ontario	2.7	1.9	2.2	1.8	1.8	2.3
Manitoba	1.8	2.0	2.7	2.0	2.0	2.3
Saskatchewan	2.3	2.2	2.2	2.1	2.8	3.3
Alberta	4.4	1.4	2.1	3.9	5.0	3.1
British Columbia	2.2	2.0	2.0	1.7	1.8	2.1
Yukon	1.9	1.1	2.2	1.4	2.5	3.6
Northwest Territories	2.3	1.5	2.3	1.4	2.9	4.0
Nunavut	..	1.0	1.7	1.7	3.2	2.3

Note: Annual average indexes are obtained by averaging the indexes for the 12 months of the calendar year.
Source: Statistics Canada, CANSIM table 326-0021.

Table 25.3 Consumer Price Index, food, 2002 to 2008

	2002	2003	2004	2005	2006	2007	2008
				2002=100			
All-items	**100.0**	**102.8**	**104.7**	**107.0**	**109.1**	**111.5**	**114.1**
Food	100.0	101.7	103.8	106.4	108.9	111.8	115.7
Food purchased from stores	100.0	101.4	103.2	105.6	108.0	110.9	115.2
Meat	100.0	101.8	106.2	108.2	107.9	111.1	113.4
Fresh or frozen meat (excluding poultry)	100.0	100.9	105.0	106.9	105.8	107.9	109.9
Fresh or frozen poultry meat	100.0	104.8	112.2	113.0	113.4	120.9	125.1
Processed meat	100.0	100.7	103.2	106.4	106.7	108.1	109.2
Fish, seafood and other marine products	100.0	99.7	99.1	99.1	98.0	100.1	101.2
Fish	100.0	99.5	99.4	100.4	100.3	103.0	105.3
Seafood and other marine products	100.0	100.2	98.3	95.8	92.0	92.7	90.8
Dairy products and eggs	100.0	103.1	105.7	111.0	115.5	119.8	124.5
Dairy products	100.0	102.9	105.5	111.1	115.7	119.9	124.6
Eggs	100.0	104.9	107.7	109.1	111.9	118.4	123.3
Bakery and other cereal products (excluding infant food)	100.0	104.3	107.0	109.8	113.6	118.1	132.4
Bakery products	100.0	105.8	109.3	113.1	118.2	123.6	137.5
Cereal products (excluding infant food)	100.0	101.6	102.8	103.9	105.3	108.4	123.4
Fruit, fruit preparations and nuts	100.0	98.2	99.3	98.8	101.3	105.7	107.4
Fresh fruit	100.0	96.5	97.9	96.2	98.4	99.6	101.2
Preserved fruit and fruit preparations	100.0	100.9	101.3	102.6	105.9	116.2	117.4
Nuts	100.0	99.4	101.6	103.0	103.5	104.9	109.8
Vegetables and vegetable preparations	100.0	94.3	92.1	93.6	98.4	98.6	100.6
Fresh vegetables	100.0	92.1	88.9	89.9	95.3	95.2	96.5
Preserved vegetables and vegetable preparations	100.0	101.8	103.4	106.8	109.2	111.0	115.3
Other food products and non-alcoholic beverages	100.0	103.3	104.4	107.0	108.9	110.1	112.8
Sugar and confectionery	100.0	106.0	107.5	107.8	112.1	112.9	115.6
Fats and oils	100.0	103.8	106.9	108.6	110.3	114.2	129.7
Coffee and tea	100.0	100.8	102.7	106.1	109.8	110.3	112.4
Condiments, spices and vinegars	100.0	100.6	100.8	103.0	103.8	104.9	107.4
Other food preparations	100.0	104.7	106.5	109.0	111.1	111.1	114.3
Non-alcoholic beverages	100.0	99.4	99.2	103.4	103.8	106.4	106.5
Food purchased from restaurants	100.0	102.5	105.2	108.2	111.1	114.1	117.0

Note: Annual average indexes are obtained by averaging the indexes for the 12 months of the calendar year.
Source: Statistics Canada, CANSIM table 326-0021.

Table 25.4 Farm Product Price Index, 2002 to 2008

	2002	2003	2004	2005	2006	2007	2008
				1997=100			
Canada	**106.1**	**101.3**	**99.4**	**97.1**	**97.7**	**108.5**	**120.7**
Total crops	109.3	105.1	100.6	88.8	93.5	117.4	141.8
Grains	111.0	105.9	94.1	76.5	84.3	133.2	157.5
Oilseeds	94.1	92.7	95.2	74.5	72.2	97.5	133.5
Specialty crops	124.5	113.4	102.5	84.6	82.3	120.7	186.7
Fruit	103.4	103.7	108.7	116.9	124.5	122.3	128.0
Vegetables excluding potatoes	115.5	116.0	116.8	116.6	122.0	113.9	119.3
Potatoes	166.8	135.4	119.4	125.9	148.6	134.9	154.5
Total livestock and animal products	103.4	98.0	98.3	104.0	101.2	101.5	103.7
Cattle and calves	117.5	98.3	87.6	103.5	102.7	99.4	99.0
Hogs	76.0	74.3	89.7	82.9	72.1	68.3	68.2
Poultry	91.9	95.7	97.9	96.4	93.0	101.9	114.6
Eggs	100.6	102.0	105.6	96.4	98.9	100.9	107.9
Dairy	112.2	119.1	119.9	128.0	130.3	137.2	139.9
Eastern Canada	**103.6**	**101.5**	**103.1**	**103.1**	**104.1**	**107.9**	**115.4**
Total crops	105.6	102.3	100.9	96.0	101.6	107.4	121.7
Grains	89.4	85.9	82.3	65.8	71.8	98.4	116.6
Oilseeds	80.9	89.9	95.2	75.1	66.2	84.3	114.8
Specialty crops	111.9	108.3	127.3	116.2	103.6	131.5	172.8
Fruit	109.3	107.6	112.8	122.0	132.7	128.4	129.5
Vegetables excluding potatoes	112.1	111.7	110.5	112.9	119.1	112.9	117.4
Potatoes	185.9	137.0	115.2	127.3	163.5	138.7	165.2
Total livestock and animal products	102.1	100.7	104.4	107.5	105.6	108.1	111.1
Cattle and calves	127.0	102.1	88.7	106.9	112.1	109.9	111.0
Hogs	74.2	72.5	88.2	80.3	68.8	65.9	65.0
Poultry	92.4	96.2	98.4	95.4	91.3	101.3	114.0
Eggs	101.8	102.2	106.6	96.7	99.6	103.9	110.9
Dairy	112.0	119.5	122.0	130.9	133.7	139.9	141.8
Western Canada	**108.1**	**101.2**	**96.1**	**93.9**	**94.2**	**110.9**	**127.1**
Total crops	111.7	106.9	99.8	83.3	87.5	122.5	153.1
Grains	115.6	110.1	96.1	78.4	86.7	142.1	168.0
Oilseeds	98.7	93.8	95.4	74.4	74.3	102.1	140.0
Specialty crops	124.6	113.2	100.7	82.2	80.5	119.7	187.9
Fruit	92.4	96.6	100.0	111.8	114.1	115.5	129.0
Vegetables excluding potatoes	124.9	128.0	128.9	111.5	114.2	102.2	109.4
Potatoes	136.2	130.8	122.8	122.8	130.1	128.8	140.6
Total livestock and animal products	105.0	95.6	92.5	106.0	102.3	100.4	101.9
Cattle and calves	114.3	96.9	87.2	110.8	108.1	104.2	103.4
Hogs	78.7	77.1	91.5	88.5	78.5	73.4	74.2
Poultry	90.7	94.6	96.7	98.2	96.1	102.8	115.6
Eggs	98.6	101.6	103.7	96.0	97.4	95.0	102.0
Dairy	113.0	117.9	113.3	118.9	119.4	128.8	133.6

Source: Statistics Canada, CANSIM table 002-0022.

Table 25.5 Farm Input Price Index, 2001 to 2007

	2001	2002	2003	2004	2005	2006	2007
				1992=100			
Canada	**129.5**	**128.5**	**132.8**	**129.6**	**134.9**	**139.3**	**149.7**
Building and fencing	120.0	122.8	122.4	137.7	136.3	137.7	138.7
Machinery and motor vehicles	143.7	143.5	157.0	155.3	163.6	168.7	171.8
Crop production	137.6	135.7	154.7	151.1	156.1	161.9	183.2
Animal production	135.1	132.3	128.2	114.4	124.2	126.5	143.6
Supplies and services	121.1	120.7	127.5	126.9	129.8	131.1	130.8
Hired farm labour	125.4	128.2	129.0	135.4	137.7	142.7	149.7
Property taxes	112.6	118.9	126.4	129.5	132.5	129.9	134.7
Interest	90.5	84.9	83.9	80.7	81.3	90.1	98.2
Farm rent	113.8	121.8	131.9	135.8	129.3	132.1	144.5
Eastern Canada	**126.6**	**126.2**	**129.0**	**127.5**	**131.3**	**135.7**	**145.3**
Building and fencing	121.9	124.3	124.2	136.2	138.6	141.4	144.2
Machinery and motor vehicles	144.4	145.9	159.3	156.4	163.6	167.7	170.4
Crop production	130.1	128.3	137.0	139.8	148.0	154.8	163.2
Animal production	129.3	128.0	125.4	117.6	120.4	122.9	143.6
Supplies and services	123.4	121.8	129.8	129.1	132.9	135.3	134.0
Hired farm labour	127.2	130.4	128.9	135.2	137.8	140.6	146.3
Property taxes	79.7	84.8	90.0	93.8	97.4	101.9	105.6
Interest	92.6	86.7	85.8	83.2	84.2	93.9	102.2
Farm rent	85.2	93.5	97.8	101.4	102.4	106.4	111.4
Western Canada	**132.9**	**130.9**	**137.5**	**131.6**	**138.9**	**143.5**	**154.5**
Building and fencing	118.5	121.6	120.9	138.8	134.2	134.6	133.1
Machinery and motor vehicles	143.3	140.7	154.4	154.3	164.1	170.7	174.0
Crop production	142.7	140.6	167.1	158.4	161.0	165.9	195.7
Animal production	141.0	136.6	131.0	111.4	127.4	129.4	143.2
Supplies and services	118.6	119.6	125.0	124.4	126.5	126.6	127.4
Hired farm labour	123.8	126.0	129.9	136.5	138.3	146.4	155.2
Property taxes	121.4	127.9	136.0	138.7	141.3	135.9	140.9
Interest	89.2	83.7	82.7	79.1	79.4	87.7	95.5
Farm rent	128.0	135.6	148.9	152.8	141.9	143.9	159.5

Source: Statistics Canada, CANSIM table 328-0014.

Table 25.6 Industrial Product Price Index, 1989 to 2008

	1989	1990	1991	1992	1993	1994	1995	1996	1997
					1997=100				
All industrial products	**84.0**	**84.2**	**83.3**	**83.8**	**86.8**	**92.0**	**98.9**	**99.3**	**100.0**
Intermediate goods	86.1	85.1	82.6	82.2	85.1	91.8	101.1	100.1	100.0
First-stage intermediate goods	97.3	90.5	81.8	79.5	76.2	92.1	118.5	100.1	100.0
Second-stage intermediate goods	82.6	83.2	82.5	82.6	86.5	91.7	98.3	100.1	100.0
Finished goods	80.7	82.9	84.4	86.1	89.4	92.5	95.4	98.0	100.0
Finished foods and feeds	84.6	87.1	88.9	89.8	91.4	93.7	95.9	98.2	100.0
Capital equipment	78.8	80.6	82.0	84.8	89.1	92.7	96.0	98.0	100.0
All other finished goods	79.8	82.1	83.4	85.0	88.6	91.8	95.0	97.9	100.0
Aggregation, by commodities									
Meat, fish and dairy products	79.7	82.0	82.8	83.7	88.3	90.3	92.5	97.0	100.0
Fruits, vegetables, feeds and other food products	86.4	86.6	86.3	87.4	88.6	93.0	95.8	99.6	100.0
Beverages	84.0	86.5	89.5	90.8	92.2	92.8	94.9	97.4	100.0
Tobacco and tobacco products	61.2	66.2	73.4	78.9	84.1	86.9	89.6	93.4	100.0
Rubber, leather and plastic fabricated products	88.9	89.3	89.0	88.1	87.7	91.4	100.2	99.4	100.0
Textile products	90.3	91.4	91.4	91.2	92.3	94.1	97.8	99.2	100.0
Knitted products and clothing	88.9	91.1	92.2	92.6	92.8	94.2	96.7	99.0	100.0
Lumber and other wood products	65.9	65.5	64.4	69.8	87.1	97.8	94.0	99.3	100.0
Furniture and fixtures	84.4	87.4	88.4	87.9	89.8	92.1	98.3	99.3	100.0
Pulp and paper products	93.4	91.9	83.0	79.7	77.3	85.8	119.5	105.7	100.0
Printing and publishing	72.7	74.8	77.4	79.1	82.9	87.7	98.6	99.4	100.0
Primary metal products	97.8	88.6	81.2	79.0	78.2	92.4	105.4	97.9	100.0
Metal fabricated products	83.3	84.0	83.9	83.7	85.6	89.1	96.4	98.5	100.0
Machinery and equipment	85.5	87.4	88.7	90.0	92.8	95.6	97.6	99.2	100.0
Motor vehicles and other transport equipment	76.3	76.7	78.2	82.3	87.8	92.2	94.9	97.5	100.0
Electrical and communications products	93.8	94.0	93.6	94.4	97.0	99.8	102.2	101.1	100.0
Non-metallic mineral products	90.5	91.5	90.8	90.3	91.0	94.5	98.9	100.1	100.0
Petroleum and coal products	86.4	97.3	94.0	86.7	85.8	85.6	90.4	100.5	100.0
Chemicals and chemical products	87.7	85.4	86.5	85.3	87.0	93.2	101.8	99.8	100.0
Miscellaneous manufactured products	84.1	85.1	86.6	86.9	90.0	95.8	98.7	100.0	100.0
Miscellaneous non-manufactured products	104.6	95.0	84.5	83.2	91.3	102.9	120.3	111.1	100.0

Note: Annual average indexes are obtained by averaging the indexes for the 12 months of the calendar year.
Source: Statistics Canada, CANSIM tables 329-0039, 329-0040, 329-0041, 329-0042, 329-0044, 329-0045, 329-0046 and 329-0048.

1998	1999	2000	2001	2002	2003	2004	2005	2006	2007	2008
					1997=100					
100.4	**102.2**	**106.5**	**107.6**	**107.6**	**106.2**	**109.5**	**111.2**	**113.8**	**115.6**	**120.6**
98.4	99.9	105.3	105.0	104.2	103.8	109.9	112.8	117.5	120.5	126.7
93.8	96.5	111.9	104.5	101.8	105.6	118.0	123.1	141.9	157.3	149.4
99.0	100.4	104.3	105.1	104.6	103.5	108.7	111.2	113.8	115.0	123.3
103.4	105.6	108.3	111.3	112.6	109.7	108.9	108.7	108.2	108.1	111.4
100.9	102.2	104.3	106.4	108.0	110.3	112.0	112.1	113.5	115.6	118.3
104.9	106.6	107.3	110.7	112.6	107.1	104.5	102.5	100.2	98.3	99.2
103.5	106.4	110.7	113.8	114.7	111.1	110.3	111.0	110.7	110.8	115.8
98.7	100.4	104.6	107.7	107.2	108.5	109.7	107.1	107.2	110.0	111.5
97.9	95.6	95.6	98.2	101.6	103.6	104.9	102.8	104.6	109.4	118.0
102.4	105.6	109.0	111.4	114.6	117.7	120.4	121.3	122.5	125.0	126.8
103.8	109.4	114.2	127.4	139.5	162.7	169.3	176.3	190.4	213.0	220.7
99.8	100.2	105.2	106.1	105.0	106.2	108.1	114.3	118.4	116.4	119.0
101.2	99.6	99.1	100.5	100.4	99.4	98.9	99.9	100.3	99.8	101.1
101.6	102.2	102.8	103.2	103.8	104.1	104.5	104.3	104.7	104.7	104.8
95.9	105.1	95.9	94.6	94.0	90.3	101.1	92.5	87.2	84.2	82.4
101.1	102.3	104.8	106.3	107.5	109.2	111.8	115.1	118.3	120.0	122.9
103.5	101.7	115.2	115.0	106.0	102.8	104.1	103.5	105.0	104.0	108.7
103.5	105.8	109.2	111.8	114.1	113.0	114.0	115.3	115.4	116.6	120.4
96.0	95.2	100.6	94.4	96.3	96.2	113.4	116.5	138.6	145.9	141.7
102.6	103.0	104.7	104.9	106.5	107.2	117.0	121.5	123.1	124.4	133.0
102.3	103.7	104.8	105.9	106.9	105.9	106.0	107.3	107.0	105.7	107.1
107.1	108.5	109.0	113.5	115.1	106.3	101.2	96.5	92.4	89.3	89.9
100.1	100.2	98.5	99.4	101.3	95.8	94.7	93.7	93.7	92.1	91.8
100.2	102.0	105.2	107.4	108.7	109.7	111.6	114.9	119.7	122.8	125.5
82.3	96.1	140.3	133.7	125.5	138.4	161.8	199.9	218.1	230.4	289.5
96.9	98.6	104.8	107.4	107.3	110.4	113.8	121.0	122.9	126.5	139.0
101.4	103.0	104.3	105.5	107.5	107.2	109.6	110.7	112.9	113.9	120.2
90.3	90.3	86.4	86.6	90.8	95.8	125.1	163.7	248.1	443.2	320.2

Table 25.7 New Housing Price Index, by region, 2002 to 2008

	2002	2003	2004	2005	2006	2007	2008
				1997=100			
Canada	**111.3**	**116.7**	**123.2**	**129.4**	**142.0**	**153.0**	**158.2**
Atlantic Region	108.7	112.5	115.9	120.5	124.9	129.6	141.8
Quebec	117.3	126.2	134.2	140.8	147.0	153.2	160.8
Ontario	114.9	120.0	126.7	132.6	137.5	141.1	146.1
Prairie Region	121.0	127.3	134.0	143.2	192.5	235.6	241.5
British Columbia	92.9	96.3	101.4	106.3	113.2	120.5	123.0
				annual % change			
Canada	**4.0**	**4.9**	**5.6**	**5.0**	**9.7**	**7.7**	**3.4**
Atlantic Region	3.1	3.5	3.0	4.0	3.7	3.8	9.4
Quebec	5.7	7.6	6.3	4.9	4.4	4.2	5.0
Ontario	3.7	4.4	5.6	4.7	3.7	2.6	3.5
Prairie Region	5.4	5.2	5.3	6.9	34.4	22.4	2.5
British Columbia	2.5	3.7	5.3	4.8	6.5	6.4	2.1

Note: Annual average indexes are obtained by averaging the indexes for the 12 months of the calendar year.
Source: Statistics Canada, CANSIM table 327-0005.

Table 25.8 Raw Materials Price Index, 2002 to 2008

	2002	2003	2004	2005	2006	2007	2008
				1997=100			
All raw materials	**112.6**	**114.8**	**128.3**	**145.3**	**161.7**	**174.1**	**196.3**
Mineral fuels	154.5	165.6	193.9	244.7	258.7	264.5	345.1
Vegetable products	97.7	92.2	88.8	80.3	84.8	102.4	129.7
Animals and animal products	103.6	100.3	101.4	104.6	104.3	106.6	108.6
Wood	83.9	82.2	83.0	75.1	77.8	84.6	81.6
Ferrous materials	92.8	95.9	125.0	125.0	125.7	134.5	162.4
Non-ferrous metals	81.3	82.0	104.8	119.7	195.7	241.7	187.3
Non-metallic minerals	110.5	116.4	122.6	133.9	141.1	148.5	168.8
All raw materials excluding mineral fuels	93.2	91.4	97.9	99.3	116.8	132.3	127.6

Note: Annual average indexes are obtained by averaging the indexes for the 12 months of the calendar year.
Source: Statistics Canada, CANSIM table 330-0006.

Table 25.9 Machinery and Equipment Price Index, domestic and imported, by industry, 2002 to 2008

	2002	2003	2004	2005	2006	2007	2008
	1997=100						
Total machinery and equipment	**109.0**	**100.8**	**96.8**	**93.9**	**90.6**	**88.3**	**91.0**
Crop and animal production	117.4	109.0	105.9	103.6	99.6	98.0	100.6
Forestry and logging	116.3	107.8	104.7	103.0	100.3	97.6	99.8
Fishing, hunting and trapping	106.4	104.2	107.5	106.4	105.6	106.3	109.4
Support activities for agriculture and forestry	114.6	106.8	104.0	101.6	97.5	95.8	99.9
Mines, quarries and oil wells	115.4	107.0	104.4	103.0	101.9	101.0	106.0
Utilities	112.6	103.6	98.5	95.6	93.8	93.2	98.6
Construction	114.9	105.6	101.6	98.9	96.0	94.0	96.4
All manufacturing	113.9	105.0	101.2	98.8	96.2	94.4	97.3
Trade	103.5	96.7	94.0	91.7	88.4	86.1	89.5
Transportation (excluding pipeline transportation)	116.0	108.8	106.6	105.1	103.0	101.4	103.5
Pipeline transportation	115.0	108.6	104.6	103.2	101.3	100.6	105.0
Warehousing and storage	111.8	106.0	104.6	103.9	101.9	100.6	106.0
Finance, insurance and real estate	106.3	97.8	93.8	90.0	84.9	81.4	83.4
Private education services	100.2	90.7	85.6	81.6	77.6	73.9	75.8
Education services (excluding private), health care and social assistance	105.4	97.6	93.4	90.1	86.4	83.6	87.3
Other services (excluding public administration)	101.7	93.3	87.2	83.5	79.9	77.0	79.5
Public administration	102.4	94.8	90.2	86.7	83.5	81.4	82.8
	annual % change						
Total machinery and equipment	**1.3**	**-7.5**	**-4.0**	**-3.0**	**-3.5**	**-2.5**	**3.1**
Crop and animal production	2.0	-7.2	-2.8	-2.2	-3.9	-1.6	2.7
Forestry and logging	2.6	-7.3	-2.9	-1.6	-2.6	-2.7	2.3
Fishing, hunting and trapping	2.3	-2.1	3.2	-1.0	-0.8	0.7	2.9
Support activities for agriculture and forestry	1.6	-6.8	-2.6	-2.3	-4.0	-1.7	4.3
Mines, quarries and oil wells	2.3	-7.3	-2.4	-1.3	-1.1	-0.9	5.0
Utilities	2.5	-8.0	-4.9	-2.9	-1.9	-0.6	5.8
Construction	2.8	-8.1	-3.8	-2.7	-2.9	-2.1	2.6
All manufacturing	1.4	-7.8	-3.6	-2.4	-2.6	-1.9	3.1
Trade	0.7	-6.6	-2.8	-2.4	-3.6	-2.6	3.9
Transportation (excluding pipeline transportation)	1.9	-6.2	-2.0	-1.4	-2.0	-1.6	2.1
Pipeline transportation	2.5	-5.6	-3.7	-1.3	-1.8	-0.7	4.4
Warehousing and storage	1.5	-5.2	-1.3	-0.7	-1.9	-1.3	5.4
Finance, insurance and real estate	0.6	-8.0	-4.1	-4.1	-5.7	-4.1	2.5
Private education services	1.1	-9.5	-5.6	-4.7	-4.9	-4.8	2.6
Education services (excluding private), health care and social assistance	1.2	-7.4	-4.3	-3.5	-4.1	-3.2	4.4
Other services (excluding public administration)	0.5	-8.3	-6.5	-4.2	-4.3	-3.6	3.2
Public administration	1.5	-7.4	-4.9	-3.9	-3.7	-2.5	1.7

Note: Annual average indexes are obtained by averaging the indexes for the 12 months of the calendar year.
Source: Statistics Canada, CANSIM table 327-0042.

Table 25.10 Composite Index, March 2003 to March 2009

	March 2003	March 2004	March 2005	March 2006	March 2007	March 2008	March 2009
Composite Leading Indicator (1992=100)	**180.7**	**191.1**	**202.4**	**213.2**	**224.1**	**227.8**	**215.9**
Housing Index (1992=100)[1]	130.4	136.5	138.1	150.1	144.9	141.6	97.5
Business and personal services employment (thousands)	2,622	2,627	2,612	2,687	2,820	2,894	2,920
Stock Price Index, Toronto Stock Exchange 300 (1975=1,000)	6,530	8,395	9,352	11,568	12,981	13,522	8,759
M1 money supply ($ millions, 1992)[2]	109,944	119,791	134,113	144,772	162,504	171,369	189,684
U.S. Conference Board Leading Indicator (1992=100)	110.3	119.3	124.6	127.4	126.9	124.5	119.7
Manufacturing							
Average work week (hours)	39.2	38.7	38.2	38.0	38.4	38.0	36.5
New orders, durables ($ millions, 1992)	20,527	22,307	25,165	26,946	27,275	27,312	19,478
Shipments to inventory ratio of finished goods	1.75	1.81	1.86	1.87	1.84	1.78	1.57
Retail trade							
Furniture and appliance sales ($ millions, 1992)	1,848	2,009	2,185	2,460	2,633	2,838	2,850
Other durable goods sales ($ millions, 1992)	7,648	7,463	7,831	8,280	8,950	9,676	9,202
Unsmoothed composite (1992=100)	**181.1**	**194.8**	**204.3**	**215.7**	**225.7**	**227.6**	**210.3**

1. Composite index of housing starts (units) and house sales (Multiple Listing Service).
2. Deflated by the Consumer Price Index for all items.
Source: Statistics Canada, CANSIM table 377-0003.

Retail and wholesale trade

Slumping auto sales, followed by the global economic downturn, weakened both retail and wholesale sales in the fourth quarter of 2008.

Consumer spending on goods—particularly durable goods such as motor vehicles and household items—and services grew 3.0% in 2008, a drop from 4.5% in 2007.

Retailers' sales totalled $426.0 billion in 2008, up 3.4% from 2007, the weakest growth since 1996. Measured by volume, total retail sales rose 2.6%, the lowest growth rate since 2003.

Wholesalers' sales rose 3.0% in 2008 to $532.5 billion. The growth in volume of wholesale sales slowed from 7.0% in 2007 to 0.4% in 2008.

Slumping auto sales were the key factor dragging down both wholesale and retail trade. On the retail side, new car dealers' sales dropped 4.5% in 2008, their largest annual decline since 1991. Unit sales of new vehicles fell 1.0% to 1.7 million vehicles, while their retail prices dropped 6.9%, the sharpest price decline in more than half a century.

Higher gas and food prices

About half the retail sales growth in current dollars in 2008 came from a 14.6% sales increase at gasoline stations, mostly reflecting higher gas prices in the first nine months of the year.

Home electronics and appliance stores posted the second highest growth; their sales rose 8.3%. Consumers bought higher volumes of commodities such as televisions, computers and telephones in 2008, as prices for these goods declined. By contrast, higher food prices were the main reason for the 4.2% gain in sales at supermarkets; food prices increased 3.9% in 2008.

Employment in the retail industry totalled 1.9 million in 2008, up 3.2%

Chart 26.1
Retail and wholesale sales

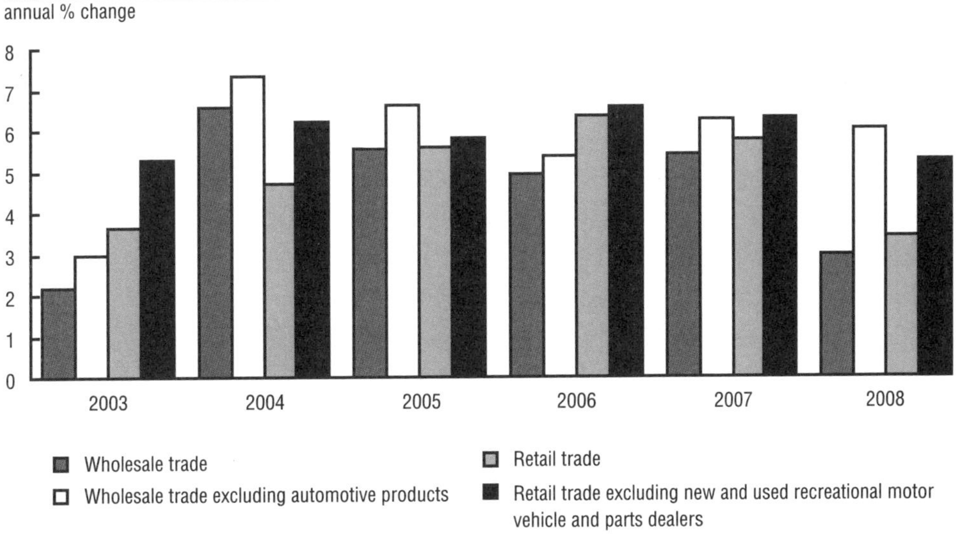

Source: Statistics Canada, CANSIM tables 080-0014 and 081-0007.

from 2007. The retail industry accounted for 13.0% of total employment in 2008. There was significant job growth in just two retail trade groups: food and beverage stores and electronics and appliance stores.

The total gross margin—the difference between total operating revenues and the cost of goods—for all store retailers was up 8.1% in 2007. Operating profit—total operating revenues minus total operating expenses and the cost of goods sold—reached $22.8 billion in 2007, up 12.5% from 2006.

Wholesalers

The wholesale industry consists of 120,000 firms whose main activity is wholesaling merchandise and providing related logistical, marketing and support services. Wholesalers employed 758,352 people in 2008.

Wholesaling's largest sector—machinery and electronic equipment, which accounts for 22% of wholesale sales—posted its fifth consecutive sales gain in 2008, up 7.1% to $117.1 billion.

Table 26.a
Employment for retail and wholesale trade

	1998	2008
	number	
Trade	**2,047,584**	**2,652,811**
Retail trade	1,399,583	1,894,459
Wholesale trade	648,001	758,352

Note: North American Industry Classification System (NAICS), 2002.
Source: Statistics Canada, CANSIM table 281-0024.

Wholesalers' gross margins increased 4.0% in 2007, compared with 13.0% in 2006. This reflected the higher cost of goods sold rather than lower revenues.

Chart 26.2
Wholesale sales, selected industries

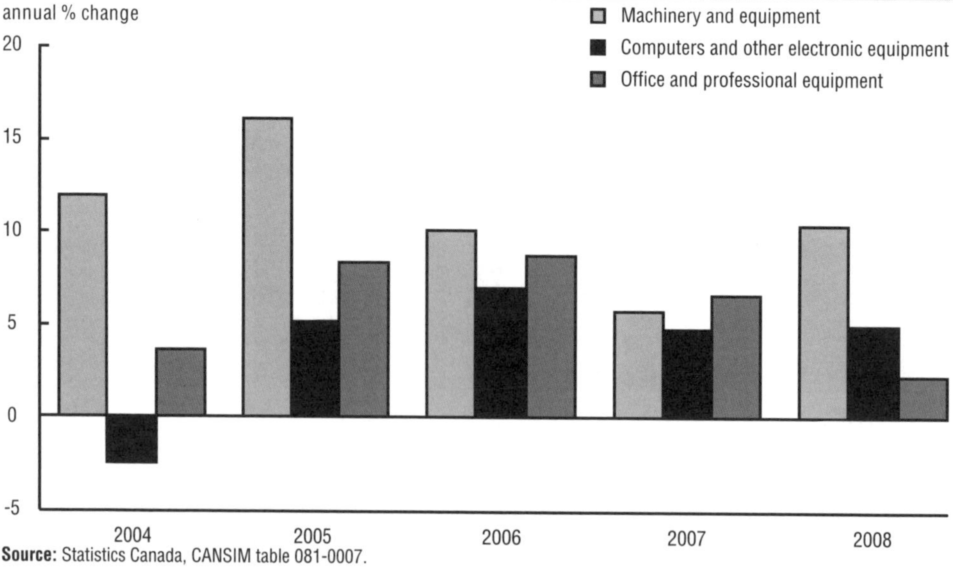

Source: Statistics Canada, CANSIM table 081-0007.

Saskatchewan is the sales leader

Saskatchewan had the top growth rate in both retail and wholesale sales for a second consecutive year in 2008. Retailers' sales increased 10.6% while wholesalers' grew 41.0%, mostly as a result of wholesalers' sales of fertilizers.

Alberta's wholesalers also did well in 2008, with the province's fourth double-digit growth rate in five years. However, retail sales in Alberta edged down 0.1%. This was mainly because of new car dealers' sales, which declined 12.4%. Still, Albertans continued to lead per capita retail spending, at about $17,000.

For the first time since 1992, Newfoundland and Labrador's population grew, contributing to a 7.6% rise in retail sales. Manitoba's retailers also benefited from population and job growth. Quebec's retailers also showed widespread gains in 2008.

Chart 26.3
Retail sales, by province, 2007 to 2008

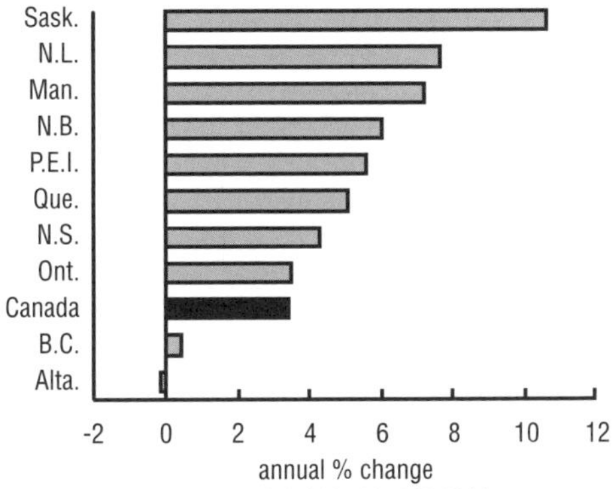

Source: Statistics Canada, CANSIM table 080-0014.

Retailers' sales in Ontario grew faster than the national average for the first time since 2000.

A key economic sector

In a year marked by a downturn in most wholesale industries, fertilizer exports provided a bright spot for Canadian wholesalers. From 2007 to 2008, fertilizer prices more than doubled as a result of higher production costs (energy, petroleum and natural gas prices) and strong demand for agricultural products and biofuels.

Canada is a leading exporter of fertilizers and fertilizer materials, accounting for 30% of world production. Most (90%) is exported to the United States, China and India, and a large proportion of those exports go through wholesalers.

Wholesalers are key participants in commercial transactions between Canadian businesses and foreign markets.

Chart 26.4
Canadian exports of fertilizers and fertilizer materials

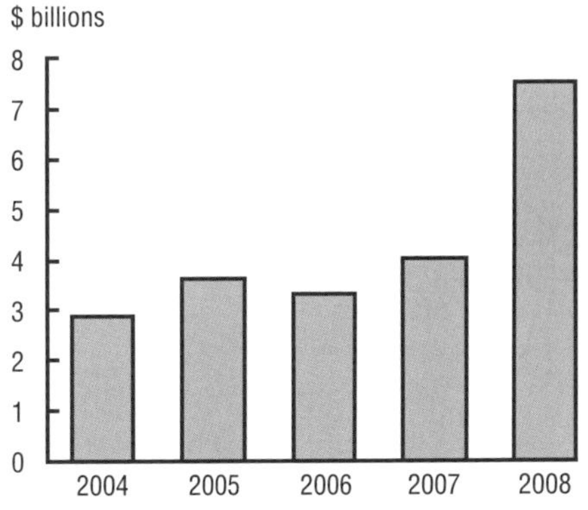

Source: Statistics Canada, CANSIM table 228-0003.

Imports account for 36% of wholesale sales and exports for 12%.

Table 26.1 Employment in retail and wholesale trade, selected industries, 1993 to 2008

	1993	1994	1995	1996	1997	1998	1999
				number			
Wholesale trade	**533,534**	**546,478**	**578,762**	**598,945**	**632,920**	**648,001**	**673,518**
Farm product wholesaler-distributors	8,146	8,548	8,385	9,819	9,773	9,437	10,876
Petroleum product wholesaler-distributors	11,512	10,756	10,249	10,831	11,084	10,894	11,370
Food, beverage and tobacco wholesaler-distributors	79,907	77,828	81,754	83,381	85,258	88,127	87,752
Personal and household goods wholesaler-distributors	63,677	66,534	70,496	72,564	80,363	81,828	84,338
Motor vehicle and parts wholesaler-distributors	53,647	53,650	59,234	60,419	62,608	62,015	63,285
Building material and supplies wholesaler-distributors	86,363	91,057	95,704	98,316	104,737	105,832	111,415
Machinery, equipment and supplies wholesaler-distributors	144,186	150,046	160,288	165,112	174,107	181,148	187,771
Miscellaneous wholesaler-distributors	59,463	61,176	64,761	69,395	74,606	77,659	84,158
Wholesale electronic markets, and agents and brokers	26,634	26,883	27,891	29,108	30,385	31,061	32,554
Retail trade	**1,342,946**	**1,335,003**	**1,368,165**	**1,361,533**	**1,396,640**	**1,399,583**	**1,411,692**
Motor vehicle and parts dealers	133,300	129,361	136,639	138,190	144,627	149,498	148,758
Furniture and home furnishings stores	45,544	47,345	45,873	44,249	46,751	49,731	52,122
Electronics and appliance stores	43,828	43,875	46,319	47,811	49,173	49,845	51,539
Building material, and garden equipment and supplies dealers	55,022	54,099	56,327	56,373	59,502	60,302	62,211
Food and beverage stores	327,764	337,591	352,807	349,419	356,810	361,556	368,053
Health and personal care stores	108,697	108,790	113,518	111,212	113,541	113,674	114,005
Gasoline stations	99,321	95,433	87,889	83,227	77,259	73,782	74,881
Clothing and clothing accessories stores	149,646	153,275	158,436	162,489	166,904	159,449	158,229
Sporting goods, hobby, book and music stores	62,125	61,254	62,936	62,831	65,335	65,486	66,700
General merchandise stores	220,637	210,541	212,064	209,386	216,462	215,399	211,153
Miscellaneous store retailers	63,413	61,520	63,457	63,683	66,728	67,432	69,566
Non-store retailers	33,649	31,920	31,900	32,662	33,550	33,430	34,475

Source: Statistics Canada, CANSIM table 281-0024.

2000	2001	2002	2003	2004	2005	2006	2007	2008
				number				
711,565	**721,924**	**722,403**	**735,691**	**731,034**	**727,592**	**739,015**	**757,881**	**758,352**
13,362	12,965	12,540	11,779	11,136	10,228	9,969	9,901	10,302
11,935	12,873	13,098	12,506	12,377	12,243	12,664	14,017	13,792
92,172	94,049	99,939	107,333	106,383	104,409	100,426	102,648	102,388
91,209	93,954	98,405	101,816	101,574	101,424	104,222	106,022	106,040
64,873	64,298	63,126	63,985	64,114	63,230	63,695	64,845	63,224
118,911	117,368	110,729	111,231	113,083	113,475	118,052	120,505	121,601
196,659	195,937	191,838	194,300	190,588	191,645	198,964	207,476	211,251
88,055	92,320	93,397	95,042	95,863	95,459	95,369	96,265	95,054
34,388	38,160	39,331	37,698	35,916	35,478	35,653	36,201	34,700
1,441,022	**1,515,965**	**1,583,324**	**1,652,488**	**1,682,775**	**1,719,798**	**1,767,437**	**1,835,502**	**1,894,459**
150,210	153,150	160,117	166,903	169,736	171,703	177,315	183,801	187,960
54,534	55,461	57,788	59,725	62,107	65,404	66,315	70,674	73,225
53,969	56,159	58,251	58,458	58,412	60,590	60,820	61,649	63,147
65,744	73,863	89,438	91,822	95,047	100,456	108,307	121,764	129,003
373,723	410,471	437,628	461,444	478,708	492,767	497,535	511,403	538,133
115,873	121,078	123,138	127,957	127,819	129,695	132,733	141,079	150,122
77,626	74,976	77,687	78,809	78,305	79,424	80,169	82,344	82,829
168,148	180,898	171,201	177,313	175,923	180,975	194,075	205,111	210,438
69,170	70,549	72,809	72,570	74,370	77,955	80,375	82,565	83,629
203,984	205,767	217,122	237,240	243,457	242,017	250,208	253,768	255,491
72,307	82,388	88,011	89,897	90,742	91,590	91,942	95,110	96,615
35,736	31,205	30,134	30,349	28,148	27,221	27,643	26,233	23,867

Table 26.2 Interprovincial trade, by province and territory, 2008

	All goods and services	Goods	Services
	$ millions		
Imports to provinces	**325,083**	.	.
Newfoundland and Labrador	**7,725**	3,446	4,279
Prince Edward Island	**2,407**	1,221	1,186
Nova Scotia	**12,389**	6,410	5,979
New Brunswick	**14,047**	8,078	5,969
Quebec	**65,800**	35,595	30,205
Ontario	**87,005**	54,700	32,305
Manitoba	**18,379**	10,477	7,902
Saskatchewan	**19,757**	9,734	10,023
Alberta	**51,395**	26,581	24,814
British Columbia	**41,757**	21,198	20,559
Yukon	**931**	405	526
Northwest Territories	**2,214**	1,008	1,206
Nunavut	**1,088**	514	574
Outside Canada	**190**	134	56
Exports from provinces	**325,083**	.	.
Newfoundland and Labrador	**10,549**	9,427	1,122
Prince Edward Island	**1,079**	603	476
Nova Scotia	**7,727**	4,703	3,024
New Brunswick	**10,163**	7,297	2,866
Quebec	**60,790**	36,258	24,532
Ontario	**113,003**	47,467	65,536
Manitoba	**14,988**	7,608	7,380
Saskatchewan	**16,034**	12,021	4,013
Alberta	**58,436**	39,724	18,712
British Columbia	**30,568**	13,552	17,016
Yukon	**273**	103	170
Northwest Territories	**1,316**	733	583
Nunavut	**149**	6	143
Outside Canada	**10**	0	10

Note: Expenditure-based gross domestic product.
Source: Statistics Canada, CANSIM table 384-0002.

Table 26.3 Wholesale trade, sales by trade group, 2004 to 2008

	2004	2005	2006	2007	2008
			$ millions		
All trade groups	**442,880.3**	**467,469.9**	**490,504.3**	**517,087.6**	**532,487.1**
Farm products	5,179.8	5,719.7	5,382.4	5,726.3	5,554.5
Food products	73,668.8	75,069.1	76,955.4	81,341.3	84,384.9
Alcohol and tobacco	7,555.2	7,398.9	8,292.1	9,042.6	9,572.2
Apparel	8,733.0	9,006.1	9,004.4	9,443.4	9,818.0
Home and personal products	27,773.5	30,024.0	30,464.3	32,559.7	32,495.3
Pharmaceuticals	28,624.0	30,285.4	31,945.1	34,516.9	38,125.0
Motor vehicles	72,632.7	73,251.8	75,370.0	76,801.4	66,367.0
Motor vehicle parts and accessories	17,431.0	17,961.5	18,599.5	18,871.9	19,191.7
Building supplies	35,605.3	39,687.1	43,001.3	46,333.1	46,664.4
Metal products	14,883.2	16,072.5	17,840.7	17,825.0	19,396.9
Lumber and millwork	13,832.8	13,762.0	13,273.2	12,040.1	10,542.3
Machinery and equipment	40,030.6	46,488.4	51,187.1	54,174.5	59,800.1
Computers and other electronic equipment	26,432.7	27,812.2	29,760.3	31,179.4	32,730.9
Office and professional equipment	19,112.7	20,725.9	22,552.4	24,037.9	24,595.2
Other products	51,385.0	54,205.2	56,876.1	63,194.0	73,248.8

Note: North American Industry Classification System (NAICS), 2002.
Source: Statistics Canada, CANSIM table 081-0007.

Table 26.4 Wholesale trade, sales by province and territory, 2004 to 2008

	2004	2005	2006	2007	2008
			$ millions		
Canada	**442,880.3**	**467,469.9**	**490,504.3**	**517,087.6**	**532,487.1**
Newfoundland and Labrador	2,285.0	2,405.2	2,569.0	2,855.8	3,177.4
Prince Edward Island	592.2	544.5	448.4	477.1	475.1
Nova Scotia	6,456.4	6,642.1	6,588.5	6,759.6	7,106.5
New Brunswick	4,683.5	4,838.1	4,861.2	5,115.4	5,353.8
Quebec	84,488.2	89,192.5	91,462.1	96,410.3	100,010.0
Ontario	235,402.6	242,633.6	251,523.7	261,476.0	259,947.0
Manitoba	10,058.7	10,765.4	11,785.6	13,361.6	13,668.9
Saskatchewan	11,039.0	12,073.0	12,322.2	14,453.3	20,372.2
Alberta	44,965.6	52,266.0	58,976.9	61,939.4	68,663.7
British Columbia	42,364.8	45,447.4	49,293.5	53,390.7	52,856.6
Yukon	77.7	91.9	118.4	140.1	146.1
Northwest Territories	439.7	544.9	531.7	657.4	638.6
Nunavut	27.0	25.3	23.1	50.9	71.3

Source: Statistics Canada, CANSIM table 081-0007.

Table 26.5 Retail store sales, by selected commodities, 2004 to 2008

	2004	2005	2006	2007	2008
			$ millions		
Total commodities	**347,704.0**	**367,182.5**	**390,553.4**	**413,145.8**	**426,560.8**
Food[1]	56,652.2	59,473.3	62,401.4	65,309.0	69,095.0
Non-alcoholic beverages	4,487.7	4,652.7	4,998.0	5,285.4	5,535.2
Alcoholic beverages	15,728.7	16,323.7	17,161.4	18,328.9	18,906.5
Personal care, health and beauty products (non-electric)[2]	9,136.4	9,348.3	9,842.6	10,330.5	10,566.5
Eyewear, prescription and non-prescription	1,299.1	1,327.2	1,432.3	1,522.4	1,539.5
Drugs,[3] vitamins and other health supplements	18,847.7	19,865.2	21,707.6	23,877.2	25,007.7
Luggage and jewellery	2,923.0	2,965.5	3,272.6	3,438.3	3,528.8
Clothing and accessories	22,193.5	23,034.0	24,488.7	25,434.0	25,670.9
Footwear	4,089.5	4,415.3	4,756.7	4,973.2	5,025.5
Furniture (indoor), household appliances and electronics	23,216.4	24,370.2	26,261.8	27,894.3	29,342.7
Home furnishings	8,388.7	8,831.8	9,658.6	10,671.3	10,551.7
New automotive vehicles	42,135.9	44,224.7	46,279.2	47,700.6	44,495.7
Used automotive vehicles	18,939.5	19,171.8	20,187.3	21,550.0	20,662.1
Automotive parts and accessories, labour receipts and rental receipts	15,524.0	16,722.0	17,753.5	18,096.0	19,306.6
Automotive fuels	28,204.5	33,428.9	36,406.6	40,849.9	47,495.3
Automotive oils and additives	811.9	856.6	961.2	989.4	1,036.0
Tableware, kitchenware, cookware and bakeware	1,748.9	1,805.3	1,950.4	1,996.2	2,056.9
Household cleaning supplies, chemicals and paper products	3,464.7	3,563.9	3,667.6	3,767.9	3,858.6
Other household supplies	2,073.4	2,110.7	2,171.6	2,091.2	1,959.5
Hardware and home renovation products	18,369.6	19,638.9	21,479.6	22,708.6	23,389.8
Lawn and garden products, equipment and plants	4,819.4	5,166.7	5,708.8	6,049.0	6,155.1
Sporting goods	3,844.8	3,958.8	4,104.3	4,329.3	4,285.8
Toys, games and hobby supplies[4]	2,642.7	2,797.0	3,188.5	3,757.2	4,116.1
Fabrics, yarns, sewing supplies and notions	740.7	682.5	662.8	669.8	608.3
Craft and artists' supplies	382.9	377.4	416.6	420.1	440.2
Prerecorded media[5]	1,940.9	2,068.7	1,986.1	1,909.1	1,904.3
Books, newspapers and other periodicals	2,740.4	2,863.1	2,946.8	2,985.3	2,944.2
Musical instruments, parts, accessories and supplies	502.3	499.4	453.8	453.3	460.9
Recreational vehicles	5,826.7	6,114.3	6,664.6	7,141.7	7,224.4
Pet food, supplies and accessories	1,767.7	1,947.4	2,120.2	2,250.0	2,559.7
Tobacco products and supplies	8,844.3	8,540.0	8,286.7	8,132.1	8,001.8
Giftware, novelties and souvenirs	1,297.7	1,200.6	1,329.8	1,312.4	1,378.4
Stationery, office supplies, cards, gift wrap and party supplies	3,329.9	3,534.0	3,674.8	3,752.9	3,783.8
Used and second-hand merchandise and antiques	1,394.3	1,471.6	1,636.4	1,794.7	1,765.0
Meals and lunches	889.1	927.8	1,049.6	1,134.4	1,220.1

1. Excludes pet food, meals and lunches.
2. Includes home health care sick room equipment and supplies.
3. Includes both prescription and over-the-counter drugs.
4. Includes electronic games.
5. Includes compact discs (CDs), digital video discs (DVDs) and video and audio tapes (excluding rentals).

Source: Statistics Canada, CANSIM table 080-0018.

Table 26.6 Retail sales by trade group, 2004 to 2008

	2004	2005	2006	2007	2008
			$ millions		
All trade groups	**346,721.5**	**366,170.7**	**389,485.1**	**412,037.3**	**426,033.7**
New car dealers	68,141.1	71,515.6	74,531.3	76,884.4	73,402.0
Used and recreational motor vehicle and parts dealers	14,559.2	15,301.4	17,286.5	18,673.8	19,412.4
Gasoline stations	33,363.8	38,356.8	41,753.3	46,387.6	53,156.8
Furniture stores	8,506.5	8,914.4	9,558.0	10,052.5	10,199.4
Home furnishings stores	4,438.9	4,686.3	5,337.6	5,990.9	6,066.8
Computer and software stores	1,581.8	1,557.5	1,502.1	1,421.3	1,397.3
Home electronics and appliance stores	9,443.1	10,164.8	11,146.2	12,305.9	13,322.1
Home centres and hardware stores	16,597.8	18,220.7	20,121.3	21,412.7	22,124.7
Specialized building materials and garden stores	4,372.8	4,340.4	4,640.9	5,057.1	5,057.1
Supermarkets	59,760.9	62,196.3	63,764.7	65,842.5	68,579.0
Convenience and specialty food stores	8,806.9	9,128.6	9,324.6	9,885.0	10,116.9
Beer, wine and liquor stores	13,789.8	14,343.9	15,095.1	16,140.0	16,875.6
Pharmacies and personal care stores	22,769.3	23,642.7	26,055.0	28,249.4	29,185.6
Clothing stores	15,311.6	16,069.3	17,226.6	18,247.5	18,385.4
Shoe, clothing accessory and jewellery stores	4,876.8	4,981.3	5,399.6	5,606.5	5,602.5
General merchandise stores	42,123.7	43,758.4	46,497.7	48,590.8	51,399.7
Sporting goods, hobby, book and music stores	8,831.4	9,379.3	9,994.3	10,553.9	10,790.7
Miscellaneous store retailers[1]	9,446.1	9,613.1	10,250.3	10,735.4	10,959.9

Note: North American Industry Classification System (NAICS), 2002.
1. Includes florists; office supply and stationery stores; gift, novelty and souvenir stores; used merchandise stores; pet and pet supply stores; art dealers; mobile home dealers; and all other miscellaneous store retailers.
Source: Statistics Canada, CANSIM table 080-0014.

Table 26.7 Retail sales, by province and territory, 2004 to 2008

	2004	2005	2006	2007	2008
	$ millions				
Canada	**346,721.5**	**366,170.7**	**389,485.1**	**412,037.3**	**426,033.7**
Newfoundland and Labrador	5,755.5	5,825.9	6,026.1	6,566.7	7,062.7
Prince Edward Island	1,384.7	1,423.9	1,512.2	1,628.9	1,720.6
Nova Scotia	10,296.5	10,526.9	11,162.5	11,636.1	12,129.3
New Brunswick	7,962.7	8,326.1	8,813.7	9,318.4	9,872.3
Quebec	78,517.9	82,532.5	86,708.9	90,663.3	95,321.2
Ontario	129,085.8	135,320.6	140,807.8	146,252.3	151,375.5
Manitoba	11,691.6	12,381.3	12,869.6	14,008.0	15,016.9
Saskatchewan	10,259.4	10,796.1	11,494.8	12,984.0	14,359.6
Alberta	43,371.6	48,493.0	55,941.8	61,159.8	61,069.2
British Columbia	47,216.6	49,286.3	52,837.1	56,365.4	56,562.4
Yukon	414.0	433.9	451.3	500.3	530.0
Northwest Territories	532.1	574.8	599.5	679.1	707.7
Nunavut	233.2	249.2	259.8	275.0	306.5

Source: Statistics Canada, CANSIM table 080-0014.

Table 26.8 Non-store retailers, financial estimates, by trade group, 2007

	All non-store retailers	Electronic shopping and mail-order houses	Vending machine operators and coffee service operators	Fuel dealers	Other direct selling establishments
	$ millions				
Total operating revenue	**13,029.4**	4,056.8	631.1	6,684.9	1,656.7
Sales of goods for resale	**12,364.9**	3,834.8	600.7	6,582.1	1,347.4E
Opening inventory	**600.5**	352.7	31.1	103.7	113.0
Purchases	**9,420.5**	2,651.2	299.1	5,691.1	779.2
Closing inventory	**868.0**	541.3	44.2	158.6	123.9
Cost of goods sold	**9,153.0**	2,462.6	286.0	5,636.1	768.3
Total operating expenses	**3,326.5**	1,436.8	313.5	825.9	750.3
Total labour remuneration	**1,121.0**	360.3	144.5	349.8	266.4

Note: North American Industry Classification System (NAICS), 2002.
Source: Statistics Canada, CANSIM table 080-0012.

Table 26.9 Retail trade, operating statistics, 2007

	Operating revenues	Operating expenses	Cost of goods sold	Gross margin
		$ millions		%
All trade groups	**438,348.7**	**95,435.5**	**320,117.9**	**27.0**
New car dealers	82,614.8	9,911.4	70,734.0	14.4
Used and recreational motor vehicle and parts dealers	22,120.0	4,736.7	16,607.9	24.9
Furniture stores	10,491.7	3,598.1	6,298.7	40.0
Home furnishings stores	6,314.2	2,379.1	3,594.4	43.1
Computer and software stores	2,176.9	554.0	1,570.4	27.9
Home electronics and appliance stores	13,469.9	3,245.1	9,486.6	29.6
Home centres and hardware stores	20,819.6	5,240.0	14,330.1	31.2
Specialized building materials and garden stores	6,090.2	1,956.2	3,881.5	36.3
Supermarkets	68,878.1	15,638.2	51,665.8	25.0
Convenience and specialty food stores	14,174.6	3,280.6	10,419.1	26.5
Beer, wine and liquor stores	15,986.1	2,449.7	8,818.7	44.8
Pharmacies and personal care stores	28,606.4	7,875.0	19,593.4	31.5
Gasoline stations	47,634.0	4,907.6	39,894.5	16.2
Clothing stores	18,821.7	7,775.4	9,357.0	50.3
Shoe, accessory and jewellery stores	6,056.9	2,470.9	3,026.5	50.0
Sporting goods, hobby, book and music stores	11,435.3	3,744.7	7,098.6	37.9
Department stores and other general merchandise stores	50,531.9	11,292.3	36,492.7	27.8
Miscellaneous store retailers	12,126.6	4,380.7	7,248.1	40.2

Notes: Gross margin is obtained by subtracting the cost of goods sold from the total operating revenues. The ratio is expressed as a percentage of the total operating revenues. This measure is also known as the return on sales.
North American Industry Classification System (NAICS), 2002.
Source: Statistics Canada, CANSIM, table 080-0011.

Table 26.10 Wholesale trade, operating statistics, 2007

	Operating revenues	Operating expenses	Cost of goods sold	Gross margin
		$ millions		%
All trade groups	**694,905.5**	**97,452.6**	**567,633.8**	**18.3**
Farm products	20,600.8	1,486.9	18,239.8	11.5
Petroleum products	132,014.4	3,247.4	125,396.9	5.0
Food products	84,515.7	11,556.8	68,972.3	18.4
Alcohol and tobacco products	8,946.1	1,344.8	7,221.8	19.3
Apparel	9,703.6	2,929.0	6,029.4	37.9
Household and personal goods	34,739.3	8,837.1	24,095.0	30.6
Pharmaceutical products	36,444.4	6,055.9	29,635.5	18.7
Motor vehicles	76,535.2	6,011.7	69,575.6	9.1
Motor vehicle parts and accessories	19,980.7	3,811.7	14,737.9	26.2
Building supplies	52,541.2	10,661.3	38,502.5	26.7
Metal products	18,277.4	2,277.4	15,116.0	17.3
Lumber and millwork	13,531.9	1,564.2	11,367.0	16.0
Machinery and equipment	53,270.5	10,830.6	39,458.6	25.9
Computers and other electronics	33,515.2	5,883.4	26,177.0	21.9
Office and professional equipment	24,195.8	6,688.7	15,802.5	34.7
Other products	70,005.3	11,925.1	55,321.0	21.0
Agents and brokers	6,088.1	2,340.7	1,984.9	67.4

Notes: Gross margin is obtained by subtracting the cost of goods sold from the total operating revenues. The ratio is expressed as a percentage of the total operating revenues. This measure is also known as the return on sales.
North American Industry Classification System (NAICS), 2002.
Source: Statistics Canada, CANSIM, table 081-0005.

Science and technology

Scientific research and innovation can improve our lives and make Canada a more competitive country. Countries with a well-supported science sector can get ahead economically by being the first to reap the benefits of new scientific discoveries and new technologies. Science and technology also employs hundreds of thousands of talented Canadians in private firms, government laboratories and university research programs.

How science is funded

How much a country spends on scientific research and development (R&D) is a good indicator—probably the best available—of how much research and innovation is taking place.

This indicator, gross expenditures on research and development (GERD), refers to all money spent on R&D in a given year. GERD is a key benchmark, not unlike gross domestic product (GDP) for the whole economy: like GDP, GERD is used for making national and international comparisons of R&D activity.

Canada's anticipated domestic spending on R&D totalled $29.1 billion in 2008, compared with $16.1 billion in 1998.

Businesses were expected to fund $14.4 billion; the federal government, $5.3 billion; and the higher education sector, $4.5 billion. Provincial governments, the private non-profit sector and the foreign sector funded smaller amounts.

Where the funding is spent

R&D performance is a measure of which sector did the work, as opposed to the source of funding for the work. Business enterprises were expected to account for $16.3 billion worth of work, more than half of total R&D performance. The higher education sector was expected to account for $9.8 billion, or one-third.

Chart 27.1
Gross domestic expenditures on R&D, by funding sector

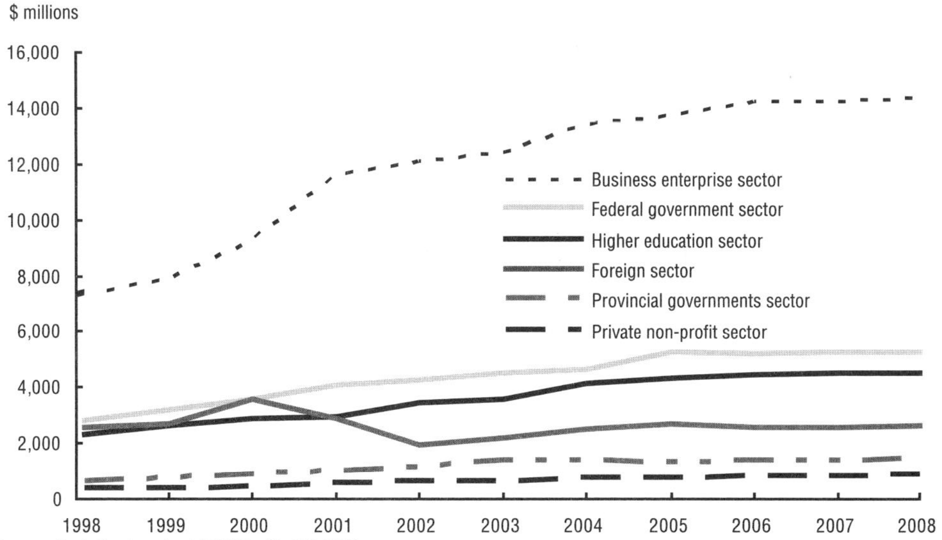

Source: Statistics Canada, CANSIM table 358-0001.

Combined, these two sectors were expected to perform 90% of Canada's R&D work in 2008, as they have since 2003.

Ontario (excluding the Ottawa region) accounted for 44% of GERD spending among the provinces in 2006, and Quebec (excluding Gatineau), 26%.

How we rank in the world

Canada's 2006 GERD spending comprised 1.9% of GDP, compared with the average among G7 nations of 2.5%. The United States spent 2.7% of GDP on GERD, the United Kingdom, 1.8%, Germany, 2.5%, and France, 2.1%. Sweden, at 3.7%, led all nations of the Organisation for Economic Co-operation and Development (OECD). Canada ranked twelfth among the 30 member nations.

Another indicator of the intensity of research and innovation is employment: according to OECD data, Canada employed 140,000 researchers in 2006, or 8.0 per 1,000 workers in the labour force.

Table 27.a
Personnel engaged in research and development, by sector

	1997	2006
	number	
Total	**145,690**	**226,250**
Federal government	13,950	15,140
Provincial governments[1]	2,970	2,820
Business enterprises[2]	82,640	148,810
Higher education	44,920	57,270
Private non-profit organizations[3]	1,210	2,210

Note: Personnel counts are reported as full-time equivalents (rounded to the nearest 10).
1. Includes provincial research organizations.
2. Natural sciences and engineering only.
3. Counts may fluctuate because of intramural research and development activities.

Source: Statistics Canada, Catalogue no. 88-001-X.

By comparison, Sweden employed 12.6 researchers per 1,000 workers in 2006; Japan, 11.1 in 2006; and the United States, 9.6 in 2005.

Chart 27.2
Gross domestic expenditure on R&D for G7 countries, 2006

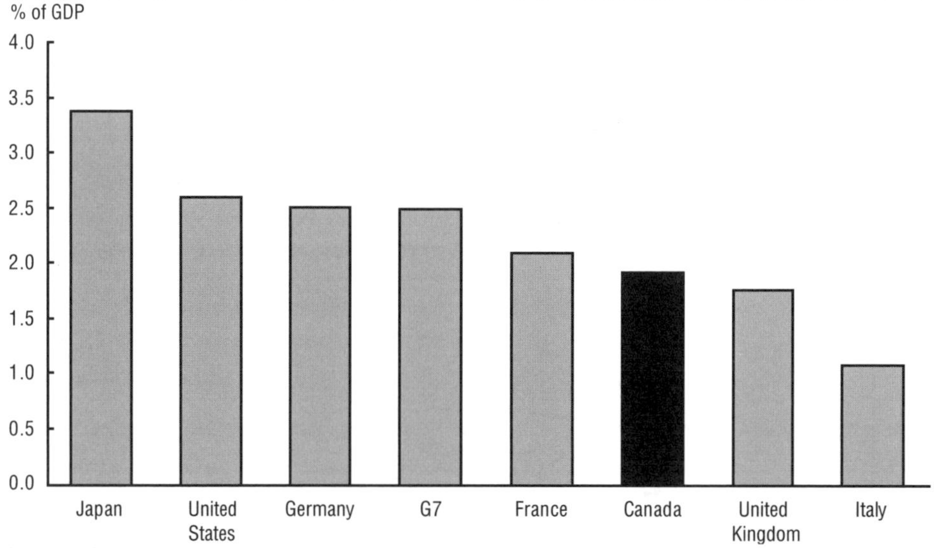

Source: *OECD in figures*, 2008.

Research and development workers in demand

The R&D that will bring tomorrow's scientific and technical advances is done by highly trained, talented people.

In 2006, 226,250 researchers, technicians and support staff worked on R&D activities in Canada, up 4.2% from 2005, and up 55% from 1997.

Researchers in natural sciences and engineering accounted for a large share of the growth over that period. Their numbers swelled 57% from 1997 to 2006: 73% of them worked in business enterprises in 2006.

The business enterprise sector employed a growing share of all R&D personnel, from 57% in 1997 to 66% in 2006.

The higher education sector gained 27% more R&D personnel from 1997 to 2006, but its share of R&D personnel shrank 6 points from 31% in 1997 to 25% in 2006.

Chart 27.3
Personnel engaged in R&D, all sectors

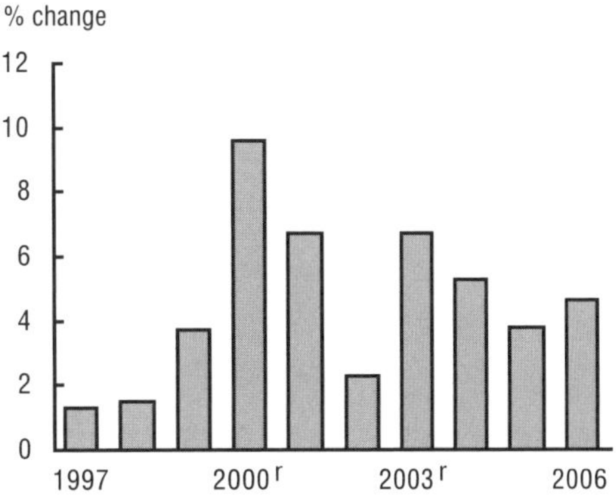

Source: Statistics Canada, Catalogue no. 88-001-X.

Three-quarters of total R&D personnel worked in Ontario and Quebec in 2006. These provinces host a significant share of the organizations that perform R&D in Canada.

Federal science and technology spending

The federal government intended to spend $9.9 billion on science and technology in the fiscal year 2008/2009. Spending intentions were down a slight 3% from the previous year, an anticipated decline after five years of growth. This activity, including R&D, takes place in the government's own laboratories and other facilities, as well as in those of companies, universities and colleges, and non-profit agencies.

Natural sciences and engineering research will receive an anticipated $7.5 billion of the total; social sciences and humanities research will receive an anticipated $2.4 billion.

Fields that are studied using federal funding include astronomy, climatology, meteorology, hydrology, geology, oceanography, energy conservation, building construction, and measurement and control of pollution.

Chart 27.4
Federal expenditures on science and technology

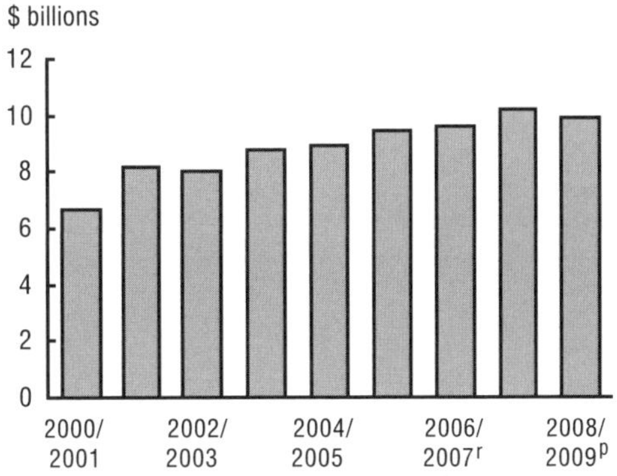

Source: Statistics Canada, Catalogue no. 88-001-X.

Table 27.1 Gross domestic expenditures on research and development, by performing sector and funding sector, 1994 to 2008

	Total	Federal government	Provincial governments	Provincial research organizations	Business enterprises	Higher education	Private non-profit	Foreign sources
	$ millions							
Performing sector								
1994	**13,341**	1,753	197	63	7,567	3,675	86	...
1995	**13,754**	1,727	186	68	7,991	3,691	91	...
1996	**13,817**	1,792	163	79	7,997	3,697	89	...
1997	**14,635**	1,720	156	58	8,739	3,879	82	...
1998	**16,088**	1,743	155	61	9,682	4,370	77	...
1999	**17,638**	1,859	173	60	10,399	5,082	63	...
2000	**20,556**	2,080	164	66	12,395	5,793	58	...
2001	**23,132**	2,103	253	23	14,266	6,424	63	...
2002	**23,531**	2,190	256	26	13,540	7,455	63	...
2003	**24,719**	2,083	254	24	14,123	8,143	92	...
2004	**26,833**	2,084	265	25	15,299	9,058	103	...
2005	**28,142**	2,414	280	23	15,791	9,518	117	...
2006	**28,715**	2,496	311	22	16,137	9,624	125	...
2007p	**28,881**	2,535	294	25	16,159	9,740	128	...
2008p	**29,071**	2,467	294	25	16,316	9,837	132	...
Funding sector								
1994	**13,341**	3,094	663	0	5,874	1,914	298	1,498
1995	**13,754**	2,989	652	0	6,288	1,926	309	1,590
1996	**13,817**	2,814	629	0	6,395	1,905	358	1,714
1997	**14,635**	2,813	656	1	7,030	1,971	367	1,795
1998	**16,088**	2,830	640	0	7,355	2,339	372	2,552
1999	**17,638**	3,216	767	3	7,917	2,649	380	2,705
2000	**20,556**	3,560	853	1	9,223	2,892	445	3,582
2001	**23,132**	4,095	1,023	0	11,636	2,928	536	2,915
2002	**23,531**	4,251	1,152	0	12,112	3,462	628	1,925
2003	**24,719**	4,526	1,354	0	12,447	3,589	637	2,167
2004	**26,833**	4,651	1,370	0	13,404	4,147	735	2,526
2005	**28,142**	5,248	1,341	0	13,756	4,341	777	2,676
2006	**28,715**	5,225	1,407	0	14,234	4,434	830	2,585
2007p	**28,881**	5,291	1,404	0	14,267	4,487	835	2,596
2008p	**29,071**	5,272	1,414	0	14,386	4,532	850	2,616

Source: Statistics Canada, CANSIM table 358-0001.

Table 27.2 Gross domestic expenditures on research and development, by province and territory, 1994, 1998, 2002 and 2006

	1994	1998	2002	2006
	$ millions			
Canada	**13,341**	**16,088**	**23,531**	**28,715**
National Capital Region	789	811	1,015	1,098
Newfoundland and Labrador	108	119	153	262
Prince Edward Island	17	24	31	70
Nova Scotia	265	311	400	502
New Brunswick	134	155	211	271
Quebec[1]	3,495	4,325	6,681	7,595
Ontario[1]	5,940	7,421	10,426	12,685
Manitoba	311	283	454	558
Saskatchewan	239	279	435	465
Alberta	966	1,174	1,709	2,412
British Columbia	1,067	1,107	1,949	2,644
Yukon, Northwest Territories and Nunavut	10	5	4	28

1. Excludes federal government expenditures for work done in the National Capital Region.
Source: Statistics Canada, CANSIM table 358-0001.

Table 27.3 Gross domestic expenditures on research and development, health sector compared with all sectors, 1988 to 2008

	All sectors	Health sector		
	$ millions	$ millions	% of all sectors	$ per capita
1988	**9,045**	1,221	13.5	46
1989	**9,517**	1,365	14.3	50
1990	**10,260**	1,551	15.1	56
1991	**10,767**	1,665	15.5	59
1992	**11,338**	1,783	15.7	63
1993	**12,184**	2,006	16.5	70
1994	**13,341**	2,105	15.8	73
1995	**13,754**	2,196	16.0	75
1996	**13,817**	2,316	16.8	78
1997	**14,635**	2,644	18.1	88
1998	**16,088**	2,930	18.2	97
1999	**17,638**	3,246	18.4	107
2000	**20,556**	3,696	18.0	120
2001	**23,132**	4,383	18.9	141
2002	**23,531**	5,273	22.4	168
2003	**24,719**	5,361	21.7	169
2004	**26,833**	6,127[r]	22.8	192
2005	**28,142**	6,298[r]	22.4	195
2006	**28,715**	6,022[r]	21.0	185
2007	**28,881**[p]	6,109[1]	21.2	186
2008	**29,071**[p]	6,162[1]	21.2	185

1. Estimate.
Source: Statistics Canada, CANSIM table 358-0001 and Catalogue no. 88-001-X.

Table 27.4 Federal expenditures on research and development, by performing province and territory and funding province and territory, 1992 to 2006

	Canada	National Capital Region	Newfoundland and Labrador	Prince Edward Island	Nova Scotia	New Brunswick
	$ millions					
Performing province						
1992	**1,716**	753	35	9	73	36
1993	**1,757**	774	36	11	75	33
1994	**1,753**	789	33	11	84	28
1995	**1,727**	805	27	9	77	29
1996	**1,792**	771	25	10	79	32
1997	**1,720**	757	23	10	71	29
1998	**1,743**	811	26	10	77	32
1999	**1,859**	808	26	12	72	32
2000	**2,080**	889	30	16	88	27
2001	**2,103**	926	27	16	70	26
2002	**2,190**	1,015	32	8	76	46
2003	**2,083**	999	23	12	66	30
2004	**2,084**	960	23	10	81	26
2005	**2,414**	1,123	28	28	66	26
2006	**2,496**	1,098	27	26	73	30
Funding province						
1992	**3,109**	748	62	10	125	54
1993	**3,156**	767	59	12	120	63
1994	**3,094**	784	52	12	127	60
1995	**2,989**	796	42	11	113	60
1996	**2,814**	755	42	12	112	44
1997	**2,813**	741	40	11	108	42
1998	**2,830**	798	45	12	113	44
1999	**3,216**	795	48	13	113	49
2000	**3,560**	872	54	19	129	42
2001	**4,095**	907	53	19	121	45
2002	**4,251**	994	63	13	131	68
2003	**4,526**	983	61	20	131	61
2004	**4,651**	945	61	18	157	57
2005	**5,248**	1,103	80	37	150	63
2006	**5,225**	1,080	75	35	158	65

1. Quebec and Ontario figures exclude federal government expenditures for work done in the National Capital Region.
Source: Statistics Canada, CANSIM table 358-0001.

Quebec[1]	Ontario[1]	Manitoba	Saskatchewan	Alberta	British Columbia	Territories
			$ millions			
234	274	81	56	78	86	1
250	276	83	54	75	88	2
225	253	79	48	93	103	7
218	259	71	52	98	81	1
226	348	77	47	94	77	5
211	302	59	74	96	83	5
227	276	49	54	94	84	4
250	322	58	60	108	106	7
350	314	69	62	116	111	9
372	328	77	63	98	97	3
370	324	72	53	92	99	3
314	351	63	54	87	80	5
320	329	73	54	110	91	6
368	395	83	68	130	91	9
371	494	81	67	133	91	5
634	848	119	89	167	252	1
660	849	121	87	164	251	2
592	799	119	82	190	270	7
580	756	108	81	207	234	1
546	714	106	74	191	204	5
546	738	85	97	194	200	5
541	732	74	78	182	198	4
665	866	92	103	218	238	7
806	899	111	120	234	262	8
999	1,126	124	123	282	290	3
993	1,114	130	113	282	338	3
1,053	1,286	131	121	321	340	5
1,067	1,323	146	123	328	409	5
1,164	1,497	157	126	405	417	9
1,146	1,563	150	122	372	419	4

Table 27.5 Federal expenditures on science and technology, by province and territory, 1999/2000 to 2005/2006

	1999/2000	2000/2001	2001/2002	2002/2003	2003/2004	2004/2005	2005/2006
	$ millions						
Canada	**5,640**	**6,084**	**7,476**	**7,300**	**7,976**	**8,156**	**8,682**
National Capital Region[1]	1,981	2,130	2,603	2,608	2,642	2,708	2,912
Newfoundland and Labrador	87	101	95	117	121	137	128
Prince Edward Island	20	29	26	24	33	39	47
Nova Scotia	197	220	225	247	257	294	261
New Brunswick	72	68	82	102	100	122	93
Quebec[2]	833	1,017	1,381	1,243	1,328	1,352	1,485
Ontario[2]	1,309	1,347	1,653	1,582	2,038	1,967	2,101
Manitoba	161	190	211	214	194	226	254
Saskatchewan	131	148	165	151	159	157	193
Alberta	301	327	476	395	469	474	484
British Columbia	528	479	525	582	588	645	673
Yukon, Northwest Territories and Nunavut	20	28	34	35	46	35	51

1. Federal intramural expenditures only.
2. Includes extramural expenditures made in the National Capital Region and executed within the province.
Source: Statistics Canada, Catalogue no. 88-001-X.

Table 27.6 Federal expenditures on research and development, by activity, 2003/2004 to 2008/2009

	2003/2004	2004/2005	2005/2006	2006/2007[r]	2007/2008[p]	2008/2009[p]
	$ millions					
Research and development and related scientific activities	**8,765**	**8,934**	**9,449**	**9,633**	**10,164**	**9,863**
Research and development	5,462	5,454	6,042	6,073	6,481	6,222
Current expenditures	5,033	5,033	5,611	5,642	6,058	5,804
Administration of extramural programs	257	269	285	279	287	302
Capital expenditures	172	152	146	152	136	116
Related scientific activities	3,303	3,480	3,407	3,560	3,683	3,641
Data collection	1,618	1,702	1,715	1,870	1,756	1,786
Information services	663	679	676	669	707	698
Special services and studies	615	666	627	576	743	665
Education support	206	230	259	298	314	326
Administration of extramural programs	56	58	59	64	66	69
Capital expenditures	145	146	70	83	96	97

Source: Statistics Canada, Catalogue no. 88-001-X.

Table 27.7 Research and development performed by the business enterprise sector, 2004 to 2008

	2004r	2005r	2006p	2007p	2008p
	All industries				
	$ millions				
Total research and development expenditures	**15,299**	**15,791**	**16,137**	**16,159**	**16,316E**
Current expenditures	14,220	14,696	15,028	15,159	15,349E
Wages and salaries	8,106	8,558	8,885	9,008	9,103E
Other current expenditures	6,115	6,138	6,143	6,151	6,245E
Capital expenditures	1,078	1,095	1,109	1,000	968E
	number of full-time equivalents				
Total research and development personnel	**138,113**	**140,610**	**148,813**	..	..
Professionals	81,295	83,689	87,577	..	..
Technicians	39,828	39,796	44,284	..	..
Other support staff	16,990	17,125	16,952	..	..

Note: Business enterprise research and development refers to research and development activities performed in Canada by the industrial (business enterprise) sector.
Source: Statistics Canada, CANSIM table 358-0024 and Catalogue no. 88-202-X.

Table 27.8 Intellectual property management at universities and research hospitals, 1999 to 2006

	1999	2001	2003	2004	2005	2006
	%					
Institutions engaged in intellectual property management	61	66	72	76	80	82
	number					
Full-time equivalent employees engaged in intellectual property management	178	221	255	280	292	323
Research contracts	5,748	8,247	11,432	14,324	15,877	13,996
Invention disclosures	893	1,105	1,133	1,432	1,452	1,356
Inventions protected[1]	549	682	527	629	761	707
Inventions declined by the institution	..	..	256	355	322	353
Patent applications	656	932	1,252	1,264	1,410	1,442
Patents issued	349	381	347	397	376	339
Patents held	1,915	2,133	3,047	3,827	3,961	4,784
New licences and options	232	354	422	494	621	437
Active licences and options	1,165	1,424	1,756	2,022	2,836	2,038
	$ thousands					
Total operational expenditures for intellectual property management	22,018	28,505	36,419	36,927	41,544	42,492
Value of research contracts	393,358	527,051	810,431	940,993	1,001,270	1,154,268
Income from intellectual property	24,745	52,510	55,525	51,210	55,173	59,689
Value of remaining equity held by the institution in publicly traded spin-offs	54,560	45,120	52,351	49,872	41,336	41,524
Investment in spin-offs raised with the assistance of the institution	..	..	54,640	56,421	23,002	x

Note: Data were not collected for 2000 and 2002.
1. Resulted in protection activity.
Source: Statistics Canada, CANSIM table 358-0025.

Table 27.9 University enrolment in natural and applied science and technology programs, by sex, 2002/2003 to 2006/2007

	2002/2003	2003/2004	2004/2005	2005/2006	2006/2007
			number		
All instructional programs					
Both sexes[1]	936,390	993,768	1,019,775	1,047,690	1,057,272
Men	398,070	419,640	431,544	442,368	445,329
Women	538,257	573,876	587,994	604,956	611,688
Physical and life sciences and technologies					
Both sexes[1]	81,804	87,261	92,199	94,497	93,564
Men	36,372	38,388	40,686	42,357	42,027
Women	45,429	48,864	51,513	52,134	51,531
Mathematics, computer and information sciences					
Both sexes[1]	45,837	43,977	40,764	36,600	33,900
Men	33,120	32,121	29,751	26,652	24,636
Women	12,714	11,832	10,971	9,945	9,255
Architecture, engineering and related technologies					
Both sexes[1]	81,096	85,785	86,529	85,503	85,755
Men	62,388	66,543	67,422	67,533	67,563
Women	18,702	19,233	19,104	17,970	18,174
Agriculture, natural resources and conservation					
Both sexes[1]	14,592	14,769	14,925	15,264	15,501
Men	6,720	6,654	6,696	6,774	6,786
Women	7,869	8,112	8,223	8,490	8,709

Notes: All counts are randomly rounded to a multiple of 3.
Historical data coded with the University Student Information System classification have been converted to the Classification of Instructional Programs 2000.
1. Figures may not add to totals because of the exclusion of the 'sex unknown' category in the table or because of rounding.
Source: Statistics Canada, CANSIM table 477-0013.

Seniors

Canada's population aged 65 and older has more than doubled in the past 35 years to 4.3 million—or 13% of the population—in 2006. Medium-growth scenarios suggest the senior population will grow to 23% in 2031.

The very elderly group (80 and older) is also growing quickly. From 1996 to 2006, their numbers swelled by 46% to reach 1.2 million. By 2031, this figure could rise by another 110% to reach 2.5 million.

Although Canada is one of the youngest of the G8 countries, the size of the baby boom following the Second World War should contribute to more rapid aging of the population than in other industrialized countries.

From workforce adjustments to retirement plans, the growing ranks of seniors will affect Canadian society. In 2006, there were just over 5 people aged 15 to 64 years for each person aged 65 years and older. This ratio gives an approximation of how many elderly people there are in relation to the pool of potential workers.

By comparison, the ratio in 1956 was almost 8 working-age adults for each person aged 65 years and older. By 2056, medium-growth scenarios indicate a further decline to 2.2 working-age persons for each elderly person.

Still working

Many seniors are continuing to work after retirement age, particularly university-educated and self-employed seniors. Women of the baby boom generation are also remaining longer in the workforce after retirement age. In 2007, women made up 35% of senior workers, a proportion expected to increase in future years.

While most near-retirees get financial advice about retirement planning and programs, almost 3 in 10 do not. Those

Chart 28.1
People aged 45 to 64 in the working-age population

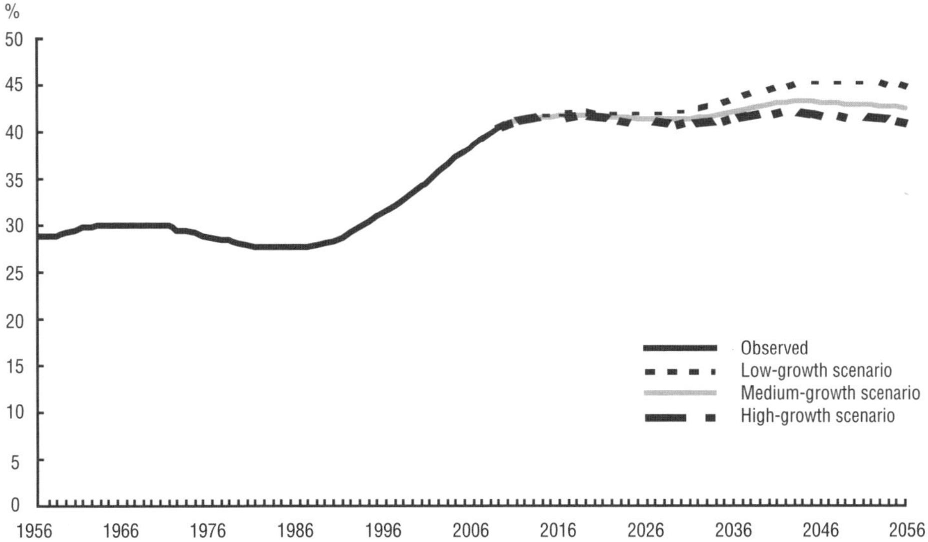

Note: Working-age population refers to people aged 15 to 64.
Source: Statistics Canada, CANSIM tables 051-0001, 051-0026 and 052-0004.

not receiving financial advice are less likely to expect their retirement income to be adequate than those who do. This relationship remains even when other characteristics such as income, pension coverage and registered retirement savings plan assets are taken into account.

Most Canadians (65%) approaching retirement anticipate that their retirement income will be adequate or more than adequate to maintain their standard of living. However, 19% of Canadians expect it to be barely adequate and 9% less than adequate.

On average, Canadian workers had family disposable incomes at age 75 (when most are retired) that were 80% of their incomes at age 55 (when they were working).

The proportion of seniors has grown more quickly in rural areas in recent years than it has in urban areas. From 1996 to 2006, seniors' share of the rural population rose 2.1 percentage points; their share of the urban population rose 1.1 percentage points. This shift may be the result of much higher immigration levels in urban areas as well as younger people migrating out of the rural areas to urban areas.

Table 28.a
Population aged 65 and older, by age group and sex

	1998		2008	
	Male	Female	Male	Female
	number			
Total	**1,585,571**	**2,138,902**	**2,007,880**	**2,555,239**
65 to 69	548,330	595,152	651,061	694,986
70 to 74	441,194	543,491	497,439	563,212
75 to 79	311,293	445,542	404,712	498,478
80 to 84	174,266	295,337	268,108	398,827
85 to 89	80,349	170,510	134,814	257,332
90 and older	30,139	88,870	51,746	142,404

Note: Estimates as of July 1.
Source: Statistics Canada, CANSIM table 051-0001.

Chart 28.2
Population, by age group and type of region

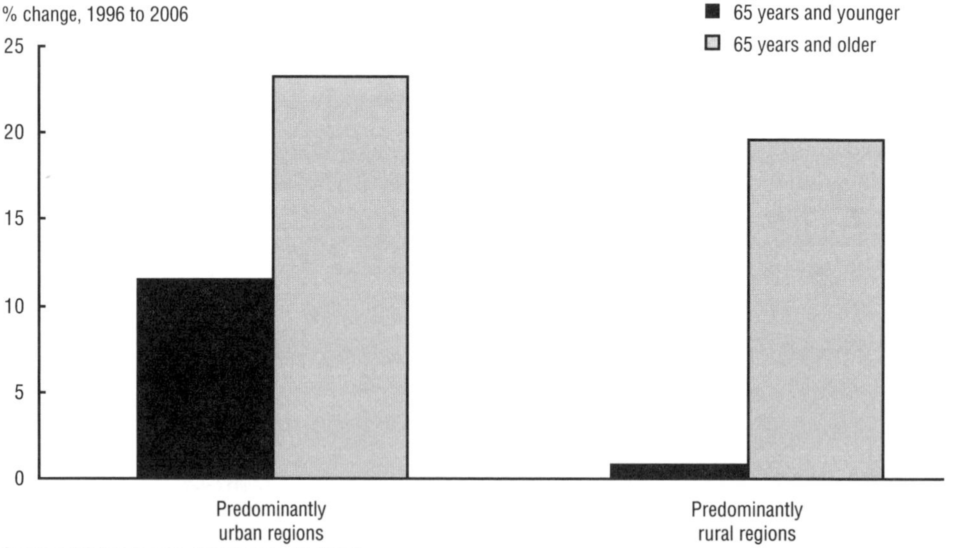

Source: Statistics Canada, Catalogue no. 21-006-X.

Retiring together, or not

Throughout much of the last century, older couples faced only one retirement decision—the husband's. However, the rise and sustained participation of women in the paid labour force since the 1970s transformed the retirement transitions of married couples. Increasingly, couples have to make two decisions and balance the preferences and constraints of partners who both made substantial contributions to household income.

Evidence indicates that, instead of retiring together, through the 1990s such dual-income couples were increasingly retiring at different times.

The opportunity to retire jointly may be constrained by factors such as age differences, health conditions, eligibility for pensions, job loss and career aspirations.

The likelihood that spouses will retire jointly is greater among older couples than younger couples. The age difference between spouses was also a factor. A wife who is much younger than her husband is more likely to continue working after he retires than a wife who is about the same age as or older than her husband.

Chart 28.3
Retirement transitions, 2001

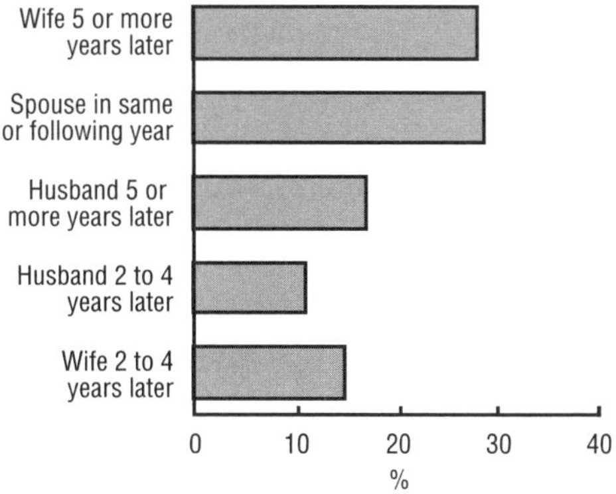

Note: Dual-earner couples in the 2001 retiring cohort.
Source: Statistics Canada, Catalogue no. 75-001-X.

Who's caring for seniors?

In 2007, about 2.7 million Canadians aged 45 and older, or approximately one-fifth of people in this age group, provided some form of unpaid care to seniors who had long-term health problems.

Fifty-four percent of caregivers reported that they were coping "very well" with their caregiving responsibilities. Another 42% said they were "generally okay" with this role.

Many people giving care to seniors balance this and other roles, such as jobs and caring for their own children. About 43% of caregivers were aged 45 to 54, a time of life when many Canadians still have children living at home.

Caregivers are more likely to be women who were employed and married. In 2007, one in four caregivers were themselves seniors; one-third of these senior caregivers were over the age of 75.

Chart 28.4
Caregiver's sources of support

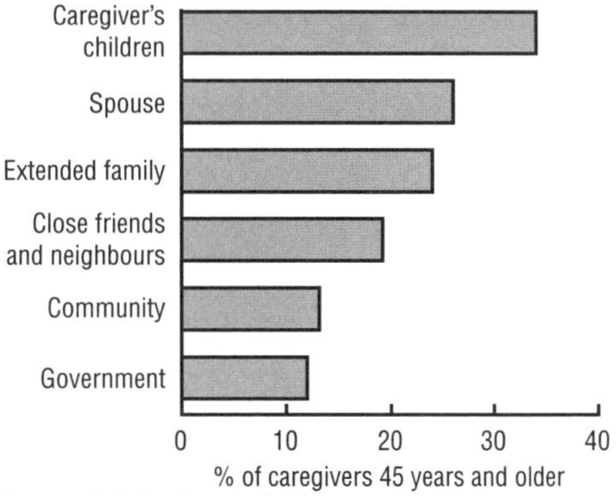

Source: Statistics Canada, Catalogue no. 11-008-X.

Table 28.1 Population estimates, by age group and by province and territory, selected years from 1983 to 2008

	1983			1988			1993		
	0 to 14	15 to 64	65 and older	0 to 14	15 to 64	65 and older	0 to 14	15 to 64	65 and older
	thousands								
Canada	**5,523.1**	**17,344.5**	**2,498.9**	**5,574.8**	**18,288.2**	**2,928.7**	**5,926.1**	**19,392.6**	**3,366.1**
Newfoundland and Labrador	160.9	371.9	46.4	139.0	383.3	52.7	122.9	399.6	57.5
Prince Edward Island	30.0	79.6	15.5	29.4	83.2	16.6	29.4	85.5	17.3
Nova Scotia	195.1	575.9	97.3	186.3	602.0	109.0	185.5	621.5	117.0
New Brunswick	170.1	470.6	74.1	157.7	488.7	83.9	150.9	506.3	91.7
Quebec	1,384.5	4,615.3	603.2	1,367.7	4,763.2	706.1	1,409.9	4,928.3	818.3
Ontario	1,900.8	6,221.5	917.2	1,981.7	6,770.1	1,086.8	2,180.4	7,241.3	1,268.3
Manitoba	240.0	692.8	127.0	241.3	719.9	140.9	244.6	722.4	150.6
Saskatchewan	244.2	635.3	121.7	247.4	646.4	134.5	237.3	625.1	144.5
Alberta	568.5	1,650.9	174.2	575.8	1,672.2	208.6	623.6	1,795.7	247.9
British Columbia	606.0	1,981.4	320.0	624.3	2,103.5	386.9	713.6	2,403.9	450.2
Yukon	6.1	16.8	0.8	6.5	19.2	1.0	7.4	21.7	1.2
Northwest Territories (including Nunavut)	16.9	32.5	1.4	17.6	36.5	1.7	..	..	..
Northwest Territories	..	..	..	..	..	..	11.4	27.1	1.3
Nunavut	..	..	..	..	..	..	9.0	14.1	0.5
	%								
Canada	**21.8**	**68.4**	**9.9**	**20.8**	**68.3**	**10.9**	**20.7**	**67.6**	**11.7**
Newfoundland and Labrador	27.8	64.2	8.0	24.2	66.7	9.2	21.2	68.9	9.9
Prince Edward Island	24.0	63.6	12.4	22.8	64.4	12.9	22.2	64.7	13.1
Nova Scotia	22.5	66.3	11.2	20.8	67.1	12.1	20.1	67.3	12.7
New Brunswick	23.8	65.8	10.4	21.6	66.9	11.5	20.1	67.6	12.2
Quebec	21.0	69.9	9.1	20.0	69.7	10.3	19.7	68.9	11.4
Ontario	21.0	68.8	10.1	20.1	68.8	11.0	20.4	67.7	11.9
Manitoba	22.6	65.4	12.0	21.9	65.3	12.8	21.9	64.6	13.5
Saskatchewan	24.4	63.4	12.2	24.1	62.9	13.1	23.6	62.1	14.3
Alberta	23.8	69.0	7.3	23.4	68.1	8.5	23.4	67.3	9.3
British Columbia	20.8	68.1	11.0	20.0	67.5	12.4	20.0	67.4	12.6
Yukon	25.8	70.8	3.4	24.4	71.9	3.7	24.5	71.6	3.9
Northwest Territories (including Nunavut)	33.2	64.0	2.9	31.6	65.5	3.0	..	..	..
Northwest Territories	..	..	..	..	..	..	28.7	68.1	3.2
Nunavut	..	..	..	..	..	..	38.0	60.0	2.0

Source: Statistics Canada, CANSIM table 051-0001.

1998			2003			2008		
0 to 14	15 to 64	65 and older	0 to 14	15 to 64	65 and older	0 to 14	15 to 64	65 and older
				thousands				
5,958.4	**20,472.3**	**3,724.5**	**5,795.7**	**21,779.6**	**4,064.3**	**5,597.7**	**23,150.6**	**4,563.1**
100.3	378.3	61.2	85.0	368.1	65.4	76.3	358.3	73.3
28.2	89.6	18.0	25.6	92.6	19.1	23.4	95.3	21.1
176.6	632.0	123.2	160.2	646.4	130.9	142.7	651.1	144.4
140.0	513.7	96.8	127.0	520.3	102.1	115.8	517.9	113.6
1,351.8	5,034.9	909.2	1,293.0	5,196.3	996.6	1,232.2	5,385.7	1,132.7
2,280.6	7,672.7	1,412.6	2,302.3	8,388.0	1,552.0	2,218.8	8,966.3	1,743.9
243.1	738.9	155.4	235.2	770.2	158.4	229.2	812.3	166.5
225.9	643.1	148.3	202.3	646.3	147.9	193.0	671.5	151.6
631.7	1,980.6	286.8	630.8	2,225.3	327.3	654.5	2,556.4	374.2
752.0	2,722.0	509.1	707.3	2,854.8	560.2	686.2	3,059.1	636.4
7.0	22.6	26.2	6.1	23.0	1.9	5.8	24.9	2.5
..	..	..	..	..	..	..	..	..
11.3	28.0	1.6	10.7	30.1	1.8	9.6	31.5	2.1
9.9	15.9	0.6	10.4	18.3	0.7	10.3	20.2	0.9
				%				
19.8	**67.9**	**12.4**	**18.3**	**68.8**	**12.8**	**16.8**	**69.5**	**13.7**
18.6	70.1	11.3	16.4	71.0	12.6	15.0	70.6	14.4
20.8	66.0	13.2	18.6	67.5	13.9	16.7	68.2	15.1
19.0	67.8	13.2	17.1	69.0	14.0	15.2	69.4	15.4
18.6	68.5	12.9	16.9	69.4	13.6	15.5	69.3	15.2
18.5	69.0	12.5	17.3	69.4	13.3	15.9	69.5	14.6
20.1	67.5	12.4	18.8	68.5	12.7	17.2	69.4	13.5
21.4	65.0	13.7	20.2	66.2	13.6	19.0	67.2	13.8
22.2	63.2	14.6	20.3	64.9	14.8	19.0	66.1	14.9
21.8	68.3	9.9	19.8	69.9	10.3	18.3	71.3	10.4
18.9	68.3	12.8	17.2	69.3	13.6	15.7	69.8	14.5
22.6	72.4	4.9	19.6	74.2	6.3	17.4	75.1	7.5
..	..	..	..	..	..	..	..	..
27.6	68.5	3.9	25.1	70.8	4.2	22.3	72.8	5.0
37.5	60.3	90.8	35.3	62.3	2.4	32.8	64.4	2.8

Table 28.2 Senior population, selected census metropolitan areas, selected years from 1987 to 2007

	1987	1992	1997	2002	2007
			%		
All census metropolitan areas	**10.2**	**11.0**	**11.6**	**11.9**	**12.5**
St. John's	9.6	9.4	10.1	10.5	11.0
Halifax	9.1	9.8	10.3	10.9	11.8
Saint John	12.3	12.3	12.7	12.9	13.4
Québec	9.6	10.8	11.9	13.1	14.5
Sherbrooke	10.6	11.6	12.3	13.1	14.2
Montréal	10.3	11.3	12.2	12.8	13.6
Ottawa–Gatineau	9.0	9.5	10.3	10.6	11.6
Toronto	9.6	10.3	10.9	10.9	11.3
Thunder Bay	11.0	13.2	14.0	14.8	15.9
Winnipeg	12.2	12.9	13.3	13.4	13.3
Regina	10.5	11.0	11.8	12.5	13.0
Calgary	7.2	7.9	8.7	8.9	9.1
Vancouver	12.0	12.0	11.6	11.9	12.3
Victoria	18.2	18.2	17.5	17.2	17.2

Note: Seniors are people aged 65 and older, based on 2001 census geographic regions.
Source: Statistics Canada, CANSIM table 051-0036.

Table 28.3 Life expectancy at birth and at age 65, by sex, selected years from 1921 to 2006

	Life expectancy at birth			Life expectancy at age 65		
	Both sexes	Males	Females	Both sexes	Males	Females
			years			
1921	**59.7**	58.8	60.6	**13.3**	13.0	13.6
1931	**61.0**	60.0	62.1	**13.3**	13.0	13.7
1941	**64.6**	63.0	66.3	**13.4**	12.8	14.1
1951	**68.5**	66.4	70.9	**14.1**	13.3	15.0
1961	**71.1**	68.4	74.3	**14.8**	13.6	16.1
1971	**72.7**	69.4	76.5	**15.7**	13.8	17.6
1981	**75.4**	71.9	79.1	**16.8**	14.6	18.9
1992	**78.0**	74.8	81.2	**18.2**	16.0	20.1
2002	**79.7**	77.2	82.1	**19.1**	17.2	20.6
2003	**79.9**	77.4	82.4	**19.2**	17.4	20.8
2004	**80.2**	77.8	82.6	**19.5**	17.7	21.0
2005	**80.4**	78.0	82.7	**19.6**	17.9	21.1
2006	**80.8**	78.4	83.0	**19.9**	18.2	21.4

Notes: Life expectancy estimates for 1921 to 1981 are based on complete life tables.
Newfoundland and Labrador is not included in the 1921 to 1941 life expectancy estimates.
Quebec is not included in the 1921 life expectancy estimates.
Source: Statistics Canada, CANSIM table 102-0511.

Table 28.4 Income of seniors, by income sources, 2002 to 2006

	2002	2003	2004	2005	2006
			number of seniors		
Total income	**3,900,870**	**3,981,550**	**4,047,910**	**4,134,590**	**4,232,680**
Total employment income	655,390	717,310	753,480	790,360	847,790
Wages, salaries and commissions	458,220	516,300	544,980	569,420	619,530
Self-employment	237,490	245,010	256,880	271,930	284,370
Investment income	2,304,320	2,297,960	2,337,730	2,385,030	2,464,280
Total government transfers	3,854,910	3,939,000	4,007,400	4,095,270	4,197,130
Employment Insurance	30,920	33,670	34,180	35,600	38,600
Old Age Security and net federal supplements	3,752,780	3,834,700	3,903,670	3,991,510	4,089,690
Canada Pension Plan and Quebec Pension Plan	3,385,960	3,485,330	3,572,590	3,672,410	3,780,480
Canada Child Tax Benefit	8,150	8,350	6,850	6,600	7,520
Goods and Services Tax Credit and Harmonized Sales Tax Credit	1,881,540	1,891,190	1,869,410	1,928,390	2,050,160
Workers' compensation	97,640	98,780	100,670	103,710	105,530
Social assistance	245,980	234,890	243,410	249,130	249,190
Provincial refundable tax credits and family benefits	1,633,980	1,701,120	1,656,500	1,691,570	2,005,630
Private pensions	2,193,560	2,267,740	2,340,170	2,415,010	2,494,340
Registered Retirement Savings Plans	385,870	384,650	388,550	415,630	382,970
Other income[1]	818,820	811,820	957,660	1,082,520	1,196,340
			$ thousands		
Total income	**105,480,835**	**110,103,805**	**116,440,076**	**123,758,734**	**134,270,968**
Total employment income	10,853,438	11,689,553	12,778,538	14,494,560	16,402,798
Wages, salaries and commissions	8,773,451	9,544,431	10,349,265	11,935,868	13,541,692
Self-employment	2,079,987	2,145,122	2,429,273	2,558,692	2,861,105
Investment income	13,274,854	13,151,553	13,253,077	13,660,905	15,790,904
Total government transfers	46,106,044	48,234,794	50,433,512	52,657,997	55,715,074
Employment Insurance	159,354	176,632	180,530	191,054	211,263
Old Age Security and net federal supplements	24,309,389	25,528,765	26,436,896	27,560,921	29,083,974
Canada Pension Plan and Quebec Pension Plan	19,225,892	20,100,873	21,264,457	22,247,273	23,397,612
Canada Child Tax Benefit	18,412	19,873	16,762	17,622	20,843
Goods and Services Tax Credit and Harmonized Sales Tax Credit	602,544	613,944	623,474	657,189	825,792
Workers' compensation	717,418	705,704	728,941	768,363	791,413
Social assistance	444,997	447,725	472,841	499,139	508,994
Provincial refundable tax credits and family benefits	628,038	641,280	709,611	716,436	875,184
Private pensions	29,537,427	31,141,959	33,514,633	35,800,725	38,520,388
Registered Retirement Savings Plans	2,377,507	2,370,551	2,467,223	2,595,343	2,611,953
Other income[1]	3,331,564	3,515,396	3,993,093	4,549,203	5,229,851
			$		
Median total income	**18,500**	**18,800**	**19,400**	**20,100**	**21,000**

Note: Seniors are people aged 65 and older.
1. Comprises taxable income not reported elsewhere, such as net rental income, support payments, retiring allowances and scholarships.
Source: Statistics Canada, CANSIM table 111-0035.

Table 28.5 Labour force characteristics, population aged 65 and older, by age group and sex, 1995 to 2008

	1995	1996	1997	1998	1999	2000
	thousands					
Males 65 and older	**1,404.2**	**1,437.3**	**1,472.1**	**1,505.6**	**1,535.0**	**1,565.8**
Labour force	139.7	140.4	144.8	154.1	150.8	148.7
Full-time employment	87.9	86.3	92.0	99.2	95.7	91.4
Part-time employment	46.4	49.1	48.5	50.7	50.5	53.6
Unemployment	5.4	5.1	4.3	4.2	4.6	3.8
Not in labour force	1,264.6	1,296.9	1,327.3	1,351.5	1,384.2	1,417.0
Males 65 to 69	513.4	521.9	531.2	536.8	538.8	538.3
Labour force	85.8	86.3	89.3	94.8	91.0	86.2
Full-time employment	56.1	54.6	58.8	63.5	60.1	53.9
Part-time employment	25.2	27.8	26.7	28.4	28.4	29.4
Unemployment	4.5	3.9	3.8	2.9	2.5	2.9
Not in labour force	427.6	435.7	441.9	442.0	447.8	452.2
Males 70 and older	890.8	915.4	940.8	968.8	996.2	1,027.4
Labour force	53.9	54.1	55.5	59.2	59.8	62.6
Full-time employment	31.8	31.6	33.2	35.7	35.6	37.5
Part-time employment	21.2	21.3	21.8	22.3	22.1	24.2
Unemployment	x	x	x	x	2.0	x
Not in labour force	837.0	861.2	885.4	909.5	936.4	964.9
Females 65 and older	**1,850.0**	**1,885.4**	**1,919.1**	**1,949.0**	**1,975.8**	**2,004.3**
Labour force	62.0	63.5	69.0	69.0	67.4	66.4
Full-time employment	24.2	24.6	27.1	28.9	30.7	27.4
Part-time employment	34.6	36.1	39.6	38.1	35.2	37.0
Unemployment	3.2	2.7	2.3	2.0	x	1.9
Not in labour force	1,788.0	1,821.9	1,850.0	1,880.0	1,908.4	1,938.0
Females 65 to 69	576.5	578.9	582.3	583.4	582.2	580.5
Labour force	42.1	40.9	45.2	43.1	41.6	41.6
Full-time employment	17.1	16.4	19.1	19.6	19.1	18.9
Part-time employment	22.1	22.8	24.4	22.0	21.3	21.2
Unemployment	2.9	1.7	1.8	1.6	x	1.5
Not in labour force	534.5	537.9	537.1	540.3	540.6	538.9
Females 70 and older	1,273.5	1,306.5	1,336.8	1,365.5	1,393.5	1,423.8
Labour force	19.9	22.6	23.8	25.9	25.7	24.7
Full-time employment	7.0	8.3	8.1	9.4	11.5	8.5
Part-time employment	12.6	13.3	15.2	16.1	13.9	15.8
Unemployment	x	x	x	x	x	x
Not in labour force	1,253.6	1,283.9	1,312.9	1,339.7	1,367.8	1,399.1

Source: Statistics Canada, CANSIM table 282-0002.

2001	2002	2003	2004	2005	2006	2007	2008
thousands							
1,598.9	**1,631.7**	**1,667.3**	**1,704.7**	**1,745.6**	**1,792.4**	**1,844.5**	**1,907.3**
150.5	168.3	192.2	200.4	210.4	216.6	239.3	270.7
95.5	105.0	118.4	123.3	132.3	131.3	146.9	171.3
50.5	58.2	67.0	70.9	71.4	75.3	83.7	91.9
4.4	5.1	6.7	6.2	6.7	10.0	8.7	7.4
1,448.4	1,463.4	1,475.1	1,504.3	1,535.2	1,575.9	1,605.2	1,636.6
538.3	537.1	540.8	550.4	561.9	578.5	601.3	630.1
86.8	98.5	113.7	120.2	129.2	134.9	149.4	169.4
56.9	64.6	73.2	80.0	85.6	84.4	94.3	112.3
26.5	29.6	35.3	35.1	39.2	43.3	48.8	51.6
3.3	4.3	5.2	5.0	4.3	7.3	6.4	5.5
451.5	438.6	427.1	430.2	432.7	443.6	451.9	460.6
1,060.6	1,094.6	1,126.5	1,154.3	1,183.7	1,213.9	1,243.2	1,277.2
63.7	69.8	78.4	80.3	81.2	81.6	89.9	101.3
38.6	40.4	45.2	43.3	46.7	46.9	52.6	59.0
24.0	28.6	31.7	35.8	32.1	32.0	34.9	40.3
x	x	1.5	x	2.4	2.7	2.3	2.0
997.0	1,024.8	1,048.0	1,074.0	1,102.5	1,132.3	1,153.3	1,176.0
2,034.7	**2,067.3**	**2,102.5**	**2,139.7**	**2,178.3**	**2,224.3**	**2,276.3**	**2,335.8**
69.8	78.1	89.2	95.1	108.1	115.2	127.0	157.9
27.6	30.5	33.2	33.7	44.4	48.1	52.4	65.4
39.2	44.9	53.2	58.2	59.6	62.4	70.3	87.8
2.9	2.7	2.8	3.2	4.1	4.6	4.3	4.7
1,965.0	1,989.1	2,013.3	2,044.6	2,070.2	2,109.2	2,149.3	2,177.9
580.0	579.9	584.2	594.8	606.5	624.1	647.2	675.6
45.3	50.9	60.1	65.4	73.5	79.3	86.5	107.1
19.0	19.9	23.1	23.8	32.4	33.2	39.3	46.2
23.7	29.0	34.5	38.8	37.6	42.8	44.3	57.3
2.6	2.0	2.5	2.8	3.5	3.3	2.9	3.7
534.7	529.0	524.0	529.4	533.0	544.8	560.7	568.4
1,454.8	1,487.3	1,518.4	1,544.9	1,571.7	1,600.3	1,629.1	1,660.3
24.5	27.2	29.1	29.7	34.6	35.9	40.5	50.8
8.6	10.6	10.1	9.8	12.0	14.9	13.2	19.3
15.6	15.9	18.7	19.5	22.0	19.7	26.0	30.5
x	x	x	x	x	x	x	x
1,430.3	1,460.1	1,489.3	1,515.2	1,537.2	1,564.4	1,588.6	1,609.5

Table 28.6 Caregivers aged 45 years and older who provide care to seniors, 2007

	All caregivers		Caregivers who provide care at least weekly	
	Men	Women	Men	Women
	%			
Personal care	17	37	75	74
Tasks outside the house	53	33	52	59
Tasks inside the house	32	57	73	73
Transportation	82	80	63	66
Medical care	14	25	77	81
Care management	33	42	62	64

Source: Statistics Canada, Catalogue no. 11-008-X.

Table 28.7 Reason a senior primary care receiver gets care, by age group, 2007

	Physical health problem only		Mental health, mental and physical health, or other	
	Men	Women	Men	Women
	%			
65 years and older	**74**	**72**	**26**	**28**
65 to 74 years	79	79	22	21
75 to 84 years	74	74	26	26
85 years and older	71	67	29	34

Source: Statistics Canada, Catalogue no. 11-008-X.

The 12 largest census metropolitan areas (CMAs) are home to 17.0 million Canadians, or 54% of the population in 2006. Most residents of these large cities do not perceive problems with physical or social incivility in their neighbourhoods.

Physical incivilities include garbage or litter lying around, vandalism, graffiti and other deliberate damage to property or vehicles. Social incivilities are defined as noisy neighbours or loud parties, people hanging around on the streets, people sleeping on the streets or in public places, people using or dealing drugs, people being drunk or rowdy in public places, and prostitution.

Differing perceptions

Three out of four Canadians aged 15 and older living in the 12 largest CMAs in 2004 felt there were no problems with incivility in their particular neighbourhoods. However, there is a wide continuum of perception among the 12 largest CMAs and even within CMAs.

About one in six individuals (16%) living in the 12 largest CMAs perceived a problem with a physical incivility in their neighbourhood. As well, one in five CMA residents (21%) perceived at least one type of social incivility to be a problem.

Eight percent of Québec residents perceived a problem with physical incivility, whereas 23% of Regina residents did; the rest of the CMAs ranged between 12% and 20%. Overall, 9% of residents in the 12 largest CMAs perceived garbage or litter lying around to be a problem in their neighbourhood, while 11% described vandalism and graffiti as a problem.

In 2004, the highest rates of perceived social incivility—with one in four residents seeing a problem where they live—occurred in Halifax, Montréal and

Chart 29.1
Perceptions of incivility, 2004

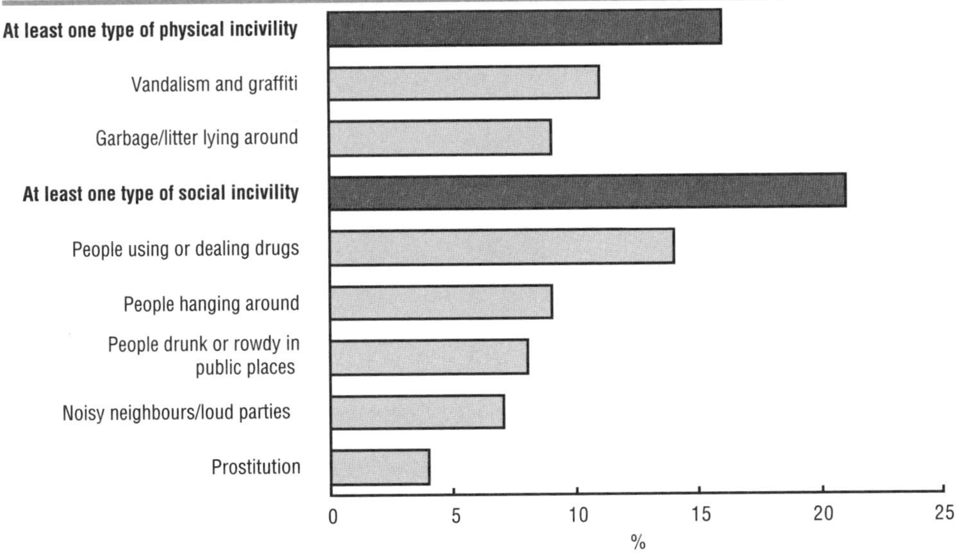

Note: Population reporting a problem with incivility in the 12 largest census metropolitan areas.
Source: Statistics Canada, Catalogue no. 11-008-X.

Vancouver. The lowest rates were in Québec, Hamilton, Winnipeg, Regina and Calgary, where one in six inhabitants observed social incivility.

In all 12 largest CMAs except Regina, using and dealing drugs was the most commonly perceived social incivility problem. With the exception of Vancouver, the social incivilities least often observed were prostitution and people sleeping on the streets.

In Toronto, Montréal and Vancouver, perceptions of both physical and social incivility rose as housing density increased. In all three CMAs, 80% or more of residents living in a suburban environment perceived their neighbourhoods had no problems with either type of incivility.

Social cohesion and community are also being affected by technological change, as the Internet continues to transform our lives. Some Canadians are using the Internet as an instrument to engage with their communities through volunteering. In 2007, about 10% of volunteers used the Internet to seek out volunteer opportunities, while 23% used the Internet in some way during their volunteer activities.

Youth aged 15 to 24 are the most likely to use the Internet to search for volunteer opportunities. Almost 18% of them do so, compared with 6% of adults aged 35 to 44. Moderate users of the Internet (one hour or less online per day) are more likely to volunteer, and they spend more time volunteering, than either non-users or people who spend more than one hour online per day.

Table 29.a
Physical and social incivilities, 2004

	Physical incivilities	Social incivilities
	% of residents reporting	
Montréal	17	24
Toronto	14	20
Vancouver	19	26

Note: This table should not be used to compare one census metropolitan area to another.
Source: Statistics Canada, Catalogue no. 11-008-X.

Chart 29.2
Incidence of volunteering and hours volunteered, Internet users and non-users, 2005

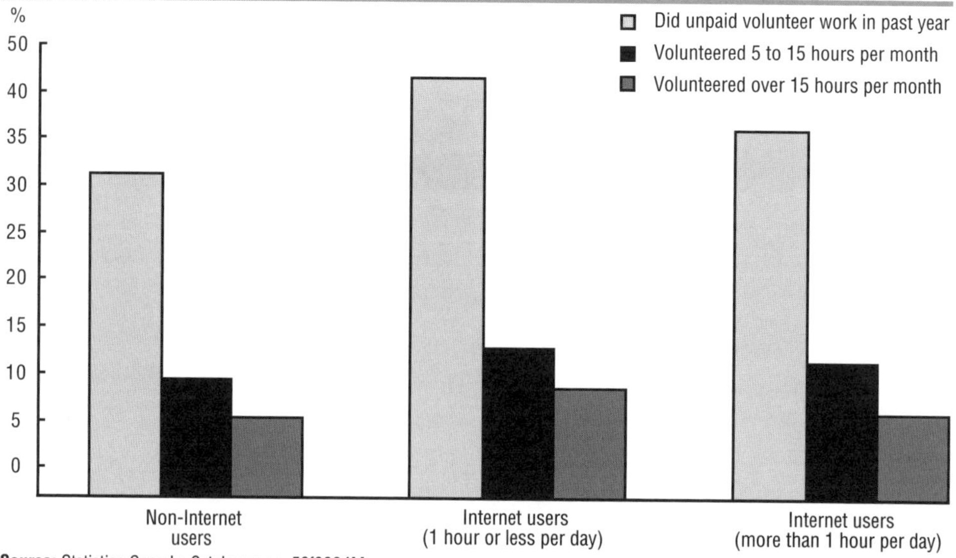

Source: Statistics Canada, Catalogue no. 56f0004M.

Unmet needs among adults with disabilities

In 2006, 2.7 million Canadian adults aged 15 and older with disabilities used or needed technical aids or specialized equipment, such as wheelchairs, Braille reading materials and communication keyboards, to help them perform daily activities. Among them, 61% had all the equipment they needed. However, 29% used such equipment but needed more, while 10% had none of the equipment they required.

Adults with the most severe disabilities, of which there were 511,670 in 2006, were the least likely to have all their needs met for such aids or equipment. Individuals with a learning limitation such as dyslexia had more unmet needs than individuals with any other disability.

The cost of purchasing or maintaining assistive devices was the most frequent reason given for unmet needs.

Chart 29.3
Adult population with disabilities, by needs met for technical aids or specialized equipment, 2006

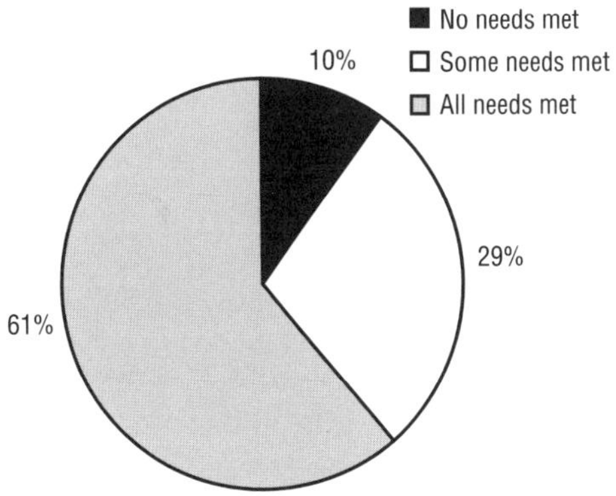

Source: Statistics Canada, Catalogue no. 89-628-X.

Even with assistive technology, half of all people with disabilities experienced difficulty participating in everyday activities at least once a week or more.

Fewer people attending religious services

Over the past two decades, the percentage of Canadians aged 15 and older who attend religious services at least once a week has declined from 30% in 1985 to 21% in 2005.

One in three people attended no services in 2005, up from one in five in 1985. About half of Canadians attend religious services less frequently than weekly, but at least once a year.

The decline in attendance is particularly noticeable among 45- to 64-year-olds, whose weekly attendance fell from 39% in 1985 to 22% in 2005. The proportion of people in that age group who had not attended religious services in the previous 12 months more than doubled from 16% to 33% over the 20-year period.

Chart 29.4
Religious attendance

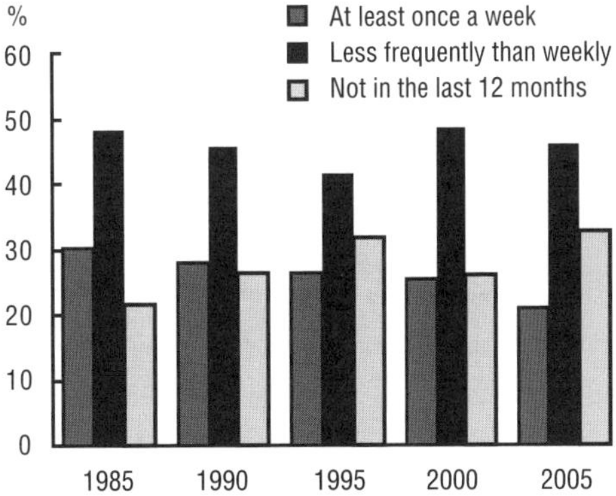

Note: Canadians aged 15 and older.
Source: Statistics Canada, Catalogue no. 89-630-X.

Table 29.1 Charitable donations, by selected characteristics of donors, and by province and territory, 2007

	Canada	Newfoundland and Labrador	Prince Edward Island	Nova Scotia	New Brunswick
	number				
All taxfilers[1]	**23,725,970**	**392,520**	**103,760**	**683,540**	**565,580**
All donors	**5,698,880**	**82,740**	**26,660**	**157,420**	**124,840**
	% of donors				
Males	**55**	58	52	53	55
Females	**45**	42	48	47	45
	years				
Average age of donors[2]	**53**	54	54	56	54
	% of donors				
Age group of donors[2]					
0 to 24	**3**	1	2	2	2
25 to 34	**12**	9	9	9	10
35 to 44	**18**	17	17	16	17
45 to 54	**24**	23	23	23	23
55 to 64	**20**	25	23	22	23
65 and older	**24**	25	26	29	25
	$				
Average donation by age group of donors[2]					
0 to 24	**510**	360	280	300	410
25 to 34	**840**	510	410	570	600
35 to 44	**1,270**	780	730	840	820
45 to 54	**1,610**	980	920	1,140	1,150
55 to 64	**1,680**	1,070	1,110	1,310	1,360
65 and older	**1,940**	1,120	1,730	1,650	1,670
Median total income of donors[3,4]	**49,310**	**37,550**	**39,180**	**43,260**	**41,150**
Median donation, both sexes[4]	**250**	**340**	**360**	**310**	**300**
Males	**270**	360	410	330	330
Females	**230**	300	320	280	260
	$ thousands				
Total charitable donations	**8,648,660**	**78,735**	**28,870**	**190,870**	**150,695**
Males	**5,728,385**	52,800	16,980	115,980	96,150
Females	**2,920,275**	25,935	11,890	74,890	54,545

Notes: Charitable donations are amounts given to charities and approved organizations for which official tax receipts were provided and claimed on tax returns.

A donor is defined as a taxfiler reporting a charitable donation amount on line 340 of the personal income tax form.

1. Taxfilers are people who filed a tax return for the reference year and were alive at the end of the year.
2. Characteristics such as age are as of December 31 of the reference year.
3. Total income is income from all sources. Median income is rounded to the nearest hundred dollars.
4. Zero values are not included in the calculation of medians for individuals.

Source: Statistics Canada, CANSIM tables 111-0001 and 111-0002.

Quebec	Ontario	Manitoba	Saskatchewan	Alberta	British Columbia	Yukon	Northwest Territories	Nunavut
				number				
5,862,570	**8,929,740**	**840,580**	**717,830**	**2,457,380**	**3,107,130**	**22,140**	**27,330**	**15,880**
1,282,210	**2,291,180**	**229,180**	**183,870**	**601,460**	**708,490**	**4,680**	**4,530**	**1,610**
				% of donors				
56	54	54	54	57	53	44	50	48
44	46	46	46	43	47	56	50	53
				years				
53	53	53	54	50	53	49	45	45
				% of donors				
3	2	4	3	5	3	3	4	4
11	12	12	11	15	11	12	19	20
17	19	18	16	19	18	21	25	24
25	23	23	24	25	23	30	29	24
21	19	19	19	17	20	22	18	20
23	24	24	28	19	25	12	6	7
				$				
180	530	740	720	710	650	420	340	570
300	920	1,060	850	1,260	1,150	640	680	830
530	1,450	1,450	1,360	1,800	1,610	890	930	1,260
600	1,930	1,950	1,540	2,540	1,890	1,580	1,430	2,130
640	1,920	1,850	1,680	3,170	1,990	1,600	1,860	2,030
960	2,250	1,950	1,790	2,910	2,230	1,440	1,850	1,920
46,110	**52,200**	**43,650**	**45,340**	**56,970**	**49,010**	**60,390**	**79,730**	**79,310**
130	**310**	**330**	**320**	**350**	**340**	**250**	**250**	**470**
140	330	370	350	400	380	270	280	450
110	280	290	290	300	300	230	220	480
				$ thousands				
814,945	**4,024,030**	**387,680**	**275,830**	**1,383,715**	**1,299,305**	**5,940**	**5,545**	**2,505**
534,525	2,644,865	253,315	176,860	996,440	832,775	3,145	3,180	1,370
280,420	1,379,165	134,370	98,965	387,275	466,530	2,795	2,365	1,135

Table 29.2 Charitable donations, by selected characteristics of donors, 2002 to 2007

	2002	2003	2004	2005	2006	2007
			number			
All taxfilers[1]	**21,979,210**	**22,465,770**	**22,725,310**	**23,311,690**	**23,338,370**	**23,725,970**
All donors	**5,520,560**	**5,588,590**	**5,781,250**	**5,833,930**	**5,752,630**	**5,698,880**
			%			
Males	57	57	56	56	56	55
Females	43	43	44	44	44	45
			years			
Average age of donors[2]	52	52	52	52	52	53
			%			
Age group of donors[2]						
0 to 24	3	3	3	3	3	3
25 to 34	12	12	12	12	12	12
35 to 44	21	21	20	20	19	18
45 to 54	23	23	23	23	24	24
55 to 64	16	17	18	18	19	20
65 and older	24	24	24	24	24	24
			$			
Average donations by age group of donors[2]						
0 to 24	380	470	460	490	530	510
25 to 34	590	700	700	820	930	840
35 to 44	940	1,000	1,000	1,200	1,300	1,270
45 to 54	1,100	1,200	1,300	1,400	1,600	1,610
55 to 64	1,200	1,300	1,300	1,500	1,600	1,680
65 and older	1,300	1,400	1,500	1,700	1,800	1,940
Median total income of donors[3,4]	**41,200**	**42,400**	**43,700**	**45,400**	**47,400**	**49,310**
Total median donations, both sexes[4]	**210**	**220**	**230**	**240**	**250**	**250**
Males	230	240	250	260	270	270
Females	180	200	200	210	220	230
			$ thousands			
Total charitable donations, both sexes	**5,847,068**	**6,513,013**	**6,922,616**	**7,879,588**	**8,529,976**	**8,648,660**
Males	3,940,147	4,389,106	4,591,471	5,293,624	5,723,000	5,728,385
Females	1,906,921	2,123,908	2,331,145	2,585,965	2,806,976	2,920,275

Notes: Charitable donations are amounts given to charities and approved organizations for which official tax receipts were provided and claimed on tax returns.

A donor is defined as a taxfiler reporting a charitable donation amount on line 340 of the personal income tax form.

1. Taxfilers are people who filed a tax return for the reference year and were alive at the end of the year.
2. Characteristics such as age are as of December 31 of the reference year.
3. Total income is income from all sources. Median income is rounded to the nearest hundred dollars.
4. Zero values are not included in the calculation of medians for individuals.

Source: Statistics Canada, CANSIM tables 111-0001 and 111-0002.

Table 29.3 Unpaid work, by sex, 2006

	Total	Males	Females
		number	
Hours spent doing unpaid housework[1]			
No hours	**2,429,695**	1,478,630	951,065
Less than 5 hours	**6,179,780**	3,777,200	2,402,585
5 to 14 hours	**8,251,255**	4,233,675	4,017,580
15 to 29 hours	**5,104,015**	1,954,050	3,149,965
30 to 59 hours	**2,559,305**	727,765	1,831,540
60 hours or more	**987,815**	223,810	764,005
Hours spent looking after children, without pay[2]			
No hours	**15,912,650**	8,154,790	7,757,855
Less than 5 hours	**2,437,875**	1,284,070	1,153,810
5 to 14 hours	**2,422,945**	1,240,970	1,181,970
15 to 29 hours	**1,717,805**	809,395	908,415
30 to 59 hours	**1,315,625**	487,970	827,655
60 hours or more	**1,704,975**	417,935	1,287,030
Hours spent providing unpaid care or assistance to seniors[3]			
No hours	**20,811,475**	10,442,800	10,368,675
Less than 5 hours	**2,911,895**	1,301,830	1,610,070
5 to 9 hours	**1,014,640**	383,625	631,020
10 to 19 hours	**380,540**	133,730	246,805
20 hours or more	**393,320**	133,145	260,170

Note: Does not include volunteer work for a non-profit organization, a religious organization, a charity or community group, or work without pay in the operation of a family farm, business or professional practice.

1. Number of hours spent doing unpaid housework, yard work or home maintenance in the week (Sunday to Saturday) prior to Census Day. This includes hours spent doing unpaid housework for members of one's own household, for other family members outside the household, for friends or neighbours.
2. Number of hours spent looking after children without pay in the week (Sunday to Saturday) prior to Census Day. This includes hours spent providing unpaid child care for members of one's own household, for other family members outside the household, for friends or neighbours.
3. Number of hours spent providing unpaid care or assistance to seniors of one's own household, to other senior family members outside the household, and to friends or neighbours in the week (Sunday to Saturday) prior to Census Day.

Source: Statistics Canada, 2006 Census of Population.

Table 29.4 Physical incivilities perceived to be a problem in the neighbourhood, 2004

	At least one type of physical incivility	Garbage/litter lying around	Vandalism and graffiti
	% of residents		
Average for 12 selected census metropolitan areas	**16**	**9**	**11**
Halifax	**17**	10	11
Québec	**8**	4^E	6^E
Montréal	**17**	11	13
Ottawa–Gatineau	**12**	7	7
Toronto	**14**	9	9
Hamilton	**16**	12^E	9^E
Winnipeg	**20**	9	17
Regina	**23**	11^E	17
Saskatoon	**18**	9^E	15
Calgary	**13**	7	9
Edmonton	**17**	9	13
Vancouver	**19**	10	15

Note: This table should not be used to compare one census metropolitan area to another.
Source: Statistics Canada, Catalogue no. 11-008-X.

Table 29.5 Social incivilities perceived to be a problem in the neighbourhood, 2004

	At least one type of social incivility	Noisy neighbours/ loud parties	People hanging around	People sleeping on the streets	People using or dealing drugs	People drunk or rowdy in public places	Prostitution
	% of residents						
Average for 12 selected census metropolitan areas	**21**	**7**	**9**	**3**	**14**	**8**	**4**
Halifax	**25**	7	12	F	17	9	3^E
Québec	**16**	5^E	5^E	F	11	8	2^E
Montréal	**24**	8	10	3	15	8	5
Ottawa–Gatineau	**21**	9	9	2^E	13	6^E	3^E
Toronto	**20**	6	9	4	13	7	4
Hamilton	**18**	4^E	8^E	F	12	8^E	F
Winnipeg	**19**	7	9	2^E	13	9	4
Regina	**17**	6^E	10^E	F	8^E	7^E	5^E
Saskatoon	**21**	6^E	8^E	F	12^E	9^E	F
Calgary	**16**	6^E	5^E	2^E	9	6^E	F
Edmonton	**22**	6	9	4^E	15	9	3^E
Vancouver	**26**	9	12	6	19	11	8

Note: This table should not be used to compare one census metropolitan area to another.
Source: Statistics Canada, Catalogue no. 11-008-X.

Table 29.6 Annual admissions to shelters, by facility type, 2008

	Total	Women	Children
		number	
All facility types	**101,019**	**61,690**	**37,902**
Transition homes	**44,639**	27,420	17,219
Second-stage housing	**3,312**	1,489	1,823
Safe home network	**817**	500	317
Women's emergency shelter	**25,530**	14,170	9,933
Emergency shelter	**19,182**	11,601	7,581
Family resource centre	**1,135**	749	386
Other types of shelter[1]	**6,404**	5,761	643

Notes: The woman–child distribution of annual admissions was unknown for about 4% of admissions; in such cases, shelters only provided the total number of admission for the year.
Precise reporting period may vary. Shelters were asked to provide information for the 12-month period ending March 31, 2006, or their own 12-month fiscal period.

1. Includes all other facilities not otherwise classified. This category may include Rural Family Violence Prevention Centres in Alberta, Interim Housing in Manitoba and other types of emergency shelters like the YWCA. These services may not be exclusive to abused women.

Source: Statistics Canada, CANSIM table 256-0013.

Table 29.7 Women residing in shelters for reasons of abuse, 2008

	number	%
Type of abuse		
Physical abuse	2,349	73
Sexual abuse	1,040	32
Financial abuse	1,550	48
Psychological abuse	2,798	87
Threats	1,658	51
Harassment	1,209	38
Other abuse	368	11
To protect children from		
Physical abuse	523	23
Sexual abuse	171	8
Psychological abuse	842	38
Threats	433	19
Neglect	314	14
Witnessing abuse of their mother	1,065	48
Unknown reasons	31	3

Note: Respondents may report more than one type of abuse.
Source: Statistics Canada, CANSIM table 256-0014.

Table 29.8 Employment, males and females, by occupation, 1987, 1998 and 2008

	1987		
	Females	Males	Females' share of total employed in occupation
	%		
Total[1]	**100.0**	**100.0**	**43.0**
Clerical and administrative	29.7	7.9	73.9
Sales and service	30.0	18.4	55.2
Occupations unique to primary industries	2.3	7.2	19.7
Trades, transport and construction	2.1	28.9	5.2
Processing, manufacturing and utilities	5.8	9.1	32.4
Management	6.0	10.5	30.1
Senior management	0.3	0.8	21.0
Other management	5.7	9.7	30.7
Professional	24.1	18.0	50.4
Business and finance	1.9	2.3	38.3
Natural sciences/engineering/mathematics	2.3	7.0	19.6
Social sciences/religion	4.3	2.0	61.4
Teaching	3.8	2.6	52.3
Doctors/dentists/other health	0.9	0.9	43.1
Nursing/therapy/other health-related	8.3	0.9	87.1
Artistic/literary/recreational	2.7	2.1	48.4
	thousands		
Total employed	**5,307.7**	**7,025.3**	...

1. Includes occupations that are not classified.
Source: Statistics Canada, Labour Force Survey.

1998			2008		
Females	Males	Females' share of total employed in occupation	Females	Males	Female's share of total employed in occupation
%					
100.0	**100.0**	**45.8**	**100.0**	**100.0**	**47.3**
24.4	7.2	74.2	23.9	7.3	74.7
28.7	18.8	56.4	28.8	19.4	57.2
2.1	6.2	22.2	1.2	4.9	18.3
2.3	26.4	7.3	2.1	27.1	7.1
5.1	9.1	31.9	3.5	6.9	31.2
8.1	11.0	38.4	7.0	11.1	36.1
0.4	0.8	27.9	0.3	0.6	29.6
7.7	10.2	39.1	6.7	10.5	36.4
29.3	21.3	53.8	32.2	23.0	55.8
3.0	2.8	47.9	3.5	2.8	52.6
2.7	9.1	20.0	3.3	10.4	22.4
6.2	2.3	68.9	7.0	2.5	71.4
5.1	2.6	62.4	5.6	2.7	65.2
1.2	1.0	50.9	1.5	1.1	55.4
8.0	1.0	86.8	9.0	1.2	87.2
3.1	2.4	52.0	3.6	2.7	54.8
thousands					
6,433.4	**7,612.9**	...	**8,104.5**	**9,021.3**	...

Table 29.9 Top occupations for males and females, 2006

	Employment	2001 to 2006 change
	number	
Males		
Retail salespersons and sales clerks	285,800	63,600
Truck drivers	276,200	40,900
Retail trade managers	192,200	-8,100
Janitors, caretakers and building superintendents	154,100	18,800
Farmers and farm managers	147,800	-21,200
Material handlers	147,000	13,900
Automotive service technicians, truck and bus mechanics and mechanical repairers	143,000	20,400
Carpenters	142,400	32,900
Construction trades helpers and labourers	133,600	47,500
Sales, marketing and advertising managers	102,600	10,200
Females		
Retail salespersons and sales clerks	400,000	68,600
Cashiers	255,500	35,500
Registered nurses	249,400	33,800
General office clerks	244,200	23,100
Secretaries (except legal and medical)	237,300	-16,500
Elementary school and kindergarten teachers	214,600	19,900
Food counter attendants, kitchen helpers and related occupations	194,800	23,100
Early childhood educators and assistants	157,700	31,700
Food and beverage servers	152,000	-2,900
Light duty cleaners	147,400	24,400

Source: Statistics Canada, censuses of population, 2001 and 2006.

Table 29.10 Employment rate of women with children, by age of youngest child, 1976 to 2008

	Total with children under age 16	Youngest child under age 3	Youngest child aged 3 to 5	Youngest child aged 6 to 15	No children at home[1]
	%				
1976	**39.1**	27.6	36.8	46.4	60.9
1977	**40.4**	29.3	37.9	47.5	61.2
1978	**42.6**	32.0	40.6	49.2	62.3
1979	**44.6**	34.6	42.9	50.9	64.1
1980	**47.1**	36.9	45.2	53.5	65.2
1981	**49.3**	39.3	46.7	56.2	66.0
1982	**48.8**	39.4	46.5	55.3	64.9
1983	**49.8**	42.2	47.9	55.0	65.7
1984	**51.6**	44.1	49.1	57.0	66.1
1985	**53.9**	46.7	52.0	59.1	67.7
1986	**56.6**	49.3	54.4	61.8	69.1
1987	**58.2**	50.2	56.1	63.8	69.8
1988	**60.4**	51.8	58.2	66.5	71.7
1989	**62.3**	52.9	59.2	69.0	72.7
1990	**63.0**	53.4	59.5	70.1	73.5
1991	**62.8**	54.4	60.1	69.0	72.6
1992	**62.1**	54.0	59.4	68.0	71.6
1993	**62.4**	54.4	59.4	68.5	71.6
1994	**62.8**	55.6	59.1	68.5	72.1
1995	**63.8**	56.0	60.2	69.8	73.0
1996	**64.5**	57.8	60.5	69.8	72.4
1997	**65.9**	58.8	62.1	71.1	73.4
1998	**67.0**	59.2	63.9	72.1	74.8
1999	**68.4**	60.1	66.0	73.4	76.0
2000	**69.2**	60.3	67.3	74.4	76.3
2001	**70.1**	61.3	67.0	75.3	76.8
2002	**71.4**	61.9	68.1	77.0	77.9
2003	**71.6**	62.7	68.5	76.7	79.0
2004	**72.4**	64.5	69.4	77.0	79.3
2005	**72.8**	64.7	70.6	77.4	78.7
2006	**72.9**	64.3	69.4	78.2	79.9
2007	**74.3**	65.1	72.6	79.4	80.9
2008	**73.8**	64.5	70.3	80.0	81.2

1. Women aged 55 and younger with no children aged 16 and younger living at home.
Source: Statistics Canada, Labour Force Survey.

Table 29.11 Need for assistive technology for children and adults, by disability type and age group, 2006

	5 to 14 years	Total, 15 years and older	15 to 39 years	40 to 64 years	65 years and older
			number		
No needs met					
Hearing	1,800E	**97,440**	6,760E	40,120	50,570
Seeing	F	**41,200**	F	19,760E	17,150E
Speech	2,420E	**F**	F	x	x
Mobility	2,220E	**180,160**	11,990	75,070	93,110
Agility	590E	**38,270**	F	19,210E	13,720E
Pain	...	**171,050**	35,310	112,650	23,090
Learning	15,650	**26,720**	13,830	12,380E	x
Other needs	1,610E	**24,750E**	3,380E	13,720E	7,650E
Some needs met					
Hearing	1,940E	**183,000**	6,010E	82,040	94,960
Seeing	2,140E	**31,960**	4,060E	18,570E	9,330E
Speech	6,010	**18,800**	5,350E	9,190E	4,260E
Mobility	1,970E	**124,810**	14,620	73,050	37,140
Agility	1,600E	**114,740**	19,080E	52,640	43,020
Pain	...	**125,850**	19,360	75,180	31,310E
Learning	17,300	**46,600**	22,100	20,750E	F
Other needs	7,720	**164,660**	29,980	78,200	56,480
All needs met					
Hearing	3,620	**408,920**	17,800	104,800	286,330
Seeing	1,470E	**184,980**	5,540E	74,930	104,510
Speech	3,250E	**6,820E**	F	F	x
Mobility	6,730	**881,820**	47,910	275,360	558,550
Agility	7,060	**259,790**	26,930	134,590	98,270
Pain	...	**688,020**	98,300	378,500	211,220
Learning	22,540	**94,930**	44,910	47,400	F
Other needs	14,330	**244,480**	37,090	125,040	82,350

Notes: Assistive technology includes wheelchairs, Braille reading materials and communication keyboards. Glasses and contact lenses are not included.
The sum of the values for each category may differ from the total because of rounding.
Source: Statistics Canada, Catalogue no. 89-628-X.

Transportation

Connecting one of the largest countries on earth, Canada's transportation system comprises more than 1.4 million kilometres of roads, 10 major international airports, 300 smaller airports, more than 72,000 kilometres of functioning railroad, and more than 300 commercial ports and harbours offering access to three oceans, as well as the Great Lakes and the St. Lawrence Seaway.

With the distances Canadians and their goods need to travel and with the importance of international trade to the economy, transportation accounts for a considerable share of Canada's gross domestic product (GDP)—4.6%, or $56.8 billion in 2008.

The sector's production grew a total 8.8% from 2004 to 2008, but just 0.3% in the last year of that period.

Transportation accounted for 691,900 jobs in 2008, or 4.7% of all jobs. Within the sector, truck transportation employed 26% of workers; transit and ground passenger transportation accounted for 17%; air transportation, nearly 10%; warehousing and storage, 6%; and rail transportation, nearly 6%.

Trucking still tops

The largest employer, trucking, also accounted for the largest share of transportation's contribution to GDP—28% in 2008. Transportation by air, water and rail combined contributed 22%.

Only trucking and air transportation saw much growth over the period 2004 to 2008: air transportation's output rose 37%; trucking's rose 11%.

Canadian trucking companies that posted annual revenue of $1 million or more hauled 607 million tonnes of goods in 2006, 3.4% more than in 2005. Domestic shipments accounted for 86% of the tonnage carried; transborder shipments made up 14%. However, transborder shipments accounted for 35% of total trucking revenue.

Chart 30.1
GDP at basic prices, selected transportation industries

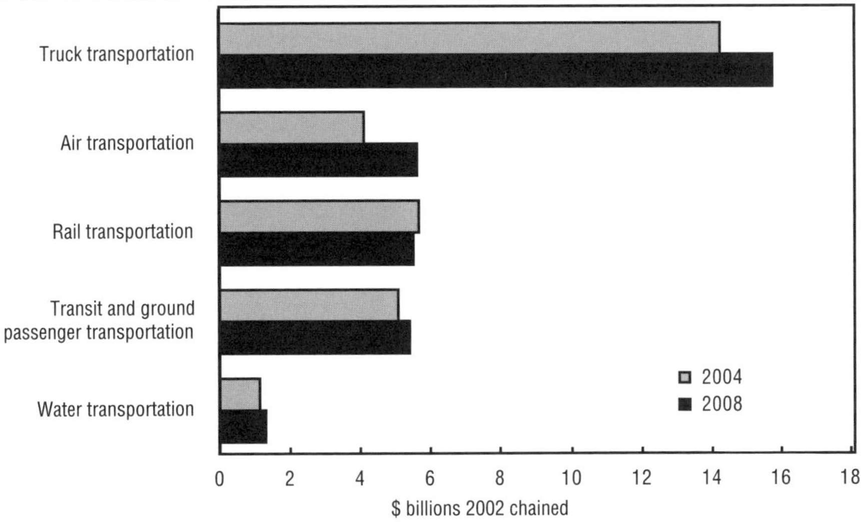

Source: Statistics Canada, CANSIM table 379-0027.

The average transborder shipment travelled 1,345 kilometres; the average domestic haul, 481 kilometres. In 2006, nearly one-quarter of the tonnage hauled originated in the Toronto, Montréal and Edmonton census metropolitan areas. Hamilton posted the fourth highest tonnage, and Vancouver the fifth highest.

Some products, such as automobiles, are carried by truck or rail, but rail transport also handles larger quantities of non-containerized commodities.

In 2008, Canada's rail carriers hauled 37 million tonnes of wheat, other grains and cereals and other food and alcoholic and non-alcoholic products; 34 million tonnes of iron ores and concentrates; 34 million tonnes of coal; and 26 million tonnes of wood and wood products.

Containerized shipping accounted for 10% of the international tonnage handled in 2006—about 33 million tonnes, or 3.9 million twenty-foot equivalent units of containers, a 40% increase since 2001.

The Port of Vancouver handled nearly 57% of the country's container traffic in 2006, making it Canada's busiest container port. It was also the busiest port overall, handling 80 million tonnes of cargo, including containers, in 2006.

Table 30.a
GDP of transportation and warehousing industries, by mode of transport, 2008

	Share of transportation and warehousing GDP	Growth rate from 2007
	%	
Air transportation	9.9	2.9
Rail transportation	9.7	-4.5
Water transportation	2.3	7.3
Truck transportation	27.7	0.3

Source: Statistics Canada, CANSIM table 379-0027.

Chart 30.2
Employment growth, selected transportation industries

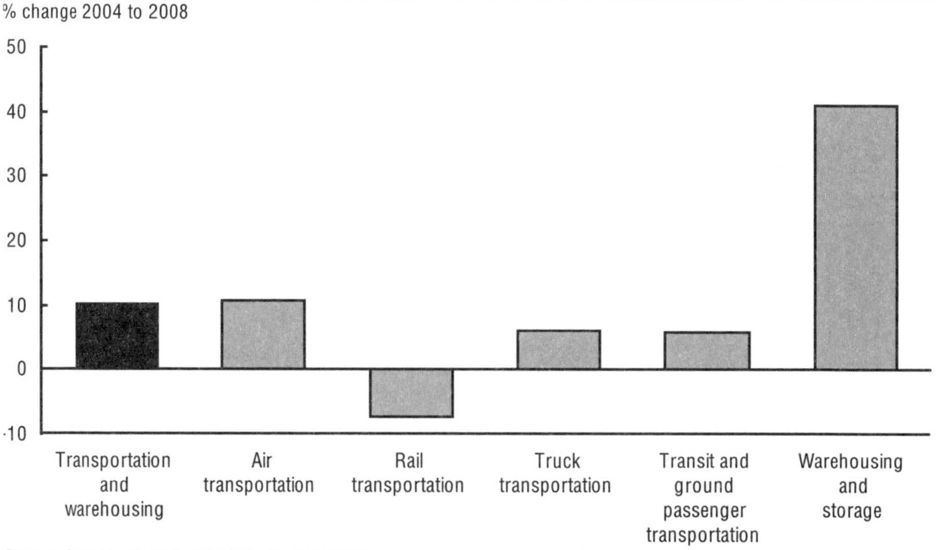

Source: Statistics Canada, CANSIM table 281-0024.

Getting around in the Arctic

The harsh climate and dispersed population north of 60 make it tough to move people and goods. Building and maintaining road or rail infrastructure is difficult in many areas. Marine transport is possible in coastal areas, but only in the warmest months. Often, air transport is the only option.

The three northern territories had about 10,500 km of roads in 2003, of which 3,100 km were paved. The Northwest Territories reported 121 km of railroad in 2007; the other territories had none.

Nunavut and the Northwest Territories send and receive cargo by sea; most of the activity is in Nunavut.

For passengers, however, aviation is key: people in the territories have a high propensity to travel by air. Citizens of Iqaluit and Yellowknife report more trips per capita than citizens of any other Canadian city. As well, the number of aircraft takeoffs and landings in Iqaluit, Yellowknife and Whitehorse generally rose from 2003 to 2007.

Chart 30.3
Air passenger trips, selected cities, 2006

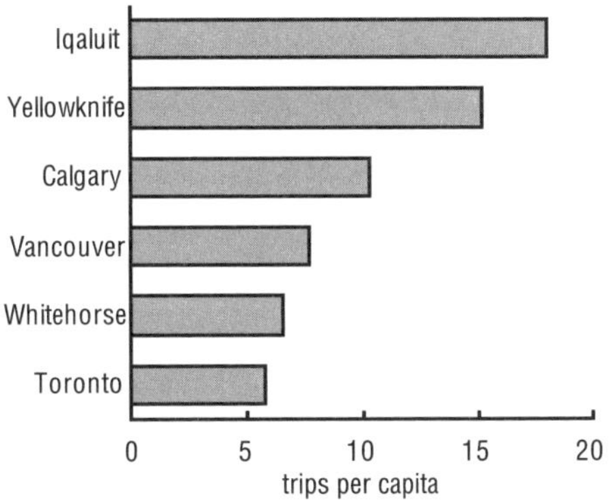

Source: Statistics Canada, Catalogue no. 16-002-X.

Getting around in Canada's suburbs

Inhabitants of the sparsely populated suburbs outside of Canada's big cities consider access to a private automobile not just convenient but, sometimes, essential.

Dependence on the automobile increased from 1992 to 2005. According to data from the General Social Survey on time use, the proportion of people aged 18 and older who went everywhere by car on the reference day—as drivers or passengers—rose from 68% in 1992 to 74% in 2005.

Conversely, the proportion of Canadians 18 and older who made at least one trip by bicycle or on foot declined from 25% in 1998 to 19% in 2005.

Suburban men, people aged 45 to 54, and people with children aged 5 to 12 were particularly likely to use their cars daily in 2005.

Chart 30.4
Time spent in the car, daily, 2005

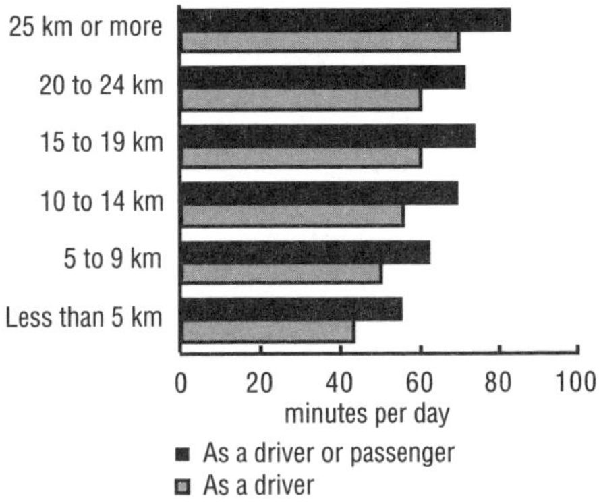

Note: Distance from city centre of census metropolitan areas only.
Source: Statistics Canada, Catalogue no. 11-008-X.

Table 30.1 GDP at basic prices for transportation and warehousing, selected industries, 2003 to 2008

	2003	2004	2005	2006	2007	2008
	$ millions 2002 chained					
Transportation and warehousing	**50,270**	**52,169**	**54,148**	**55,690**	**56,624**	**56,756**
Air transportation	3,668	4,119	4,710	5,116	5,467	5,623
Rail transportation	5,151	5,648	5,780	5,750	5,769	5,508
Water transportation	1,123	1,135	1,205	1,191	1,226	1,316
Truck transportation	13,531	14,235	15,085	15,530	15,692	15,741
Transit and ground passenger transportation	4,885	5,071	5,088	5,154	5,278	5,402
Pipeline transportation	5,380	5,066	4,952	5,007	4,846	4,523
Scenic and sightseeing transportation and support activities for transportation	9,033	9,152	9,460	9,872	10,247	10,438
Postal service and couriers and messengers	5,834	5,883	6,110	6,218	6,248	6,391
Warehousing and storage	1,648	1,915	1,903	2,040	2,083	2,064

Note: North American Industry Classification System (NAICS), 2007.
Source: Statistics Canada, CANSIM table 379-0027.

Table 30.2 Canadian railway carriers' operating statistics, 2002 to 2007

	2002	2003	2004	2005	2006	2007
	$ thousands					
Operating revenue	**8,213,346**	**8,307,268**	**8,861,767**	**9,821,994**	**10,397,871**	**10,481,566**
Freight revenue	7,256,434	7,354,925	7,879,379	8,759,069	9,344,811	9,435,757
Passenger revenue	287,394	255,776	265,192	282,881	294,529	291,784
All other operating revenue	669,518	696,567	717,194	780,044	758,530	754,026
Operating expenses	**6,621,037**	**6,713,296**	**6,951,895**	**7,506,354**	**7,787,544**	**7,989,137**
Ways and structures expenses	1,229,852	1,221,768	1,283,774	1,311,510	1,340,936	1,459,704
Equipment expenses	1,396,081	1,430,549	1,371,147	1,440,876	1,466,059	1,507,953
Rail operating expenses	2,718,701	2,776,794	2,929,148	3,216,111	3,385,043	3,621,517
General expenses	1,276,401	1,284,185	1,367,826	1,537,857	1,595,506	1,399,963
	thousands					
Transportation and other cost-generating sources						
Tonnes of freight transported	335,830	343,304	361,606	369,943	353,346	350,487
Tonne–kilometres of freight transported	317,806,584	318,263,125	338,897,938	352,139,700	352,342,829	357,444,398
Passengers transported	4,251	3,958	4,048	4,269	4,243	4,336
Passenger–kilometres of passengers transported	1,596,947	1,433,643	1,420,804	1,478,454	1,450,481	1,444,656
Litres of diesel oil consumed for all trains	1,969,741	2,007,813	2,097,070	2,130,224	2,119,082	2,193,684
	number					
Employees	37,282	36,312	35,591	34,995	34,062	34,281

Source: Statistics Canada, CANSIM tables 404-0004, 404-0005, 404-0013, 404-0016 and 404-0019.

Table 30.3 Shipping activities at Canadian ports, tonnage loaded and unloaded, 1994 to 2006

	Total	Domestic	United States	Other international
	thousands of tonnes			
Total handled				
1994	**351,316**	104,368	78,801	168,147
1995	**360,455**	100,740	85,198	174,518
1996	**357,513**	97,649	88,484	171,379
1997	**376,067**	93,418	94,313	188,337
1998	**376,032**	96,607	100,060	179,364
1999	**385,597**	104,398	101,983	179,216
2000	**402,783**	109,020	108,794	184,969
2001	**394,701**	107,842	107,955	178,904
2002	**408,141**	125,407	114,310	168,424
2003	**443,779**	137,079	123,366	183,335
2004	**453,280**	138,206	123,329	191,746
2005	**471,268**	140,356	128,681	202,231
2006	**466,277**	136,210	126,717	203,350
Loaded				
1994	**222,222**	52,184	49,520	120,518
1995	**226,910**	50,370	49,939	126,601
1996	**223,096**	48,825	52,399	121,873
1997	**234,653**	46,709	56,891	131,054
1998	**227,346**	48,304	58,872	120,171
1999	**231,847**	52,199	59,727	119,921
2000	**242,351**	54,507	64,744	123,099
2001	**228,663**	53,939	62,038	112,685
2002	**237,051**	62,780	72,867	101,404
2003	**259,872**	68,485	81,180	110,207
2004	**265,126**	69,096	83,720	112,310
2005	**271,978**	70,224	85,767	115,987
2006	**274,088**	68,080	84,378	121,629
Unloaded				
1994	**129,094**	52,184	29,282	47,629
1995	**133,546**	50,370	35,259	47,917
1996	**134,416**	48,825	36,085	49,506
1997	**141,414**	46,709	37,423	57,283
1998	**148,686**	48,304	41,189	59,194
1999	**153,750**	52,199	42,256	59,295
2000	**160,432**	54,513	44,050	61,869
2001	**166,038**	53,903	45,917	66,219
2002	**171,091**	62,626	41,444	67,020
2003	**183,908**	68,594	42,186	73,128
2004	**188,155**	69,110	39,609	79,436
2005	**199,290**	70,132	42,914	86,245
2006	**192,190**	68,130	42,339	81,720

Source: Statistics Canada, Catalogue no. 54-205-X.

Table 30.4 Employment in transportation and warehousing, selected industries, 1994 to 2008

	1994	1995	1996	1997	1998	1999
	number					
Transportation and warehousing	**549,518**	**553,249**	**555,148**	**566,196**	**582,593**	**588,436**
Air transportation	45,461	48,399	49,823	55,414	60,367	62,400
Rail transportation	54,907	52,226	48,659	46,099	46,323	45,989
Water transportation	11,143	12,886	13,274	11,744	11,018	11,636
Truck transportation	137,754	141,304	145,125	155,044	156,256	156,362
Transit and ground passenger transportation	95,453	91,245	91,752	91,173	91,776	93,039
Pipeline transportation	5,310	5,086	4,842	4,943	4,694	4,653
Scenic and sightseeing transportation	1,791	1,931	1,872	1,786	1,780	1,903
Support activities for transportation	69,741	69,385	66,534	68,732	71,285	76,532
Couriers and messengers	36,070	36,815	37,047	38,160	39,215	38,501
Warehousing and storage	25,949	25,568	27,584	27,144	28,350	29,033

Note: North American Industry Classification System (NAICS), 2002.
Source: Statistics Canada, CANSIM table 281-0024.

Table 30.5 Major Canadian airlines, selected operating statistics, 1994 to 2008

	1994	1995	1996	1997	1998	1999
	thousands					
Passengers transported	19,126	21,428	23,164	24,363	24,571	24,047
Passenger–kilometres	45,281,336	51,798,045	57,015,549	62,479,410	64,426,065	65,711,146
Kilograms of goods transported	395,674	386,560	405,975	449,828	431,150	451,801
Tonne–kilometres of goods transported	1,537,977	1,728,762	1,882,803	2,058,953	2,340,594	2,016,503
Hours flown	638	723	785	826	843	904
Litres of turbo fuel consumed	3,055,616	3,417,802	3,349,814	3,631,436	3,855,178	3,571,445

Source: Statistics Canada, CANSIM table 401-0001.

Table 30.6 For-hire trucking operating statistics, 1993 to 2007

	1993	1994	1995	1996	1997	1998
	$ millions					
Operating revenues	8,944.9	10,976.2	12,054.9	12,764.0	14,224.1	14,885.8
Operating expenses	8,561.0	10,145.6	11,256.9	12,019.4	13,223.8	13,877.8
	%					
Operating ratio	0.96	0.92	0.94	0.94	0.93	0.93

Source: Statistics Canada, CANSIM table 403-0002.

2000	2001	2002	2003	2004	2005	2006	2007	2008
				number				
599,227	**595,098**	**600,305**	**608,331**	**627,973**	**644,095**	**663,583**	**685,332**	**691,909**
62,751	61,991	57,576	60,508	59,576	60,978	61,159	68,453	65,971
47,275	45,991	46,005	44,545	43,256	42,669	41,429	40,496	40,151
12,765	11,939	12,055	x	x	x	x	x	x
157,250	166,409	168,389	166,207	172,019	176,893	179,588	181,942	182,376
97,161	92,757	101,602	104,617	112,311	115,571	116,925	119,760	118,881
4,949	4,369	4,344	x	x	x	x	x	x
2,051	2,855	2,879	x	x	x	x	x	x
78,978	77,103	79,489	83,381	85,313	87,872	92,206	96,283	97,601
38,271	38,685	37,046	37,432	38,909	40,914	43,794	45,862	46,894
29,436	28,477	28,044	29,586	31,096	32,437	41,013	43,365	43,822

2000	2001	2002	2003	2004	2005	2006	2007	2008
				thousands				
24,480	23,414	23,430	20,042	28,159	32,091	33,439	35,568	37,494
68,516,738	67,018,521	69,254,337	59,508,960	76,122,855	83,909,440	88,323,198	93,363,940	96,677,633
407,876	361,834	355,493	298,990	297,246	268,947	265,470	242,511	218,944
1,934,683	1,725,325	1,800,415	1,419,988	1,478,716	1,378,548	1,425,103	1,301,260	1,260,823
921	856	806	703	926	981	1,010	1,078	1,119
3,871,274	3,678,966	3,453,486	2,999,282	3,660,671	3,855,953	3,980,077	4,137,528	4,178,965

1999	2000	2001	2002	2003	2004	2005	2006	2007
				$ millions				
16,943.4	19,469.1	21,002.8	20,617.8	22,744.7	25,162.0	27,028.6	28,771.3	28,094.1
15,759.6	18,130.9	19,466.0	19,215.0	21,297.7	23,345.6	24,918.5	26,905.7	26,544.8
				%				
0.93	0.93	0.93	0.94	0.94	0.93	0.92	0.94	0.94

Table 30.7 Vehicle registrations, 2003 to 2008

	2003	2004	2005	2006	2007	2008
	number					
All vehicle registrations	**24,687,511**	**25,196,428**	**25,838,309**	**26,684,822**	**27,577,524**	**28,466,275**
Road motor vehicle registrations	18,883,584	19,156,055	19,515,295	20,065,171	20,593,251	21,087,014
Vehicles weighing less than 4,500 kilograms	17,768,773	17,989,919	18,275,275	18,738,941	19,198,960	19,612,935
Vehicles weighing from 4,500 kilograms to 14,999 kilograms	379,079	393,528	415,764	442,607	461,144	490,147
Vehicles weighing 15,000 kilograms or more	282,420	285,942	301,574	318,272	328,128	332,873
Buses	79,948	77,842	78,962	80,447	82,583	84,163
Motorcyles and mopeds	373,362	408,822	443,718	484,903	522,433	566,894
Trailers	4,315,996	4,513,641	4,722,563	4,961,184	5,231,114	5,527,800
Off-road, construction and farm vehicles	1,487,930	1,526,731	1,600,450	1,658,466	1,753,158	1,851,460

Source: Statistics Canada, CANSIM table 405-0004.

Table 30.8 Road motor vehicle fuel sales, 2002 to 2007

	2002	2003	2004	2005	2006	2007
	thousands of litres					
Net sales of gasoline	37,949,600	38,421,608	38,911,752	38,484,324	38,653,955	39,640,225
Gross sales of gasoline	39,205,669	39,797,315	40,146,013	39,845,934	39,918,335	40,854,912
Net sales of diesel oil	13,737,648	14,720,634	15,671,144	16,216,420	16,611,819	17,196,304
Net sales of liquefied petroleum gas[1]	323,935	313,019	358,459	324,286	325,747	316,239

Note: Gross is the total volume sold and net is the volume on which taxes were paid.
1. Data for British Columbia are not included.
Source: Statistics Canada, CANSIM table 405-0002.

Travel and tourism

31

Whether it is the dinosaur bones in Alberta, the restaurants in Montréal or the 2010 Olympics in Vancouver, Canada offers tourists a variety of interesting sights and experiences.

Tourism contributed to Canada's economy an average $24.0 billion each year in the past decade, and provided 663,000 jobs in a range of tourism-related industries.

In 2008, American and overseas visitors spent $16.1 billion in Canada. Canadian travellers spent about $28.7 billion outside Canada—a $12.6 billion travel deficit, the highest level ever. Over the past 20 years, Canadian spending overseas has decreased only twice—in 1994 and 2002.

Canadian travellers

Almost two-thirds of our tourist revenue is generated within Canada. In 2008, 214.5 million trips were taken by Canadians within Canada. The vast majority of these trips—92%—were within the traveller's home province.

When Canadians venture abroad, the United States is the number one destination. In 2007, Canadians made 17.8 million overnight visits to the United States: the top five American states were New York, Florida, Washington, Michigan and California.

After the United States, the top five most-visited overseas countries in 2007 (in order) were Mexico, United Kingdom, France, Cuba and the Dominican Republic. Overnight visits to Mexico were up 21.1% in 2007 from 2006. Spending by Canadian tourists in overseas countries was also up, reaching a record $10.9 billion in 2007.

Visitors to Canada

In 2008, 37.5 million passengers passed through Canada's airports. The busiest airports were Toronto (Pearson), Vancouver and Montréal (Trudeau). Trains carried

Chart 31.1
Tourism gross domestic product

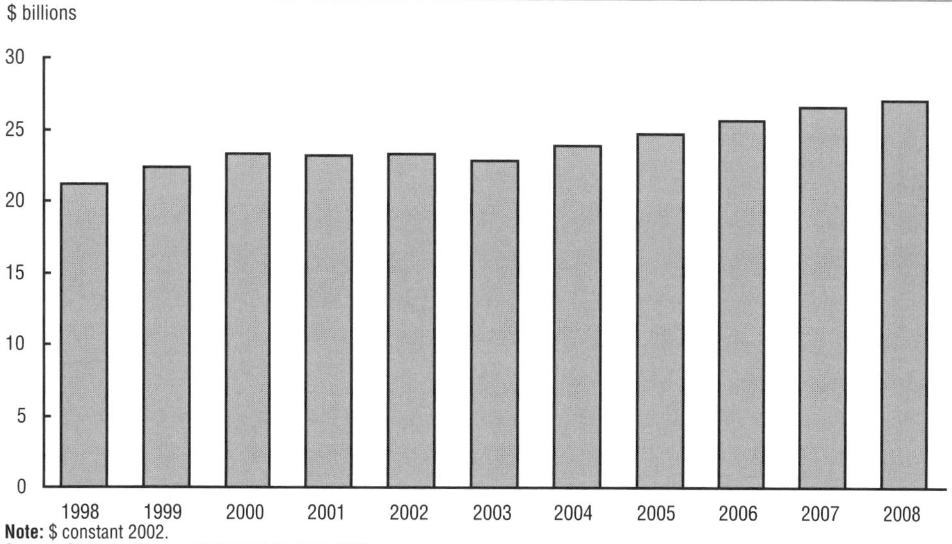

Note: $ constant 2002.
Source: Statistics Canada, CANSIM table 387-0001.

4.3 million passengers in 2007, up 2.2% from 2006. Ferry traffic was estimated at 39.0 million passengers, and cruise traffic at 1.4 million.

Visitors increase

Travel from overseas nations into Canada (same day and overnight) numbered 4.8 million people in 2008, an increase of 85,000 international travellers from the year before.

The number of overnight trips to Canada from countries other than the United States increased 1.7% to 4.6 million. Toronto, Vancouver, Montréal, St. Catharines–Niagara and Québec, in that order, were the main tourism hot spots for overseas visitors in 2008.

Most tourists to Canada came from the United Kingdom, followed by France, Germany, Japan, Mexico and Australia.

Eight of the top 12 overseas markets registered increases in overnight trips to Canada in 2008. The strongest growth was from Hong Kong (13.1%), followed by Mexico (11.7%) and France (10.5%). Meanwhile, Japan posted the largest decrease in travellers to Canada with a 16.6% drop.

Travel across the border from our American neighbours also decreased. Overnight travel from the United States to Canada declined 6.6% from 2007 to 2008.

Table 31.a
Non-resident travellers entering Canada

	2004	2008
	number	
Total	**38,844,666**	**27,370,109**
From the United States	34,626,114	22,605,645
By automobile	27,254,823	16,469,856
By plane	4,328,939	3,805,849
From other countries	4,218,552	4,764,464
By land	537,734	541,897
By air	3,565,560	4,060,855

Source: Statistics Canada, CANSIM table 427-0001.

Chart 31.2
International travellers entering or returning to Canada, 2008

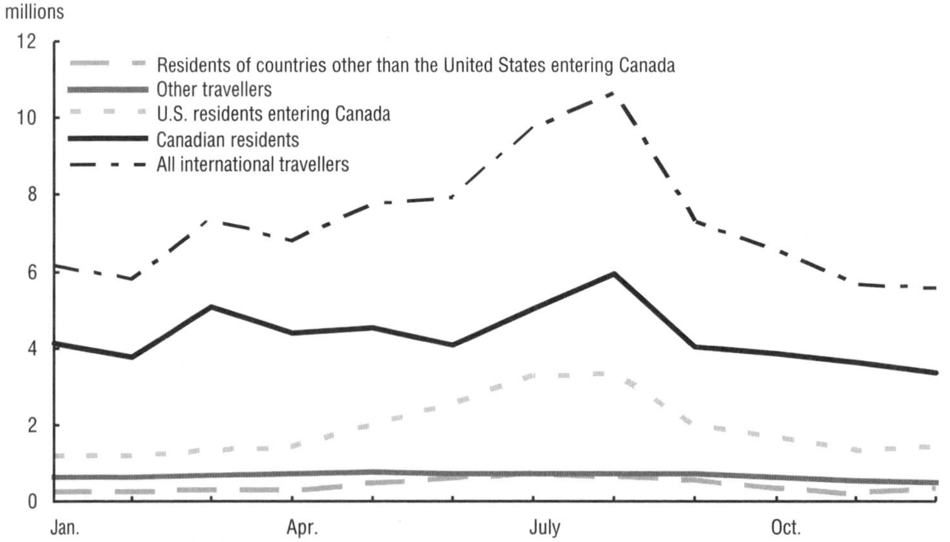

Source: Statistics Canada, CANSIM table 427-0001.

Cross-border travel, the loonie and oil prices

A rising Canadian dollar usually encourages more cross-border travel and shopping.

In November 2007, the dollar appreciated to US$1.03 and the number of trips to the United States rose to 3.8 million. By November 2008, the dollar depreciated to US$0.82, and the number of Canadians' cross-border trips retreated to 3.1 million.

Oil prices, which significantly affect the transportation costs of cross-border travel, played a role. Gasoline prices in Canada climbed 84% from January 2002 through May 2008: in the United States, prices jumped 176%. This increase was mostly the result of the 57% rise of the loonie against the U.S. dollar over that period.

Chart 31.3
Canadian residents returning from the United States

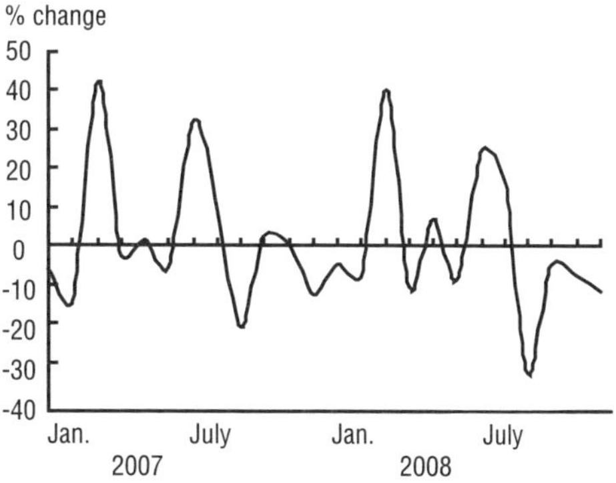

Source: Statistics Canada, CANSIM table 427-0001.

In other words, it could have been worse for travellers if the loonie had not appreciated while oil prices were rising.

Canadians in search of warmer climates

Travelling overseas, particularly to warmer climates, is a growing favourite among Canadians.

The relatively open border between the United States and Canada has historically meant extensive travel between the two countries. While we visit New York and other border states more often, we tend to travel farther and stay longer in the warmer states. In 2007, Canadians stayed a total of 42.9 million nights and spent $2.8 billion in Florida; in California, we stayed 9.8 million nights and spent $1.0 billion.

Beyond the United States, we are making more trips to other warm spots around the globe. Mexico was our number two destination in 2007; Canadians stayed 11.1 million nights and spent over $1.1 billion. Cuba ranked fifth and the Dominican Republic, sixth.

Chart 31.4
Canadians' top 5 non-U.S. destinations, 2007

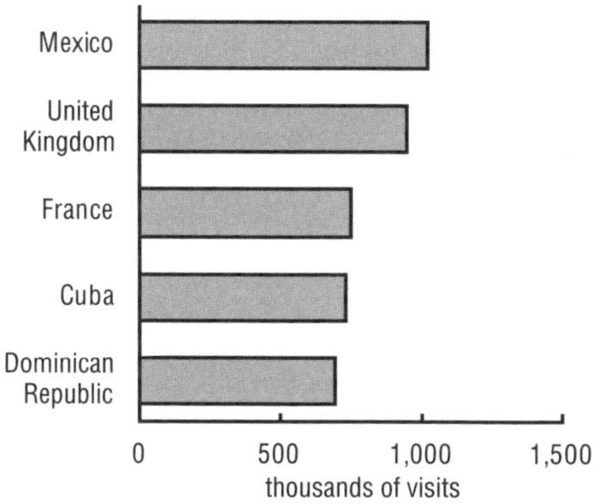

Note: Visits of one night or more.
Source: Statistics Canada, Tourism and the Centre for Education Statistics.

In 1994, by comparison, the six most popular destinations were, in order, the United States, Mexico, France, Germany, Italy and the Netherlands.

Table 31.1 Tourism gross domestic product, 1993 to 2008

	1993	1994	1995	1996	1997	1998	1999
	$ millions 2002 constant						
Tourism gross domestic product	**16,861**	**17,646**	**18,034**	**18,426**	**20,014**	**21,164**	**22,410**
Total tourism industries	13,370	14,019	14,278	14,556	15,782	16,475	17,517
Transportation	3,918	4,230	4,194	4,430	5,163	5,390	5,982
Accommodation	4,760	4,905	4,935	4,951	5,114	5,285	5,320
Food and beverage services	2,265	2,309	2,388	2,322	2,478	2,587	2,767
Other tourism industries	2,427	2,576	2,760	2,853	3,027	3,212	3,450
Other industries	3,491	3,628	3,754	3,870	4,233	4,688	4,893

Source: Statistics Canada, CANSIM table 387-0010.

Table 31.2 Receipts and payments on international travel account, 1993 to 2008

	1993	1994	1995	1996	1997	1998	1999
	$ millions						
Spending in Canada by foreign residents (receipts)	8,479	9,558	10,819	11,748	12,221	14,018	15,142
Spending in foreign countries by Canadians (payments)	14,358	13,679	14,092	15,353	15,873	16,029	17,092
Receipts minus payments, international travel account	-5,879	-4,121	-3,274	-3,603	-3,652	-2,009	-1,950

Source: Statistics Canada, CANSIM table 387-0005.

2000	2001	2002	2003	2004	2005	2006	2007	2008
				$ millions 2002 constant				
23,266	**23,222**	**23,319**	**22,827**	**23,836**	**24,729**	**25,619**	**26,559**	**27,045**
18,196	18,002	17,920	17,458	18,123	18,787	19,507	20,142	20,517
6,272	5,905	5,526	5,477	5,838	6,135	6,421	6,687	6,808
5,404	5,461	5,709	5,619	5,798	6,050	6,283	6,460	6,623
2,864	2,857	2,898	2,771	2,855	2,915	3,017	3,051	3,094
3,656	3,778	3,787	3,589	3,633	3,688	3,790	3,944	3,993
5,071	5,219	5,400	5,371	5,714	5,941	6,112	6,418	6,528

2000	2001	2002	2003	2004	2005	2006	2007	2008
				$ millions				
15,997	16,437	16,741	14,776	16,980	16,674	16,609	16,469	16,119
18,444	18,487	18,402	18,727	20,236	21,864	23,402	26,511	28,734
-2,447	-2,050	-1,659	-3,952	-3,257	-5,191	-6,792	-10,043	-12,616

Table 31.3 Employment generated by tourism, 2003 to 2008

	2003	2004	2005	2006	2007	2008
	thousands					
Tourism activities	**612.2**	**616.8**	**622.8**	**635.8**	**653.4**	**662.9**
Total tourism industries	491.4	495.5	500.8	511.2	525.2	532.6
Transportation	78.4	79.1	79.7	81.5	83.6	84.8
Air transportation	51.5	52.1	52.6	53.6	55.5	56.6
Railway transportation	2.6	2.5	2.6	2.5	2.4	2.4
Water transportation	1.7	1.6	1.6	1.6	1.6	1.6
Bus transportation	9.9	9.8	9.8	9.9	10.1	9.8
Other transportation industries	12.7	13.0	13.2	13.9	14.0	14.4
Accommodation	158.8	161.5	162.0	163.9	168.3	166.0
Food and beverage services	146.2	145.0	146.1	151.1	157.3	163.4
Other tourism activities	108.0	109.9	113.0	114.8	116.0	118.3
Recreation and entertainment	67.2	68.2	68.6	70.4	70.8	70.8
Travel agencies	40.8	41.8	44.4	44.4	45.2	47.6
Other industries	120.7	121.2	122.0	124.6	128.3	130.3

Source: Statistics Canada, CANSIM table 387-0003.

Table 31.4 Travel arrangement and reservation services, 2003 to 2007

	2003	2004	2005	2006	2007p
			$ millions		
Travel agencies					
Operating revenue	1,480.0	1,501.1	1,592.3	1,668.7	1,755.5
Operating expenses	1,455.6	1,414.7	1,509.0	1,551.0	1,657.2
Operating profit margin (%)	1.6	5.8	5.2	7.1	5.6
Tour operators					
Operating revenue	6,105.8	6,288.0	6,971.7	7,217.0	7,524.6
Operating expenses	6,130.9	6,188.6	6,894.2	7,118.1	7,460.0
Operating profit margin (%)	-0.4	1.6	1.1	1.4	0.9
Other travel arrangement and reservation services[1]					
Operating revenue	229.5	240.7	264.7	279.0	908.6
Operating expenses	211.2	221.7	243.8	257.1	881.9
Operating profit margin (%)	8.0	7.9	7.9	7.8	2.9

Notes: North American Industry Classification System (NAICS), 2007.
Operating revenue excludes investment income, capital gains, extraordinary gains and other non-recurring items.
Operating expenses exclude write-offs, capital losses, extraordinary losses, interest on borrowing, and other non-recurring items.
Operating profit margin is derived as follows: operating revenue minus operating expenses, expressed as a percentage of operating revenue.
1. Please note a change in methodology: starting with 2007, the annual data for NAICS Code 56159 cannot be compared with those for previous years.
Source: Statistics Canada, CANSIM table 351-0003 and Catalogue no. 63-018-X.

Table 31.5 Accommodation services, 2003 to 2007

	2003	2004	2005	2006	2007
			$ millions		
Operating revenue	12,314.6	13,197.8	14,193.0	14,667.9	15,482.2
Operating expenses	10,993.6	11,243.9	12,009.2	12,215.2	13,056.1
Salaries, wages and benefits	3,926.9	4,238.1	4,473.5	4,684.8	4,899.5
			%		
Operating profit margin	10.7	14.8	15.4	16.7	15.7
			number		
Active establishments	16,355	15,576	16,293	F	F

Notes: North American Industry Classification System (NAICS), 2007.
Estimates for the most recent year are preliminary, and subject to revision.
Components may not add to total because of rounding.
Operating revenue excludes investment income, capital gains, extraordinary gains and other non-recurring items.
Operating expenses exclude write-offs, capital losses, extraordinary losses, interest on borrowing, and other non-recurring items.
Salaries, wages and benefits include vacation pay and commissions for all employees for whom a T4 slip was completed and the employer portion of employee benefits for items such as Canada/Quebec Pension Plan or Employment Insurance premiums.
Operating profit margin is derived as follows: operating revenue minus operating expenses, expressed as a percentage of operating revenue.
Source: Statistics Canada, CANSIM table 351-0002 and Catalogue no. 63-018-X.

Table 31.6 Canadians travelling in Canada, by province and territory of destination, 2002 to 2007

	2002	2003	2004	2005	2006	2007
	thousands					
Canada	**198,366**	**183,167**	**185,134**	**203,976**	**207,470**	**214,559**
Newfoundland and Labrador	4,211	3,631	3,583	3,251	3,068	2,939
Prince Edward Island	1,299	1064	1048	1,092	1018	1057
Nova Scotia	6,963	6,155	5,985	7,265	7,318	7,087
New Brunswick	5,226	4,884	4,379	5,293	5,254	5,349
Quebec	42,754	44,171	44,674	51,611	57,278	57,240
Ontario	81,417	73,323	77,236	82,700	83,036	86,903
Manitoba	7,544	7,308	7,151	6,983	7,275	7,294
Saskatchewan	8,415	7,781	7,797	7,814	7,874	8,164
Alberta	16,231	13,163	13,125	18,727	17,364	20,052
British Columbia	24,273	21,656	20,112	18,931	17,908	18,418
Yukon, Northwest Territories and Nunavut	..	..	..	..	77	56^E

Note: All trips with destinations to Canada.
Source: Statistics Canada, Canadian Travel Survey–Travel Survey of Residents of Canada Bridging Project.

Table 31.7 Expenditures by Canadians on trips in Canada, by province and territory of destination, 2002 to 2007

	2002	2003	2004	2005	2006	2007
	$ thousands					
Canada	**27,212,704**	**25,375,064**	**26,299,571**	**29,349,441**	**30,370,293**	**31,512,813**
Newfoundland and Labrador	624,662	609,003	580,359	556,702	578,466	613,323
Prince Edward Island	160,140	150,294	149,013	184,515	256,255	210,645
Nova Scotia	833,685	809,078	780,325	996,174	1,072,260	984,719
New Brunswick	828,965	714,206	703,055	747,261	767,427	732,070
Quebec	5,438,700	523,764	5,531,487	6,348,527	6,802,911	7,002,866
Ontario	9,373,178	8,938,867	9,237,284	10,285,870	10,637,175	11,006,038
Manitoba	787,764	790,535	827,254	833,557	902,279	987,116
Saskatchewan	1,103,753	1,059,449	1,149,117	1,184,540	1,140,990	1,168,570
Alberta	3,312,461	2,564,234	2,876,157	3,621,678	3,664,737	4,107,182
British Columbia	4,692,612	4,440,335	4,403,611	4,370,479	4,483,499	4,642,885
Yukon, Northwest Territories and Nunavut	..	..	..	..	64,294^E	57,397^E

Note: Excludes spending done in Canada for foreign travel or spending for interprovincial trips, spending done in the province of origin of the trip when there is no overnight visit reported in that same province and both the point of origin and portion of airfare allocated to the province of origin of the trip.
Source: Statistics Canada, Canadian Travel Survey–Travel Survey of Residents of Canada Bridging Project.

Table 31.8 International travellers entering or returning to Canada, 2004 to 2008

	2004	2005	2006	2007	2008
	thousands				
Total international travellers	**89,824.9**	**89,310.4**	**89,120.8**	**89,103.1**	**87,146.0**
Total non-resident travellers	38,844.7	36,160.1	33,390.2	30,373.5	27,370.1
United States residents entering Canada	34,626.1	31,655.0	28,872.7	25,694.6	22,605.6
Residents of countries other than the United States entering Canada	4,218.6	4,505.1	4,517.5	4,678.9	4,764.5
Total Canadian residents	41,786.3	44,030.9	46,912.3	50,044.6	51,737.3
Canadian residents returning from the United States	36,047.3	37,794.0	40,173.4	42,640.7	43,613.2
Canadian residents returning from countries other than the United States	5,739.0	6,237.0	6,738.9	7,403.8	8,124.0
Total other travellers	9,194.0	9,119.4	8,818.2	8,685.1	8,038.7
Immigrants and former residents	322.5	314.2	287.1	268.2	263.4
Non-resident crews	3,163.9	3,146.9	3,080.7	3,143.2	2,989.3
Canadian crews	5,707.6	5,658.2	5,450.4	5,273.7	4,786.0

Source: Statistics Canada, CANSIM table 427-0001.

Table 31.9 Non-resident travellers entering Canada, by country of residence, 2003 to 2008

	2003	2004	2005	2006	2007	2008
	thousands					
Total non-resident travellers, countries other than the United States	**3,393.2**	**4,218.6**	**4,505.1**	**4,517.5**	**4,678.9**	**4,764.5**
Europe	1,859.9	2,213.4	2,372.9	2,334.7	2,430.3	2,492.1
Africa	60.5	68.1	71.9	83.2	86.7	91.4
Asia	922.8	1,272.4	1,321.3	1,327.6	1,307.8	1,265.3
North America, Central America and Caribbean	283.0	334.2	354.7	381.4	425.2	450.9
South America	78.0	105.2	131.2	141.8	152.7	163.5
Oceania and other Ocean Islands, total	189.0	225.2	253.0	248.8	276.3	301.2

Note: United States residents are excluded.
Source: Statistics Canada, CANSIM table 427-0003.

Table 31.10 Travel by Canadians to foreign countries, top 15 countries visited, 2007

	Overnight visits		
	Visits	Nights	Spending in country
	thousands		CAN$ millions
United States	17,759	130,801	11,545
Mexico	1,019	11,146	1,084
United Kingdom	947	11,608	1,149
France	745	9,287	973
Cuba	724	6,136	629
Dominican Republic	690	5,871	599
Germany	370	3,526	323
Italy	352	3,836	514
Netherlands	258	2,094	210
China	258	5,452	455
Spain	187	2,027	246
Hong Kong	177	2,757	209
Republic of Ireland	166	1,787	203
Switzerland	148	1,058	107
Austria	137	761	98

Source: Statistics Canada, Tourism and the Centre for Education Statistics.

Table 31.11 Travel by Canadians to the United States, top 15 states visited, 2007

	Overnight visits		
	Visits	Nights	Spending in state
	thousands		CAN$ millions
New York	2,968	8,195	918
Florida	2,485	42,857	2,812
Washington	1,995	5,591	432
Michigan	1,410	3,562	305
California	1,148	9,764	1,006
Nevada	937	4,236	825
Maine	888	2,887	262
Pennsylvania	769	1,815	145
Vermont	765	2,207	159
North Dakota	625	1,286	163
Massachusetts	604	2,315	262
Ohio	592	1,540	142
Montana	578	1,764	183
Minnesota	573	1,517	193
Virginia	513	1,552	113

Source: Statistics Canada, Tourism and the Centre for Education Statistics.

List of maps, charts and tables

Maps

Charts

Tables

Glossary

Aboriginal identity: People who identify with at least one Aboriginal group (i.e., North American Indian, Métis or Inuit), who are Treaty Indians, Registered Indians as defined by the *Indian Act*, or who are members of an Indian band or First Nation.

Allophones: People whose mother tongue is neither English nor French.

Anglophones: People whose mother tongue is English.

Assault levels 1 to 3: Level 1 or common assault includes behaviours such as pushing, slapping and punching, but does not involve a weapon or any serious injury. Assault levels 2 and 3, or major assault, include aggravated assault and assault with a weapon to cause bodily harm.

Balance of international payments: Covers all economic transactions between Canadian residents and non-residents. It includes the current account and the capital and financial account. The current account covers transactions on goods, services, investment income and current transfers. The capital and financial account is mainly composed of transactions in financial instruments.

Balance of payments (BOP): *See* Balance of international payments.

Body Mass Index (BMI): Measure of an individual's weight in relation to his or her height. BMI is highly correlated with body fat and is widely used to indicate health risks. BMI is classified into six categories, each representing a different level of risk: 'Underweight' is less than 18.5 BMI; 'Normal weight' is from 18.5 to 24.9 BMI; 'Overweight' is from 25.0 to 29.9 BMI; 'Obese Class I' is from 30.0 to 34.9 BMI; 'Obese Class II' is from 35.0 to 39.9 BMI; and 'Obese Class III' is greater than or equal to 40.0 BMI.

Building permit: Permit required in most jurisdictions for new construction, adding onto pre-existing structures and, in some cases, major renovations.

Canada Pension Plan (CPP): Contributory, earnings-related social insurance program that provides a stable and dependable pension that can be built on for retirement. It also provides people and their dependants with basic financial protection in the event of disability or death.

CANSIM (Canadian Socioeconomic Information Management System): Database that enables users to track trends in virtually every aspect of Canadian life. It contains over 26 million time series (observations for a subject at regular intervals).

Capital investment: Includes all expenditures on buildings, engineering construction and machinery and equipment.

Census: Survey that includes all units in a population (people, events, businesses, etc.).

Census agglomeration (CA): Area consisting of one or more neighbouring municipalities situated around a major urban core. A CA must have an urban core population of at least 10,000.

Census Division (CD): Group of neighbouring municipalities joined together for the purposes of regional planning and managing common services (such as police or ambulance services). These groupings are established under laws in effect in certain provinces of Canada. For example, a census division might correspond to a county, or a regional district. In other provinces and the territories where laws do not provide for such areas, Statistics Canada defines equivalent areas for statistical reporting purposes in co-operation with these provinces and territories.

Census family: Married couple (with or without children of either or both spouses), couple living common-law (with or without children of either or both partners) or lone parent of any marital status, with at least one child living in the same dwelling. A couple may be of opposite or same sex. Children in a census family include grandchildren living with their grandparent(s) but with no parents present.

Census metropolitan area (CMA): Area consisting of one or more adjacent municipalities situated around a major urban core. The CMA must have a population of at least 100,000, of which 50,000 or more live in the urban core.

Census of Agriculture: Survey conducted by Statistics Canada every five years to produce data on the agriculture industry.

Census of Population: Survey conducted every five years to produce data on the population and dwelling counts for Canada, each province and territory, and smaller geographic units such as cities or districts within cities.

Constant dollars: Dollars of a particular base year that are not adjusted (by inflation or deflation) to show changes in the purchasing power of the dollar.

Consumer Price Index (CPI): Measure of the percentage change over time in the average cost of a large basket of goods and services purchased by Canadians. The items contained in the basket are divided into eight broader categories: food, shelter, household operations and furnishings, clothing and footwear, transportation, recreation, education and reading, and alcoholic beverages and tobacco products. The quantity and quality of the items in the basket are held constant. As a result, changes in the cost of the basket are due to pure price movements and not to changes in the basket's composition.

Core Consumer Price Index: A variant of the CPI that excludes eight of its most volatile components: fruit, vegetables, gasoline, fuel oil, natural gas, mortgage interest, intercity transportation, and tobacco products. These fluctuating components are found within the broader taxonomy of the consumer index, which includes food, shelter and transportation. The core index also excludes the effect of changes in indirect taxes on the remaining components. *See* Consumer Price Index.

Core public administration (CPA): The group of federal public servants who work for the Treasury Board Secretariat of Canada.

Crude oil: Naturally occurring liquid mixture of hydrocarbons; liquid petroleum. The liquid hydrocarbons may be mixed with natural gas, carbon dioxide, saltwater, sulphur compounds and sand. Most of these substances are separated from the liquid hydrocarbons at processing facilities near the producing field.

Employment: People who, during the Labour Force Survey reference week, did any work at all at a job or business, that is, paid work in the context of an employer–employee relationship, or self-employment (also includes unpaid family work, which is defined as unpaid work contributing directly to the operation of a farm, business or professional practice owned and operated by a related member of the same household); or had a job, but were not at work because of factors such as own illness or disability, personal or family responsibilities, vacation, labour dispute or other reasons. Excludes people on layoff, between casual jobs, and those with a job to start at a future date. *See also* Unemployment and Labour force.

Employment rate: Refers to the number of people employed, expressed as a percentage of the total population aged 15 and older.

Ethnic origin: Ethnic or cultural group(s) to which an individual's ancestors belong.

Exchange rate: Value of the Canadian dollar against the currencies of other countries.

Farm Input Price Index (FIPI): Measures the annual price movement of specific farm inputs at the farm gate; that is, the annual price movement of the goods and services that comprise basic agricultural overhead costs. The specific farm inputs are building and fencing, machinery and motor vehicles, crop production, animal production, supplies and services, hired farm labour, property taxes, interest and farm rent.

Farm Product Price Index (FPPI): Measures the change through time in prices received for agricultural commodities at the first transaction point. These agricultural commodities include both crops and livestock and animal products, including grains, oilseeds, specialty crops, fruit, vegetables, potatoes, cattle and calves, hogs, poultry, eggs and dairy products.

Fertility rate: Number of live births occurring in a given time period relative to the number of women of childbearing age.

Francophones: People whose mother tongue is French.

Full-time equivalent (FTE): A measure of employees or jobs based on a standard work week or year. Thus, an employee who works for half a year, or half the week all year, has a full-time equivalence of 0.5.

G8: Top eight industrialized countries in the world: Canada, France, Germany, Italy, Japan, Russia, the United Kingdom and the United States.

General government: Administrative part of governments. Excludes units that deliver services, such as schools and hospitals.

General Social Survey (GSS): Statistics Canada survey that gathers data on social trends to monitor changes in the living conditions and well-being of Canadians over time and to provide information on specific social policy issues of current or emerging interest.

Generation status: Indicates for how many generations a person and their family have been in Canada. It is derived from place of birth of respondent, the place of birth of the father and the place of birth of the mother and further, it only pertains to the population aged 15 and older. People are defined as either 'first generation,' 'second generation' or 'third generation or more,' which are defined as follows. First generation refers to people born outside of Canada. Second generation refers to people born in Canada with at least one parent born outside of Canada. Third generation and more refers to people who were born in Canada and whose parents were both born in Canada.

Goods-producing sector: Sector of the economy that is composed of agriculture, forestry, fishing and hunting; mining, oil and gas extraction; utilities (electric power, gas and water); construction; and manufacturing.

Greenhouse gases (GHGs): A group of gases that trap heat in the atmosphere by reflecting solar energy back toward the surface of the Earth. The most significant greenhouse gases produced by economic activities are carbon dioxide (CO^2), methane (CH^4), nitrous oxide ($N^{2}0$) and chlorofluorocarbons (CFC).

Gross domestic product (GDP): Total unduplicated value of goods and services produced in the economic territory of a country or region during a given period. GDP can be measured in three ways: 1) as total income earned in current production; 2) as total final sales of current production; or 3) as total net values added in current production.

Heritage institutions: Institutions whose purpose is to acquire, preserve, study, interpret and make accessible to the public, for its instruction and enjoyment, objects, specimens, documents, buildings and land areas of educational and cultural value, including artistic, scientific, historical, natural and technological material.

Home language: Language spoken most often at home.

Homicide: A homicide occurs when a person directly or indirectly, by any means, causes the death of a human being. Homicide is either culpable (murder, manslaughter or infanticide) or non-culpable (not an offence and, therefore, not included in the Homicide Survey). Deaths caused by criminal negligence, suicide and accidental or justifiable homicide (e.g., self-defence) are not included.

Household maintainer status: Refers to whether or not a person residing in the household is responsible for paying the rent, the mortgage, the taxes, the electricity or other services or utilities. Where a number of people may contribute to the payments, more than one person in the household may be identified as a household maintainer.

Industrial production utilization rate: The ratio of an industry's actual output to its estimated potential output.

Industrial Product Price Index (IPPI): Measures price changes for major commodities sold by Canadian manufacturers.

Inflation: Upward movement in the average level of prices or a persistent rise in the average price of goods and services; affects cost of living. The most widely used measure of inflation is the Consumer Price Index (CPI).

Information and communications technology (ICT): Any products or services provided by the telecommunications industry, including cellphones, personal computers, telephones and Internet and cable services.

Intellectual property: Form of creative endeavour that can be protected through a trademark, patent, copyright, industrial design or integrated circuit topography.

Interprovincial migration: Movement from one province to another involving a permanent change in residence. A person who takes up residence in another province is an out-migrant with reference to the province of origin, and an in-migrant with reference to the province of destination.

Labour force: Civilian, non-institutional population aged 15 and older who, during the Labour Force Survey reference week, were employed or unemployed. *See also* Employment and Unemployment.

Labour productivity: Real output per hours worked.

Low income cut-offs (LICOs): Income thresholds below which families will devote a larger share of income to food, shelter and clothing than the average family would. To reflect differences in the costs of necessities among different community and family sizes, LICOs are defined for five categories of community size and seven of family size.

Machinery and Equipment Price Index (MEPI): Measures price changes for machinery and equipment purchases, relative to the gross annual accumulation of wealth as represented by the purchase of new machinery and the development and expansion of infrastructure.

Median: Value of the middle number of a series ranked in order of size.

Mortality rate: Number of deaths from all causes per 100,000 population.

Mother tongue: First language an individual learns at home and still understands.

Multiple visible minority: Respondent who reports more than one visible minority group as ethnic origin (e.g., "Black" and "South Asian").

Natural gas: Gaseous petroleum consisting primarily of methane with lesser amounts of (in order of abundance) ethane, propane, butane and pentane, and heavier hydrocarbons, as well as non-energy components such as nitrogen, carbon dioxide, hydrogen sulphide and water.

Natural gas liquids: Natural gas liquids are those hydrocarbon components in natural gas recovered from raw natural gas by processing through extraction plants, or recovered from field separators or other gathering facilities. These liquids include propane, butanes, ethane and pentanes plus.

New Housing Price Index (NHPI): Measures price changes for contractors' selling prices of new residential houses.

Non-contributory registered pension plan: A pension plan in which all required contributions are made by the employer.

North American Industry Classification System (NAICS): Industry classification system developed to provide common definitions of the industrial structures of Canada, Mexico and the United States. Its hierarchical structure is composed of sectors (two-digit code), subsectors (three-digit code), industry groups (four-digit code), and industries (five-digit code).

Obese: *See* Body Mass Index.

Off-reserve: Aboriginal people not living on a reserve.

Operating expense: Wages, salaries and supplementary labour income, intermediate purchases, capital consumption allowances and net indirect taxes on factors of production.

Operating revenue: Revenue from the sales of goods and services; rental and operating lease revenue; and revenue from commissions, franchise fees and royalties.

Organisation for Economic Co-operation and Development (OECD): A group of 30 member countries sharing a commitment to democratic government and the market economy. The OECD produces internationally agreed upon instruments, decisions and recommendations to promote rules of the game in areas where multilateral agreement is necessary for individual countries to make progress in a globalized economy.

Overweight: *See* Body Mass Index.

Participation rate: Represents the labour force expressed as a percentage of the population aged 15 and older. The participation rate for a particular group (age, sex, etc.) is the labour force in that group expressed as a percentage of the population for that group.

Per capita: For each person or per person.

Petajoule: A unit of energy equalling 1,015 joules. A joule is a unit of energy equal to the work done when a force of one newton acts through a distance of one metre.

Petroleum products: End result of the petroleum refining process. They include fuels like gasoline, aviation fuel, diesel and heating oil; products such as solvents and lubricants; and raw materials for manufacturing petrochemicals.

Population density: Number of people per square kilometre.

Profit margin: The difference between the cost of buying or producing something and the price for which it is sold.

Public sector: Public administration at the federal, provincial or municipal levels of government, as well as Crown corporations, liquor control boards and other government institutions such as schools (including universities), hospitals and public libraries.

Raw Materials Price Index (RMPI): Measures price changes for the purchase of raw materials by Canadian industry. The term 'raw material' refers either to a commodity that is sold for the first time after being extracted from nature, or a substitutable recycled product (e.g., metal scrap).

Registered Pension Plan (RPP): Pension plans for employees sponsored by employers or unions and usually funded through contributions by both employees and employers. RPPs must satisfy certain conditions and be registered for the purposes of the federal *Income Tax Act*.

Registered Retirement Savings Plan (RRSP): Program that allows savings for retirement to grow tax free in a special savings plan registered by the Canada Revenue Agency. Contributions to RRSPs can be made up to December 31 of the year the contributor turns 69.

Rural area: Area of a country not falling into either the large urban or small urban categories. See also Small urban area.

Sandwich generation: Individuals caught between the often conflicting demands of caring for children and caring for seniors.

Services-producing sector: Sector of the economy composed of the following: trade; transportation and warehousing; finance and insurance, real estate and renting and leasing, and management of companies and enterprises; professional, scientific and technical services; information and cultural industries; arts, entertainment and recreation; administrative and support services; waste management and remediation services; educational services; health care and social assistance; information, culture and recreation; accommodation and food services; public administration; and other services.

Small urban area: Urban area not part of a CMA that has a minimum population of 1,000 people and a population density of at least 400 people per square kilometre. *See* also Rural area.

Social assistance: Transfer payments (including refundable tax credits) to help individuals and families maintain a socially acceptable level of earnings.

Terms of trade: The price of exports relative to the price of imports.

Time stress: Measure of sleep deprivation used in the General Social Survey.

Tourism: The activities of people travelling to and staying in places outside their usual environment for less than one consecutive year for leisure, business or other purposes.

Tourism industries: Industries that would cease to exist or would continue to exist only at significantly reduced levels of activity in the absence of tourism.

Trade surplus: Positive trade balance occurring when a country exports more goods than it imports.

Twenty-foot equivalent (TEU): Standard unit describing a ship's cargo carrying capacity or a shipping terminal's cargo handling capacity. A standard forty-foot (40x8x8 feet) container equals two TEUs (each 20x8x8).

Unemployment: People who, during the Labour Force Survey reference week, were on temporary layoff expecting recall and were available for work; were without work, had actively looked for work in the past four weeks, and were available for work; or had a new job to start within four weeks from the reference week, and were available for work. *See also* Employment and Labour force.

Unemployment rate: Number of unemployed people, during the Labour Force Survey reference week, expressed as a percentage of the labour force (unemployed plus employed). The unemployment rate for a particular group (age, sex, province, etc.) is the number unemployed in that group expressed as a percentage of the labour force for that group.

Visible minority: People, other than Aboriginal people, who are non-Caucasian in race or non-white in colour.

Visitors: People travelling to and staying in places outside their usual environment for not more than one consecutive year for leisure, business or other purposes. They are referred to as either tourists (those who stay overnight or longer in the place visited), or same-day visitors. *See also* Tourism.

Sources

All sources are from Statistics Canada except those noted as "Other."

Begin your research from the Statistics Canada home page at www.statcan.gc.ca/start-debut-eng.html.

Chapter 1: Aboriginal peoples

Aboriginal Children's Survey 2006. Occasional. 89-634-X
The Aboriginal Labour Force Analysis Series. Occasional. 71-588-X
Aboriginal Peoples in Canada in 2006: Inuit, Métis and First Nations, 2006 Census. Occasional. 97-558-X

Chapter 2: Agriculture

Agriculture—Population Linkage Data for the 2006 Census. Every five years. 95-633-X
Cattle Statistics. Semi-annual. 23-012-X
EnviroStats. Quarterly. 16-002-X
Farm Cash Receipts - Agriculture Economic Statistics. Semi-annual. 21-011-X
The Financial Picture of Farms in Canada. Every five years. 2006 Census of Agriculture
Hog Statistics. Quarterly. 23-010-X
Sheep Statistics. Semi-annual. 23-011-X

Chapter 3: Business, consumer and property services

Cable and Satellite Television Industry. Annual. 56-209-X
Corporations Returns Act. Annual. 61-220-X
Financial and Taxation Statistics for Enterprises. Annual. 61-219-X
Quarterly Financial Statistics for Enterprises. Quarterly. 61-008-X

Chapter 4: Business performance and ownership

Canadian Business Patterns. Semi-annual. 61F0040X
Financial Performance Indicators for Canadian Business. Annual. 61-224-X
Insights on the Canadian Economy. Occasional. 11-624-M
Financial Statistics for Enterprises. Quarterly. 61-008-X

Chapter 5: Children and Youth

2006 Census: Family Portrait: Continuity and Change in Canadian Families and Households in 2006. Occasional. 97-553-X

The 2006 Participation and Activity Limitation Survey: Disability in Canada. Occasional. 89-628-X

Canadian Demographics at a Glance. Irregular. 91-003-X

Canadian Social Trends. Irregular. 11-800-X

Children and Youth Research Paper Series. Occasional. 89-599-M

Health reports. Quarterly. 82-003-X

Other

Bio Med Central (BMC) Public Health. www.biomedcentral.com

Chapter 6: Construction

Building Permits. Monthly. 64-001-X

Canadian Economic Observer. Monthly. 11-010-X

Capital Expenditure Price Statistics. Quarterly. 62-007-X

Perspectives on Labour and Income. Monthly. 75-001-X

Chapter 7: Crime and justice

Canadian Centre for Justice Statistics Profile Series. Occasional. 85F0033M

Family Violence in Canada: A Statistical Profile. Annual. 85-224-X

Juristat. Irregular. 85-002-X

Police Resources in Canada. Annual. 85-225-X

Chapter 8: Culture and Leisure

Canadian Social Trends. Quarterly. 11-008-X

Culture, Tourism and the Centre for Education Statistics—Research Papers. Occasional. 81-595-M

Government Expenditures on Culture: Data Tables. Annual. 87F0001X

Chapter 9: Economic accounts

Canadian Economic Accounts Quarterly Review. Quarterly. 13-010-X

Canadian Economic Observer. Monthly. 11-010-X

Gross Domestic Product by Industry. Monthly. 15-001-X

National Balance Sheet Accounts, Quarterly Estimates. Quarterly. 13-214-X

National Income and Expenditure Accounts, Quarterly Estimates. Quarterly. 13-001-X

Provincial and Territorial Economic Accounts Review. Semi-annual. 13-016-X

Chapter 10: Education, training and learning

Culture, Tourism and the Centre for Education Statistics— Research Papers. Occasional. 81-595-M

Education Highlight Tables, 2006 Census. Occasional. 97-560-X

Education Indicators in Canada: Report of the Pan-Canadian Education Indicators Program. Occasional. 81-582-X

Education Matters: Insights on Education, Learning and Training in Canada. Bi-monthly. 81-004-X

Educational Portrait of Canada, 2006 Census. Occasional. 97-560-X

Chapter 11: Energy

Electric Power Generation, Transmission and Distribution. Annual. 57-202-X

Energy Statistics Handbook. Quarterly. 57-601-X

EnviroStats. Quarterly. 16-002-X

Other

National Energy Board

Chapter 12: Environment

Canadian Environmental Sustainability Indicators. Annual. 16-252-X

EnviroStats. Quarterly. 16-002-X

Households and the Environment. Biennial. 11-526-X

Human Activity and the Environment: Annual Statistics. Annual. 16-201-X

Chapter 13: Ethnic diversity and immigration

Analytical Studies Branch Research Paper Series. Occasional. 11F0019MWE

Canada's Ethnocultural Mosaic, 2006 Census. Occasional. 97-562-X

Canadian Social Trends. Irregular. 11-008-X

The Immigrant Labour Force Analysis Series. Occasional. 71-606-X

Immigration and Citizenship Highlight Tables, 2006 Census. Occasional. 97-557-X

Perspectives on Labour and Income. Monthly. 75-001-X

Chapter 14: Families, households and housing

Changing Patterns in Canadian Homeownership and Shelter Costs, 2006 Census Occasional. 97-554-X

Matter of Fact. Occasional. 89-630-X

Chapter 15: Geography

Maps and geography. Every five years. http://www.statcan.gc.ca/mgeo/index-eng.htm

Other

Central Intelligence Agency, Washington D.C; Environment Canada; Natural Resources Canada

Chapter 16: Government

Public Sector Statistics. Annual. 68-213-X

Chapter 17: Health

Health Indicators. Semi-annual. 82-221-X
Health Reports. Quarterly. 82-003-X
Health Reports—Supplement. Annual. 82-003-S
Leading Causes of Death in Canada. Annual. 84-215-X

Chapter 18: Income, pensions, spending and wealth

Canadian Economic Accounts Quarterly Review. Quarterly. 13-010-X
Canadian Social Trends. Irregular. 11-008-X
Income in Canada. Annual. 75-202-X
Income Trends in Canada. Annual. 13F0022X
Pension and Wealth Research Paper Series. Occasional. 13F0026M
Spending Patterns in Canada. Annual. 62-202-X

Chapter 19: Information and communications technology

Broadcasting and Telecommunications. Irregular. 56-001-X
Canadian Internet Use Survey—Public Use Microdata File. Biennial. 56M0003X
Innovation Analysis Bulletin. Irregular. 88-003-X
Quarterly Telecommunications Statistics. Quarterly. 56-002-X

Chapter 20: International merchandise trade

Canadian Economic Accounts Quarterly Review. Quarterly. 13-010-X
Canadian Economic Observer. Monthly. 11-010-X
International Merchandise Trade Annual Review. Annual. 65-208-X

Chapter 21: Labour

Annual Demographic Estimates: Canada, Provinces and Territories. Annual. 91-215-X
Employment, Earnings and Hours. Monthly. 72-002-X
Labour Force Historical Review. Annual. 71F0004X
Labour Force Information. Monthly. 71-001-X
Perspectives on Labour and Income. Monthly. 75-001-X
Workplace and Employee Survey Compendium. Occasional. 71-585-X

Chapter 22: Languages

Canadian Demographics at a Glance. Irregular. 91-003-X
Canadian Social Trends. Irregular. 11-008-X
Education Matters: Insights on Education, Learning and Training in Canada. Bi-monthly. 81-004-X
Language, 2006 Census. Occasional. 97-555-X

Chapter 23: Manufacturing

Analysis in Brief. Occasional. 11-621-M
Canadian Economic Observer. Monthly. 11-010-X
The Canadian Productivity Review. Occasional. 15-206-X
Gross Domestic Product by Industry. Monthly. 15-001-X
Perspectives on Labour and Income. Monthly. 75-001-X

Chapter 24: Population and demography

Annual Demographic Estimates: Canada, Provinces and Territories. Annual. 91-215-X
Annual Demographic Statistics. Annual. 91-213-X
Canadian Demographics at a Glance. Irregular. 91-003-X
Canadian Social Trends. Quarterly. 11-008-X
Health Reports. Quarterly. 82-003-X

Chapter 25: Prices and price indexes

Analysis in Brief. Occasional. 11-621-M
Capital Expenditure Price Statistics. Quarterly. 62-007-X
The Consumer Price Index. Monthly. 62-001-X
EnviroStats. Quarterly. 16-002-X
Farm Product Price Index. Monthly. 21-007-X
Industry Price Indexes. Monthly. 62-011-X

Chapter 26: Retail and wholesale trade

Analysis in Brief. Occasional. 11-621-M
Canadian Economic Accounts Quarterly Review. Quarterly. 13-010-X
Retail Trade. Monthly. 63-005-X
Wholesale Trade. Monthly. 63-008-X

Chapter 27: Science and technology

Federal Scientific Activities. Annual. 88-204-X
Gross Domestic Expenditures on Research and Development in Canada and the Provinces. Annual. 88-221-X
Innovation Analysis Bulletin. Irregular. 88-003-X
Science Statistics. Irregular. 88-001-X

Other

Organisation for Economic Co-operation and Development

Chapter 28: Seniors

Canadian Demographics at a Glance. Irregular. 91-003-X
Canadian Social Trends. Irregular. 11-008-X
Income Security and Stability During Retirement in Canada. Occasional. 11F0019M
Perspectives on Labour and Income. Monthly. 75-001-X
A Portrait of Seniors in Canada. Occasional. 89-519-X

Chapter 29: Society and community

Canadian Social Trends. Irregular. 11-008-X
How Canadians' Use of the Internet Affects Social Life and Civic Participation. Occasional. 56F0004M
Matter of Fact. Occasional. 89-630-X
Participation and Activity Limitation Survey 2006: A Profile of Assistive Technology for People with Disabilities. Occasional. 89-628-X

Chapter 30: Transportation

Canadian Social Trends. Irregular. 11-008-X
EnviroStats. Quarterly. 16-002-X
Monthly Railway Carloadings. Monthly. 52-001-X
Rail in Canada. Annual. 52-216-X
Shipping in Canada. Annual. 54-205-X
Trucking in Canada. Annual. 53-222-X

Chapter 31: Travel and Tourism

Canadian Travel Survey: Domestic Travel. Annual. 87-212-X
International Travel. Annual. 66-201-X
International Travel: Advance Information. Monthly. 66-001-P
National Tourism Indicators, Quarterly Estimates. Quarterly. 13-009-X
Rail in Canada. Annual. 52-216-X
Travel-log (Touriscope). Quarterly. 87-003-X

Index

Notes: Statistics for provinces and territories are mainly under "Provincial/territorial statistics"; those for urban areas are mainly under "Census metropolitan areas (CMAs)." Page references in *italics* denote a chart or table. CMA stands for "census metropolitan area"; CPI, for "Consumer Price Index"; GDP, for "gross domestic product"; GERD, for "gross domestic expenditures on R&D"; GHG, for "greenhouse gas"; ICT, for "information and communications technology" and R&D for "research and development."

G

Q

R

U

Y